TRIUMPH OF

A
SHAAR
PRESS
PUBLICATION

SURVIVAL

THE STORY OF THE JEWS IN THE MODERN ERA 1650-1990

BEREL WEIN

Published by SHAAR PRESS
in conjunction with
MESORAH PUBLICATIONS, LTD.
4401 Second Avenue / Brooklyn, N.Y 11232 / (718) 921-9000 / www.artscroll.com

Distributed in Israel by SIFRIATI / A. GITLER
6 Hayarkon Street / Bnei Brak 51127 / Israel

Distributed in Europe by LEHMANNS
Unit E, Viking Business Park, Rolling Mill Road / Jarrow, Tyne and Wear, NE32 3DP / England

Distributed in Australia and New Zealand by GOLDS WORLD OF JUDAICA
3-13 William Street / Balaclava, Melbourne 3183, Victoria / Australia

Distributed in South Africa by KOLLEL BOOKSHOP
Shop 8A Norwood Hypermarket/ Norwood 2196 / Johannesburg, South Africa

ISBN: 0-89906-498-1

Printed in the United States of America by Noble Book Press
Custom bound by Sefercraft, Inc. / 4401 Second Avenue / Brooklyn N.Y. 11232

To my wife, Jackie

Contents

Section VI   Treacherous Hopes
1920-1930

Section VII   The Holocaust and the State
1938-1958

Preface

It has truly been noted that history is too important to be left to the historians. This is certainly true in the case of Jewish history. Jewish history as a discipline and Jewish history books in general did not come into vogue until the late nineteenth century. Jewish historiography, therefore, has been almost exclusively the product of secular Jews,[1] who held a strong bias against rabbinical Torah Judaism. Thus, the irony of most Jewish history texts is that they have been written with condescension, if not hostility, to the basic beliefs and true heroes of Jewry over the centuries. It would not be an exaggeration to say that many books on Jewish history by non-Jews[2] have been much more insightful, sensitive, and sympathetic to their subject matter than those written by "objective-minded," secular Jews. Thus, almost by default, a great deal of current "Jewish history" books, articles, and texts are not truly Jewish, and are barely accurate history.

I am not a historian, nor the son of a historian. I have, however, spent years reading, researching, writing, and lecturing about the Jewish people and their place in the world. All authors write from a personal bias. Mine is that I am an Orthodox Jew who believes in the divinity of Jewish tradition and in the uniqueness of the people of Israel. There exists within the Jewish people a collective memory of its history. This collective memory operates independently of research materials, books, and other "acceptable" historical evidence. One benefit of being an Orthodox Jew is having access to this memory bank of events, insights, world views, and life-giving legends. My education in a yeshivah, my good fortune in knowing and conversing with some of the last great Eastern European rabbis, and my family tradition and its members have combined to allow me a glimpse of this collective memory treasure of Israel.

This collective experience has shaped my view of events, past and present, and my judgments regarding people, movements, and directions among the Jewish people. Perhaps more than anything else, it has been my guide to the choice of facts, occurrences, and people I have included in my narrative. It is why I consider this book to be a *Jewish* history book. Nevertheless, I have quoted extensively from non-Jewish sources, as well as non-Orthodox Jews, because I believe that for a history to be fair and accurate, its author must take into account what others have to say and their view of events. It is also illuminating to find that many non-traditional Jews are aware of the verities of Torah and traditional Jewish life and how they affect the way Jewish history unfolds and should be

---

1. The main exception being the fourteen-volume series on Jewish history by Zev Yavetz, first published in the 1890s.

2. Paul Johnson, *A History of the Jews,* and Conor Cruise O'Brien, *The Siege,* are only two examples of this phenomenon.

understood, thus, confirming much of the traditional outlook on Jewish events. Finally, the ancient Jewish doctrine of accepting truth from whoever says it must be honored in a book like this.[3]

Superficially at least, the history of the Jewish people is an unrelieved litany of disaster, persecution, and horror. Perhaps it is precisely this that lends a peculiar fascination to the story of the Jewish people. Once the raw facts are digested, three essential questions remain to plague the student of Jewish history: (1) Why did such a fate befall Jewry? (2) How has the Jewish people persevered and survived against such brutal forces? And (3) What is the ultimate meaning of its struggle for survival?

To me, the answer to these three questions can be found only in the realm of the supernatural. These are matters of theology and soul and not merely of politics and human conditions. There are no laws of natural history nor any rules of civilized development that can adequately answer the paradox of Jewish persecution and survival. "Behold it is a people that shall dwell apart and not be reckoned among the nations."[4]

The more I read and study Jewish history, the clearer it becomes that there is an Author and Planner, Who guides Israel to its destiny. It is my prayer that this book will help its readers share this vision.

Acknowledgments

This book is my responsibility solely, but its appearance and publication is due to the encouragement and efforts of many. Rabbis Nosson Scherman and Meir Zlotowitz provided me with wise counsel from the inception of this project. I am also greatly appreciative of the fact that we have become good friends as a result. I also wish to thank Rabbis Leibel Reznick and Yacov Hain for their interest and comments. Mr. Joseph Friedenson provided me with valuable information about pre-World War II Eastern European Jewry, various scholars read portions of the manuscript and made erudite comments, and an anonymous friend was the source of material for the chapter on the Gaon of Vilna.

Rabbi Sheah Brander designed the book, in yet another demonstration of his graphics artistry, ably assisted by Mordechai Golding, as well as Eli Kroen and Yitzchok Saftlas.

I must thank Mrs. Ethel Morrow and Mrs. Shulamith Rosenblatt who typed some of the first drafts of this book. I am grateful as well to the typesetters and proofreaders who performed so competently and conscientiously: Judi Dick, Bassie Goldstein, Nina Indig, Zissi Landau, and Faygie Weinbaum.

My students and congregants, wittingly or otherwise, helped me formulate my ideas and helped strengthen my resolve to complete this book.

My family, and especially my wife, showed me their usual forbearance during the long and sometimes emotionally volatile process of writing this book. And I close with thanks to the God of Israel who has granted me life and perseverance to see this day.

Cheshvan, 5751 / October, 1990

Berel Wein

---

3. See Maimonides' introduction to his commentary to *Ethics of the Fathers* ('*Shemonah Perakim*'), where he states that he has gleaned information even from non-Jewish philosophers, both ancient and more recent, because "one should hear the truth from whoever states it."
4. Numbers 23:9.

TRIUMPH OF SURVIVAL

Prologue

HERE IS A PATTERN TO THE story of the people of Israel. The Bible itself provides the early chapters and foretells the future. After slavery in Egypt and the miraculous exodus from the land of their bondage, the Jewish people at Sinai enter into the covenant of the Torah. This unique people, with beliefs and practices far different from the peer civilizations of their time, conquered and settled an inhospitable bit of land that is strategically important as the bridge connecting Asia, Europe, and Africa.

Their Torah and prophets taught them that the source of their strength and security was spirituality; that they would prevail by the spirit, not by the spear. But they strayed from the strictures of their Divine covenant and thus proved themselves unequal to their Divine mission. King Nebuchadnezzar of Babylon conquered the land, destroyed the Temple, and exiled the people. Though taking up residence throughout the Mediterranean basin, the Jews lived mainly in Babylonia and Persia. Seventy years after their exile, many returned to their homeland, though the majority remained in their new-found homes, far from the Land of Israel.

Back in their land, they rebuilt the Temple, formulated methods and scholarly disciplines for the preservation of their faith and its Torah as represented by the Mishnah and Talmud, and became the visible enemy of paganism and its philosophies. The Jews also became the focal point in the development of Western civilization. They defended themselves against the pagan Syrian-Greeks and defeated them. They even held their own for a time against the vaunted Roman Empire until they were finally defeated and subjugated. In 70 C.E., the Jews were exiled, after losing their sovereignty and independence and seeing their Second Temple destroyed.

The Jews now lived all along the rim of the Mediterranean Sea. A new religion, Christianity, formed originally by a sect of Jews, swept paganism before it and became the dominant influence in Western life for millennia, but the Jews gave little notice and scant approval to their prodigal offspring, persisting in their own eternal beliefs and rituals.

After the brutal Roman suppression of the Bar Kochba rebellion in 135 C.E., the Jewish community in the Land of Israel declined and the stereotype of the "wandering Jew" was created and confirmed. From then on, the center stage of Jewish history continually moved, as the scenes shifted from Babylonia to North Africa, to Spain and Portugal, to France and the German Rhineland, and stretched eastward into the Balkans, Poland, and Russia.

Another new monotheistic religion, Islam, became a powerful military and spiritual force. It, too, was based on Jewish theological concepts and social order, but it did not affect internal Jewish life and behavior. Indeed, for a long time Jews would feel freer in the society of Islam than in the Christian West. The Jews lived in a self-created vacuum, but were nevertheless part of the sweep of history that surrounded them. Their role was mainly of thought and ferment, rather than of active participation, but the Jews were prime participants in the drama of Western civilization's development. Though they were innocent bystanders in the contest between Islam and Christianity for world dominance, the Jews, and not the Moslem targets of Christian piety, were often the main victims of the Crusades.

Along with the general burden of humanizing civilization, the Jews bore another crushing yoke — the resolution of their own destiny as a people. As the centuries passed in exile and degradation, the gnawing question at the root of the so-called Jewish problem was: "How can we achieve our national redemption and thus escape from our difficult position vis-a-vis the rest of humanity?" The lengthening exile and the bleak tomorrow converged to crush Jewish life in a vortex of pressures and stress, some of them self-manufactured. The cumulative effect of the exile began to take its toll. Events and tragedies like those that had been suffered in stoic silence by the Jews in the thirteenth century were too great to be borne quietly in the sixteenth century, for every generation lives not only with its troubles but with the accumulated horrors of preceding times as well. Each new cut reopened all the old scars and wounds. The burden of the ages became increasingly heavy, and a sense of near panic besieged parts of the house of Israel as the centuries passed.

The Inquisition and expulsions of the Jews from the Iberian Peninsula in 1492 and 1496 triggered a desperate reaction in the

Jewish world. Spain and Portugal, which had provided home and haven to the intelligentsia and aristocracy of Israel for five centuries, became the graveyard of Jewish hopes and lives. Almost 250,000 Jews converted to Christianity — most of them originally only pretending to do so — in an attempt to save their homes, fortunes, families, and way of life. An equal number of Jews chose exile and dislocation rather than betray their faith, conscience, and tradition.

In an irony of history, Columbus' voyage to the New World was delayed by the density of ship traffic evacuating hapless Jews from Spanish harbors. King Ferdinand and Queen Isabella decreed a deadline beyond which all Jews remaining in Spain must either convert or die at the stake — a day that fell on the ninth day of the Hebrew month of Av, the anniversary of the destruction of both Temples in Jerusalem. To the tens of thousands of Jews crossing the border to lives of suffering and uncertainty, the date was a Divine omen, signifying that though God was angry with them, He had not forgotten them.

Many Spanish and Portuguese Jews escaped to Holland, Italy, Turkey, and even to the Land of Israel. Many others crossed Europe and eventually found home and refuge with the Jews of Poland and Russia, assimilating into the Ashkenazic lifestyle and rite. The shock of Spanish Jewry's tragedy reverberated throughout the Jewish world. The disaster that befell the wealthiest, most sophisticated and stable section of world Jewry plunged the Jewish people everywhere into a state of depression.

Kabbalistic ideas and values gained public popularity in the Jewish world as the secrets of the ages, zealously guarded and reserved over untold generations exclusively for people of utmost scholarship and piety, now became part of the public domain. These teachings provided comfort because they imparted meaning and purpose into events that were otherwise incomprehensible. But there was a downside. Unscrupulous people would capitalize on the lack of sophistication of the Jewish masses in such metaphysical matters, and wreak havoc with traditional Jewish life and mores. Great internal stresses developed within the Jewish people, and there was mounting pressure for change and alleviation of the Jewish condition in the exile of Europe.

The outside world, too, did not stand still. The fifteenth and sixteenth centuries brought great and violent changes to Europe, now emerging from the enforced piety of the Middle Ages. The ideals of the Renaissance took hold and refashioned Europe. The foundation for the future reformation of Christianity, for the rebellion against absolute monarchy, and for the colonial expansion of Western civilization into all parts of the world was laid during those two centuries. The hope of Western civilization for a better tomorrow and the soaring — almost arrogant — optimism upon which Western man would build his new world eventually infected the people of Israel, as well.

The story of the Jewish people from the 1640s onward is a history of drastic change and unswerving loyalty, of great achievements and monumental defeats. The most decisive events of current Jewish life were formed by the larger historic currents of the last 350 years. The emergence of a large and wealthy American Jewish community, assimilation and religious ferment, the Holocaust, the resurgence of Torah life and scholarship, the State of Israel, the people and the Land are the products of these years.

The impetus towards the light of the future stems from the knowledge of those forces and struggles that have so recently shaped our immediate, dark past. To know the past of the Jewish people is to believe in its future.

Section I

The Abyss of Despair

1648-1730

1

Tach V'Tat

Winds of Change

HE YEARS OF THE LATE Middle Ages were a time of wrenching turmoil. The Renaissance, the Reformation, and the changing imperial and economic alliances within Europe all served to destabilize the old order. The Church's grip on Western man was loosened imperceptibly at first, but irreversibly. The new world that would emerge held hopes and promises and also terrible dangers. Gunpowder and more modern weapons of death, combined with the wealth of new colonial empires, were to change Europe. To most of the Jews of Europe, the demise of the old order and the coming of the new society went almost unnoticed. Jews generally were in no way part of ongoing European life or culture, and to the average Jew neither pope nor anti-pope, Luther nor Loyola, were of concern or difference. Physically, the Jews were locked into their ghettos and small villages, while spiritually they soared to the greater heights of scholarship, Kabbalah, and piety.

By the start of the seventeenth century the Jews of Western Europe, nevertheless, may have become more aware of the changing tides of history that beat about them. But the Jews of Poland, Lithuania, and Russia remained completely unaware of the occurring world changes. Isolated among an ignorant, hostile, and unlettered peasantry, protected only by autocratic whim, the Jews of Eastern Europe as a whole were nevertheless mildly secure in their lifestyle and social position. They had no desire for equality or assimilation but rather sought only a de facto autonomy by which they could continue to conduct their lives and communities according to their faith and tradition.

The winds of change that were bringing more liberal attitudes to Western Europe did not reach Eastern Europe. Poland and Lithuania remained staunchly Roman Catholic and Russia's faith in the Orthodox Church was unchallenged. Most of the Jews were content with their dangerous status quo, convinced that no major upheavals were in store for them. Their precarious plight in Christian Europe was not an abnormal situation to them. The expulsion of the Jews from Spain in 1492 had proven how illusory were the hopes of the Jews for religious, political, and economic stability. Every governmental eruption in Europe shook the Jewish people to its foundation, and Europe in the sixteenth and seventeenth centuries was replete with wars, revolutions, and turmoil. Yet no one was prepared for the devastating events that befell European Jewry in 1648.

After the demise of Spanish Jewry, the center stage of Jewish history shifted to Eastern Europe. The following descriptions of that quality of life places Eastern European Jewish life into perspective:

> There was scarcely a [Jewish] house in all the kingdom of Poland where its members did not occupy themselves with the study of Torah . . . Thus, there were many scholars in every community . . . With the coming of dawn, the members of the *Chevrah Tehillim* (a group devoted to reciting the Book of Psalms) would rise to recite Psalms for about an hour before prayers. Each week they would complete the recitation of the entire Book of Psalms. And far be it that any man should oversleep the time of prayer in the morning and not go to the synagogue, except under unusual circumstances . . . Never was a dispute among Jews brought before a Gentile judge or before a nobleman or before the king, and if a Jew took his case before a Gentile court he was severely punished and chastised . . . All the six pillars[1] upon which the world rests were in existence in the (Jewish Communities of the) Kingdom of Poland . . .[2]

> There were many who lived in appalling poverty and many who were pinched by never-ending worries; and there were plenty of taverns with strong spirits. But drunkards were never seen among Jews. When night came and a Jew wanted to while away his time, he did not hurry to take a drink; he went rather to his books or joined a group that, either with or without a teacher, gave itself over to the pure enjoyment of study. Physically worn out by their day's toil, they sat over open volumes and intoned the austere music of the Talmud.

---

1. Torah, prayer, and charity; truth, justice, and peace. Mishnah *Avos* 1:2,18.
2. *Yeven Metzulah* by Nassan Nata Hanover (reprinted Tel Aviv, 1945), a history of Jews in Poland, Lithuania, and Rasein during 1648-9.

Poor Jews, whose children knew only the taste (as one of the songs has it) of "potatoes on Sunday, potatoes on Monday, potatoes on Tuesday," sat there like intellectual princes. They possessed whole treasuries of thought — the knowledge, ideas, and sayings of many ages. When a problem came up, there was immediately a crowd of people to offer opinions, proofs, quotations. One raised a question on a difficult passage in Maimonides' work and many vied in attempts to explain it, outdoing one another in the subtlety of dialectic distinctions. The stomachs were empty, the houses overcrowded — but the minds were replete with the riches of the Torah.[3]

This inner life of the Jews was tenuously balanced on the key assumption that no major political or military upheavals would occur in Poland, Lithuania, or Russia. In the seventeenth century, as in later times, this could hardly be guaranteed. Since the Jews were not integrated into the general society, and since they were at best tolerated but never accepted, turmoil would only serve to further isolate and endanger them. They were always present as the necessary scapegoat, the tinderbox upon which the sparks of revolution and war could feed.

The year 1648 (corresponding to the Jewish calendar year 5408)[4] was to be an auspicious year for captive Israel, the Jews were told by masters of Kabbalah. By mathematical computations based upon statements of the *Zohar*[5], many Jews came to believe that the coming of the Messiah would occur during that year. Since the advent of the Messiah according to Jewish tradition would be prefaced by dangers, uncertainty, and even war, the Jews were subconsciously prepared for turmoil and discomfort. However, they were not prepared for the systematic barbarity and mass murder that would be their fate.

---

3. Introductory Essay to Roman Vishniac's photographic record of Eastern European Jewry, "Polish Jews" (Schocken Books, N.Y. 1973).

4. In common parlance, the year 5408 was identified as 408, omitting the number 5000, since knowledge of the millennium was presumed. In Hebrew, 408 and 409 are represented by the Hebrew letters *tav-chet* and *tav-tet*, which, when combined in speech, is pronounced "*tach*" and "*tat*." Thus the years 5408 and 5409 (1648-49) were called *Tach V'Tat*.

5. Rabbinic tradition ascribes authorship of the *Zohar* to Rabbi Shimon bar Yochai, who flourished in Israel during the second century C.E.

The Rise of Chmielnicki

N 1635 AND AGAIN IN 1636, there had occurred uprisings of the local peasants and Cossacks in Preyeslov, in the Ukraine. The Cossacks, natives of the area, were skilled and warlike horsemen. These unfortunates, exploited and oppressed by Polish landlords in a manner representative of the worst excesses of the feudal system, revolted against their masters. The eternal cry of the masses for land, bread, and the power to direct their own lives soon turned into a shriek of madness and frustration. Grafted onto their traditional, fierce anti-Semitism, these factors led to a tragedy of epic proportions.

For a few months, the Cossacks took control of the area and proclaimed themselves free men. The Jews of the area, some of whom were the tax collectors of the absentee Polish landlords, bore the full brunt of the Cossacks' new-found freedom. Forced by the Polish masters of the land into the most unpopular areas of work (as tax collectors, tavern keepers, estate administrators, and moneylenders), unprotected by any form of governmental controls, despised because of their alien rituals and beliefs, the Jews were the most visible and accessible — as well as defenseless — representatives of the hated Polish oppressor. Within a week's time, two thousand Jews were killed and the remainder of the Jewish community of the area was sent reeling westward into Poland as refugees.

Bogdan Chmielnicki

After three months the rebellion was put down and the Polish masters returned to power. Once again Jews were imported into the area to serve the feudal nobles, collecting ever higher taxes and lending money at even more usurious rates, while attempting somehow to rebuild their shattered Jewish community. They viewed this incident, which centered about the town of Preyeslov, not as a harbinger of the future but rather as an isolated event that fit into a long history of sporadic persecution, death, and torture. This analysis was far too rosy.

By 1648, the Cossacks and their peasant allies of the Ukraine and Middle Russia had found a leader. Bogdan Chmielnicki, then in his early fifties, had led a rather ordinary existence. As a young man he had served as a cavalryman in the forces of the Poles and the Cossacks fighting the Turks. After numerous unsuccessful financial endeavors and disappointments over his inability to attain any significant rank within the Polish military, he found himself with an enormous ego, and a great deal of pent-up rage and frustration, but with seemingly nowhere to go. No stranger to personal misfortune, a strong Greek Orthodox who despised his Roman Catholic mentors, he was stoic, unafraid, and willing to risk all in order to vindicate his religion, talents, and ambition.

In 1647 he suffered personal abuse from the Polish governor of Czehryn, and his wife was carried off by marauding Polish irregulars who invaded his home at the behest of the governor. In fury and hate, he deserted the Poles and joined the Cossack Zaporozhian group. This rabble consisted mainly of highwaymen, escaped criminals and dispossessed serfs. They were, however, skilled soldiers, equipped with intrepid ingenuity, and all had nothing to lose.

With his cunning, personality and military acumen, Chmielnicki welded these people into a potent fighting force. Raising the banner of freedom, he fanned the hatred of the masses against the Roman Catholic Polish oppressor, and soon almost all of the Ukraine joined the uprising. The Tartars of Crimea — an Asiatic tribe that had come west into European Russia centuries before — also allied themselves with him, and in April 1648 he crossed the Dnieper westward. Initial successes in the battles at Zheltye Vody and Korsun won Chmielnicki widespread support from the peasant masses who now saw him as their potential

THE CHMIELNICKI
MASSACRES 1648-1656

savior and leader. In the autumn of 1648, his Cossacks swept all before them and invaded Poland proper, capturing Pilawce and, finally, Lwow. A truce was called and the Poles hastily granted Chmielnicki a noble title and autonomy for a Cossack state in return for his commitment to pay at least lip service to Polish sovereignty and to halt the war.

This war left a legacy of latent violence and enmity between the ethnic groupings of Poland and the Ukraine. It was not only the Jews who suffered at the hands of the marauding Cossacks. Their revolt was an orgy of hate against established authority and representatives of religions other than their own. Roman Catholic clergymen were beheaded, nuns violated, and their churches pillaged and burned by their Eastern Orthodox fellow Christians. Polish nobles were held for immense ransoms and, more often than not, tortured to death, even after the ransoms were delivered. Numerous quarrels between the Cossacks and the Tartars always left death and destruction amidst those former allies. But no one suffered as cruel a fate as did the Jews. They were decimated and uprooted. According to Jewish chronicles, between 1648 and 1653 almost one hundred thousand Jews and three hundred communities[6] died at the sword of the Cossacks and from the resulting chaos, famine and disease. The cruelties that the Cossacks practiced upon the helpless Jewish population were horrific, even for that barbarous time.

> Some were skinned alive and their flesh was thrown to the dogs; some had their limbs and hands chopped off and their bodies thrown on the road to be crushed by wagons and horses; some had wounds cut deep into them and were then thrown on the street to die a slow death, writhing in their blood and agony until they breathed their last; others were simply buried alive. The Cossacks slaughtered infants in the laps of their mothers. They were sliced open and skewered like fish. [Women, even pregnant women, were tormented horribly] . . . Children were pierced with spears, roasted on open fires and brought to their mothers to be eaten . . . Holy scrolls of the Torah were torn to pieces and turned into boots and shoes.[7]

It is no wonder that thousands of Jews preferred to fall into the hands of the Tartars who, though no less bloodthirsty than their Cossack allies, had a better business sense about the matter. Knowing that Jews the world over would ransom their captive brethren, even for

---

6. The total world Jewish population at that time is estimated to have been 3,500,000. Eastern European Jewry numbered 1,300,000.

7. *Yeven Metzulah*, Chapter 4.

exorbitant prices, they sold thousands of Jews to Turkish slave dealers who, in turn, "distributed" them to the Jewish communities of the Mediterranean coast. Rome, Bologna, Venice, Padua, Casablanca, Tunis, Salonika, Aleppo, and Jerusalem became the new homes of these Eastern European Jews. Thirty thousand of them were saved in this fashion.[8] Thousands of others died in captivity and transit, but on the whole this uprooted segment of Eastern European Jewry was considered fortunate and many of them later gained prominence in their new surroundings.

Overwhelming Slaughter

INITIALLY, THE COSSACKS ANNOUNCED that Jews who were willing to convert would be spared. Out of hundreds of thousands of potential converts, few took up the offer. After the Battle of Tulchin, at which the treacherous Polish gentry sold out their Jewish "allies" to the common Cossack enemy, one hundred and fifty Jews died with the *Shema* on their lips. Not one of them embraced Christianity. This poor showing enraged the Cossacks. And thus even many of the previous converts were slaughtered. Later, the ruler of Poland allowed all those Jews who had been forcibly converted to return to the religion of their fathers. Most did so. They were reaccepted into the Jewish community and were officially pardoned by the rabbinic authorities for their lapse. However, their apostasy, though temporary and pathetic, caused many of those Jews who remained loyal in the face of death to treat their lapsed brothers with coolness, if not open disdain.

The history of the people of Israel in its long exile should have shown the Church that honey catches more flies than vinegar. Faced with death or conversion, most Jews chose death. This was true in third- and fourth-century Rome, in eighth-century Syria and Mesopotamia, during the Crusades of the Rhineland in the eleventh, twelfth, and thirteenth centuries, and in fifteenth-century Spain and Portugal. It remained true in seventeenth-century Poland and Russia. However, in later times, when faced with the choice between the hope for a better life through voluntary assimilation or loyalty to their religion, vast numbers of Jews

---

8. *Yeven Metzulah*, Chapter 4, puts the figure at only twenty thousand. However, in later chapters Rabbi Hanover mentions other such instances, thus raising the total significantly.

would opt out of Judaism. Whether the Cossacks understood this lesson is an academic question. They hated Jews so much that even a mass conversion of all Israel would not have prevented this slaughter, though it may have mitigated its size and intensity. Thus, the obstinacy of the Jews was welcomed by the murderous Cossack mob, who obliged them with the greatest single slaughter of Jews from the times of the Roman conquests of Israel in 70 and 135 C.E. until the time of Hitler in 1940.[9]

So the Jews went to their deaths. They attempted to flee before the invading armies, and at times there were hundreds of thousands of them on the roads of Poland. However, those who were trapped in the besieged cities or surrounded by the marauding bands in the open fields and on the roads could offer little or no organized resistance.[10]

The Jews had been fierce fighters in earlier times. The wars of the Jews against the Romans had tested the imperial legions as did no other set of campaigns. Cowardice was never a Jewish trait and military skill was a Jewish talent from Biblical times. Against the Cossacks, too, Jews fought fiercely to save themselves when the opportunity arose. In fortified cities such as Ostroh and Lwow, Jewish resistance was strong and effective. Many Jews were able to escape death because of this armed defense. But the opportunities for such armed resistance were few.

Nevertheless, the people of Israel always were aware of the futility of martial arts, no matter how strong they knew they were. "Not by might nor by strength, but by My spirit, says the Lord of Hosts"[11] was the true slogan of Israel.

Now in an open-ended exile, beset by overwhelming enmity, in a time when individual freedoms and the rights of man were not even acknowledged, they assumed that the best defense was no defense. A low profile, a turned cheek, an unobtrusive presence, and an adjustment to the status quo, no matter how degrading and dangerous it was, were the main weapons of the Jewish arsenal. Ultimate reliance upon Godly favor, and a firm belief in the eternal promise of the survival of Israel over its enemies, buttressed this attitude. Jews would defend themselves bravely whenever they could. They would not proceed to

---

9. One must take into account that the means for mass slaughter available to the Cossacks in 1648-49 were rather primitive. Everyone had to be dispatched individually by sword or musket. Concentration camps, machine guns, gas chambers and crematoria would have to await a later and more advanced form of civilization.

10. Quoted by Hanover, *Yeven Metzulah*, Chapter 7.

11. Zechariah 4:6.

their deaths willingly as sheep to the slaughter, but they realized that prayer, piety and Torah scholarship were better guarantors of life and continuity than walls, muskets, or sabers.

The helplessness of the situation also influenced the behavior of the Jews. Their routes of escape were severed, and the reception they would receive from the Polish defenders, even if they escaped, was at best uncertain. Alone and despairing, the holiness of martyrdom held less terror for them than the misery of continued life under inhuman conditions. It was an act of sanctification and not of surrender, of ultimate bravery and belief.

Another consideration tinged the Jewish response to the slaughter of its people. It was an old Jewish tradition dating back to Biblical times that the death of the righteous and innocent served as an expiation for the sins of the nation or the world. The stories of Isaac and of Nadav and Avihu, the prophetic description of Israel as the long-suffering servant of the Lord, the sacrificial service in the Temple — all served to reinforce this basic concept of the death of the righteous as an atonement for the sins of other men.

Jews nurtured this classic idea of death as an atonement, and this attitude towards their own tragedies was their constant companion throughout their turbulent exile. Therefore, the wholly bleak picture of unreasoning slaughter was somewhat relieved by the fact that the innocent did not die in vain and that the betterment of Israel and humankind somehow was advanced by their "stretching their neck to be slaughtered." What is amazing is that this abstract, sophisticated, theological thought should have become so ingrained in the psyche of the people that even the least educated and most simplistic of Jews understood the lesson and acted upon it, giving up precious life in a soaring act of belief and affirmation of the better tomorrow. This spirit of the Jews is truly reflected in the historical chronicle of the time:

> Would the Holy One, Blessed is He, dispense judgment without justice? But we may say that he whom God loves will be chastised. For since the day the Holy Temple was destroyed, the righteous are seized by death for the iniquities of the generation.[12]

---

12. *Yeven Metzulah*, end of Chapter 15.

Rabbinic Leaders Suffer With Their Flocks

HE TRUCE BETWEEN CHMIELNICKI and the Poles was of short duration. In the spring of 1649, he and his Cossack army returned to the offensive. Marching northward, elements of his army reached southern Lithuania. However, his forces were now scattered and he could not defend himself at every point along the broad front. To further complicate Bogdan's life, his scheming allies, the Tartars, determined that they had gained all that they could from the rebellion and, in a lightning shift of sides — aided by gold and expansive Polish promises — they betrayed the Cossacks and joined the Polish forces. Realizing the hopelessness of his military position, Chmielnicki entered into negotiations with the Poles, and in August of 1649, the compact of Zborow was signed. During the winter of 1650, The Council of Four Lands[13] proclaimed the twentieth of Sivan as a public fast day. It was on that date in 1649 that 6,000 Jews were massacred in Nemirov, turning the river waters red. But the Cossacks were too restless after years of fighting and looting to settle down on the farm; in 1651 the revolution flickered anew but this time was put down by the Poles in the battle at Berestczko.

In a reversal of roles that is common in Jewish history, the victorious Poles now vented their wrath upon the hapless Jews of the area, accusing them of collaborating with the Cossack invader! In 1652, the Tartars again reversed themselves and rejoined Chmielnicki and the rebellion gained momentum once more. To further compound the chaos, a plague of cholera swept Poland in the summer of 1652 and in Cracow alone thousands of Jews died of the dreaded disease. The Jews,

---

13. The Council of Four Lands was an autonomous Jewish governing body which had limited governmental functions over Jewish communities in Poland, Lithuania, White Russia, and Volhynia (northwest Ukraine). Founded in 1527, it flourished in the sixteenth and seventeenth centuries. It sponsored a high court of appeals for judicial matters, and convened regular congresses of rabbinic and lay leaders. These congresses generally coincided with the great semi-annual mercantile fairs that usually took place in Lublin or Yaroslav. The congresses dealt with legislative, administrative, judicial and spiritual matters. The Council represented the Jewish community before the Polish monarchy, and policed internal Jewish matters. The council also had powers to tax and even inflict corporal punishment. It disbanded in 1764 when its power was revoked by the Polish authorities. The subsequent dispute between chassidim and misnagdim prevented its revival at a later time. An extensive record of the activities of the Council has been preserved in the *Pinkas Vaad Arba Aratzos* — the Record-Books of the Council of Four Lands.

reeling from almost five years of constant hell, abandoned their Polish communities and institutions and many fled to Russia, Lithuania, Germany, and the Balkan countries.

Among the great leaders of Jewish Poland at this fateful time was Rabbi Yehoshua Heschel of Cracow (1596?-1664). He was popularly known as the *Rebbe* Reb Heschel (this, one hundred years before the rise of chassidic *rebbeim*), and was a genius and charismatic personality. In Lublin, he headed one of Poland's largest yeshivos. In 1649 he was forced to flee Lublin, and the yeshivah disbanded. In 1654 he was able to reestablish it in Cracow, and it became the center of Torah learning in post-Chmielnicki Poland. However, his major efforts were directed at improving the welfare of the Jewish refugees in Poland, and he even traveled to Vienna to appeal to the Emperor for aid in this cause.

Reb Heschel's leading disciple in the pre-pogrom years was Rabbi David Halevi Segal,[14] the author of the commentary, *Taz* (acronym of *Turei Zahav*), to the *Shulchan Aruch* (Code of Law). Rabbi David was the Rabbi of Ostroh, Volhynia, when the Cossacks struck. He escaped with his family to Moravia, where he lived in poverty and pain until he returned to Lwow, Poland in 1658. There he re-established his yeshivah and continued to produce his works of prodigious scholarship. Though old and in ill health, he was one of the great shapers of the future of Polish Jewry through his efforts as one of the leaders of the Council of Four Lands. In 1664, a pogrom in Lwow killed over one hundred Jews, among them two of his sons. In 1667 Rabbi David died, mourning over his personal tragedies and the tragedies of his generation.

Rabbi Heschel's other great disciple, who was almost fifty years younger than Rabbi David HaLevi, was Rabbi Shabsai Cohen, known as the *Shach* (acronym of his halachic work *Sifsei Cohen*). This remarkable personage was a genius and an author of immense intellect, having published part of his famous commentary to the *Shulchan Aruch Yoreh Deah* when he was barely twenty-four years old. Forced to flee Vilna in 1655, he too eventually became a rabbi in Moravia. In his Moravian exile, he longed for his native Vilna, helped establish the twentieth of Sivan as the memorial fast day for the martyrs of 1648-49, and composed memorial prayers and poems to commemorate the occasion. He died a young man, far from his roots, with his greatness stilled in its prime by the terrible events of his generation.

Among the other rabbinic leaders who were uprooted by the

---

14. Segal is a common name used by Levites. However, he is usually known only as Rabbi David Halevi.

disaster were Rabbi Ephraim Cohen,[15] his son-in-law Rabbi Yaakov Zak,[16] Rabbi Menachem Mendel Krochmal,[17] and Rabbi Nathan Hanover.[18] All of them escaped to Moravia and eventually became prominent rabbinic leaders there and in Hungary. All suffered personal tragedy. Their absence weakened the Polish Jewish community even after the defeat of the Cossacks. It was a difficult time for all Jews, and the foremost rabbis of the time suffered mightily with their people.

Resolving Controversies

 HE POGROMS BEGINNING IN 1648 set off a chain of internal events among the Jews of Eastern Europe that would color their thinking and influence their pattern of life for centuries to come.

First of all, they brought about the settlement, once and for always, of certain controversies of the preceding century. In the middle of the 1500's, the definitive law book of the people and religion of Israel was published. The *Shulchan Aruch* (literally, *Set Table*) was written by Rabbi Yosef Karo of Safed, in the Land of Israel, and enhanced with glosses by Rabbi Moshe Isserles (*Rama*) of Cracow, Poland, to reflect the customs and opinions of the Ashkenazic Jews of Eastern Europe. Thus the completed work could be accepted as authoritative by both Sephardic and Ashkenazic Jews, and it was an instant success. As a result of the *Shulchan Aruch,* knowledge of the complexities of Jewish law and a definitive opinion regarding the practical behavior of a Jew became accessible to the masses. Many felt that having a *Shulchan Aruch* in one's house was, to a great extent, like having one's own private rabbi available for consultation. The advent of the printing press made the book a mass seller and it took immediate root in the soil of Jewish life.

However, every action begets a reaction. Many Talmudic scholars opposed the authority of the *Shulchan Aruch* and claimed that it would interfere with true scholarship and research, since scholars would not investigate the sources as rigorously as before. They also objected to its easy availability to the masses, who, they felt, would defeat the intent of

---

15. The author of *Shaar Ephraim*.
16. The father of Rabbi Tzvi Ashkenazi, the Chacham Tzvi.
17. The author of *Tzemach Tzedek* and eventually the rabbi of Nicholsburg and of all Moravia.
18. The author of *Yeven Metzulah,* quoted above.

the book due to their ignorance. Finally they were concerned that the effect of the *Shulchan Aruch* would be to undermine the authority and position of the local rabbi, who could either be ignored because of the accessibility of rabbinic decision through the use of the *Shulchan Aruch* or be refuted if his opinion did not appear to conform directly with the written word of the *Shulchan Aruch.*

The worth of the book was proven beyond argument during the terrible years of pogrom and exile. At a time when the great sages were being slaughtered or put to flight, when the Talmudic academies were disbanded and closed, when Jewish courts ceased functioning, Jewish law and tradition were preserved in the main by the presence of this extraordinary law book. Two of its foremost commentators, Rabbi David Halevi (the *Taz*) and Rabbi Shabsai Cohen (the *Shach*), suffered exile and near death in 1648 and 1649, but, ironically, their immortality was guaranteed by the terrible events of those years, since the *Shulchan Aruch,* together with their notes and commentaries to it, was now irrevocably installed as the basic post-Talmudic code of Jewish law and behavior.

Another controversy that had raged within Ashkenazic Jewry in the 1500's was how to interpret the events of the Spanish Inquisition and expulsion. Many thought that the terrible end of Jewry on the Iberian peninsula was a form of Divine retribution for the accommodation of Sephardic Jewry to the mores of Spanish life.[19] The dress, manners, and educational tolerance of Sephardic Jewry were roundly criticized by much of Ashkenazic Jewry as being non-Jewish. The echoes of the fourteenth-century struggle between the Ashkenazic and Sephardic Jews over the permissibility of the study of philosophy had still not died down. The Ashkenazim began to feel themselves superior in matters of Jewish law, scholarship and observance.

The shock of the debacle of 1648-49, which in ferocity and casualties far overshadowed the cruelty of the Spanish Inquisition, gave pause to Ashkenazic Jewry. They were unable to ascribe their troubles to any particular failing in Jewish observance, and assimilation with the local populace of Eastern Europe was both unwanted and impossible. They had no easy answers for the cause of the Lord's wrath against them. Just as they accepted the events of 1648-49 as God's will, they now came to accept its earlier manifestation in 1492 Spain.

Finally, tragic events of the time served to further spread and

19. See *Iggeres HaMussar* by Rabbi Shlomo Alami, quoted in *Toldos HaDoros* Vol. 2, p. 238, for a bitter description of the laxness of behavior of Spanish Jews.

popularize the concepts of the Kabbalah among Eastern European Jewry. The spread of the ideas of the Kabbalah among the masses of Israel had received its greatest impetus in the middle of the sixteenth century through the efforts of Rabbi Yitzchak Luria (the Holy *Arizal*) of Safed, Israel, and his disciples. At the time, however, the proliferation of these old-new ideas did not receive universal approbation. Traditionally, the study of Kabbalah had been limited to mature scholars who had mastered the Talmud. In the hands of the unlearned, unsophisticated masses, the mystical and metaphysical ideas of the Kabbalah could be dangerous.[20] For this reason, many great scholars opposed the spread of these esoteric teachings, and were frightened that such ideas would eventually lead to irrational behavior and heretical thought among the unsophisticated masses of Israel.

The horror of 1648-49, however, was not subject to rational explanation or cold, scholarly analysis. To be borne, it had to be understood on a completely different plane. The world of murder and cruelty could not be the real world. That real world, therefore, had to be a mystical existence that masked itself in the symbols of everyday living. The symbols could be unbearably evil, but the true world that they represented was glorious and worthwhile. Ultimately, one lived in a world of souls and spirits and not of bodies. Pain, death, and anguish could touch only bodies; nothing that Chmielnicki's hordes did could touch souls, which were the only lasting existence.

The sacrifices of the pogroms were necessary somehow to raise the potentially holy sparks of humanity from their lowly physical hosts and exalt them to the throne of Heaven. Thereby the terrible evil would be expunged and transformed into the general improvement of humankind — this was the real world and only by its particular, "unworldly" logic could one survive the onslaught on faith and reason loosed by Chmielnicki. After surveying the wreckage of their lives and communities, Eastern European Jews decided that the outer world was cold, unfriendly, deadly, and frightening. The inner kabbalistic world held out hope, comfort, and purpose. Thus, as the troubles increased, fewer voices were heard to oppose the spread of kabbalistic studies and beliefs among the masses of Eastern European Jewry.

---

20. See *Rama* to *Yoreh Deah* 246:4 and *Shach* ad loc. See also *Chavos Yair* 210.

Chmielnicki's Demise

N 1654, CHMIELNICKI TURNED to the Russian Czar for aid in his rebellion against the Poles, agreeing to place his Cossacks under Russian rule in return for a great deal of autonomy for his Cossack state. However, he proved a most unreliable vassal, for when the Russians invaded Poland later in 1654, he did not march with them. Instead, he now maneuvered for an alliance with Sweden, which then controlled large areas of Poland and Prussia and had an army on Polish soil. By joining with the Swedes, Chmielnicki hoped to achieve complete independence for his Cossack state and to deal mortal blows to both his Polish enemy and his Russian ally. The negotiations with the Swedes became protracted, and before they were completed, Chmielnicki died in August of 1657. The Russians and the Poles patched up their differences shortly thereafter, with Russia gaining greater dominance in the lands west of the Dnieper River. In a few years, the Cossack autonomy was curtailed completely by Russia. Fifteen years after its beginning, the Cossack revolution ended, having caused hundreds of thousands of deaths but achieving none of its goals. A great heroic statue of Bogdan Chmielnicki stands in Kiev today as a monument to one of the leading butchers of mankind.[21] As is often the case in human history, one man's butcher is another's hero.

By 1655, Jewish life in Poland began to return to normalcy. Pogroms became more sporadic, though they remained bloody, and Jewish refugees began to return to their previous dwelling places. Painfully, communities were rebuilt, Talmudic academies were reopened, the dead were buried and the living turned to the task of salvaging something from the cruel world. However, life would never be the same for Eastern European Jewry. The scars of 1648-49 were not healed even three hundred years later, when European Jewry ultimately met its Final Solution. *Tach V'Tat* was the harrowing watershed of Jewish history in Eastern Europe. Jews now knew that bad could become worse and that survival would be no small task in the Eastern European environment. That lesson would not be easily forgotten.

---

21. There is, as of now, still no monument in Kiev to the 35,000 Jews the Nazis murdered at Babi Yar. Statues are for the killers, not the victims.

2
Shabtai Tzvi

Formative Years

NREALIZED EXPECTATIONS LEAD TO dire disappointments. It had been thought by many Jews that 1648 was to be the Messianic year. Instead, in Eastern Europe it brought flames and agony to the Jewish population. Similarly, in Smyrna, Turkey, the year would bring the unveiling of the "Messiah," raising hopes for redemption that would prove false. It would be many years before Eastern European Jewry would regroup after the tragedies of 1648 and the Cossack revolution. It would also be many years before the debacle of the false messiah could be faced and overcome. The disappointment of being so badly duped by a false messiah would haunt the people of Israel ever afterward; in response to this, the public display of enthusiasm in later times for those promising messianic deliverance would be muted and hesitant. Once burned, twice warned. Never again would Israel take such claims at face value.

The facts of the story are clear and sad. Shabtai Tzvi was said to be born on the Ninth of Av,[1] the gloomiest day of the Jewish calendar, the day both Temples were destroyed and numerous other tragedies occurred. His parents were originally from Greece and probably descended from Spanish exiles, though this is not conclusively clear. Shabtai's family was undistinguished in scholarship and social standing, though his father did eventually become a rather prosperous merchant and was a commercial agent for a number of wealthy European traders.

The young boy received a traditional Jewish education. Possessed of a good mind and a diligent nature, he excelled in his studies. Before

---

1. Whether this date is accurate or legend is not certain. The Midrashic statement that the Messiah will be born on the Ninth of Av may have caused Shabtai's followers to choose that birthdate retroactively at his behest.

his twentieth birthday, he was reportedly ordained a *chacham* (the Sephardic rabbinic title) and apparently was well regarded in the scholarly circles of his community. Even though the study of the Kabbalah was usually reserved for people of greater maturity, Shabtai was initiated into the mysteries of that study early in his scholastic career. However, his bent toward mysticism was more deeply rooted in the tradition of the *Zohar*, the basic book of Kabbalah, than in the more contemporary mode of Lurianic Kabbalah.[2] He gained a wide reputation as a budding Talmudic scholar, and as an aspirant of note to the Kabbalah. He also began to practice ascetic ways: self-flagellation, total isolation from other human beings for long periods of time, innumerable immersions in ritual baths of purification, and other forms of behavior that caused his acquaintances to first consider him strange, then strangely holy, and, finally, purely pious and almost godly.

The young Shabtai evidenced a charismatic air that blinded others to his faults and encouraged abnormal adulation. Though all were aware of his strange behavior, he was widely respected. Eventually he was held in awe, revered, and feared. By the time he was twenty-two he had been married twice, though both marriages ended quickly in divorce because they were not consummated.[3] Apparently, by then he was also afflicted by the classic mental disturbance that would hound him all of his life, the recorded symptoms of which, as described by his contemporaries, suggest a manic-depressive psychosis. Although this illness sheds light on his future behavior, nevertheless his charisma, shrewdness, and attraction to others were sufficient to convince a great deal of the Jewish world that this insanity was really a gift of prophecy.[4]

In 1648 Shabtai first began to experience messianic delusions. The horrors suffered by Polish Jewry and the Messianic expectations for that year may have triggered the idea in his mind. In one of his manic moments he had an apocalyptic vision of himself saving Israel as its messiah. He told the dream to his immediate relatives and friends and they properly dampened his ardor. In 1650, he almost drowned while

---

2. Rabbi Yitzchak Luria — called the Arizal in Jewish history — flourished in Safed, Israel, in the middle of the sixteenth century and, through the revelations transcribed by his chief disciple, Rabbi Chaim Vital, was responsible for the explosion of kabbalistic study and practice among the Jews of the next generation.

3. See *Zos Toras Hakan'us* by Rabbi Yaakov Emden, Altona, 1752, quoting Leib ben Oyzer's Yiddish collections.

4. Jewish tradition maintains "that after prophecy was taken from the prophets it was given to the mad" (*Talmud Bavli, Bava Basra* 12b). His followers, however, hardly considered him mad. They considered him a *genuine* prophet.

swimming off Smyrna, and proclaimed that his deliverance was miraculous. Then he claimed to have warred with dogs, wolves and serpents, always miraculously prevailing. By 1651, his behavior and wild claims reached the ears of the rabbinical authorities of Smyrna. They threatened him with excommunication, but Shabtai mocked them publicly. They finally banished him from the community to the accompaniment of a thorough thrashing.

For the next seven years Shabtai wandered through the major Jewish communities of Greece, Albania, and Turkey. His charm and scholarship always stood him in good stead, and he made many friends wherever he went. However, the bizarre nature of his behavior continually caught up with him, and he was driven out of many Jewish communities, sometimes even undergoing the pain and humiliation of public flogging. During this period, Shabtai publicly violated many precepts of basic Jewish law and was guilty of behavior insulting to the holy Torah scroll. In 1658, Shabtai arrived in Constantinople and immediately earned the ire of the local rabbinate, which also attempted to excommunicate him. He then returned to his home in Smyrna where he remained for a number of years. It is there that his messianic pretensions gained wide publicity and the "new faith" was born.

Title page of Nathan's Tikkun Keriah which depicts Shabtai Tzvi as messiah, sitting on the kingly throne.

Strange Bedfellows

Y HIMSELF, SHABTAI TZVI COULD NOT have realized the coup of deceiving myriads of people. He was abetted by one of those strange characters who appear on the stage of history and, in spite of their lunacy, affect and influence a world that prides itself upon being sane and realistic.

That man was Nathan of Gaza, who became the "prophet" of the new messianic movement. In 1658, Shabtai revealed a new faith centered about his messianic pretensions. In 1662 he left Smyrna, traveled to Egypt, and from there embarked upon a pilgrimage to the Holy Land. The year 1663 found Shabtai in permanent residence in Jerusalem. There, Nathan, a young man still in his twenties, met the man

whom he would proclaim as the messiah. In 1665, the first and most grandiose of Nathan's messianic "prophecies" overtook him:

> . . . I was undergoing a prolonged fast in the week before the feast of Purim. Having locked myself in a separate room in holiness and purity, and reciting the penitential prayers of the morning service with many tears, the spirit came over me, my hair stood on end and my knees shook and I beheld the "*merkavah*"[5] and I saw visions of God all day long and all night and I was granted true prophecy like any other prophet, as the voice spoke to me and began with the words: "Thus speaks the Lord." And with the utmost clarity my heart perceived toward whom my prophecy was directed (that is, toward Shabtai Tzvi).[6]

Nathan, who, despite his relative youth, was well known as a Talmudist and kabbalist of talent, now spent a number of months convincing Shabtai Tzvi that he was indeed the messiah. By the summer of 1665, the team of Nathan and Shabtai was firmly established, and on the holiday of Shavuos of that year, Nathan proclaimed Shabtai the messiah at a public gathering in Gaza. Shabtai first demurred modestly, but then, adopting the role of leader and savior, he publicly admitted his "true" messianic nature and began tinkering with the observances and rituals of traditional Judaism.

His proclamation of messianic kingship spread in Israel and he returned to Jerusalem in triumph. The rabbis who had previously opposed or mocked him were now powerless even to criticize him, for the masses idolized him. Nathan adroitly explained away all inconsistencies and aberrations in Shabtai's personal behavior,[7] and also developed the theology of the movement, "proving" by Scripture and tradition that Shabtai was the true messiah. A wave of imagined cures, ostensible miracles and "supernatural events" followed. The bandwagon gained momentum. The millennium had seemingly arrived.

Shabtai's fame spread throughout the world. The Jews living around the Mediterranean basin were the first to flock to his banner. Jews in Greece, Italy, Syria, Egypt, and Turkey began to rid themselves

---

5. The Talmudic and kabbalistic term used in describing the celestial court and the throne of the Lord, as described in Ezekiel ch. 1.

6. Quoted by G. Scholem in his *Shabtai Sevi: The Mystical Messiah*, p. 204. Scholem, generally, is very biased against rabbis and traditional Judaism and this colors his scholarship. See Chapter 3, footnote 8.

7. A strange marriage in 1665 by Shabtai to the mysterious and adulterous "Queen Sarah" was only one of Nathan's problems.

of their earthly possessions preparatory to their trip to the Holy Land. Soon the good news spread to Western Europe. Wild rumors concerning the advent of the messiah reached Amsterdam and were believed by both the Jewish and non-Jewish communities. The wealthy, sophisticated and intellectual Jewish communities of Amsterdam, Hamburg, Altona, and Frankfurt am Main all fell victim to the Shabtai hysteria. Caution was thrown to the winds and "non-believers" were abused and punished. Fundamental changes in liturgy and religious practice were allowed because of the alleged messianic quality of Shabtai Tzvi.[8] Despite Shabtai's personal aberrations and heresies, many genuine religious leaders supported the movement he spawned, since they saw in it a vehicle for returning many lax and back-sliding Jews to the observance and knowledge of their faith.[9]

Rabbi Yaakov Sasportas

Rare were those who sensed the nature of the tragedy that was unfolding and were willing to take action to prevent it. Foremost among the opponents of the new messiah was Rabbi Yaakov Sasportas of Amsterdam. A concerned and imposing person, he polemicized against Nathan, Shabtai, and all their followers. Exiled from his home because of his opposition to Shabtai, Rabbi Sasportas continued the battle and rallied the doubters to publicly question the authenticity of Shabtai Tzvi. Nevertheless, to a great extent, his was a voice in the wilderness. Jews in Western Europe also began to sell and dispose of their homes and businesses. They chartered boats for the trip to the Land of Israel, engaged in flagrant penitential behavior, and openly threatened painful retaliation against their non-Jewish neighbors for past abuses.

Exposure as False Messiah

By the end of 1665 the messianic furor reached the Jewish communities of Poland and Russia. There too, all was swept aside by the fanatical belief in the messiah. Many of the most famous rabbis of the time were trapped in the snare of Nathan and Shabtai. Rabbi David Halevi[10] sent his son and

---

8. For many generations thereafter, the priestly blessing was recited on the Sabbath by *Kohanim* in the Spanish-Portuguese Synagogue in Amsterdam, an innovation of Shabtai Tzvi's time.

9. See for example, Rabbi Yaakov Sasportas, *Tzitzas Novel Tzvi* p. 121, for his criticism of this short-sighted policy.

10. The author of the *Taz*, he was one of the foremost commentators and legal authorities on the *Shulchan Aruch*. See Chapter 1, Tach V'Tat.

stepson to interview the messiah, and when they returned to Poland with purportedly magical gifts from Shabtai to the aged scholar, the venerable Rabbi David's name was enlisted in the cause of the new messiah by Shabtai's followers. This was fraudulent on their part, because Rabbi David never gave permission for the use of his name, although he never publicly repudiated Shabtai as a fraud. Apocalyptic propaganda abounded, and institutionalized life in the Jewish communities of Eastern Europe became chaotic. Everyone held his breath waiting for the inevitable climax of the drama to unfold, but no one foresaw the surprising and tragic end of this spectacle.

Shabtai installed himself as an emperor and held court in Smyrna and in Constantinople. Tribute, gifts, and emissaries were sent to him from all over the Jewish world. The Sultan of Turkey became aware of Shabtai's activities. The Sultan looked at all of these events with first a quizzical and later a jaundiced eye, but he took no action, since all of the activity was beneficial to the Sultan's purse and to the general economy of the Ottoman Empire. The Sultan also noted that Shabtai Tzvi was circumspect in his public statements and as of yet had not proclaimed himself to be superior to the sovereignty of the Sultan.

Shabtai, however, overstepped this boundary in the summer of 1666. He abolished the Jewish fast days of the Seventeenth of Tammuz and the Ninth of Av, days which commemorated the destruction of Jerusalem and the Holy Temple. He also engaged in public licentious sexual behavior, ate non-kosher foods, pronounced a newly formulated benediction "Who has permitted that which has previously been forbidden," and publicly announced that he would soon march upon Jerusalem to liberate it from the Sultan's rule. Complaints against Shabtai reached the Sultan from both Jewish and non-Jewish sources.

Alarmed at the seditious nature of Shabtai's behavior, the Sultan removed him to Gallipoli where he was technically under arrest. By bribing his wardens, Shabtai continued to act as an emperor and held court in the prison where he was confined. He was allowed unusual freedom and luxuries and continued to receive large delegations from many countries. His detention was explained by Nathan as being part of the developing stages of the Redemption, the "pangs of birth" of the Messianic Era. However, in September 1666, the Sultan tired of the game and had Shabtai brought before him to Adrianople.

In the middle of September 1666, Shabtai denied before the Sultan and his court any messianic pretensions on his part. The council of the Sultan then presented him with the choice of martyrdom or conversion to Islam. Shabtai Tzvi, "the messiah of Israel, the hope of the ages, the scion of David and the culmination of Jewish destiny," chose apostasy at the age of forty. He now adopted a new name, Aziz Mehmed Effendi, and accepted a royal stipend as well as an appointment as an officer at the Sultan's court.

The charade had come to an end. History had exposed the hoax. The news regarding the apostasy of the messiah spread throughout the Jewish world like a punishing plague. The skeptics were sickened by the accuracy of their prediction. The believers were shocked and paralyzed. The non-Jewish world hooted with derision.

After the initial trauma, the true believers, under the guidance of Nathan, developed a new theology and proclaimed that Shabtai's conversion to Islam was the concluding scene in the first act of the messianic drama and in no way canceled his efficacy as the redeemer of the Jews. However, even the naivete of the masses of Israel had limits and the rejection of Shabtai and his cult became widespread and strong. Hard-core pockets of believers would remain until the beginning of the eighteenth century, but by 1670 the messianic movement of Shabtai Tzvi had lost its credibility and popularity among the vast majority of Jews. The Jewish people put on as brave a face as possible about the situation, but their hearts were broken. Shamed, disillusioned, and frightened, they retreated within themselves to continue to wrestle with the age-old problem of guaranteeing Jewish meaning and survival.

Shabtai Tzvi and his movement were major elements in the great internal Jewish tragedy of the modern era. False hopes dashed prevented real hopes from being pursued and realized. A renegade messiah weakened faith among many in the basic validity of the idea of the true redeeming Messiah. The failure of intensely loyal Jews, who were innocently duped by the fraud, to triumph over their enemies would cause many passive Jews to look for their personal future elsewhere, by infiltrating and imitating the hostile non-Jewish environment. For some, the debacle of Shabtai Tzvi closed the door upon their Jewish commitment, and now their faith and their talents would be expended outside the confines of traditional Judaism. Thus, in a not too indirect fashion, Shabtai Tzvi was a factor in setting in motion those forces of history that introduced Reform, secularization, and assimilation to the masses of European Jewry. The bitter fruits of his long-severed tree are still to be tasted in the modern Jewish world.

3
Regrets and Recriminations

Heretics and Excommunication

SIDE FROM THE IMPACT of Shabtai Zvi's conversion on his immediate followers, the consequences of this act would be deeply felt by his contemporary opponents and by later generations as well. A spirit akin to vigilantism swept the Jewish world. Not only would former supporters of Shabtai Tzvi be scrutinized as to their current beliefs and behavior, but anyone not conforming to "acceptable" standards of behavior would feel persecution. The misuse of Kabbalah by Shabtai and his followers brought suspicion upon many learned and pious men. As often happens in times of danger and crisis, good men came to be tarred by the sins of miscreants. In order to eradicate once and for all the scourge of the false messiah, zealous men — even great men — could unwittingly trample on the lives of other great men who were innocent of Shabtai's guilt. Too often, the legitimate and necessary fight against Shabtaiism led to excesses, even to the stifling of creativity and individuality within the traditional Jewish world.

In order to further set the scene of the time, one must take into account previous breaches in the wall of traditional Judaism that centered in the city of Amsterdam. After their expulsion from Spain in 1492, great numbers of Spanish Jews settled in Amsterdam. They achieved stability, success, and security in their new home. The growth of the city from a small sleepy port to one of the major cities of Europe coincided with the rise and growing strength of its Jewish residents.

The Sephardic Jewish community of Amsterdam experienced many rumblings, however. The dislocation of exile took its toll, and the traditional authority of the rabbi and the communal authorities was not as all-pervasive as it had been in Spain. In spite of their weakening power, the rabbis acted quickly and decisively when they felt that Torah life was threatened. The first example of this was in the case of Uriel Acosta.

Born in Spain to a family of Jews converted to Roman Catholicism, Acosta early in life became disenchanted with Christianity, and, with his mother and brothers he fled to Amsterdam, where he returned to Judaism. Soon he lost his passion for Judaism as well, and published a rambling treatise accusing rabbinic Judaism of being non-Biblical and non-Jewish! In 1616 the rabbis of Amsterdam excommunicated him. Acosta recanted and was reaccepted into the Jewish community, but in 1624 he lapsed again, publishing an even broader and more disjointed work denying the immortality of the soul. He was immediately excommunicated again. He later recanted once more, but, depressed by his public humiliations, he committed suicide in 1640.

Acosta was the forerunner of a more famous heretic, Baruch Spinoza. Recipient of a traditional Jewish education, Spinoza rebelled against many of the fundamental beliefs of Judaism. He formulated his own metaphysical philosophical system which was at variance with basic Jewish beliefs; it was pantheism, the doctrine that identifies God with natural forces. Not being one to keep his views private, Spinoza created a furor in the local Jewish school by debating his beliefs with the students.

Spanish-Portugese Synagogue in Amsterdam

The rabbinic authorities attempted to have him retract his heretical viewpoint or, at the very least, remain silent. However, Spinoza's stubbornness forced them to take drastic action and, in July of 1656, he was officially excommunicated by the Jewish community of Amsterdam.[1] Spinoza went on to international fame and repute but always remained a renegade as far as Jews were concerned. Even an attempt by David Ben-Gurion, first Prime Minister of Israel, three hundred years after Spinoza's death, to posthumously rehabilitate him and remove the ban of excommunication, was greeted universally within Jewry by frosty silence and unforgiving apathy.

---

1. A visitor to the archives section of the library of the Spanish-Portuguese Synagogue in Amsterdam can see the ledger sheet which lists the members of the community in 1656 with a line drawn through the name of Baruch Spinoza.

Yavetz Versus Ramchal

THE RABBINIC AUTHORITIES OF Amsterdam and other Western European cities were not prepared to be tolerant of non-conformists in the aftermath of Shabtai Tzvi. The belief in him had now been proven to be a major, damaging heresy, and his apostasy loosed a flood of invective and vigilance against his believers and followers. This was legitimate and necessary, but, inevitably, in the zeal to uproot any vestige of Shabtai's beliefs and followers from the national body of Israel, many innocent people would also be punished. In excising the tumor of Shabtai, healthy tissue was also cut away.

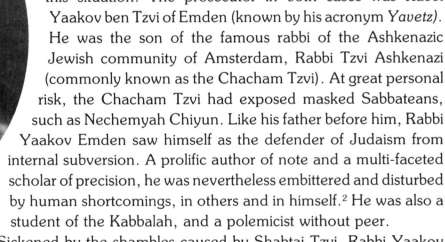

The Chacham Tzvi

There are two separate incidents that most clearly reflect this situation. The prosecutor in both cases was Rabbi Yaakov ben Tzvi of Emden (known by his acronym *Yavetz*). He was the son of the famous rabbi of the Ashkenazic Jewish community of Amsterdam, Rabbi Tzvi Ashkenazi (commonly known as the Chacham Tzvi). At great personal risk, the Chacham Tzvi had exposed masked Sabbateans, such as Nechemyah Chiyun. Like his father before him, Rabbi Yaakov Emden saw himself as the defender of Judaism from internal subversion. A prolific author of note and a multi-faceted scholar of precision, he was nevertheless embittered and disturbed by human shortcomings, in others and in himself.[2] He was also a student of the Kabbalah, and a polemicist without peer.

Sickened by the shambles caused by Shabtai Tzvi, Rabbi Yaakov Emden searched out suspected followers of the false messiah and sought to remove them from public Jewish leadership. He also included in his list of enemies those who publicly or privately practiced kabbalistic rituals and ceremonies, and distributed amulets to the populace. He felt that excesses of the kabbalistic fervor of the last century had contributed greatly to the original success of Shabtai Tzvi and were the basis of his appeal to the masses of the Jewish people. Although he himself was a distinguished kabbalist, he felt that the study of Jewish mysticism must

---

2. See his own autobiography, *Megillas Sefer,* Jerusalem, 1979, for many examples of this.

3. The study of Kabbalah in an intense fashion was usually reserved for married men over the age of forty who had first proved their prowess in mastering the traditional Torah and Talmudic studies.

once again be restricted to mature scholars, as had been the historic Jewish practice.[3] He was convinced that in order to snuff out the last embers of Shabtai's conflagration, the public practical use of Kabbalah among the masses of Israel must be stopped.

His first attack was upon a then almost unknown young scholar, Rabbi Moshe Chaim Luzzato (known by his acronym *Ramchal*). *Ramchal* was born in Padua, Italy in 1707. A man of insight and brilliance, who early on gained a reputation for Talmudic scholarship and analysis, he was quiet, introverted, serious, and studious. While he was yet an adolescent, his knowledge and the breadth of his intellectual horizons gained him adherents and students. However, his spiritual bent and his expertise in Kabbalah while he was yet young and unmarried brought him the suspicious glances of others.

At an early age (approximately twenty), *Ramchal* claimed powers of communication with a spirit from heaven that taught him many kabbalistic secrets and viewpoints. He was a prolific writer and, among other works, wrote a book of religious poetry, a Hebrew lexicon and grammar, books on Kabbalah, Jewish philosophy, metaphysics and theology, as well as his magnum opus, "The Path of the Righteous" (*Mesilas Yesharim*), which became the premier book in the field of Jewish ethics. He was, however, a nonconformist in his appearance, behavior, and even in his style of writing. His grasp of the Hebrew language was phenomenal and innovative. In his simple, sparse but haunting style, he broke with the accepted pattern of medieval rabbinic Hebrew. His language was a throwback to the classical style of clarity and simplicity exhibited by Maimonides and the Mishnah, yet *Ramchal* was innovative as far as vocabulary and sentence structure were concerned.

> Rabbi Moshe Chaim Luzzato was a pathfinder and pioneer, and this was the true reflection of his inner spirit and heart. He was the scout who came before the army. In every field of knowledge to which he contributed, he came as though he was the first to plow that ground. He reawakened the dawn of Jewish poetry after centuries of silence. He was the first to fully and clearly explain the rules of analytic thought as applied to theology. He was also able to pick up the thread of Jewish ethics woven by Rabbi Bachya in his *Chovos Halevavos*[4] centuries earlier, and thereby to combine in the study of ethics, scholarly

---

4. *The Duties of the Heart* — a primer of Jewish ethics and one of the premier works of Jewish thought, by Rabbi Bachya ibn Pakuda, who flourished in the eleventh century.

analysis with clarity of practical purpose, thus making ethics a definitive way of life and school of thought.[5]

It was *Ramchal's* love of Kabbalah that brought him to the attention of those committed to uproot the Shabtai heresy by opposing the public study and practice of mysticism. In 1729, a disciple of *Ramchal*, Yekusiel Gordon of Vilna, published a letter describing the ability of *Ramchal* to communicate with a heavenly teacher who introduced him to the intricacies of practical Kabbalah and also describing the "new *Zohar*" composed by *Ramchal*. This came to the attention of Rabbi Moses Hagiz of Altona, another famous son of a famous father, Rabbi Yaakov Hagiz, both of whom fought the Sabbatean heresy. Together with leading rabbis of Venice, Rabbi Moses Hagiz demanded that *Ramchal* be condemned. The rabbis of Padua forced him to agree to forsake some of his kabbalistic activities as long as he lived outside the Land of Israel, and not to publish his works without their approval. He surrendered his manuscripts to them as well. When, however, *Ramchal* continued to write works of kabbalistic study for his personal use, he was so severely criticized that he could no longer remain in Italy, and in 1734 his books were banned by the rabbis of Italy. Traveling north in Europe, *Ramchal* was humiliated by the leaders of Frankfurt am Main in 1735, and forced to take an oath that he would end his further study and practice of Kabbalah. He visited Altona and then moved to Amsterdam, where he became an optical lens grinder and diamond polisher.

Like Rabbi Moses Hagiz, Rabbi Yaakov Emden resided in Altona, and this virtually guaranteed that he would take a leading role in the opposition to *Ramchal*. Although he cleared *Ramchal* of suspected Sabbatean tendencies, Rabbi Yaakov Emden attacked him publicly and in writing for the kabbalistic activities that Rabbi Hagiz found objectionable. However, *Ramchal* remained silent in the face of the diatribe against him, and the onslaught abated. He lived in Amsterdam for a number of years, publishing many works, including the *Mesilas Yesharim*[6] which would give him undying fame, and reviewing his study and teaching of Kabbalah. In 1743, he and his family embarked for the Land of Israel and settled in the holy city of Tiberias. There, in his fortieth year, he met his untimely end in an epidemic of plague that swept the city. He is buried in the ancient Jewish cemetery in Tiberias near the grave of Rabbi Akiva.

---

5. *Tzintzenes HaMan,* Volume II p. 158, by Eliezer Shteinman, Tel Aviv.

6. *The Path of the Just*. This book on Jewish ethics became a basic text of the Mussar Movement one hundred and fifty years later.

Rabbi Yaakov Emden later regretted his campaign against *Ramchal*. Recalling that he was not asked to sign Rabbi Hagiz's original ban against *Ramchal* because of political machinations, Rabbi Yaakov Emden commented:

> I am grateful that he did me the favor of not having me sign the ban [against *Ramchal*]. I am willing to accept truth from any source even if it be from the smallest of the small, and if the only sin of *Ramchal* was in revealing secrets told him by a heavenly voice, may my share be like his share . . . and the mere fact that the he was yet so young and not married (while studying Kabbalah) is a slight transgression on his part — but it is not of so heavy a weight as not to be borne . . . Nevertheless, no intentional persecution was brought upon him . . . From Frankfurt he traveled to Amsterdam and settled there, and he became a diamond polisher, and is to be complimented for supporting himself gainfully. He published here two small works, *Mesilas Yesharim* and *Daas Tevunos,* and after living here for a few years, he traveled to Israel and it is reported that he died there.[7]

Rabbi Yaakov Emden
and Rabbi Yonasan Eybeshitz

HOWEVER, RABBI YAAKOV EMDEN'S main war was conducted against one of the great rabbis and scholars of the time, Rabbi Yonasan Eybeshitz. A great commentator on the Talmud and Jewish legal codes, Rabbi Yonasan was world famous for his wisdom and Torah knowledge. In 1711, when he was yet a very young man, he headed the Talmudic Academy in Prague, and later served in rabbinic posts there. In 1740 he moved to Metz, in the province of Alsace, and ten years later he became rabbi of Rabbi Yaakov Emden's home city, the great Jewish tri-community of Altona, Hamburg and Wandsbeck (known by its acronym AHU).

Rabbi Yonasan was known not only for his intellectual accomplishments, but as an active kabbalist as well. He was especially famous for distributing amulets, and his amulets were in great demand. This

Rabbi Yonasan Eybeshitz

---

7. Quoted by Abraham Bick in his book, *Rabbi Yaakov Emden*, Jerusalem 1974, Mosad Harav Kook, pp. 21-22.

practice raised the ire of Rabbi Yaakov Emden. In 1751, Rabbi Yaakov Emden discovered an amulet authored by Rabbi Yonasan Eybeshitz, which Rabbi Yaakov believed to contain veiled references to the apostate false messiah, Shabtai Tzvi. Rabbi Yaakov immediately called for a ban of excommunication against the "author" of the amulet, though he did not name Rabbi Yonasan explicitly. The Jewish community of Altona split in defense and condemnation of their rabbi, Rabbi Yonasan. The leaders of the community defended Rabbi Yonasan, closed Rabbi Yaakov's synagogue and printing press, and forced him on the defensive.

Rabbi Yonasan rallied his disciples and colleagues to his side. Such great personages as Rabbi Yechezkel Landau (known as the *Noda B'Yehudah*) of Prague, and Rabbi Elijah, the Gaon of Vilna, defended him. However, Rabbi Yaakov Emden continued his attack and also gained the support of the rabbis of Frankfurt am Main and Alsace in his battle against Rabbi Yonasan. Rabbi Yaakov was forced to leave his home in Altona and move to Amsterdam. The battle was so bitter and public that it reached the attention of Emperor Frederick of Denmark, in whose jurisdiction the city of Altona lay. The Emperor "decided"[8] that Rabbi Yaakov Emden was justified in his accusations and removed Rabbi Yonasan from his rabbinical post. However, the matter was appealed to the Emperor once again, and, in 1756, Rabbi Yonasan was returned to his post as Rabbi of Altona and the dispute finally died down.

Traditional Jewry viewed this tragic dispute with sad understanding. The innocence of Rabbi Yonasan Eybeshitz has been established[9] and his great works on the Talmud and Jewish law are still studied and admired. Rabbi Yaakov Emden has also been forgiven for his strong polemics. His great literary works, such as his wide-ranging books of responsa on Jewish law, his commentary on the prayers, and his glosses on the Talmud, gained him the admiration of his contemporaries and later generations. He suffered a life of sickness and pain, and the tragedy of the deaths of close relatives dogged him throughout his years. Both he and Rabbi Yonasan sought the truth and fought for its revelation with all of their talents. They both attempted to revive the people of Israel from the paralysis of Shabtai Tzvi. To some extent, they

---

8. Rumors were rampant that bribery and undue influence affected the Emperor's decision.

9. The acute bias against all traditional rabbis and rabbinic thought of such secular Jewish scholars as Graetz, and in modern times, Gershon Scholem, shows through in their strident accusations that Rabbi Yonasan was a secret follower of Shabtai Tzvi, even though all available evidence is to the contrary.

were both heroes and simultaneously victims of their time and of the historic events that preceded them.

One of the great men of Jewry, surveying the dispute from the vantage point of history one hundred and seventy-five years later, declared, "Were their dispute to have been contained among the leadership element of the Jewish people there is no doubt that the two great antagonists themselves would have resolved the dispute in their lives. Unfortunately, however, outside parties became involved and maximized the dispute."[10]

Rabbi Yaakov Emden died in 1776 on a Friday afternoon and was buried in the Jewish cemetery in Hamburg within hours. In the press of the necessarily quick burial, before the Sabbath, he was buried in an already opened grave only a few spaces away from the final resting place of Rabbi Yonasan Eybeshitz. Those who appeared to be so far separated in their lives were joined in their deaths in immortality.[11] But the struggle over the false messiah had not yet ended.

Jacob Frank

THE FINAL NOTEWORTHY EVENT of this sad time was the last gasp of the messianic movement of Shabtai Tzvi in Poland. Under the leadership of Jacob Frank, a Polish Jew who traveled extensively in the Middle East, the remnants of the Shabtai movement rallied and once again asserted their messianic mission. The behavior of Frank and his associates was scandalous and licentious, and the rabbis were quick to respond with bans and excommunications.

The Frankists complained about the rabbis and the Jews generally to the local authorities and tricked the leaders of the Polish Catholic Church, especially the Bishop of Kaminetz-Podolsk, into believing that the Frankists could and would convert the Jews of Poland to

---

10. This statement has been attributed to Rabbi Abraham Kook, the late Chief Rabbi of Israel.

11. There is a Chassidic tradition that, in his last moments, Rabbi Yaakov welcomed a vision of Rabbi Yonasan, who had died in 1764. On that basis, Rabbi Yechezkel Landau [the *Noda B'Yehudah*], who was in Altona at the time, concluded that Rabbi Yaakov could be buried in the same row with Rabbi Yonasan, even though the local custom followed the exhortation of Rabbi Yehudah HaChassid that "enemies" not be buried in the same row. Zunz, *Gedulas Yonasan*, Israel, 1968.

Catholicism. The Bishop forced the local rabbis to meet the Frankists in a public debate in 1757. The rabbis were adjudged to have "lost" this contest and were ordered by the local authorities to pay a fine to the Frankists. In addition, many copies of the Talmud were confiscated and burned, mostly in Podolia. In 1759 the Frankists again forced their rabbinic opponents into a debate. This debate, however, was held under more impartial auspices, and the Frankist doctrines were refuted. Nevertheless, the Church continued its pressure on the Frankists to carry out their promises to convert themselves and to lead Polish Jewry to the baptismal font. In desperation, Frank himself led five hundred of his followers in being baptized at ceremonies of great solemnity held in Lwow. However, the Church soon sensed the fraudulent nature of Frank and his conversion, and, like his hero, Shabtai Tzvi, Jacob Frank was arrested and imprisoned. He was released in 1772, and together with his daughter, Eve, continued to propagate his messianic nonsense until his death in 1791.

Thus ended the saga of the last of the major false messiahs. However, the damage inflicted by Shabtai Tzvi and Jacob Frank was severe and lasting. New winds were now blowing and the old protective walls were tottering. Internal dissension, mental fatigue, and unending poverty and persecution were the lot of the Jews in Europe. Radical new solutions for the Jewish problem were on the way as the Jewish people were propelled into the modern age.

Section II

Enlightenment,
Reform,
and Modernity

1730-1830

4

The New World
and the Changing Old World

HE JOURNEY OF CHRISTOPHER COLUMBUS across the frightening Atlantic must be reckoned as one of the turning points in the history of civilization. The age of exploration and discovery would now also become the age of hope and stirring. Notwithstanding the rapacity of the colonial empires, the cruelty of the pioneers of settlement, and the annihilation of ancient and worthy peoples and civilizations — the net result in the eyes of the Western world of the colonization of America was progress, wealth, and freedom from the medieval bonds of serfdom, clericalism, and hopelessness. The New World, especially North America, was not only a new stage for the drama of civilized man, but its discovery created a new dimension for his yearnings and struggles. America, and all that it would later come to represent, would master Europe, inexorably change it, and itself usurp the dominant role in the story of man. But all of this was not yet visible even to the most far-seeing savants of Europe, in 1492.

It was not an accident of events that Columbus sailed from Palos on August 3, 1492, the very same day when Jews the world over were completing their mournful observance of the Ninth of Av, the anniversary of the destruction of both the First and Second Temples in Jerusalem. That doleful day had even more tragic implications that year than usual for the people of Israel, for it marked the final deadline for the expulsion of the Jews from Spain. It was the last day by which Jews had to leave Spain or convert, on pain of death at the stake.

On that Ninth of Av, the great Biblical commentator and Spanish-Jewish statesman, Don Isaac Abarbanel, led approximately 80,000

Jews across the Spanish border to Portugal. Now the reign of terror of the Inquisition and the torture of the Marranos grew in scope and fury. Only later would the irony of the Divine plan be seen: on that very day when Spain chose to close out six centuries of intense and productive Jewish life on its soil, Columbus sailed to discover a new continent where there would be a safe haven for Jews (and others) and where the people of Israel would once again be able to rise to a preeminent role in general society. That black day in August 1492 had a ray of brightness to it. Pity that this did not become apparent for another four centuries.

The discovery of the New World caused many new tensions in Europe. The competition between England and France for domination of North America brought the French and Indian War to the American colonists. However, it also was an integral part of the great Seven Years' War in Europe, where it involved not only England and France but Austria, Prussia, and Russia as well. Any European war caused great panic among the Jews of Europe. Their lot in life was so bitter that the issues over which monarchs and statesmen sent young men to die had no meaning to the Jews; they really had nothing more to lose (but their lives). Thus they were not in the forefront of change in the eighteenth century. Yet, while not being overtly disloyal, they were hardly interested in the perpetuation of the status quo. Thus, in the eyes of European Jewry, the enlightened despotism of Frederick the Great and the growing strength of democratic parliamentary forces in England were certainly preferable to the black despotism of the Czars.

Jews had had relatively little experience with England over the centuries. They had been expelled from the country during the Crusades,[1] but their memories of England were not nearly as sad as were those of France, Germany, Spain, and Russia. Thus the growing success of British imperialism the world over, and England's emergence as one of the major continental powers, were viewed with admiration and hope by European Jewry. From the middle of the eighteenth century until the middle of the twentieth century, Jews in Europe would look to England to champion many of their interests and aspirations.

The discovery and settlement of America also accelerated the diminution of the role of the Church in European life. The Reformation, Counter-Reformation, and the wars of the sixteenth and seventeenth centuries severely undermined the hegemony of the Catholic Church.

---

1. In 1656, Oliver Cromwell allowed the Jews to return to England. It is interesting that Shakespeare, whose portrayal of the Jew Shylock is far from flattering, probably never saw a Jew.

Modern Christian man was specifically going to be less Catholic, and generally less formally religious, and certainly less interested in theology and other-world problems. The Church was still far too strong to be openly opposed or even safely ignored, but it was certainly a sign of the times that the leaders of colonial America were not known for their religious beliefs or piety.[2]

The New World did not wish to reimpose the religious tyranny of Europe on its shores. Freedom *of* religion meant freedom *from* religion as well, and even though discrimination and persecution based on religion would continue to exist in America, the noble ideals of tolerance and equality found expression in practical terms in the New World as they never had in Christian Europe. Thus, at a time when the Church was forced on the defensive in Western Europe, Europe's Jews began to imagine a freer and more open society in which they too could function.

However, the greatest influence of America on European life generally, and the Jews particularly, lay in the mere fact that it was there. It stood for a new beginning, a continent without history, an undeveloped colossus there for the taking. It provided the first physical alternative to the squalor and pain of European ghetto life. In the emerging independence of the United States lay the hopes of the masses of Europe. There were very few Jews in the original American colonies, though during the time of the Revolution there were some Jewish Patriots (as well as Jewish Tories). The Jewish population in North America was barely more than a thousand in 1776 and not really a factor in the Revolutionary War. Most of the Jews in the thirteen British colonies were Spanish-Portuguese. The original Jewish families — Seixas, Mendes, Levy, Touro, Solomon, and others — had little communication with their Jewish brethren in Europe. But the fact that they existed was known to the Jews of Europe, and the knowledge that America could become a place of immigration and refuge was stored in their collective brain. A century later this would be translated into mass action and movement.

Thus, the freedom of the colonies and the establishment of the United States signaled a new age for Europe. The new American experience would ultimately demand that Europe also attempt to reform itself. Western man would now have the opportunity to build a society free of the old chains of monarchy, Church, feudalism,

---

2. Jefferson, Hamilton, Paine, Franklin and others were agnostics, if not atheists.

and despair. The struggle between the old and the new, between authoritarianism and democracy, would throw Europe and the world into turbulent chaos for the next two centuries. But modern Western man believed that the hoped-for result was worth the pain and suffering. The Jews of Europe would have to react to these new realities. Full of hope and fear, they would also adjust to the forces of change unleashed in Europe by "the shot heard round the world" at Lexington and Concord.

For the Jews living in the Old World in the seventeenth and eighteenth centuries, these changes were yet imperceptible. The age of "reason," the time of "enlightenment," had not yet taken hold in Western Europe, while Eastern European Jewry was still in the process of recovery from the scourge of Chmielnicki. Great rabbinical figures still were the norm of Jewish society. However, the old forms of life were under attack in Christian Europe. With the collapse of the bastions of the monarchy, the Church, and the privileged nobles, would also come the collapse of the walls of the ghetto.

In Western Europe first, new ideas and new forms began to take hold. These external upheavals would rock internal Jewish structures and bring challenges to the very uniqueness of Israel as a religion, culture, and society. The responses to that challenge, the restructuring of Jewish life, the salvation of the Torah and its people now become our story. Just as the description of war requires the reader to view many isolated incidents individually before he can grasp the totality of its horror and purpose, so, too, must we recognize the individual events, personalities and directions of the eighteenth and nineteenth centuries in order to appreciate the overall challenge that the entrance of the modern era brought to Jewish life.

5
Moses Mendelssohn

NE OF THE FUNDAMENTAL DIFFERENCES between the traditional Jewish perspective of history and the secular humanist perspective is in their divergent views of the causal relationship of historic change. Modern historiography, as developed through the period of the Enlightenment, postulated the theory that there are historic imperatives that govern all human life. The individual in no way controls or shapes human history; he is barely a participant in it. There are huge, impersonal, cataclysmic forces that sweep away nations, civilizations, and eras, and the efforts of puny individuals to stem the tide or even influence its direction are meaningless.

Not so, states the Jewish view of history. All historic forces are of Divine origin and are implemented by man, according to his free choice and will. Judaism has always thus been able to reconcile man's freedom of action with God's will, which guides all historic events. God rules all, initiates historic change, and shapes all human behavior. Yet, He does so through man, and man's free choice and personal ideas are the instruments of the Divine purpose. Thus man creates history, shapes destiny, and fosters change. The visible force in history is man and his behavior, wisdom, and folly — it is constrained only by the general indefinable parameters of God's universal rule. Therefore, though the events of eighteenth- and nineteenth-century Europe — which are so central to the story of the Jewish people — are certainly in consonance with God's purpose, they were the products of human beings, of people, and not of formless, inexorable historic forces.

One of these human beings was a German Jew named Moses Mendelssohn. His personal biography reflects the story of one of the first

Jews in the Western world to win a place for himself in the alien non-Jewish world. But, as later events would so sadly prove, the triumph of Mendelssohn would prove to be hollow, temporary, and ultimately deceiving. Mendelssohn and his contemporaries sowed the wind; European Jewry would reap its whirlwind two centuries later.

All of the falseness of the Enlightenment[1] and its "benefits" for Jewry would be mirrored in the story of Mendelssohn. He loosed forces that would be destructive to myriads of Jews individually and to the Jewish people as a whole. The harshness of Jewish history's judgment upon him is a reflection of the incipient disaster that he was so prominent in fashioning. He saw himself as a hero to his people. History would cast him differently.

Moses Mendelssohn

Moses ben Menachem Mendel (hence his family name, Mendelssohn) was born in Dessau in 1729 (hence his frequently used appellation, Dessauer). He was a wonder child, possessed of great intellectual powers and enormous diligence.[2] He received a thoroughly traditional Jewish education and was very well versed in the Talmud and Bible. However, at the age of fourteen he traveled to Berlin and there, under various Jewish tutors, acquired a broad secular education which influenced him in attempting to reformulate the truth of traditional Judaism. He eventually found employment with a rich Jewish silk merchant, became his bookkeeper, tutor, and eventually his partner. But he was not to earn his fame in the mercantile world.

He became acquainted with Gotthold Lessing, one of the great German men of letters of his day, and through him came to the attention of the leading German intelligentsia of the time, including members of Prussian King Frederick's court. Mendelssohn's philosophic works, written in brilliant German, began to appear in print, and by 1763 he was one of the most honored and noted scholars in Germany. Nevertheless, he remained an outwardly observant Jew, even after his acceptance in German philosophic and intellectual circles. In his own eyes, Mendelssohn never seriously compromised his Jewish faith or practice.

Initially, he received rabbinic approbation for many of his works and corresponded with some of the leading rabbis of Germany, Bohemia

---

1. The Enlightenment was a movement of thought and belief which was popular in eighteenth-century Europe. Its dominant conviction was that correct reasoning and scientific understanding would lead to true knowledge, human peace, and social progress without the necessity for religion as a factor in human life.

2. His unremitting application to his studies brought on an illness that left him permanently disfigured by a severe curvature of the spine. *The Jewish Encyclopedia*, Vol. 8, p. 479, Funk and Wagnalls, 1916.

and Poland on a regular and friendly basis.[3] However, he later would be isolated from all rabbinic approval and, still later in his personal life, he strayed from the meticulous observance of tradition that marked his youth. Mendelssohn translated the Hebrew Bible into German, fought tenaciously for Jewish civil rights as an integral part of the reforms of the Age of Reason and Emancipation, and defended Judaism against the attacks, intellectual and otherwise, of the non-Jewish world. His *Phaedon* and his later work, *Jerusalem*, represented vigorous apologia for Judaism and the Jews.

Yet Mendelssohn is viewed, and correctly so, as the father of Reform Judaism.[4] Some of his own children and most of his grandchildren became Christians. He opened the gates to the torrent of assimilation and intermarriage that characterized Western European Jewry in the eighteenth and nineteenth centuries. His name became a symbol of change and controversy, and eventually of a cruel hoax. The seeds of this bitter fruit can be seen in Mendelssohn's own writings and in his approach to Judaism and the Jewish people. Though he did not coin the phrase, Mendelssohn was the spiritual father of the famous motto of the nineteenth-century *Haskalah,* or Jewish Enlightenment: "Be a cosmopolitan man in the street and a Jew in your home." Time and events would prove the impossibility of that dichotomy, but in the eighteenth century, at the height of the Enlightenment, Mendelssohn believed it possible. He mistakenly saw himself as the prime example of the realization of this goal.

Like many other geniuses, he assessed his exceptional qualities naively and did not appreciate his uniqueness. He was convinced that since he, Mendelssohn, could remain moderately observant and openly

---

3. Among them, Rabbi Yonasan Eybeshitz of Hamburg and Rabbi Hirsch Lewin of Berlin. However, he was severely criticized from the outset by other great rabbis of the time, such as Rabbi Pinchas Horowitz of Frankfurt am Main (see p. 79), Rabbi Yechezkel Landau of Prague, and Rabbi David Tevele of Lisa. *Jewish Education in Germany in the Period of Enlightenment and Emancipation* by Mordechai Eliav, Sivan Press, Jerusalem, chapter 1, quotes the polemics against Mendelssohn by the rabbis of the time.

4. Current Reform spokesmen are resistant to claim him as their spiritual father. "Only in the broader sense may it be said that Mendelssohn was the spiritual father of Reform, in that he attempted to make his contribution to human thought and at the same time live as a Jew. He was meticulously observant, deeply learned, and confessed proudly that he was a member of his people. Living in two worlds had its problems . . . but on the whole he succeeded and thereby showed that it could be done." W. Gunther Plaut, *Judaism*, Vol. 36 Number 2, Spring, 1987 "Living in Two Worlds — Reform Judaism in the Diaspora."

Jewish at the court of the Emperor and in the leading intellectual salons of Europe, all other Jews could and would do so as well. However, when the Enlightenment was loosed on the masses of Jewry, many of whom were ill prepared to deal with the new world unless they could discard their old one, it would have tragic consequences.

Mendelssohn did not appreciate this clear danger and therefore was personally hurt and stung by the opposition of many of the great rabbis of his day to his approach to modernity and Judaism. He mistook their opposition for vindictiveness and obscurantism. The opportunity for equality and civil rights, for intellectual and economic advancement, blinded Mendelssohn to the terrible risk and danger inherent in the complete acceptance of the tenets of the Enlightenment. His rabbinic opponents were more cautious and more perceptive and events proved them wiser. The dictum of the Talmud,[5] "Who is a wise man? — One who foresees what will yet be born," was their yardstick of events. The rabbis saw in Moses ben Menachem Mendelssohn not the superficially devout Jew fighting for Jewish rights, but rather Mendelssohn's grandchildren, who were converts to Christianity, and already suffering the pangs of self-hatred that is the lot of all apostate Jews. The rabbis recoiled from that sight.

Mendelssohn's own premises about Judaism were tainted by his acceptance of the philosophies of the Enlightenment. He was not only wrong practically, but theoretically as well. He was guilty of poor judgment, but, far worse, of not realizing where his errors would lead. Though he himself believed in Sinai and Divine revelation, he explained that the ritual laws of the Torah applied only to Israel, and were to lead to the understanding of the moral and philosophical ideas of the Torah, which were universal and subject to human reasoning and understanding.

This basic attitude regarding the faith of Israel was his ultimate undoing. His followers took his ideas to their ultimate conclusion. Since the great moral ideas of the Torah were meant for all of mankind, and since now in the Age of Enlightenment all mankind was united in the pursuit of good, there was no need for Israel to retain its observance of the Torah's particular ritual laws. Rather, Jews should join the rest of society in implementing the moral truths of the Torah. Furthermore, since the Enlightenment, and especially the philosophy

---

5. *Talmud Bavli*, *Tamid* 32a.

of Immanuel Kant,[6] proposed man as the sole arbiter of human universal moral ideas, the Torah was binding only to the extent that man was willing to accept its individual teachings. From this flowed the rejection of traditional Jewish life and of ritual observance, the stripping of Divinity from the Bible, and the loss of respect for the ancient truths of Judaism.

This theory of personal moral judgment, encouraged by Mendelssohn, grew into Reform Judaism. It declared that reason, rather than faith, is the source of truth and that human intelligence and experience alone are capable of guiding human destiny and moral behavior. Reform, through Mendelssohn, but more strongly later through Abraham Geiger and Samuel Holdheim in the post-Mendelssohn generation, became the ultimate Kant — Mendelssohn's rationalism extended to its illogical extreme. It may have been rational, it may have been ethical culture, it may have been humanist, but it was no longer Judaism.

Mendelssohn also firmly believed in the inherent positive efforts of Western culture and the Enlightenment. He did not see culture as a "handmaiden of Torah,"[7] rather he viewed it as an end in itself. Culture would uplift and ennoble Jews, just as he felt this enlightened culture had already begun to redeem general society. Mendelssohn therefore saw his German translation of the Bible not only as a medium to make the Torah understandable to estranged and non-Hebrew-speaking Jews, but rather more importantly, as a means to educate Torah-knowledgeable Jews in the use and understanding of the German language!

In effect, he was the first of a long line of apologetic Jews in the modern era. Mendelssohn wanted Jews to have an aesthetic view of the world, an appreciation of the arts, a knowledge of literature and poetry and a philosophic harmony regarding life. He was certain that his

---

6. German philosopher (1724-1804). He was the leading philosopher of modern times, the exponent of "critical," "transcendental," or "formal" idealism. His *Critique of Pure Reason* and his *Inquiry to the Distinctness of the Principles of Natural Theology and Morals* are works of influence and prestige even today. Dayan I. Grunfeld's trenchant essay-introduction to the English edition of Rabbi S.R. Hirsch's *Horeb*, Soncino Press, London 1962, p. LXXIV, explains Kant's philosophy as follows: "Kant, whose moral philosophy is the culmination of nineteenth-century individualism, insisted on moral autonomy to such an extent that any law coming from the outside (heteronomy), even if that outsider (heteros) is God Himself, must be subjected to the scrutiny of man's own conscience and moral self-legislation. To Kant, only autonomy was the basis of true morality."

7. The traditional medieval rabbinic term used to describe secular arts and sciences.

commentary on the Torah, the *Beiur*, was a "necessary first step towards culture." He was convinced that Judaism could survive in an enlightened cultural world, only if it was part of that culture. Jewish worth was to be measured by outside criteria, by Esau's opinions of Jacob, by what the standards of European Enlightenment would allow. What would not pass the standards of contemporary German Enlightenment would be discarded from Jewish thought and practice.

"Mendelssohn's purpose was to gain approval by the non-Jewish world, and therefore he would not accept the ideas and legends of the rabbis unless they were in conformity with the general beliefs of the nation (Germany) and its inhabitants."[8] This viewpoint of a Jewish inferiority-complex vis-a-vis general culture would have strong echoes in the house of Israel over the next two centuries.

His own weakening observance of a Torah lifestyle, combined with his slavish imitation of Enlightenment values and ideas, distanced him from Jewish perspective and tradition. By the end of his life, he was the grandfather of Christians, both literally and figuratively. His experience should have been an example for later "reformers" and "enlighteners" as to the true results of non-Jewish thought and behavior. Perhaps it was. When Mendelssohn died in 1786, Europe was poised on the edge of momentous change. Revolution, constant war, the Industrial Revolution, and radical new doctrines concerning social change all were on the way. The old Europe was disappearing and the new one would topple the ghetto walls. But the Jews would emerge innocently into a much more dangerous world than Mendelssohn ever envisioned.

---

8. Flekele's criticism of Mendelssohn quoted by Mordechai Eliav, p. 38 note 69.

6

Reform Sweeps All — Almost

Emancipation and Its Options

HE INTOXICANT OF PERCEIVED freedom caused many Western European Jews to lose their historic perspective. In their headlong dash towards emancipation and equal rights, the sacred "baggage" of the ages was perforce discarded. Much of it was willingly abandoned, but some of it disappeared almost unnoticed by its owners. The impetus for this radical change in Jewish life was the equally radical change in political Europe.

Beginning in the 1780's, liberalizing laws — "Edicts of Toleration" — were put into effect in Prussia, the German States, the Austro-Hungarian Empire, and even in Italy and the Papal States. In 1781, the Emperor Joseph II of Austria began the process of removing restrictions on Jews attending universities and opened new avenues for them in the trades and the market place. In 1784, Louis XVI of France, in one of the last acts of the dying monarchy of the Bourbons, abolished onerous special taxes on Jews. In 1781, the great German thinker, Christian Wilhelm Dohm, published his famous treatise "On the Improvement of the Jews as Citizens." Dohm's basic thesis was that Jewish people were on the whole pretty despicable, but that granting civil rights and freedom of opportunity to them would help improve and civilize them. Dohm maintained that full civil liberties for Jews was the method "by which they can be cured of this corruption so as to become better people and more useful citizens."[1] Thus, the case for Jewish freedom was stated in terms that would still pander to the German distaste for the Jew and yet appear to be in harmony with the new liberal tenor of the times.

---

1. *Encyclopedia Judaica*, Volume VI, p. 153.

The greatest impetus to political emancipation of Jews in Western Europe was provided by the French Revolution and its Napoleonic aftermath. Voltaire and Rosseau were no friends of the Jews; in fact, their writings were laced with derogatory and defamatory statements about Jews and Judaism. But they were trapped into "tolerance" by their own radicalism. "Liberty, Fraternity, and Equality" had to somehow apply to Jews as well, so the fall of the monarchy and the rise of the Republic brought a degree of political equality to French Jews. On September 27, 1791 the new National Assembly of France passed, by a narrow margin and only after a heated and bitter debate, the law of complete emancipation of the Jews. The virus of French anti-Semitism was still strong and prevalent, but the ideas of the French Revolution, spread throughout Europe, would bring the Jews a measure of physical freedom and social and economic opportunities heretofore unknown. In those heady times, many Jews and non-Jews felt that "the Jewish problem" was now amenable to solution.

Benjamin Disraeli

In spite of the upheavals of the Napoleonic era,[2] Jews continued to make steady progress in the areas of civil liberties and economic opportunities in the early nineteenth century. But as the outer world opened for Jews, their inner world began to crumble. Many Jews were convinced that Judaism in its traditional form was outmoded and irrelevant in the new, modern era. Above all, they saw their Jewishness as an obstacle to their economic and social advancement.

To these Jews only two options were open. The first was apostasy, usually in the form of conversion to the local dominant Christian denomination. Some of the most famous Jewish apostates of the early nineteenth century have left an enduring legacy, for good or evil, on world developments. Disraeli, in England, was the great architect of Victorian imperialism and enshrined the British Empire as the dominant force in nineteenth-century world affairs. Heinrich Heine became the muse of modern German literature. His genius of language and thought made him the leading literary figure in Europe. Though he was an expatriate from Germany for most of his life and died and was buried in Paris, he remains even today one of the strongest literary figures for Germans and Germany. Karl Marx unleashed the doctrines of dialectical materialism, capitalism versus communism, the dictatorship of the proletariat and class warfare on Europe and the world. His great work *Das Kapital* and his other works (*The Communist Manifesto*, et

Heinrich Heine

Karl Marx

---

2. See the later chapter regarding Napoleon and the Jews.

al.) became the bible of the atheist Left, and Marxism itself remains an undefinable ideal that still stirs passion in millions and panic in other millions today.

These famous apostates, along with many others of their day, were all cursed by terrible feelings of guilt which they translated into virulent self-hatred and base anti-Semitism. Disraeli, the most moderate of the apostate Jews, stated: "I look upon the Church as the only Jewish institution remaining. The Jews owe everything to the Church."[3] Disraeli's father, upon converting to Christianity, said that "the Talmud was a complete system of the barbarous learning of the Jews. The Jews have no men of genius or talent to lose. I can count all their men of genius on my fingers. Ten centuries have not produced ten great men."[4] Heine was even more vitriolic. But he was also terribly cynical about his own conversion. He stated that "baptism was the entrance ticket to European culture. I should not like if you saw my baptism in a favorable light. I can assure you, if our laws allowed stealing of silver spoons, I would not have done it."[5] Yet he also said that the Jews believed "there is only one god — Mammon; and Rothschild is his prophet."[6] He condemned "the three evil maladies: poverty, pain, and Jewishness."[7] His statements of self-hatred would become part of the literature of the new anti-Semitism of nineteenth- and twentieth-century Europe.

Most demented of all the Jewish apostates in his opinion of Jews and Judaism was Karl Marx. His small book of concentrated venom, *A World Without Jews*, is full of ranting hatred. Marx dangerously crossbred anti-Semitism with his new theories of economic and social revolution. The enemy of all progress was now the Jew. It was the Jew who was responsible for all the ills of the world, for the Jews somehow had forced this value system and social ideas on the non-Jewish world. "Money is the jealous god of Israel, besides which no other god may exist. Money abases all the gods of mankind and changes them into commodities. It has therefore deprived the whole world, both the human world and nature, of their own proper value. Money is the alienated essence of man's work and existence; this essence dominates

---

3. M.N.C. Salbstein, *The Emancipation of the Jews in Britain* (New Jersey, 1982).

4. Salbstein, op. cit.

5. Jeffrey L. Samorens, *Heinrich Heine; A Modern Biography* (Princeton, 1979).

6. Op. cit.

7. Op. cit.

him and he worships it. The God of the Jews has been secularized and has become the god of this world."[8]

Marx, like many apostate Jews, suffered terrible pangs of guilt and violent anger regarding his situation.[9] He lashed out virulently and vituperatively at Jews and Judaism. But, ironically, his foes nevertheless tarred him with the brush of Judaism. The Russian exile, Bakunin, criticizing Marx's social engineering ideas, attacked Marx personally. He wrote, "Marx is by origin a Jew. He unites in himself all the qualities and defects of the gifted race. Nervous, some say, to the point of cowardice, he is immensely malicious, vain, quarrelsome, [and] is intolerant and autocratic."[10] Apostasy may indeed have been the ticket of entry to modern nineteenth-century European society, but the apostate never really finished paying for that ticket. Nevertheless, the nineteenth century saw the highest number of Jewish conversions to Christianity since the days of the forced conversions of the Spanish Inquisition. It is estimated that more than 250,000 Jews converted in the nineteenth century in Central Europe alone.[11] Thus, the specter of large-scale desertion of Judaism by emancipated Jews haunted the thoughts of Western Jewish leaders.

---

8. T.B. Battenove, *Karl Marx, Early Writings* (London 1963).

9. "The hostility of [Marx] to everything connected with religion, and in particular with Judaism, may well be partly due to the peculiar and embarrassed situation in which such converts sometimes found themselves. Some escaped by becoming devout and even fanatical Christians, others by rebelling against all established religion. They suffered in proportion to their sensitiveness and intelligence. Both Heine and Disraeli were all their lives obsessed by the personal problem of their peculiar status; they neither renounced nor accepted it completely, but alternately mocked at and defended the religion of their fathers, incapable of a single-minded attitude toward their ambiguous position, perpetually suspicious of latent contempt or condescension concealed beneath the fiction of their complete acceptance by the society in which they lived." Isaiah Berlin, *Karl Marx,* Oxford University Press, 1963, p. 22.

10. Op. cit. p. 90.

11. Paul Johnson, *A History of the Jews,* Harper and Row, 1987, p. 312.
". . . Christianity was not so much a name for a religion as 'the only word expressing the character of today's nineteenth-century international civilization in which numerous millions all over the many-national globe felt themselves united.' A man felt he had to become a Christian in the nineteenth century in the same way he felt he had to learn English in the twentieth. It applied to countless non-white natives as well as Jews."

Accommodating to the Times

THE SECOND OPTION, THEREFORE, Reform Judaism, seemed to be a more reasonable one for many of these Jews. Convinced that traditional Torah Judaism had no future in the modern world, and frightened by the conversion of so many Jews to Christianity, the leaders of Reform feverishly sought to accommodate an ancient faith to a swiftly changing society. They wagered their future on the ideals of the nineteenth century, sacrificing the hard-won national experiences and historic truths of three thousand years in the process. They lost the wager. The first Reform temple was dedicated in Seesen, Germany in 1810. Israel Jacobson, who headed that temple, introduced an organ, a mixed choir, German sermons, German songs, German prayers and ecclesiastical robes to the ritual.[12] A Reform temple opened in Berlin in 1815, but was closed in 1823 by a government edict that stated, "the Divine services of the Jews must be conducted in accordance with the traditional ritual and without the slightest innovation in language, ceremonies, prayers or songs."[13] Reform, however, continued to grow and, despite great rabbinical opposition,[14] gained control over many of the Jewish communities of Germany.

Abraham Geiger

The leader in this thrust of power by Reform was Abraham Geiger, who was active in the Jewish community of Breslau. An avowed radical, he espoused complete rejection of Talmudic Judaism. Indeed, he spoke of the need to abolish all the institutions of Judaism.[15] Samuel Holdheim, even more radical than Geiger, eventually headed the

12. *The Jewish Encyclopedia*, Volume X, p. 354.

13. Op. cit. The government was then afraid of the liberalizing influences in the society and thus opposed reform with regard to religion and society. Orthodox Jews would soon learn by bitter experience that appealing to government to enforce tradition was a dangerous if not foolhardy expedient. Government is fickle, if not sometimes malicious. Thus, from 1824 onward, all edicts of the states of Germany regarding Jewish matters were now to "remove the abuses which had crept into the synagogues and to introduce reforms." The government then had changed to a more liberal mode and was in favor of changes in society.

14. Led by Rabbis Baruch Oser, Moses Jaffe and Yechiel Speier, all of Hamburg; S.A. Tiktin of Breslau, Isaac Bernays, also of Hamburg; Solomon Trier of Frankfurt, and Mayer Weil of Berlin.

15. Paul Johnson, *A History of the Jews*, p. 334. Also see Dayan Grunfeld's essay (footnoted here in Chapter 5 of this book, footnote 6) for a more thorough treatment of Geiger's reforms.

Reform congregation in Berlin. He argued against circumcision, covered heads during worship, wearing a *talis*, the blowing of the *shofar* on Rosh Hashanah, the use of the Hebrew language, the belief in a Messiah, the mention of Zion, Jerusalem or the Land of Israel in the services ("we know of no fatherland except that to which we belong by birth or citizenship")[16] and Saturday as the Jewish Sabbath (he changed it to the Christian Sunday).

German Reform also abolished the "automatic assumption of solidarity with Jews everywhere."[17] Thus German Reform took no active role of protest in 1840 over the Damascus blood libel and resulting pogrom there.[18] By the middle of the nineteenth century, Reform had dethroned Jerusalem in favor of Berlin.[19] Adherents of Reform described themselves as "Germans of the Mosaic persuasion" but no longer as Jews.[20]

The initial success of Reform sent shock waves through the traditional rabbinate. All of their efforts to stem the spread of the new movement had failed. In effect, the vehemence of the rabbinate's opposition seemed to confirm the accusations of their emancipated foes that traditional Jews were intolerant, backward and doomed to social extinction. This was especially true when the German state governments began to back Reform in the 1830's.[21]

It was not only the substance of traditional Judaism that Reform rejected. Even more, it abhorred the image, the distinctiveness, of traditional Jews. Jewish beards and black clothes, certain mannerisms of hands and eyes, and Jewish speech dialects all had to be eliminated before Jews could take their rightful place in modern European society. Therefore, almost in the spirit of evangelical fanaticism, Reform undertook to rid the Jewish people of its old image. The

---

16. *The Jewish Encyclopedia,* Volume X, p. 357.

17. Paul Johnson, *A History of the Jews,* p. 334.

18. This was not true of the Reform movement in France which actually took up the cause of the Syrian Jews.

19. See the frighteningly prophetic comment of Rabbi Meir Simchah Hacohen of Dvinsk in his Biblical commentary *Meshech Chochmah* (written in 1909) to Leviticus 26:44, regarding the fate of "those who call Berlin their Jerusalem."

20. Zechariah Frankel, who himself was "enlightened" (Conservative Judaism claims him as its spiritual progenitor), commented that "the [Reform] society cannot be considered Jewish; it belongs to Judaism as little as to any other religion."

21. It became the policy of some of the separate state governments of Germany to liberalize society and religion in order to bring about a more enlightened atmosphere in the country.

traditional Jew, or better put, the image of that traditional Jew, became a target of Reform's efforts and enmity. As could be expected, traditional Judaism and Jews responded in kind. The lines of division and opposition were clearly and irrevocably drawn. Eventually the increasing tempo of assimilation and Enlightenment drove Reform to an even more radical, less Jewish bent. Reform attitudes and intentions took on a more universalistic, socially political hue, and distanced themselves completely from Jewish traditional values and life.

Nineteenth-century German and American Reform so significantly diminished Jewish liturgical, ritualistic and theological distinctiveness that it was left with precious little with which to provide a collective Jewish purpose. Unwilling to maintain the traditional notion of the "Chosen People," Reform thinkers sought some other compelling justification for perpetuating a distinct communal entity, when even Christian liberals persuasively urged assimilating Jews to convert to more "enlightened" and "progressive" (read: Christian) religions. To address this issue, Reform rabbis conceptualized Judaism as one of several enlightened religions whose chief purpose was to instruct Jews in the same universal moral principles embodied in Christianity. In so doing, they invested "Chosenness" with new meaning. The corporate Jewish raison d'etre now became a mission to bring higher moral ideals to the wider society by leading an exemplary ethical life and by participating extensively in socially useful causes and movements. For only in laying special claim to leading an ethical life and doing justice could Reform thinkers argue for the continuity of a distinctive and identifiable Judaism that they had stripped of "unreasonable" features: its ancient legalisms, primitive rituals, outmoded symbols, as well as the historic quasi-national self-image.[22]

Failure of Expectations

EFORM'S EARLY SUCCESS also ultimately proved to be the source of its own undoing. For even in its most radical form, Reform did not provide the solution for the "Jewish problem." The greatest appeal of a new idea is the hope

---

22. Stuart M. Cohen, *American Modernity and Jewish Identity* (Tavistock Publications, New York and London 1983), pp. 28-9.

that it provides for the solution of current problems and its promise of an improved future. The greater the idea, the more radical its proposals, the higher the expectations it engenders. Therefore, the inability of the new proposal to truly solve the already existing problems automatically throws the new solution on the ash heap of history.[23] By the end of the nineteenth century, European Reform had exhausted itself of any regenerative powers. It never represented the majority of Jews in the world; it was divorced from the mainstream of Jewish history, tradition and destiny; it never "normalized" the Jewish situation in Europe; and it became little more than a conduit for further assimilation, intermarriage, and conversion to Christianity. Reform's main growth would be achieved later, in America.[24]

Leopold Zunz

Beginning in 1819, Reform also spawned a new type of Jewish scholarship, which, it hoped, would give greater acceptance in the non-Jewish world to its new "modern" form of Judaism. It was a secular scholarship, based upon research of Jewish works of literature and scholarship throughout the ages, unencumbered by belief in Divinity, sacredness of text or the observance of traditional respect for the ancient rabbis and their disciples and spiritual heirs. This movement reached its apex in the *Society Feur Die Wissenschaft des Judentums* — the Society for the Science of Judaism. While the society disintegrated due to the conversion to Christianity of its members, this type of scholarly pursuit continued. The secularization of the holy would later appear in Jewish Eastern Europe under the style and guise of *Chochmas Yisrael* — the "Wisdom of Israel." Isaac Jost, Leopold Zunz, Edward Gans, and Heinrich Graetz were the main scholars who propagated the new Jewish science. Moritz Steinschneider, Marcus Jastrow, and David Friedlaender, together with Rabbi Zechariah Frankel of Breslau, also endorsed the new effort to remake Judaism in the form of secular scholarly study. Despite its voluminous research and scholarship, the movement made no vital or lasting impression in the Jewish or the non-Jewish world. It treated Judaism as a museum piece, as an ancient, dying religion, and attempted to explain it to the world before it completely passed from the scene. It was a science in the nature of being an autopsy on traditional Judaism. Its primary, though not

Heinrich Graetz

Moritz Steinschneider

Rabbi Z. Frankel

23. One is reminded of the caustic remark of Rabbi Moshe ben Nachman (*Ramban*) in 1267, at his debate with Pablo Christiani before King James of Aragon regarding the promise of Christianity — "Woe to a world such as ours is now, if this is how it appears after the coming of the Messiah."

24. See the later chapters: "Emigration to America" and "Assimilation Forever."

exclusive, error was its failure to realize that the corpse was not yet dead. Eventually, the Science of Judaism would lose popularity while traditional Judaism, which it attempted to dissect and analyze coldly and scientifically, Divinely survived.[25]

25. There are still major Judaic studies departments in many universities in the Western world but the number of traditional Talmudic students in world Jewry today far outnumbers the remaining disciples of the Science of Judaism. In the words of Rabbi Dr. Ezriel Hildesheimer, the Rector of the great Orthodox Rabbinical Seminary of Berlin, "Jews are more interested in knowing what *Rashi* has to teach us than in knowing what were the color of the clothes *Rashi* wore."

7
Orthodoxy Responds

Rabbi Isaac Bamberger

RTHODOX JEWRY RESPONDED to the new society of Emancipation and Reform in varied fashion. Initially, it was overwhelmed by the rapidity of Reform's advance. The majority of Western European Jews were blinded by the light of the new freedom and, in leaving the ghetto, they were willing to leave the traditional Jewish life practiced in the ghetto as well. By 1850, Reform had become dominant in the official *kehillah* life of many communities throughout Western and Central Europe. However, Orthodoxy had by then mounted a strong counter-attack. This rejuvenated Orthodoxy was the product of the prodigious efforts of many powerful rabbinic leaders,[1] who represented the varying responses to the challenge posed by Reform.

One of these men was Rabbi Isaac (Seligman Baer) Bamberger[2], known as the Rav of Wurzburg, in Bavaria. In his community he strengthened Orthodoxy in the time-honored fashion, forming a large synagogue congregation, opening and maintaining a yeshivah as well as a rabbinical training program, and, in 1855, establishing a complete Jewish educational system from elementary school to higher education. He was a Talmudic scholar of note, and a prolific author of books on *halachah*, Talmud, customs and Hebrew grammar and exegesis.[3] He also had a broad secular education, though it was informal and non-university oriented. Because of his personality, education, great

---

1. Among the leaders of German Orthodoxy who fought Reform tenaciously were Chacham Isaac Bernays (1792-1849), the rabbi of Hamburg; and Rabbi Yaakov Etlinger (1798-1871) of Altona, author of the famous Talmudic work *Aruch LaNer*. They were the primary early mentors of Rabbi Samson Raphael Hirsch.

2. 1807-78.

3. One of his more popular works was *Amirah L'Veis Yaakov*, published in Furth in 1858.

rabbinic stature and moderate behavior, he proved an elusive target for Reform and helped stem the tide of Reform in Germany.

With almost no exceptions, German state and city law required all Jews to belong to a single religious community. When Reform came to dominate most of these *kehillah* structures, Orthodox Jews were forced to remain tax-paying members of the Reform community, even in cases where the new leaders closed such institutions as the yeshivah and the *mikveh* (ritual bath). Many Orthodox leaders fought for the right to secede and form their own communities. Gradually, the German legislatures granted these rights, and in 1876 it became the law in Frankfurt am Main, as well. Once German law permitted Jews to secede from the Reform religious community and form their own *Austritts Gemeindes*, or separate Orthodox communities, such independent communities were established in several cities.

Rabbi Bamberger was a pragmatist. Where it was possible for the Orthodox to maintain their autonomy within the general community, he opposed secession. However, in those communities where Reform had prevailed and would not accommodate Torah Judaism, Bamberger advised the formation of an *Austritts Gemeinde*. He firmly believed that by positive deeds — building synagogues, yeshivos, and schools — Reform would itself be influenced and that the traditional forms of Judaism would eventually prevail. For this reason, once the Reform community of Frankfurt am Main offered to moderate its hostility and accommodate the needs of the Orthodox, Rabbi Bamberger came out publicly against secession. In this he opposed Rabbi Samson Raphael Hirsch, who led his followers into an independent *Austritts Gemeinde*. Rabbi Bamberger's stand caused Frankfurt Orthodoxy to split. Bamberger's pragmatic view was adopted by many of the Orthodox Jews in Germany, who viewed him as a champion of Orthodoxy.

Rabbi Samson Raphael Hirsch

 MAJOR FIGURE AND great leader of German Orthodoxy was Rabbi Samson Raphael Hirsch.[4] This remarkable person was the father of what came to be called Neo-Orthodoxy, a movement which Hirsch himself more correctly characterized as *Torah im Derech Eretz* — "Torah with the ways

4. 1808-1888.

of the world." At the age of twenty-two, he became rabbi of Oldenburg and there, in 1836, he published his first famous work, *The Nineteen Letters of Ben Uziel*.[5] This original work, written in German, made a profound impact on many rootless young German Jews, and provided a focus for an intelligent examination of traditional Judaism in the light of the new Enlightenment. Hirsch's later works — *Horeb*, his commentaries to the Bible, to Psalms, and the *Siddur,* and countless articles and letters — all were in the same vein. They were written in flawless, literary German, and were cogent and relevant to the times. Hirsch was incisive and fiercely protective of traditional Judaism, its values and customs.

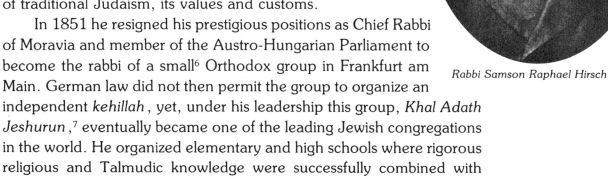

Rabbi Samson Raphael Hirsch

In 1851 he resigned his prestigious positions as Chief Rabbi of Moravia and member of the Austro-Hungarian Parliament to become the rabbi of a small[6] Orthodox group in Frankfurt am Main. German law did not then permit the group to organize an independent *kehillah*, yet, under his leadership this group, *Khal Adath Jeshurun*,[7] eventually became one of the leading Jewish congregations in the world. He organized elementary and high schools where rigorous religious and Talmudic knowledge were successfully combined with thorough secular studies. His congregants fully integrated themselves in German economic and professional life. They attended universities, dressed stylishly and were good citizens. But they were fiercely loyal, observant, uncompromising Jews who did not discard any custom or law of Judaism.

Hirsch attacked Reform head-on. He borrowed all of its "positive" aspects — education, social acceptance in manners and dress, and the veneer of Western culture — and integrated them into a thoroughly traditional, punctiliously observant Jewish community. He not only refused to compromise with Reform, he refused to associate with it. He had no inferiority complex regarding Orthodoxy.

In 1876, a new German law finally permitted Jews to secede from the official community. Hirsch took this opportunity to separate himself and his congregation from the larger German-Jewish community which

5. First translated into English by Rabbi Dr. Bernard Drachman, New York, 1899.

6. Eleven families had petitioned for the right to establish a separatist Orthodox community. They represented more than one hundred and fifty families in this endeavor.

7. In German, it was known as the *Israelitische Religions Gesselschaft,* or Israelite Religious Society. Thus, since it could not become a "congregation" under German law, it functioned as a "society."

was so heavily dominated by Reform. Unlike Rabbi Bamberger, he championed the case of the *Austritts Gemeindes* in Frankfurt and wanted not so much to influence Reform as to free himself and his community of Reform. As a matter of religious principle and intellectual honesty, he refused to extend any form of communal recognition to Jewish organizations that denied the Divinity and authority of the Torah. His *austritt* was a declaration of the invalid nature of Reform-dominated communal organizations. He articulated the principle that any "Judaism" that denied the authority of the Written and Oral Torah was inherently false; therefore, as a matter of principle, Orthodox Jews could not give it the recognition implied by membership.

Hirsch never saw Western culture as being more than a "handmaiden of the Torah law."[8] It was not an end, but rather a means to an end — that end being a fully Torah-observant life and value system. His system demanded *Torah im Derech Eretz* — Torah *with* the ways of the world, but never *Derech Eretz*, the ways of the world, alone. Hirsch's philosophy of life, the raison d'etre of man, is "Not to see God, but to see the earth and earthly condition, man and human conditions, from God's point of view. It is the loftiest height that can be reached by human minds here on earth, and that accordingly is the one good to which all men should strive."[9] Culture is not the goal. The goal is Godly service and Godly perspective. Culture, knowledge, the arts, Enlightenment are all legitimate tools in the pursuit of this goal, but they are never more than tools. Hirsch preached the doctrine of Jewish self-worth[10] in the face of Reform's Jewish self-abasement. He stated that Torah had nothing to be ashamed of in its relationship to human civilization. It did not need to be "reformed." On the contrary, it alone represented the ultimate goal of that civilizing process.

---

8. See Hirsch's commentary to Leviticus, 18:5, for a brief essay regarding the understanding of the value of secular studies within the framework of a Torah life. His major thrust there is " . . . the permission to occupy oneself also with other spheres of knowledge (outside Torah studies) is assumed. Only, the knowledge of the Torah and the understanding we derive from it is to be our principal concern and to regard it as having been given to us as the absolute and firmly established truth, . . . so that when we study and occupy ourselves with other spheres of knowledge we still never leave the basis and aims of the Torah to which alone our intellectual work is dedicated . . ."
9. Hirsch's commentary to Exodus 23:20.
10. See Hirsch's commentary to Genesis 49:7.

The Chasam Sofer

NOTHER MAJOR ORTHODOX counter-force against Reform was Rabbi Moses Schreiber-Sofer.[11] Known as the Chasam Sofer (the name given to his great works of Torah scholarship and rabbinic responsa), he was born and raised in Frankfurt am Main. At an early age he was known to the scholars of Frankfurt as a *wunderkind*. The rabbi of Frankfurt then was the famous Talmudist, Rabbi Pinchas Horowitz.[12] He and other great scholars in Frankfurt were influential in shaping the young genius. One of them, Rabbi Nosson Adler,[13] became the young man's primary teacher, guide, and mentor. Rabbi Adler was a giant of intellect and piety, but he ran afoul of the communal and rabbinic authorities in Frankfurt due to his sponsorship of prayers and meditation sessions in his home, which were conducted according to kabbalistic principles and rituals, and in contradiction to the accepted custom and ritual of Frankfurt Jewry. The young Moses Sofer was initially shielded from the dispute when Rabbi Adler sent him away to study in Mainz at the yeshivah of Rabbi Tevel Sheier. There, the young man grew great in Torah scholarship and also gained knowledge in biology, anatomy, botany, astronomy, mathematics and history,[14] all of which knowledge is evident in his later writings.

The Chasam Sofer

In 1779 he returned to Frankfurt to continue his Torah studies with Rabbi Adler. However, shortly thereafter, Rabbi Adler, who continued with his own private prayer house and kabbalistic practices in spite of warnings from the leaders of the *kehillah* to desist, was placed in *cherem*, or public ban, by the communal authorities. Thus in 1782, when his mentor, Rabbi Adler, left Frankfurt to become the rabbi of Boskowitz, Moses Sofer accompanied him there, never to return to Frankfurt.[15]

Rabbi Sofer led schools and communities in Boskowitz, Prustitz, Dresnitz, and Mattersdorf. He saw the attempts of Reform to overrun the Jewish communities of the Hapsburg Empire. He sensed the

---

11. 1763-1839.

12. Commonly known as the *Hafla'ah*, after the name of one of his great Talmudic commentaries (see p. 79).

13. 1741-1800.

14. Yehudah Nachshoni, *Rabbi Moses Sofer,* p. 53, Jerusalem 1981, quoting Rabbi Leib Landsberg's biography of Rabbi Sofer.

15. However, he always signed his responsa "Moses Sofer of Frankfurt am Main."

problems of his time and saw the gifts of the Emancipation to Central European Jewry — limited civil rights, greater economic opportunity, and a freer personal life — as a Trojan horse that would destroy communal Jewish life and Jews individually. Thus, when in 1804 he was offered the position of rabbi in the famous imperial city[16] of Pressburg,[17] he sensed an opportunity to turn the tide against Reform. His accomplishments in Pressburg were legendary. He built a great yeshivah which was the bulwark of Orthodoxy in Central Europe for the ensuing century. His disciples became the rabbinic and communal leaders of Austria, Rumania, and Hungary. And their watchword was that Reform "would not pass" through the gates of their communities.

The Chasam Sofer styled a motto that symbolized his attitude toward Reform and Enlightenment: *Chadash asur min haTorah,* or "Newness is forbidden by the Torah." By this he meant that any innovation not sanctioned by Jewish tradition was dangerously harmful to Judaism. The Chasam Sofer was no obscurantist. He was not opposed to positive developments in Jewish life, education, and demeanor. His yeshivah in Pressburg, its curriculum and educational way, was in itself an innovation for its time.[18] He spoke and wrote fluent German, represented the interests of Jewry at the court of the Emperor, took part in the defense of Pressburg against the armies of Napoleon in 1809, and was thoroughly conversant with the social trends of his age. But he was primarily a giant in piety, Talmudic stature, and rabbinic leadership, who reminded all of an earlier and greater era.

He was a kabbalist of eminence,[19] a halachic judge of boldness and decisiveness, a defender of the poor, the widow and the orphan, a poet and person of deep sensitivity, a pliant and soft-hearted person, and yet a fierce, iron-willed defender of Jews and traditional Judaism. He saw that what today seemed attractively modern could tomorrow be fatal

---

16. The Hapsburg dynasty maintained a number of imperial cities in their empire, foremost being the capitals of Vienna and Budapest.

17. In today's Czechoslovakia, it bears the Slavic name of Bratislava.

18. For a marvelously human and incisive picture of life at the yeshivah in Pressburg see *Olamo shel Abba,* by Rabbi Anshel Miller, Jerusalem, 1984, beginning at p. 44. Among the many innovations of the yeshivah in Pressburg was an ordered curriculum of study, emphasis on training in public speaking, communal educational projects with the laity of the city, and a rigid and set system of exams on the Talmudic subjects covered in the classroom; but the parameters of Torah study and piety that characterized the yeshivah were part of the ancient tradition of Israel.

19. See the stories regarding his amulets and other kabbalistic mystical workings in Nachshoni, p. 100.

to Jewish survival. He fought tenaciously for the retention of the most minute *minhag* (custom) of Israel. Any departure from the observance of *halachah,* any compromise in ritual or outlook, was a conduit to eventual assimilation, conversion, and disappearance. Assimilation, he felt, was an internal urge of the person to deny his Jewishness. Therefore any form of public pardon or condoning of that negative inner urge by Orthodoxy was foolish, self-defeating, and eventually treacherous. Hence, *"Chadash asur min haTorah."* He was wont to say, "He who mocks Jewish customs cast doubts on his own Jewishness."[20]

The Chasam Sofer advocated complete separation from any Reform element within the Jewish community. His views on separation were even stronger than Hirsch's. "If it were left to me," he wrote, "I would remove [Reform] completely from the Jewish camp. We should not marry their children, nor should we follow them in any fashion. They are like the Sadducees, the Karaites. We will remain with our tradition and let them leave."[21] He used his influence at the court of the Hapsburgs to oppose the granting of further rights or recognition by the government to Reform. He steadily opposed the Reform preacher, Aron Horin, the leader of Reform in Austro-Hungary, and exposed him as an ignorant charlatan.[22] He accused Reform of behaving in an un-Jewish manner and pounded home this theme relentlessly. And his tenacity won the day and preserved most of Central European Jewry in its traditional form for many years. Only later in the nineteenth century did the Reform movement make significant progress in Hungary.

The Chasam Sofer was not a polemicist. He did not write books or articles in his battle with Reform,[23] yet his deeds spoke loudly and lastingly, and his attitude and tactics toward Reform served as a model for later generations and set a standard of loyalty to tradition in Jewish life that has survived till today. The modern era has brought terrible divisiveness to the Jewish world. But it would be in the crucible of this internal struggle that the Jewish people would be annealed, and its fate and survival depended on the outcome of that struggle.

---

20. Nachshoni, p. 23.

21. Nachshoni, p. 209, based on a text quoted in the biographical work on the Sofer family, *Chut Hameshulash.*

22. Horin's children converted to Christianity. See the responsa that the Chasam Sofer devoted to Horin and his innovations, *Responsa of Chasam Sofer,* vol. 6, Responsa 84-92.

23. See his *Likkutei Teshuvos,* Responsa 84 for his reasons not to publicize his war against Reform.

8

The Rothschilds
and Moses Montefiore

Mayer Amshel Rothschild

Mayer Amshel Rothschild

THE EMANCIPATION BROUGHT new winds of thought and practice into the Jewish world, and with them new opportunities for individual Jews, though not yet for the Jewish people as a whole. The prototype for all Jewish success in the modern era preceded the Emancipation, which in fact it helped fashion. It was the family of Rothschild. The name Rothschild eventually became synonymous with great wealth, private multi-national banking, and shrewd political judgment. To the masses of poverty-stricken Jews, Rothschild was a hero, the Jew who finally made good in the outside world. To non-Jews, the name Rothschild awakened feelings of envy, suspicion, resentment, grudging admiration, and the realization that individual Jews would now appear in positions of prominence in general society.

The family of Rothschild thus came to represent something far more important than their own personal lives and experiences. They came to represent world Jewry in the eyes of many. But they were unprepared for such an enormous historic burden, and, therefore, most of them were irresponsible both in fulfilling their historic responsibilities and to their Judaic roots and destiny.[1] In fact, the Rothschilds set the standard and created the mold for almost all of the later "Jewish rich" in general society, who in the nineteenth and twentieth centuries undertook to represent Jewish interests in the world, even though they were

---

1. The main exceptions to this judgment are the first Rothschild, Mayer Amshel, and the later Barons Edmund de Rothschild of Paris and Benjamin Wolf Rothschild of Frankfurt, as well as some members of the English branch of the family.

unelected, unchosen, and usually intellectually, morally, and religiously unfit for the task. This dangerous, often counter-productive and arrogant assumption of leadership by wealthy Jews would damage the Jewish cause mightily over the ensuing centuries.[2]

The founder of the house of Rothschild[3] was Mayer Amshel Rothschild.[4] Originally intended for the rabbinate, he studied at the yeshivah in Furth. However, in 1760, after his father's death, he returned to Frankfurt and began his career as a general mercantile agent, and eventually became a banker. A religiously observant Jew, he benefited from the more tolerant spirit of his time and made important connections with German nobility and especially with William IX of Hesse. This led him to work on behalf of the Crown Prince of Prussia, and by 1806 he had become Hesse's official court agent for investments and loans. His fortune became immense, and his reputation as an astute, loyal, and ingenious financier grew on the European continent.

Two of Mayer's sons, Salomon Mayer of Vienna and Nathan Mayer of London, were the linchpins on which the dynasty developed and flourished. In England, Nathan was able to duplicate the German success of his father, and, on the strength of his dealings in the time of the Napoleonic wars, became one of the leading capitalists in the British Empire. His brother Salomon in Vienna became a confidant of the Hapsburgs, and helped finance the first Austrian railway. His branch of the firm also benefited greatly from the turmoil and unending need for funds by governments, generated by the Napoleonic wars. Thus, by 1815 the Rothschilds were firmly established in Germany, Austria, and England, and wielded strong influence throughout Europe. Two other sons, Karl Mayer of Naples and Jacob Mayer of Paris, though overshadowed by the success of their older brothers, also established permanent branches of the firm in Italy and France. Thus was international private banking born.

The Rothschilds built their own exclusive system of communications,[5] and though they were loyal to the governments of each of their branches in the business dealings of that particular branch, they were

---

2. Barons de Hirsch and Gunzberg are two prominent nineteenth-century examples of this misguided assumption of public service by unqualified magnates, as were many leaders of American Jewry in the nineteenth and twentieth centuries.

3. The name Rothschild was derived from the sign of a red shield on the family home located then at 148 Judengasse in Frankfurt am Main.

4. 1743-1812.

5. Carrier pigeons, couriers, and eventually coded telegraph wire messages.

basically supranational in spirit and concept. As such, they were a steadying and calming influence in post-Napoleonic Europe, for they were on the side of profitable peace and security, and opposed to the risks of war and narrow interests. In the nineteenth century, they became the premier banking family in Europe. In Jewish eyes, this soon grew into myth and legend. Most of the family departed from the ways of Jewish observance and several of them — mainly females — married non-Jews. Nonetheless, the Jewish people, as a whole, turned a blind eye to these defects of character and behavior. The Rothschilds became folk heroes of Israel.

The emergence of successful, non-apostate — and identifiably Jewish, albeit not observant — Jews was an important ingredient in the new self-view of secular Jews in the nineteenth century. In Jewish folklore of the time, both in Eastern and Western Europe, the dream of becoming "richer than Rothschild" was a common theme. But the dream was not only that of wealth for wealth's sake. It had a deeper vision and a more ephemeral goal. It was for physical freedom from persecution and fear, for acceptance and toleration by the non-Jewish world, for the right to use a Jewish talent in the broad arena on a grand scale, and for the right to remain Jewish while doing so. The hero, the idol, the goal was Rothschild, not Disraeli, Heine, or Marx. This dream, rooted in European Jewry throughout the nineteenth century, explains the agenda of American Jewry in the twentieth century. It was in America that this dream came to reality and where many Jews did come to feel themselves "richer than Rothschild."

Moses Montefiore

PERHAPS EVEN GREATER in Jewish folklore than Rothschild was the name Montefiore, which also stood for Jewish success and behavior in the nineteenth century. Moses Montefiore[6] was a leading money agent and stockbroker in London and, through his business acumen and family and political connections, amassed a vast fortune at an early age. When he was forty, he retired from active business pursuits and devoted his life thenceforth to the service of the Jewish people. He was the great defender of his people, an unapologetic Jew who was scrupulously

6. 1784-1885. Born in Leghorn, Italy and a scion of an ancient and respected Sephardic family, he married a sister of Nathan Rothschild's wife.

observant of his religion, respectful and subservient to its rabbinical leaders, and humble and kind in character.[7]

He first rose to international prominence in the Jewish world in 1840, when he spearheaded the Jewish defense against the Damascus blood libel. In February 1840, a Capuchin priest and his servant were murdered in Damascus. The local Church charged that Jews committed the crime in order to obtain Christian blood for the coming celebration of Passover.[8] A number of Jews, subjected to barbarous tortures, "admitted" the crime and implicated others. The French consul in Damascus solemnly upheld the truth of the blood accusation. Montefiore, who was friendly with Queen Victoria[9] and Lord Palmerston,[10] mobilized a delegation of Jews from England and France, and under official British prodding, was granted an audience with the Ottoman ruler of Syria, Mohammed Ali.[11] Montefiore succeeded in having the Jewish captives in Damascus released and even had the Sultan issue a ban against all such further blood libels against Jews living within the borders of his empire. This electrifying success achieved for Montefiore instant fame and acclaim throughout the Jewish world.

Moses Montefiore

Montefiore traveled the world on behalf of justice for his people. His trips to Russia in the 1850's, and later to the Holy Land, became legendary. He made the first Jewish purchases of land outside the walls of Old Jerusalem and, in effect, began the process of colonization which would restore Jewish sovereignty in Palestine.[12] All of the Jewish world

---

7. One of the great legends regarding him was that every night before retiring, he would descend to his cellar, don his death shrouds, and lie in the coffin he had prepared for himself. This, he was purported to have said, gave him a balanced and realistic view of himself, his importance, and his vast wealth. Legends are not necessarily factually accurate, but they are very important, nonetheless, because they do accurately characterize and delineate the behavior and attitudes of the person who is the subject of the legend.

8. The calumny of the blood libel, fostered by the Church so diligently in the Middle Ages, dies hard. As late as the 1920's there was such a blood libel accusation against the Jews of Massena, New York!

9. An unlikely but forceful friend of the Jews and Jewish interests throughout her long reign.

10. Henry John Temple (1784-1865), foreign minister and prime minister of England.

11. 1769-1849.

12. The neighborhoods of Mishkenot Shaananim and Yemin Moshe, as well as the symbolic windmill outside the walls of Jerusalem, are the result of Montefiore's visit and capital investment.

joined him in celebrating his centennial in 1884. A special volume[13] of approbation containing letters from all of the great rabbinic leaders of the time and from the Jewish communities worldwide was presented to him, together with commemorative secular honors from governments and political notables. After his death, numerous Jewish institutions of learning, social welfare, and humanitarian aid were named after him. It would be difficult for anyone after him, in terms of social service to the Jewish people, to be "more magnificent than Montefiore."

---

13. This volume is currently in the collection of a Jewish bibliophile in Toronto, Canada.

9
Napoleon

Liberal Attitude

F THE ROTHSCHILDS WERE the heroes of the nineteenth-century secular Jewish world, a non-Jew served as the main catalyst for change in that world. Napoleon Bonaparte[1] was the central character in European life at the beginning of the nineteenth century. Not only did he inflict war, radical changes, and his blood relatives upon all of the neighboring European countries, but Napoleon also changed European Jewish life as well. His remarkable rise and spectacular fall loosed shock waves throughout Jewish Europe, and contributed mightily to the dismantling of traditional Jewish life and beliefs beginning with the nineteenth century.

Napoleon Bonaparte

Napoleon rose to power amidst the chaos and anarchy of the French Revolution and the resultant "Reign of Terror." A famed and feared general since 1795, Napoleon became consul of France in 1799 at the age of thirty, and immediately embarked on a career of empire-building. In the Italian campaigns preceding his rise to dictatorial power, Napoleon displayed a policy of great sympathy and tolerance toward Jews.

Wherever his sword advanced, Jews were given civil rights, ghetto walls were literally torn down,[2] and Jews were given positions of some importance in his administrations. Jews therefore initially flocked to his banner and held him in great esteem as a benevolent ruler and sincere benefactor. Though Jews were given equal rights of citizenship by the revolutionary French National Assembly in 1791, it was only under Napoleon, a decade later, that they began to exercise these rights freely. This coincided with the rise of Reform and thus, in the early

---

1. Born on Corsica in 1769 and died on St. Helena in 1821.
2. Paul Johnson, *A History of the Jews*, p. 306.

nineteenth century, much of French Jewry, drunk on the heady wine of civil freedom, cast away their religious traditions. First they joined Reform, and eventually attempted to assimilate completely into French society. Napoleon's liberal attitude towards Jews proved to be a major factor in this process of assimilation.

The reaction to the new Jewish freedom by the non-Jewish population, however, was often violent and hate-filled; centuries of religious anti-Semitism could not be ended by mere imperial fiat. In the first decade of the nineteenth century, even though the Church was in decline and itself persecuted by the Jacobins[3] and the radical wing of French libertarians, it still stood for religious and economic repression of the Jew. The Royalist party, hoping to restore the Bourbons to power in Paris, in the early 1800s railed against the Jews and accused them of fomenting rebellion and anarchy. Thus was born the damning fiction of the Jew as a subversive, a traitor, a radical, and a political incendiary. Modern anti-Semitism invented a new Jew to replace the old traditional religious one as the enemy of the people.

Still, Napoleon's influence on the matter of Jewish rights was felt throughout Europe, even beyond his empire. Civil rights were granted

---

3. The name given to the most famous political faction in the French Revolution. It was the group that launched and sustained a "reign of terror" against opponents of the Revolution, and especially against the Catholic Church.

Napoleon's Great Sanhedrin

to Jews in Prussia in 1812,[4] and Austria soon followed suit. Considerable freedom, though certainly not without genteel discrimination, was also granted to the Jews of England. Under Napoleon, the Jews of Western Europe had their legal disabilities lifted and were ushered into the Age of Reason and Enlightenment. Most Western Jews now envisioned for themselves an opportunity for a life of dignity, economic advancement, and social acceptance. Napoleon's brilliant military victories in Europe from 1799 to 1810 seemed to guarantee survival of the new spirit of the age. Jewish Europe seemed poised at the edge of a new horizon of hope and equality.

Coin of Napoleon and the Great Sanhedrin

Ulterior Motive

NAPOLEON, HOWEVER, WAS NOT the Judeophile that many Jews felt he was. Jews soon came to realize that their early euphoric assessment of Napoleon may have been wrong. In the session of the Imperial Council on April 30, 1806, Napoleon stated that it was dangerous to allow a large number of Jews to continue to live in the border province of Alsace, since their loyalty to France was questionable ("Jews are a state within a state").[5] Yet, the next month he convened an Assembly of Notables to determine the best way to open the general economy to Jews, so that they would be able to earn respectable livelihoods. He also forgave many onerous taxes previously placed on Jewish communities in newly conquered areas of the empire. But he was clearly intent on solving the Jewish "problem," in ways that did not augur well for the Jewish future. He was proving to be an enigma to the Jewish people.

Napoleon's outward tolerance and fairness toward Jews was actually based upon his grand plan to have them disappear entirely by means of total assimilation, intermarriage, and conversion. In effect, his was a benign "final solution" to the Jewish "problem." To that end, Napoleon convened the Assembly of Jewish Notables in May, 1806, and followed up by establishing a "Sanhedrin," which met in Paris in February, 1807.

The Assembly of Jewish Notables included one hundred and eleven leading Jews from France, Germany and Italy. It met to provide

---

4. Revoked under the terms of the Treaty of Vienna in 1815.
5. *The Jewish Encyclopedia,* Vol. 9, p. 168.

satisfactory answers to twelve questions which Napoleon put to it.[6] The answers were then submitted to Napoleon who convened his mock Sanhedrin to ratify the answers and grant them binding legal standing. He hoped thereby that his program for assimilation would be acceptable to Jewry at large, and be presented as having been legally ratified by the Jewish "assembly" itself. However, traditional Jews saw the "Sanhedrin" as a bad joke, a mockery of the sacred, and a trial to be endured. Reform Jews welcomed it in the hope that it would aid Napoleon in solving the Jewish "problem."

The Sanhedrin had seventy-one members — all appointed, at least indirectly, by Napoleon. Twenty-five members were laymen and the remaining forty-six were rabbis.[7] Not all the rabbis were traditional Jews. Reform rabbis from Amsterdam, Hamburg and Italy were also members of the Sanhedrin. The head of the tribunal was, however, a great rabbi and renowned Talmudic scholar, Rabbi David Sinzheim,[8] the rabbi of Strasbourg. He was forced into the position of being the head of this ill-advised and strangely constituted group, but nevertheless, with skill, diplomacy, patience, and wisdom, he was able to dilute any halachic effects of the group's decisions. He severely limited the participation of the Reform representatives and attempted to narrow the scope of the Sanhedrin's deliberations.

---

6. The twelve questions were:

(1) Is it lawful for a Jew to have more than one wife?

(2) Is divorce allowed by the Jewish religion? Will the divorce be valid if it is issued by virtue of laws in contradiction to the French Judicial code?

(3) Are Jews prohibited from intermarrying with Christians?

(4) In the eyes of the Jews, are non-Jewish Frenchmen considered as brethren or strangers?

(5) What line of conduct does Jewish law prescribe toward non-Jewish Frenchmen?

(6) Do French-born Jews, treated by France as citizens, consider France their country? Are they bound to defend it? Are they bound to obey its laws and civil code?

(7) Who elects rabbis?

(8) What type of police jurisdiction and power do the rabbis exercise over the Jews? What judicial powers do the rabbis possess?

(9) Are these police and judicial powers of the rabbis, as well as the form of their election, regulated by binding Jewish law, or is it only a matter of custom?

(10) Are there professions from which Jewish law itself precludes Jews?

(11) Does Jewish law forbid Jews to take interest on a loan between Jews?

(12) Does Jewish law permit Jews to take interest on a loan made to non-Jews?

7. All attended, since an "invitation" from Napoleon was a summons that no one dared refuse.

8. 1745-1812. He was the author of the esteemed Talmudic commentary, *Yad David*.

Eventually the Sanhedrin approved nine articles of Jewish "dogma,"[9] and together with the Assembly of Notables submitted them in a final report to Napoleon. On April 6, 1807, the charade ended and Napoleon dissolved both the Sanhedrin and the Assembly of Jewish Notables. The Sanhedrin provoked a great deal of public attention and was viewed negatively and suspiciously by the non-Jewish masses. The myth of secret international Jewish assemblies which ruled the Jews and the world now seemed to be fleshed out in reality.[10] The theory of the conspiracy of the Jews for world domination began to gain credence, and the Sanhedrin was its prime example. Thus did Napoleon's efforts to mitigate the physical discomfort of the Jews under his rule and speed their assimilation into non Jewish-society inadvertently aid in the birth of modern anti-Semitism.

Ultimate Defeat

APOLEON WAS INVOLVED WITH Jews in his military life. In 1798 he embarked from France to the Middle East on a mission of conquest. The Ottoman Empire of Turkey was still reeling from the loss of part of the Crimean peninsula to Russia in 1791, and Turkey itself was rocked with riots and disaffection with the government. Napoleon saw an opportunity to dislodge Turkey from Palestine and rushed toward the fray. He saw it as a new crusade and longed to add Jerusalem to his list of military conquests. His army captured Malta, and then proceeded to Egypt.

---

9. They were:
    (1) Polygamy is forbidden to Jews in conformity with the decree of Rabbeinu Gershom.
    (2) A Jewish divorce would be valid only after a previous decision on the matter by the French civil authorities.
    (3) Religious marriage must be preceded by a civil contract.
    (4) Marriages between Jews and Christians are binding civilly, though they cannot be celebrated with any religious ceremony.
    (5) Jews were bound to view their non-Jewish fellow citizens as brethren and to aid and protect them equally with Jews.
    (6) Jews consider the land of their birth or adoption as their fatherland and will fight to defend it when necessary.
    (7) Judaism does not forbid any type of productive handicraft or occupation.
    (8) Jews find it commendable to engage in agriculture, manual labor, and the arts as well.
    (9) Jews are forbidden to exact usury from Jew or non-Jew alike.
10. Paul Johnson, *A History of the Jews*, p. 310.

There he attempted to rally Moslem support to his cause against Turkey,[11] even going as far as suggesting that he and his army were willing to forsake Christianity and embrace Islam. The Egyptians were wily enough not to commit themselves to Napoleon's goal, and he finally left Alexandria in early 1799 to invade Palestine.

In the Land of Israel he met fierce military opposition from the Turkish governor, Jezem Pasha.[12] This governor had a Jewish adviser, Chaim Parchi, who encouraged him in his spirited defense of the country against Napoleon. The Jews of the country were united in their loyalty to Turkey and their opposition to Napoleon. The Sephardic Jews of the Moslem countries did not suffer as greatly as their Ashkenazic brethren. The Sephardim had a strong sense of loyalty to the rulers of their countries, and were generally much less enamored of Western culture and ideas than were the Jews of Europe.

The great leader of Jewish Jerusalem of that time, Rabbi Yom Tov Algazi, and his court, publicly offered prayers on behalf of the Turks and voiced great fears about a Napoleonic conquest.[13] Napoleon approached Jerusalem, thought better about challenging its forbidding walls by siege, and turned west to the coast. He captured the city of Jaffa, massacred 4,000 of its defenders and then turned north, moving up the seacoast. On the Sabbath preceding Purim 1799, Napoleon began the siege of Acre. The legendary Rabbi Nachman of Breslav was in Acre that Sabbath and miraculously escaped the siege the next day, placing a curse on Napoleon. Napoleon was unable to prevail and was forced to lift the siege of Acre and withdraw from the Middle East. The opposition to him of Palestine's Jews rankled and helped contribute to his ambivalent feelings about the Jewish people.

In 1812 Napoleon made the fatal error of turning east for new conquests. In 1807, at Tilsit in Northern Prussia, he had signed peace treaties with both Russia and Prussia. By the terms of these treaties, Prussia gave up its Polish provinces and they were formed into a new entity, the Duchy of Warsaw. The Duchy was bound to France by treaty and Napoleon helped fan Polish hopes for the eventual national freedom of all Poland. The Duchy of Warsaw contained a large Jewish population which, like its Western European brothers, initially welcomed Napoleon and the French as their new masters. Anything was better

---

11. Much as England would in 1915.

12. Who suffered mightily at the hand of his cruel master, the Sultan, and was in fact mutilated by him on whim. *See Toldos HaDoros,* Vol. 3, p. 379.

13. *Toldos HaDoros,* Vol. 3, p. 44.

than being handed over to the cruelty of Czar Alexander! By the terms of the treaty of Tilsit and its secret appendix, Alexander and Napoleon were to become allies, dividing Europe between them. There was a vague understanding between the two emperors that somehow Russia would attack portions of the British Empire in order to abet Napoleon's aims for world domination. However, the Czar soon lost appetite for the alliance and refused to implement many of its terms. Napoleon sulked, and tried to cajole Alexander into fulfilling the terms of his bargain. By 1812, Napoleon was frustrated and angry at his erstwhile ally.

In the spring of 1812, Napoleon massed an enormous army of close to 500,000 soldiers in Poland, hoping thereby to intimidate Alexander into a more cooperative mood. By the end of June, Napoleon had exhausted his patience and his "grand army" struck eastward, reaching Moscow on September 14. But Alexander refused to sue for peace. The Russians practiced "scorched earth" tactics the whole length of their retreat. This strategy called for the total destruction of crops and towns so that nothing would be left for Napoleon's army, and the practice culminated in the burning of Moscow itself on the day of its capture. Napoleon and the "grand army" were by now exhausted, and they were ill prepared for the onslaught of the ferocious Russian winter. He was forced to withdraw westward, and the disastrous retreat sounded the death knell to Napoleon's dream of European domination. Fewer than 10,000 able-bodied soldiers survived the sad march home, and the mighty French army was destroyed.

By 1814, Napoleon was forced to abdicate and was exiled to Elba. However, in 1815 he escaped to France and ruled for The Hundred Days, but he was defeated at Waterloo and abdicated once more. He was then exiled to St. Helena where he died in 1821.

Lasting Effects

HE JEWS IN EASTERN EUROPE were divided in their appraisal of Napoleon and the war he unleashed upon them. Many of them had welcomed his coming. Great chassidic leaders endorsed his aim of defeating Russia and felt the war against the Czar could be the prophesied battle of Gog and Magog, which would herald the coming of the Messiah.[14] However, a great leader and defender of Chassidus of that age, Rabbi Shneur Zalman,[15] opposed Napoleon and demanded that the Jews remain loyal to the Czar and Russia, this in spite of the brutal treatment and imprisonment he himself had suffered at the hands of the Russian government. His reasoning in this matter was crystal clear: "If Bonaparte triumphs, wealth will increase amidst Israel and the cause of the Jewish people would be uplifted, but they [the Jews] would separate themselves [from Torah] and the heart of Israel would be far from its Father in Heaven."[16]

Rabbi Shneur Zalman accurately assessed the dangers to traditional Jewish life posed by the French Enlightenment now sweeping east with Napoleon. All of the physical benefits for Jews that may have come in the wake of Napoleon's victory would be canceled by the loss of Jewish identity, purpose, and religious beliefs and practices. Rabbi Shneur Zalman recognized the great confrontation between secular, Western values and freedoms and the traditional Jewish Torah way of life. This struggle is really the essence of the story of the Jews in the nineteenth century.

Though Napoleon was defeated, his invasion of Russia created a new Eastern Europe. The ideas and goals of the French Revolution, the hopes of a secular, humanist society for a better tomorrow, now invaded Poland and Russia. These ideas would also assault traditional Jewish life there as well. Thus, Napoleon served as the conduit for *Haskalah* (Enlightenment), helping it to gain a foothold in the ranks of Eastern European Jewry. Just as he had succeeded in uprooting the old societies of Europe, so did Napoleon alter Jewish society throughout Europe and leave within that Jewish society a legacy of ferment, discontent, and radicalism that would severely test its long-proven ability to survive and flourish.

---

14. See *Toldos HaDoros*, Vol. 3, p. 143. Rabbi Menachem Mendel of Rimanov led the group of Jews who favored Napoleon in his war. The Seer of Lublin (the *Chozeh*) was much more cautious in his assessment of the situation, and attempted to dampen the rising messianic fervor engendered by the invasion of Napoleon's "Grand Army".

15. For a more detailed description of this renowned leader, see the *"Chassidus,"* chapter 11.

16. Letter to Rabbi Moshe Meisels from Rabbi Shneur Zalman, quoted in *Toldos HaDoros,* Vol. 3, p. 139.

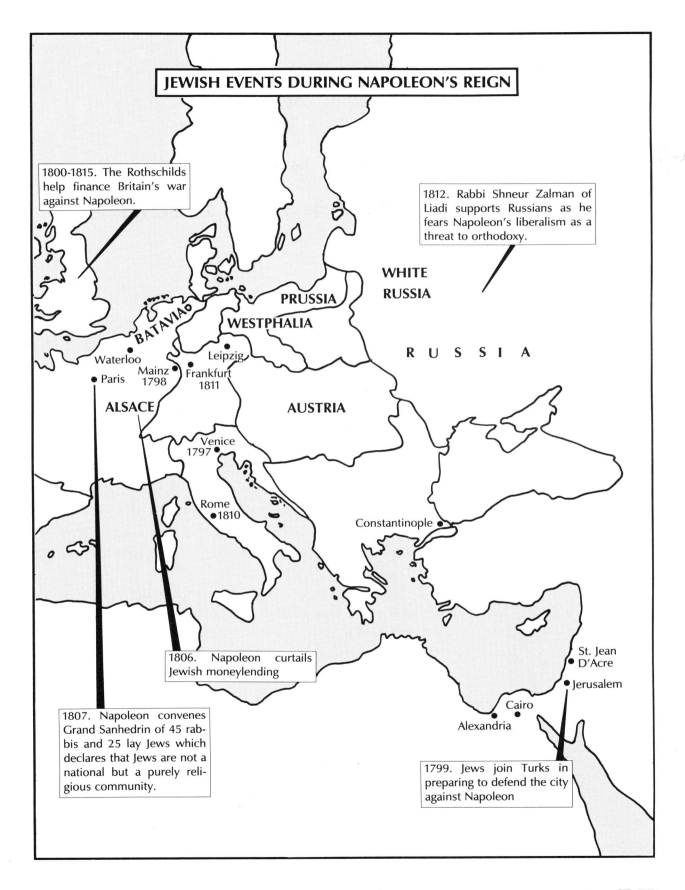

JEWISH EVENTS DURING NAPOLEON'S REIGN

1800-1815. The Rothschilds help finance Britain's war against Napoleon.

1812. Rabbi Shneur Zalman of Liadi supports Russians as he fears Napoleon's liberalism as a threat to orthodoxy.

WHITE RUSSIA

PRUSSIA

WESTPHALIA

R U S S I A

BATAVIA

Waterloo

Leipzig

Paris

Mainz
1798

Frankfurt
1811

ALSACE

AUSTRIA

Venice
1797

Rome
1810

Constantinople

St. Jean
D'Acre

Jerusalem

1806. Napoleon curtails Jewish moneylending

Cairo

Alexandria

1807. Napoleon convenes Grand Sanhedrin of 45 rabbis and 25 lay Jews which declares that Jews are not a national but a purely religious community.

1799. Jews join Turks in preparing to defend the city against Napoleon

10

Torah Scholarship
and Survival of Tradition

N THE MIDST OF THE TRAGEDY and turmoil of Jewish life engendered by pogroms, false messianism, Reform, and the political and social realignment of Europe, there was one bright constant that guaranteed the continuity of Jewish life and tradition. That was the proliferation of Torah study, scholarship, and books. It was as though Israel's inner voice reconfirmed to itself that the surest defense against the onslaught of outside events was the intensification of Torah study and the strengthening of Torah scholarship. The explosion of sacred knowledge and creativity reinforced the primacy of Torah in Jewish life and rallied the forces of tradition and faith. Jews repeated the sentiment of King David: "If it were not for the joy-giving quality of Your Torah, I would have been lost in my anguish."[1]

The streams of Torah scholarship in the eighteenth century were diverse and free-flowing. The traditional scholarship of interpretation of the Talmud, based on the work of *Rashi*,[2] *Tosafos*[3] and the *Rishonim*,[4] was intensified and widened by many scholars of this age. It is

1. Psalms 119:92.

2. Rabbi Shlomo Yitzchaki (1030-1096), the teacher of Israel and the main commentator to the Bible and the Talmud.

3. Several hundred French and German scholars — many of them students, grandchildren, and disciples of *Rashi* — who, in the twelfth and thirteenth centuries, developed a commentary to the Talmud that became the basis for didactic Talmudic study.

4. The "early ones" — the other commentators to the Talmud, mainly Spanish, North African, German, and French, from the eleventh through the fifteenth centuries. For biographies of these rabbinic personalities see *The Rishonim*, ed. by Rabbi Hersh Goldwurm; ArtScroll History Series; Mesorah Publications, Ltd., N.Y. 1982.

impossible to give a complete listing of the major sages of the seventeenth and eighteenth centuries and their accomplishments. As is usually the case, some of the premier scholars of the period are virtually unknown to us because they did not leave written works. Countless manuscripts were unpublished because the authors lacked the financial resources to print them. Those manuscripts, as well as untold rare and currently out-of-print books, were destroyed in the Holocaust, this being yet another of the incalculable losses of this century's catastrophe. The following incomplete listing, therefore, is intended as no more than a glimpse of the intellectual majesty of a golden era of Torah creativity.

Among the major Talmudic commentators of the era was Yaakov Yehoshua Falk,[5] the rabbi of Frankfurt am Main. His work *Pnei Yehoshua* remains a basic text of Talmudic interpretation. Another leading example of such Talmudic commentary was the work of Rabbi Yechezkel Landau[6] of Prague. His book *Tzelach*[7] gained wide popularity and acceptance. He was also one of the greatest decisors of questions of rabbinic law. His responsa were collected and published under his own auspices[8] and those of his son,[9] under the name *Noda B'Yehudah*. This book became a classic in rabbinic literature and served as the basic starting point for many later rabbinic discussions of new halachic problems[10] raised by the technology and society of modern Europe. Rabbi Landau took an active role in attempting to end the strife engendered by the accusations of Rabbi Yaakov Emden against Rabbi Yonasan Eybeshitz.[11] He also bitterly opposed the translation of the Bible into German by Moses Mendelssohn, and he correctly foresaw Mendelssohn's reforms as the forerunner of assimilation and intermarriage.[12]

Another great scholar of the time was Rabbi Pinchas Horowitz,[13] who became rabbi of Frankfurt am Main in 1771. Born in Lithuania, he became a follower of the early chassidic masters and an author of note.

---

5. 1680-1754.

6. 1713-1793.

7. The acronym of the Hebrew words *Tziyun L'Nefesh Chayah*.

8. The first section.

9. The second section.

10. Such as autopsies, shaving one's beard, wearing "non-Jewish" clothing, and other subjects.

11. See earlier chapter, "Regrets and Recriminations."

12. See chapter on Mendelssohn.

13. 1730-1805

His two main commentaries to the Talmud, *Hafla'ah*[14] and *HaMakneh*,[15] are outstanding examples of scholarly analysis and incisive interpretation, as is his commentary on the Torah, *Panim Yafos*. These works became staple texts for later generations of Talmudic students.

Two thorough commentaries to the *Talmud Yerushalmi* (Jerusalem Talmud) were published during the eighteenth century. That Talmud had hitherto been a sealed book to most because it had never been the subject of extensive commentary, as had the Babylonian Talmud. Rabbi Moshe Margolies[16] of Kaidan, Lithuania authored *Pnei Moshe*, which filled a real need for students of that Talmud. After its appearance a second major commentary, *Korban HaEdah,* was published by Rabbi David Frankel of Dessau (and later of Berlin). It covered approximately half of the *Talmud Yerushalmi*, and was more detailed in its explanation of the text than was *Pnei Moshe*. The two commentaries taken together enabled the student to understand the Talmudic text. Almost all editions of the *Talmud Yerushalmi* produced after the eighteenth century include both of these commentaries on the printed page.

One of the major scholarly contributions of the age was written by Rabbi Aryeh Leib HaCohen Heller[17] of Stry, in Galician Poland. In 1788 he published his great work, *Ketzos HaChoshen*, a commentary to the section of the *Shulchan Aruch* dealing with monetary and legal matters. His work is a classic of legal analysis and a fine dissection of abstract legal concepts into their basic component parts. His ability to delineate conceptual differences between apparently analogous cases resolved many difficult textual problems regarding passages of the Talmud and the Codes, and reconciled apparent conflicts in the law itself. The brilliance of this work made it immensely popular with his contemporaries and later generations. The book became one of the basic texts for the yeshivos in Lithuania in the next century and is still used as a model of rabbinic thought and Talmudic reasoning. Rabbi Heller produced other major scholarly works, but none equaled *Ketzos HaChoshen* in acceptance and popularity.

Rabbi Yaakov Lorberbaum of Lissa[18] produced *Nesivos HaMishpat*, which serves as a companion work to *Ketzos HaChoshen*. The two works, *Ketzos* and *Nesivos,* were included in the Lemberg edition of the

---

14. A commentary to Tractate *Kesubos*.
15. A commentary to Tractate *Kiddushin*.
16. An early teacher of the Gaon of Vilna.
17. 1754-1813.
18. 1760-1838.

Codes in the nineteenth century and are now considered to be basic texts of rabbinic jurisprudence. Rabbi Lorberbaum also authored numerous other works on the Talmud, Codes, and Scripture, as well as a halachic commentary on the order of prayers.

Yet another major commentary to the Codes was published in the 1760s. It was entitled *Pri Megadim* and authored by Rabbi Yosef Teomim[19] who was originally an elementary school teacher in Lemberg, and later became the rabbi of Frankfurt am Oder. His work was a super-commentary to *Orach Chaim* and *Yoreh Deah*, in that it explained the commentaries of Rabbi David HaLevi (the *Taz*), Rabbi Shabsai Cohen (the *Shach*) and Rabbi Avraham Abale Gombiner (the *Magen Avraham*). *Pri Megadim* interpreted the difficult passages in these commentaries and provided comprehensive overviews of the subject matter under discussion. Rabbi Teomim was not only a Talmudic scholar of great stature, but he was well versed in Hebrew language and grammar, and was a rigorous logician. His introductions to the sections of the Codes are models of analytic logic and of an orderly exposition of the fundamental principles and concepts underlying the groups of laws. Again, from the nineteenth century onward, almost all editions of the Codes included the *Pri Megadim* as a standard commentary text.

The proliferation of scholarly commentaries to the *Shulchan Aruch* threatened to overwhelm the simplicity of the work itself. Since so much effort was expended by scholars in studying and analyzing the brilliant and stimulating super-commentaries, the authoritative character of the *Shulchan Aruch* tended to be diminished. Especially for people who were not scholars, there was a need for a short code, which, in plain un-equivocal language, described practically the rules of conduct and law.

The first to fill this new need was Rabbi Avraham Danzig,[20] who composed the first great abridgment of the Codes. He was a disciple of Rabbi Yechezkel Landau of Prague, and served as a rabbinical judge in Vilna during the time of the Gaon of Vilna. His two main works were *Chayei Adam* and *Chochmas Adam*. The former deals with all religious laws bearing upon prayers, benedictions, the Sabbath, festivals and the like. The latter covers the dietary laws, ritual purity, mourning, and burial of the dead. The two books together became the basic law for much of Eastern European Jewry. They were written in an ethical tone and imparted to their readers the enthusiasm of piety and Godly service.

---

19. 1712-1792.

20. 1748-1820.

They became the model for later abridgments of the commentaries on the *Shulchan Aruch*.

Another one of the major scholars of the century was Rabbi Akiva Eiger,[21] who served as rabbi of Posen, in Prussia. His profoundly analytical responsa and novellae on the Talmud are still important parts of all yeshivah curricula, and new editions and arrangements of them are published regularly. As great as he was in scholarship, so he was unsurpassed in personal behavior and humility. He was the father-in-law of Rabbi Moses Sofer, the *Chasam Sofer,* whose accomplishments have been discussed previously in this book.

Rabbi Yaakov Reisher[22] was the author of the famous book of responsa *Shevuth Yaakov*, and the commentary to *Shulchan Aruch, Chok Yaakov*. Rabbi Yechezkel Katzenellenbogen,[23] the rabbi of Altona-Hamburg, was the author of *Knesses Yechezkel*, a book of rabbinic responsa. Rabbi Meir Eisenstadt[24] helped rebuild the tradition of Jewish scholarship in Hungary after the ravages of the invading Austrian army had destroyed much of Jewish life there. He was the author of *Panim Me'iros*, an authoritative book of responsa. Rabbi Chaim Cohen Rapaport,[25] rabbi of Lvov, a strong opponent of the Jacob Frank heresy in Poland and one of the leading scholars of the age, was the author of a book of responsa bearing his name. The brief commentary to the *Shulchan Aruch*, *Ba'er Hetev*, authored by Rabbi Yehudah Ashkenazi, the rabbinic judge of Tiktin, appeared in 1725, and the commentary to *Shulchan Aruch* by Rabbi Hezekiah de Silva,[26] *Pri Chadash*, in 1705.

The first famed rabbinic encyclopedia, *Pachad Yitzchak*, was authored by Rabbi Isaac Lampronti,[27] who served as rabbi of Ferrara, Italy, and was a physician, linguist, and philosopher. He undertook to arrange in alphabetical order all subjects discussed in Talmudic and rabbinic literature. The work became a standard reference text in the rabbinic world, for almost every subject in rabbinics is included and indexed with the appropriate references to the Talmud, Codes and responsa. The first six volumes of the work appeared during the author's lifetime, with the rest remaining in manuscript until the middle

---

21. 1761-1837.
22. Flourished 1715-1730.
23. Flourished 1713-1740. He died in 1749.
24. He died in 1744.
25. Flourished 1750-1780.
26. 1659-1695.
27. 1679-1756.

of the nineteenth century, when they were published in Germany. This great encyclopedic work, written without the aid of computers, research assistants, and other later publishing aids, remains a classic and is the basis for all later works of similar form and purpose.

Eminent Sephardic rabbinic figures of the eighteenth century included Rabbi Yehudah Rosanes[28] of Constantinople, the author of *Mishneh L'Melech*, a commentary to the code of Maimonides; Rabbi Yom Tov Algazi[29] of Turkey and Israel, the author of responsa, *Rit Algazi*; and the great bibliophile and scholar, Rabbi Chaim Yosef David Azulai,[30] known as the *Chida*. The latter was a prolific writer and authored many works of scholarship. As a fundraiser for the Sephardic *yishuv* in Jerusalem, he traveled widely. He visited libraries throughout the world,[31] identifying long-lost Hebrew manuscripts and copying lost classics. His influence on Jewish scholarship was far reaching and long lasting. Rabbi Chaim ibn Attar[32] emigrated from Fez to Jerusalem in 1742 and died there one year later. His great work was *Or HaChayim*, a commentary to the Bible which received universal approval and became a basic text for the interpretation of Torah, both in its plain meaning and through the prism of kabbalistic thought.

The test of the vibrancy and vitality of a civilization is its intellectual and spiritual force during times of duress and stress. While the Jewish world was shaken badly during the eighteenth century, the study of Torah and the creativity of Torah scholarship during that century was almost unmatched,[33] except for the great achievements of the eleventh and twelfth centuries. This remarkable achievement was a testament to the vitality of traditional Jewish life in the face of the new and unexpected onslaughts upon it. A pattern of Jewish survival, and of Torah survival within the Jewish people, was thereby set for future centuries. In spite of all odds against it, Israel would survive and the intensification of Torah study within it would remain the vehicle that would guarantee this survival.

---

28. 1657-1727.

29. 1727-1802.

30. 1724-1806.

31. Including that of the Vatican.

32. 1696-1743.

33. The cursory review of Torah scholarship in this chapter has not included the works of the great chassidic masters and of the Gaon of Vilna, who also flourished during this century. Their contributions are discussed in the next section of this book.

Section III

Chassidim, Misnagdim, and the Response to Reform

1730-1870

11
Chassidus

Baal Shem Tov

THE EIGHTEENTH-CENTURY turbulence in Jewish life was not restricted to Central and Western European Jewry. Even though the winds of "emancipation" and "reason" did not easily penetrate the domain of the Czars, great changes nevertheless occurred in Jewish life in Eastern Europe. The grinding poverty and the hostile and vicious behavior that engulfed Eastern European Jewry forced it to look for new avenues of revitalization and hope. Whereas Western European Jewry turned to the outside world for meaning and purpose, Eastern European Jewry, in the main, would turn inward, finding new hope and strength in preserving its ancient traditions and beliefs, but in a revolutionary and vibrant fashion. The movement that provided this change in Jewish life and provoked a century-long bitter controversy was called Chassidus.

The facts of the history of Chassidus, like the movement itself, are shrouded in legend, mystery, contention, and wonder. While espousing definite philosophies and directions, the movement was basically one of individuals, not of theories and historical forces. These individuals were so imaginative and persuasive, and possessed such power of spirit and personality, that they built Chassidus into the largest mass movement of Jews in the modern era. That movement is so varied and complex that it is difficult to describe it or trace its history as a whole. In fact, it is not a "movement" in the sense of having a unified program and organizational structure. It must be glimpsed in the miniature, in the detail, in the story of its *tzaddikim*[1] and leaders in order to be understood in its totality.[2]

Rabbi Yisrael ben Eliezer — the Baal Shem Tov (Master of the Good Name) — was the founder of Chassidus. There were a number of people in Jewish history who also had the appellation of Baal Shem Tov,[3] but Rabbi Yisrael is *the* Baal Shem Tov. He was born on the eighteenth day of Elul, 1698,[4] in the village of Okopy in the Polish province of Podolia, near the Dniester River. Here the legends begin.

His father was aged when he was born, and Yisrael was soon orphaned. He was an unusual child, and at the age of twelve was the Hebrew-school teacher's *bahelfer*, or assistant, whose responsibility it was to "shepherd" little school children, fetching them to school and returning them home after classes. He also served at various times as an assistant sexton, a ritual slaughterer, a common laborer, and an itinerant holy man. He wandered from village to village seemingly without purpose or goal. He married the sister of the famed scholar Rabbi Gershon Kitover, who, at first, considered his new brother-in-law to be an embarrassment. The Baal Shem Tov joined roving groups of pious men and then lived in isolation for some years in the Carpathian mountains near Kitov. Eventually he settled in the small town of Tluste in Polish Galicia. There, at the age of thirty-six he "revealed" himself, and became widely known as a healer and holy man. He then visited the Jewish towns and hamlets of Podolia, Volhynia, and Galicia, and attracted a large following.

---

1. The righteous men, who are representatives of the soul of Israel; the leaders and the patrons, the friends, the counselors, the representatives of God to man and of man to God.

2. A varied but vital bibliography on Chassidus, its founders and leaders, includes, but is certainly not limited to, *Be'er HaChassidus*, by Eliezer Steinman, Bnei Brak, 1970; *HaChassidus*, by Yitzchak Alfasi, Tel Aviv, 1977; *Zeramim V'Kitos B'Yahadus*, by Avraham Korman, Tel Aviv, 1967; *Chassidim U'Misnagdim*, by Mordecai Wilensky, Jerusalem, 1971; *HaChassidus*, by Aron Marcus, Bnei Brak 1980. The latter book is a work on Chassidus and its masters by a German Jew, a colleague of Rabbi Samson R. Hirsch, who traveled to Poland to observe Chassidus and eventually became a chassid himself. The book was originally published in German, in 1901, and was translated into Hebrew in this generation. However, Marcus showed great bias against certain chassidic leaders and groups, and he unwittingly accepted slanderous information in some cases. Consequently, the translator was advised to take the liberty of editing, changing and even omitting parts of the original work in order "to give satisfaction to the soul of the author."

3. Eisenstein, in his encyclopedia, *Otzar Yisrael*, lists five other *Baal Shems*. Even Rabbi Hai Gaon and the *Kuzari* discuss *Baal Shems*.

4. There is a conflicting tradition that he was born in 1700.

He began to preach the basic tenets of Chassidus: the Omnipresence of the Creator and the greatness of His creation; the importance and significance of man in creation and the universe; the influence that man and his actions have even upon God Himself;[5] that evil always contains good within it, because nothing can exist without an inner spark of holiness; that prayer is the key to God and is the primary means of Israel's spiritual self-elevation and, as such, is entitled to sustained and primary emphasis in a Jew's life; that regular daily physical purification in a *mikveh*[6] is a prerequisite to spiritual purification; that joy is the required background for Jewish life and that pessimism and depression cause sin and spiritual apathy; that fervent enthusiasm and an awareness of God's presence are essential components of Torah study and performance of commandments; that commandments must be performed with emotion and a feeling for their sacred character; that prayer must be conducted with intense concentration (*kavanah*); that Torah study and performance of commandments must be performed with only the purest intentions, without any ulterior motive, for the sole sake of fulfilling God's will; and, finally, that the *tzaddik* (the holy man) binds the Jewish people together into the corporate national body of Israel, and serves as a link between God and the masses who may be incapable of such spiritual elevation on their own.

None of these ideas were new to Judaism;[7] however, the emphasis Chassidus placed upon them, and their combination, created a new program that was little short of revolutionary. Coupled with this was the strong projection in Chassidus of kabbalistic thought and behavior. Since the middle of the sixteenth century, the *Arizal's* Kabbalah had grown in influence in all rabbinic circles, but the sad experience of the Shabtai Tzvi debacle forced the study of Kabbalah underground. Its knowledge and use was deemed to be forbidden to the masses of Jewry. This aversion to the study of Kabbalah was further strengthened in the aftermath of the Frankist debacle, during which episode the study of Kabbalah was abused.

---

5. See *Kedushas Levi*, by Rabbi Levi Yitzchak of Berditchev, *Parshas Naso,* where it is written that the verse "The Lord is your protective shadow" can be interpreted to mean that just as the shadow of a person mimics his actions, so too does God respond to us and is influenced, so to speak, by our actions.

6. A ritual bath necessary for purification from uncleanliness according to Torah law.

7. However, the idea of God's goodness being found in everything, including seeming evil, was vigorously disputed by Rabbi Chaim of Volozhin in *Nefesh HaChayim,* 3:3. This idea could be misinterpreted as coming too close to the heresy of Spinozian pantheism and, perhaps more than any other philosophical idea of Chassidus, caused the schism with the misnagdim — the opponents of Chassidus.

In 1756, the *Vaad Arba Aratzos,* or Council of Four Lands, adopted an edict restricting the general study of Kabbalah to men over the age of forty. This was now reversed by Chassidus, which brought the Kabbalah and its primary book, the *Zohar,* to the forefront of Jewish life.[8] Chassidus introduced new customs and folkways to general Jewish life based upon a mystical view of life and Torah, at times favoring the Kabbalah over the traditionally accepted *halachah*. It also changed the basic *nusach*[9] of prayer of its adherents from the traditional Ashkenazic form, in vogue for centuries, to a "Sephardic" form, which it preferred since it was more kabbalistically oriented.[10] The Baal Shem Tov also

8. Chassidus was not a monolith in this matter. See *HaChassidus* by Marcus, p. 66, for a description of the strong opposition within Chassidus itself to Rabbi Nachman of Breslav because of his popularization of kabbalistic secrets among the masses who, his opponents felt, were too unsophisticated for such studies.

9. Ritual order of prayer. The changes in the ritual by the Chassidic masters was a major cause of the opposition to them. A halachic discussion of the conflicting views is found in *Yabia Omer* (VI:10) by Rabbi Ovadiah Yosef.

10. The Sephardic *nusach* was not accepted in its entirety by the chassidim; rather, only those changes were accepted that were necessary to conform Nusach Ashkenaz to the *Arizal's* kabbalah. This led to much confusion, since the *Arizal's* view on many matters were not known with certainty, nor was there agreement regarding to what extent the *Arizal* should be followed. The founder of the Chabad/Lubavitch group, Rabbi Shneur Zalman of Liadi, was the first and almost the only one of the early chassidic leaders to publish a *siddur* incorporating those changes in the *nusach* which he deemed necessary. Because most of the changes proposed in this *siddur* are based on the *Ariz*al's views, it came to be known as *Nusach Ari*.

The synagogue of the Baal Shem Tov

introduced a new and improved method of manufacturing and sharpening knives for ritual slaughter (*shechitah*). This innovation was strenuously opposed by the opponents of the new movement, who were known as misnagdim, but in time it came to be accepted universally. In sum, by the time of his death, 6 Sivan, 1760, the Baal Shem Tov had unleashed a whirlwind in Eastern European Jewish life. It would sweep the masses of Eastern European Jews with it and, with revolutionary fervor and pious zeal, forever change Jewish society.

Maggid of Mezeritch

HE BAAL SHEM TOV WAS the founder of Chassidus, but the architect who built, shaped, and spread the movement was Rabbi Dov Ber,[11] the *Maggid* of Mezeritch. Born in Lukatch,[12] he was attracted to the Baal Shem Tov as a young man and became his foremost disciple and spiritual heir. Rabbi Dov Ber was a *maggid* — a preacher[13] — and, as the pre-eminent chassidic leader of his time, became known simply as "The *Maggid*". Contemporaries testified that he was both a brilliant Talmudic and kabbalistic scholar.

He held the post of preacher in many smaller communities in Poland until finally settling in Mezeritch, where he founded a center of chassidic study and inspiration for his generation. The Baal Shem Tov had many great disciples and contemporaries,[14] but the man who organized and broadened the chassidic movement and produced tens of great leaders was the *Maggid*. By the time of his death in 1772, the *Maggid* had attracted to his center of learning in Mezeritch some of the

---

11. His definite year of birth is unknown; it has been given variously as 1704 and 1710.

12. According to another version, he was born in an unknown village in Volhynia.

13. Reb Dov Ber was a *maggid* in Koretz and Rovno. Many towns and cities had a resident *maggid* who preached, while the rabbi was responsible for halachic rulings. Often, a *maggid* would be an itinerant preacher who supported his family by traveling from town to town and delivering his sermons.

14. A partial list would include Rabbi Yaakov Yosef of Polnoa (author of *Toldos Yaakov Yosef*), Rabbi Pinchas Shapiro of Koretz, Rabbi Shabsi of Rashkov, Rabbi Meir of Premishlan, Rabbi Tzvi Hirsh of Kaminka, Rabbi Chaim of Krasna, Rabbi Leib of Shpole (the *Shpoler Zayde*), Rabbi Menachem Mendel of Vitebsk, Rabbi Avraham Gershon Kitover (the brother-in-law of the Baal Shem), and Rabbi Yisrael of Satanov (an early and vociferous foe of Chassidus whom the Baal Shem himself converted into a disciple and follower).

most brilliant minds, extraordinary personalities, and strongest men of his day. There he molded them into great leaders, far-seeing visionaries, practical dreamers, hardened but humble protagonists, inspired teachers and holy men. It was the *Maggid* who, more than anyone else, was able to take a man of outstanding potential and develop him into a *tzaddik*, the personality who was to become the key to the success of Chassidus.

The names of the disciples and colleagues of the *Maggid* are legend. The great people who were touched and taught by him included Rabbi Elimelech of Lizhensk and his brother — the holy man disguised as simple Jew — Rabbi Zusia of Onipoli; Rabbi Shneur Zalman of Liadi, the founder of Chabad[15] Chassidus; Rabbi Yisrael of Kozhnitz (the Kozhnitzer *Maggid*); Rabbi Nachum Twersky of Tchernobel; Rabbi Aharon Perlow of Karlin, the founder of Chassidus in Lithuania; Rabbi Yaakov Yosef of Ostroh; Rabbi Levi Yitzchak of Berditchev;[16] Rabbi Chaim of Amdure; Rabbi Avraham Abba Weingarten of Luboshow; Rabbi Meshulam Feivish Heller of Z'baricz; Rabbi Shlomo Gottlieb of Karlin; Rabbi Avraham of Kalisk;[17] Rabbi Pinchas HaLevi Horowitz[18] and his brother, Rabbi Shmelke of Nicholsburg.

Rabbi Shneur Zalman of Liadi

This most impressive group of individuals would, of necessity, take diverse roads in their service of God and Israel, but they would tolerate and respect each other personally. However, the movement would begin to suffer the pangs of success, that are common to all triumphant

---

15. Chabad is the acronym of the Hebrew words, *Chochmah, Binah, Daas*, the three levels of wisdom as explained in kabbalistic thought. Rabbi Shneur Zalman was the founder of the dynasty of Lubavitch (hence the family name of the Lubavitcher *Rebbes* is Schneerson — son of Shneur). His **Sefer HaTanya** is likely the seminal work of Chassidic/Kabbalistic philosophy.

16. A legendary figure in Jewish life, famous for his love of Jews and his defense of the Jewish people against its enemies. In his prayers on behalf of the Jewish people, he always sought to show their innate goodness and find excuses for their misdeeds. He even went so far as to symbolically summon God to a *din Torah* — a court case — to justify Israel and free it from its exile; this **din Torah mit Gott** was later immortalized in song.

17. Originally a disciple of the Gaon of Vilna and fierce foe of Chassidus, he was "converted" to Chassidus by the *Maggid* and later, together with Rabbi Menachem Mendel of Vitebsk and Rabbi Gershon Kitover, founded the chassidic community in the Land of Israel at the end of the nineteenth century.

18. Later, rabbi in Frankfurt am Main, where he was a known but publicly unobtrusive chassid in that bastion of Ashkenazic, non-chassidic Jewry (see p. 79).

revolutions. Thus their adherents among the masses would often quarrel, sometimes violently, with one another. Chassidus would prove hardy and healthy, but the different customs and styles that arose among the various chassidic dynasties often fueled sharp disputes between them. As in all idealistic movements, the lofty nobility of theory was strained many times by the attempt to translate it into daily lifestyle and behavior. Also, as a movement that appealed not only to scholars and spiritually lofty people, but equally to the unlearned masses, it suffered from the conduct of adherents who were incapable of differentiating between the inner struggle for spiritual elevation and the truculent battle for the supremacy of one's group. In most cases, the *rebbes* tried to restrain the infighting, but not always were they successful.

Despite these growing pains, Chassidus would prove to be an ennobling and sure method for insuring Jewish continuity, commitment, and Torah observance for its multitude of adherents.

The *Maggid* and his disciples trained the next generation of *tzaddikim* and they continued to spread Chassidus throughout Eastern Europe. The biological descendants of the Baal Shem himself,[19] Rabbi Baruch of Mezibuzh, Rabbi Moshe Chaim Ephraim Sedikov,[20] Rabbi Yisrael the Dead,[21] and Rabbi Nachman of Breslav[22] brought the message of Chassidus to all parts of Poland and the Ukraine. These descendants of the Baal Shem, however, did not command the primary leadership of the chassidic movement; this authority was invested in the *Maggid*.

Chassidus in its first century was a meritocracy, and its leaders were

---

19. His daughter, Aydel, was herself considered a *tzadekes,* a holy woman and miracle worker, who, in effect, served as a leader under the imprimatur of her father, the *Besht* (the acronym of ***Baal Shem Tov***). In the first century of Chassidus, there would be other famous women who would be accorded great leadership status. Aydel's own daughter, Feige, was one of those women.

20. 1740-1800.

21. So called because of his apparent revival from the dead when he was a child.

22. One of the most famous personages in Chassidus. He was born in 1772 and died in 1810. Upon his death, his chassidim vowed never to have another *rebbe* as his successor. The Breslaver chassidim regularly visit his grave in Uman, Russia, in spite of all physical and governmental obstacles, and, especially under the Communists, at great personal danger. As recorded by his great disciple, Nassan, Rabbi Nachman's stories, sermons (*Likkutei Maharan*), and his informal talks (*Sichos Maharan*) form the main thrust of Breslaver Chassidus. His chair was smuggled out of Communist Russia, sliver by sliver, and reassembled to sit in the great Breslav synagogue in Jerusalem today. Many refer to the Breslaver chassidim as the "dead chassidim," because their *Rebbe* is no longer alive. However, their tenacity and survival to this day belie this title.

chosen because of their own personal greatness and rarely because of dynastic lineage.[23] Such leaders brought the movement to new lands, by force of their scholarship, zeal, holiness, and personalities. The *Maggid's* own great-grandson, Rabbi Yisrael Friedman of Rizhin,[24] would become a legend who contributed greatly to the spread of Chassidus to the Austro-Hungarian Empire. Rabbi Shabsi of Rashkov brought Chassidus to Bessarabia, Rabbi Avraham Yehoshua Heschel of Apt moved to the Ukraine, Rabbi Asher of Stolin came to Polish Lithuania, Rabbi Dov Ber Schneerson migrated to White Russia, and Rabbi Yitzchak Taub of Kaliv innovated Chassidus in Hungary. By 1810, Chassidus dominated Jewish Eastern Europe, with the exception of the Baltic states of Prussia, Lithuania, Latvia, and Northern Russia. After 1815, chassidic leaders were chosen almost invariably on the basis of family descent. This was one indication of the end of the revolutionary period of Chassidus and its evolution into the "establishment" for most of Eastern European Jewry.

---

23. See *Divrei Chaim* by Rabbi Chaim Halberstam, the famous *Rebbe* of Sanz, *Choshen Mishpat* §32. "Concerning the question of the inheritance of honor of being a *rebbe* . . . is it to be supposed that the authority of chassidic *rebbes* is a public office, like that of a rabbi, where it is accepted that the son can inherit his father's post? [The chassidic *rebbeim*] were men of Divine inspiration and their holy prayers and words produced results . . . I do not know how the idea of inheritance can enter into such matters."

24. Born in 1797, he lived like royalty, with servants, livery, retinue and gold carriage, but this was only his public persona, his way of gaining respect for his position. Privately, however, he avoided pleasure and even tended toward asceticism. He attracted thousands of followers to Rizhin but also provoked many powerful opponents among other chassidic groups. He was falsely accused of ordering the death of two Jewish informers, and imprisoned for twenty-two months. After his release, he was still in grave danger, until he managed to move his court from the domain of the Czar, in Rizhin, to Sadigur, under the rule of the Hapsburgs. His arrival in Bukovina vitalized Chassidus there, and tens of thousands of Jews became his disciples. However, his extravagant public lifestyle made him the subject of many bitter disputes and biting criticism. One of those disputes, that between Sanz chassidim and Sadigur chassidim, has assumed legendary status. Rabbi Yisrael died in 1850 (3 Cheshvan 5611). At his death he testified that he took with him no enjoyment at all from this world. Many great chassidic and non-chassidic contemporaries testified to his greatness, piety, and inspired leadership.

Counter-Revolution

THOUGH CHASSIDUS SPREAD throughout Eastern Europe, its main home and vitality were in Poland. And there Chassidus encountered inner turmoil and counter-revolution. After the death of the *Maggid,* the leadership of Polish Chassidus passed into the hands of Rabbi Elimelech of Lizhensk, and then to his disciple, the *Chozeh* (Seer) of Lublin, Rabbi Yaakov Yitzchak Horowitz.[25] The *Chozeh* initiated his own court even before the death of his teacher, Rabbi Elimelech of Lizhensk. Many criticized him for this and considered him guilty of lese majesty towards Rabbi Elimelech. However, it was part of the nature of Polish Chassidus in that era to expand and look for deeper meanings and new spiritual nuances, even if that meant discarding some of the hard-won gains of previous *rebbes* in particular and Chassidus in general. The *Chozeh* became the leader of Polish Chassidus in the last decade of the eighteenth century. He infused Chassidus with a new vigor, pursued intellectual Torah study strongly, and pushed for even greater expansion of Chassidus within the Jewish people. As had the *Maggid,* he also attracted many of the greatest young men of Polish Jewry to himself, and Lublin now became the spiritual home of Chassidus.

The *Chozeh* was the leader of a corrective counter-revolution within Chassidus, and his favorite disciple and most brilliant student and namesake, Yaakov Yitzchak Rabinowitz of P'shis'cha, called "The *Yid HaKadosh,*" or "The Holy Jew," continued this counter-revolution in a more radical form. During the lifetime of the *Chozeh,* "The Holy Jew" established his own court and gathered around him a group of dynamic personalities willing to sacrifice all, in order to discover for themselves the inner truth of Chassidus. Thus, what the *Chozeh* had previously done to his master, Rabbi Yaakov Yitzchak of P'shis'cha did to the *Chozeh.* Even though he personally remained loyal to the *Chozeh* and would visit Lublin regularly, he and his group were soon ostracized by the partisans of the *Chozeh.*

P'shis'cha opposed the institutionalization of Chassidus, and set standards that others considered unreasonably high. In P'shis'cha they refused to honor leaders whom they considered unworthy, mocked customs and observances performed by rote, shunned the unlettered

---

25. Born in 1745; died on the Ninth of Av, 1815.

and ignorant, and demanded honesty above all else. P'shis'cha abhorred physical luxury, dynastic rights, holiness based on miracles, pomp, and form. It ridiculed comfort, quiet, and placidity. It searched only for sacrifice, truth, and simplicity. It was direct, sharp, and abrasive. It took the hard road and, to many, it appeared bizarre, angry, and dangerous. Some of the great chassidic leaders of the time feared the new radicals, and Chassidus faced a great inner crisis that threatened its vitality and very survival. The abyss of schism beckoned. When "the Holy Jew" died during Succos, 1813, the brake holding back the open rift in Chassidus was removed. It was a dangerous time.

As his successor, "the Holy Jew's" followers chose his outstanding disciple, Rabbi Simchah Bunim, who had left the vibrantly Jewish P'shis'cha to take up residence in the religiously backsliding German city of Danzig. The *Rebbe* Reb Bunim, as he was called, tried to attract the wayward Jews of wealthy, modern Danzig, who were then succumbing to modernity and Enlightenment. To do so, he made himself accessible to them, visiting them and adopting mannerisms and dress that made them feel comfortable in his company. He acted as a lumber dealer and later became a pharmacist. He played chess and other games, loved music and musical instruments. This was his way of outreach — meeting Jews who had strayed and using his magnetic personality to draw them back.

Rabbi Bunim of P'shis'cha was a *rebbe par excellence*. He provided wisdom with fire, guidance with vision, hope with withering self-criticism. A man of piercing intellect, he understood that not everyone could or should be a P'shis'cha chassid. He searched for an elite group — a few good men — and he drew them to P'shis'cha. Among his disciples were three giants: Rabbi Menachem Mendel Morgenstern, who became the Kotzker *Rebbe*; Rabbi Yitzchak Meir Alter, later the founder of the Gerrer dynasty;[26] and Rabbi Yitzchak Kalish, who became the *Rebbe* of Vorki. Close to three hundred other superior young men forsook their homes and careers to warm themselves at the fire of P'shis'cha. But Rabbi Bunim also understood that he had to reconcile himself with mainstream Chassidus. The

---

26. Reb Mendel's original family name was Halperin, but because of his support of the Polish national revolution, he changed it to Morgenstern to confuse and escape the punishment of the Russian conqueror. Rabbi Yitzchak Meir's original name was Rottenberg but he changed it to Alter for the same reason as Reb Mendel. Whether their support of the Poles was voluntary or coerced is still a debate among scholars.

opportunity to do so occurred at the great wedding at Ustila.[27]

At Ustila, over two hundred leading *rebbes* gathered to celebrate the wedding of the children of two great *rebbes*. The elder statesman of Chassidus, Rabbi Avraham Yehoshua Heschel of Apt, convened a court at the wedding to hear the charges that P'shis'cha was deviating in an unacceptable manner from the accepted norms of Chassidus. The *Rebbe* Reb Bunim chose not to attend the wedding and he sent Rabbi Yitzchak Meir to represent him. He did so ably, and Rabbi Avraham Yehoshua Heschel of Apt decided not to publicly condemn P'shis'cha.[28] The confrontation was avoided, and though the muttering continued for decades, a schism never materialized.

The *Rebbe* Reb Bunim died just before Rosh Hashanah in 1827. He was succeeded by the most radical, enigmatic, and awe-inspiring figure in Chassidus, Rabbi Menachem Mendel Morgenstern of Tomashov. Born in 1787, he was a genius of rare proportions. His colleagues, Rabbi Yitzchak Kalish, who became the *Rebbe* of Vorki, and Rabbi Yitzchak Meir Alter, who would later become Reb Mendel's brother-in-law, deferred to him as the successor of the *Rebbe* Reb Bunim.

Later, Reb Mendel would move to Kotzk and would be known immortally as the Kotzker *Rebbe*. He had no equal in intellect. His knowledge of Torah was awe inspiring. His personality, however, was so dynamic and his standards of honesty and discipline so demanding that he was feared by his adherents and disciples as no other *rebbe* ever was. His incisive aphorisms became a book of Chassidus by themselves.[29] He was the epitome of the counter-revolution of Chassidus,

---

27. The wedding was that of Rabbi Shmuel Yechiel, the son of the *Rebbe* Dan of Radvil, to the daughter of the *Rebbe* Yosef of Ustila.

28. See Marcus, p. 134, for the advice that the Apter *Rav* gave to Rabbi Yitzchak Meir. "The *Shulchan Aruch* is the King's highway for us. Because of the bitter exile, obstacles were placed on the King's highway that blocked this road for many. The Baal Shem Tov found a detour that was hidden between mountains and forests, and that detour eventually led back to the main road. Since the Baal Shem, many marchers have damaged that detour itself and it has become more difficult to traverse it. You at P'shis'cha are now attempting to force a new detour over even more dangerous terrain. I doubt your success in this. Instead, attempt to return to the King's highway directly." When R' Yitzchak Meir became the *Rebbe* of Gur, he would follow this advice.

29. Some of his famous statements are: "Where can God be found? Wherever man allows him in." "If I am and you are, because I am myself and you are yourself, then I am I and you are you; but if I am because you are, then I am not I, and you are not you." "I prefer an evil person who knows he is evil to a pious person who thinks he is pious." "It is possible to bring the dead back to life. Still better is it to bring the living back to life." "All that is thought should not be said, all that is said should not be written, all that is written should not be published, all that is published should not be read." "The

and in him did the search for the inner soul of Chassidus culminate. He did not wish to be *rebbe* for the masses; he despised the world, its wealth and pettiness. He was not tolerant of fools and he raged at injustice. He was an angry person in the most positive sense of the word, because he raged at imperfection and slothful pursuit of less than the ideal. He was a difficult *rebbe* to serve. Ordinary people needed warmth and comfort, a human *rebbe*, and not a fiery avenging angel.

In 1839, Reb Mendel withdrew from public life and, though thousands still considered him their *rebbe*, he remained a recluse until his death in 1859. He suffered many reverses and disappointments in his later years. His disciple, Rabbi Mordechai Yosef Leiner, broke with him, and led a large number of chassidim from Kotzk to a new center at Izhbitze. A milder version of Reb Mendel, Rabbi Mordecai Yosef founded the dynasty of Radziner Chassidus. His grandson, Rabbi Gershon Henoch Leiner,[30] was a genius and a renowned leader, but a controversial personality whose great achievements aroused violent opposition.

Reb Mendel's son-in-law, Avraham Bornstein of Sochatchov,[31] refused to continue the Kotzker dynasty; instead, Sochatchov became a separate movement. Reb Mendel's son, Rabbi David, was unable to successfully inherit his father's mantle. Rabbi Yitzchak Meir Alter, Reb Mendel's brother-in-law, resided in Warsaw and in its suburb, the small town of Gura Kalavaria, where he founded the great chassidic dynasty of Gur, which grew to become the normative Polish Chassidus in the twentieth century. Other disciples of Kotzk became the forerunners of prominent Polish courts. Among them were Rabbi Yitzchak Kalish, the *Rebbe* of Vorki, many of whose disciples, led by Rabbi Shraga Feivel Danziger, became the chassidim of Alexander. The *Rebbes* of Vorki, their cousins, the *Rebbes* of Amshinov,

---

purpose of man is to raise the sky." " 'Thou shalt not steal' means thou shall not steal from yourself — do not deceive yourself."

Many of his sayings are recorded in the great chassidic work *Emes V'Emunah*, and are quoted by his disciples in their own works.

30. Born in 1839, he died in 1891. He wrote a "Gemara" for the Mishnah, *Seder Taharos,* and called it *Sidrei Taharos.* He also claimed that he had identified the amphibious creature known as *chilazon,* from whose blood came the blue dye — *techeles* — for *tzitzis.* Both of these major achievements were hotly disputed by other chassidic and non-chassidic rabbinic circles.

31. 1839-1910. He was a great scholar and his books, *Eglei Tal* and *Avnei Nezer*, are Talmudic and halachic classics.

and the court of Gur, formed the bulk of Polish Jewry. Thus did the school of P'shis'cha prevail, and its revolutionary zeal helped stamp the ultimate form on Polish Chassidus.

Chassidic Leaders

OTHER MAJOR CHASSIDIC DYNASTIES flourished in Galicia, Poland, Rumania, and Hungary. Though a detailed description of them is beyond the purview of this book, mention must be made of some of the great men who revitalized Jewish life in different parts of Europe, all of them imposing chassidic masters, but each unique and different in the nuances of his service to God and man.

Rabbi Menachem Mendel Hager of Kossov[32] founded the Hager dynasty in 1802. His grandson and namesake,[33] who was the son-in-law of Rabbi Yisrael of Rizhin, established the chassidic court at Vizhnitz in 1854. After World War I, it moved to Grosswerdein (Nagy-Vardan/Oradea) in Hungary/Rumania. It numbered tens of thousands of adherents in Europe, and after the Holocaust reestablished itself in Israel and in the United States, where it is famed for its love of Jews and its many educational and social institutions.

Rabbi Shalom Rokeach of Belz[34] was a disciple of the famed *Chozeh* of Lublin, of Rabbi Shlomo of Lutzk, and of Rabbi Uri of Strelisk. The Belzer dynasty was one of the main chassidic groups in Galicia and Hungary. It was very popular, influential, and powerful in Europe, and now is headquartered in Jerusalem, with branches in the United States and elsewhere. Like most chassidic dynasties, it is intertwined by marriage with many other dynasties, and is known for its dynamic projects in the Jewish world.

The Teitelbaum family were chassidic leaders in Sighet and later in Satmar. The founder of the dynasty was Rabbi Moshe Teitelbaum of Ujhel.[35] Today it is one of the largest and most powerful groups in world Jewry, due mainly to the late Satmar *Rav,* Rabbi Yoel Teitelbaum, who

---

32. 1778-1826.

33. Menachem Mendel of Vizhnitz (1830-1885).

34. 1779-1855.

35. 1759-1841.

survived the Holocaust. He combined great Torah genius with charismatic leadership ability to rebuild the Satmar community. Its acts of charity and social welfare are legendary, as is its fierce opposition to the secular policies and influence of Zionism. Satmar is currently centered in New York, but is well represented in Israel and in almost every Jewish community in the world.

Another very influential Rumanian/Hungarian dynasty was that of Rabbi Yosef Meir Weiss[36] of Spinka. The descendants of Rabbi Tzvi Elimelech Shapiro[37] of Dinov became leaders in Rumania/Hungary. His great-grandson, Rabbi Chaim Elazar Shapiro,[38] was the head of the dynasty of Munkacz, the city where he also maintained a large yeshivah. His strongly held views in opposition to Zionism and on other Jewish organizational issues were controversial. The combination of all of these great personages gradually converted Rumania and Hungary into bastions of Chassidus, with the *rebbes* sharing power and influence with the disciples of Rabbi Moses Sofer.

Finally, Rabbi Chaim Halberstam of Sanz[39] spawned many different dynasties of chassidic masters, concentrated mainly in Galicia and Hungary. One of the leading scholars of his time and an uncompromising fighter for Jewish tradition, he was in the forefront of many struggles for Jewish life in the nineteenth century. The chassidic courts of Klauzenberg and Bobov are offshoots of the house of Sanz, as were many others that were wiped out by the Nazis. These centers of Chassidus are currently in Israel and New York, and number many thousands of followers and supporters.

Chassidus did not occur in a vacuum. In order to appreciate the movement, one must also be aware of its opponents and the historical forces at work during the time. The hundred years from 1750 to 1850 were times of flux and change for Eastern Europe and its Jews. Only against the backdrop of the developments of the century can the appearance and achievements of Chassidus be measured. Hence, the following chapters, though not directly discussing the history of Chassidus, nevertheless illuminate the movement and its historic destiny.

---

36. 1839-1909.
37. 1738-1841.
38. 1871-1937.
39. 1793-1876.

12

The Gaon of Vilna

A Non-leading Leader

HE EARLY CHASSIDIC MASTERS were great and unusual people who were able to revitalize much of Eastern European Jewry within the parameters of tradition, Torah, and *halachah*. Their modus operandi was a mass movement that brought Judaism to the people, thereby succeeding in attracting them to its teachers. During that same era there was another master, one who was private and secluded, but who, in his own unique way, was the towering force of that age and whose influence and scholarship remains eternally vital. This man was Rabbi Eliyahu of Vilna, known as the *Gra*, acronym of the *Gaon Rabbeinu Eliyahu*, or simply as **the** *gaon*, or genius *par excellence*.[1]

Historically, he was the standard for all Jewish tradition and scholarship of his age. All other luminaries of intellect that lived in the eighteenth-century Jewish world were dimmed by the light of his presence.[2] He was reminiscent of an age long gone, comparable to scholars deemed superhuman, to the time of the great *Rishonim* of Spain, France, and Germany.[3] Even the leaders of Chassidus, which

---

1. Though many people in Jewish history have been described as *geonim*, or geniuses, when someone speaks of "*The* Gaon," it is understood that he refers to Rabbi Eliyahu of Vilna.

2. See approbation of Rabbi Yisrael Lipschitz (*Tiferes Yisrael*) to *Choshen Mishpat*, Koenigsberg 1863, and of Rabbi Chaim of Volozhin to *Orach Chaim*. See Landau, *HaGaon HaChassid MiVilna*, for many examples of this.

3. It is reported that the Gaon's disciple, Rabbi Chaim of Volozhin, compared Rabbi Eliyahu to *Rashba*, Rabbi Shlomo ben Aderes, a pre-eminent Torah scholar of fourteenth-century Spanish Jewry.

he strenuously opposed, regarded him with the utmost respect.[4]

Rabbi Eliyahu was a very complex and dazzling person. Such geniuses cannot be assessed by those who did not know them and therefore cannot comprehend their true standard.[5] There are many paradoxical qualities concerning him as well. Yet, we know enough about him from his writings, contemporaries, and disciples to sketch some likeness of this towering personality.

Eliyahu, the son of Shlomo Zalman, was born in 1720, in Vilna. During his lifetime, he acquired two titles conferred sparingly by Jews and, even when granted, rarely if ever bestowed simultaneously on the same person. He was called "the *Gaon*" — the ultimate Torah scholar, and "the *Chassid*" — the truly pious servant of God. Throughout the ages, Jewish scholarship has always been entwined with ritual observance and moral piety. But the reputation of Rabbi Eliyahu in the areas of both scholarship and piety is an amazing testimony to his lofty moral character and intellectual genius.

The Vilna Gaon

He was never a rabbi in any official sense, and never held public office or headed any Jewish school, institution, or community. In fact, he was a very private, reticent, and solitary person, who achieved his fame and influence by reputation and not primarily by personal contact. This paradox of a "non-leading leader" only further emphasizes the titanic dimensions of his personality and accomplishments. Within the uniqueness of his person, the Gaon embodied all of the variant strains of Jewish knowledge, scholarship, and historical tradition.

Perhaps the Gaon's most enduring historical contribution to the nation was his restoration of the Torah scholar to his traditional position of primacy in Jewish life. The effects of *Tach V'Tat* and Shabtai Tzvi, coupled with unrelenting war, dislocation, and pogroms, combined to weaken the infrastructure of Jewish life and Torah study. By his personal example and efforts, the Gaon strengthened the status of Torah scholarship. The hero of Jewry was to be the scholar and not the

---

4. "The *Gaon* and *Chassid* . . . is renowned to all as peerless in his time . . . We hear that there is no one in Lithuania who will dare to challenge the *Gaon* and *Chassid's* view . . ." So wrote the great chassidic master, Rabbi Shneur Zalman of Liadi, whom the Gaon had relentlessly opposed. *Letters of the Baal HaTanya*, by D.Z. Hillman (ed.) § 56,57,85.

5. Rabbi Aharon Kotler, famed scholar and rosh yeshivah, felt that all attempts to describe and assess the Gaon are beyond us. See his approbation to *Ruach Eliyahu*, Jerusalem, 1949.

miracle worker. By aligning oneself to scholarship, one would automatically have a more rational, less other-worldly and miraculous view of Jewish life and Torah.

To many of the unlearned, downtrodden masses of Eastern European Jews, this scholarly portrait of Judaism was much less appealing than was the soaring, emotional, and supernatural vision of Chassidus. It promised no instant results nor did it always lighten the burden of life. It was, however, a realistic, fundamental approach to Torah and life, in consonance with the tradition of Israel. It may have dampened exorbitant hopes and lessened dreams, but it provided the firm basis upon which the Gaon's disciples built the modern yeshivah educational system and revitalized the Jewish ethical approach to life through the Mussar movement. The Yeshivah and Mussar Movements in Jewish life, born of nineteenth-century Eastern European circumstances, were spiritually fathered by the Gaon. The preservation of the priority of Torah scholarship as the focal point of Jewish life was thus perhaps his greatest achievement.

Herculean Task

RABBI ELIYAHU UNDERTOOK and completed a daunting task that only someone of his intellect and stature could have accomplished, and he gained the universal acceptance of even his greatest peers: he edited and standardized an accurate text of the Mishnah and Talmud. His immense knowledge, scholarly intuition, and prodigious research of texts and manuscripts, coupled with his unerringly holy instinct for the truth,[6] enabled him to eliminate hundreds of copyists' errors that, through the centuries, had entered the books of the Talmud, Midrash, and later rabbinic literature. So numerous and inclusive were the benefits of this herculean task — done without research staff, assistants or modern technology — that only outstanding scholars could begin to appreciate its enormous benefits, and much of the Gaon's work has not yet been fully appreciated in Jewish scholarship. The reverence in which the traditional texts were held was such that only the Gaon's great reputation

---

6. His disciple, Rabbi Chaim of Volozhin, stated that the Gaon fasted in prayer and penance many days before finally undertaking any single emendation in the then-accepted text of the Talmud. See also Rabbi Yisrael of Shklov who, in his introduction to *Taklin Chadtin*, describes the Gaon's painstaking work in this area.

for piety — for being the "chassid" — could serve as the wedge of acceptance for his corrections in the texts of the basic books of Jewish scholarship. His textual emendations solved many puzzles, answered many questions, and reconciled many scholarly conflicts. They also eliminated, in many instances, seemingly erroneous pilpulistic[7] interpretations that had distorted ideas and decisions of Torah and *halachah*.

Through intense Talmudic scholarship, strict adherence to Jewish tradition, loyalty to — and respect for — the holiness of the previous generations of Jewish scholars, the Gaon achieved great changes in Talmudic texts and methods of study, and his changes have been accepted as true and faithful to the original intent of the Sages. The mainly secular "scholars" of later generations who attempted to "scientifically" reorder the Talmud and its literature to conform to then-fashionable standards of scholarship have, with the passage of time, more often than not been proven wrong. Not so with the works of the Gaon. Subsequent to the Gaon, all meaningful Talmudic scholarship had to take into account the Gaon's glosses and notes to the text.

The private entrance to the study of the Vilna Gaon

7. *Pilpul* is defined as a form of innovative, ingenious reasoning, sometimes almost circuitous in nature, used in Talmudic thought and logic. It was always popular in Jewish scholarship, especially in Polish circles. It was sharp, bright, and sometimes even breathtaking in its ability to bind together disparate subjects and reconcile the apparently irreconcilable. In time, however, beginning in the seventeenth century, such leading authorities as *Maharal* of Prague, Rabbi Yeshayah Horowitz (the *Shelah*), Rabbi Yair Bachrach (*Chavos Yair*), and Rabbi Aryeh Leib of Minsk (*Sha'agas Aryeh*) felt that the development of *pilpul* had reached a point where it had become too much of a good thing, and the excesses of this system of logic sometimes bordered on the extreme. As it had evolved, this method of study was roundly criticized as not being truly representative of accurate Torah study. The Gaon, whose basic commitment was to the accuracy of the text, and the thoughtful, rational, in-place analysis of the subject matter, was paramount in discouraging the use of this method of study in Lithuania. *See* the introductions of Rabbi Chaim of Volozhin, of R' Yisrael of Shklov, ibid., Rabbi Asher Tiktiner at the end of his *Kesser Rosh*, Rabbi Pinchas of Plotsk, in his *Kesser Torah*, *Aliyos Eliyahu*, gloss 77, as well as *Darchei Noam*, Koenigsberg 1764. In today's yeshivos the word "*pilpul*" is used to denote a scholarly lecture grounded in the style of analysis and textual accuracy promoted by the Gaon, and thus should not be confused with the *pilpulistic* method of the seventeenth and eighteenth centuries criticized by the Gaon for its illogical excesses and irrelevant hair-splitting.

Disparate Reasons

NLY TWICE IN HIS LIFETIME did the Gaon leave the privacy of intense study, once when he was relatively young and once toward the end of his life, and both times his motives for so doing were known only to him.

While he was probably in his thirties, he embarked on a self-imposed exile.[8] For almost five years he was absent from his beloved Vilna, during which time he wandered westward from city to city, traveling incognito, suffering all the hardships and deprivations of travel, accepting the abuse meted out to strange wayfarers (especially Jewish ones), until he finally reached Germany. There his true identity was discovered and revealed; with his anonymity ended, he began his return home. His journey through Prussia, Poland, and Lithuania took on the festive air of a royal tour, as scholars and laymen alike strove to see and pay tribute to the monarch of Torah knowledge. [9]

The Gaon never explained his motives for undertaking a project as troublesome, disturbing, and dangerous as anonymous exile. However, his disciples (in hindsight, some years later) saw in his journey a practical attempt to achieve three main objectives: (a) to expiate his sins[10] by the penance of exile; (b) to discover and publicize unknown great Torah scholars who were isolated and hidden in the small Jewish villages of Eastern Europe, so that the masses of Jewry could benefit from their scholarship and erudition; [11] and (c) to have the opportunity to examine, compare, and study rare manuscripts and books of Torah scholarship, scattered throughout the Jewish communities of Eastern Europe, in his quest of sources for his redaction of many major texts of Torah and rabbinic literature.[12]

---

8. In Yiddish, this was known as *praven golus*. Many great holy figures in Jewish history undertook the dangers and privation of travel and exile as a pilgrimage to spiritual elevation.

9. Maimon, *Sefer HaGra*, p. 68.

10. Maimon, *Sefer HaGra*, p. 61, relates that he heard from the elders of Vilna that one of Eliyahu's "sins" was pulling out a hair of his father's beard when he was yet a child!

11. Rabbi Yeshayah Zuchivitzer and Rabbi Moshe of Ivya were two of the Gaon's "discoveries."

12. In *Sefer HaGra*, p. 68, Maimon offers an ingenious verification of this hypothesis.

In these reasons for his self-imposed exile, Rabbi Eliyahu was able to mirror in his own private life the unique, purposeful experience of Israel in its long national exile. For the Jew had always seen in the exile not only punishment for sin and expiation, but also the opportunity to prove conclusively that millions of people could live a holy and pious life for centuries even under the most abject physical circumstances, and that great contributions to education, scholarship, civilization and the quality of human life could stem from a transient and persecuted minority.

In his later years, the Gaon attempted to realize another Jewish dream — to settle in the Land of Israel. He made the necessary arrangements, wrote letters of farewell and an ethical will to his family and community, and left Vilna once more, this time bound for the Land of Israel. He never arrived there. Physical difficulties, frailties of health, and the lack of adequate transportation forced him to turn back after almost two months on the road. He later was heard to say that "the hand of Heaven restrained him" from successfully completing his journey.[13] However, his attempt, though aborted, left a deep imprint on his followers and bore positive fruit in the next generation, as large numbers of his disciples settled in Israel and became major components of the *Yishuv* in Jerusalem, Tiberias, and elsewhere in the country.

The Value of Wisdom

 HE GAON WAS THE MICROCOSM of the nation of Israel and, therefore, he served as the prism in which all Jews loyal to Torah and tradition could see the reflection of their own particular point of view against the infinite backdrop of traditional Jewish life and values.

If it could be said of any single human being that he knew everything, it was the Gaon. He knew the Torah in all its breadth and depth, but he was also expert in the sciences, mathematics, philosophy, music, and medicine, among other disciplines. To him, however, all fields of knowledge were found in the Torah and defined in the discipline of Torah. He could not countenance any pursuit that was divorced from Torah, much less opposed to Torah. He felt such

---

13. See introduction to his *Beur L'Orach Chaim,* as reported by his sons.

pursuits to be ephemeral, with no positive reality. Consequently, scholarly pursuits that in others would have been questioned, or even attacked as deviations or innovations, were accepted when they emanated from the Gaon, because there was no doubt that coming from him they were valid expressions of the Torah's infinite wisdom. Though others may have failed to perceive these expressions, the vision of the Gaon was deeper. A number of examples will help illustrate this.

The Gaon was acquainted with the theses of Plato and Aristotle through the works of Maimonides, Yehudah HaLevi, Saadiah Gaon, Moshe Chaim Luzzatto, and other great Jewish philosophers. His method of Torah study and interpretation was intensely analytical and logical — that of a rationalist of the first order. Yet no one would accuse him of demeaning the sanctity and mystery of the Torah or the primacy of its teachings.

He was the greatest Jewish expert on philosophy in his age — "he knew philosophy to its ultimate level"[14] — but he was never criticized for this even by those who regarded philosophical rationalism suspiciously, if not scornfully. The Gaon himself rejected philosophy as being a necessary discipline with its own inherent value, independent of its utility in understanding the Torah. He stated that he "learned only two good things" from his study thereof, and that "the balance [of philosophic thought] should be discarded."[15] Of attempts to reinterpret Talmudic passages that conflicted with philosophical teachings, the Gaon wrote, "All the statements [of the Sages] are to be understood in the simple meaning; however, they do have an inner meaning that is not the inner meaning of the philosophers — which is superficial — but [the inner meaning] of the masters of truth."[16] This attitude towards the sophistry and fantasies of philosophy, combined with his indisputable piety, earned him immunity to controversy on this issue of his own knowledge and use of philosophy, something that even the greatest of his predecessors often failed to achieve.

The Gaon of Vilna was a leading protagonist of the study of natural sciences as an indispensable adjunct to the correct understanding of the Torah itself. His disciple, Rabbi Yisrael of Shklov, stated that "upon completing his commentary to the 'Song of Songs,' the Gaon declared

---

14. The introduction to the famous scholarly work, *Pe'as HaShulchan*, by Rabbi Yisrael of Shklov, one of the Gaon's pre-eminent disciples. See note 36 below.

15. *Pe'as HaShulchan*, ibid. See *Letters of Chazon Ish*, vol. II, §171.

16. *Beur HaGra, Yoreh Deah* 179:13, where he strongly disagrees with a ruling of Maimonides and criticizes his overly positive attitude towards philosophy.

that all of the disciplines are essential for the understanding of our holy Torah, for they are all included in the Torah, and that he had mastered them all. He mentioned algebra, geometry, engineering, and music, praising the latter greatly . . . and he explained the essence of all the sciences. With regard to medicine, he studied only surgery, anatomy, and related topics. Though he wished to study pharmacology from contemporary doctors, his saintly father restrained him because it would cause his Torah study to be interrupted."[17]

The Gaon also told Rabbi Yisrael that if one did not appreciate musical composition he would be unable to understand "most of the accentuation and cantillation of the Torah, the secrets of the Levitic songs, and the secrets of the *Tikkunei Zohar,*"[18] and that through music, man could achieve spiritual elevation and ecstasy.[19] The Gaon himself wrote on the natural sciences[20] and instructed his disciples to translate into Hebrew certain books of history and the scientific disciplines.[21]

However, it is clear that the Gaon saw all of this wisdom as being valuable only as a means to one end — that of attaining fuller knowledge and appreciation of Torah and God's will on earth. This caveat was clearly evident from his writings and personal conduct. Furthermore, he did not move to incorporate such study into the curricula of Jewish education. Nor did his most famous disciple, Rabbi Chaim of Volozhin, include any secular studies in the program of his great yeshivah in Volozhin. Clearly, the Gaon held that it was essential for a Jew to devote himself to Torah studies until he became an accomplished Torah scholar. Then, the greatest scholars could perfect their Torah knowledge through acquaintance with other disciplines, but these disciplines were not on a plane with Torah study itself.

17. *Pe'as HaShulchan,* ibid.

18. Ibid.

19. Hence, perhaps, the emphasis on music in Chassidus!

20. The Gaon wrote *Ayil Meshulash*, a work on algebra and trigonometry. *Sefer HaT'chunah*, a work on astronomy, is ascribed to him by some, but this is disputed by others. See Landau, *HaGaon . . .* p. 374.

21. Rabbi Baruch of Shklov wrote that he translated Euclid, and Rabbi Avraham Simchah of Amitzlov wrote that he translated Josephus Flavius' *War of the Jews*, both at the Gaon's behest.

Studying Kabbalah

N HIS TIME THE GAON OF VILNA was the foremost student and exponent of the study of Kabbalah.[22] The secrets of the *Zohar,* as well as the holy traditions of Jewish mysticism, were explored, unraveled and explained by him. He delved into Kabbalah with a focus unmatched by any of his contemporaries, including many of the famed founders of Chassidus. Many of his commentaries to the Biblical books were phrased and expressed in terms of kabbalistic interpretation and insight. Although there were many who opposed the mass study of Kabbalah — a legacy of the sorry outgrowth of the Shabtai Tzvi excesses — their criticism never visited the Gaon because he clearly limited its study to those who were mature scholars and, therefore, qualified to delve into the secrets of the Torah.[23]

The Gaon's own followers severely criticized the chassidic masters for emphasizing Kabbalah and mysticism among the masses and for stressing these teachings, seemingly at the expense of Torah study and rational Halachah. Kabbalah study was never studied formally in the Lithuanian yeshivos that were later founded by the heirs of the Gaon's school. Nevertheless, the same opponents of these studies as they were developed in Chassidus never doubted the truth of the Gaon's exposition and use of this very same subject matter and technique. The fact that he combined the mystical and the rational in his approach to Torah and to life, and showed their true harmony, ranks as one of his greatest accomplishments.[24]

Ironically, the Gaon himself acquired a reputation as a miracle worker and legends abound, many of them well documented by unimpeachable sources, concerning his supernatural powers and his

---

22. See *Rav Pe'alim,* by the Gaon's son, Rabbi Avraham, who quotes on p. 29 his father as saying that he authored thirty books of commentary on the *Zohar* and that he would not be embarrassed to relate their contents to Rabbi Shimon bar Yochai, the author of the *Zohar.*

23. Two of his great contemporaries, Rabbi Yonasan Eybeshitz and Rabbi Moshe Chaim Luzzatto, had been criticized because of their kabbalistic activities. See *Luchos HaEidus,* p. 76, and Rabbi Yitzchak Moltzin's introduction to *Derech Hashem.* The Gaon strongly defended them both and was instrumental in their vindication. See Maimon, *Sefer HaGra,* p. 150.

24. See Landau, *HaGaon . . .,* pp. 141-42 n.12.

miraculous acts.[25] It is important to note that, in reporting these extraordinary occurrences, his sons and disciples attribute all such powers exclusively to the Gaon's astounding diligence and knowledge of Torah.[26] The sons of the Gaon stated explicitly, "The greatness of God upon this great man came by crowning him with the crown of Torah." This enabled him to know and control events in a supernatural fashion.[27]

In the summer of 1794, Vilna was besieged by the Russian army, then engaged in one of its regular attempts to conquer Poland and Lithuania. As the Jews prayed in the main synagogue of Vilna during the fierce bombardment of the city, the Gaon publicly reassured them that they would be spared. At that instant, a cannon ball struck the roof of the synagogue and remained lodged in the roof beam, neither penetrating nor exploding. This miracle of the Gaon was commemorated in Vilna for many decades after his death.[28]

The Gaon is correctly remembered as the leading foe of the chassidic movement, but, ironically, it may be maintained that, in one sense, he was its savior. Through his criticism of the excesses of its early years, he isolated and discredited its extremists and reemphasized the primacy of intellectual Torah study and *halachah* in Jewish life. In that sense, he was the antidote to the raging virus of unbridled change that was sweeping the Jewish world of the eighteenth century. By insuring that Chassidus remained in the mainstream of Jewish life and tradition, he helped prevent it from becoming an aberrant movement which would have earned the opprobrium of history.[29]

---

25. Among his inner circle, amazing stories were known such as his aborted attempt to create a *golem* before his bar-mitzvah! (Introduction of R' Chaim of Volozhin to *Sifra D'Tzniasa*); his study with celestial mentors (ibid.); his assistance to departed souls (approbation of Rabbi Shaul of Vilna to ibid.), he and his disciples feasting on a sumptuous bird which was "sent from Heaven" (*Aliyos Eliyahu* p. 24).

26. Landau, HaGaon . . ., p. 263.

27. Introduction to *Beur HaGra, Yoreh Deah.*

28. Noach Hillel Steinschneider, *Ir Vilna,* p. 50.

29. In *Sefer HaGra,* p. 73, Mosad Harav Kook, 1947, Maimon relates that his mentor, Rabbi Yechiel Epstein of Novardok, quoted one of the great *rebbes* of Lubavitch, the *Tzemach Tzedek,* as having said that the chassidic movement would have drifted off and out of the orbit of Torah discipline and halachic practice were it not for the Gaon's opposition to it in its formative stage. It should be noted, however, that this story comes from an opponent of Chassidus.

The Gaon died on the nineteenth of Tishrei, the fifth day of Succos, in 1797, and was buried in the great cemetery of Vilna.[30] His legacy was guarded by his children and brothers. His sons: Rabbi Yehudah Leib, Rabbi Avraham,[31] and Rabbi Shlomo Zalman; his sons-in-law, Rabbi Moshe of Pinsk, Rabbi Uri of Dubrov, Rabbi Tzvi Hirsch Dunchin; his brothers, Rabbi Avraham,[32] Rabbi Yissachar Ber, Rabbi Meir of Yanishak and Rabbi Moshe of Padzelva, all preserved his thoughts and works. They edited and published his writings and spread his ideas and

---

30. The Gaon's remains were removed from the old cemetery in 1953 when the local authorities converted the Jewish burial ground into a sports park. Even dead Jews are included in the hateful program of anti-Semitism. His new grave was refurbished and the monument rebuilt in the 1960s through the efforts of Rabbi Pinchas Teitz of Elizabeth, N.J. Reportedly the Gaon's "Ohel," or mausoleum, also contains the remains of his wife, his son, Rabbi Avraham, and Avraham ben Avraham, the Ger Tzeddek (Righteous Convert) of Vilna.

31. The author of Rav Pe'alim, an encyclopedia to Midrash, and other works. He published and introduced several of the Gaon's works.

32. Author of Maalos HaTorah and a well-known rabbinic figure in Lithuania.

Old Tomb of the Vilna Gaon

influence throughout Lithuania, Latvia, White Russia, Lithuanian Poland, and Prussia. The Gaon's main disciples built upon his legacy and thereby changed the face and direction of much of Jewry.

These disciples included the brothers Rabbi Zalman and Rabbi Chaim of Volozhin,[33] Rabbi Binyamin Rivlin of Shklov,[34] Rabbi Yisrael Rivlin of Shklov,[35] the brothers Rabbi Menachem Mendel[36] and Rabbi Simchah Bunim of Shklov,[37] Rabbi Shlomo of Wilkomir,[38] and Rabbi Yaakov Kahane.[39] Many contemporaries considered him their mentor though they did not study under him. Among them were Rabbi Avraham Danzig,[40] Rabbi Shmuel Avigdor,[41] Rabbi Aryeh Meites,[42] and Rabbi Baruch Schick of Shklov.[43]

But in a greater sense all of Jewry became his disciples. Rarely has one individual had such a profound influence upon his people. The Gaon was in the tradition of *Rashi*, Maimonides, Rabbi Yosef Caro and Rabbi Moshe Isserles. A giant in an age of giants, his benevolent shadow was cast over world Jewry, and his tradition served as an exemplary haven for Jewish scholarship, ethics, and behavior, and as a guide for the future of the Jewish people.

---

33. The brothers were legendary figures in Lithuanian Jewry. Rabbi Zalman was regarded as the leading disciple of the Gaon, both in Torah and in piety, but he died as a very young man. His older brother, Rabbi Chaim, came closer than anyone to being the Gaon's "successor" as the leading Torah authority in Lithuania and White Russia. He was the founder of Volozhin Yeshivah and the spiritual father of the modern yeshivah movement.

34. Author of the rabbinic work *Gevi'i Gevia HaKesef*, and the leader of the disciples of the Gaon in the city of Shklov, Lithuania.

35. Author of *Pe'as HaShulchan* and spiritual father of the *Yishuv HaYashan*, the reborn Jewish settlements in Safed and Jerusalem in the nineteenth century.

36. He was responsible for the publication of many of the Gaon's manuscripts, such as his commentary to Proverbs.

37. See *Aliyos Eliyahu*. These two brothers were also among the founders of the *Yishuv HaYashan* in Palestine in the 1800s.

38. The Gaon's sons listed him as second only to Rabbi Chaim Volozhin among the disciples. See Landau, *HaGaon . . .*, p. 275.

39. Author of *Geon Yaakov* on tractate *Eruvin*, son-in-law of the Gaon's brother, Rabbi Yissachar, and regarded as one who accurately comprehended his mentor's teachings; see Rabbi N.N. Rabinowitz's introduction to *Geon Yaakov*.

40. Author of the famous halachic work, *Chayei Adam*.

41. The last Chief Rabbi of Vilna and the leader of the offensive against Chassidus in the 1780s.

42. A famous "lobbyist" (*shtadlan*) on behalf of the Jews of Vilna.

43. More an acquaintance of the Gaon than a disciple, he was the grandfather of two of White Russia's greatest Torah luminaries: the brothers Rabbi Yaakov, author of *Mishkenos Yaakov,* and Rabbi Yitzchak Friedman, author of *Keren Orah,* of Karlin.

13

Misnagdim —
The Reaction to Chassidus

Strong Opposition

LL REVOLUTIONS BEGET REACTIONS. The sweeping changes that Chassidus wrought changed the basic fiber of Jewish life in Eastern Europe. Chassidus brought with it wrenching social upheaval, a new egalitarian spirit and a vastly different societal hierarchy. But such changes were not made in a vacuum. The established leadership of the Jewish communities in Eastern Europe did not take kindly to the radical changes in Jewish society proposed by the early chassidic masters. Amazed by the instant popularity and success of the new movement, frightened by its apparent radicalism and mystical bent, the established Jewish leadership reacted strongly and negatively. However, the rapid spread of Chassidus throughout Poland, Galicia, and the Ukraine soon muted many voices of effective opposition. Not so in Lithuania and White Russia. There, in that bastion of intense Torah scholarship under the sway of the gigantic personality of the Gaon of Vilna, the opposition to Chassidus was organized, intensive, and unyielding. The opponents to Chassidus were called misnagdim[1] and they attempted to eliminate the new movement from the national body of Israel.

The organized opposition to Chassidus occurred in four main waves: 1772, 1781, 1797, and 1813. There are extensive records of

---

1. Literally, "opponents." It is not clear as to whether this name was chosen by the "opponents" themselves or was given them by their chassidic rivals. The word misnagdim has a negative ring to it; nevertheless, the misnagdim bore this identity with fierce pride.

the bitter debate between the two camps.[2] The leaders on both sides were saintly, scholarly, and idealistic, but many of the followers who leaped into the fray were of decidedly lesser caliber. The ferocity of the confrontation eventually degenerated into violence, treachery, informing on one another to the Czar's government, and other forms of unethical behavior. There is no fight like a family fight. There is no war like a religious war. Hence a dispute that is both familial and religious easily spirals out of control.

The opening salvo was the ban on Chassidus issued in April, 1772 by the leadership of the Vilna Jewish community.[3] This ban[4], signed by the Gaon himself, made strong and detailed accusations against Chassidus. The main complaints contained in that ban were:

(1) They separated themselves from the central synagogue of their communities and formed their own prayer groups in private homes — known as *shtiebels*.

(2) They changed the prayer ritual from the Ashkenazic rite to the more kabbalistically oriented *Nusach Sefard,* or Sephardic rite.[5]

(3) They shouted, danced, and indulged in acrobatics and other unacceptable behavior during prayer.

(4) They did not respect accepted Torah scholars or, even worse, Torah scholarship.

(5) They evinced strange social behavior, bordering on the bizarre.

(6) They advocated the use of tobacco and liquor to induce "happiness."

Later bans included other charges: that the chassidim had a lax attitude toward the proper halachic time of the morning and evening prayers,[6] and that they introduced a new method of sharpening

---

2. Mordecai Wilensky's monumental work, *Chassidim and Misnagdim,* Mosad Bialik, Tel Aviv, 1970, contains an extensive review of the literature of the conflict. Wilensky, however, displays an antagonism to the chassidim that is not always justified by his sources.

3. Strong criticism of Chassidus had already surfaced in the 1760s and sporadic publications denouncing the movement appeared as early as 1746. See Wilensky, p. 27. It is also apparent that the militant misnagdim of Shklov instigated their brethren in Vilna to issue the ban from Vilna.

4. The text of the ban is quoted by Wilensky, p. 60.

5. As noted above, this rite is not the same as that used by the Jews of Spain and the Middle East.

6. This matter was the subject of great controversy among chassidim themselves and was one of the major causes of the older chassidic opposition to the new school of P'shis'cha-Kotzk Chassidus.

the knives for kosher slaughter.[7]

Some of these complaints were picayune in themselves and seemed important for what they seemed to reveal about the tenor of the movement. Others were serious charges. But the main cause of the war against Chassidus, especially as far as the Vilna Gaon and his disciples were concerned, was the suspicion that Chassidus was soft on the primary principle of Judaism — the study and knowledge of Torah, especially the Talmud. Suspicion, wrath, and indignation were stirred by such statements as those of the chassidic leader, Rabbi Yaakov Yosef of Polnoa, that "One should not accustom himself to be constantly diligent in his studies; rather he should also mingle with people, but that the fear of God should be upon his face";[8] or that "his [the Baal Shem Tov's] soul told the Rabbi (Baal Shem Tov) that he achieved communication with the heavenly spheres not because he studied much Torah from the Talmud and the commentators, but rather because of sincere prayer."[9]

The primacy of the Torah scholar was a sacred tenet of the Eastern European Jewish public. This position was guarded zealously by the scholars themselves and by the general Jewish society. This status was already being threatened, though yet mildly, by the nascent movement of *Haskalah*/Enlightenment moving slowly eastward from Germany. But it was Chassidus that provided the main challenge to the established hierarchy. Positions, attitudes, and lifestyles that had been built and formed over centuries were overthrown in a few decades. If not for the continuity of Torah study, the troubles of exile would long ago have destroyed Israel. Now, the new movement of Chassidus apparently shifted the focus and the emphasis of Jewish life to different nuances of halachic Judaism at the apparent expense of pure Torah study. This, the misnagdim considered to be mortal heresy and national suicide.

The ban of 1772, powerful though it was, resulted in only being a temporary blow to Chassidus. The misnagdim were unable to press their advantage and turn back the tide; the main effect of the ban was to prevent further expansion of Chassidus in Lithuania and White

---

7. The chassidim honed their slaughtering knives to a razor-sharp edge, which many of their opponents contended increased the danger of imperfections (*p'gimos*) in the blade. The Gaon of Vilna was not opposed to this new custom per se, but only to the departure from the accepted norm. See Wilensky, p. 46, note 11. See also the words of Rabbi Shneur Zalman, *Shulchan Aruch Harav*, at the end of Vol. 6, p. 1788, in defense of the new knives. In time, this innovation was accepted universally as a superior method of ritual kosher slaughter.

8. *Toldos Yaakov Yosef, Parshas Vayetzei.*

9. *Tzava'as HaRivash* (quoted by Wilensky, p. 19).

Russia. But the ban was counter-productive, as well: It helped unite otherwise quarreling chassidic groups. By making Chassidus the underdog, it gained sympathy and supporters for the movement, and it forced Chassidus to respond strongly to its detractors.

Reconciling the Difference

HE CHASSIDIC *TZADDIKIM* WERE compelled to reassess the situation in light of the firm opposition to them. They attempted to negotiate with their critics, to defuse the issues, to defend themselves from the onslaught. However, the time was not yet ripe for acceptance or peace. As long as the misnagdim were still not convinced that Chassidus was a permanent fixture within the framework of Jewish tradition, they granted it no quarter. The results of the ban, however, were disappointing. Even in Vilna itself, the chassidim continued to function.

Extremists on both sides continually fanned the flames of hatred. Finally, in 1781, an even more stringent ban[10] was published, again over the signatures of the Gaon and Rabbi Shmuel Avigdor, the chief rabbinic judge of Vilna. Other bans were issued by the communities of Grodno, Pinsk, Brisk and Slutzk. These bans were made public jointly at the *yarid* (periodic market fair) of Zelve. But after the death of the *Maggid* of Mezeritch in late 1772, the chassidim had regrouped and strengthened themselves, and thus were better prepared for the new onslaught against them. Their main defender was Rabbi Shneur Zalman, the founder of Chabad. He traveled unceasingly,[11] wrote and spoke in defense of Chassidus, and became its chief spokesman and the lightning rod for the attacks of its antagonists.

Rabbi Shneur Zalman was a brilliant Talmudist and an original thinker of the highest order. He composed a famous and authoritative halachic work, *Shulchan Aruch Harav*,[12] that ranks among the classic works of Torah law. His magnum opus, however, was a book of

---

10. Wilensky, p. 101.

11. He himself traveled to Vilna to personally mollify the Gaon, but was refused a meeting. See Wilensky, p. 161, and also *Toldos HaDoros,* Feder, Bnei Brak 1985, p. 136.

12. First published in Shklov, 1814, though handwritten copies of the work were already available for many years before that date.

philosophical and kabbalistic treatment of the basic ideas of Chassidus. Entitled *Likkutei Amarim,* but popularly known as *Tanya* (after its first word), this work was first published in 1796[13] and became one of the basic texts of Chassidus. Its erudition, style, and clear presentation of abstract mystical ideas raised the level of the debate with the misnagdim to a much higher plane. The book was based on the clear acceptance of the validity of Rabbi Yitzchak Luria's *(Arizal's)* system of Kabbalah. Privately, to his chassidim, Rabbi Shneur Zalman was critical of the Gaon for questioning aspects of this system of Kabbalah and for his refusal to publicly grant it the status of Divine revelation.

Rabbi Shneur Zalman's book was of such high caliber that it demanded a response in kind from the misnagdim. No ban or curse could wish it away. The response was slow to come. It eventually was written by the leading disciple of the Gaon, Rabbi Chaim of Volozhin. His famous work, published posthumously in 1824, was called *Nefesh HaChayim.*[14] The book was not only an answer to *Likkutei Amarim,* though it never referred to it, but in many ways it complemented and mirrored it.[15] It was a seminal interpretation of classic rabbinic thought and brought into sharp focus the new departures of Chassidus from the previously accepted norm. But it is clear from both works that the chassidim and misnagdim had now much more in common than in dispute. The appearance of these two works marked the beginning of a slow rapprochement between the two camps, though the twenty-five years separating their appearances were bitterly tumultuous ones.

The Government Intervenes

 HE BAN OF 1781 WAS REINFORCED in 1797 by a new development. The Gaon had died on 19 Tishrei/October 9 of that year and many among the chassidic masses, though not among the leaders, marked his passing with public glee. This insult to the memory of the Gaon provoked the misnagdim to issue an even more bitterly worded ban against the chassidim. In Vilna itself, the Council of the Jewish Community took

---

13. Less than a year before the Gaon's death. The book was published in Slavita.

14. The book was named by the author's son, Rabbi Yitzchak of Volozhin.

15. See *Torah Lishmah,* Norman Lamm, Mosad Harav Kook, 1972, p. 42.

an extremely hostile position against the local chassidic movement and persecuted them incessantly.[16]

The chassidim in Vilna looked desperately for an escape from their diminishing state. Foolishly, they turned to an unlikely champion for aid. In the spring of 1798, the chassidim of Vilna filed a complaint with the Russian government over the behavior of the Jewish Council of Vilna. They complained not only about their unfair treatment at the hands of the Council, but they accused the members of the Council of misappropriating public funds and of prejudice in the collecting of the tax monies that the Jewish community was required to pay the Czar's government. The Russian government reacted with alacrity to this opportunity. On April 26, 1798, the governor of Vilna Province issued a proclamation justifying the claims of the chassidim and severely limiting all the governing powers of the Jewish Council of Vilna.

This victory of the chassidim tempted some people to go even further. They delivered to the Russian authorities a copy of a secret letter that the Jewish Council of Vilna had distributed in an attempt to raise funds for certain "lobbying efforts" at the royal court in St. Petersburg. In July 1798, the members of the Jewish Council of Vilna were arrested and interrogated by the Russian authorities.

Now, terrified of the consequences of the Russian government's interference on the side of the chassidim, the misnagdim fought fire with fire. In late summer 1798, a complaint against chassidim in general, and Rabbi Shneur Zalman in particular, was sent to the Russian authorities. Among the alleged crimes was the collecting of money for the purpose of sending it to a foreign country (the Land of Israel, then under Turkish rule), which was a serious crime in Czarist Russia.[17] In October 1798, Rabbi Shneur Zalman was imprisoned in the Peter and Paul Fortress in St. Petersburg. Rabbi Shneur Zalman was interrogated there by a high official — according to a chassidic tradition, it was the Czar

---

16. See Wilensky, pp. 21 and 212. Public floggings, forced public confessions, and the humiliating forced recanting of Chassidus are some examples of the persecution of the chassidim.

17. Almost every rabbi in Czarist Russia was "guilty" of sending money to *Eretz Yisrael,* a "criminal act," and thus they were always in jeopardy of being informed upon by disgruntled dissidents. Rabbi Shneur Zalman defended himself on the grounds that aiding Jews in the Holy Land was an old religious practice. His accuser, Rabbi Avigdor of Pinsk, responded that the chassidim were sending amounts far in excess of the customary amounts. This was true, because a large group of chassidim had settled in *Eretz Yisrael* in 5537/1777, and their comrades in Poland were assisting them. Aside from them, there were hardly any Ashkenazic Jews in the Holy Land at that time.

himself disguised as a prison officer — who became convinced of his innocence and released him on November 27, 1798 — the nineteenth day of Kislev.[18] His release triggered a new wave of accusations against the Jewish Council of Vilna by the chassidim. In January 1799, the members of that council were dismissed by the Russian government, and in new, government-sponsored elections held under the watchful eyes of the police, eight new council members — all chassidim — were "elected." Thus did Vilna, the home of the Gaon and the bastion of the misnagdim, come under the rule of the chassidim.

The Battle Subsides

HE MOST IMPLACABLE FOE of Chassidus was Rabbi Avigdor of Pinsk. He was instrumental in driving Rabbi Levi Yitzchak (later of Berditchev) from the rabbinic position in Pinsk because of his chassidic beliefs. He then succeeded to the position himself.[19] In 1786, however, the chassidim counter-attacked and Rabbi Avigdor himself was finally deposed in 1794. Thereafter he devoted himself on a full-time basis to the struggle against the chassidim. He was instrumental in the ban of 1797, issued in Vilna. He lobbied in St. Petersburg against the chassidim and became a familiar figure in government offices. Finally, in the spring of 1800 he submitted a long detailed protocol of accusations against Chassidus and Rabbi Shneur Zalman.

Rabbi Avigdor's underlying accusation was that Chassidus promoted social and religious anarchy — and he knew that the Czar was petrified of anarchy. Rabbi Aharon of Karlin had spread Chassidus in Lithuania in the 1770s and his activities there made him "subversive" in the eyes of the Russian government. That was now also the general charge against Rabbi Shneur Zalman. However, the specific accusation against him was once more that of transmitting money illegally to Turkey (i.e., Palestine). On Nov. 21, 1800, Rabbi Shneur Zalman was arrested and again sent to St. Petersburg where he was held in prison. After interrogation, he was released on December 9, 1800, but was

---

18. Chabad chassidim refer to this day as the "Holiday of Redemption," and celebrate it annually.

19. Wilensky, p. 230, implies that he "bought" the position for a large sum of money paid to local notables and the town council.

required to remain in St. Petersburg since the matter was still under investigation by the Russian Senate. As a consequence of the assassination of Czar Paul and the attendant governmental confusion, Rabbi Shneur Zalman was finally allowed to leave St. Petersburg on April 20, 1801. The matter dragged on in the Russian bureaucracy, and it was not until 1804 that the government dismissed all charges against him and vindicated the rights of the chassidim in Vilna and elsewhere.

By now, both sides were exhausted by the quarrel and its attendant consequences. The chassidim realized the futility of trying to govern Jewish Vilna with its overwhelmingly non-chassidic population and withdrew from that fray. Rabbi Shneur Zalman used all of his influence with the chassidim to prevent further violence and treachery.[20] The misnagdim came to the slow realization that Chassidus was here to stay and that it was useless to continue the violent struggle against them. Rabbi Chaim of Volozhin was a calming influence and the battle seemed to be over.

In 1813, however, the fire flickered to life once again. In the wake of the Napoleonic war in Poland and Russia, the Jewish community was divided in its national loyalties and thus was viewed with suspicion by the Russian authorities. The misnagdim then accused some of the chassidic leaders of favoring Napoleon — a charge which was partially true[21] — and forwarded that new accusation to the Czar. In addition, they formulated and published a new ban reiterating all of the accusations of the original Vilna ban of 1772. Once again, Rabbi Shneur Zalman was able to deflect the blow. He had remained a staunch supporter of Russia in the Napoleonic war and his efforts were noted by the governmental authorities. The last ban had no effect on the chassidim who, by now, were immune from such attacks.

The Russian government was no longer viewed as particularly anti-chassidic, but equally anti-Semitic toward both groups. And both chassidim and misnagdim were now being challenged by a new and strong enemy — *Haskalah,* or Enlightenment. Instead of fighting one another, they had to present some sort of common front among themselves on behalf of traditional Judaism. Thus the great struggle dimmed, as both sides gradually learned to accommodate each other, even though they still disagreed on many fundamental issues of theory and practice.

---

20. See Wilensky for copies of the letters of Rabbi Shneur Zalman to his chassidim, pp. 296, 299, 305 and 306.

21. See the earlier chapter on Napoleon.

14

The Yeshivos

A Departure from Tradition

NE OF THE PRIMARY DEVELOPMENTS in Eastern European Jewish life in the nineteenth century was the establishment of the great houses of Torah learning — yeshivos.[1] These institutions eventually became the nucleus for vibrant Jewish communities and provided the spark of genius and commitment necessary to preserve the traditional way of Jewish behavior, originally for the misnagdim and eventually for the chassidim as well. The rise of these yeshivos was, in itself, also a new departure from the traditional methods of Torah study in Eastern Europe in vogue in the seventeenth and eighteenth centuries. In that era, the centers of Torah study were scattered and small. The rabbi of the community was responsible for the education of the younger men[2] in his town. More prominent scholars would attract greater numbers of students, but, essentially, a yeshivah was a private unstructured affair, conducted in the local synagogue or around the rabbi's table. The new movement introduced the yeshivah as an "institution," in the mode of contemporary centers of Torah learning.

---

1. It is noteworthy that in almost all of the modern history books regarding the Jewish people, the role and importance of the yeshivos is virtually ignored. For example, *Toldos Am Yisrael,* edited by C. Sassin, Tel Aviv 1969, devotes two paragraphs to the yeshivah movement of the nineteenth century, while spending chapters on secular Jewish movements which, less than a century later, are already extinct.

2. Formal education for women in Orthodox circles in Eastern Europe first came into vogue during the 1920s, though there were always individual women of great education in all generations. In earlier times, women were educated in the home to fulfill their roles as wives and mothers and had no formal educational structure.

Most Jewish boys studied in *cheder*[3] from the age of three until they were ten. After that, some continued their formal education, usually to the age of bar mitzvah, thirteen, by attending communal classes or having a private tutor. Once achieving adolescence, the overwhelming majority of Jewish youth joined the local labor force, becoming apprentices to local artisans or tradesmen, or left home to fend for themselves in a difficult, impoverished, and hostile environment. Others continued their studies until they were sixteen or

3. Literally, "a room." This was the traditional name for primary school education among Eastern European Jews.

The Cheder

seventeen, by which time they would be Talmudic scholars, since Torah study had been their sole preoccupation since early childhood. It was common that people would participate in study groups for several hours a day, before and after work.

Only a certain select few, who showed great promise in their Torah studies and intellectual development, remained in full-time Torah study and, invariably, the rabbi of the community was their teacher or mentor. Those truly outstanding young men who exhausted the talents and/or knowledge of the local rabbi were then advised to leave and study at the homes of greater rabbis throughout Eastern Europe. These rabbis accepted, taught, molded, and eventually ordained the young men who came to them. In the middle 1700s, however, this system began to break down. The partition of Poland, from 1772 till 1794, devastated Jewish economic and social life in Lithuania, northern Poland, and White Russia. The chaos of war and the societal instability fostered in its wake undermined the traditional Jewish educational system. Great rabbis were forced to leave their homes, travel was dangerous, and the study of Torah declined sharply.

A nostalgic myth persists regarding nineteenth-century Eastern European Jewry. It depicts that world of our ancestors in an idyllic fashion.[4] Everyone was pious. The study of Torah abounded. Jewish social life was free from strife. And even though life was poor physically and anti-Semitism abounded, Jews in the *shtetl*[5] were happy, tolerant, and accepting of their lot in life. Myths are usually exaggerated at best and wildly inaccurate at worst, and this myth about nineteenth-century Eastern European Jewish life is no exception. As the 1800s progressed, the Enlightenment[6] had begun to make serious inroads on traditional Jewish life in Lithuania, northern Poland, and White Russia, especially in the large cities, but in the *shtetels,* as well.

"The Gaon of Vilna saw clearly the dangers inherent in the unprecedented growth of the new movement [the Enlightenment] and was greatly concerned by the likelihood of disastrous effects [upon religious observance] by the continuing development and widening of this new movement [the Enlightenment]."[7] The level of Torah study

---

4. The glorification of that world in literature, drama, and music is all-pervasive. *Fiddler on the Roof* is an excellent example of this trend.

5. Literally, "small village." This word became synonymous with Eastern European Jewish life before the urbanization of the Jewish masses and their eventual emigration from Eastern Europe in the nineteenth century.

6. See Section III, Chapter 16, "The Haskalah."

7. *Etz Chaim*, Moshe Sinonvitz, Tel Aviv 1972, p. 16.

had sunk precipitously in the countryside, even in the vicinity of Vilna, the "Jerusalem of Lithuania." Many Jewish young men no longer pursued Torah study as enthusiastically as before. The status of the Torah scholar declined in the eyes of society. In the eyes of many, Torah had lost its preeminent role in the Jewish society. In 1864 Rabbi Moshe Joseph, the rabbi of Krinak, Lithuania, wrote a letter in support of Volozhin Yeshivah, describing in detail Jewish life in Lithuania at the beginning of the nineteenth century:

> I am seventy-eight years old today and when the holy rabbi [Chaim Volozhin] founded the Yeshivah [of Volozhin] I was fifteen or sixteen years old. I was an intelligent youth and very observing of the world around me. Before the house of God [Volozhin Yeshivah] was founded by him, the world [of Lithuanian Jewry] was desolate, empty, and formless, for no one then knew even of the name — yeshivah — and what was its purpose and way of life. No longer was there any fame of scholars or popularity for Talmudic scholarship, for the world was devoid of intensive Torah [study]. Even the holy books, such as copies of the Talmud, were not to be found anywhere, except in the possession of certain exceptional people who were wealthy. Even in the synagogues of large communities there was not a complete set of the Talmud to be found, nor did the [populace] find such [books] necessary, because they were not used.[8]

It is undoubtedly true that the above letter may have presented a picture that was bleaker than the reality; witness the large numbers of outstanding scholars that were still to be found in every hamlet. However, it is true that the traditional, misnagdic world was in danger of being engulfed by ignorance, secularism, and apathy. It needed a viable alternative to Chassidus[9] and a strong counterforce to Enlightenment. It found a solution in the establishment of yeshivos throughout Europe and the creation of a movement of youth and scholarship that still is one of the most vital forces in Jewish life today.

A complete review of all of the yeshivos of the nineteenth century (and their twentieth-century successors) is beyond the ken of this book. Nevertheless, a historical sketch of a number of these institutions is necessary for an understanding of nineteenth-century Eastern European Jewish life. It will also help explain the origins of much of the vitality and

---

8. Ibid., p. 15.

9. The rationalistic, conservative, and unemotional nature of most Lithuanian Jews made Chassidus a non-viable option for them.

also the tensions in the internal modern Jewish world, for the yeshivos were, and still are, in the felicitous phrase of a famous non-orthodox Jewish poet, "the national creative workshop of the Jewish people."[10]

Rabbi Chaim of Volozhin

he yeshivah in Volozhin was the "mother" of all the yeshivos of the nineteenth century. It was founded by the famed disciple of the Gaon of Vilna, Rabbi Chaim Itzkowitz of Volozhin.[11] This great personality opened the yeshivah in Volozhin in 1803. In preparation for this revolutionary undertaking he sent a letter to all of the Jewish communities and their rabbis in Lithuania.[12] In it he meticulously explained the necessity for a central, national house of learning that would attract the highest caliber of student to Torah study and would provide a proper physical and spiritual environment of support for intensive Torah study. He stated:

> There are those who wish to study and have no financial means to do so, and those who wish to study and are financially able to do so but have no teacher to guide them in the true path of analytical Torah study . . . and they are all like sheep without a shepherd . . . and even though I am unworthy of a crown that does not truly befit me . . . nevertheless, [I see] a time not far distant when the Jewish people will be without leaders . . . and the doors of the house of study will be locked . . . Therefore do I call all of my beloved brethren to hear the truth . . . to repair the breach in our wall and to support God's Torah [through this yeshivah] with all our might, whether by supplying proper students, whether by providing the necessary financial support.[13]

The letter brought a strong response from Lithuanian Jewry. The

---

10. Chaim Nachman Bialik (1873-1934), a former yeshivah student of Volozhin who later became the secular poet laureate of political Zionism.

11. Born 1749 in Volozhin and died there in 1821.

12. The text of this famous letter appears in *Etz Chaim*, p. 33; also in *Hapeles*, vol. 2 number 3 (Teves, 1902); and in *Jewish Institutions of Higher Learning in Europe — Their Development and Destruction*, edited by Samuel Mirsky, New York 1956, p. 2.

13. *Etz Chaim*, pp. 33-34.

finest young minds vied for acceptance to the yeshivah.[14] Rabbi Chaim sent *meshulachim*[15] — fund raisers — to the Jewish communities in Lithuania to help maintain the yeshivah financially. Though the yeshivah never achieved true financial independence, it nevertheless did receive support from hundreds of communities throughout the Jewish world. In this also, Volozhin was a departure[16] from the accepted norm in Eastern Europe that institutions were supported exclusively by the local community.

Rabbi Chaim was not only the head of the yeshivah; in a deeper respect, he was the yeshivah itself. His method of pedagogy, his analytical style of studying Talmud, his scholarly nuances and attention to detail, his philosophy of life and education, and finally his piety of character and his integrity of personality, all became the hallmarks of Volozhin. He was not merely a lecturer or an administrator. He was the guide and mentor of all of the students and the guiding force behind all educational progress. He was all things to the students — father and mother, teacher and confidant, friend and adviser, critic and boss.

In this he became the prototype and standard setter for those who came after him and claimed for themselves the modern version of the title of *Rosh Yeshivah*. His educational philosophy was based on four main principles: (1) the necessity for personal influence and interaction between the teacher and the student; (2) communal study, rather than private isolated study and research; (3) the building of self-confidence and personal self-worth among the students and their psychological and spiritual elevation; and (4) the infusion of the feeling of joy and accomplishment in Talmudic studies.

As the true disciple of the Gaon of Vilna, Rabbi Chaim was determined to counteract the trend of *pilpulistic*[17] study that had been

---

14. Volozhin eventually established a geographical "quota system" to parcel out the limited number of admissions in an equitable fashion.

15. Literally, "those who are sent." They were also known by the name *shadar*, an acronym for *shluchei d'rabbanan* — those who are sent forth by the rabbis.

16. However, the precedent for far-reaching international fund raising had already been set by the great Babylonian communities from the sixth to eleventh centuries, but had disappeared from the Jewish scene in Eastern Europe in the sixteenth and seventeenth centuries.

17. *Pilpul* — literally, "pepper, spicy." See note 7, p. 103. The following is a further explanation. In this chapter the term is used in its narrowest sense, as a technical method of study. It was a sophistry of logic that allowed disparate subjects to be joined together by sometimes specious logic in order to arrive at a given conclusion or solution. Though *pilpul* had and has a legitimate place in the spectrum of methods

in vogue among Talmudic students in Eastern Europe for centuries. This study system had unfortunately been abused to the extent that in the hands of the non-adept it now represented the most negative sides of the field of Talmudic study of the time.

The Enlightenment had a field day ridiculing the sophistry and circuitous reasoning prevalent in some unsophisticated circles of Talmudic students of the day. First the Gaon and later Rabbi Chaim were determined to restore balance to the methodology of Torah study. This was not due to the criticism of the *Haskalah,* but rather from their deep understanding of true methodology of Torah study. Accuracy of the text, thorough knowledge of all the basic commentaries of the Talmud, logical reasoning, probing analysis, intellectual honesty, and an openness to hear and understand conflicting viewpoints became the hallmarks of the "Lithuanian way"[18] of study. Thus analytical skill, honest textual study and rigidly logical conclusions replaced the quick, mercurial responses and unlikely comparisons that technical *pilpul* sometimes overemphasized.

This was the way of Rabbi Chaim, and this became the way of Volozhin. Coupled with tremendous devotion to study,[19] a brisk pace of learning[20] and the holy competitiveness of brilliant personalities, Rabbi Chaim built Volozhin into the premier intellectual institution of his time. His yeshivah bred tolerance of others' opinions, and humility of spirit, along with tenacity of purpose, and originality of thought and decision.[21] Under Rabbi Chaim, Volozhin revitalized Lithuanian Jewry

---

employed in Talmudic study, it often was overused and abused and became a symbol of lightning genius sometimes coupled with less than complete intellectual honesty. This technical definition of *pilpul* should not be confused with the use of that word today, when it now denotes deeply analytical and far-ranging comparisons of Talmudic opinion and reasoning.

18. The "Lithuanian way" of Talmudic study has become the dominant form of study in most of the major yeshivos today.

19. A twelve-hour study-day was the norm for Volozhin, while the *masmidim* — the diligent ones — would spend eighteen to twenty hours per day in study! There were "shifts" of learning in the yeshivah at all times, even immediately after the fast day of *Yom Kippur,* so that Torah would be studied around the clock, seven days a week. See *Etz Chaim,* p. 47.

20. My grandfather, Rabbi Chaim Tzvi Rubenstein of blessed memory, came to Volozhin as a young student in 1888. He told me that in the first winter semester at Volozhin his learning group completed a thorough and detailed study of two major tractates — *Gittin* and *Kiddushin* — in seven months!

21. See Rabbi Chaim's letters on these matters as quoted in *Etz Chaim,* p. 45, and Mirsky, p. 21.

and returned the crown of Torah to its ancient glory. It raised the banner of the Vilna Gaon on high — the banner that proclaimed: "Only through Torah study will Israel survive."

The Mantle Passes On

RABBI CHAIM DIED IN 1821 and the mantle of leadership passed on to his son, Rabbi Yitzchak of Volozhin, who succeeded his father as rabbi of the community and head of the yeshivah.[22] He was a wise and able person, and under his direction the yeshivah grew. His main fame, however, was associated with his leadership regarding the negating of the educational decrees of the Czar regarding Russian Jewry.[23] He was also the great reconciler between the misnagdim and the chassidim and joined forces a number of times with the great chassidic leaders of his day in the struggle against Enlightenment, as well as against the tyranny of the Czar.

Eventually he was preoccupied by these overriding communal duties, somewhat to the detriment of the yeshivah. During the later years of his life the continuing oppression of Russian Jewry by the Czar led to a severe downturn in Jewish economic life, and the yeshivah suffered severe financial problems. These problems caused a reduction in the number of students accepted to the yeshivah and brought poverty into the physical life of the students still in attendance.[24] But the spirit and influence of the yeshivah remained strong and vital. Rabbi Yitzchak died in 1849, and his untimely death caused crisis and tension in the great institution.

The dynasty of the *Bais HaRav* — the house of the Rabbi (Chaim of Volozhin) — now was continued through sons-in-law. Rabbi Yitzchak had three sons, two of whom died in their youth. His surviving son, Rabbi Eliyahu Zalman, made no claim to his father's

---

22. In Eastern and Central Europe, in the smaller Jewish communities, the offices of the communal rabbi and the *rosh yeshivah* were combined in the body of one person. The benefit of such an arrangement is easily apparent to all. However, this grand tradition did not emigrate to Israel or the United States, and, with only a few exceptions, the roles of the community rabbi and *rosh yeshivah* nowadays are mutually exclusive.

23. See the later chapter on Jewish Russia in the 1800s in this book.

24. *Etz Chaim*, p. 195.

The Netziv

titles.[25] Rather, it was Rabbi Yitzchak's oldest son-in-law, Rabbi Elazar Yitzchak Fried,[26] who succeeded to the leadership of Volozhin Yeshivah and the rabbinate of the community. His significant duties in the yeshivah had already begun years earlier, as Rabbi Elazar Yitzchak assisted his father-in-law and gradually became the main educator in the yeshivah, delivering the Talmudic lectures and lending his creative genius to enhance the level of Torah study. It was only natural, therefore, that his de facto leadership of the yeshivah became de jure in 1849 upon the passing of his father-in-law. However, Rabbi Yitzchak was himself already gravely ill when he assumed the positions of Rabbi and *Rosh Yeshivah,* and his health continued to decline thereafter. After four years, he died in 1853, at the age of forty-four, leaving a potential vacuum of leadership for Volozhin and its yeshivah.

Conflicting Styles

ABBI YITZCHAK'S SECOND son-in-law was the legendary Rabbi Naftali Tzvi Yehudah Berlin — the *Netziv*.[27] Born into a well-known rabbinic[28] family in 1817, in 1831 he married the daughter of Rabbi Yitzchak and entered Volozhin. Throughout his father-in-law's lifetime, he maintained a low profile and was seemingly overshadowed by his brilliant brother-in-law, Rabbi Elazar Yitzchak Fried. However, during this period of seeming reticence, he authored one of the great works of rabbinic scholarship of that century, *Ha'amek She'eiloh* — a commentary to the then little-known work of the Babylonian geonic era, *Sh'eiltos d'Rabbi Achai Gaon*.[29] During Rabbi Elazar Yitzchak Fried's illness,

---

25. Rabbi Eliyahu Zalman's son-in-law, Rabbi Yehudah Heshel Levin, would claim the right to a position in the yeshivah after the death of Rabbi Yitzchak's successor, Rabbi Elazar Fried, but his claim was rejected by the board of the yeshivah.

26. He was the nephew of Rabbi Yitzchak, born in Volozhin in 1809.

27. The acronym of his name, as well as the Hebrew noun meaning "prince" and/or "leader."

28. His father, Yaakov, was not a rabbi, though he was a great Talmudic scholar.

29. Literally, "Questions directed to Rabbi Achai Gaon." Rabbi Achai was the leading scholar of the great Talmudic school in Pumbedisa, Babylonia, in the ninth century, and his book served as a means of transmission of the Babylonian Torah heritage to the then newly emerging Jewish centers in North Africa, Spain, France and Germany.

the *Netziv* began to deliver Talmudic lectures in the yeshivah. When his brother-in-law died, a governing board of rabbis and trustees met to realign the leadership of the yeshivah. The *Netziv* was appointed as Rabbi of Volozhin and the head of the yeshivah. As his associate in the leadership of the yeshivah, the board appointed a great-grandson of Rabbi Chaim Volozhin, Rabbi Yosef Dov Ber HaLevi Soloveitchik.[30]

Rabbi Yosef Dov Ber was a genius; brilliant, sharp, incisive, with lightning creativity in Talmudic learning. His lectures were fiery, alive with confrontations and paradox, stimulating, innovative, and reminiscent of the *pilpul* school of study. In contrast, the methodology and presentation of the *Netziv* was more placid, thorough, wide ranging in scope and sources, and more pedantic in nature. These two great people complemented each other educationally, socially, and personally, and Volozhin now grew and developed into an even greater institution of learning.

The conflicting styles of the *Netziv* and Rabbi Yosef Dov Ber, as well as their divergent educational philosophies, eventually caused a split within the student body. Both the *Netziv* and Rabbi Yosef Dov Ber acted quickly to prevent a more serious situation from developing; in 1857, they themselves convened a *Din Torah*[31] to decide the direction of Volozhin. The ruling of the rabbinical court confirmed the *Netziv* as the head of the yeshivah and Rabbi Yosef Dov Ber as his assistant. From that time forward, the *Netziv* shaped and developed Volozhin. In 1865, Rabbi Yosef Dov Ber left Volozhin and became the rabbi of Slutzk, from where he went on to his greatest fame as the rabbi of Brisk.

In 1865, a great fire swept Volozhin, whose wooden homes and thatched roofs were quickly consumed. The yeshivah building was burned to the ground together with its library and many original

---

30. Later also known as the *Bais HaLevi,* after his great books of Torah thought and responsa. For a thorough and complete biography of him, *see HaRishon L'Shalsheles Brisk,* by Chaim Karlinsky, Jerusalem 1984. Rabbi Yosef Dov Ber was born in 1820 and died in 1892.

31. The members of the Rabbinical Court that decided these matters were Rabbis David Tevil of Minsk, Yosef Peimar of Slutzk, Zev Wolf of Vilna and the young Yitzchak Elchanan Spector, then of Novardok and later of Kovno. For the details of the proceedings and the rabbinic decisions, *see Etz Chaim*, pp. 228-230; *Zichron Yaakov,* by Yaakov HaLevi Lipschutz, Vol. 2, p. 36; *Mekor Baruch*, by Baruch HaLevi Epstein, Vol. 4, p. 846; and *HaRishon L'Shalsheles Brisk,* by Karlinsky, p. 128. Though there are minor discrepancies in the versions told by these four authors, all are in agreement on the major facts and decisions in the matter.

manuscripts of Rabbis Chaim and Yitzchak of Volozhin. The *Netziv* devoted his entire energies to the rebuilding of the yeshivah and a new three-story structure was built. More students arrived and the yeshivah grew to four hundred students.

A new driving force was now added to the staff of the yeshivah, who, together with the *Netziv*, made Volozhin the magnet that attracted the greatest minds of Jewish Russia in the 1870s and 1880s. He was Rabbi Yosef Dov Ber's son, Rabbi Chaim HaLevi Soloveitchik,[32] who arrived in Volozhin in 1873, and in 1880 was appointed associate head of the yeshivah with the *Netziv*. Rabbi Chaim completed the revolution in Torah-learning methodology that became the hallmark of the "Lithuanian Yeshivos." Keen intensive analysis, the dissection of the subject under discussion down to its fundamental components, clarity of thought, unswerving logic, a new set of linguistic terms to define abstract legalisms, and, above all, rigorous intellectual honesty,[33] were the basics of Rabbi Chaim's "way" — *derech* — of learning.

Once again the two personalities of Volozhin — the patriarchal *Netziv* and the young Rabbi Chaim — and their disparate approaches to Talmudic learning complemented each other and enhanced the yeshivah. Under the leadership of Rabbi Chaim and the *Netziv*, Volozhin nurtured and produced almost three generations of Jewish leadership: rabbinic, lay, and even secular. The influence of Volozhin on Jewish life, in all of its forms and manifestations, was enormous.

Czarist Authorities Interfere

HE EXPERIENCE OF VOLOZHIN in its dealings with the Czarist authorities mirrored the plight of Russian Jewry generally. Beginning in 1827, the Russian government began its insidious interference in the educational policies and institutions of the Jews. In its effort the government was abetted, willingly or naively, by the efforts of the nascent *Haskalah* in Russia. In

---

32. Born in 1853 in Volozhin and died in 1918 in Warsaw, Reb Chaim was a child prodigy. He married the granddaughter of the *Netziv,* and thus the Soloveitchiks compounded their connection to the *Bais HaRav*.

33. See *Etz Chaim*, p. 258, where it is stated that Rabbi Chaim often postponed his scheduled Talmudic lectures by saying, "My friends, I have nothing new to tell you. Upon reflection, everything that I prepared for today's lecture is in reality worthless!"

1835, new laws were passed to define the role of the rabbi and to require him to be fluent in Russian. In 1844, the Russian government, again with the cooperation of the leaders of the *Haskalah* movement, founded two "rabbinical colleges," one in Vilna and the other in Zhitomir. These institutions were meant to produce the new style of rabbi that the Czar demanded. In 1853, the government announced that only graduates of these two "official" seminaries would be allowed to function as rabbis.[34] In 1859, the government proclaimed that secular studies — mathematics, geography, Russian language and culture — were to be included as part of the curriculum of the yeshivah.

The *Netziv* himself had no intention of allowing forced secular studies to become an official part of the yeshivah curriculum [35] and he would not bow to the official fiat of the government in this matter. There were periods when secular studies were taught in Volozhin — in a separate building, to a limited number of students, and by non-Jewish teachers.[36] This was done to satisfy the local authorities, who were also continually given bribes to overlook the broad non-compliance of the yeshivah with governmental regulations. However, the pressure of the leaders of the *Haskalah,* as well as that of the Russian government, continued to increase, regardless of these attempts to mollify them.

In 1877, a disgruntled student of Volozhin falsely informed the authorities that the *Netziv* personally, and Volozhin generally, were engaged in anti-government activities. As "proof" of his spurious charge, he produced a forged letter, purportedly signed by the *Netziv*. The *Netziv* was arrested and interrogated but finally freed.[37] But this event took its toll, both on the yeshivah and on the *Netziv*. From that day forward the authorities focused their attention on Volozhin. Regular inspections of the yeshivah by the education ministry, new laws and regulations, and continual harassment of the yeshivah by all local and regional authorities ensued.

To further complicate the situation in later years, another great fire raged in Volozhin in the summer of 1886, destroying the village and the "new" yeshivah building as well. Through superhuman efforts, the

---

34. The experiment in "official" rabbinic seminaries ended ignominiously with the closing of the two schools in 1873, while the yeshivos they were meant to replace, prospered and expanded.

35. See the long article on the subject by the *Netziv* himself in his book of halachic responsa, *Meishiv Davar,* Section One, Chapter 44, published in 1893 in Warsaw.

36. *Etz Chaim,* p. 322.

37. For further details of this sad story, see *Etz Chaim*, p. 321.

Netziv kept the yeshivah in session in temporary quarters, and was able to raise the necessary funds to rebuild the yeshivah for a second time, twelve months later. The success of the yeshivah in surviving all of its difficulties eventually proved its own undoing. The government, in wonderment at the tenacity of the yeshivah, now realized that Volozhin stood in the way of the implementation of its new, radically brutal policies towards the Jews. It therefore redoubled its efforts to control the yeshivah, and, failing this, resolved to close it.

In 1877 the director of schools for the Vilna district inspected Volozhin. He found many "illegal"[38] students in the yeshivah. Most students were found deficient in their knowledge of Russian language and culture. Even though he did not call for the closing of the yeshivah, he made further demands concerning the faculty and curriculum of the school. The yeshivah was now surrounded by inimical forces — the Czar, the *maskilim*, rebellious students who had been influenced by the winds of change sweeping Russia, and the grinding poverty that sapped its strength.

Nevertheless, the yeshivah somehow continued to prosper scholastically and spiritually. It grew to four hundred and twenty-five students, many of them destined to be the leaders of the Jewish people for the next fifty years. Under Rabbi Chaim Soloveitchik and the aging *Netziv*, the level of Torah study reached great heights of diligence, creativity and accomplishment. The vast majority of the students remained loyal to Volozhin and to its goals, ideals, and system. However, there were fissures from within.

From 1860 onward, an active *Haskalah* cell operated within the yeshivah. Though only a small minority of students were associated with it, its existence was a divisive force within the yeshivah. In this, it reflected, in microcosm, the pressures then punishing Russian Jewry. Many of these students who formed the cell of *Haskalah* within Volozhin went on to become the leaders of various Jewish and non-Jewish secular movements. These opinionated and talented people damaged the people of Israel severely.

There also existed another clandestine group in the yeshivah, called *Nes Tziyonah*.[39] This group was tolerated by the *Netziv* who, himself, was a supporter of the *Chovevei Zion*, or "Lovers of Zion"[40]

---

38. Those without proper identification papers; those of army age without proper exemption certificates; foreigners, etc.
39. "Flag of Zion."
40. See later chapter on Zionism for details regarding this group.

organization. *Nes Tziyonah* was formed in 1885, and its activities raised the suspicions of the governmental authorities, who regarded its activities as anti-state. This caused the administration itself to object to the group's existence within the yeshivah and, in 1889, to disband it.[41]

In 1890, a new organization called *Netzach Yisrael* was formed in the yeshivah, which again espoused the cause of the Land of Israel among the student body. This organization also demanded of its members an intensive love of the Jewish people, of Jewish scholarship, observance of all Torah precepts, and a dedication to the cause of Jewish leadership. Many future rabbis and leaders were members of this group.[42] After the closure of Volozhin the group disbanded, but some of its members provided the leadership for other new organizations.

The *Netziv* attempted to bring his eldest son, the famed rabbi of Moscow, Rabbi Chaim Berlin, into the administration and direction of the yeshivah. In 1890, Rabbi Chaim moved to Volozhin, bringing with him his world-famed library of Judaica and rabbinics,[43] and began to deliver Talmudic lectures in the yeshivah. However, his style was not popular with many of the students who were accustomed to the genius and style of Rabbi Chaim Soloveitchik, and opposition to him grew slowly within the student body. Saddened and burdened, the *Netziv* did not pursue the issue of succession and Rabbi Chaim Berlin left soon after for Berlin, Paris, Amsterdam, London and other communities. There he raised funds to help defray the deficit of the yeshivah. He eventually settled in Jerusalem, where he served as an honored rabbi until his death.

On December 22, 1891, the Russian government made new official demands of the yeshivah that rendered its existence impossible.[44] The governmental requirements in this package were so extreme that they

41. The *Netziv's* attitude towards it was summed up in his comment "that good works can just as well be accomplished by others outside of the yeshivah and do not require those in the yeshivah to divert themselves from the study of Torah on their behalf." See Mirsky, p. 65.

42. Among the members were Rabbis Shmuel Aharon Tameret, Yitzchak Nisenbaum, Moshe Mordechai Epstein, Isser Zalman Meltzer, Avraham Dov Ber Kahane Shapiro, Menachem Krakovsky, Avraham Yitzchak Kook, Yehudah Leib Dan Yichye. See Mirsky, p. 64, and *Etz Chaim*, pp. 311-314.

43. Today, this library is the property of, and housed in the annex of, Yeshivah Etz Chaim in Jerusalem.

44. See Mirsky, pp. 70-1. The four main requirements were: 1) no Talmudic studies allowed at night; 2) secular studies to be taught from 9:00 A.M. to 3:00 P.M.; 3) the school day to be no longer than ten hours per day; and 4) all of the faculty must have diplomas from recognized Russian educational institutions.

made it impossible for the *Netziv* to keep the yeshivah open. The demand of the government was a cynical one; in effect it demanded that Volozhin cease to function as a yeshivah. Understandably, the administration of the yeshivah refused to consider this. In January 1892, the Russian inspectors came to Volozhin to enforce the decree. The *Netziv* refused to accommodate them. The yeshivah was closed, its students exiled, the Jewish world saddened.[45]

From its destruction, however, all of the other yeshivos now grew. Torah learning continued to spread in Lithuania and new students were recruited. But it was never the same. Every yeshivah following it was a piece of Volozhin, but there was only one Volozhin.

---

45. See the eyewitness description of the closing of Volozhin in *Mekor Baruch*, p. 2026. Also *Etz Chaim*, p. 333.

15

The Yeshivah
Movement Expands

Mir

DOZEN YEARS AFTER THE FOUNDING of Volozhin Yeshivah, a second yeshivah of its type was founded in the small town of Mir[1] in Lithuania. It was opened in 1815 by a leading scholar of the community, albeit a layman, Shmuel Tikitinsky. For the first eight years of the yeshivah's existence he supported the yeshivah singlehandedly, and Shmuel's son, Avraham, soon joined his father as the head of the yeshivah. Mir soon gained popularity and stature and by 1840 it numbered one hundred students.

In 1835 both Shmuel and Rabbi Avraham Tikitinsky died tragically. Rabbi Yosef David Mirrer, the rabbi of Mir, then assumed the leadership of the yeshivah. In 1850, Chaim Leib Tikitinsky, the grandson of the founder, returned to Mir and became the leading educator in the yeshivah. Rabbi Chaim Leib was an outstanding pedagogue, and, under his tutelage, Mir established itself firmly as a leading yeshivah, second only to Volozhin in numbers and reputation.

Rabbi Chaim Leib died in 1899, leaving his youngest son, Avraham, as his only heir capable of assuming the mantle of leadership in Mir. Avraham was appointed titular head of the yeshivah, but he immediately began to search for a charismatic figure who could inspire and expand the yeshivah. At the same time, in 1899, Rabbi Eliyahu David Rabinowitz-Tumim[2] left the post of rabbi of Mir to emigrate to

---

1. Literally, Mir means "village." The town was called "Da Mir," or the village, because of its central location and importance.

2. Commonly known by the acronym of his name, *Aderes.* He was the father-in-law of Rabbi Avraham Yitzchok Kook, and a well-known and respected scholar and leader. See his fascinating autobiography, *Seder Eliyahu,* Mosad Harav Kook, Jerusalem, 1983.

Jerusalem. Thus, the possibility of finding one person to head both the community and the yeshivah arose. That person was Rabbi Eliyahu Boruch Kamai, who served as the rabbi of Mir, and joined Rabbi Avraham Tikitinsky as head of the yeshivah.

It was under Rabbi Kamai that Mir became the leading yeshivah of Lithuania, having survived the Czar's persecution while its sister yeshivah, Volozhin, succumbed. It grew in numbers and stature, and before the first World War had a student population of almost two hundred fifty. It produced many great rabbinic leaders[3] and was strongly influential on Jewish life in Lithuania. Rabbi Kamai's style of study, deeply analytical, yet combined with constant flashes of pilpulistic brilliance, proved attractive to prospective students, as did his magnificent personality and friendly, soft attitude towards his students.

After a number of years, Rabbi Avraham Tikitinsky departed Mir. He suffered from a retinal disease that robbed him of his sight, though he continued to deliver Talmudic lectures from memory. He eventually moved to Minsk and died there in 1921. Rabbi Kamai thereupon brought his son-in-law, Rabbi Eliezer Yehudah Finkel,[4] into the

---

3. Such as Rabbi Selig Baruch, head of Lomza Yeshivah; Rabbi Reuven Grozovsky, of Kaminetz in pre-war Poland and later head of Bais Medrosh Elyon, Monsey, N.Y.; and Rabbi Yosef Farber, head of Heichal Hatalmud in Tel Aviv.

4. The son of Rabbi Nosson Tzvi Finkel, the "Alter" of Slobodka Yeshivah. The son inherited many of the attributes of his great father.

yeshivah, and by 1907 he was recognized as Rabbi Kamai's heir apparent. He possessed not only great scholarly attributes but also was an administrator, fund raiser, and leader of unusual quality. In 1911 the village of Mir, together with its yeshivah building, burned to the ground.[5] The young Rabbi Finkel was the driving force in the rebuilding of the yeshivah as well, and helped mold it into the primary yeshivah of the time.

Rabbi Eliezer Yehudah Finkel

During the First World War, the yeshivah was forced to abandon Mir in 1916. Rabbi Eliyahu Baruch remained with his community in Mir, but fell seriously ill and died in Minsk, in 1917, after unsuccessful surgery. His son, Rabbi Avraham Tzvi Kamai, succeeded to the post of rabbi in Mir and was also appointed to an associate leadership role in the yeshivah. The yeshivah returned to Mir, now part of Poland, in 1921, under the leadership of Rabbi Finkel. Rabbi Yerucham Levovitz, a famed teacher of *mussar,* became the *mashgiach,*[6] and this combination of three great personalities — Rabbis Finkel, Kamai, and Levovitz — proved a magnet to students.

For the next eighteen years young men streamed to Mir. Not only students from Poland and Lithuania were in attendance, but also large contingents from Germany, the United States, South Africa, Switzerland, Czechoslovakia, Belgium, England, Rumania, Hungary, and even from Australia.[7] Thus Mir became the first truly international yeshivah of modern times.

In miraculous fashion, nearly the entire student body of the yeshivah escaped Europe during the Second World War and spent the war years as refugees in Kobe, Japan and Shanghai, China. After the war ended, the yeshivah reestablished itself in two branches: one in Brooklyn, N.Y. and the other in Jerusalem. Mir, in both branches, remains among the major yeshivos in the Jewish world.

---

5. These periodic conflagrations were part of Eastern European *shtetl* life. Mir had burned to the ground in 1878, and again in 1892. See Mirsky, p. 93.

6. Literally, "supervisor." The *mashgiach* in Lithuanian yeshivos had a special role. He looked after the spiritual and emotional growth of the students and was their counselor and adviser. He also delivered a *mussar* lecture in ethics and Jewish *weltanschaung* on a regular basis in the yeshivah. Rabbi Yerucham Levovitz and Rabbi Nosson Tzvi Finkel of Slobodka were the outstanding *mashgichim* in the yeshivah world of Lithuania.

7. See *Yahadus Lita,* vol. 1, p. 217, Tel Aviv 1959.

Slobodka

Rabbi Moshe Mordechai Epstein

Rabbi Isser Zalman Meltzer

 NE OF THE LARGEST AND MOST influential yeshivos in Lithuania after the closing of Volozhin was the famed Yeshivah Knesses Israel in Slobodka.[8] In 1863 a small yeshivah was founded in Slobodka, a suburb of Kovno, by Rabbi Tzvi Levitan.[9] In 1877, Rabbi Nosson Tzvi Finkel[10] joined Rabbi Levitan as the leader of the yeshivah. It was at this time that Rabbi Finkel, joined by Rabbi Yitzchak Blaser[11] and others, founded the "Kovner Kollel" for advanced Talmudic studies. The influence of the *kollel* was great and, with increased appreciation for the importance of Talmudic scholarship, the community perceived the necessity for a larger yeshivah. In response to this perception and the efforts of Rabbi Finkel, the Yeshivah Knesses Yisrael came into being.

In 1889, Rabbi Yitzchak Yaakov Rabinowitz[12] came to the yeshivah, and under his Talmudic genius it flourished. His analytic qualities and creative insights into the structure of the Talmud and *halachah* placed him on a special level of greatness and popularity. He often was compared[13] to the great Rabbi Chaim Soloveitchik of Volozhin. In 1890, Rabbi Dov Heller became the *mashgiach* of the yeshivah, and in 1894, two brothers-in-law, Rabbis Moshe Mordechai Epstein and Isser Zalman Meltzer, joined the faculty of Slobodka. These two great scholars, both products of Volozhin, helped Slobodka achieve new heights in popularity and recognition.

Eventually, all of the above-named scholars left Slobodka, except for Rabbi Nosson Tzvi Finkel and Rabbi Moshe Mordechai Epstein.

---

8. Slobodka was an all-Jewish suburb of Kovno (Kaunas), the capital of Lithuania between the wars. Aside from the famed Yeshivah Knesses Yisrael, there was a second large yeshivah, Knesses Bais Yitzchak, in Slobodka. See more on these yeshivos in the later chapter on *mussar*.

9. Also known as Rabbi Hershel Slobodker.

10. Born in 1849 in Rasein, Lithuania. Known as the "Alter (Elder) of Slobodka." He was the father and patron of most of the Lithuanian yeshivos of the late nineteenth and early twentieth centuries.

11. The great disciple of Rabbi Yisrael Salanter, the founder of the *Mussar* Movement. He served as rabbi of the Czarist capital, St. Petersburg, and therefore became known as Reb Itzele Peterburger.

12. Later to be known as Reb Itzele Ponivezher, when he became the rabbi of Ponivezh, the second city of Lithuania.

13. Mirsky, p. 143.

Rabbi Nosson Tzvi Finkel

These two built Slobodka into the major "*mussar* yeshivah"[14] of Lithuania and into the major producer of rabbis, teachers, and religious leaders of the twentieth century. Rabbi Finkel — known as the *Alter,* or Elder — had an uncanny insight into individual students; they, in turn, revered and loved him. It is remarkable that most of the great figures in the post-war American yeshivah world were molded by the *Alter:* Rabbi Aharon Kotler, Rabbi Reuven Grozovsky, Rabbi Yaakov Kaminetzky, Rabbi Yitzchak Yaakov Ruderman, and Rabbi Yitzchak Hutner. In 1909, Rabbi Isaac Sher, son-in-law of Rabbi Finkel, joined the faculty of the yeshivah. The yeshivah continued to function throughout the First World War, though it was temporarily exiled from its home in Slobodka.

Rabbi Yitzchak Elchonon Spector

After the war, in 1924, Rabbis Finkel and Epstein left Slobodka with most of their students and founded a new yeshivah in Hebron, in the Land of Israel. Rabbi Sher remained in Slobodka and maintained the yeshivah there until World War II. The Hebron yeshivah was destroyed by an Arab pogrom in 1929, but stubbornly reestablished itself once more in Jerusalem. Rabbi Sher himself escaped Slobodka in 1941 and reestablished another branch of the Slobodka yeshivah in Bnei Brak. Thus, Rabbi Finkel's great yeshivah still thrives and grows in its branches and in those spawned by his disciples.

Rabbi Baruch Ber Leibowitz

A second large yeshivah in Slobodka was founded in 1897, and was named Knesses Beis Yitzchak, in memory of the famed Rabbi Yitzchak Elchanan Spector, Rabbi of Kovno. It was a "competitor" of Rabbi Nosson Tzvi Finkel's yeshivah, in that it was explicitly a non-*mussar* yeshivah, while Rabbi Finkel's Knesses Yisrael was the prototype of the *mussar* yeshivah. The famed Rabbi Chaim Rabinowitz[15] was its first head, but in 1904 he left and was replaced by one of the central figures of the yeshivah world, Rabbi Baruch Ber Leibowitz.[16]

Rabbi Leibowitz was the premier disciple of Rabbi Chaim Soloveitchik and one of the leading Talmudists of his time. He combined a charismatic personality with personal integrity and holy piety. Rabbi Baruch Ber headed the yeshivah in Slobodka until the first World War, when it was disbanded. He reestablished it, first in Krementchug, Russia, and finally, after the war, in Kaminetz, Poland, where it became known as Yeshivas Kaminetz. There, the yeshivah

14. See chapter on the *Mussar* Movement in this book.
15. Also known as Rabbi Chaim Telsher.
16. 1870-1940.

Rabbi Reuven Grozovsky

grew and prospered. Rabbi Baruch Ber was aided by his son-in-law, Rabbi Reuven Grozovsky,[17] who served as assistant *Rosh Yeshivah* and in the administration of the yeshivah. Students from many foreign lands flocked to its study hall and Rabbi Baruch Ber became the mentor of many. After its destruction in the Second World War, the yeshivah was able to reestablish itself in Jerusalem and Brooklyn, where it exists today.

Radin

LL OF THE YESHIVOS WERE PRODUCTS of great people who, through their sacrifice, ingenuity, and tenacity, gave life to their own institutions and to the yeshivah movement generally. More than most, however, the yeshivah in Radin was identified with one man. He was Rabbi Yisrael Meir HaCohen Kagan,[18] who moved to the small hamlet in Vilna Province in 1869. There he gathered around him young men of note and scholarship, and the yeshivah began to develop. Many of the early students of Radin were married men[19] and Rabbi Yisrael Meir was their patron and teacher. He was a rare individual: a strong personality who was a saint, a gregarious person who never spoke a forbidden word, an everyday Jew who was one of the great creative and scholarly geniuses of his time, a humble and self-effacing person who was the effective leader of traditional Jewry. At the time of his death in 1933, at the age of ninety-five, he was beloved and respected by all of world Jewry, and his influence was felt in all circles and factions of the Jewish people.

The main impetus to the growth of the yeshivah came in 1904 when Rabbi Naftali Trop became its rosh yeshiva. It grew to over three hundred students, but it was caught in the battles of the First

---

17. 1896-1958. Later, the head of Bais Medrosh Elyon in Monsey, N.Y.

18. Popularly known as the *Chofetz Chaim*. This was the name of his first major work, published anonymously in the 1870s. It was a book regarding the laws and attitudes pertaining to slander, deceit, verbal and oral communication, and conversation generally. It established its author in the forefront of scholars and holy men of the generation.

19. *Perushim* who left their families for extended periods of time to pursue their Torah studies in an unencumbered, if lonely, fashion. The largest group of such *perushim* was found in the little Lithuanian village of Aishishok.

World War. The yeshivah and Rabbi Yisrael Meir wandered in exile in Russia, splitting into three groups, but somehow surviving the horrors of the war and the ensuing Bolshevik revolution and civil war. In 1921, the yeshivah reopened in Radin, then part of the new Poland, and once more it grew and prospered.

Rabbi Elchanan Wasserman

In 1929 Rabbi Naftali Trop died suddenly, at the age of fifty-nine, and was succeeded by Rabbi Baruch Faivelson and Rabbi Menachem Mendel Zaks,[20] a son-in-law of Rabbi Yisrael Meir. Rabbi Faivelson died soon thereafter and Rabbi Zaks became the head of the yeshivah, assisted by Rabbi Avraham Trop, the son of Rabbi Naftali. Among the many great students of Radin who spanned different times and places were Rabbi Elchanan Wasserman,[21] Rabbi Yosef Kahaneman,[22] Rabbi David Leibowitz[23] and Rabbi Eliezer Levin.[24] The yeshivah was closed by the Communist authorities in 1940, and the students and faculty were later annihilated by the Germans in the early 1940s. The names of Radin and the *Chofetz Chaim* survive in a number of different institutions in the United States and Israel.

Rabbi Yosef Kahaneman

Telshe

LTHOUGH THE POPULATION OF TELSHE was under 10,000, half of it Jewish, it was considered a major city in Lithuania, close to Prussia, on the crossroads between Germany and Western Europe and Russia and Eastern Europe. Its yeshivah was formed in 1875. In 1881, Rabbi Eliezer Gordon, one of the great students of Volozhin and a disciple of Rabbi Yisrael Salanter,[25] was chosen as the rabbi of Telshe. He immediately took responsibility for the yeshivah and assumed its leadership. He

---

20. Later, a member of the faculty of Rabbi Isaac Elchanan Theological Seminary of Yeshiva University in New York.

21. Head of the great yeshivah in Baranowitz and one of the leaders of the Jewish world in pre-World War II Poland.

22. The famed Ponivezher *Rav* and the founder of the great Ponivezh yeshivah, first in Lithuania, and then in Bnei Brak, Israel.

23. The founder of the Rabbinical Seminary of America, known as Yeshivas Chofetz Chaim, in Forest Hills, N.Y.

24. The head of the Orthodox Rabbinate of Detroit, Michigan, for over fifty years, beginning in 1938.

25. See chapter on the *Mussar* Movement in this book.

Rabbi Eliezer Gordon

Rabbi Shimon Shkop

recognized the serious inroads of the *Haskalah* movement[26] among traditional Jewish youth, and struggled to raise both the yeshivah student's level of education and his prestige in the eyes of the community.

Telshe was the most "progressive" of all the Lithuanian yeshivos. It had an organized educational philosophy, curriculum, and structure. Rabbi Gordon was a great leader, a compassionate father to his students, and a tireless worker for the cause of his yeshivah.[27] In 1882, Rabbi Yosef Leib Bloch, Rabbi Eliezer's son-in-law, joined the faculty of the yeshivah. He was a dynamic, forceful personality who left his indelible stamp on the yeshivah. He, in fact, became the eventual educational architect of Telshe Yeshivah, its forms and classes, divisions and order. Rabbi Yosef Leib was joined in the yeshivah faculty by Rabbi Shimon Shkop,[28] a nephew by marriage to Rabbi Gordon, and one of the leading young Talmudic geniuses of Lithuania. In addition, Rabbi Chaim Rabinowitz[29] joined the faculty.

This formidable array of greatness in knowledge and educational leadership made Telshe one of the largest and most popular yeshivos in Lithuania. Rabbi Yosef Leib left the yeshivah for several years but returned in 1910, succeeding his father-in-law as the rabbi of the town and the head of the yeshivah. The First World War slowed the development of the yeshivah, but immediately after the war, Rabbi Yosef Leib revitalized the yeshivah and expanded its educational projects. Rabbi Yosef Leib was an extraordinary personality whose energy, creativity, and industry were legendary. He was aristocratic in appearance, bearing, and personal habits. Punctual, regal in dress and manners, and most forceful in his presentation of ideas and policies, he was a formidable leader. He, more than anyone else, formed and molded Telshe.

In 1920, the yeshivah founded a preparatory school for younger students as an adjunct of the yeshivah. This *mechinah*[30] became the prototype for today's secondary school yeshivos. In 1929, a special *kollel* for rabbinic students was opened. In 1926, a *Beis Medrash*

---

26. See below, Chapter 16, on the *Haskalah* Movement.

27. He died in London in 1910, while on a fund-raising mission for the yeshivah, and is buried there.

28. Later, *rosh yeshivah* of the famed yeshivah in Grodno. He was also a student of Volozhin.

29. See note 15 above and the section on Slobodka.

30. Literally, "preparatory."

L'Morim ,[31] or teachers' seminary, was opened with thirty students from the yeshivah forming its nucleus. In 1927, a Hebrew Gymnasium for Girls[32] was opened in Telshe. This was the first school of its type under Orthodox auspices in Lithuania. In 1930, a teachers' seminary for young women was established. This network of Jewish education proved a model for all Jewish communities and its influence was felt far beyond Telshe itself.

In late 1929, Rabbi Yosef Leib died and his son, Rabbi Avraham Yitzchak Bloch, succeeded to his father's positions as rabbi of the city and head of the yeshivah. A large American and Western European contingent joined the student body, and it continued to grow until its destruction during the Second World War. Rabbi Avraham Yitzchak's younger brother, Rabbi Eliyahu Meir Bloch, and his brother-in-law, Rabbi Chaim Mordechai Katz, escaped to America and reestablished the yeshivah in Cleveland, Ohio. It also has branches in Chicago, Riverdale, N.Y. and Israel.

Slutzk-Kletzk-Lakewood

HE YESHIVAH ETZ CHAIM was founded in Slutzk, a town in Lithuanian Russia, in the 1890s. Its head and founder was the famed Rabbi Yaakov David Willowski,[33] the rabbi of the town. In 1897, Rabbi Nosson Tzvi Finkel of Slobodka sent fourteen of his prime students and faculty members to Slutzk, to help build and strengthen the yeshivah. One of these newcomers to Slutzk was Rabbi Isser Zalman Meltzer,[34] who became the

---

31. A teacher's college — a school to train educators. This was a new, almost radical, departure for traditional Jewry generally and for a yeshivah particularly.

32. This paralleled the opening of the Bais Yaakov girls' school system in Poland at the same time by the pioneer Jewish woman educator, Sarah Schneirer.

33. 1845-1914. Known by his acronym, *Ridvaz*. He was the author of one of the basic commentaries on the Jerusalem Talmud. He was, for a period of time, the Chief Rabbi in Chicago and later settled in Safed, Israel, where he died and is buried. He was a brilliant, outspoken battler for Torah Judaism, whose life was filled with accomplishment as well as controversy.

34. 1870-1953. He served as a member of the faculty at Slobodka itself from 1894 to 1897. His career as a *rosh yeshivah,* beginning in Slobodka and ending in Jerusalem, spanned sixty years! He was a student of Volozhin and favorite of Rabbi Chaim Soloveitchik. He was the brother-in-law of Rabbi Moshe Mordechai Epstein, the *Rosh Yeshivah* of Slobodka. In 1925 he emigrated to Jerusalem, where he served as the *Rosh Yeshivah* of Etz Chaim until his death in 1954.

mainstay and leader of the yeshivah. When Rabbi Willowski left Slutzk in 1903 to emigrate to America and eventually to the Land of Israel, Rabbi Isser Zalman Meltzer became the rabbi of Slutzk and the official head of the yeshivah. A person of remarkable character and selfless dedication, Rabbi Meltzer built the yeshivah into a major educational force.

The First World War and the attendant Bolshevik Revolution caused great disruption of Jewish life in Slutzk, which was in Soviet Russia. The yeshivah was forced to abandon Slutzk and reestablish itself in Kletzk, Poland, under the direction of Rabbi Aharon Kotler,[35] Rabbi Meltzer's son-in-law. Rabbi Meltzer himself suffered imprisonment and degradation at the hands of the Communist oppressors and finally, in 1923, succeeded in escaping across the Polish border to rejoin his yeshivah and family in Kletzk. However, he soon emigrated to Jerusalem and the effective leadership of the yeshivah passed to Rabbi Kotler. The yeshivah students in Kletzk numbered two hundred and sixty[36] in 1939 on the eve of the war. Rabbi Kotler[37] escaped to America in 1941 and reopened the yeshivah of Kletzk in Lakewood, New Jersey, under the name Beis Medrash Govoha. From humble beginnings, it grew into one of the largest and most influential yeshivos in the world. It maintains a branch in Jerusalem and has been instrumental in the founding of numerous yeshivos throughout the United States.

---

35. Born in 1892 and himself one of the leading students in Slobodka and later in Slutzk, Rabbi Kotler was one of the outstanding leaders of Jewry in the post-World War II era. He was a great Talmudic genius and a leader of vision and tenacity. He was the founder of the illustrious Talmudic yeshivah in Lakewood, New Jersey, and pioneered the concept of *kollelim* in America. He was also the driving creative force behind such organizations as Agudath Israel, Torah Schools for Israel, Vaad Hatzolah, and Torah Umesorah. His influence on all sectors of Jewish life and factions was immeasurable and his strength of character and intensity of vision were major factors in rebuilding and revitalizing Orthodox Jewry after the war.

36. Mirsky, p. 235.

37. A further assessment of the great career of Rabbi Kotler is provided in the later chapter on American Jewry after World War II.

Novardok — Beis Yosef

NE OF THE MOST FAMOUS of the *mussar*[38] yeshivos in Lithuania was that of Novardok. This yeshivah later was the mother of an entire network of yeshivos scattered throughout Lithuania, northern Poland and Russia. The yeshivah was founded by one of the most unique and different personalities of Jewish Lithuania, Rabbi Yosef Yoiz'l Horowitz.[38] A disciple of Rabbi Yisrael Salanter,[39] he was a strong advocate and practitioner of *mussar* and he became the target of many of the opponents of the movement.

The yeshivah was founded in 1896 and soon gained the support of the local community of Novardok[40] and of its famous rabbi, Rabbi Yechiel Michel Epstein.[41] In spite of the then-vehement opposition to *mussar* and especially to the practices and intensity of Rabbi Horowitz, the yeshivah grew and prospered. Nevertheless, the struggle against the yeshivah and Rabbi Horowitz did not abate and in 1908, upon the death of Rabbi Epstein,[42] the yeshivah was forced to leave the city. However, it returned in 1909 and by 1912 it was housed in its own newly built school building.

Novardok Yeshivah helped found many other yeshivos and incorporated most of them into a unified educational group known as Yeshivos Beis Yosef. Aside from Rabbi Horowitz himself, the yeshivah and its affiliates were led by Rabbi Avraham Yaffen, his son-in-law. The number of major yeshivos of Beis Yosef eventually rose to over twenty. They were characterized by intense Torah study combined with the study and practice of *mussar* in a public and overt fashion. The students were trained to pursue truth and justice, disregarding public opposition and disdain; to be unimpressed by the prevailing social conventions of

---

38. 1850-1920.

39. Again, see chapter on the *Mussar* Movement.

40. A county seat in Lithuania with a population of five thousand. Its Jewish community was founded in the sixteenth century and it was famous because of the great rabbis and scholars that served the community over the years.

41. A brother-in-law of the *Netziv* of Volozhin and the author of a famous, authoritative halachic work, *Aruch HaShulchan*, which became a handbook for Torah decisions in rabbinic circles.

42. Rabbi Epstein had been one of the main defenders and supporters of the yeshivah.

society; and to be fearless in spreading Torah and *mussar* amongst the Jewish people. Novardok, its institutions and affiliates, and its students were the shock troops of the *Mussar* Movement.

With the advent of the German army's occupation of Novardok in 1915, the yeshivah was transferred to Homel in Russia. During its stay in Russia, branches of the yeshivah were formed in many Russian towns and cities including Kharkov, Zhitomir, Rostov, Astrachan and Kiev. The yeshivah also became a central rallying point for many students of other yeshivos who had fled into Russia due to the ravages of the war and were isolated from their home yeshivos.[43]

The outbreak of the Russian revolution in 1917 and the attendant civil war in Russia damaged the Beis Yosef movement severely. The Communists persecuted these yeshivos and their students cruelly and relentlessly. By 1920, most of the yeshivos in Russia were forcibly shut and the students of Novardok attempted, singly and in groups, to escape to Poland. Rabbi Horowitz died in an epidemic in Kiev in 1920, and Rabbi Yaffen reestablished the yeshivah in Bialystok and Mezeritch in Poland. Eventually, large yeshivos of Beis Yosef existed in Warsaw and Pinsk as well. The network of yeshivos, schools, and institutions once again expanded, this time in Poland and Lithuania, during the decades between the wars, and finally encompassed over eight different schools numbering over four thousand students.[44] The yeshivos also published books, pamphlets, magazines and periodicals, as well as scholarly journals of Torah and *mussar*.

The Second World War destroyed the yeshivah and its affiliates in Poland and Lithuania. Those students not killed by the Germans were exiled by the Russians to Siberia, where they faced seemingly inevitable death due to malnutrition and the harsh elements. Miraculously, Rabbi Yaffen and a number of students escaped. They reestablished the yeshivah in New York after the war, and smaller branches were founded in Israel as well.

---

43. One of the outstanding students at Homel during this time was the young Yisrael Yaakov Kanievsky, later one of the giants of Torah in Israel. He was known as "The Steipler" after his home town of Hornosteipl.
44. Mirsky, p. 277.

Pressburg

O F COMPLETELY DIFFERENT NATURE and history were the yeshivos in the Austro-Hungarian Empire. They were founded earlier, in the main, than the Lithuanian yeshivos, and developed independently of their Eastern European counterparts. The largest and most influential yeshivah in Central Europe was in Pressburg. This imperial city of the Austro-Hungarian Empire (now known as Bratislava, Czechoslovakia) had a long and rich Jewish history. Jews first settled there in the fourteenth century, and the Jewish community there served as a bridge between Hungary and Rumania on the east and Germany and Austria on the west. However, the situation of Jewish life and education in the Austro-Hungarian Empire in the eighteenth century was bleak. One of its rabbis wrote: "This country is being destroyed by the arrogance of those ignorant of Torah who undertake to decide matters of *halachah* . . . and they pervert what is just . . . and desecrate the Torah."[45] Attempts to improve the situation proved fruitless until the arrival of Rabbi Moses Sofer,[46] the *Chasam Sofer,* as rabbi of Pressburg.

In 1807, the *Chasam Sofer* established a great yeshivah in Pressburg on the ruins of previous small institutions of learning.[47] Through the charisma of his gigantic personality, he caused a revolution in Jewish life. He elevated the cause of Torah, educated a generation of leaders, built a spiritual dam that contained the tide of Reform, raised the dimensions of Torah scholarship and made his yeshivah the central institution of Jewish life in the Austro-Hungarian Empire. The Pressburg community undertook the maintenance of the yeshivah,[48] and it soon

---

45. Quoted in Mirsky, p. 451, from a letter written by the elder Rabbi Akiva Eiger, who was rabbi in Pressburg.

46. See chapter on Reform for a description of his life, views, and programs.

47. Mirsky, p. 450, quoting Rabbi Avraham Shmuel Binyamin Sofer, the son of the *Chasam Sofer,* who said, "It is well known that before my father, the *Chasam Sofer,* came to Pressburg, there was only a small yeshivah here with but a few students."

48. In this respect, Pressburg was unlike the Lithuanian yeshivos which required national and even international support, and never were maintained locally. The reason for this was that the Lithuanian yeshivos produced, in the main, rabbinic and scholarly persons, and thus never had a base of financial support from its alumni. However, the Hungarian yeshivos produced a much higher proportion of laymen

grew into an institution of two hundred and fifty students. It bred Jews of great piety and profound faith, whose unswerving loyalty to Torah and *mitzvos* took precedence over all else in life.[49]

Almost all of the great non-Chassidic rabbis and teachers of Austro-Hungarian Jewry were graduates of the yeshivah in Pressburg. "Oberlander"[50] Jewry was Pressburg. Not only was Pressburg a school for rabbis, it was a school for Torah accomplishment in its purest fashion. It was meant to produce Torah personalities of the highest order, people who — no matter what their trade or profession — were accomplished Torah scholars, pious, observant, uncompromising in faith, and gentle in human relations. Pressburg and its students truly reflected the life and behavior of its leader, the *Chasam Sofer.*

Though some of the graduates of Pressburg came to be pre-eminent in the rabbinate, many of them participated in all avenues of commerce and careers; they spoke and were fluent in German[51] and were familiar with Western culture; they were strong personalities and of great communal influence. But primarily, all of their lives, they were yeshivah students, and though they may have long ago left the halls of learning, the spirit and influence of the yeshivah never left them.

In 1826, the governor-general of Pressburg, on the instigation of local Reform leaders, who correctly saw in the *Chasam Sofer* their most dangerous foe, sent him a long questionnaire regarding the yeshivah. He replied to the questionnaire in perfect German and satisfactorily answered its ten questions.[52] The governor-general was satisfied with the reply, and, in spite of the continued pressure of the Reform leaders, he took no action against the yeshivah.[53]

---

whose business careers allowed them to be the financial mainstays of the yeshivos they had attended. In general, the methods of the Lithuanian and Hungarian yeshivos differed as to the intensity and depth of Talmudic study, and the life and career goals of their students. The Lithuanian yeshivos were more intense, elitist, and rigorous as to their students, curriculum, and educational goals than were the Hungarian schools. It has been noted by leaders of both schools that the Lithuanian academies existed primarily to produce great scholars while the Hungarian academies strove to produce strong Torah communities. Both succeeded.

49. For a fascinating and entertaining description of Pressburg, its yeshivah and the life of its students, see *Olamo shel Abba* by Pinchas Miller, Jerusalem, 1984, beginning at page 44.

50. The name for the geographical region west of the main Carpathian mountains in Rumania-Hungary and north of the Danube River.

51. The *Chasam Sofer* even allowed Orthodox rabbis to preach in German if the occasion arose and circumstances required it. See *Olamo shel Abba*, p. 86.

52. See Mirsky, p. 464.

53. See Mirsky, p. 466.

In 1839, Rabbi Moshe Sofer died and was succeeded as the rabbi of Pressburg and the head of the yeshivah by his beloved son, Avraham Shmuel Binyamin Sofer.[54] Like his father, he was a man of great character, talent, knowledge, and charisma. His quiet diplomacy and aristocratic demeanor made him an accepted force even in the court of the Austro-Hungarian emperor, and he won for the yeshivah recognition as an official theological college. This status exempted its students from military service, which, by the 1860s, had become mandatory for the Jews living in the Austro-Hungarian Empire. He also was the driving force behind the construction of new study buildings for the yeshivah, all of which enhanced its fame and enlarged its enrollment. As a result, the Orthodox community was supplied with constant and gifted leadership by the yeshivah in Pressburg.

Rabbi Avraham Shmuel Binyamin Sofer was a gifted orator, a man of wit and style, and an author and scholar of note. In 1869 he organized a convention of the Orthodox Jewish congregations in Hungary, and gained governmental recognition of the independent authority of these "separate" congregations. This allowed for three distinct, recognized Jewish communities in Hungary. They were the Orthodox, the Reform, and the Neolog.[55] In 1872, Rabbi Avraham Shmuel Binyamin Sofer died at the age of fifty-seven,[56] and was succeeded by his son, Rabbi Simchah Bunim Sofer.[57] He in turn served as the head of the yeshivah and the rabbi of Pressburg until his death in 1907.

After his death, his son, Rabbi Akiva Sofer, became the rabbi of Pressburg and the head of the yeshivah. The First World War and the resultant breakup of the Hapsburg Empire brought tumultuous times to the yeshivah. Pressburg became Bratislava and passed to the dominion of the new country of Czechoslovakia. Hungary, Austria, Germany, and Poland hampered the growth of the yeshivah by creating difficulties regarding passport control, customs, and visas to students attempting to reach Pressburg/Bratislava. The economic support for the yeshivah

---

54. Known as the *Ksav Sofer*.

55. Not as radical as the Reform, but bitterly opposed by the Orthodox for their willingness to compromise on matters of *halachah*, Jewish customs and practices.

56. The story is told that when he was seriously ill as a child at the age of seven, young Avraham Shmuel Binyamin's mother implored her husband, the *Chasam Sofer,* to intercede by prayer with the Heavenly court to save their dying son. The *Chasam Sofer* prayed and then reported to his wife, "I have prevailed for a stay of fifty years."

57. Known as the *Shevet Sofer.*

dwindled in the wake of the precarious financial situation in Europe between the wars. But, in spite of all obstacles, the yeshivah continued to flourish and grow. Pressburg remained the example par excellence for all the yeshivos in Central Europe.[58]

After the Czech crisis of 1938 and Hitler's invasion of that country, Rabbi Akiva Sofer escaped to Jerusalem. There, he once again opened the doors of the Pressburg Yeshivah.

There were numerous other great institutions of Jewish learning in Europe. Space in a work such as this cannot allow for the detailed and in-depth analysis to which each of these institutions is entitled. They varied in size, method, outlook, and student body. But they were united in purpose, that being the preservation of Jewry on the basis of Torah study, knowledge, and observance. A brief and superficial list of these institutions would include those of Lomza,[59] Slonim,[60] Grodno,[61] Kobrin,[62] Baranowitz,[63] Warsaw,[64] Lublin,[65] Heide, Belgium,[66] Berlin,[67] Frankfurt am Main and Radomsk, among

---

58. Both Rabbi Shalom Ber Schneerson, the Lubavitcher *Rebbe,* and his son, Rabbi Yosef Yitzchak Schneerson, visited Pressburg in connection with plans for their new yeshivah. Also, at a later time Rabbi Meir Shapiro of Lublin visited Pressburg regarding his own plans for the great Yeshivas Chachmai Lublin (see Mirsky, pp. 494-5); he also visited the great yeshivos of Lithuania and patterned much of his educational program and method on their example.

59. Rabbi Yechiel Mordechai Gordon was its head.

60. Headed by Rabbi Shabsai Yogel.

61. Yeshivas Shaar HaTorah was headed by the famed Rabbi Shimon Shkop, originally from Telshe. It has been reestablished in the United States by Rabbi Zelik Epstein.

62. Headed by Rabbi Pesach Pruskin.

63. Headed by the great disciple of the *Chofetz Chaim,* Rabbi Elchanan Wasserman. Though in America in 1939, he returned to his yeshivah to be with his students in their hour of trial and destruction. He was trapped by the Nazi invasion and was murdered by Lithuanian collaborators.

64. The Mesivta of Warsaw was headed by Rabbi Meir Don Plotzki. The Tachkamoni of Warsaw was headed by Rabbi Moshe HaLevi Soloveitchik, the son of Rabbi Chaim. There were many *shtieblach yeshivos* in Warsaw, led by men of great scholarship. Most of the yeshivah students in Warsaw were chassidim, in contradistinction to the students of the other yeshivos who were *misnagdim.*

65. Led by the legendary Rabbi Meir Shapiro.

66. Founded in 1931 by Rabbi Shraga Feivel Shapiro.

67. Popularly called Hildesheimer's Seminary, after its gifted founder, Rabbi Ezriel Hildesheimer. It was not strictly a yeshivah in the Lithuanian definition of the term, and its purpose was to produce rabbis and thinkers to represent Orthodoxy in Germany and Western Europe, but not necessarily great Torah scholars in the Eastern European tradition. Its later leaders included Rabbi David Tzvi Hoffman, Rabbi

others.[68] There was also a great yeshivah in Ponivezh,[69] a network of yeshivos associated with Lubavitch,[70] as well as Torah schools of higher learning in Yasi,[71] Kishinev,[72] Chernowitz,[73] Vizhnitz,[74] Sered,[75] Toshnad,[76] Satmar,[77] and Sighet.[78] The Chassidic court of Gur[79] also operated a large system of yeshivos throughout Poland.

All of the yeshivos of Continental Europe were destroyed in the Second World War, but many of them have since reopened in Israel and the United States. The importance of the yeshivah movement to the survival of the Jewish people over the past one hundred and fifty years cannot be overemphasized. It remained the creative life force — the "factory" — of the Jewish people.

Avraham Eliyahu Kaplan, and Rabbi Yechiel Yaakov Weinberg (*Sridei Eish*). See the previous chapter, "Reform Sweeps All — Almost."

68. A network of Chassidic yeshivos founded and led by the *Rebbe* of Radomsk, Rabbi Shalom Chanoch HaCohen Rabinowitz. The yeshivos were called Kesser Torah and eventually numbered thirty-six, with three thousand students in various sections of Poland.

69. Lithuania, founded and headed by Rabbi Yosef Kahaneman. He reopened the yeshivah in Bnei Brak, Israel, in 1942. It is one of the largest yeshivos in the world. See note 22 above.

70. Yeshivos Tomchei Tmimim, led by the *Rebbe* of Lubavitch.

71. Rumania.

72. Headed and supported by the great Rabbi Y.L. Zirelsohn, who was also a member of the Rumanian Parliament.

73. Founded by Rabbi Daniel Sternfeld in 1923.

74. Founded and led by the great dynasty of Vizhnitz Chassidus, the Hager family.

75. Also founded by the Vizhnitz dynasty.

76. Founded by Rabbi Moshe Brisk and continued by his son-in-law, Rabbi Shmuel Greenberg. It was one of the larger yeshivos in Hungary, numbering well over three hundred students.

77. There were four yeshivos in Satmar, the largest one led by Rabbi Yoel Teitelbaum, the Satmar Rav. See Mirsky, p. 547.

78. Led by Rabbi Yekusiel Yehudah Gross. There was also a textile-weaving plant associated with the yeshivah, allowing its students to acquire a trade within the environment of the yeshivah.

79. Founded by the *Chiddushei HaRim,* Rabbi Yitzchak Meir Alter, and led by the Rabbis of Gur Chassidus.

16

The Haskalah

Enlightenment and Reform

 HE IDEAS OF THE ENLIGHTENMENT and Reform made their way east to the Jews of Poland and Russia in the late eighteenth and early nineteenth centuries, but, in their Western and especially Germanic forms, Enlightenment and Reform were basically unpopular among Eastern European Jews. In Western Europe, these movements were seen as the means for assimilation and acceptance of the Jew into the non-Jewish society. If baptism was "the ticket for admission to Western society"[1] in the 1700s, Enlightenment and Reform were the entry pass in the 1800s. However, the official hostility of the Czar and his government to the Jews — coupled with the terrible bigotry and unreasoning hatred of the local population towards their Jewish neighbors, and with the unattractive, boorish and uncultured way of life of the peasantry — made mass assimilation in Eastern Europe an unpopular option. Assimilation in Jewish history was always possible — but usually occurred only when the non-Jewish society was open and attractive, and sanctioned and encouraged it.[2] The Jews of Eastern Europe knew that the true goals of Enlightenment and Reform were unrealizable in their milieu, and therefore the movement itself was irrelevant.

However, the ideas loosed by the events of the eighteenth and nineteenth centuries in Western Europe were the proverbial genie, and they could not be returned to the bottle. In Eastern Europe there were now Jews who were no longer satisfied with the old ideas and mores of

---

1. Heinrich Heine's bitter assessment of his generation.

2. Spain in the middle ages, Western Europe in the nineteenth century, the United States in the current era.

Jewish life. They searched for an escape from the terrible physical circumstances of their life in Eastern Europe,[3] and they were convinced that "Jewish culture" would provide an answer to the "Jewish problem." If the Jews were "cultured," anti-Semitism would be ameliorated, hatreds would diminish, and the Jew would eventually be accepted by the Czar, his government, and his subjects as a productive and necessary element in society.

The *Haskalah* Movement represented this drive to create, disseminate and popularize Jewish "culture." If this drive towards "culture" would eventually destroy religious observances and beliefs — then so be it. The old, after all, has to make way for the new.[4] Thus, there arose the myth of the "modern" Jew who always claimed to advance the Jewish cause while proclaiming that the "old-style" Jew was the dead-weight anchor who held back all Jewish progress.[5]

Haskalah was not a monolith; it came in different forms and guises and in different shades of radicalism. Certain forms of *Haskalah*, therefore, eventually gained wider acceptance among Eastern European Jews, though *Haskalah*, as a whole, never became a strong mass movement in Eastern Europe.

There was a Hebrew *Haskalah,* based on the revival of the Hebrew language as the cornerstone of culture. There was a Yiddish *Haskalah,* determined to create a secular literature and art form in Yiddish and harness the free-style flow of expression of this most folk-reflective language of Ashkenazic Jews. There was Russian *Haskalah,* based on the conviction that the centrality and primacy of the Russian language and literature was necessary for Jewish cultural survival in Russia. There was a Biblical *Haskalah* that created a Jewish culture by the use of intense non-traditional Biblical scholarship and even Biblical Criticism. There was the *Haskalah* of *Chochmas Yisrael* — the Science of the Wisdom of Israel — which defined Jewish culture through the scholarly study of all facts of Judaism and Jewish life gone by, as a means of

---

3. See Chapter 17.

4. One of the popular slogans of the *Haskalah* was the paraphrase of the Biblical text in Leviticus: "And the old shall be removed for the new." This is a prime example of their ability to distort Biblical meaning by quoting phrases out of context.

5. The *Haskalah* in its writings always characterized itself as the forces of "light," while the traditional Jew, especially chassidim and the leading rabbinic figures of the time, were characterized as the forces of "darkness." Rabbi Yaakov Lipschutz, the secretary of Rabbi Yitzchak Elchanan Spector of Kovno, and his associates, were always smeared by the *maskilim* as being the *lishkah hashchorah,* the "black office," due to their unremitting opposition to the *Haskalah.*

preserving it in a museum-like status.[6] Western, academic, scholarly methods were to be used to explain the Bible, Mishnah, Talmud, Jewish customs, personages, and events. This culture would preserve the "old Judaism and the Jew" as a historical relic, while the *new* Jew made his way blithely into the welcome world of the modern era. Later, there would arise the labor, or socialist, *Haskalah,* which tied Jewish culture and destiny to the revolution of the proletariat. Much of the energy and goals of the *Haskalah,* as well as most of its adherents, would eventually be absorbed in the movement of political Zionism at the end of the nineteenth century.

The *maskilim*[7] used the pen to popularize their ideas. The sanctity of the written and printed word among Jews[8] gave credence to non-Jewish and even anti-Jewish printed polemics, especially if they were written in the Jewish languages of Hebrew and Yiddish. Thus *Haskalah* was able to wield an influence among Eastern European Jews disproportionate to its actual numbers and strength.

Secular Hebrew Literature

 HE FATHER OF THE LITERATURE of the *Haskalah* was Yitzchak Ber Levinson (*Ribal*).[9] In 1828 he published a pamphlet called *Teudah B'Yisrael,*[10] in which he advocated drastic reforms in the traditional method and curriculum of Jewish schools. He supported the ideas of Jews becoming farmers and not merchants or tradespeople, and of conducting Jewish studies and Jewish life generally in the Russian language.[11] In the

---

6. See chapter on Reform and Enlightenment for the description of the work of Zunz, Geiger, Gans, and others in the Society for the Science of Judaism in nineteenth-century Germany. Many of the members of this society eventually converted to Christianity!

7. Literally, "wise ones." Traditional Jews used the word sarcastically and the followers of *Haskalah,* proudly.

8. A product of the long association of literacy with Torah and holy writings.

9. He was known as the "Russian Mendelssohn." He was born in 1788 and died in 1869.

10. "Meaning for Israel."

11. He chose Russian because that was his mother tongue but he would also have settled for French or German.

1820s and 1830s, he was instrumental in establishing *Haskalah* schools in Warsaw, Oman, Odessa, Kishinev, and Riga,[12] in which the language of instruction was German.

The *Haskalah* schools were not popular. In fact, most of the support for the *Haskalah* came only from the infinitesimally small group of very wealthy Russian Jews who were ashamed of their poor relatives and their different folkways. These wealthy Jews, though few in number, were again disproportionate in influence, and their material and moral support gave *Haskalah* a stronger standing with the Russian government than it would otherwise have achieved. The *maskilim* would exploit this relationship with the government to the detriment of Jewish society in Russia.[13] The *Haskalah* imported much of its leadership from Germany, and this foreign flavor eventually turned it even more radical.

Avraham Dov Lebensohn,[14] Avraham Mapu,[15] Mordecai Aaron Ginzberg, Yehudah Leib Gordon,[16] and Moshe Leib Lilienblum[17] were the famous authors of the new secular Hebrew literature. Their works were laced with ridicule and criticism of rabbis, tradition, folk customs, and the old Jewish life. They concentrated upon and exaggerated the faults and foibles of their observant brothers and traditional fathers. They wished to destroy the old world before the new one was yet built.[18] Their works obtained a wide readership and they were known and read clandestinely in the yeshivos as well. They became the founders of the first secular Judaism in the history of Israel.

12. *Toldos Am Yisrael,* Vol. 3, edited by S. Ettinger, Tel Aviv 1969, p. 124.

13. The nefarious complicity of the leaders of the *Haskalah* in some of the worst decrees of the Czar against nineteenth-century Russian Jews guaranteed its unpopularity among Eastern European Jews. See *Zichron Yaakov* by Yaakov HaLevi Lipschutz, Vols. I and 2, for numerous examples.

14. Known as Adam Dov HaCohen (1794-1878).

15. 1808-1867. Author of the infamous *Eyit Zavua — The Hypocritical Vulture,* an acidic work portraying rabbinic Judaism as the villain of Jewish history.

16. Known by the acronym *Yalag* (1831-1892).

17. Later a leading Zionist writer and activist (1843-1910).

18. The *Haskalah* itself realized this fatal shortcoming. Eduard Gans, one of the founders of the Society for the Science of Judaism, wrote: "The break with the intimacy of the old existence has indeed occurred, but the deeper return to this intimacy has not taken place. The enthusiasm for religion and the genuineness of the old relationships has vanished, but no new enthusiasm has broken forth, no new set of relationships has been built" (quoted in *Zakhor,* by Y.H. Yerushalmi, University of Washington Press, 1982, p. 86).

In Yiddish, there arose other secular Jewish authors. Yisrael Achsenfeld, Shlomo Ettinger, Yitzchak Yoel Linitzky, Shlomo Yaakov Abramowitz,[19] Shalom Rabinowitz,[20] and Yitzchak Leib Peretz[21] all became famous and widely influential in their time. However, with the exception of Odessa, which became a center for *Haskalah*, the movement did not strike deep roots within the Eastern European community. Though *Haskalah* was not successful in creating the new Jewish culture and people it desired, it was quite successful in destroying the ancient values of Judaism, especially in the eyes of the young. The later successes of Zionism, Bundism, Socialism, Communism and Anarchism in Jewish society all were based on the destruction of the old value system by *Haskalah*. Inadequate communal Jewish education and the grinding poverty of life also strengthened the influence of *Haskalah*. Yet the Jewish establishment remained overwhelmingly observant and traditional, and opposed the *Haskalah* forcefully. The chassidim, who were the main targets for the ridicule of the *maskilim*, fought the *Haskalah* tenaciously and with every means at their disposal. Even traditional, Talmudic scholars who espoused a more modern educational approach, such as Rabbi Shlomo Yehudah Rapaport,[22] Rabbi Tzvi Hirsch Chajes,[23] and others, were strongly opposed by the chassidim.[24]

---

19. His pen name was Mendele Mocher Sforim (1835-1917).

20. His pen name was Sholom Aleichem, of *Fiddler on the Roof* fame (1859-1916).

21. 1852-1915. The father of Yiddish culture. Many of his works portrayed chassidim in a nostalgic, though anachronistic light.

22. 1790-1867. Known by his acronym *Shir*, he was a well-known Talmudic scholar and the son-in-law of the renowned author of *Ketzos HaChoshen* (one of the great rabbinic works of the nineteenth century and a mainstay in the curriculum of the yeshivos), Rabbi Aryeh Leib HaCohen. His rabbinic career was beset by fierce opposition from chassidim, because he was accused of being a *maskil*. He was opposed by the German leaders, Rabbi S.B. Bamberger and Rabbi S.R. Hirsch, as well, because of his tolerance of Reform.

23. 1805-1855. A famous Hungarian rabbi and well-known Talmudic scholar who corresponded with the *Chasam Sofer*. However, his works on the Bible and Jewish thought were laced with philosophy and a critical approach that was deemed too liberal by many. He too suffered a troubled rabbinic career because of this, though his views were far more traditional than those of Rapaport.

24. It is an irony of history that the example of Chassidus, in successfully opposing and eventually replacing the traditional Jewish leadership in Eastern Europe, inadvertently served as a model for the *Haskalah's* attempt to do the same. Whereas Chassidus dethroned personalities and councils, *Haskalah* attempted to dethrone traditional Judaism itself. Political Zionism would later also attempt to do so and would have greater success than did *Haskalah*.

In the bitterness of the battle, the *maskilim* turned to the Russian government for aid. The government passed many decrees to strengthen the hands of the *maskilim*. In 1848 it established new rabbinic academies under the auspices of the *Haskalah* in Warsaw, Vilna, and Zhitomir. The government ordered that only graduates of those seminaries could hold official rabbinic positions in Russia.[25] But in spite, or perhaps because, of governmental sanction and support, these seminaries proved to be a dismal failure. Many of their graduates eventually converted to Christianity, and the schools and their students proved to be an embarrassment to the *maskilim* themselves.[26] By 1873 the "new" seminaries were closed by the same "benevolent" government that had opened them twenty-five years earlier.

Lasting Influence

HE Russian Minister of Education, Oborov, was a notorious anti-Semite. He attempted by fiat to close the traditional Jewish schools and replace them with "modern education." The *maskilim* backed Oborov, hoping thereby to "civilize" their more traditional brethren and hasten the solution of the "Jewish problem." Oborov chose a German Jew to implement the new decree. Dr. Max Lilienthal had come to Russia in 1839 to serve as director of the "enlightened" Jewish school of Riga. In 1842, Oborov appointed Lilienthal Inspector-General over the Jewish schools.[27] He attempted to convince the Jewish communities of Eastern Europe of the Czar's benign intent in the establishment of the new educational system. In 1843, the Russian government convened a conference on the subject of Jewish education. There, Lilienthal was forcefully opposed and bested by Rabbi Yitzchak of Volozhin and Rabbi Menachem Mendel Schneerson,[28] and traditional Jewry retained the right to operate its "old" school system in competition with Lilienthal's new schools. Within a decade, the new school system closed because of

---

25. A rabbi appointed as a result of this governmental decree was known as a *Rav Mitaam*. See Chapter 17.

26. Ettinger, p. 126.

27. For fascinating anecdotes regarding Oborov, Lilienthal, and the new schools, see *Mekor Baruch*, by Rabbi Baruch Epstein, Vol. 2, Chapter 17, and Vol. 4, Chapter 45.

28. The *Rebbe* of Lubavitch, known for his famous rabbinic work, *Tzemach Tzedek*.

lack of administrators, faculty, and students. Dr. Max Lilienthal left Russia in shame, but soon resurfaced in the United States where he became a leading Reform rabbi.

While not very successful in realizing its dream of reshaping the Jewish people, the *Haskalah* still had a profound and lasting impact upon the nation. It not only influenced its adherents, but perhaps, more importantly, it shaped its opponents. It forced traditional Jewry on the defensive and caused it to discard some of its precious assets[29] in its zeal to at least save Torah and observant Judaism.

Whereas Reform created the classic assimilationist Jew, the "non-Jewish Jew,"[30] who would likely never see Jewish grandchildren in his family, *Haskalah* created the secular Jew. He was also a "non-Jewish Jew," but he was, in the main, not prone to convert or to even abandon Jewish society, though he professed no Jewish faith and observed no Jewish ritual. He attempted to redefine Jewish life and Judaism itself in his own image and by his own terms. He created a secular Judaism of intellect and scholarship, ideals and dreams, social welfare and political progress, devoid of the Jewish past and irrelevant to Jewish destiny. Thus, the secular *Haskalah* laid claim to the Hebrew language, to Biblical literature and study, to Jewish history and historiography, and contested the traditional vision of the Jewish future.

The bitterness of the *maskilim*, their limitless self-hatred, and their rage against the Jewish past drove them to behave despicably. As often happens in revolution, the activist radicals defined the movement, thus leaving those traditional Jews who were also interested in a modernization of means of education and social welfare no room for compromise or gradual acceptance. The positive elements of *Haskalah* — the ferment of new ideas and talent, the creativity of scholarship and new methodology — all were present in the traditional camp as well. But in the popular mind, the traditional Jewish establishment, in their struggle against the unbridled hatred and excesses of many of the *maskilim*, was depicted as obscurantist and reactionary.

The *maskilim* encouraged a revitalization of the Hebrew language and its popular use. They favored a thorough knowledge of the Bible, especially of the Prophets, and its more intensive use in the curriculum

---

29. Such as any further educational emphasis on the study of the Prophets, Hebrew language, and Jewish philosophy.

30. A most felicitous term used by Paul Johnson in his *History of the Jews,* and by many other writers both before and after him.

of the traditional Jewish school.[31] They encouraged the use of different and newer techniques in the classroom, of more attention to the hygiene of the students and the school facility, and demanded less learning by rote and pure memory. They were interested in promoting a knowledge of Jewish history, of the thought and philosophy of the great medieval sages of Israel, and of the intricacies and beauty of Hebrew grammar.

Each of these goals, taken individually, was a positive and worthy one. But *Haskalah* generally preached that the achievement of these goals was possible only if internal Jewish religious life was significantly altered. Thus, the agenda of the *Haskalah* was apparently conditioned on this false and destructive premise of the more radical *maskilim*. This forced a negative reaction to all ideas and plans of the *maskilim* by the defenders of Jewish tradition. "If the *maskilim* are for it, then we are against it" became the platform of much of traditional Jewry. In Galicia and in Hungary, in Lithuania and in Russia, the battle for and against *Haskalah* raged throughout the nineteenth century.

Outside forces, new persecutions, mass migrations all contributed to the chaos of that struggle. The old Jewish world was breaking up and the Jewish people, its Torah, and its faith were put to the test as perhaps never before. New issues and struggles were now to arise, but the backdrop of *Haskalah's* destabilizing influence insured the bitterness and divisiveness of these coming new conflicts. The sweet seeds of Enlightenment were to bear bitter fruits indeed.

---

31. Though how they reconciled acceptance of the Bible with the rejection of the God of the Bible remains a puzzle.

Section IV

The Pale of Settlement

1820-1880

17

Russian Oppression Under the Czars

Czar Alexander I

Y THE BEGINNING of the nineteenth century, the largest concentration of Jews in the world lived under the oppressive shadow of the Russian Czar. The Russian government was never anxious to incorporate Jews among its subjects and, until the virus of imperialism infected the Czars in the eighteenth century, very few Jews lived in "Mother Russia" proper.[1] However, the first partition of Poland in 1772 added 600,000 Jews to Russia. These Jews, living in Lithuania and eastern Poland, were an unwelcome addition to Russia, and the Russian government immediately began to consider their new subjects as the "Jewish problem." The second partition of Poland, in 1793, added an additional 400,000 Jews to Russia and the third partition of Poland, two years later, netted an additional 250,000 Jews. Thus, there were 1,350,000 Jews under the Czar's control by 1800. After the Napoleonic wars and the subsequent political and territorial divisions of Europe, the Czar was the "proud" ruler of almost 1,500,000 Jews. Even though most Jews proved themselves loyal to Russia during the Napoleonic invasion, the Czar was convinced that his Jewish subjects

---

1. Best estimates are that there were about 100,000 Jews living in Russia itself in 1770. See Martin Gilbert, *Atlas of Jewish History*, Dorset Press, 1985, p. 49 for the statement of Czar Ivan IV in 1550: "It is not convenient to allow Jews to come with their goods into Russia, since many evils result from them." This attitude of the Russian rulers and much of the Russian populace did not really vary in the next 435 years.

were perfidious, disloyal, and useless. He and his successors were determined to solve their "Jewish problem."[2]

Alexander Pavlovich, Czar Alexander I,[3] succeeded to the throne of the Romanovs in 1801. "Modern history knows few more tragic figures than that of Alexander I. His early years had been full of brilliant promise . . .; but in the end he left a terrible legacy to Russia: a principle of government which . . . veiled a tyranny supported by spies and secret police; an uncertain succession; an army permeated by organized disaffection; an armed Poland, whose hunger for liberty the Czar had whetted but not satisfied; . . . an educational system rotten with official hypocrisy; a church in which conduct counted for nothing, orthodoxy and ceremonial observance for everything; economic and financial conditions scarcely recovering from the verge of ruin; and serfdom."[4]

If this was the situation of Russia generally, the state of Jewish affairs was even more appalling. A despot who ruled by the knout and sword, Alexander I was an anti-Semite, determined to crush his newly acquired Jewish vassals. In 1795, under the reign of Paul I, the Pale[5] of Settlement came into being. This area was drawn beyond the western frontier of Russia proper and limited the area where Jews were allowed to settle. By 1812, Alexander I had finalized the borders of the Pale, which consisted of twenty-five western provinces stretching from the Baltic to the Black Sea, and included most of eastern Poland, Lithuania, White Russia, the Ukraine, the Crimea, and Bessarabia. Jews could not leave the Pale without special governmental approval.

In 1804, Alexander I issued further decrees limiting Jewish population and residence within the Pale itself. Jews were now forbidden to live in incorporated villages or to work there, and in addition were prevented from selling liquor[6] to the local peasant population. The Czar justified this decree on the basis of the necessity of

---

2. The accepted solution, succinctly stated in the late nineteenth century by Vyacheslov Plehve, K.P. Pobedonostsev and Nicholas Ignatiev, among other leading advisers to the Czars, was "one-third conversion, one-third extermination, one-third emigration."

3. 1777-1825, son of Czar Paul I.

4. *Encyclopedia Britannica,* Vol. 1, 1968, p. 568.

5. "Pale," from the Latin palus, meaning a stake or other symbol of demarcation. It is a historical term denoting a district marked off from the surrounding country by a definite boundary, or operating under a different legal and/or administrative system.

6. The liquor trade was a traditional Jewish business in Eastern Europe. This decree affected almost one-third of the Jewish population. See Johnson, *A History of the Jews,* p. 358.

forcing Jews to engage in "productive" labor — farming and timber — and to wean them from "exploitative" occupations. This often-heard calumny of the anti-Semite was drummed into the Russian and Jewish psyche to such an extent that, by the end of the century, "enlightened" and secular Jews repeated it as though it were true.[7] However, the Czar's real intent was to force the Jews to convert or leave. The Jews in the Pale became completely impoverished, and they were not yet able to engage in meaningful migration. Nevertheless, their rate of conversion was virtually non-existent.[8]

Czar Nicholas I

LEXANDER I DIED in 1825 and was succeeded by his younger brother Nikolai Pavlovich,[9] who became Czar Nicholas I. A xenophobic tyrant, physically powerful and cruel, he had great fears of foreign contamination of "Holy Mother Russia." He was known as the "Iron Czar" and his capacity for work and responsibility was prodigious. His attitude towards Jews was even more depraved than his brother's.

In 1827, he formulated the infamous decree of the "Cantonists."[10] This decree placed a levy on all Jewish communities to provide young men for service in the Russian army. They were conscripted at the age of twelve (sometimes even younger) and "trained" and educated at the local canton, or military depot. Then, at the age of eighteen, they were formally inducted into the Russian army for a term of twenty-five years! Many of these children died from malnutrition, beatings, loneliness, and disease. Others broke under the pressure and converted to Christianity, though, on balance, this did little to improve their lot. But the majority remained steadfast in their Jewishness under the most trying conditions.[11] Less than half of the Cantonists ever returned home.[12]

---

7. A symptom of the terrible disease of self-hatred that ravages much of secular Jewry.

8. In fact, there was even a small counter-movement of Gentiles who were interested in converting to Judaism! See Ettinger, Vol. 3, p. 99.

9. 1796-1855.

10. A "canton" was a small military camp, usually used for training or schooling.

11. See Ettinger, p. 100, for a heartrending description of Jewish youths who killed themselves rather than succumb to the pressure to convert.

12. See Louis Greenberg, *The Jews in Russia,* Schocken Books, 1944, Vol. 1, pp. 48-52, for a graphic description of the Cantonist system.

The Cantonist system also undermined Jewish communal life. The quota of conscripts had to be filled by the leaders of the Jews, or their own children would be conscripted.[13] Wealthy families would pay to safeguard their own sons, and well-connected families took advantage of their political influence, and thus the children of the poor, the orphans, the defenseless and downtrodden, were usually the ones to be drafted. To compound the horror, Jewish kidnappers[14] — bounty hunters — stalked the streets in search of their small prey, delivering them to the Russian depots for a fee. The organized communities were powerless to control this Jewish underworld,[15] and the rabbinic and religious leaders of the town were often unable to fight this moral depravity. Their inept behavior, coupled with the unceasing agitation of the *maskilim,* aroused a fury and frustration among the lower classes of Jews — who were the most directly affected — against religious leaders in general and rabbis in particular. This fury would later vent itself in a rebellion against the representatives of Torah and tradition, given the catalyst of secular Zionism and Socialism, at the close of the nineteenth century.

In 1839, the Czar decreed that the money collected by the Jewish community for its internal maintenance should be given to the government for "proper distribution to the necessary Jewish institutions."[16] The basis for the financial support of many of the Jewish communities was a voluntary tax on kosher poultry and meat. This tax was paid to the local *kehillah* organization, and the proceeds were then used to support Jewish education and other charitable and social organizations, as well as the salaries of Jewish religious functionaries. Thus, if enforced, the Czar's decree would have destroyed the Jewish communal organizations, which were the backbone of Jewish life itself.

In 1840, a special governmental commission was appointed to undertake "the fundamental restructuring of Jewish society in Russia." In line with this, new restrictions were now decreed against the Jews. The Pale of Settlement was shrunk, traditional Jewish clothing was prohibited or heavily taxed, non-Jews could no longer be employed as

---

13. A forerunner of the tactics employed by the Germans in the next century with the Judenrat.

14. Known in Yiddish as "*khoppers*" — grabbers.

15. Life in the *shtetl* was not as idyllic as the later nostalgia purveyors would have one believe.

16. *Toldos HaDoros*, Vol. 3, p. 216.

domestics by Jews, Jews were prohibited from marrying before the age of eighteen, Jewish agricultural settlements — originally encouraged by Alexander I — were now curtailed. Thousands of Jews were capriciously exiled from their homes to new locations, Jewish education was stringently supervised, the Jewish quota for the Russian army was tripled, and decrees against the Talmud and its study were promulgated. Jewish printing presses were limited,[17] and Jews were divided into new categories — "useful" Jews[18] and "useless" Jews.[19] Jews were forbidden to engage in many professions unless they first converted to Christianity.[20] Quotas were imposed to hold down their enrollment in all Russian schools of higher learning. The government instituted a new categorization of religious functionaries, forcing the Jewish councils to accept criminals, child-nappers, and informers into their ranks. This further lowered the reputation of traditional Jewish leadership in the eyes of the Jewish masses.

The government insisted on "official rabbis"[21] who would be responsible for keeping the local registry of births, deaths, marriages, and divorces. These "official rabbis" were to be literate in Russian and meet the standards of the government for the clergy. These standards effectively excluded almost all of the traditional rabbis in Russia from being officially recognized as rabbis. Thus, the basis of their salaries and their official powers were stripped away by the governmental fiat. The "official rabbis" were often sincere people who bowed to the authority of the recognized rabbis, but many times they were men of low character, and ignorant in Jewish law.[22] Some of them were "enlightened" Jews, whose loyalty to tradition and Torah observance was tenuous at best.

---

17. In all of Russia, only two Jewish presses (Kiev and Vilna) were legal. All Jewish books printed in Russia required the imprimatur of the Russian censors (many of whom were apostate Jews).

18. Farmers, artisans, skilled workers, and the "educated."

19. Teamsters, unskilled laborers, rabbis, teachers, the unemployed, the sick, the orphans — these were subjected to a higher conscription quota to the army.

20. A famous anecdote of the time concerns a Jewish scholar who, upon converting to Christianity, was made a professor at the university in St. Petersburg. When asked whether he was convinced of the truth of his new religion he ruefully replied, "Yes, I am convinced of the truth that it is better to be a professor at the university in St. Petersburg than a *melamed* (an elementary school teacher) in my *shtetl*."

21. Known by the infamous description as *Rav Mitaam* — a rabbi sanctioned by governmental authority.

22. There were notable exceptions, such as Rabbi Jacob Maazeh of Moscow, and others. Most "official rabbis" attempted to be of good service to their people and ameliorate the difficulties of Jewish life in Russia.

Others were simply charlatans. This development further undermined the authority and standing of the traditional rabbi, and contributed to the continued unraveling of the traditional *kehillah*-community structure.

The endless structure of laws and codes, changes and amendments, senate hearings, ministry circulars, bureaucratic forms, and administrative decisions created an impossible task of enforcement. All of the laws could not be universally enforced against all of Russian Jewry at one time. Selective enforcement bred corruption of the police and local authorities. Thus, the already inefficient, venal, and capricious system of Russian law enforcement was now further corrupted, as individual Jews and Jewish communities resorted to bribes to avoid the unfair and cruel enforcement of the restrictive laws.[23] This wide spread corruption had dire consequences for the Czar's police, and for the Jews as well. In a cesspool, no one smells like roses.

Czar Alexander II

 N 1855, IN THE MIDST of the Crimean War, Nicholas I died and was succeeded by his eldest son, Alexander II. The effects of the Crimean War on Russia served to discredit Nicholas' policy of sacrificing all other national interests to the cause of militarism and imperialism. Russians groaned under the weight of bureaucratic inefficiency and ruthless coercion. Their cry for reform had to be heeded, and Alexander II became the unlikely reformer. He officially abolished the class of serfdom and emancipated the serfs. He reorganized the military, formulated a new and fairer penal code, a more orderly and efficient judicial procedure, and some self-government for the populace. He also became the great reformer in Jewish matters as well. On the day of his coronation, March 2, 1855, Alexander revoked the hated and feared decree of "Cantonism," conscription of young Jews. The Jews sighed in relief and jumped for joy.[24]

This major reform was followed by other minor but important improvements. The Pale of Settlement was widened for all Jews and eventually even abolished for certain classes of Jews. The pressure on

---

23. See Johnson, pp. 360-1.

24. See Greenberg, p. 75, for an emotional description of the freeing of the potential conscripts on that day.

Jewish soldiers to convert to Christianity was lessened, controls in Jewish schools were relaxed, and educational opportunities for Jews in Russian trade schools, gymnasia, and colleges were enhanced. By 1865, many Russian Jews were convinced that a fundamental change of attitude towards them by the Russian government had occurred. It appeared that the sun of enlightenment and liberalism, which rose in the West a century earlier, was finally making its way east, and many Jews were anxious to cheer its arrival.

The danger with any governmental reform that is too little and too late is that it provokes unrealizable dreams, and is a catalyst for revolution and anarchy. This state of affairs invariably prevents further necessary reforms from occurring, and turns the professedly liberal ruler into a reactionary tyrant. This was the trap into which Alexander II and his government fell.

A general feeling of disappointment overtook Russia. In the educated classes, two extreme groups appeared: the disappointed liberals who desired greater and speedier reform, and the displaced conservatives who wanted to return to a more authoritarian regime.[25] A general feeling of discontent permeated the populace. Alexander sensed that the support which had originally buoyed him was slipping away. As the liberals turned more radical, and secret societies advocating violence as the means of reforming Russia grew, the Czar abandoned his program of reform and began to return to the traditional repressive policies of his predecessors.

This change in Alexander's attitude reflected itself in the Jewish Russian world as well. Many of the secret, violent revolutionary organizations that the Czar so feared were disproportionately Jewish in their composition. The Jews, who took advantage of the liberalization of educational opportunities and flocked to the gymnasia and colleges in ever-increasing numbers, did so at the price of cutting loose from their traditional values; yet they were still envied and despised by their non-Jewish fellow students.

The non-Jewish world viewed the Jews as "pushy," and moved quickly to foreclose their opportunities for advancement in the professions and commerce. The Czar supported these social restrictions against the Jews. The policy of Russia in the late 1860s was represented by a disillusioned Jewish intellectual of the time: "Education, even that of a university, gives you the civic rights of honorary citizenship, but not

---

25. *Encyclopedia Britannica,* Volume 1, p. 85.

An elderly wanderer and his grandson

those of ordinary citizenship. Go to your 'Moshkes' and 'Berels' (the traditional non-Jewish derogatory use of Jewish names), for with them and among them is your place."[26]

Alexander himself was a product of his upbringing and environment, and thus unabashedly a virulent anti-Semite. He never intended to give the Jews civic acceptability and equal rights.[27] The Jews would have to earn any improvement in their situation, and the method of earning such gain was by becoming less Jewish. Even in Alexander's concessions to the Jews, he made certain to specify limitations and conditions. By the late 1860s it was apparent to all that no major amelioration of the oppression of the Jews was now likely.

The Polish revolution against Russia in 1863, brutally crushed by Alexander's army and police, sparked even greater anti-Semitism. The struggle against this revolution intensified Russian patriotism and reinforced its xenophobic view of the world, at the expense of all liberal tendencies towards non-Russian minorities, and especially regarding the Jews. In 1870 Alexander revived the decree of 1850 against the traditional form of Jewish dress. In 1871, a special committee on Jewish affairs was established at the Ministry of the Interior. All Jewish government schools were closed, including the infamous official rabbinical seminaries that were established to produce the new rabbis who would modernize Judaism. A blood libel trial occurred in the Russian Caucasus in 1879.[28] The Czar categorically refused the advice of many of his ministers to completely abolish the Pale of Settlement. By 1880, reactionary Russia intensified its anti-Jewish stand and the great hopes of the 1860s were dashed by the realities of the 1880s.

Religious Jewry observed these events with a wry sentiment of acceptance. It had expected little of Alexander, and hence was immune to great disappointment. However, the *maskilim* and secular Jews were distraught by the negative turn of events. All of their efforts to ingratiate Jewry in the good graces of Russian society were fruitless. The press turned increasingly anti-Jewish. The quota for Jewish students in Russian schools was again introduced and enforced.

In 1871 a major pogrom took place in Odessa, the bastion of

---

26. A. Dumoshevsky as quoted in Greenberg, Vol. 1, p. 85.

27. Greenberg, ibid., p. 98.

28. Greenberg, ibid.

Haskalah influence in Russia. In their periodicals,[29] the *maskilim* had preached knowledge of the Russian language and culture by Jews, an identity of spirit and goals with the intelligentsia of Russia, and an abandonment of traditional Jewish studies, dress, and lifestyle. The reward for this assimilation was to be full and equal rights under Russian law, and acceptance in Russian society. How cruel was their disappointment when becoming "Russians of the Mosaic Faith" did not change them from being "dirty Zhids" in the eyes of the populace and the government.

29. *Razsvet* (Odessa) began publishing in 1860. *Razsvet* (St. Petersburg) began publishing in 1829 under the editorship of M. Kulishner. These periodicals were printed in Russian. *HaMelitz*, published in Hebrew under the editorship of Alexander Zederbaum (*Erez*), began publishing in Odessa in 1860. A German supplement of this paper was under the editorship of Dr. Aaron Goldenblum. The basic thread of thought unifying all these journals was their goal of Russifying Jewry and making it "useful" to the Russian state and society.

A typical flooded main street in Poland

18
Unrest and Anti-Semitism

HE "ENLIGHTENED" JEWS had repudiated their history, forgotten their traditions, and come to despise everything that made them conscious of belonging to an eternal race. Without an intelligent understanding of Jewish ideals, considering their Judaism to be a burden — as an escaped convict is hampered by heavy chains — what could compensate for their belonging to a tribe of "Christ killers" and "exploiters"? How pathetic was the position of those who advocated fusion with the Russian people through national self-destruction. Life and the logic of events demanded that the Jew define his position, for it had become impossible to occupy a seat between two chairs. "Either one openly declared himself a renegade or one decided to share the sufferings of his people."[1] Thus, the bankruptcy of the policy of *Haskalah* was clear by the end of the reign of Alexander II.

Czar Alexander III

N MARCH 13, 1881, while he was returning to the Winter Palace from a drive in central St. Petersburg, Alexander II was mortally wounded by a bomb thrown into his carriage. This assassination brought to the throne his son, the ultimate autocrat and boor, Alexander III (Aleksander Aleksanderovich, 1845-1894). When his elder brother died in 1865, Alexander became the heir apparent and was placed under the tutelage

---

1. Correspondence from the town of Berezovka in *Russky Evrei* (St. Petersburg, 1881) no. 41, as quoted in Greenberg, Vol. II, p. 56.

of K.P. Pobedonostsev, a reactionary and fanatical person. He instilled in his ward hatred for democratic reform, a firm belief in the principle of the divinity of autocratic government, unswerving loyalty to the narrowest interpretation of Russian Orthodox Christianity, and a mystical trust in the *narodnost* (belief in the Russian people) system, in which there was no place for the Jews in Russia, let alone Jewish civil rights or political advancement.

Alexander III

"Alexander's political ideal was a nation containing only one nationality, one language, one religion, and one form of administration, and he did his utmost to prepare for the realization of this ideal by imposing the Russian language and Russian schools on his German, Polish, and Finnish subjects, by fostering Russian Orthodoxy at the expense of other confessions, by persecuting the Jews, and destroying the remnants of German, Polish, and Swedish institutions in the outlying provinces."[2] Pogroms, new disabilities imposed on the Jews of Russia, anti-Semitic cabinet ministers and administrators all combined to make the reign of Alexander III one of the most tragic times in Eastern European Jewry's history.

Expulsions, deportations, arrests, and beatings became the daily lot of the Jews, not only of their lower class, but even of the middle class and the Jewish intelligentsia. The government of Alexander III waged a campaign of war against its Jewish inhabitants.[3] When the great synagogue in Moscow was built in 1891, with the permission of the local authorities, it was constructed in Byzantine style with a cupola having the star of David topping it. After the completion of the building, the Czar's administration ordered the removal of the entire cupola, and finally in 1894 the building was closed and the Jews were given the option of selling it or converting it into a "philanthropic institution."[4] The Jews were driven and hounded, and emigration appeared to be the only escape from the terrible tyranny of the Romanovs.

---

2. *Encyclopedia Britannica,* Vol. I, p. 571.

3. Greenberg, Vol. II, p. 38.

4. Greenberg, Vol. II, p. 47.

Czar Nicholas II

N NOVEMBER 1, 1894, Alexander III died, unmourned and unloved by most of his subjects, and hated by the Jewish community. His eldest son, Nicholas II (Nikolai Aleksandrovich, 1868-1918), the last of the Romanov Czars, succeeded his father. An inept, shallow person, timid and shy in public, given to admiration of the military and its pomp, he was married to Alexandra, the granddaughter of Queen Victoria of England.

Alexandra was a strong-willed woman who dominated her meek husband. She was also a fanatic believer in the mysticism of Russian Orthodoxy, and was convinced that her task in life was to prop up her husband in his unrealistic insistence on the divine right of kings and the heavenly decree of absolute autocracy for Russia's rulers. She would brook no compromise on these matters, and thus Nicholas II, the Czar who led Russia into the twentieth century, was doomed from the outset.

Nicholas also was greatly influenced by Pobedonostsev, the tutor of his father, and a staunch supporter of Russian Orthodoxy and Czarist autocracy. However, even Pobedonostsev would eventually prove too liberal for Nicholas and Alexandra. The Czar's main ministers were staunch monarchists and anti-democrats, but Nicholas and Alexandra distrusted them all. Eventually they turned for counsel and guidance to one of the great "con-men" of all time, Grigori Rasputin. The fact that their only son, the Czarevich, was a hemophiliac, influenced them to pursue faith healers and spiritual quacks for cures and sustenance, and Rasputin exploited this to his personal benefit. Thus did the Russian monarchy lose all touch with reality as it lurched towards its demise.

Famine and War

ICHOLAS WAS A BITTER anti-Semite. Therefore, his ministers, who might have otherwise supported policies ameliorating the Jewish desperation in Russia, vied with each other for the Czar's favor by promulgating new anti-Jewish decrees.[5] The Jews became the means for political advancement and power in the court of the Czar. Even the most notorious

---

5. Greenberg, Vol. II, p. 85.

anti-Semitic officials opposed expelling the Jews from Russia, since that would remove the main issue upon which their power base could be expanded.[6] Pogroms raged throughout Russia, many of them organized and supported by the government itself. New expulsions, the removal of even the most basic human rights from Jews, enforcement of the admission quotas in schools, and the restrictions now placed on Jewish learning and observance made Jewish life intolerable. Coupled with grinding poverty, a high infant mortality rate, and a hostile society, these conditions caused many Jews to turn in desperation from traditional life and values.

A small section of Russian Jewry became radicalized, continuing the trend established under Alexander III. Feeling that they could only benefit from a change of government, Jews were disproportionately represented in all of the revolutionary movements of the time. Thus, the tide of anarchy, socialism, social revolution and "just" violence seeped into the life of Eastern European Jewry. It proved to be a major source of Jewish bitterness and discord, not only in Russia but later in Israel and the United States as well. This influx of radicalism naturally led to the continuing secularization of the adherents of revolution, and their goal was to change Jewish life and destiny permanently and forcefully. To them the old way had no message, no hope, no right to exist any longer. Only in destroying the old could the new utopian era begin. And destroy they would.

Two great disasters befell Russia in this period, which would accelerate violent change. In 1891, at the end of Alexander III's reign, a fearsome famine struck Russia. Terrible weather and drought, inept transportation, and governmental corruption and inefficiency all combined to cause a severe shortage of food in Russia that year. Ironically, the peasants, who were the producers of the food, suffered most; over 400,000 peasants died in the famine of 1891.[7] Misery among them deepened and their resentments began to grow. Eventually these feelings would be released in violence, vengeance, and hatred.

The second disaster was the Russo-Japanese war of 1904. The completion of the Trans-Siberian railway made Russia a Pacific power, and inexorably, this led to competition with Japan, which was just then embarking on its expansionist imperialistic policies that would so

---

6. Ibid.

7. *In War's Dark Shadow*, W. Bruce Lincoln, New York 1983, p. 25.

influence the twentieth century. Russia saw itself as a Christian bulwark against the encroachment of the heathen Japanese. The internal problems of Russia were so encompassing and intractable that the Czar resorted to the time-honored ruse of diverting internal discontent by means of a patriotic war. Frightened by workers' strikes and revolutionary violence, Plehve, his chief minister, advised Nicholas that "in order to suppress revolution we need a small victorious war, [which] would get the masses' attention away from political questions."[8] Russia lost the war,[9] and Nicholas lost the remaining trust of the Russian people in an autocratic monarchy. Sailors in his navy mutinied, the army's loyalty to the Czar was suspect, and revolutionary dissent and violence flared anew. Plehve himself was assassinated, as was the Grand Duke, Sergei Aleksandrovich, the Czar's brother.

The year 1905 was a time of supreme crisis for the Czar. Strikes, civil war, and peasant riots all combined to give Russia an air of anarchy. In the fall of 1905, faced by the prospect of all-out war and revolution, Nicholas made important concessions to democracy. He declared himself a constitutional monarch. He granted all Russians civil rights and agreed to a duly elected (though not yet by universal suffrage) parliament, or Duma, that would approve all laws. The October Manifesto, as it was called, provoked varying reactions. The revolutionaries claimed that it was indecisive and insincere, and demanded more and now. The moderates, mainly organized in the political group called the Kadets, were grateful but cautious. The monarchists and conservatives were appalled by the Czar's concessions.

The Duma

MITRI PIKHNO, AN EDITOR of a rural conservative paper, together with many other supporters of the old order, quickly found the culprit responsible for the revolution and the Czar's capitulation. "It's the Jews!"[10] There arose an organization of thugs and bigots called the "Black Hun-

---

8. Ibid., p. 225.

9. Jacob Schiff, a German-Jewish immigrant who became one of the leading financiers on Wall Street, financed a major part of the Japanese war effort in retaliation against Russia's anti-Semitism. This contributed to the exaggerated Japanese view of Jewish power which benefited the Jews under their rule in World War II.

10. Lincoln, p. 303.

dreds."[11] They hounded S.Y. Witte, the Czar's chief minister, claiming that he was in the employ of the Jews, and eventually were successful in convincing Nicholas himself of this nonsense. They took bloody revenge for their political defeats on the hapless Jews. Many Jews were killed in the wave of pogroms that swept Southern Russia in November, 1905. A four-day pogrom in Odessa culminated in unspeakable acts of bestiality against the Jews. Nicholas not only refused to punish the murderers, he welcomed the leaders of the Black Hundreds to his summer palace, where he accepted badges of membership in the organization for himself and his son. "Because nine-tenths of the troublemakers are Jews," he explained to his mother, "the people's whole anger turned against them. That is how the pogroms happened."[12]

11. Its political party name was the more prosaic "Union of the Russian People."
12. Lincoln, p. 336.

Black Hundreds

In 1906, the first Duma met. The Kadets were the largest party and, together with the representatives of the peasants, wished to promulgate new laws that would bring greater freedom to the Russian masses. At the same time the Czar, however, began to renege on his promise for the end of autocracy. Witte was now gone from the government and new men appeared in power, whose goal was to prevent the implementation of the October Manifesto. The Czar dissolved the Duma in preemptory fashion, though promising to recall a second Duma. Most of the Kadet party fled into Finnish exile, and the opposition to the Czar now fell into the more radical hands of the Socialists and Communists.

In 1907, the Second Duma was convened with very strong leftist representation, as well as with a large number of extreme right members, and a greatly weakened center. The resulting chaos brought about the dissolution of the Second Duma as well, and under the crafty leadership of Petr Stolypin, the Czar's chief minister, Nicholas was able to return to almost complete autocratic rule. The revolutionaries were exiled to Siberia or fled from Russia, and the ultra-conservatives regained power. They had Stolypin assassinated, and forced the Czar to rely upon them for advice and aid. The revolution of 1905 was dead, and the last chance for the survival of the Romanov dynasty also died with it.

Changing Times

THE EVENTS OF THE 1890s and the early 1900s continued to radicalize a significant number of Russian Jews, especially among the young. Despairing of peaceful change and sickened by the bloody persecution of their fellow-Jews, many young Jews now became convinced that the solution to the Jewish problem lay in the transformation of all Russian society and government. They refused to see the persecution of Jews as a particularly Jewish problem, as did traditional religious Jewry, but rather as a symptom of the general malaise of Russia. Thus, these young Jews flocked to the parties of the left, and Jews were very strongly represented in all of the radical socialist, communist, and anarchist parties of Russia. This only provoked greater anti-Semitism from the government and the reactionary parties, which in turn contributed to the further radicalization of the Jews. This creation of a large, idealistic, revolutionary cadre of young Jews would have far-reaching consequences in the later history of Zionism and other events of the twentieth century.

Mendel Beilis

In 1911, a council of noblemen, at the behest of the Black Hundreds, suggested to the Czar that he should "purify" Russia by expelling its Jewish population.[13] In support of this request, the ancient canard of the "blood libel" was revived. An unfortunate, obscure Jew from Kiev by the name of Mendel Beilis was thus propelled into history. A Christian child was murdered in Kiev and Beilis was arrested for the crime, on the grounds that he needed the child's blood for Jewish ritual. The police soon became aware of the identity of the actual murderers, but, under instructions of the Minister of Justice, continued to gather "evidence" against the hapless Beilis. Protests against this travesty were lodged with the Russian government by agencies and organizations in Western Europe and the United States, but they were ignored. Beilis was brought to trial at the end of 1913, but he was found not guilty because of lack of evidence, though the presumption of the "blood libel" itself was never refuted.

The Beilis trial was, in effect, the concluding incident in a series of such fabrications. At Passover time in 1903, a vicious four-day pogrom had occurred in the Bessarabian city of Kishinev. Forty-five Jews were murdered,[14] over six hundred were severely injured, and over thirteen hundred homes were destroyed. Rapes, beatings, torture, and atrocities overtook the Jewish community while the authorities encouraged the mob in their evil.[15] A general of the Russian army commented upon the outrage at Kishinev: "From the Czar and Plehve, I heard that the Jews needed to be taught a lesson because they have been putting on airs and leading the revolutionary movement as well."[16] As the disapproval of the world poured in

---

13. *Toldos Am Yisrael,* Ettinger, Vol. 3, p. 174; Greenberg, Vol. II, p. 87.

14. In 1903, the murder of only forty-five Jews was enough to stir the entire world! The price for the attraction of the world's sympathy escalated greatly during the unfolding of the twentieth century.

15. Lincoln, *In War's Dark Shadow,* p. 221, states ". . . was appalled to learn from Jewish and Christian sources that the Bishop of Kishinev actually had blessed a crowd of pogromists as he passed them in the street, while not far away the mob was raping sixteen women and girls they had found . . ."

16. Ibid.

on the Czar's government (the President of the United States protested formally), the Russian government shifted the blame for the pogrom to the Jews themselves.[17] Making the victim the culprit for his own destruction is one of the great psychological ploys of oppressors. The Jews were thus deprived of even the comfort of sympathy usually reserved for the innocent victim.

The Jewish world of Eastern Europe was fast disintegrating. The shock of the Great War that lay only a few years distant would complete the destabilization process. Nevertheless, the Jews of Russia were still able to maintain a robust culture and a devotion to their tradition. They would yet nurture new movements and supply unexpected vitality for the Jewish world. In retrospect we see that, somehow, they triumphed over the Czar and his autocratic government, though at tremendous cost.

Burial of Torah Scrolls destroyed during the pogrom in Kishinev

17. Ibid., p. 222. "You are yourselves to blame for all that has happened."

19
Tradition Embattled

Pressures on Two Fronts

NE OF THE GREAT IRONIES of the nineteenth century was that Jewish traditional life was threatened by both the Enlightenment and liberalism on one hand, and repression and autocracy on the other. The Enlightenment promised Jews a brave new world of equality and opportunity if only they would discard their outmoded garb, their irrelevant life style, and their antiquated faith. The oppression of the Russian Czars was particularly harsh upon traditional Jews, their social and communal infrastructure, and their prosperity and physical well-being. The Czars wanted to break the Jewishness of their Jewish subjects, and, in despair and frustration, there were Jews who accommodated themselves to that reality by bowing to the wishes of their cruel Russian masters. Thus, the pressures of both the new liberal ideas of Western Europe and the reactionary policies of Eastern Europe combined to undermine the basic traditional way of life that had been the story of Jewish Europe for almost a millennium.

For the first time since the ascent of the Sadducees in the time of the Second Temple, and of the Karaites in the seventh century, traditional Torah Jewry was forced on the defensive. Although it still was by far the largest and most vital force in Jewish life and the Jewish population, it suffered significant defections. Bitter words from other Jews were heard about rabbis, Torah scholars, the Talmud, and the traditional Jewish way of life.

The leaders of *Haskalah* turned into ferocious foes of Chassidus particularly, and Jewish tradition and observance generally. The leaders of the *Haskalah* were convinced that time and circumstance were on their side. They were also convinced that the government and the general society were their allies in modernizing the Jewish people. Hence they followed the path of cooperation with the non-Jewish governmental authorities in persecuting their traditional brethren.[1]

Another factor that weakened the traditional Jewish community was its loss of governmental sanction. For centuries, the government dealt with the original traditional Jewish community — the *kehillah* — as the representative of Jews. This government recognition automatically strengthened the power of the *kehillah* and allowed it to foster traditional Jewish values and lifestyle in its members. All important matters of life — from the cradle to the grave — were governed by the *kehillah;* thus, deviations from traditional Jewish behavior were intrinsically unwelcome and, therefore, rare and restrained. However, the policies of the Czar and his officials in the 1800s undercut the authority of the traditional community. The government dealt with alternate "leaders" — "official rabbis,"[2] *maskilim,* informers, sycophants and charlatans. The government forced the traditional leaders to enforce its onerous decrees against the Jews, thus further diminishing the respect for, and authority of, the traditional *kehillah* in the eyes of its own constituents. Thus, the *kehillah* fast became an anachronism, and its main prop for centuries — the government — now became its opponent.

Distorted Ideals

URTHERMORE, THE ENEMIES of tradition were using the weapons of Judaism itself against the ancient religion. Secular humanism, Enlightenment, Marxism, and the social philosophies of the new age were all partially based upon ancient, basic Jewish ideals. These ideals were distorted in their new form, but the basic outline of their Torah origins was still recognizable. What traditional Jew could oppose the ideals of human equality, civil rights, universal education, the rights of the working man, the elimination of economic exploitation, and the right of self-government? These lofty ideals were lifted from their

---

1. *Toldos Am Yisrael,* Ettinger, Vol. III p. 128.
2. *Rav Mitaam* — see the previous chapter.

Torah context and installed in an alien environment that turned hostile to Torah Judaism and eventually to Jews themselves.

> God tells the Israelites that they must be a "light unto nations," setting a moral and ethical example for all people. The destruction of the Temples . . . and the ensuing diaspora of the Hebrews offered them a very practical opportunity to be such an example. Unfortunately they (the world) have not taken advantage of it. Having accepted the dualism prevailing in the West, the legacy in the industrial nineteenth century, descendants of the Hebraic tradition lost their connection with their divine root and assumed the same pessimistic materialistic world view as their European host nations. In psychology, for example, Sigmund Freud assumed correctly that the mind could influence the body to create disease, but he neglected the Hebraic notion that the same mind that destroys can also heal, if it does not isolate itself from ethics, the commandments [of the Torah] and the social context of experience. In economics, Marx similarly disassociated himself from his Hebraic roots, secularizing its ethical concern for the community and rejecting its spiritual component in his entirely economic view of human redemption. Einstein's scientifically "objective" release of the power of the atom, cut off from moral or ethical considerations, likewise opened the door to a kind of secular humanism that ignores the divine healing powers in the human mind and instead creates an atom bomb.[3]

Secular Versus Traditional

N COMBINING THE OPPOSING trends of assimilation and nascent Jewish nationalism, secular Jewry created a new Bible, a new nation, a new language, a new religion, and a new Jew: A new Bible, in which God's name appears hundreds of times, but God Himself is eliminated from the meaning and lessons of the book. A new nation, based upon nineteenth-century

---

3. *Hebraic Medicine* by Gerald Epstein, *Advances,* Institute for the Advancement of Health, vol. 4, No. 1, 1987, p. 63. The main thrust here is that Freud and Marx despaired of correcting or controlling man's basest behavior and therefore abolished the concept of moral guilt, and encouraged revolution and the justification of violence and licentiousness.

nationalism, but devoid of the intrinsic unity of tradition and shared values. A new language, Hebrew, that was revived from the ancient holy tongue, but stripped of its ethical veneer and holy purpose.[4] A new religion of secular humanism, agnosticism, and even atheism, was meant to substitute for the rigorous demands and daily discipline of traditional Jewish life. And a new Jew was to be created, who would be able to take his place as a full member of the world society, without inhibition and restriction, but at the sacrifice of his uniqueness, and, eventually, his soul.

The response of traditional Jewry to this challenge was diverse, defensive, and, on the whole, not very effective. The secularists captured the tools of modernity immediately. The Jewish newspapers, from the *Archives Israelites,*[5] to *HaMaggid*[6] *HaMeilitz,*[7] *Carmel,*[8] and *Tzefirah,*[9] were all unabashedly secular and opposed to the millennia-old message of Judaism.[10] The printed word was holy to Jews because of their long tradition of scholarship and books; no one treated the printed word indifferently. Thus, though these newspapers had a very limited readership, they had a very large influence on Jewish life. The fact that many of them were printed in Hebrew added to their authenticity, even though their message was essentially anti-traditional, if not anti-Jewish.

Traditional Jewry was also riven with internal strife. Rivalries between different chassidic courts and dynasties were frequent and vitriolic. The strife between chassidim and misnagdim, though muted and sub rosa, was still present. And within the camp of the misnagdim, the struggle regarding *mussar*[11] proved quite bitter. Thus, traditional Jewry found itself under severe attack from its adversaries and was to a great extent unable to effectively counter the ominous threat that secular Jewry posed.

---

4. A modified "Sephardic" method of pronunciation was introduced among Ashkenazic Jewry in order to make clear that the new Hebrew was not to be seen as the same language as the old traditional, rabbinic, holy Hebrew.

5. Began publishing in Paris in 1840.

6. Began publishing in Prussia in 1856.

7. Began publishing in Odessa in 1860.

8. Began publishing in Vilna in 1860.

9. Began publishing in Warsaw in 1862.

10. A situation that in the main still pertains today. There were traditional Jewish newspapers and periodicals published in Western Europe and later in Eastern Europe as well, but the media battle was won early by the secularists.

11. See the next chapter for details of the *Mussar* Movement, its struggle and opponents.

Finally, traditional Jewry suffered from the breakdown of the old geographic and economic infrastructure of its society. The process of urbanization was well under way in the nineteenth century. Jews, whose families had lived for centuries in the rural areas of Poland and Russia now migrated to the cities. Jews now constituted almost a third of the population of Warsaw, a quarter of the population of Lodz, and lived in much increased numbers in Vilna, Bialystok, Odessa, Kiev, Memel, Riga, and Minsk.

Urbanization has always been an unsettling experience. The Talmud characterizes urban living as "difficult,"[12] spiritually and physically debilitating. New surroundings, crowded living conditions, the spiritual squalor and accepted immorality of life in the big city, the more hurried pace and frantic activity of the metropolis, all combined to erode the old faith and its value system and life style. The city has always been the place for the young, the new, the experimental, and even the deviant side of life.

Traditional Jewry suffered mightily from the transition from the rural world of the village to the new mores of the city. Family bonds were loosened, the *kehillah* was weakened, the opportunity to stray was now more available, and the new, secular way proved attractive, exciting, and more in tune with city life. The synagogue lost its hold as the central institution of life. Small prayer groups — *shtieblach*[13] — became the norm, especially among chassidic Jews in the large cities, and thus further undermined the centrality of the synagogue. These smaller prayer groups contributed to further fractionalization of traditional Jewry and the diffusion of its strength and influence.

Effects of Industrialization

HE RAPID INDUSTRIALIZATION of Russia in the latter nineteenth century was wondrous. In spite of all of the inefficiencies and corruption of the Czar's government, Russia converted herself into a modern industrial power.[14] But with the progress came the pain. Squalor, inhuman

---

12. *Talmud Bavli, Kesubos* 110b.

13. Literally, "small house" (of prayer), in Yiddish.

14. See Lincoln, *In War's Dark Shadow,* Dial Press, New York 1983, p. 16.

working conditions, long hours, low wages, industrial accidents, and the demoralization that machinery works upon man were the lot of the working class. Many Jews in the cities of Poland and Russia became such working men. They toiled in the textile industry, in tobacco factories, in metal-working shops and in the timber, lumber, and woodworking trades. They worked long hours of physically exhausting labor for very low wages. Disease, dirt, and depression were rampant in their lives. It was more difficult to devote time to study and prayer, to be meticulous in observance of the commandments, to concentrate on the spiritual nature of life.

Secularism's promise of a better life proved very alluring. Labor unions and socialism addressed people's immediate needs and hopes, and the old way became less dominant and real. Though most urban Jews remained nominally traditional and observant of commandments, their commitment to the Jewish way of life was eroding. This commitment may have appeared to be a mile wide but it was only an inch deep. The centers of Torah strength, the yeshivos and chassidic courts, became more remote for many Jews. The traditional Torah community was slowly turning more inward, seemingly reconciled to its loosening grasp on the masses of Eastern European Jewry. Because of its own internal problems and the changing world about it, traditional Jewry would appear to have accepted defeat by default.

20
The Mussar Movement — Ethical Rebirth

Rabbi Yisrael Salanter

OT EVERYTHING IN Eastern European Jewish life, in the nineteenth century, was sad and dark. The Jewish people have a unique talent to be productive, optimistic, and vital, even in the worst of times. The record of scholarship, ideas, literature, and commerce that the Jews compiled in the Dark Ages, the Crusades, the Inquisition, and the constant wars of Europe staggers the mind and strains credulity. Thus, in the midst of Czarist persecution, vicious pogroms, grinding poverty, and inner defections, the creation of a new movement of ethical rebirth within Eastern European Jewry should not be seen as completely surprising or even unexpected.

This new movement — the *Mussar*[1] Movement — began in

---

1. Literally, chastisement. In the vernacular it has come to mean ethics. There are a number of excellent books and articles regarding the *Mussar* Movement. The author has relied heavily on the article of Rabbi Yaakov Yechiel Weinberg published originally in Vol. 1 of *Yahadus Lita*, Am Hasefer, Tel Aviv 1960, p. 320, and later reprinted in Volume 4 of *Seridei Aish*, Mosad Harav Kook, Jerusalem, 1969, p. 276. For valuable insights into Reb Yisrael and the leaders of the *Mussar* Movement, see Hillel Goldberg, *The Fire Within*, Mesorah Publications, Brooklyn 1987. In addition, one should read Rabbi Dov Katz' four-volume work, *T'nuas HaMussar*, Tel Aviv 1952. Of immense value is the work of Emmanuel Itkes, *Rabbi Yisrael Salanter*, Hebrew University Press, Jerusalem 1982. Dr. Jacob B. Glenn's *Rabbi Israel Salanter*, Jewish Publication Society, Philadelphia 1948, also contains valuable information and insights. The source for much of their material is *Ohr Yisrael*, a compilation of some of Rabbi Yisrael's thought, by one of his main disciples, Rabbi Yitzchak Blaser (Peterburger). In recent years, many works of leading *mussar* personalities have been published, both in English and Hebrew, and have achieved a wide readership.

Lithuania in the 1850s and exerted a long and lasting influence on Jewry and its institutions of learning and society. By its very nature, *mussar* could not become a mass movement,[2] but its force and vitality were felt at every level of Jewish society. It molded Jewish leadership — especially rabbinic leadership — for generations.

The movement was the product of the mind and efforts of one of the great personalities and seminal thinkers of Eastern European Jewry, Rabbi Yisrael Lipkin[3] of Salant,[4] Lithuania. He was known throughout the Jewish world as Rabbi Yisrael Salanter, after the name of the town where he gained maturity. He was born in Zaager, Lithuania[5], in 1810, and his father, Rabbi Zev Wolf Lipkin, personally educated him in

2. Although Rabbi Yisrael expected the masses to adopt and join the movement, in reality, it was a movement that appealed primarily to scholarly, intellectual people. One of the main areas of concentration of *mussar* was in the Lithuanian yeshivos of the nineteenth and twentieth centuries.

3. 1810-1883.

4. This small Lithuanian village produced three giants of the Jewish world in the 1800s. Rabbi Zundel (see below), Rabbi Yisrael and Rabbi Shmuel, all named Salant or Salanter. Rabbi Shmuel was the Ashkenazic rabbinical leader of Jerusalem for over seventy years, until his death in 1909.

5. Itkes, p. 77.

Salant

Torah. A genius in intellect, blessed with a phenomenal memory, the young Yisrael soon became famous for his prowess in Talmudic scholarship and adopted a pilpulistic style of study. However, his father, who disapproved of *pilpul* [see the note on *pilpul* on page 125], sent him to Salant to study with the rabbi of the village, Rabbi Tzvi Hirsch Broida, who was famous for his analytic method[6] of Torah study. Rabbi Yisrael remained in Salant for over fifteen years. He married there[7] and began to gain new fame for his knowledge and genius.

In Salant, Rabbi Yisrael underwent a personal transformation. He forsook the pilpulistic method of study and intensified his search for simplicity and intellectual accuracy in his studies.[8] He matured in his outlook and goals, and began his career as a teacher and leader. But most importantly, he found for himself a mentor, the great Rabbi Zundel of Salant[9], who became Rabbi Yisrael's role model.

It was Rabbi Zundel who directed Rabbi Yisrael to the path of *mussar* and convinced him that this was the way to personal greatness and Godly service. Rabbi Yisrael described the self-effacing, secretive, holy man Rabbi Zundel as "a ladder established on earth with its head reaching heaven."[10] Rabbi Yisrael's assessment of himself in later years, vis-a-vis Rabbi Zundel, was "that till now I have not reached his ankles."[11]

Rabbi Zundel occupied no official rabbinic position, yet was widely known for his scholarship, piety, and erudition. It was undoubtedly his influence that encouraged Rabbi Yisrael never to accept any official rabbinic post.[12] And it was Rabbi Zundel who commanded Rabbi Yisrael,

---

6. Itkes, p. 78.

7. His wife, Esther Eisenstein, died in 1871 in Vilna. They were the parents of four sons and two daughters. See Itkes, p. 337, note 3 for details.

8. Rabbi Yisrael then undertook never again to involve *pilpul* in his Torah studies, a commitment that he honored all his life. His emphasis in Talmudic study now was textual, analytic, and strongly rooted in developing the correct understanding of the Talmud and its commentaries by study in depth, rather than by extraneous comparisons of differing cases.

9. This giant of the spirit was born in 1786 and was one of the main disciples of Rabbi Chaim of Volozhin. Rabbi Zundel moved to Jerusalem in 1838, together with his famous son-in-law, Rabbi Shmuel Salant. He died there in a cholera epidemic that swept Jerusalem in 1866.

10. Itkes, p. 80.

11. Ibid.

12. Itkes, p. 81. He quotes the tradition that Rabbi Yisrael and Rabbi Shmuel Salant committed themselves never to accept any official rabbinic post, never to author books, and not to engage in kabbalistic studies!

"Study *mussar* and then you will be God fearing!"[13] The primary book of *mussar* studied by Rabbi Zundel himself[14] was the *Mesilas Yesharim* of Rabbi Moshe Chaim Luzzatto.[15] Rabbi Yisrael made this book the basic primer of *mussar* study, and so it has remained. In short, it can be said that if Rabbi Yisrael was the father of the *mussar* movement, Rabbi Zundel was its grandfather.

In 1840, Rabbi Yisrael left Salant and moved to Vilna. Originally, he came there without his family, as a Torah student.[16] Within a short period of time, however, he was joined by his wife and children and took a position as *rosh yeshivah* in the Vilna yeshivah called "Remailles."[17] Because of internal faculty frictions in the yeshivah, Rabbi Yisrael soon left and founded his own school in Zorace, a suburb of Vilna.[18]

His rare combination of a charismatic, holy personality, a talent for oratory, a logical and coherent approach to unraveling Talmudic difficulties, and his exemplary personal behavior attracted many great students. He conducted classes not only in Zorace, but visited many of the synagogues and study houses of Vilna on a regular basis and taught Torah to many different groups in Vilna. His fame spread and his reputation as one of the leading Talmudic scholars of the age was solidified. From this position of achievement and respect, he turned to his life's work — the establishment of the *Mussar* Movement.

In 1845 in Vilna, Rabbi Yisrael outlined his program for the ethical rejuvenation of traditional Jewry. A century after the Chassidic revolution, *mussar* was to be the parallel revolution of the misnagdim. Rabbi Yisrael sought to elevate Jewish religious life by restoring the primacy of ethical precepts as the key to meaningful religious observance and Torah study. He envisioned the defeat of the forces of Reform and *Haskalah,* not so much by attack and dispute, as by the

---

13. *Ohr Yisrael*, Rabbi Yitzchak Blaser, p. 31.

14. *Ohr Yisrael*, p. 124.

15. See Chapter 3 regarding him.

16. A *porush*, a scholar separated from his family and the world. The *perushim* were well known and accepted in nineteenth-century Lithuanian society.

17. This yeshivah was founded in 1827 and was one of the established yeshivos in Vilna. In 1831, the yeshivah was granted a building to house the school in the courtyard of a well-known Vilna Jew, Reb Maille. The two words "Reb Mailles" were usually slurred together and pronounced "Remailles," which became the yeshivah's popularly used name.

18. See Itkes, pp. 91-3, for details regarding this incident.

inner restructuring of the traditional camp on superior ethical and behavioral grounds. He sought to deepen the religious commitment and value system of Jews individually and the Jewish community generally. All aspects of Jewish life — education, commerce, family, community relations with the government and non-Jews generally — were to be measured by the standards of *mussar,* traditional Jewish ethics.

To accomplish this, his plan consisted of four parts: 1) The printing and dissemination of *mussar* books, 2) lectures and speeches to be delivered regularly in synagogues and houses of study on *mussar* topics, 3) the establishment of special "*mussar* houses" in all communities and neighborhoods, where *mussar* would be taught and studied, and 4) the development of a select cadre of disciples who would commit themselves to spread and strengthen the *Mussar* Movement.[19] This ambitious program began to take root in Vilna, and Rabbi Yisrael and his ideas achieved wide popularity, not only among the scholars, but even among the masses of Vilna's Jews as well.[20]

In the 1840s, the *Haskalah* movement was on the ascent. Nowhere was this more evident than in Vilna, where a number of *Haskalah* leaders lived and were active in propagating their cause. The leaders of the *Haskalah* were fascinated by Rabbi Yisrael, his personality and philosophy. They somehow felt that he could be their ally. This fatal misreading of Rabbi Yisrael by the *maskilim* would eventually force him to leave Vilna.

In 1848, the Russian government established, under the auspices of the *Haskalah,* two new official, rabbinic seminaries, whose goal was to produce "modern" rabbis. One of these seminaries was opened in Vilna,[21] and Rabbi Yisrael was asked to teach Talmud in the new institution. Because of his fame, the *maskilim* gleefully anticipated that his participation in the new seminary would automatically grant it legitimacy in the Jewish world. They had the right idea but they chose the wrong man. The *Haskalah* had the backing of the Russian government in its program for these new seminaries, and because of this governmental pressure involved in the seminary's offer,[22] Rabbi Yisrael found it impossible to remain in Vilna. He was a sworn opponent of the

---

19. Itkes, p. 95.
20. *Seridei Aish*, Weinberg, Vol. 4, p. 288.
21. See the previous chapters on yeshivos, *Haskalah*, and Russian oppression.
22. Itkes, p. 158 and 160; Yaakov Lipschutz, *Zichron Yaakov*, Vol. 1, p. 176.

Haskalah and would never cooperate in their seminary venture. He therefore saw no other course for himself but to leave Vilna and flee to Kovno. By early 1849, Rabbi Yisrael was already residing permanently in Kovno.

Observance With a Soul

N MUSSAR, ITS DEVELOPMENT and dissemination, Rabbi Yisrael saw the means to revitalize Torah Jewry from within. His keen historical insight led him to realize that alien ideas and movements would not help Jewry adjust to the new, modern, secular world. He was aware that *Haskalah* would lead eventually to Reform, assimilation, conversion and self-annihilation. But he was also aware of the social and educational failings present among traditional Jews, and that these failings were emphasized and exposed by the changing conditions of the modern era. Poor social manners, discourteous behavior, societal class imbalance, a neglect of the spirit of the law as opposed to its letter, and a disregard of the ethical nature of Torah and its personal, character-building nature were the accusations heaped on traditional Jewry by the *Haskalah*. Chassidus, which also attempted to address these accusations, was not a viable option for the misnagdim (as previously explained in chapter 14 on "Yeshivos"). Rabbi Yisrael now advanced *mussar* as the solution, the uplifting answer to the external degradation and internal weakness of Jewish life in Russia.

Mussar was not merely piety. It was psychology, sociology, and philosophy as well. It defined Jews on the ethical plane of Torah standards and stressed individual development and achievement, independent of the level and standards of the general society. *Mussar* came to build the individual, knowing that thereby it would change and improve general society as well. It saw the world in microcosm and taught that salvation lay in a Torah society founded on moral standards set by the Torah and Jewish tradition. Much like Chassidus, the language and outer garb of *mussar* were new, but its internal core was as old as Sinai.

Rabbi Yisrael felt that the traditional Jewish community was becoming delinquent in its response to social and human responsibilities. He demanded ethical improvement in society, and personal commitment to moral values. He required punctilious observance of the law and its commandments, but with a soul: with the understanding that good deeds are necessary to create a good person, and that becoming that good person was the end goal of Jewish life.

Mussar, therefore, lent a new dimension to all of the time-honored aspects of Judaism. It was to be prayer with *mussar*, Torah study with *mussar*, communal activity with *mussar*, charity with *mussar*, domestic relations and family life with *mussar*, life itself with *mussar*. *Mussar* was meant to successfully challenge the blandishments of the secular humanism of the nineteenth century and to infuse Jews with internal pride and self-worth in an age of Czarist oppression. Its scope and influence was felt in the Jewish world, and the movement shaped traditional Jewish society in a fashion far stronger than the mere number of its adherents might indicate.

Offshoots of Mussar's Growth

N KOVNO, RABBI YISRAEL originally served as a public preacher.[23] By 1851, however, he had retired from that position and began to conduct a yeshivah. He attracted great personalities as his students and disciples. Among them was Rabbi Yitzchak Blaser,[24] Rabbi Naftali Amsterdam,[25] Rabbi

---

23. "*Maggid Meisharim.*" In the tradition of Eastern European Jewry, the rabbis of the community spoke publicly only twice a year — the Sabbath before *Yom Kippur* and the Sabbath before *Pesach*. The oratorical void was thus filled by paid community preachers — *maggidim* — who spoke on a regular basis at various local synagogues. Depending on the personage of the *maggid*, this could be a position of great honor and dignity or, alternatively, a very menial and degrading occupation.

24. 1837-1907. He was known as Rabbi Itzele Peterburger because of his service as rabbi in St. Petersburg, then the capital of Russia, for a number of years. He was sent there by Rabbi Yisrael to serve the city's Jewish community. Most of the Jewish inhabitants of that city had no legal permission to live there, but there was also a wealthy class of assimilated Jews who did possess the necessary governmental approval to reside there. Rabbi Yitzchak Blaser was very effective in a very difficult position. He later returned to Kovno where he became one of the trustees of the Kovno *Kollel*. In 1904 he emigrated to Jerusalem, where he died.

25. 1832-1916. One of the distinguished men of *Mussar*. For a time, he was the rabbi of Helsinki, Finland, though most of his career was spent in Kovno. He emigrated to Jerusalem in 1906 and died there, ten years later.

Simchah Zisel Ziev,[26] Rabbi Eliezer Gordon,[27] and Rabbi Jacob Joseph.[28] Hundreds of others came under his tutelage and influence, and his educational prowess was great. He was the role model, the pedagogue, the inspiration, and the master. His followers and students were loyal to him and they built the *Mussar* Movement and its attendant yeshivos and institutions in his spirit.

From 1851 to 1857 in Kovno, the *Mussar* Movement centered in the study hall that Rabbi Yisrael occupied in the courtyard of Tzvi Hirsh Navyozer.[29] In 1858 Rabbi Yisrael published his famous monograph, *Iggeres HaMussar*,[30] in which he expounded his entire philosophy of *mussar* and life. The humility and longing for improvement which, according to Rabbi Yisrael, are the hallmarks of the truly pious, are evident in this remarkable pamphlet. Rabbi Yisrael later continued to expound on these ideas in rabbinic periodicals and letters. But the main thrust of his ideas and program was to be found in the lives and writings of his students and in the yeshivos they founded.

The *mussar* yeshivos of Lithuania became the prototype of the modern yeshivah. Telshe, Slobodka, Radin, Mir, Kelm, Novardok, Kletzk, Slutzk — all were products of the *Mussar* Movement[31] and its disciples. Even after the *Mussar* Movement had become less influential in general Jewish life, its imprint on yeshivah education remained indelible. A sweeping inner reform of Jewish life took place and, though it was less drastic than the Chassidic revolution, its effects were just as permanent and positive.

---

26. 1824-1898. The renowned pedagogue of the *Mussar* Movement. Early in his career, he established a famous yeshivah in Grubin in Prussian Lithuania. That school included some courses in mathematics and sciences in its curriculum. The yeshivah closed after a number of years. Rabbi Simchah Zisel moved on then to Lithuania proper and there established the great "Talmud Torah" at Kelm, Lithuania. It became one of the foremost *mussar* yeshivos in the world, and some of the prominent leaders of the Torah world of the next generation were his disciples.

27. 1841-1910. The esteemed rabbi of Telshe, Lithuania and the founder of Telshe Yeshivah.

28. 1842-1902. A founder of a number of yeshivos in Lithuania, he was known as the *Maggid* of Vilna. In 1888, he was appointed as the Chief Rabbi of New York City. His tenure was tumultuous and painful. The Rabbi Jacob Joseph Yeshivah, established on the Lower East Side of New York City and one of the oldest Jewish institutions in America, was named after him. It is now located on Staten Island, N.Y. and in Edison, N.J.

29. It was known as Navyozer's Kloiz.

30. *The Letter of Mussar*.

31. See above, Chapter 14.

Opposition

 NEW MOVEMENT MUST evoke a reaction. Not everyone viewed the *Mussar* Movement benignly. Originally, the *Haskalah* hoped that *mussar* would be its ally, but when *Haskalah* was rebuffed by Rabbi Yisroel, the *maskilim* opposed *mussar* with derision, scorn, and bitter enmity. Some traditional Torah forces also disagreed with certain aspects of the movement. They were concerned that *mussar* would divert the yeshivah student from the exclusive pursuit of Torah study, as well as subverting the traditional eminence of the scholar in favor of the new creature — the *baal-mussar* or *mussar* personality. They firmly believed that good character traits could be achieved through Torah study exclusively.

As long as Rabbi Yisroel still lived in Lithuania, this opposition to the *Mussar* Movement from the traditional Torah camp was muted. However, when he left Lithuania in 1857, first to settle in Memel and other Prussian communities, and finally to travel to Berlin and Paris, the opponents of *mussar* became more vocal. The vehemence of their objections can be traced directly to the success of the *Mussar* Movement and its widespread influence in the Torah world of the time.[32]

The *Mussar* Movement caused an upheaval in the yeshivos of the time, and a number of institutions became embroiled in internal controversy for many years over the issue. Like all young idealistic believers in a new ideal, many of the *mussar* advocates proselytized openly, tenaciously and successfully. Some of them undermined the authority of the established rabbis and *roshei yeshivah*, and cast themselves as an elitist, exclusive group. The opposition of many established rabbinic and yeshivah leaders to their movement and theories eventually had a salutary, calming effect upon them. It dampened their ardor, quieted the shrillness of their campaign, and reversed their bent towards extremism.

Thus, the rabbinic opponents of *mussar* forced its proponents to examine their tactics, strategy and ideals in the light of the very *mussar* ethics they claimed to represent. Henceforth, the battle for *mussar* would be waged within the ethical parameters of behavior propounded

---

32. See Rabbi Dov Katz, "*Pulmus HaMussar*," Jerusalem 1972, for a detailed study of the controversy over *mussar*.

by the movement itself. As has often been the case in Jewish history, the sincere opponents of seemingly positive innovations and new movements proved to be the best friends of the new movement, saving it from excesses and channeling it into the mainstream of tradition and Jewish life.

While the opposition of some of the rabbis to *mussar* was to have a positive effect, the opposition of *Haskalah* to *mussar* was mainly negative and malicious. The *maskilim* dreaded the success of *mussar*, fearing that its ability to reform traditional Jewry on a more ethical and idealistic plane would rob them of their chief weapon against traditional Jewish life. The *maskilim* ridiculed the piety and exactitude of *mussar*[33] and used every means at their disposal, including governmental pressure and broad media propaganda, to attempt to crush the movement.

Rabbi Yisrael responded to the broadsides of the *maskilim* by founding a weekly newspaper, *T'vunah*, which appeared for twelve issues in the autumn of 1861. Rabbi Yisrael had by then moved to Prussia and the paper was published in Memel and Koenigsberg. The great rabbis of the time[34] supported the paper and contributed to its columns. Sadly, the venture was short lived, but it was one of the first attempts to respond to the attack of the *maskilim* by the use of the new methods of publicity and newspapers. Though disappointed by the early demise of *T'vunah*, Rabbi Yisrael correctly assessed that its mere appearance was in itself a success for tradition in its battle against *Haskalah*.

Rabbi Yisrael and *mussar* also competed with the *Haskalah* for the elite of Jewish youth. Rabbi Yisrael realized early on that *mussar* would remain a movement small in numbers and therefore concentrated his efforts on establishing a cadre of talented people who would then become the leaders of Eastern European Jewry. These elite young men were the very same people that the *Haskalah* hoped to attract to its camp. The *Haskalah,* itself basically an elitist movement, reacted

---

33. The school of *mussar* of Novardok, founded by Rabbi Yosef Y. Horowitz (the Alter of Novardok), specialized in social behavior that openly indicated contempt for "worldly standards." It was the target of much criticism and a special object of ridicule by the *maskilim*.

34. Such as Rabbi Yitzchak Elchanan Spector of Kovno, Rabbi Yosef Shaul Nathanson of Lvov, Rabbi Shlomo Kluger of Brod, Rabbi Alexander Moshe Lapidus of Rassayn, Rabbi Yosef Ber Soloveitchik, then of Volozhin, and later of Slutzk, and Rabbi Shmuel Salant of Jerusalem. Other great rabbinic figures also participated in *T'vunah*.

violently to the success of *mussar* in attracting the young men of promise and intelligence that *Haskalah* had been certain would be its adherents.[35] This war against *mussar* was waged on a personal and low plane, with much polemics and little philosophy and thought, and was very vicious.

As evidence of the nature of the conflict, the following incident is most revealing.

Rabbi Yisrael's youngest son, Yom Tov Lipman Lipkin, was a mathematics prodigy. Though he had no formal education, he was accepted at the age of seventeen as a student at the University of Koenigsberg. His father opposed his choice, but was powerless to prevent its exercise. The young Lipkin eventually achieved a Ph.D. in mathematics at the University of Vienna and discovered a technological breakthrough in applied mathematics, known until today as the "Lipkin parallelogram." Lipkin moved to St. Petersburg, where he was showered with honors by the Russian government. By this time, he had forsaken much of traditional Jewish life, and had become a hero for the *maskilim* and an example of how the new, modern Jew could succeed even in anti-Semitic Russia, if only he would accommodate himself to the new realities of life. The *maskilim*, bearding the lion in his den, announced the honor to Lipman Lipkin in their newspaper *HaMaggid*[36] and congratulated "the great rabbi and teacher, Rabbi Yisrael Salanter of Kovno . . . [whose son, Lipman] is a crown to his sainted and learned father, who did not prevent his son from studying in the university, so that thereby Torah and wisdom will be united in the person of his son, for the glory of our people."

Four issues later the following letter appeared in *HaMaggid:*[37]

> Since truth has been the guiding light of my life, I am compelled to publicly announce that my son is not the "crown" to me as the editor indicated, but rather the opposite is true. He is a source of disappointment and sadness to me and my heart weeps over his way of life. Anyone who loves him and can influence him to change his way and not go counter to my soul and wishes will do

---

35. For a striking similarity to this syndrome, Menachem Begin's short autobiography, *White Nights,* recounts the hatred that the Communist interrogator of Begin felt for the Zionist youth organizations, because he claimed that Zionism robbed Communism of an elite class of intelligent, idealistic Jews who would have otherwise been perfect commissars.

36. 1865, Vol. 7, p. 49.

37. 1865, Vol. 11, p. 83.

a great favor to me this very day. Yours in faith, Yisrael of Salant.

This vignette sums up the struggle of *mussar* and *Haskalah*. It also illustrates the deep inroads that the ideas of *Haskalah* and secular humanism had made in the traditional Jewish community. It would not be unheard of for rabbis' sons to become members and leaders of the secular community, and this defection in the ranks of some of the leading families of traditional Jewry served to legitimatize *Haskalah* and its aims. The *Haskalah* continued to attempt to create the impression in the minds of traditional Jews that Rabbi Yisrael himself was a secret admirer of *Haskalah*. [38]

Rabbi Yisrael, his disciples, and the yeshivos that were the products of their efforts and spirit may have been a new and modern innovation in Jewish life — but they were not *Haskalah*. They were authentically Jewish and their program stemmed only from Torah and tradition. Even ideas that were adopted from outside Judaism were thoroughly Judaized in their presentation to the Jewish people and filtered carefully through the prism of Torah. The *Haskalah,* on the other hand, derived its ideas and goals almost exclusively from outside Judaism, and even the Jewish ideas and content that became part of *Haskalah* were secularized and de-Judaized in their presentation and goals. [39]

This basic difference was readily apparent by the beginning of the twentieth century, but in the 1850s and 1860s, the formative years of the *Mussar* Movement, this difference was not yet perceived by many members of the Jewish public. The greatness of *mussar* and its influence on its society became more readily recognizable in later generations, when the movement itself was past its peak, than in its early stages, when the movement's popularity and dynamism were surging.

---

38. Itkes, pp. 341-2.

39. Such as Biblical studies that became Bible criticism, and Hebrew language that was severed from its roots as a "holy tongue."

21

New Yearnings

Jewish Nationalism

HE NEW WORLD OF the modern era loosed the pent-up feelings of Europe's masses. Social revolution, economic change, shifting alliances, new ideas — some brilliant, others fatuous — were the order of the day. The vast changes — diplomatic, technological, and political — of the twentieth century were still hidden from view, but the peoples of Europe in the 1880s and 1890s sensed their subtle presence and stirred, in anticipation of change. Much of the new world would be channeled by the thoughts and ideas of three Jews — Karl Marx, Sigmund Freud, and Albert Einstein. For better or for worse, they would have a profound influence on the twentieth century. In the new world now being born, the Jewish people would be both catalyst and victim, creator and product, aggressor and survivor.

In the ferment of the nineteenth century, two small books were published that were of great influence in the Jewish world. One was *Rome and Jerusalem* by Moses Hess.[1] The other was *Auto*

---

1. 1812-1875. Hess received a traditional Jewish education in Torah and Talmud from his Polish grandfather who had emigrated to Germany, but he joined Marx and Engels, and was known as the "communist Rabbi Moses." The Damascus blood libel of 1840 reawakened within him his Jewish concerns, and in 1862 his book, *Rome and Jerusalem,* was published. The leading postulates of the book were that (1) Jews would never be fully accepted in Europe, (2) the Jewish national feeling is indestructible and inseparable from Judaism itself, and (3) Jews would sacrifice the gains of Emancipation and Enlightenment in order to maintain their spirit of Jewish nationalism. He saw the Jewish colonization of Palestine as the only solution to the "Jewish problem." Hess was also an unremitting foe of Reform Judaism, although in his personal life he was not a traditional Jew by any means.

Moses Hess

Leon Pinsker

Emancipation by Leon Pinsker.[2] Both books represented the prevalent ideas of the nineteenth century, as applied particularly to the Jewish people. Nineteenth-century man's confidence in his ability to solve all human problems was now to be applied to the "Jewish problem."

The basic tenet of these works was that the future of the Jewish people lay exclusively within the powers of determination of the Jewish people itself.[3] The "Jewish problem" would be solved not by Divine intervention, nor by governmental charity, but by Jewish effort and self-improvement. The development of a productive Jewish laboring class, of a strong and vibrant and idealistic middle class, of a national sense of purpose and goal — all defined in secular terms — would force the nations of the world to see the Jewish people in a more objective and benign light.

This view was completely representative of nineteenth-century secular humanism, which naively fostered the notion that education, productivity and ideals alone could overcome the basic evils of human society. It cruelly propagated the myth adopted by so many killers and haters that the persecution of the victim is basically the fault of the victim himself.[4] Thus, a new solution — Jewish nationalism, with all the pride and productivity inherent therein — was advanced to solve the "Jewish problem." It would find a strong and vibrant echo in the hearts of the masses of Eastern European Jewry.

Even though Western European Jews such as Hess, Herzl,[5] Zangwill[6] and others were the architects of Jewish nationalism, the

---

2. 1821-1891. Pinsker was a Jewish Russian physician, who belonged to an assimilated Jewish family, and rose to become one of the most respected doctors in Odessa. He despaired of the condition of Russian Jews. At one and the same time, he begged the authorities for greater freedom and rights for the Jews, and begged the Jews to become more assimilated and Russian. Neither appeal bore fruit, and in 1881, his book *Auto-Emancipation* stated that the "Jewish problem" had to be solved by the Jews themselves and that the solution lay in acquiring a land of their own for colonization and settlement.

3. This was the Jewish version of the prevalent nineteenth-century philosophy of complete reliance on human effort and the belief that the victim always possessed the power to somehow save himself, if he only so desired.

4. This distortion has been perpetuated in our time in the analysis of the Holocaust by such scholars as Bruno Bettelheim and Hannah Arendt, and, to a lesser extent, Raoul Hilberg.

5. The founder of political Zionism. See below, Chapter 24, for details on his life and work.

6. Israel Zangwill (1864-1926) was a well-known author on Jewish subjects. An apologist for Jews and Judaism, he specialized in books about Jewish ghetto life. In the

movement itself was basically an Eastern European phenomenon. The Jews in Western Europe did not feel that they had a "Jewish problem." Though anti-Semitism in Western Europe was rampant in the late nineteenth century,[7] Western European Jews were confident that it was a transitory situation given to amelioration through humanism and enlightenment.

The granting of civil rights to Jews in Western Europe, the rise of Jewish wealth and station in France, England, and Germany, and the new democratic procedures of government, all combined to convince the Jews in Western Europe that the "Jewish problem" was restricted to the domain of the Czars. This attitude was all pervasive in Western European Jewry, reflecting the beliefs of the Reform movement and Jewish Enlightenment.

Thus, Jewish nationalism never achieved in Western Europe the popularity or impetus that it did among Eastern European Jews. Convinced of their secure position in the new Europe, internationalist and universalist in world view, optimistic and confident of their future as citizens of the most powerful and progressive states in the world, Western Jews felt no need to achieve a "Jewish solution" to their aspirations, since they were convinced that the improvements inherent

---

early stages of Zionism he was one of the leaders of the movement, and later headed his own organization, The Jewish Territorial Organization for the Settlement of the Jews Within the British Empire.

7. The Dreyfus Trial, the election of Karl Luger as mayor of Vienna on a platform of openly anti-Semitic promises, and other public displays of enmity to Jews, all were manifestations of the underlying antipathy of the Western European population to their Jewish fellow-citizens.

Conference of Jewish leaders in St. Petersburg. They attempted to ameliorate the Czar's decrees.

in the progress of Western civilization would automatically benefit them as well.

Agriculture and Labor

SIDE FROM THE NASCENT idea of Jewish nationalism, the mystique of returning to the land also took hold in Eastern European Jewish society. Perhaps as a reaction to the trauma of the rapid industrialization[8] and urbanization of Jewish Russia, many Jews longed for a simpler and more satisfying life style. There had always been Jewish farmers in Europe, but the peasant farmer of Russia, with his coarseness, illiteracy, and brutality, was hardly a role model for Jews. Yet, a new philosophy of life arose among Jews, granting farm work and agricultural labor an almost holy aura.

Writers such as A.D. Gordon[9] and Y.C. Brenner[10] extolled the virtues of the toil of farming in terms of nobility and messianic fervor. The Jewish people could never solve the "Jewish problem" if they persisted in remaining artisans, merchants, money agents and loggers. Only in the back breaking struggle of wresting food from the recalcitrant ground would Jews find fulfillment and the Jewish people salvation. Jewish farming communes, Jewish agricultural training centers, and Yiddish and Hebrew books on farming all gained popularity. Societies to encourage agricultural settlements for Jews in Russia, Palestine, Argentina, the United States and elsewhere were created and funded.[11]

---

8. Russia industrialized more rapidly than any other European country in the late nineteenth century. It was far behind the rest of Europe at the beginning of the nineteenth century, but by the end of the century it was one of the leading industrial powers of the world.

9. Aaron David Gordon (1856-1922) was the "prophet" of the return of the Jewish people to agricultural pursuits. An agnostic *maskil,* he had an almost supernatural view of the importance of farming and manual labor to the Jewish condition. The intensity of his belief in this idea fueled the Kibbutz movement in the early twentieth century.

10. Yosef Chaim Brenner (1881-1921) was a radical socialist and a brilliant poet and writer. The famous kibbutz, Givat Brenner, named after him, was the experimental laboratory for some of his social and agricultural plans. He died a violent death in the Arab pogroms of 1921.

11. Baron Maurice de Hirsch (1831-1896) was a leading philanthropist and a sponsor of Jewish colonization the world over. He believed that "All our miseries come from the Jews who want to climb too high. We have too many intellectuals!" The Alliance

The romance of agriculture[12] became part of the Jewish dream of the nineteenth century.

The longing for social justice, one of the prime contributions of Judaism to civilization, also translated itself into active Jewish movements in the nineteenth century. The establishment of labor unions, which coincided with the rise of Socialism and the intense industrialization of Europe, proved especially attractive to Jews.

The Jewish Labor Federation — the Bund[13] — was popular,

Baron Maurice de Hirsch

Israelite Universelle, based in Paris and founded in 1860 "to defend the civil rights and religious freedom of the Jews," was also active in Jewish colonization efforts. It founded the first agricultural school for Jews in Palestine, *Mikveh Yisrael,* in 1896.

12. John Kenneth Galbraith in his fascinating autobiography, *A Life In Our Times* (Houghton Mifflin Co., Boston 1981), makes the astute comment that "farmers were studying agriculture (in agricultural colleges) more or less without exception in order to escape it. The countrymen, in contrast, intended to farm. They were the sons of affluent . . . families possessed of land somewhere adjacent to the city. The son in question had become enamored of the horses, cattle and . . . acres and had decided to make them his career." This attitude explains in part why the Jews, who were forbidden in the main to farm in Russia, embraced farming in the early twentieth century, and why their children fifty years later fled farming in droves.

13. In the United States, the counterpart of the Bund was the *Arbeiter Ring* — the Jewish Workmen's Circle. Like the Bund, it was Yiddishist in language and culture, socialist in politics and economics, and bitterly anti-religious. It sponsored dances and banquets that took place on *Yom Kippur*. Its main media organ was the newspaper *The Jewish Daily Forward*, and it also sponsored a network of Yiddish/socialist clubs and schools.

The Eighth National Conference of the Bund, Petrograd, 1917

strong, and very effective in advancing the rights of the Jewish working man. Even though its leftist, socialist philosophy and aggressive posture made it a divisive force in Jewish life, it wielded great power and influence. Its bitter anti-religious tone would eventually propel it outside of the mainstream of Jewish life, but in its heyday, the Jewish labor movement had hundreds of thousands of members and sympathizers. Its commitment to reform society, to minimize the exploitation of the many by the few, and its attempt to balance the privileges of capital with the rights of the human laborer served to attract idealistic Jewish youths to its banner. Jews were also prominently represented in all of the major national labor organizations in Russia, Western Europe, and the United States.[14] In the twentieth century, Jewish involvement in the worldwide rise of labor organizations had profound political consequences for the Jewish people in the Land of Israel and in the Diaspora.

Changing the Balance of Power

 LTIMATELY, THE NEW-FOUND mobility that resulted from the availability of railroads, steamships, and new countries and colonies stirred the physical movement of Jews. Emigration, which had always been at least a partial answer to Jewish troubles, now loomed even larger in the Jewish mind. The masses of Eastern European Jews knew that the fulfillment of their aspirations was impossible under the Russian Czar. The deterioration of life and society in Czarist Russia forced Jews to seriously consider leaving the "Old Home."[15]

Beginning in the 1870s, waves of immigrants left the Pale of Settlement. The number of Jews in Russia continued to grow at a rapid rate, so that the Jewish population remained stable, or even increased slightly, in spite of the emigration. Nevertheless, the sense of new movement, of great opportunities and different locations, inspired a

---

14. The founder of the American Federation of Labor was an immigrant Jew, Samuel Gompers. The textile workers' unions, such as the ILGWU, were dominated by Jews, both in membership and leadership. David Dubinsky, Sidney Hillman, and other Jews were powerful and influential labor leaders in the United States until the middle of the twentieth century. Leon Blum in France, Leon Trotsky in Russia, and Rosa Luxemburg in Germany were all leaders in the trade union movement and avid socialists and social revolutionaries.

15. The "old home" — in Yiddish, "der alter heim" — was the nostalgic name that Eastern European Jews used to refer to the birthplace from which they fled.

long-latent feeling of "wanting to move on" among Eastern European Jews. Even though inertia, religious fears, quotas on immigration, lack of money, and the dangers of travel would temper enthusiasm for leaving the "Old Home," emigration from Russia would become a dominant factor and influence in Jewish life world wide. The beginning of the end of European Jewry had started.

The Great Synagogue in St. Petersburg (Leningrad)

In all of these yearnings and new directions, secular Jewry played a leading role. Jewish nationalism, agricultural interest, labor organizations and immigration societies all became the province of the secular element of the Jewish people. These organizations, which were essentially substitutes for religious Judaism, changed the balance of power within Jewry. It is ironic to note that the new social agenda, rooted in idealism and justice, was based primarily on fundamental Torah values and perceptions. Yet, as was to happen later regarding Zionism in the twentieth century, the essential Torah ideas and values that fueled these movements, did not prevent them from becoming anti-Torah vehicles.

The vehemence of the secular attack against traditional Jewry remains one of the great mysteries of modern Jewish history. The Jewish world, never monolithic or free from internal strife, entered the twentieth century bitterly divided and furiously warring within itself. No united Jewish approach to any problem or opportunity in the modern world was apparently possible. Intoxicated by the new, secular Jewry attempted to destroy the timeless value of the old heritage. Frightened and appalled by this new attack against its fundamental beliefs, traditional Jewry guarded its ancient treasures and way of life by every means at its disposal. The pieces would fall where they would.

Synagogue in Samara, built in 1908, which had 1,000 seats

Section V

Leaving the
"Old Home"

1880-1920

22

Emigration to America

The Safe Shore

IF AMERICA WAS THE "golden land"[1] of opportunity for all of the poor and oppressed of Europe, to much of European Jewry it was the only fortress for safety and security in the world. By the early 1830s, America's fame as the land of freedom and opportunity had solidified in the minds of Europeans. The original waves of immigration to the United States in the early 1800s were from the British Isles. Among them in the 1820s was a small wave of Jews from England, most of whom were traditional in nature and practice.

But in the 1830s large-scale emigration began from Germany to the United States. German Jews, too, then began to arrive in significant numbers on American soil. In 1826 there were 6,000 Jews in the United States.[2] By 1840, the year of the Damascus blood libel, there were 15,000 American Jews, but by 1860 the German-Jewish immigration had pushed that number to 150,000 Jews. The Jews settled in New York and Cincinnati,[3] Chicago, Cleveland, Detroit, St. Louis, New Orleans, Minneapolis, Savannah, Atlanta, and Philadelphia. The California gold rush in 1848-9 drew thousands of Jews to the west coast of the continent.

The original American Jews of the colonial and Revolutionary War eras were Sephardic, assimilated, and unobtrusive. But the German Jews were more noticeable, more numerous, and socially aggressive. In the main, they were Reform, "enlightened,"[4] and determined to adopt

Waiting in Ellis Island

---

1. Or, as Eastern European Jews would refer to it when their own wave of immigration began late in the century, the *goldeneh medinah*.

2. Johnson, *A History of the Jews*, p. 366.

3. Cincinnati became the home of Reform Judaism in the U.S.

4. Many of them were active participants in Germany's social revolutions of the 1830s and 1840s, and thus were liberal, reform, and radical in their political as well as religious beliefs.

the protective coloration of their new society. Their Temples and communal organizations mimicked those of their Christian counterparts.

The Reform movement in the U.S. spawned very liberal, if not radical, rabbinic leadership, in the persons of David Einhorn, Samuel Hirsch, Isaac Mayer Wise, and Samuel Adler. The original lay leaders of American Jewry were also fashioned in this Reform mold. Joseph Seligman, Jacob Schiff,[5] August Belmont, the Bamberger family and others cut a wide swath for other Jews in the financial world.[6] The basic infrastructure of American Jewry was thus fashioned by Reform Jews and used for the express purpose of "Americanizing" Jews through persistent assimilation and disregard of tradition. This Reform orientation of official, organized American Jewry would have profound influence on the later waves of Jewish immigration to the United States.

Beginning in 1881, the disasters of Russian Jewry forced a tide of refugees to flow to the United States. In the decade of the 1880s, almost 200,000 Jews from Russia came to the United States. In the next decade, the number swelled to 360,000 and in the decade that preceded the outbreak of the First World War, almost 800,000 Eastern European Jews arrived in America. By the time of the Great War, the Jewish population in America had grown to more than two million.

Judah P. Benjamin. U.S. Senator from Louisiana. Attorney General, Secretary of War, and Secretary of State of the Confederacy

Isaac Mayer Wise

5. He was personally much more traditional than his counterparts, and attempted to preserve Judaism in America in a fashion that he thought would be viable.

6. See Stephen Birmingham's book, *Our Crowd,* for a description of these titans of finance and merchandising, and a fascinating revelation of the lives of the early German-Jewish settlers in the United States, including the reluctance on the part of most of them and their offspring to acknowledge their Jewishness.

The Building of R.H. Macy & Co. at the corner of Sixth Avenue and West Fourteenth Street. Isador Straus entered the firm in 1888 and bought it eight years later with his younger brother, Nathan.

The route to the United States led first through Brody, a town in Polish Galicia, and then to such rail centers and ports as Lemberg, Cracow, Breslau, Berlin, Bremen, Hamburg, Brest, Le Havre, and Antwerp. Steerage accommodation, a long and usually nauseous voyage across the Atlantic, unscrupulous ticket agents, bemused and overly bureaucratic immigration officers, and the bewilderment of facing the unknown, all combined to make the journey to America an unforgettable and mainly unpleasant one for most of the immigrants.[7]

Russian Jewry, spurred by the "storms of the south"[8] and by unremitting cruelty and poverty, began to leave. It was encouraged in this exit by the Russian government itself which saw in America a convenient dumping ground for its unwanted Jews. Count N.P. Ignatiev, a member of the inner cabinet of Czar Alexander III, stated: "The Western frontier is open for the Jews. The Jews have already taken ample advantage of this right and their emigration has in no way been hampered." Another official remarked ". . . the Western frontier is open for the Jews. Why don't they take advantage of it?"[9] Vast numbers of Russian Jews, especially the poor, the young, the adventurous and the secular, took the hint.

Helping Hands

HE ATTITUDE OF GRASS-ROOTS America to the new immigration, and more importantly to the new immigrants, was mixed. In spite of being the freest and most cosmopolitan of all societies in the history of civilization, the United States has never been free of bigotry, prejudice, and violence. Jew-baiting became common, and as Jews became more numerous and affluent, the public reaction against them in America increased. It is ironic that Jews suffered the ignominy of the quotas in colleges, and of restricted areas of residence in the United States in the same way as they did in Russia, though certainly in a more genteel,

---

7. An excellent account of the rigors of immigration to the United States appears in Ronald Sanders' book, *Shores of Refuge*, Henry Holt & Company, N.Y. 1988.

8. The euphemistic name given to the pogroms in southern Russia.

9. S.M. Dubnow, *History of the Jews in Russia and Poland*, Philadelphia 1916, Volume 2, pps. 285 and 265.

discreet and less painful manner.[10]

Nevertheless, there were many Americans who welcomed the new immigrants. Not only their Jewish fellows who had arrived earlier in the 1800s were sympathetic to the new Jewish Americans, but even the vast non-Jewish community proved, in the main, hospitable. Many Americans seemed to recognize that these poor, frightened, different people could prove to be a valuable asset. The amorphous, diffused, but basically friendly reaction of America to her new role as the "golden land" for the persecuted of Europe found expression in the words of a young Jewish poet of the time, Emma Lazarus:[11]

> *"Give me your tired, your poor,*
> *Your huddled masses yearning to breathe free,*
> *The wretched refuse of your teeming shores.*
> *Send these, the homeless, tempest-toss't to me.*
> *I lift my lamp beside the golden door."*

Jews sensed this inherent warmth and welcome. They grasped the opportunity that now appeared, and were convinced that this new exile would differ materially from the old one they fled. They wrote their relatives in Europe and told them, "Come!" The new immigrants, though themselves still struggling economically in their new surround-

---

10. Johnson, p. 370.

11. A descendant of an old line, wealthy Sephardic family, she was born in 1849 and died in 1887. Her sonnet, "The New Colossus," later was enshrined in bronze at the foot of the Statue of Liberty in New York harbor.

Castle Garden, the first major reception center in New York for arriving immigrants, in 1896

In the front courtyard of the HIAS building — after receiving their emigration papers

ings, sent money, tickets, and encouragement to their relatives, friends and *landsleit*[12] to facilitate their immigration to America. And come they did! In retrospect, the Divine hand that moved the Jews from one exile to another now signaled a new exodus. It would prove to be a salvation. It would become the "remaining camp"[13] that would survive and prosper when the Old World annihilated the Jewish population that had lived in its midst for more than a millennium.

Not all Eastern European Jews were enthusiastic about Jewish immigration to the United States. The rigors of travel and resettlement wreaked havoc with their spiritual commitment and traditional way of life. The Reform infrastructure of existing American Jewry undermined the attempts of the new Jews to rebuild their traditional Jewish life in America. It would be decades before traditional Jewry would feel comfortable and strong in the United States.[14] The Hebrew Immigrant Aid Society (HIAS),[15] the Federation of Jewish Philanthropies, the American (and especially New York City) Public School system, all helped to "Americanize" the Jewish immigrants.

Many of these immigrants, in their rush to assimilate successfully, "threw their *tefillin* into the New York harbor," to quote a phrase of the time. Scrupulous observance of the law, intensive Torah and Talmudic study, holiness and sanctity of personal life, all fell casualty before the process of "Americanization." The six-day — and sometimes seven-day — work week, the lack of the traditional Jewish infrastructure, and the

---

12. People from the same town or area.

13. Genesis 32:9.

14. See Irving Howe, *World of our Fathers,* Harcourt Brace Jovanovitch, New York 1976. In this otherwise excellent work on immigrant Jewish life in the United States during the period from 1880-1930, there is almost no mention of traditional religious Jewish life. This is partly due to Howe's secular bias and socialist upbringing, but it is also a sad testament to the bewilderment, pessimism, and defeatism of much of traditional Jewry in its early attempt to find a role for itself in America.

15. It was the leading Jewish organization concerning itself with the problems of Jewish immigration and immigrants. See *Shores of Refuge,* Chapter 31, for a history of this organization.

emphasis on material achievement weakened the religious resolve of many. Even when parents fought to preserve it, children would reject a tradition they associated with alien-status, backwardness, and poverty. This phenomenon was not lost on traditional Jewry and its leaders in Eastern Europe. And thus, with rare exceptions, the great rabbis of Russia counseled against emigrating to America.[16] As a consequence, most of the giants of Jewish

At the information desk

spirit who could have molded American Jewry at its beginning did not then come to the United States, leaving a vacuum in strong Orthodox leadership that showed itself in an almost total absence of yeshivah and day school education.

The attitude of organizational American Jewry to the rising tide of Jewish immigration from Eastern Europe was also mixed. These already American Jews — German, cultured, and assimilated — viewed their coarse, Yiddish-speaking, Jewish-looking, and more traditional brethren with condescension, sympathy, consternation, and bewilderment. These established Jews were fearful that their own major social accomplishments would be jeapordized by their uncouth relatives. They attempted to screen the newcomers and to prevent "undesirables" from arriving in America.

On March 20, 1882, the Hebrew Emigrant Aid Society (not to be confused with the later HIAS) sent a telegram to the European committee[17] "supervising" Jewish immigration to the United States saying: "Send only young unmarried refugees to emigrate hither. Send neither families nor farmers."[18] The United Hebrew Charities' report of 1888, on the subject of Jewish immigration, pointedly stated:

---

16. This attitude of the great rabbis of Europe towards America was prevalent even in the 1930s. See *The Collection of the Letters of the Chazon Ish* (Rabbi Avraham Y. Karelitz), edited by Rabbi S. Greineman, Jerusalem 1955, letter 177: "I do not agree with any Jewish soul moving to that country (America)."

17. This committee was mainly sponsored by the Alliance Israelite Universelle of Paris and operated in Brody and other main centers of Jewish embarkation to the United States.

18. Sanders, *Shores of Refuge*, p. 97.

Young boy delivering bundles of clothes, 1910

Few of the European Jews who have arrived here within the past few years may be styled exiles for religion's sake; and sympathy that was generously extended without question or reservation to the saddened victims of oppression prior to 1884, cannot be expected to be offered to people who rush to America merely to better their financial and social conditions . . .[19]

However, the traditional values of brotherhood and human concern, so deeply ingrained in the Jewish character and Torah lifestyle for millennia, prevailed. The help afforded the newcomers to America on a personal and communal basis was massive. HIAS, the Hebrew Sheltering House Association, the Yiddish press, the Federation of Charities, the local settlement houses, all labored mightily to ameliorate the plight of the new arrivals. The tradition of Jewish caring and help was the single most apparent social trait of the time. Jews attempted to take care of their own. And this certainty of a brotherly reception and substantive help served to encourage Russian Jewry to keep on coming.

Mixed Messages

HE EMIGRATION OF JEWS from Russia, though welcomed by the Czar's government, proved troubling to the "Russified" Jew. There was a small percentage of Jews who had "made it big" in the country of their oppression. These non-Jewish Jews were frightened by the mass exodus from Russia of their much less fortunate brethren. They were afraid that the headlong flight would put them in a bad light, vis-a-vis the Russian society to which they hoped to gain entrance. They heard the whispers that Jews were not — and therefore even they themselves could not be — loyal Russians. They were afraid as well that the mass flight of Russian Jewry would be viewed as a surrender of their struggle for equal civil rights in Russia.

---

19. Ibid., p. 185. An attitude repeated vis-a-vis Russian Jewish immigration to America in 1989 by the United States State Department.

OPPOSITE: The Jewish Lower East Side of Manhattan, circa 1900

In April 1882, Baron Horace Gunzberg[20] convened a council of Jewish "leaders" in St. Petersburg, with the agreement of the Czar's ministers, to discuss the problem of Jewish emigration. Their resolution, passed at the end of the conference, stated that they "reject completely the thought of organizing emigration (of Jews from Russia), as being subversive of the dignity of the Russian body politic and of the historic rights of the Jews to their present fatherland (Russia)."[21]

Thus, a striking and almost inexplicable pattern of public behavior began amidst world Jewry, one that would repeat itself often in the next century. The deeply pious and most traditional element of Jewry and the most assimilated element of Jewry apparently shared a common behavior pattern about major events in the Jewish world.[22] However, Orthodoxy had neither organized policy nor a guide on the matter, its behavior pattern being established by rabbinic responses to personal questions by hundreds of different individuals. The assimilated Jews, however, acted out of a planned and organized program. In addition, the motives of the Orthodox rabbis and of secular Jewry were dramatically opposed to one another. The Orthodox rabbis in their personal responses fought to preserve traditional Judaism, while the assimilationists wanted to systematically weaken or destroy it. The masses of Jewry in the middle seemingly ignored both and adopted new policies and agendas, based on their own perception of self-preservation and advancement.

From 1881 until the start of the First World War in 1914, America remained the goal for millions of Jews in Eastern Europe. There were Jews who were unable to find comfort in their new environment and returned to Europe. There were many others who found the "Golden Land" disappointing, harsh, and alien, and who wrote home to their families expressing these negative reactions. Nevertheless, there was almost nothing that could dim the general enthusiasm of Eastern European Jewry about America. Cynics among the Jews did not even feel it sacreligious to conclude their Passover Seder by saying, "Next

---

20. A secular leader and spokesman for Russian Jewry. Assimilated, pompous, enormously wealthy, he contributed huge sums of money to help Jews resettle in Russia itself. He was born in 1833 and died in 1909.

21. Sanders, *Shores of Refuge,* p. 90.

22. Emigration from Europe, support of political Zionism, public demonstrations against discriminatory governments — these are just some of the many issues that are examples of this curious phenomenon in Jewish life of the last century. Naturally, there were exceptions to this behavior pattern on certain issues and by certain individuals, but in the main, the phenomenon has held.

year in America."[23] The famous Yiddish secularist author and humorist, Sholom Aleichem,[24] wrote in one of his novels:[25]

> . . . One could surmise that these were emigrants, because one could hear the words, "escort," "Hamburg," "ship ticket," "America." The word "America" was heard more often than any other. The word "America" had for them a special magnetism, a kind of magical meaning. It stood for an ideal of which many, many had long dreamed. They imagined America to be a kind of heaven, a sort of Paradise.

The impetus for this swelling immigration was, naturally, the terrible situation of Jews in Russia. The pogroms, poverty, discrimination, and horror that marked the Jewish condition in Russia convinced hundreds of thousands of Jews to vote with their feet. In historical retrospect, it is clear that only disaster lay ahead for Eastern European Jewry. America provided opportunities unimagined in Jewish Russia, and that basic fact soon was perceived by the masses of Jewry groaning under the yoke of the Czar. The flood of immigrants to America would be stemmed only when the United States adopted restrictive immigration policies in the 1920s. By then, it would already be too late for millions of Jews imprisoned in the new Russia and persecuted in resurrected Poland.

---

23. Quoted by Sanders, p. 151, from Mary Antin's memoirs, *The Promised Land* (Boston 1912) p. 141.

24. The pen name of Solomon Rabinowitz (1859-1916). He left Russia in 1905, and died and is buried in New York. He was known as the "Jewish Mark Twain," and was a very popular Yiddish author. Though he was thoroughly secular in outlook and anti-traditional in behavior, he nevertheless captured much of the essence of traditional Eastern European Jewish life in his characters and writings.

25. Quoted in *Shores of Refuge*, p. 227, from Sholom Aleichem's novel *In the Storm* translated by Aliza Shevrin, pp. 215-216 (New York 1984).

23
Return to Zion

The First Aliyah

N THE 1880S NOT ALL Russian Jews leaving Europe were heading for America. A small but steady stream of Jews were bound for home — the Land of Israel. The Jewish presence in Palestine had been small but constant throughout all the centuries of exile. Major Jewish immigration into Palestine occurred after the expulsion of the Jews from Spain. In the late eighteenth and early nineteenth centuries, Eastern European Jews, mainly the students of the early Chassidic masters and the disciples of the Gaon of Vilna, settled in Safed, Tiberias, Hebron, and Jerusalem. They soon became an important force in the country, not only as far as their Sephardic brethren were concerned, but they were also noticed by the Turkish authorities, who then ruled the country in their usual corrupt and cruel manner.

These Eastern European Jews laid the foundation for what would be known as the *Yishuv HaYashan*.[1] These pious, holy people, who sacrificed so much to realize their personal dream and preserve the historic link of Jewry to its homeland, acted as spiritual agents for all Jews and thus understandably expected to be spiritually and financially supported by the Jews of the Exile.[2] Few of them could maintain themselves financially in the backward economy and under the despotic Moslem rule in the Holy Land.

---

1. The *Old Settlers*. This name was meant to differentiate them from the *Yishuv HaChadash* — the new settlers, who were to come at the end of the nineteenth century and who represented completely different social, religious, and national values.

2. See Menachem Friedman, *Chevrah V'Dat* (Jerusalem 1978), Chapter 1, for a detailed analysis of this sometimes strained symbolic relationship between the *Yishuv HaYashan* and the Jews who remained in Eastern Europe or emigrated to America.

In 1890, Rabbi Yosef Chaim Sonnenfeld, later rabbi of Jerusalem, likened the *Yishuv HaYashan* to an army stationed away from home to defend its nation's interest. Clearly, the troops are entitled to be supported by the country they serve. The famous charity known as Rabbi Meir Baal Haness[3] was the vehicle of financial support for much of the *Yishuv HaYashan*. Various *kollelim*[4] existed in Palestine, and each received money regularly from the Jewish communities of the Exile, particularly from their hometowns and native countries. This money was distributed by the elders of the *Yishuv HaYashan* to the constituent families of the separate *kollelim*. This system, by which the *Yishuv HaYashan* subsisted, was called *chalukah* — the Hebrew word for distribution or dividing.

This program was an expression of the historic Jewish concepts of supporting Torah scholars and also assisting the needy, but in the

3. Named after the legendary *tanna* Rabbi Meir, (second-century Palestine,) who was famous for his miraculous protective powers and his love of the Land of Israel.

4. Study and social groups, usually organized according to the different countries of origin in Europe, who together formed the *Yishuv HaYashan*.

*Ashkenazic Jews of
Yishuv HaYashan
at the
Western Wall,
circa 1900*

Rabbi Shmuel Salant

propaganda broadsides of the enemies of the *Yishuv HaYashan*, *chalukah* became a derisive term somewhat akin to "living on the dole" or "welfare." Naturally, there were severe defects in the *chalukah* system of support of the *Yishuv HaYashan*. In some instances, not all funds were distributed equitably, not all recipients were honest and sincere or worthy, and not enough money was ever raised and sent to Palestine to support the community in even a minimal fashion. But these were human and organizational failings that are indigenous to all social programs that distribute money broadly. Nevertheless, the system did function after a fashion, and it was the mainstay of Jewish life in Palestine in the 1800s.

By 1840, when Rabbi Shmuel Salant assumed the leadership of the *Yishuv HaYashan* in Jerusalem, the Jews were already a majority of the population in the Holy City.[5] Jewish immigration to Palestine continued slowly but regularly, and by 1880 there were 25,000 Jews in Palestine, with almost 17,000 of them living in Jerusalem.[6] They were approximately 10% of the entire population of Palestine at that time.[7]

The Jews lived under terrible physical circumstances. Poverty, disease,[8] and the barrenness of the land itself all combined to make life

5. See the remarkable book by Joan Peters, *From Time Immemorial*, New York 1984, p. 485, note 126, referring to 1840: "The population of the City of Jerusalem is computed at 15,000, of whom about 4,500 are Moslems, 8,000 Jews, and the rest Christians of various dominations."

6. Conor Cruise O'Brien, *The Siege* (New York 1986), p. 31.

7. Peters, p. 161.

8. The eye disease trachoma was especially prevalent among Jews in Palestine, in the nineteenth century. Cholera epidemics were also balefully common.

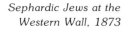

Sephardic Jews at the Western Wall, 1873

extremely difficult for the inhabitants of Palestine. But the worst cruelty for Jews was the Moslem institution of *dhimmi*.[9] A *dhimmi* is an infidel, anyone who is not a Moslem. The prophet Mohammed proclaimed in the Koran that "two religions may not dwell together." This was pragmatically interpreted in the Moslem world as meaning that two religions may not dwell together in equal status.[10] Though non-Moslem religions and its adherents were allowed to exist in the Moslem society, they could do so only in an inferior role and purely in a subsidiary state, many times being outside the protection of the law. Therefore, it is completely logical that, in 1858, when a Moslem in Hebron was confronted with his theft and vandalism of Jews, he would state that it was "his right derived from time immemorial in his family to enter Jewish houses, and take toll or contributions at any time without giving account."[11]

The persecution of the defenseless Jewish minority in Palestine by the Turkish rulers and the Arab inhabitants of the country was constant, vicious, capricious, and violent. In 1839, the British Consul in Jerusalem, W.T. Young, reported: ". . . scarcely a day passes that I do not hear of some act of tyranny and oppression against a Jew . . . In two instances, I have succeeded in obtaining justice for Jews against Turks — but it is quite a new thing in the eyes of these people to claim justice for a Jew . . ."[12] Yet the Jews continued to come, impelled by their inner awakening to the possibility of realizing in person the dream of the ages.

---

9. See below, Chapter 31, for more details about this.
10. Peters, p. 175.
11. Ibid., p. 175.
12. Ibid., p. 187.

Mishkenot Shaananim

Jewish structure in the Land of Israel began to take shape in spite of all the obstacles of poverty and discrimination. In 1855, Sir Moses Montefiore purchased land in Jerusalem for a Jewish settlement west of the walls of the Old City.[13] In 1854, the Misgav Ladach Hospital was opened, followed by the Bikur Cholim Hospital and the Chabad Beit Menachem Study House in 1858. A Jewish poorhouse, Batei Machseh, was also in operation before 1860. In 1864, the famous Hurva Synagogue was rebuilt and rededicated in the heart of the Jewish quarter of the Old City of Jerusalem. In that same year the Evelina de Rothschild Girls School was opened. In 1868, Jewish Jerusalem boasted twenty-one synagogues while the Moslem population had only eleven mosques and the Christians twenty-one churches and convents.[14]

The Jews, however, as is their wont, were badly divided among themselves. Not only was there palpable tension between the Ashkenazic and Sephardic communities, but the competition between the various *kollelim* and segments of the Ashkenazic community itself was highly divisive and unaccountably fierce. The *maskilim* also attempted to establish "new" schools in Jerusalem and infiltrate the community, thus adding to the Ashkenazic strife. Even though Rabbi Shmuel Salant was the titular rabbinic leader of Jerusalem, he found it hard to establish harmony.

The famous British archaeologist and explorer, Charles Warren, in his memoirs concerning his Jerusalem project, wrote in 1876: "There is an irrepressible pride and presumption about this fragile wayward people of Ashkenaz that I could not help but admire; dressed in greasy rags they stalk about the Old City with as much dignity as though they were dressed in the richest garments and give way to no one; years of oppression have in no way quelled their ancient spirit and if they could only be induced to work and become united, they would be a very formidable race, for their courage and fortitude makes up for the want of [physical] stamina."[15] Great rabbinic figures[16] from Europe continued to arrive in Jerusalem throughout the 1800s and this constantly

---

13. Now the neighborhoods of Mishkenot Shaananim and Yemin Moshe in Jerusalem. Located nearby is the legendary Montefiore windmill.

14. Martin Gilbert, *Jerusalem History Atlas*, New York 1977, p. 47.

15. Ibid., p. 50.

16. Among them were Rabbi Meir Auerbach (*Imrei Binah*), Rabbi Chaim Berlin (the son of the *Netziv* of Volozhin), Rabbi Yitzchak Blaser (disciple of Rabbi Yisrael Salanter and former rabbi of St. Petersburg), Rabbi Yehoshua Leib Diskin (rabbi of Brisk), and Rabbi Eliyahu David Rabinowitz-Tumim (the *Aderes,* formerly rabbi of Slutzk and Ponivezh and the father-in-law of Rabbi Abraham Y. Kook).

revitalized the community, though also indirectly contributing to its further fragmentation and divisiveness.

The Jews of Jerusalem saw themselves as a holy community. They lived a life of piety, simplicity, self-help and goodness. In spite of persecution and poverty, they felt themselves fortunate and were joyously honored at being Jerusalemites. They felt themselves charged with the holy task of preserving, through Torah, prayer, and piety, the Jewish presence in the Holy City until the Messianic age would arrive.

Rabbi Tzvi Hirsch Kalischer

The disciples of the Gaon of Vilna and the Baal Shem Tov had planted a holy seed in Jerusalem and their descendants were determined to have it survive, grow, and flourish. Understandably, they were fiercely protective about their Jerusalem, seeing it not only as a physical place, but equally as an ideal of holiness and Godly service. Jerusalem had once again become a living center for the Jewish world.

In the late 1870s and early 1880s there arose in Russia a strong support movement for emigration to Palestine. The movement itself was called the *Chibath Zion* and it adherents were *Chovevei Zion* — Lovers of Zion. Thus, twenty years before the advent of Herzl and political Zionism, an organization devoted to Jewish emigration from Russia to Palestine was formed. Its purpose was not only to support the Jews who had already arrived in Palestine and settled there, but to encourage and facilitate large-scale group emigration from Russia to the Land of Israel. The goal was not political, but to foster Jewish agricultural settlement in the Land wherever possible.

In 1884, the loosely formed local groups of the *Chovevei Zion* gathered in Katowice, Poland, to form a united national organization. The titular leader of the movement was Dr. Leon Pinsker.[17] The movement benefited from strong rabbinic participation as well. Rabbi Tzvi Hirsch Kalischer,[18] who died before this meeting in Katowice, was nevertheless universally recognized as one of the leaders of *Chovevei Zion*. Rabbi Naftali Tzvi Yehuda Berlin of Volozhin was also known as a strong supporter of the goals of *Chovevei Zion*. Many famous rabbis of Russia regularly signed public letters on behalf of *Chovevei Zion*,[19] and

17. The author of *Auto-Emancipation*. He was a secular Jew. See Chapter 21.

18. 1795-1874. He was the man who convinced the Alliance Israelite Universelle to found the first new Jewish agricultural school and farming community in Palestine in 1870. It was called Mikveh Yisrael, and was located near Jaffa.

19. Among them were Rabbi Yitzchak Feigenbaum of Warsaw, Rabbi Yosef Dov Ber Halevi Soloveitchik of Slutzk and later of Brisk, Rabbi Yisrael Morgenstern, the Chassidic *Rebbe* of Pilov-Kotzk; Rabbi Meir Leibush Malbim, and Rabbi Akiva Yosef Schlesinger (Lev Halvri) of Hungary and later of Jerusalem. See *Sorbanei Geulah* by Chaim Koolitz, Jerusalem 1987, pp. 69-72, for further details.

Rabbi Shmuel Mohilever

Baron Edmond
de Rothschild
on a visit
to Palestine

perhaps the most dynamic leader of the movement was Rabbi Samuel Mohilever of Bialystok. It was he who interested Baron Edmond de Rothschild[20] in the cause of Jewish colonization in Palestine.

Beginning in 1881, Rothschild founded or adopted numerous Jewish settlements in Palestine. These included Ekron, Gadera, Rishon LeZion, Zichron Yaakov, Rosh Pina, Yesod Hamaala, Metulla and Hadera, all established before the age of political Zionism. In 1878, Petach Tikva was founded, and peopled principally by Orthodox Jews from Jerusalem. The Carmel Wine Company[21] was founded in 1882 and Rothschild gave it the necessary financing and patience that allowed it to develop successfully.[22]

All of this spurred a group of Jews to begin systematic emigration from Russia to Palestine. The group called itself BILU[23] and formed the nucleus of what was the First Aliyah[24] — the first wave of modern major immigration to Palestine. Between 1881 and the beginning of the First

---

20. Known as the *Nadiv HaYadua* — "the renowned philanthropist," Rothschild invested over seventy million gold francs in his "colonies," which he eventually turned over to the colonists themselves. He was born in 1845 and died in 1934.

21. Called Carmel Oriental (Eastern Carmel) to differentiate it from Rothschild's other, western, Carmel Wine Company in France.

22. He also provided vine cuttings from his French vineyards to begin the grape plantings in the Land of Israel.

23. The acronym for the Hebrew words of the Bible *"Bais Yaakov Lechu V'nailchah"* (Isaiah 2:5): "House of Israel, let us go forth." The balance of that verse, *Be'or Hashem*, "in the light of God," was significantly omitted from their slogan.

24. The First Aliyah lasted approximately from 1881 to 1903. The emigration from 1904 to 1914 is characterized as the Second Aliyah.

Chovevei Zion, 1880

World War, over 60,000 Jews left Eastern Europe and settled in Palestine.

The influence of *Chovevei Zion* was itself very strong, especially in the circles of the young, idealistic, and secular Jews. The older, more traditional Jews continued to emigrate to Jerusalem, Jaffa, Safed, Tiberias and Hebron under the aegis of the *Yishuv HaYashan* and the *chalukah* system. But they were inundated by the great flow of new immigrants that arrived, imbued with the ideology of *Chovevei Zion*, and later, political Zionism.

Petach Tikva, the first moshavah, 1883

Chovevei Zion itself was torn by internal dissension. The issues that caused its division have remained acutely alive for a century. They go to the heart of the Jewish existence in the nineteenth and twentieth centuries. Shall Jews be traditional, observant, and in continuity with all previous Jewish history, or shall they be secular, humanist, and radically different from all previous Jewish generations? Shall Jews struggle to have an independent, political state only in Palestine, or may it be elsewhere? Shall they endeavor to create an autonomous, spiritual, or cultural center for themselves under the sovereignty of a benevolent non-Jewish political entity and forsake national sovereignty? Shall the Jewish nation strive to be a "light unto the nations" or shall it be a "normal" people — "like all other nations shall be the house of Israel"?

Asher Ginsburg,[25] better known by his pen name *Achad Ha'am,* was the enfant terrible of *Chovevei Zion.* He ridiculed the national aspirations of the movement and its support of colonies, farms, and nation-building in Palestine. He contended that the solution for the Jewish problem lay in "preparing and uplifting hearts," creating a new Jewish culture based on Hebrew language and literature, and erecting in Palestine a Jewish spiritual center that would re-educate the Jewish people in the light of the new ideas of the modern world.

He believed that no Jewish state in Palestine, by itself, could alleviate the Jewish problem. In fact it would probably exacerbate it. Only secular spirituality, cultural excellence, and moral probity would impress the world with the correctness of the Jewish position in society, and thus ameliorate anti-Semitism and solve the "Jewish problem." This naive and fanciful view of the Jewish situation did not appeal to the masses of Israel. But *Achad Ha'am* wielded great influence among the small, vital, influential Jewish intelligentsia of his time, and his unlikely prescription for Jewish success still had its adherents in the Jewish world a century later.

Many of the secular and religious Jewish leaders who supported the ideal of *Chovevei Zion* strove mightily to prevent the spirit of messianism from permeating the movement and its efforts. Most of the founders of *Chovevei Zion* saw Jewish settlement in Palestine as a realistic, attainable, and logical method of helping alleviate the "Jewish problem" in the late 1800s, but they recognized that the lesson of the false messiah was irrevocably a part of the collective Jewish psyche. As such, there was great caution in characterizing the ongoing emigration from Russia

---

25. 1856-1927. His main base of support and operations was in Odessa, Russia.

and the new settlements in Palestine as being part of the process of "the end of days."[26] Pinsker and the secularists, who did not believe in the Messiah, could not, in good conscience, dress the return to Zion in messianic garb. Their denial of tradition forced them to take a cold, realistic, evolutionary approach to Jews resettling Palestine. They were bound to think of the project in Western, secular terms — nationalism, economic development, and social progress. There was no room for the Son of David in their world or plans.

Initially, the religious Jews who supported *Chovevei Zion*, in the main, also refused to encourage messianic hopes. But the situation of the Jews, both physically and spiritually, was far too fragile to support such a wild dream of nationhood on a purely secular and logical basis. The true strength of the idea and its public popularity rested on a spiritual and traditionally religious foundation. It was the Torah of the Jew, its commandments and customs that made Jerusalem and the Land of Israel central and unique to Jews in distant exiles. It was the mystery, the spirituality, the supernatural character of Jerusalem that drove Jews towards it. And *Chovevei Zion*, therefore, was basically a "religious" movement, even though it possessed a clear majority of secular, agnostic leadership. This paradox would haunt *Chovevei Zion* and lead to its undoing, as a mass movement, in the late 1800s. It would also be the cause of the schizophrenia of its successor, political Zionism.

Because of the "religious" basis of the movement, the spirit of messianism could not be completely contained. The main prophet of the return to Zion as being not merely a practical answer to the "Jewish problem," but as the beginning of the messianic process, was the Yugoslavian rabbi, Yehudah Alkalai.[27] He was active in promoting the projects of Sir Moses Montefiore and of the Alliance Israelite Universelle in the Land of Israel. In his major work, *Raglei M'vasser*,[28] he called for "tithing" by the Jewish people. Ten percent of the Jews in Europe should now emigrate to the Land of Israel and ten percent of all Jewish material assets should be invested in the new Jewish settlements in Palestine. In

---

26. The phrase of the Prophets of Israel that describes the Messianic Era. However, both Rabbis Kalischer and Alkalai did write and speak in terms of "hastening the messianic redemption."

27. 1798-1878.

28. *The Footsteps of the Bearer of Good Tidings.* This book, written in flawless Hebrew, contained a great deal of mystical and kabbalistic thought. It was a spiritual call for the rebirth of messianism among the Jewish people. As such, it was naturally controversial and received very mixed reviews from the rabbis of Israel. Rabbi Tzvi Hirsch Kalischer also spoke in terms of "hastening the Messianic redemption."

his words, "All of the time limits [for the arrival of Messiah] have already expired. Only the return of the Jewish people to the Land of Israel is lacking — that will be the national repentance of the Jewish people, and through this, Israel will accept God's sovereignty and rule. Let us only return to our Holy Land."[29]

This message struck deep echoes in the Jewish public.[30] The longing for Zion, the hope for the appearance of the long-delayed Messiah, the supernatural belief in the redemption of Israel from its long and painful exile, all combined to give the *Chovevei Zion* movement a messianic quality that its leaders had striven to avoid. Jews identified with the romanticism of Rabbi Alkalai more than with the prosaic and pedantic plans of Dr. Pinsker.

Boon or Bane

HERE WAS AN INTENSELY NEGATIVE reaction to Jewish emigration to Palestine in general, and to *Chovevei Zion* in particular. This was brought on by the movement's tinge of Messianism, its belief that the redemption would be brought closer by practical efforts alone, without spiritual renewal and Torah observance, its close association with agnostics and atheists, and the prominent role of the philosophy of secularism in the return to Zion.

Rabbi Moshe Teitelbaum[31] of Uheli, Rumania/Hungary, had already declared in the early part of the nineteenth century, "I am convinced that it is the will of God that we should not emigrate to the Land of Israel now, of our own volition. Rather we are to wait here in the exile until the day when our righteous Messiah will lead us to our land."[32] It must be noted that this statement was made over sixty years

---

29. Koolitz, p. 66.

30. The great seminal thinker of Chassidus in the late nineteenth century, Rabbi Tzadok HaCohen of Lublin, wrote of these times that "it is the period of the footsteps of the Messiah." See his *Tzidkas HaTzaddik*, §46. Yet he was determinedly anti-Zionist after the founding of that movement, stating, "I fear lest my departure and ascent to Jerusalem might seem like a gesture of approval for Zionist activity . . . I will not move from my place. I will not ascend for the sake of the Zionists." See Johnson, p. 403.

31. 1759-1841. Known by the title of his famous books of *halachah* and Chassidus, *Yismach Moshe*. The founder of the famous Teitelbaum dynasty, which is today represented primarily by the followers of the *Rebbe* of Satmar.

32. Koolitz, p. 69.

before the birth of secular, political Zionism. Thus, the later opposition to Zionism by sections of traditional Jewry was one of principle, and not a mere reaction to the secular leadership of that movement. Rabbi Teitelbaum's grandson, Yekusiel Yehudah of Sighet,[33] attempted to forcibly prevent Jews from emigrating to Palestine. When Rabbi Akiva Yosef Schlesinger[34] planned his journey, the rabbi of Sighet ordered, according to Schlesinger, that "whoever will help me emigrate to the Land of Israel is to be likened unto one that helps strengthen paganism!"[35]

Thus was the issue of the return to Zion the source of divergent visions. Was it messianism or paganism? Was it the salvation or the destruction of the Jewish people? The answers to these questions were in doubt, and became the source of bitter dispute among Jews for the next century. But in spite of all of the controversy, Jews kept on coming to the Land of Israel. Between 1883 and 1887, eight new Jewish suburbs were established west of the walls of old Jerusalem. In 1888, Kfar Hashiloah, a Jewish Yemenite[36] village, was founded south of Jerusalem. Another ten new Jewish villages were formed in the early 1890s and the Jewish presence in Palestine generally, and around Jerusalem specifically, became more pronounced. The fateful return to Zion was irrevocably in motion by the early 1890s. With the coming of the Zionist movement, it would take on a new impetus, a different direction, and a great urgency.

The impending struggle over the nature of the Jewish colonization of Palestine was reflected in the halachic dispute over the observance of *Shemittah*[37] — the Sabbatical year of agricultural rest — which fell in the year 1889. In 1882, the previous *Shemittah* year, there were very few Jewish farmers in Palestine, and those few farmers did indeed allow their fields to lie fallow during the Sabbatical year. However, the rapid increase in new Jewish farming settlements in the mid-1880s, forced

---

33. 1808-1883. Known by his works on Torah called *Yetev Lev*. One of the eminent Chassidic leaders of his era.

34. Author of *Lev Halvri* and a prominent Hungarian rabbi.

35. Koolitz, p. 70. See also *Chassidus V'shivas Tzion* by Yitzchak Alfasi, Tel Aviv, 1976, p. 14, for the opinions of other great Chassidic leaders in support of Rabbi Teitelbaum's opposition to Jewish emigration to Palestine.

36. A harbinger of the great Yemenite emigration to Israel in the twentieth century.

37. The seventh year, the Sabbatical year, when the land in Israel was biblically ordained to lie fallow for that year. Various halachic opinions as to the theoretical validity of that biblical law after the destruction of the Temple have always existed, but the question never became a real one, practically speaking, until the 1880s, with the new advent of the agricultural settlements of Baron Rothschild and *Chovevei Zion*.

the rabbis aligned with *Chovevei Zion* to face the problem of the forthcoming *Shemittah*, 1889. The settlers, their sponsor, Baron Rothschild, and most of the leadership of *Chovevei Zion* claimed that the entire project of new agricultural settlements for Jews in Palestine would collapse if the land of the existing settlements would not be tilled that year.

The threat of the closure of the existing settlements and of the withdrawal of Baron Rothschild's continued support forced a meeting of the rabbinical trustees of *Chovevei Zion* in Vilna, in the fall of 1887.[38] Two of these trustees, Rabbis Mordechai Eliasberg of Brisk and Shmuel Mohilever of Bialystok, undertook to publish a halachically sound *heter*[39] to allow the fields to be tilled in 1889.[40] The third trustee, the renowned *Netziv*[41] of Volozhin, opposed any such *heter*. The *heter* was nonetheless published over the signatures of Rabbi Yehoshua of Kutna,[42] Rabbi Shmuel Mohilever, and Rabbi Shmuel Zanvil Klepfish of Warsaw. The *heter* was further strengthened by a long, legal, halachic discourse supporting it, which was published in 1888 by Rabbi Yitzchak Elchanan Spector of Kovno.[43] However, it was bitterly opposed by the Rabbis of Jerusalem, as well as by the *Netziv*,[44] Rabbi David Friedman of Karlin, Rabbi Yosef Dov Ber Soloveitchik of Brisk,[45] and Rabbi Samson Raphael Hirsch.

The furor over this *heter* weakened the organization of *Chovevei Zion*. It also revealed the basic division in the attitude of religious Jewry to the new settlements, and especially to the nature of the "new Israel"

---

38. For a detailed description of this meeting and an excellent review of the entire dispute over the *Shemittah*, see Rabbi Shlomo Shternberg, *Heter 5649,* Tel Aviv 1986.

39. Literally, permission.

40. It is beyond the parameters of this book to discuss this matter in detail, since it is a most intricate halachic problem. Suffice it to say that the *heter* is based on the temporary sale of the Jewish land to a non-Jewish buyer for a period of time overlapping the *Shemittah* year itself. The *heter* itself, originally, was portrayed as being temporary in nature and duration, and not self-renewing for future Sabbatical years.

41. Rabbi Naftali Tzvi Yehuda Berlin.

42. One of the renowned rabbinic figures of Poland.

43. The acknowledged leading rabbinic expert, or *posek*, in Jewish law of his age.

44. Whose credentials as a prominent supporter of *Chovevei Zion* removed any suspicion of political or public policy motives.

45. For more particulars, see Rabbi Yechiel Michel Tykocinsky, *Sefer HaShemittah,* Jerusalem, 5th printing, 1980, pp. 59-62.

being then formed in the Holy Land. Underlying the purely halachic question of the possibility of the observance of the *Shemittah* in the new settlements were the great social questions of the viability of the *chalukah* system, Jewish labor as somehow being self-redemptive, and "accommodating" Judaism to new realities.[46] The *heter* was renewed in 1896 — this time to less objections, a third time in 1903 — to even fewer objections, and again in 1910. Those who opposed it on halachic grounds were not won over, but the practice had become routine among those who employed it.[47] However, the controversy continued to surface and has never really been settled, neither halachically nor politically.[48] This merely indicates how intractable the problems of *Chovevei Zion* remain even a century later. Thus, the return to Zion would be a perilous one, physically, socially, and religiously. But the return was on.

---

46. See Shternberg, pp. 1-13 in his introduction.

47. To support the *heter* of 1910, Rabbi Avraham Yitzchak Kook, who was then the rabbi of Jaffa in Palestine, wrote his famous book, *Shabbas HaAretz*. Rabbi Kook was bitterly criticized for his support of this *heter* by some of the rabbis of Jerusalem and by Rabbi Yaakov David Willovsky (known as the *Ridvaz*) of Safed.

48. Since the establishment of the State of Israel, the *heter* has been institutionalized by the Chief Rabbinate of Israel and has become, for all practical intent, self-renewing. However, the number of farms and farmers not relying on the *heter*, and the percentage of Jewish land left fallow on the *Shemittah*, has steadily increased. The trend away from the *heter* began with the arrival of the *Chazon Ish* in the 1930s and his original research work on the laws of the Sabbatical year. The trend accelerated sharply in the 1970s and 80s until, during the *Shemittah* of 1987, the State of Israel imported large quantities of grain to satisfy the needs of those who would not rely on the *heter*.

24
Political Zionism

The Dreyfus Affair

HE END OF THE NINETEENTH century brought great drama and significant events to world Jewry, but almost all of these were enormously sad. The arena for these events was not Eastern Europe as would have been expected, but rather Western Europe. The Jews of France, Germany, and Austria had already enjoyed equal rights for decades. The process of Reform and assimilation had accelerated in these countries. Only some five hundred Jews out of the entire Jewish population of France, excluding Alsace, were Orthodox in the 1890s.[1] Christian rituals were introduced into the Reform Temples of France. By 1865, an organ was part of the religious services, rabbis dressed like priests, and Sabbath services were held on Sunday.[2] In spite of becoming more French than the French, the Jews of France were very uncomfortable, because organized political, national anti-Semitism became part of French life in the 1880s.

In 1886, Edward Drumont[3] published a virulently anti-Semitic book, *La France Juive,* and the book ran into one hundred and twenty-one editions within one year of its first publication, and became the most widely read book in France.[4] In 1892, he founded a successful anti-Semitic daily newspaper, *La Libre Parole.* He perpetuated the blood libel, the "fact" that the Jews were still crucifying

---

1. Desmond Stewart, *Theodor Herzl,* London 1974, p. 143.
2. Ibid.
3. 1844-1917.
4. Conor Cruise O'Brien, *The Siege*, New York 1986, p. 63.

Christianity in the nineteenth century, and the myth of the Elders of Zion controlling the world.[5]

Le Pouvoir Civil

A cartoon representing the anti-French Jewish "conspiracy"

His views were accepted in many strata of French society, but nowhere was his work more popular than with the officer corps of the French army. The three hundred Jewish officers of the French army were subjected to regular ridicule, insult, and discrimination by their professional colleagues. Stung by the anarchists and pacifists of the left, humiliated by its complete defeat in the Franco-Prussian War of 1870, the French army was frustrated, malevolent, and paranoid. One of its main enemies was the "Jewish influence" in French life. This made the military the logical candidate for an anti-Semitic incident. It would not be long in coming.

In October, 1894, Drumont's *La Libre Parole* published a report accusing a high-ranking officer of the French General Staff of providing military secrets to Germany. That officer was a Jewish captain of artillery, Alfred Dreyfus.[6] The French General Staff truly believed Dreyfus to be guilty, but it lacked the legal evidence necessary to confirm its suspicion.[7] Under the leadership of Major Hubert Joseph Henry and General Mercier, the Minister of War, a "secret file" was prepared of documents tying Dreyfus to the treason, and he was court-martialed. The file was based on fabricated and forged documents.[8] Nevertheless, the defense was never shown the "secret file" and the court-martial was heavily influenced by its secret introduction.

On December 21, 1894, the French court-martial, meeting *in camera*, found Dreyfus guilty of treason and sentenced him to life imprisonment on Devil's Island (the harsh penal colony in the Caribbean Sea), forfeiture of his military rank, and to public military

---

5. Ibid., p. 64.

6. 1859-1935. Dreyfus was a most unlikely villain and an even more unlikely hero. Cold, officious, pompous, wearing a pince-nez, he was not much of an officer and even less of a Jew. He was bewildered by the whole scandal surrounding him, and was pitiful in humiliation, and passive in promoting his own rehabilitation. Nevertheless, his name became synonymous with the Jewish problem, and his personal vindication became the barometer of Jewish democratic rights in Europe.

7. For a brilliant analysis of the Dreyfus trial and affair, see Barbara Tuchman, *The Proud Tower*, New York 1966, the chapter entitled "Give Me Combat."

8. Henry would commit suicide when the crime of his forgeries was uncovered.

Emile Zola

degradation. On January 3, 1895, Dreyfus was paraded through the streets of Paris to the jeers and abuse of the mob, many shouting "Death to the Jews," and in the courtyard of the Ecole Militaire he was stripped of his sword, his epaulets and his honor. Shipped off to the Caribbean hell-hole of Devil's Island, Dreyfus believed the incident had ended, as did his antagonists.

However, the matter was far from settled. France was divided into two camps — the Dreyfusards and the anti-Dreyfusards. Inexorably, the conflict about Dreyfus, the role of the Church and clericalism, and the acceptance of anti-Semitism as a fashion in French society drew the French intelligentsia and political leadership into active controversy. Emile Zola,[9] a leading Parisian journalist, published his famous "J'accuse"[10] in 1898, uncovering the miscarriage of justice and demanding the release and exoneration of Dreyfus. The furor over Dreyfus drove France close to open civil strife.

At last, in 1899, Dreyfus was returned from Devil's Island to stand trial at a second court-martial. In spite of the revelation of the forgeries

---

9. 1840-1902. Contrary to the anti-Semitic propaganda of the time, he was not Jewish.

10. Literally, "I accuse." On January 12, 1898, in the Parsian newspaper, *L'Aurore*, Zola accused, by name, leaders of the government and the military, charging them with illegal actions and conspiracy in the matter of the Dreyfus trial. Zola himself was tried for libel on the basis of his article, was convicted seven-to-five by the jury, and escaped to England to avoid the consequences of that conviction.

Dreyfus being stripped of his rank

and the conspiracy, and the public unmasking of the true culprits, the French army could still not admit its error publicly. The second trial also ended with a verdict of guilty against Dreyfus. However, the new sentence was no longer life imprisonment, but only five years — and the time he had served on Devil's Island was accepted as fulfillment of the terms of his penalty.

This second miscarriage of justice evoked international condemnation. It also continued the political and social turmoil in France itself. Eventually the Dreyfusards prevailed, as the Left came to political power and led the government. In 1906, Dreyfus was pardoned and promoted to major. However, his troubles had not ended. He was slightly wounded in an assassination attempt in 1908, and his attacker was acquitted in the trial that followed.[11] Dreyfus served as an artillery officer in the French army during World War I. He eventually retired from the army and died at the age of seventy-six, never appreciating the role Providence assigned him in history.

In Vienna, a new political party, the Christian Social Party, arose. It was headed by an urbane but malevolent Austrian, Karl Lueger,[12] who campaigned for mayor of Vienna on an openly anti-Semitic platform. He was elected mayor in May 1895, by an overwhelming

11. Tuchman, *The Proud Tower*, p. 262.
12. 1844-1910.

Dreyfus being reinstated as major

Theodor Herzl

majority. Though Lueger's bark was far worse than his bite, and he did prove to be an effective and fair administrator, his election chilled the ardor of many European Jews for the "new Europe." As a recent historian has stated so well: "The liberal reformist current of the nineteenth century, in which the Western Jews had put all their trust, had finally brought democracy to Vienna. And Viennese democracy had made it plain that it had no use for the Jews."[13]

Theodor Herzl

UT IT WAS TO BE another citizen of Vienna who would affect the course of Jewish history. Among the foreign press correspondents who witnessed Dreyfus' degradation was a journalist for Vienna's *Neue Freue Presse*,[14] Theodor Herzl.[15] Herzl himself was an assimilated Jew. He was born in Budapest and raised in Vienna, and he was the epitome of the new Jew of Europe, unfettered by tradition and Jewish observances. His grandfather, Simon Loeb Herzl,[16] was an observant Jew and a devoted disciple of Rabbi Yehudah Alkalai, the spiritual mentor of the *Chovevei Zion*. Theodor's father, Jacob,[17] and his mother, Jeanette,[18] were no longer observant, nor was Judaism an overriding concern in their lives. Though Theodor was the beneficiary of both the circumcision and *bar-mitzvah* ceremonies,[19] his attachment to Judaism was superficial. He knew no Hebrew and was ignorant of even the most rudimentary customs and traditions of Israel. There is even some doubt as to whether Theodor's wife, Julie,[20] was Jewish. In any event they were never married in a Jewish religious wedding ceremony.[21]

---

13. O'Brien, *The Siege,* p. 71.

14. A leading liberal newspaper, owned by assimilated Jews. It never acknowledged Herzl's role in the Zionist movement, or the movement itself, for that matter. It was *The New York Times* of its day.

15. 1860-1904.

16. 1805-1879.

17. 1835-1902.

18. Née Diamant, 1839-1911.

19. Theodor Herzl's only son, Hans, was not circumcised by his father, nor did he celebrate a *bar-mitzvah.*

20. Née Naschaner, 1868-1907.

21. See Desmond Stewart, *Theodor Herzl,* Appendix II, p. 373.

Herzl was a mediocre playwright but a journalist of note, a man of handsome visage and imposing presence. His height, high forehead, piercing eyes and great black beard combined with his personal grace, great intelligence and aura of authority to make him a most charismatic figure. As late as the early 1890s, Herzl himself advocated conversion to Christianity of all young Jewish children as the only solution to anti-Semitism and the "Jewish problem."[22] Ever the dramatist, Herzl even conceived of a grand parade and conversion ceremony that would include the princes of the Church and the leading Jewish citizens of the world (himself included).[23] However, the Dreyfus trial, with its public release of virulent anti-Semitism, changed Herzl's view of the "Jewish problem" and altered his professional life and career.

Herzl's solution to the "Jewish problem" was now simple, though yet apparently unrealistic — the Jews must have their own land. He composed a short book, *Der Judenstaat (The Jewish State)*,[24] in which he outlined in dramatic and utopian strokes the new Jewish homeland.

The state would resemble Venice, with a Rothschild as its first leader. The cities would be spacious, beautiful, well kept and filled with grand plazas and parks. The Jewish quarters from all of the cities of the world would be transported and rebuilt in their new land. German would be the official language of the new state and formal dress would be the vogue for all state functions.[25] All of this preposterous detail and sophomoric posturing did not dampen the ardor of the Jewish dreamers who read his book and responded to its message.

Many Jews instinctively felt that Herzl's solution was the only practical one to the "Jewish problem." A homeland was in fact possible and the Jews would set about to make the unrealistic real. Herzl called for a meeting of Jewish leaders to discuss the new homeland concept. A new name, "Zionism,"[26] was given to Herzl's concept. On August 29,

---

22. *The Complete Diaries of Theodor Herzl,* edited by Raphael Patai, Herzl Press, New York, p. 7.

23. Stewart, p. 142.

24. Published in Vienna by M. Breitenstein in 1906. A condensed version of the book appears in Arthur Hertzberg, *The Zionist Idea; a Historical Analysis and Reader,* Harper & Row, New York, 1959.

25. This fetish of Herzl for formal dress, top hats and tails, etc. was actually enforced by him at the first six Zionist Congresses. It was partially a reflection of his worship of imperial Germany and its ways.

26. The name was coined by Nathan Birnbaum, a leader of Jewish university students in Vienna in 1893, four years before the Zionist Congress met. Birnbaum later broke with Zionism and became one of the leading theoreticians and the general-secretary of the non-Zionist Agudath Israel movement.

1897, in the Municipal Casino of Basel, Switzerland,[27] the first Zionist Congress convened. Delegates from sixteen countries attended. Among them was Max Nordau,[28] of France, who would succeed Herzl as the head of the Zionist movement.

Much of Zionism's early program was the work of Nordau, who was shrewd, politically astute, and adept at language and compromise. Like Herzl, Nordau was an agnostic, if not an atheist. Both he and Herzl were elitists. Paradoxically, however, at the heart of the Zionist movement, even in its inception and certainly throughout its history, were the plain, simple, visionary Jews of Eastern Europe. Herzl deprecatingly called them his "army of *schnorrers* (beggars),"[29] but they, more than the assimilated, wealthy, sophisticated leaders of the Zionist movement, grasped the opportunity of Zionism. By combining this new political venture with their ancient belief in Zion and restoration, they eventually gave the Zionist movement its success.

The First Zionist Congress defined the purpose of Zionism: "To create for the Jewish people a home in Palestine secured by public law."[30] Herzl was not a particular patriot of Palestine as the Jewish State, as his later flirtation with Uganda reveals. Nevertheless, the "schnorrers" never really considered anywhere else but Jerusalem and the Land of Israel, and Herzl initially deferred to them.

The First Zionist Congress electrified the Jewish world, especially the Jews of Eastern Europe. Vast segments of Jewry disputed Zionism and its goals, but from 1897 on, no one could ignore it. Herzl was in a state of euphoria — "Were I to sum up the Basel Congress in a word — which I shall guard against pronouncing publicly — it would be this: At Basel, I founded the Jewish State. If I said this out loud today, I would be answered by universal laughter. Perhaps in five years, and certainly, in fifty, everyone will know it."[31]

Herzl gloried in the adulation extended to him. His ego was enormous, growing into a messianic view of himself. Though he never became an observant Jew, he did become more Jewish. He began to attend synagogue (though he still could not read Hebrew) and acquaint himself with rabbis and with Jewish tradition.

---

27. Herzl's original intent was to hold the meeting in Munich, Germany, but the Jewish community of the city, fearing that their German loyalty would be compromised, protested officially and Herzl withdrew.

28. 1849-1923.

29. Johnson, p. 399.

30. Stewart, p. 255.

31. *The Complete Diaries of Theodor Herzl,* p. 581.

Orthodox Opposition to Zionism

THE OPPOSITION TO ZIONISM by a great section of religious Jewry was uncompromising and fierce. Though there were many observant Jews among the delegates to the First Zionist Congress, including a number of famous rabbinic personalities, the Zionist movement itself, and its Congresses and organizations, was overwhelmingly secular. Eventually, the movement would become radically secular and anti-religious.[32]

Pious Jews had a number of philosophic and practical considerations for opposing Zionism. Foremost was the fear that the new movement would prove to be the substitute for the traditional spirit of Torah among the masses of Israel. This fear was fully realized in the

---

32. Johnson, p. 404, states, "This wide, though by no means universal, opposition of pious Jews to the Zionist program inevitably tended to push it more firmly into the hands of the secular radicals."

Second Zionist Congress in Basel, 1898

ensuing years of Zionist organization and publicity, during which the struggle to settle Palestine dominated Jewish life almost to the exclusion of all else. It would be brought into sharper focus when later Zionist Congresses proposed and enacted educational efforts, schools, camps, and seminars designed to promote a new "culture" among the Jews.[33] This new "culture" was, in the main, anti-religious, disrespectful of the Jewish past, and committed to create a "new Jew," who would be unfettered by the experiences of the Exile and the strictures of the Torah.

At the early Zionist Congresses, the Zionist movement professed to be neutral on matters of religion, but neutrality in halachic matters of religion automatically means opposition; to deny the authority of *halachah* on the basis of "neutrality" is to oppose it. So it was that Zionism became the vehicle that the remnants of the defeated *Haskalah* movement used to once again mount their attack against Jewish tradition. This time it was done in a much more successful and telling fashion. For basically, Zionism hijacked a religious idea, treasured and preserved by the Jewish people over long millennia of exile. Zionism cloaked this religious idea now in a purely secular guise. As such, it could prove lethal to the faith of Torah and the supremacy of *halachah* in Jewish life.

Zionism redefined the Jewish people. It was no longer a people based upon Sinai and revelation, upon Torah and tradition. It was rather to be a people with a shared "culture," this said "culture" being non-Jewish in origin and outlook, and dedicated to a goal of nationhood for the sake of nationhood itself.

Rabbi Saadyah Gaon's ancient statement that "our people is a nation by the virtue of our acceptance of the Torah" had been the foundation of Jewish life for millennia. Zionism denied this premise. "Our people is a nation because of culture, geography, nationalism, and persecution" was the new slogan of Zionism. It was an idea that religious Jewry could not accept. Even the Religious Zionist movement never agreed with this philosophy of Zionism, but rather attempted to adopt a pragmatic program of cooperation with the Zionist movement to bring about Jewish statehood and physical security. But many religious Jews shied away from even such a program, seeing only the new philosophy of Zionism, which they regarded as being wrong, dangerous, and ultimately self-destructive.

A second objection to the Zionist movement resulted from the assimilationist, agnostic backgrounds of its leaders. Could it be that

---

33. The "culture" program was adopted at the Second Zionist Congress in 1898.

salvation would come to Israel from people who did not eat kosher food, who did not observe the Sabbath, and who were illiterate in Jewish scholarship and Hebrew language? Not likely, said the leadership of religious Jewry. Whereas the *Chovevei Zion* — the Lovers of Zion — had strong rabbinic leadership, and even the *maskilim* who were part of that movement were mostly publicly observant Jews, the Zionist movement, with the exception of Ussishkin,[34] Reines,[35] and Fishman,[36] was led almost exclusively by non-observant Jews. This personal stigma of non-observance caused large numbers of Jews, who were pro-Zionist in their love of *Eretz Yisrael,* to turn away from the Zionist movement

---

34. Menachem Mendel Ussishkin (1863-1941) was a leading Russian Zionist. He opposed Herzl's brand of political Zionism and was much closer in spirit to the ideas of Achad Ha'am. Nevertheless, he took a powerful role in the development of the Zionist movement, the Jewish National Fund, and the Jewish Agency for Palestine. He was a most imposing figure, a gifted orator, and an observant Jew.

35. Rabbi Jacob Reines (1839-1915) was the Rabbi of Lida, Lithuania. A graduate of the Volozhin Yeshivah, he was a fine orator and a supporter of *Chovevei Zion*. In 1909, he founded the Mizrachi movement and can therefore be called the father of "Religious Zionism." In spite of his early enthusiasm for the Zionist movement, he later withdrew from public activity on its behalf, and devoted himself to the yeshivah that he established in Lida. That yeshivah, like its founder, was controversial. It included secular studies as part of its curriculum, and it was also Zionistically oriented. The famed "Meitcheter *Illui,*" Rabbi Shlomo Polatchek, was its *Rosh Yeshivah* for a time.

36. Rabbi Yehudah Leib Fishman (later Maimon) (1875-1952) was one of the founders and leaders of Mizrachi. A prolific writer and scholar, he devoted his life to the cause of Zionism, and was the Minister of Religions in the first Israeli government. He was also the founder of the famed publishing house, Mosad Harav Kook, and the editor of the scholarly Torah journal, *Sinai.* He owned one of the largest rabbinic, Hebraic libraries in the world and was a most influential person in Zionist and rabbinic circles. A strong fighter for his positions and a skilled political leader, he was also a most controversial person.

Early Mizrachi leaders. Rabbi Reines wears the top hat, and Rabbi Fishman is seated at extreme right

Rabbi Reines

itself. The very people who made Zionism appealing to the *maskilim* made it anathema to masses of pious Jews.

A third factor that led religious Jewry to reject political Zionism was its unclaimed and unspoken, but nevertheless inherent, messianic quality and message. Herzl himself did not believe in the idea of the Messiah but he did not shirk from the compliment of being called the Messiah.[37] In his public pronouncements, Herzl was careful to describe Zionism as a purely secular, nationalistic movement formed to solve a specific pragmatic problem — the homelessness and persecution of Jews. Zionism "was the solution of a human problem by secular human means."[38] However, the masses of Israel did not see the matter that way. To them, it was a movement that would somehow restore them to their ancient greatness and fulfill the lofty promises of the prophets. As such it had to be connected with the supernatural, with the messianic process, if not with the Messiah itself. Rabbi Reines, the founder of Mizrachi,[39] also explicitly denied the messianic nature of Zionism, *even of religious Zionism.*[40] In spite of this, the messianic element of Zionism preached by Alkalai and Kalischer was not stifled in the Mizrachi. The prevailing opinion in its circles eventually concurred with the later view of Rabbi Avraham Y. Kook,[41] that Zionism was somehow part of the Divine process of redemption that would lead to the coming of the Messiah. In the eyes of other great rabbinic leaders, therefore, Zionism could only be another false messiah in the guise of a national movement. There was nothing about Zionism that fit the traditional ideas of Jewry about the Messianic Era. The Messiah would have to be a person, and not an organization. That person would be a scholarly, observant Jew descended from the House of David. He would represent Torah and lead Jewry and the world towards spiritual repentance. None of the primary leaders of Zionism remotely fit that description. Therefore, Zionism had to be a false messiah, whose demise would be beneficial for the Jewish people.

---

37. Johnson, p. 399. See also Stewart, p. 201, quoting Herzl as being told on his visit to a synagogue in Sofia that he could turn his back on the Torah since — "you are holier than the Torah!" Herzl believed the blasphemy.

38. Johnson, p. 403.

39. The name of the largest political faction of religious Jewry within the Zionist movement.

40. See *Ish HaMoaroth* by Geulah Bat Yehudah, Jerusalem 1985, p. 81. "Our efforts towards settlement [of Palestine] have nothing to do with the [idea] of the [messianic] redemption of Israel."

41. See Chapter 28, "Palestine for Whom?" for more about him and his philosophy.

Herzl Makes Headway

IONISM WAS INDIGNANTLY REJECTED by Reform and assimilated Jews. They felt threatened by the charge of "dual loyalty," and had long ago discarded any attachment to Zion and Jerusalem. Afraid of the unknown, ashamed of their heritage and history, the Reform movement bitterly assailed Zionism as being anti-Jewish(!) and a throwback to ancient discredited aspirations. Reform was convinced that the solution to all Jewish ills lay in rapid and thorough assimilation. The Jews must become more European.

The return to Zion was opposed at every turn by Reform. Even the secular Zionists were too Jewish for Mendelssohn's heirs. They were joined in their opposition to Zionism by the assimilated, pseudo-Jewish establishment. The wealthy, philanthropic class of Jews led by Barons Hirsch and Rothschild opposed Herzl's scheme and considered Zionism dangerous to Jewish interests (as well as to their personal fortunes). Moritz Benedikt, the owner of Herzl's newspaper in Vienna, stated the case for Reform and assimilationist fears thus: "No individual has the right to take upon himself the tremendous moral responsibility of setting this avalanche in motion. We shall lose our present country (Austria) before we get a Jewish state."[42]

However, though unable to attract the Reform and assimilated, Herzl and Zionism nevertheless made considerable headway among the masses of Israel, who were traditional and strictly observant. The main reason for this was Herzl's ability to bring the problem of Jewish persecution and the solution of Zionism to the fore of the world scene. In less than a decade of public activity, Herzl met with the leaders of the world's great empires and actually negotiated with them on matters of Jewish interest.

Herzl was a master showman, and his efforts gave an appearance of movement, achievement, and success, even if no substantive accomplishments could be recorded. He used the anti-Semitism of Europe to convince his imperial hosts of the necessity for a Jewish homeland far from their borders. Vyacheslov Plevhe, the Czar's Minister of Interior and the enforcer of pogroms and discrimination

---

42. Johnson, p. 398. Benedikt's prediction was disastrously correct, though not quite in the way that he meant it.

against Russia's hapless Jews, told Herzl, "You are preaching to a convert . . . we would very much like to see the creation of an independent Jewish state capable of absorbing several million [Russian] Jews." [43]

The Kaiser of Germany, Wilhelm II, met twice with Herzl, once in Palestine itself.[44] He made vague promises to Herzl to try and influence his erstwhile ally, the Sultan of the Ottoman Empire, to allow a Jewish homeland in Palestine. Naturally, nothing came of this, and, in fact, the Kaiser himself was more interested in German colonization of Palestine than in a Jewish presence there. Herzl's visits to the Sultan achieved nothing, and they were almost lost in the Byzantine haze of corruption, sloth, and inertia that characterized the court of the Ottoman Emperor in the last decades of his empire. It was clear that no Moslem ruler of Palestine could look favorably on a Jewish national presence on "Moslem" territory.[45] Herzl was privately discouraged by his failures with the Sultan and the Kaiser. Publicly, however, he put an optimistic face on matters and continued his frenetic high-level diplomacy.[46]

---

43. Quoted by Johnson, p. 400.

44. There is a famous photograph of Herzl and the Kaiser in Palestine. Stewart, p. 272, feels that this photograph was not only contrived but actually doctored by Herzl to show him with the Kaiser, and thus to put him in a favorable political light.

45. In fact, as a consequence of Herzl's attempts to influence the Sultan, the rights of the Jews already living in Palestine in 1898 were severely curtailed by the Ottoman authorities. See Stewart, pp. 275 and 276. Turkey was much more accommodating in its negotiations with the non-Zionist Agudath Israel regarding the rights of Jews under its domain. During these discussions in 1917, the Turks committed themselves to the concept of post-War Jewish *religious* autonomy in Palestine. The Ottoman Empire was deathly afraid of Zionism, but the Turks lost the war — and Palestine.

46. Herzl also visited Pope Pius X who informed him: "We cannot give approval to this movement [Zionism]. We cannot prevent the Jews from going to Jerusalem but we can never sanction it. Jerusalem must not get into the hands of the Jews . . . If you will settle in Palestine and bring the other Jews with you we will prepare enough churches and priests to baptize all of them." See Koolitz, p. 73.

Uganda Unacceptable

ROM GERMANY AND TURKEY, Herzl now turned to England. There had been a great deal of romantic pro-Jewish feeling in certain aristocratic and literary circles in Victorian England.[47] Heroic Jewish figures appeared in the literature of England of the time and there was a fascination among many with the idea of a Jewish homeland. In the summer of 1902, Herzl met with Lord Rothschild in London and later with Joseph Chamberlain, the colonial secretary. These meetings provided the germ of the idea that a Jewish colony could be established, under British auspices and protection, in East Africa.[48] The place was called Uganda.[49]

At the Sixth Zionist Congress in 1903, Herzl announced that England had offered the Jews territory in British East Africa and that the colony there would be under Jewish autonomous control within the confines of the British Empire. This news split the Zionist movement. The Eastern European Jews, led by Chaim Weizmann,[50] revolted against Herzl. To them Zionism had only one meaning — Jerusalem and the Land of Israel. In holding this position, they reflected the feeling of the masses of Jewry.

Herzl, however, controlled the Congress, and it was agreed that the matter would be pursued and decided at the next Congress. In the interim, Herzl's health began to decline. He had heart trouble, his famous black beard was beginning to grey, his boundless energy began to flag, and his spirit was subdued. He had spent most of his sizable family fortune on the cause of Zionism and now money woes were an additional concern to him. By the time of the Seventh Zionist Congress

---

47. The prosaic, real Jews who lived in England during the nineteenth century were still subject to a great deal of bigotry, discrimination and abuse by English society. However, English anti-Semitism was much more discreet and less dangerous than the variety then in vogue in continental Europe.

48. Stewart, pp. 202-3.

49. The area under discussion approximates the borders of the current-day state of Kenya.

50. 1874-1952. Born in Motele, in the Pale of Settlement, Weizmann received a traditional Jewish education. As a young man he left for Berlin, where he graduated college as a chemist. He soon became an ardent Zionist and would devote his life to the cause of a Jewish state. In 1948 he was elected the first president of the State of Israel.

in the summer of 1905, when the Ugandan proposal would be voted upon, Herzl would be dead, and England itself would have had second thoughts. However, even after Herzl's death, England never formally rescinded its offer to consider Jewish colonization of Uganda.

The opposition to Uganda at the Seventh Congress, once again led by Weizmann and the Eastern European Zionists, was extremely strong, and for the first time in Zionist circles, Herzl — after his death — was attacked and bitterly criticized. Herzl, the assimilated Jew, who came to Zionism only as a result of the Dreyfus trial, never appreciated the depths of loyalty to Palestine and Jerusalem that fueled the Zionism of his Eastern European colleagues. To him, Zionism was not a religious concept nor an offshoot of Jewish history and tradition, but a new, pragmatic approach to the problem of Jewish suffering. Therefore, Uganda was acceptable, as any other possible territory would have been acceptable, as a Jewish home. He was committed to the Jewish State but not to the Jewish Land. His opponents, all of whom came from the traditional way of life of Jewish Eastern Europe, saw Zionism only in terms of the Land of Israel. They were not enticed by the prospect of a Jewish state anywhere else in the world, and rejected such a colony out of hand.[51]

Many delegates abstained from the Uganda vote out of respect to Herzl's memory,[52] but the final decision of the Congress was not to support any Jewish colonization efforts anywhere in the world except the Land of Israel. Herzl himself had concluded before his death that "Palestine is the only land where our people can come to rest."[53] Thus did the fulcrum of the Zionist movement move irrevocably east. Even though Max Nordau, the assimilated Western Jew, succeeded Herzl as the head of the movement, the control and policies of Zionism were now in the hands of Weizmann and the Eastern European Jews. Herzl's "army of *schnorrers*" had taken control of his aristocratic organization.

On July 3, 1904, Herzl died. The story of the fate of his family is one of unrelieved tragic and avenging irony. The Zionist movement established a large trust fund on behalf of his family. Not wanting to

---

51. Hence, this serves as a partial explanation of the failure of the so-called Jewish state of Birobidjan, established by the Bolsheviks in the 1920s — no echo whatsoever of the project survived among the masses of world Jewry. The fact that it was Communist, controlled by Stalin, and only artificially Jewish, also guaranteed its failure.

52. Among them, many members of the Mizrachi! See Geulah Bat Yehudah, *HaRav Maimon B'Doratav*, Jerusalem 1979, p. 126, and *Ish HaMoaroth*, p. 200.

53. Quoted by Johnson, p. 402.

endanger the investment, the Herzls bypassed the trust funds of their own Zionist movement, such as the Jewish National Fund and the Keren Hayesod, and invested the money in gilt-edged bonds of the Austro-Hungarian empire which, within a decade, would be worthless.

Herzl's widow died in 1907. His daughter Pauline suffered from illnesses, was addicted to morphine, and died in 1930, childless and alone. His son, Hans, suffered from mental disorders, was baptized as a Catholic in 1924, returned to Judaism, and committed suicide soon after Pauline's death.[54] He, too, died without progeny. Herzl's youngest daughter, Trude, was killed by the Germans in the "model" concentration camp, Theresienstadt, in 1943. Her sole son, Herzl's last descendant, committed suicide in 1946. Herzl's remains were removed from his Viennese tomb and reinterred in his grave on Mount Herzl in Jerusalem by the government of Israel.

---

54. Stewart, p. 339.

25

Social Revolution

Changing the World

HE DECADE PRECEDING World War I was more tumultuous than usual in the Jewish world. As the great powers jockeyed for position, provoked needless confrontations, and armed themselves for the coming struggle, oblivious to the consequences of their belligerent behavior, the Jewish reality in Europe was the continuing presence of unremitting, implacable anti-Semitism.

The pogroms in Russia were becoming more numerous and more savage. After the defeat of the Russians in the Russo-Japanese War, and the abortive revolution against the Czar, such organized anti-Semitic groups as the Black Hundreds held sway in the Pale of Settlement. Kishinev, Gomel, Kiev, and other Russian cities rocked to the violence and atrocities of the mindless enmity against the Jews. Vienna had elected an openly anti-Semitic mayor. The Kaiser of Germany vociferously expressed his disdain of Jews, even the assimilated ones of Germany. When the German press dared criticize one of his courtiers, Kaiser Wilhelm responded by blaming the press attacks on "Jewish insolence, slanders, and lying."[1] France was reeling from the Dreyfus struggle. And the most sinister form of European anti-Semitism — the "Jewish problem," the "conspiracy theory," the religious personification of Jews as being the social and economic Satan, while still guilty of deicide — was exported to the Ottoman Empire.

The diplomat, social critic and author, Conor Cruise O'Brien, is

---

1. Alan Palmer, *The Kaiser,* New York 1978, p. 125.

correct in stating that "The net result of the importation of European forms of anti-Semitism into the Middle East was to prove even more damaging to the Arabs than to the Jews."[2] It would prevent the Arabs from viewing the Jews and Zionism realistically and rationally. The myth of the conspiratorial, all-powerful and malevolent Jew became fixed in the Arab mind. It would haunt their psyche for the next century.

But initially and primarily it was the Jews who would suffer physically from this new attitude of malevolent conspiracy. The Jews worldwide, therefore, seemingly had no way out, and, in their despair, many of them adopted radical new means to change the situation. It was not sufficient for Jewish society to change, these radical Jews said, but rather that all of the old, corrupt world society would have to be uprooted. Only through the destruction of the old and all of its evils could the new and all of its promises blossom.

The majority of Eastern Europe's Jews still remained faithful to their traditions and lifestyle. They made a strong attempt to improve their own society by placing new emphasis on the social and interpersonal aspects of the *halachah* and Jewish tradition. It was the minority of Jewry, the secular Jews, who publicly advanced the causes of anarchy, revolution, socialism, communism, trade unionism, and

---

2. *The Siege,* O'Brien, p. 111.

The funeral of Rabbi Eliyahu Chaim Meisel (1821-1912) in Lodz. Rabbi Meisel built a factory for handweavers who were unemployed as a result of the mechanization of the textile industry

democratic governments as solutions to the problems of the Jewish and the general world. Traditional Jewry, however, chose to concentrate not on the forms of society but on the substance of its citizens.

The Chofetz Chaim

THE MUSSAR MOVEMENT founded by Rabbi Yisrael Salanter had grown, until, by the late 1800s, it was a powerful impetus to a quiet revolution within traditional Jewish life in Lithuania and White Russia. The strength of this ethical strain in traditional life was enhanced and expanded by the personality and works of the saintly scholar of Radin, Rabbi Yisrael Meir HaCohen Kagan.[3] This person of gigantic spirit, intellect, and vision attempted to improve the quality of life in Jewish society. His magnum opus, by which he was was identified ever after,[4] was *Chofetz Chaim* .[5]

This book was a compilation of the laws and attitudes of the Torah towards slander, libel, verbal abuse, and the like. The ethical Jewish society always viewed gossip, malicious or benign, as forbidden,

---

3. 1839-1933. See Chapter 14, "The Yeshivos" for the section on Yeshivas Radin, which he founded and headed.

4. It is very common in Jewish life for an author to be known by the name of his book, once that book attains recognition and popularity.

5. Literally, "wanting life." The book was published in Vilna in 1873, and has been reprinted numerous times since then.

dangerous and unacceptable. It was the root cause of divisiveness and much societal negativism. It cloaked bigotry, protected prejudices, and justified discrimination, oppression, and social and economic exploitation. By raising the subject, the *Chofetz Chaim* attempted to put emphasis on the ethical and Torah restraints on speech, writing, newspapers, and other forms of communication. He was careful never to preach withdrawal from society — indeed, those close to him remember him as an engaging conversationalist — but he taught that speech must be employed carefully and scrupulously.

The Chofetz Chaim

To the *Chofetz Chaim*, there were values higher than unrestrained freedom of speech. Quietly and patiently, he spread the message of peace, social harmony, and justice in Jewish Lithuania, Poland, and White Russia. In the decades before World War I, his influence and presence rallied the forces of fairness and equity within the traditional Jewish community, and his personal example of simple faith and rectitude inspired a fundamental improvement in the social fabric of Eastern European Jewish life.

The *Chofetz Chaim* wrote many other works on the Torah view of an ethical society. He also wrote special books and pamphlets for Jewish soldiers serving in the army of the Czar, for Russian Jewish emigrants to America and South Africa; for Jewish women in a rapidly changing world; for Jewish students sorely in need of spiritual direction and support. He preached hygiene, health, public charity, welfare, and free-loan funds for the indigent. He emphasized the rights of the laborer to fair and timely wages, and publicly denounced the excesses of the owners of factories, land, and capital, especially when they were seemingly observant Jews. He fought for the retention of the sanctity of the Sabbath as the foundation of Jewish life. He placed the yeshivos at the center of the Jewish world and described them as the only hope for the Jewish future. Indeed, he founded and directed one of the world's major yeshivos in his own town of Radin.

A halachic scholar of the first order, he was the author of the six-volume *Mishneh Berurah*, perhaps the definitive commentary on *Shulchan Aruch Orach Chaim*. His three-volume *Likkutei Halachos* proved him to be an equally erudite scholar of the Talmud. His gentle nature belied his iron will. This man, small of stature, dominated his generation.

The chassidic leaders of Poland also exerted strong pressures on their flock for social improvement. One example of the great chassidic leaders at the time was Rabbi Yehudah Aryeh Leib Alter, the *Rebbe* of Gur.[6] He himself was the example for modesty, humility, and a renewed egalitarian approach to chassidic life.[7] His compassion for the working man,[8] his disdain for worldly power and luxuries,[9] his fierce sense of justice, and his search for truth and honesty, inspired his tens of thousands of followers to self-improvement and social conscience. He bade them to "look beneath the *shtreimel* and into the head."[10] His son and successor, Rabbi Avraham Mordechai Alter,[11] encouraged Orthodox newspapers and political action, organized social institutions, and gave Chassidus a strong organizational structure and a resolute societal program.

In general, in spite of the continuing ravages of secular Jewry, Polish Jewry remained overwhelmingly observant and, for the most part, chassidic before World War I.[12] The strength and charisma of Rabbi Avraham Mordechai Alter, and the loyalty and cohesiveness of his disciples, were major factors in the rebuilding of Polish Jewry after the displacement and destruction of World War I. The Chassidic Movement's program for Jewish self-improvement and social development was no less progressive or successful than that of secular Jewry, but its means of implementation were far more gentle, peaceful, and much less destructive. Its successes, however, are less known, since

6. 1846-1905. He is known as the *Sefas Emes*, after the name of his works of Biblical and Talmudic interpretation. See Aharon Sorasky, *Dmuyot Hod*, Bnei Brak 1968, vol. 2, pp. 21-53, and *Rebbes of Ger*, Mesorah Publications, 1985, for examples of his behavior and leadership.

7. He never sat at the head of the table, but rather together with his chassidim.

8. He once gave his grandson a large amount of money, but in pennies. "How can I carry the money away?" complained the young man. "It is beyond human endurance to bear such heavy pails of coins." The *Sefas Emes* replied, "Think about how many years the poor water-carrier, who receives three cents a pail for carrying it up many flights of stairs, had to work to amass this amount of money. You have achieved it so quickly!" Sorasky, p. 34.

9. His slogan was "This world is no world."

10. Sorasky, p. 35.

11. 1866-1948. Known as the *Imrei Emes*.

12. However, it is apparent that large numbers of the people were only superficially pious, and more Jews were becoming radicalized and secular even before World War I. As a result, the upheavals and displacements of the war, which destroyed leadership structures and made refugees of many heads of households, caused serious, virtually irreparable breakdowns in religious life.

nineteenth-century Orthodoxy was notorious for not recording or publicizing its achievements and projects.

The Radical Left

HE QUIET REVOLUTION in Jewish life begun by the *Mussar* Movement and continued by traditional Jewry at the turn of the century was publicly overshadowed by the violent revolution imposed by the revolutionary secular forms of Jewish society. This small minority of Jews — radical, idealistic, violent, and consumed by self-hatred — proclaimed themselves the leaders of the new Jewish people. In essence, their program stated that there was no necessity for a Jewish people, for in the "new" Russia, the "new" Poland, the "new" Germany, the "new" world, all problems would fall away, all differences would disappear and all social ills would be healed. In such a "brave, new world," a Jewish people, with its uniqueness, special identity, and Torah way of life, would be unnecessary, counter-productive, and anachronistic. Hence, as a necessary prerequisite for the formation of the *new* Jewish people and the *new* world, the *old* Jewish people and the *old* world would have to disappear.

This was the program of the Jewish Left, the *Bund*,[13] the socialists, the communists, the labor Zionists, the anarchists, and the universalists. Their loose personal behavior, irresponsible public posture and statements, and frenetic energy frightened their fellow Jews. But even more ominously, it enraged and struck terror in the hearts of most of their non-Jewish European neighbors. It established a new Jewish stereotype, that of the revolutionary radical. It competed with the old canard of the "capitalistic, money-grubbing, venal, opportunistic Jew." Both stereotypes, contradictory as they were, remained alive in Europe with dire historic consequences. In the nineteenth and twentieth centuries, Jews have been attacked and slaughtered for being both capitalists and communists, conservatives and revolutionaries.

With perfect hindsight we are now able to see the basic failing of the violent Left. The true nature of the Left has become clear only now at the end of the twentieth century.

---

13. The Socialist-oriented Jewish trade union organization in Poland. Its counterpart in the United States was the "Workman's Circle" organization.

Compassion is not what motivates the Left, which is oblivious to the human suffering its generations have caused. What motivates the Left is the totalitarian Idea. The Idea that is more important than reality itself. What motivates the Left is the Idea of the future in which everything is changed, everything transcended. The future in which the present is already annihilated. In which its reality no longer exists.

What motivates the Left is an idea whose true consciousness is this: Everything human is alien. Because everything that is flesh and blood humanity is only the disposable past. Because all that exists deserves to perish. This is the consciousness that makes mass murderers of well-intentioned humanists and earnest progressives, the Hegelian liberators of the socialist cause.[14]

The Jewish Left, fleeing at all cost from their background of Judaism dominated by the Idea of Divine Torah, subscribed to this new human, Idea-philosophy wholeheartedly and, eventually, heartlessly.

The unsuccessful revolution of 1905 by the Left against the Czar hardened the oppressive anti-Semitic attitude of the Russian government. This, in turn, served to radicalize even more Jews. In addition, the Russian government now employed many Jewish agents in the *Okhra*, its oppressive internal secret police force. Many of these Jews were double agents, and their sinister behavior vis-a-vis other Jews and the Jewish population of Russia cast a further pall of fear over Jewish Russia. In addition, the recent ascendancy of a few Western European Jews in the arts, sciences, and commerce, fields from which they had previously been barred, fueled Russian anti-Semitism and a negative reaction against the masses of Russian Jews who were themselves mostly unaware even of the existence of these areas of human endeavor.

Modern-minded Jews in Russia wished to emulate the successes of their Western cousins, while the xenophobic ruling class of Russia became even more suspicious of all Jews. Such Jews as Rathenau,[15]

---

14. Taken from David Horowitz's essay in *Political Passages, Journeys of Change Through Two Decades, 1968-1988*, edited by John H. Bunzel, The Free Press, New York 1988.

15. 1867-1922. German industrialist and foreign minister. Assassinated by right-wing, anti-Semitic, German nationalists for his role in negotiating the Armistice Agreement ending World War I.

Mahler,[16] Schonberg,[17] Pissaro,[18] Chagall,[19] Modigliani,[20] Freud,[21] Bergson,[22] Kafka,[23] Sontine,[24] Bakst,[25] and Einstein[26] all combined to revolutionize the modern world. Since all of these men were publicly identified as Jews, they also focused the attention of the old world and all of those forces resistant to change and its accompanying ferment on the "Jewish problem," with sad results.

Agudath Israel

WARE OF THE CHANGING social circumstances of Europe, and troubled by the challenges of secularism, Zionism, and the Left, traditional Jewry attempted to organize for the battle. In the Polish-Prussian city of Katowice, in 1912, representatives of the major groupings within traditional Jewry met to form an international movement dedicated to the preservation of

16. 1860-1911. Musical composer and conductor. Head of the court opera in Vienna. He converted to Catholicism in order to be appointed to this prestigious post. A great innovator and musical genius, but a renegade Jew.

17. 1874-1951. A protege of Mahler's and a leading influence on modern classical music composition. He was born a Jew, raised as a Catholic, converted to Protestantism, and returned to Judaism with the rise of Hitler.

18. 1830-1903. One of the greatest French impressionist painters.

19. 1887-1985. A world famous painter of Jewish and nature scenes. Best known in the Jewish world for his stained glass windows of the Twelve Tribes of Israel, executed for the synagogue of the Hebrew University in Jerusalem.

20. 1884-1920. Italian impressionist painter.

21. 1856-1939. The father of modern psychiatry and psychology. His influence on modern-day society is almost immeasurable. Though many of his ideas and insights originated in traditional Jewish thought and sources, he was a self-hating Jew who had no use for his tradition or heritage. Physician, heal thyself!

22. 1859-1941. French philosopher who advanced the idea of intuition as the basis for scientific discovery and understanding of the natural world.

23. 1883-1924. Austrian author whose feverish, surrealistic view of the world and its events evoked the horrors of the twentieth century in a haunting fashion.

24. 1893-1943. Impressionist and modernistic painter.

25. 1866-1924. Designer of costumes and sets for the Russian ballet, famed painter, and producer of some of the most innovative and daring ballets of the time. He was Chagall's teacher and mentor.

26. 1879-1955. The genius who revolutionized our understanding of time, space, and physical laws. Though never observant, he was proudly Jewish, and, in 1951, was proposed by Ben Gurion to be the second president of Israel. He declined the honor.

tradition and Torah values within Jewish life. This organization was called Agudath Israel. Its leadership was formed from the followers of Rabbi Samson Raphael Hirsch in Germany, the great Chassidic leaders of Poland, and many of the leading representatives of the misnagdic Lithuanian *kehillos* and yeshivos, as well as leaders of Hungarian Jewry.

Nathan Birnbaum,[27] originally a secular Zionist, became one of the leading theoreticians of Agudath Israel. Jacob Rosenheim,[28] an intellectual from Frankfurt, and a skilled administrator and orator with a Western education and outlook, became the effective administrative head of Agudath Israel. Rabbi Chaim Ozer Grodzenski[29] of Vilna and the *Rebbe* of Gur, Rabbi Avraham Mordechai Alter, were its spiritual leaders and ideological authorities in Eastern Europe, and mobilized the masses of traditional Jewry on its behalf. The Agudah also had the blessing and support of the great sage and holy man, the *Chofetz Chaim*.

The Agudah itself was composed of different factions and theories. The Westernized German Jews were not in complete social and political harmony with their Chassidic Polish or intellectual Lithuanian brethren. The Agudah also encompassed the *Yishuv HaYashan* in Jerusalem, though the World Agudah organization would often find itself in conflict with this group.[30] In order to preserve the unity of the organization and to maintain its primary role as an umbrella group for all traditional Jews, the Agudah agreed that each community of Jews had a right to maintain its own lifestyle and traditions, and was not subject to the authority of any other group, community or rabbinic leadership (even fellow-Agudists).[31] The Agudah did not see itself as a worldwide movement or alliance of disparate Orthodox groups, but rather as the voice of the Torah nation of Israel, and thus all groupings of Jews adhering to tradition were conceived of as potentially belonging to its natural constituency.

The Agudah did not receive universal approval and support in traditional circles. The Mizrachi, the religious Zionist movement founded in 1909 by Rabbi Jacob Reines, enjoyed wide support among rabbis and the masses. The non-Zionist stance of the Agudah caused a natural

---

27. 1864-1937. His philosophy was that "Israel (the people) comes before Zion (the land)."

28. 1870-1965.

29. 1863-1940. A Talmudic genius, and a man of exceptional warmth, wisdom and compassion, he was universally recognized as the active leader of traditional Lithuanian Jewry.

30. See Menachem Friedman, *Chevrah V'Dat*, pp. 281-2.

31. Ibid., p. 220.

ideological conflict between the two movements. Although many rabbinic figures who were sympathetic to the Mizrachi also attempted to play a role in the Agudah,[32] it became clear, early on, that such fence-straddling was unrealistic.

The Agudah would not condone the anti-religious activities of the Zionist movement, and conducted an all-out struggle against the acceptance of the new prototype of Jew that Zionist culture was producing. It refused to acknowledge that a secular organization, not based upon the Divinity of Torah and tradition, could somehow represent the Jewish people, no matter how positive its goal. It resented the willingness of the Mizrachi to cooperate with the Zionist movement and did not share the Mizrachi ideology that Zionism, in and of itself, was a positive, if not even a messianic, force. Moreover it felt that the Zionist Movement could not be moved toward tradition by working from within, as Mizrachi hoped. The schism within traditional Jewry between the Mizrachi and Agudah would run very deep and long.

Also opposed to the Agudah were a number of great independent rabbinic and Chassidic leaders. Some felt that the organization, by its nature and composition of constituents, was too prone to compromise with its traditional (Mizrachi) and secular (Zionist) opponents. Others were opposed to the very concept of imposing an organizational structure upon a nation that is defined exclusively by the traditional standards of Torah scholarship and piety. They argued that organizations are, by nature, wooden and non-spirited, and thus the structured Agudah would contribute to a loss of vitality in Orthodox life, as well as sanctioning a "new" way to solve the ancient Jewish problem.

Foremost among this group of opponents were a number of Hungarian rabbis[33] and some rabbis, originally of the *Yishuv HaYashan* in Jerusalem.[34] Though not numerous, they were quite outspoken and, as such, greatly inhibited the actions and policies of the Agudah. Like its rival, the Mizrachi, the Agudah found itself constantly engaged in a two-front war. This would contribute to its lack of overall strength in

---

32. Rabbi Avraham Yitzchak Kook, who was to become Mizrachi's spiritual leader, was on his way to Europe to attend an Agudah meeting when World War I began, thus canceling the meeting and exiling him from Palestine for the duration of the war.

33. Such as Rabbis Tzvi Elimelech Shapiro of Munkacz and his son, Rabbi Chaim Elazar Shapiro, Rabbi Yoel Teitelbaum of Satmar and a number of other famous rabbinic personalities.

34. These dissidents, led by Rabbis Amram Blau and Raphael Katzenellenbogen, eventually broke with the established rabbinic leadership of the *Yishuv HaYashan* and formed a group called *Neturei Karta* (Guardians of the City).

opposing the encroachment of secular Zionism in the traditional Jewish world.

Also, the Agudah, more than the Mizrachi or secularists, would be damaged by the events of World War I and the subsequent weakening of Eastern European Jewry and the popularization of Zionism. In spite of all of its handicaps, the Agudah remained the home organization for a very large segment of Orthodox Jewry and many of its greatest rabbinic figures. The emergence of such an organization in the period before the outbreak of World War I mirrored the shifting forces in the Jewish world and the necessity for new forms to safeguard the traditions of Israel. The war forced cancellation of Agudath Israel's first Great Congress (*Knessiah Gedolah*), scheduled for the summer of 1914. Due to the dislocations of the war, it did not take place until 1923.

The Second Aliyah

Tel-Aviv's founders meet to draw lots for land on the sand dunes outside Jaffa — site of the proposed Jewish suburb

THE DECADE PRECEDING World War I marked the time of the Second Aliyah from Eastern Europe to Israel. This immigration to Israel differed from the First Aliyah at the end of the nineteenth century, in that the new immigrant was basically secular, socialist, idealistic, and zealous in his belief that he was not only building a new land, but also creating a new Jew and a new nation. There was a continuous and often extreme effort to break with the old Jewish tradition and religious faith.

The theme of the Second Aliyah was "Jewish labor." These colonists were the core of Labor Zionism, the movement that founded and led the State of Israel for its first three decades. They believed in the sanctity of labor and the rights of the proletariat, and were opposed to the excesses of capitalism, and the power of religion. They were convinced of the irrelevance of Jewish history to their lives and goals. They looked forward to the utopian Marxist tomorrow and the ultimate triumph of the international workers' movements. In a practical vein, they founded agricultural communes known as *kibbutzim*, where everyone contributed according to his abilities and everyone received according to his individual needs, where there was no private property and where even the privacy of the family was submerged in collective living. Degania, Ein-Harod, Givat Brenner, Nahalal, and other communal settlements were built with their sweat and blood. Swamps were drained, eucalyptus trees were planted to prevent the swamps' return, rocks were cleared, barren land was plowed, and, grudgingly, the soil began to respond to the efforts of its new tenants. In 1908, Jews moved north from Jaffa to begin building a new Jewish suburb, which they called Tel-Aviv. It has since become the largest exclusively Jewish city in the world.

The men of the First Aliyah employed Arab labor to till the soil of Baron Rothschild's colonies. The men of the Second Aliyah stated, "Let Israel clearly know that Jewish landlords will never restore the land to Israel, unless there be Jewish workers."[35]

David Ben Gurion, Yitzchak Ben Tzvi, and others who were

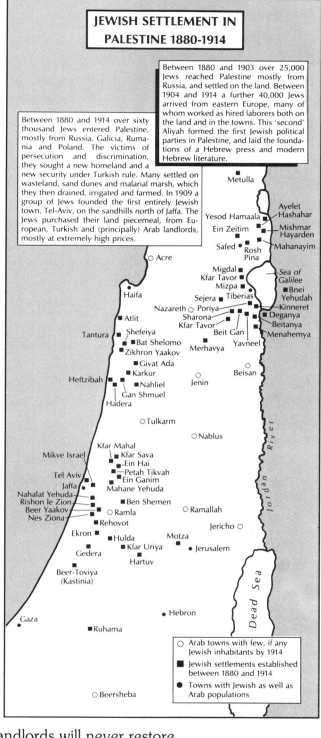

JEWISH SETTLEMENT IN PALESTINE 1880-1914

Between 1880 and 1903 over 25,000 Jews reached Palestine mostly from Russia, and settled on the land. Between 1904 and 1914 a further 40,000 Jews arrived from eastern Europe, many of whom worked as hired laborers both on the land and in the towns. This 'second' Aliyah formed the first Jewish political parties in Palestine, and laid the foundations of a Hebrew press and modern Hebrew literature.

Between 1880 and 1914 over sixty thousand Jews entered Palestine, mostly from Russia, Galicia, Rumania and Poland. The victims of persecution and discrimination, they sought a new homeland and a new security under Turkish rule. Many settled on wasteland, sand dunes and malarial marsh, which they then drained, irrigated and farmed. In 1909 a group of Jews founded the first entirely Jewish town, Tel-Aviv, on the sandhills north of Jaffa. The Jews purchased their land piecemeal, from European, Turkish and (principally) Arab landlords, mostly at extremely high prices.

○ Arab towns with few, if any Jewish inhabitants by 1914
■ Jewish settlements established between 1880 and 1914
● Towns with Jewish as well as Arab populations

---

35. *Israel, a Personal History.* David Ben Gurion, N.Y., 1971, p. 40.

destined to be the leaders of the State of Israel forty years later were members and prototypes of the Second Aliyah. Their fiery idealism and unlimited capacity for work and sacrifice was mixed with an abiding contempt for the Jewish past, and a vitriolic hatred of the mode of Jewish life known in the exile of Europe.

The new Jew, whom they idealized, would speak Hebrew, not Yiddish, Ladino or Arabic,[36] be a farmer, laborer, warrior, and intellectual. He would be idealistic, selfless and honest, indifferent to material wealth, concerned with the society and not the individual. He would also be irreligious (if not anti-religious) and view Jewish tradition as an anachronism and an unnecessary burden. The communes of these new Jews knew nothing of Sabbath or *Yom Kippur,* and had no synagogue or kosher kitchen. A new Passover Seder service based upon Marx and Engels was composed, *Shavuos* became a purely

---

36. Hebrew was the spoken language of few of the people of the First Aliyah, among whom Yiddish dominated. The adoption of Hebrew as the "official" language of the Jewish *Yishuv* in Palestine was an accomplishment of the settlers of the Second Aliyah, forced upon them by the unwavering insistence and prodding of one man — Eliezer ben Yehudah.

Tel-Aviv in 1920

agricultural holiday, the Bible became literature, and religious ritual was deemed repulsive and hence prohibited.

The *Yishuv HaYashan* and the rabbis of Palestine attempted to somehow influence the lifestyle of the new communities. In the late summer of 1913, a "Journey of Repentance" was organized by the leading rabbinic figures of the country to visit these new settlements and speak to the people of the Second Aliyah about tradition and Jewish values.

This mission was led by Rabbi Avraham Y. Kook, then the rabbi of Jaffa, Rabbi Yosef Chaim Sonnenfeld,[37] the leading rabbi of the *Yishuv HaYashan* in Jerusalem, Rabbi Ben Tzion Yadler,[38] the famed *Maggid* of Jerusalem, and Rabbi Yaakov Moshe Charlop,[39] a confidant of Rabbi Kook and rabbi of the Shaarei Chesed neighborhood in

---

37. *See* Chapter 28, "Palestine for Whom?" for details regarding these great rabbinic personages.

38. A noted orator, scholar, educator and leader of the *Yishuv HaYashan*.

39. 1883-1952. Author of the famous halachic work, *Beth Zvul*, and later *rosh yeshivah* of Yeshivath Mercaz Harav in Jerusalem.

Tel-Aviv today.

Jerusalem. The visit of the rabbis to the new settlements achieved mixed results. In some places they were received coldly, while in others, enthusiastically. Some settlements agreed to install a kosher kitchen and maintain a synagogue, while others refused all of the requests of the rabbis.[40]

The mixed results of the visit were reflected in the different attitudes of the rabbis who embarked on the mission. Rabbi Kook was strangely encouraged by the experience and felt for all his life that a return to traditional Jewish life was near for the leftists of the Second Aliyah and their descendants. However, Rabbi Sonnenfeld was profoundly saddened and shocked by what he had seen, and was thus strengthened in his previous resolve not to compromise with or accommodate the secular Zionist forces in any fashion. Thus, this common experience shaped the attitudes of these two great rabbinic leaders in completely opposite fashions.

Jews in Name Only

THE TURMOIL OF THE EARLY twentieth century was part of the American Jewish experience as well. Many of the revolutionary Jewish figures of the 1905 uprising against the Czar fled to the sanctuary of America.[41] They stirred the latent embers of Jewish socialism among the Russian immigrants to America, and made it a vital and abrasive force in American Jewish life. *The Jewish Daily Forward*, edited by Abraham Cahan,[42] became the Yiddish newspaper with the largest circulation, most forceful influence, and greatest longevity. It was intensely socialist, anti-religious, and anti-Zionist in its original form, but time and circumstances mellowed its stance, though it always retained its pro-labor and socialist bias. In fact, much of Jewish culture in America — the Yiddish theater, art, dance,

---

40. For details of the mission, see Shmuel Avidor, *HaIsh Neged HaZerem*, Jerusalem 1970, and S.Z. Sonnenfeld, *HaIsh Al HaChomah*, Jerusalem 1971; English edition published as *Guardian of Jerusalem*, ArtScroll History Series, Mesorah Publications, Ltd., 1983.

41. Among them were men who would help build the American trade union labor coalition, such as David Dubinsky and Sidney Hillman. Irving Howe, *World of Our Fathers*, Harcourt Brace Jovanovitch, New York 1976, pp. 287-324, describes the idealism and socialist inclination of this group.

42. 1860-1951.

and literature — was predominantly left-leaning in outlook and purpose.

These Jewish socialists "accepted the breakup of the traditional Jewish world view; they favored the fracturing of opinion and pluralism of tendencies within Jewish life that followed upon the end of religious hegemony; yet they strongly resented all proposals toward a further assimilation into the gentile world. They wanted to remain Jews — non-believing, radical, modern — but Jews."[43]

In this they paralleled the goals of their brothers of the Second Aliyah. In America, the achievement of this goal — just being Jews without belief — would prove impossible. In the Land of Israel, however, because of different circumstances, such as the coming of statehood and constant war, the results of the attempt to "just be Jewish" would be much more ambiguous. The undoing of Jewish socialism lay in the fact that it could not deliver on its promise of "a new society in which all men would live without want, in freedom and fulfillment."[44]

Despite its pronounced antipathy toward Judaism, Jewish socialism in the Land of Israel was supported by Jews, most of them traditional, if not observant, who wanted to remain Jewish. They were also helped by the fact that there was no predominantly gentile culture into which to assimilate. Thus, though abysmally ignorant of basic Judaism, the children and grandchildren of the Second Aliyah often remained "Jewish" despite themselves, a phenomenon that diminished generations later, as the State of Israel sought ways to cope with the alienation of its founders' grandchildren. However, it has correctly been noted that "Jewish socialism and Zionism also transformed the posture of Jewish life, creating a new type of person: combative, worldly, spirited, and intent upon sharing the future of industrial society with the rest of the world."[45] Yet Hitler, Stalin, and Arafat would later cause a reexamination of the efficacy of this new posture and new type of Jew.

---

43. Howe, p. 293.

44. Ibid., p. 323.

45. Ibid.

The Reform Movement

ASIDE FROM THE PRESSURES of the revolutionary Left, both against and within the Jewish people, other new movements developed within Jewry, especially in the United States.

In the 1800s and the early 1900s, Reform Judaism was dominant in America, if not in numbers, certainly in organization and influence. Reform, which sought to assimilate Jews quickly and completely into American society, found a hospitable climate in the Unites States. The "melting pot" theory of assimilation of immigrants and all ethnic groups was then much in vogue. Though religious freedom and tolerance were embedded in American intellectual thought, the practical world of "getting ahead" allowed little room for deviation from the white, Anglo-Saxon, Protestant norms and lifestyle. Thus, the goals of Reform — assimilation and less overt Jewish identity — closely matched the aims of the social and economic leaders of American society of that time. The early success of Reform in America was a natural product of this unspoken alliance.

The main driving force in organizing and institutionalizing American Reform Judaism was Isaac Mayer Wise.[46] Born in Czechoslovakia, educated in the Rabbinical Seminary of Prague,[47] he came to the United States in 1846. Wise held a number of pulpits and gained a well-deserved reputation as an extreme "Reformer."

His innovations included a mixed choir, mixed pews, counting women as part of the prayer quorum (minyan), a new modernized prayer book in English, practically omitting all Hebrew prayers, and an abolition of many of the main rituals of Judaism such as kashruth, religious divorce (get), and Sabbath observance.[48] He published a newspaper called The Israelite which, by default, became the media spokesman for American Jewry.

In 1875, Wise established and headed Hebrew Union College in Cincinnati, Ohio, which remains the main seminary for Reform

---

46. 1819-1900.

47. He was ordained by Rabbi Solomon Y. Rapaport, a noted rabbinic scholar and *maskil*, who was the controversial rabbi of Prague in the middle 1800s.

48. All this in the 1850s!

Judaism. In 1889, he established and became president of the Central Conference of American Rabbis, the rabbinical arm of Reform Judaism. He was a prolific writer and lecturer and a genius at organization. In 1873, he united the individual American Reform temples of the country into the Union of American Hebrew Congregations.

Thus Reform Jewry at the beginning of the twentieth century in America was powerful, well organized, united, and had a strong infrastructure and a clear program of goals. It was also, as always, well financed and had access to the most powerful Jews in America, who were almost always personally non-observant and assimilated, and thus comforted by Reform's abrogation of the basic tenets of Torah and Judaism. In contrast, Orthodoxy, which, in its Ashkenazic form, arrived in America fifty years after Reform, was divided, disorganized,[49] poorly financed, and suffered from an inferiority complex in dealing with the new reality of American life. It is no surprise, therefore, that Reform in America believed itself to be the wave of the future and was confident that traditional Jewry and Torah observance were doomed in the new world.

The Reform movement made official its clean break with the Judaism of the past at a conference of its rabbis held in Pittsburgh in 1885. Known as the Pittsburgh Platform, this credo said, among other things:

> We hold that all such Mosaic and rabbinical laws as regulate diet, priestly purity, and dress, originated in ages and under the influence of ideas entirely foreign to our present mental and spiritual state . . . their observance in our days is apt rather to obstruct than to further modern spiritual elevation.

It also stated:

> We consider ourselves no longer a nation, but a religious community, and therefore expect neither a return to Palestine, nor a sacrificial worship under the sons of Aaron, nor the restoration of any of the laws concerning a Jewish state.[50]

That conference also confirmed Sunday services as a replacement for Saturday services "in localities where the necessity for such services appears or is felt."[51] And finally, it removed the requirement of circumcision for male converts to Judaism.[52] Thus did Reform

---

49. Orthodoxy somehow had (and still has) an abhorrence of organization and unity.
50. *The Jewish Encyclopedia*, Vol. 4, p. 215.
51. Ibid.
52. Ibid.

misinterpret its role and distort the lessons of Jewish history, to the later detriment of myriads of its American adherents.

Conservative Judaism

THE EARLY 1900S SAW the rise of a movement that eventually called itself Conservative Judaism. Though it claimed descent from the schools of *Haskalah* of Eastern Europe,[53] this movement originated and remained basically a product of American society and conditions. A group of founders, including Sabato Morais,[54] established the Jewish Theological Seminary of America in New York in 1886. They hoped that the rabbis trained and ordained there — all of whom would have to be English-speaking college graduates — would be a positive influence on the immigrants and their children. They were convinced that traditional Jewish life as it existed in Europe could never take root in America, and therefore a new form of Judaism was necessary.

The school also accepted the aid of spiritual leaders such as Alexander Kohut,[55] Marcus Jastrow,[56] and Benjamin Szold,[57] all of whom were non-observant Jews, but were nevertheless opposed to the Reform movement. The school had great financial difficulties in its first decade, but by 1902 it was reorganized on a stable financial basis.

---

53. The Conservative movement claims Zechariah Frankel (1801-1875), the rector of the Rabbinical School of Breslau, a bastion of *Haskalah* thought and influence, as its spiritual founder.

54. 1823-1897. He was the spiritual leader of Mikveh Israel Congregation of Philadelphia and was a strictly Orthodox Jew of the Sephardic tradition. However, he was never recognized as a Talmudic scholar, and the Eastern European immigrants had no rapport with and little respect for him and his new institution. He served as the first president of the Seminary.

55. 1842-1894. Ordained by the Rabbinical School of Breslau, he was the rabbi of Congregation Ahavath Chesed in New York City. He authored the *Aruch HaShalem*, a famous lexicon of the Talmud.

56. 1829-1903. Served as a rabbi of a Reform congregation, though not personally Reform. Author of a famous and widely used Aramaic-English dictionary of Talmudic words. He himself was non-observant.

57. 1829-1902. Originally a student of the yeshivah at Pressburg, he left for Breslau. He was the rabbi of Congregation Ohev Shalom in Baltimore and allowed innovations in ritual.

Professor Solomon Schechter[58] of Cambridge University in England was then brought to America to head the Seminary. He built the Seminary into an imposing institution[59] with one of the largest Judaica libraries in the world. He popularized a theory called the "Historical School" of Judaism, which maintained that Judaism was a human and not a Divinely revealed institution, and therefore had developed through the ages in response to the will and needs of the Jews under varying circumstances. In this, he broke with traditional Jewish belief in the Divinity of Torah and *halachah*, and set Conservative Judaism on its slippery course of trying to maintain Jewish ideals, traditions, and actions, while yet denying their Divine origin.[60]

Search For Leadership

 N 1886, THE IMMIGRANT JEWS of New York appealed to the leading rabbis of Europe to send a superior rabbinic personage to serve as the *Rav HaKollel* — Chief Rabbi — of New York. By this, they meant that he be the rabbi for their Russian immigrant community, since he certainly would not be an acceptable rabbinic leader for the assimilated, Americanized, old-line Jewish community of New York. In 1888, the famed *Maggid* of Vilna, Rabbi Jacob Joseph, accepted the call and moved to New York.

A noted student of Rabbi Yisrael Salanter, he was a man of great talents and energy, superior scholarship, and refined and moral character. But he was crushed by the problems and chaos of the immigrant Jewish community of New York at the turn of the century. His struggle to control and stabilize the kosher poultry and meat area of Jewish life in New York brought him into open conflict with

---

58. 1847-1915. He was the true founder and educational architect of the Seminary. In fact, the institution is still known by many as "Schechter's Seminary." He was a Talmudic scholar of Eastern European origin and education. However, he was a follower of *Haskalah* and was greatly influenced by the values and beliefs of nineteenth-century Europe. He gained international fame though his discoveries and studies of ancient Hebraic documents found in the Cairo *genizah* (storage place) in the 1890s.

59. Among the scholars Schechter brought to the Seminary were Louis Ginzburg, Israel Davidson, Israel Friedlander and Alexander Marx.

60. The wits at the Seminary maintained that "it was an institution with an Orthodox faculty established to train Conservative rabbis to serve a Reform laity."

Rabbi Margolies

unscrupulous butchers, greedy meat purveyors, corrupt politicians, and self-appointed "religious leaders." His attempts to organize and control Jewish religious life were undone by the active opposition of some and the general apathy of most of the community. This struggle seriously affected his health and in 1894 he suffered a paralytic stroke that removed him from public life. In 1902 he died, and his funeral was one of the largest ever seen in New York. With his death, the office of Chief Rabbi for New York was buried as well.

At this time, Orthodox Jewry in America had no organizational structure whatsoever. A synagogue had its rabbi or lay leadership, but it was an island unto itself. The community structures of European and Sephardic Jewry, which provided for education, kashruth, and general welfare, had never been established in the amorphous, immigrant Jewish population centers of the United States.

Traditional Jewry slowly began to organize itself at the beginning of the twentieth century in America. Under the leadership of Rabbis A. Pereira Mendes[61] and Bernard Drachman,[62] the Union of Orthodox Jewish Congregations of America[63] was founded in 1898. Rabbis Hillel Klein and Herbert Goldstein founded Orthodox communities of great strength and viability. In 1902, Rabbis Bernard Levinthal[64] and Moses Zebulun (Ramaz) Margolies[65] helped found the Union of Orthodox Rabbis of the United States and Canada, commonly known as the Agudath Harabonim. This organization attempted to bring some order into the chaos of Jewish religious life in America. The heterogeneous

---

61. 1852-1937. He was the spiritual leader of the prestigious Spanish-Portuguese Congregation, Shearith Israel, of New York.

62. 1861-1945. A native American Orthodox rabbi, he was the Rabbi of Congregation Zichron Ephraim on the Upper East Side of New York. He was also the first translator into English of the Nineteen Letters of Rabbi Samson Raphael Hirsch.

63. Popularly known as the OU.

64. 1865-1952. He was the leading Orthodox rabbi of Philadelphia and was the most "Americanized" of the Eastern European rabbis then in the United States. He was a very influential rabbinic figure, whose leadership extended far beyond the confines of his synagogue and community.

65. 1851-1936. The first rabbi and effectively the founder of Kehilath Jeshurun Congregation in New York. His grandson-in-law, Rabbi Joseph Lookstein, and great-grandson, Rabbi Haskell Lookstein, have since succeeded him in the spiritual leadership of that community. The community's Ramaz school is named after him.

nature of the newly arrived Jewish communities hindered these efforts, but the organization served as the beginning of an Orthodox rabbinic infrastructure in the United States.

Birth of the American Yeshivah

HE TIMES AND THE MORES of American Jewry were inimical to traditional observance and Jewish behavior. It was estimated that by 1906 over ninety percent of the Eastern European Jewish immigrants to America had ceased to be strictly observant in their religious behavior and practices.[66] The field of kashruth lay in shambles, charlatans masqueraded as "rabbis" or "reverends," there was no meaningful Jewish education in America, and the radical attacks of the Jewish Left on religion took their toll.[67] But the main propellants towards complete abandonment of the old ways and headlong assimilation into the general society were the difficulty of Sabbath observance and the new freedom and opportunity that America presented to Jews who blended into its culture.

Jewish education in the United States was often in the hands of malevolent and incompetent private teachers — *melamdim* — and any meaningful attempt at Jewish education was mainly confined to "Hebrew Schools,"[68] which, after a full day of public school attendance, most children found burdensome, unfair, and irrelevant to their new society. These schools met four or five times per week for two or three hours per session. Their curriculum included Hebrew prayer, Bible, *Rashi,* Mishnah, and even Talmud. They also prepared boys for their *bar-mitzvah* ceremony. Most of them used Yiddish as the language of instruction, though, by the 1920s, English began to dominate.

The subjects of instruction were largely irrelevant in a non-Orthodox society, and the quality of education was uneven. Though the much-maligned "Hebrew teacher" was not as inept as American Jewish legend describes him, Jewish novelists and social historians

---

66. Aaron Rothkoff, *Bernard Revel,* (Jerusalem) p. 25.

67. "A ticket to an 1890 Yom Kippur Ball read: Grand Yom Kippur Ball with theater. Arranged with the consent of all new rabbis of liberty . . . The Kol Nidre will be offered by John Most. Music, dancing, buffet, Marseillaise and other hymns against Satan." Ibid. p. 6.

68. Usually called a "Talmud Torah."

have portrayed him as a mercenary fool or sadist, or both. Only a handful of students continued their Jewish studies after *bar-mitzvah* age, and most "graduates" of these Hebrew schools soon forgot what they had learned and became part of the assimilatory drift of the time.

Against this dismal backdrop, a number of Orthodox rabbis and laymen organized the first American yeshivah for advanced Talmudic study. Rabbi Moshe Mayer Matlin[69] organized private classes in Talmud for adolescent boys. Originally these classes met in his home and later a building was purchased to house the new school.[70]

The Etz Chaim Hebrew School, founded in 1886, and strengthened and supported by Rabbi Jacob Joseph, was the "feeder" of students to Rabbi Matlin. When, in 1896, Rabbi Yitzchak Elchanan Spector, the great rabbi of Kovno, Lithuania, died, Etz Chaim and Rabbi Matlin's academy united to form one institution, named Yeshivah Rabbi Yitzchak Elchanan, in memory of that great sage. The majority of its students were young men who had previously attended European yeshivos, and the curriculum and atmosphere of the new American school closely mirrored its Eastern European counterparts.

69. He was a rabbi in Slutzk, Lithuania, before emigrating to the United States, and was a member of Chief Rabbi Jacob Joseph's rabbinical court in New York.

70. The building was located at 156 Henry Street, New York City.

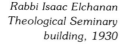

Rabbi Isaac Elchanan Theological Seminary building, 1930

Other Orthodox schools of learning also were established at that time, including the Rabbi Jacob Joseph School, named after the deceased great rabbi of New York. It was founded in 1903, a year after his death. Mesivtha Tifereth Jerusalem opened its doors in 1906. In that same year, Rabbi Margolies became the president of Yeshivah Rabbi Yitzchak Elchanan. Some time thereafter, a young man by the name of Rabbi Bernard Dov Revel[71] entered the yeshivah, and in a relatively short period of time rose to become its president. Revel was the driving force that made the yeshivah an American institution, rather than a copy of the traditional Lithuanian yeshivah, and prepared the way for the eventual growth of Torah scholarship and resilient Orthodoxy in America.

Reaching for the Silver Ring

N THE DECADE BEFORE the First World War, many American Jews gained wealth, prominence, and public office. Oscar Strauss[72] was named ambassador to Turkey and later served as Secretary of Commerce in Theodore Roosevelt's administration. His older brother, Isidor,[73] was a congressman from New York and a well-known philanthropist and Jewish communal worker. Their brother, Nathan,[74] made Macy's the flagship of United States department stores. Julius Rosenwald[75] became the head

---

71. 1885-1940. He was a genius of note, a student of the great yeshivah of Telshe in Lithuania. However, he was later attracted to *Haskalah*, became self-taught in secular studies, and soon lapsed into revolutionary radicalism. He participated in the 1905 revolution against the Czar and was arrested and imprisoned. In jail, he rethought his situation in life, returned to Jewish tradition and Talmudic study, and decided to dedicate his life to Torah and the Jewish people. In America, he married an Oklahoma oilman's daughter and moved to Tulsa to be part of the family oil business. He soon tired of the business world, and, thanks to his secular education and degrees, Talmudic erudition and love of Torah, as well as his charismatic personality, he was chosen in 1915 to head the Yeshivah Rabbi Isaac Elchanan. For more about him and the yeshivah, see Chapter 30, "American Jewry in the 1920s" in the next section.

72. 1850-1926.

73. 1845-1912. He was also a partner in the famous department store, Abraham and Strauss. He and his wife went down with the Titanic (April 1912).

74. 1848-1931. He was also a well-known philanthropist and contributed to Jewish causes in Jerusalem, where a street is named for him.

75. 1862-1932. Opposed Zionism vociferously and was a strong supporter of Reform Judaism.

of Sears Roebuck and Company, eventually America's largest retail merchandiser. He was a committed philanthropist, especially to causes that supported the education of blacks in America.

Louis Marshall[76] founded the American Jewish Committee and, together with Jacob H. Schiff,[77] fought for Jewish rights the world over. Benjamin Cardozo[78] and Louis Brandeis,[79] both future Supreme Court Justices, were making their mark in the legal world, as was Judge Mayer Sulzberger[80] of Philadelphia. Sulzberger's cousin, Cyrus L. Sulzberger,[81] became one of America's greatest industrialists and also led the Jewish Agricultural Society.

Out of the turbulent decade at the beginning of this century, American Jewry was beginning to rise and take its own form. It would yet dominate the Jewish world in this century, but in 1914 no one knew that. The century had begun with high hopes for the world and the Jewish people. The world did not then see the hideous smirk of the angel of death lurking just beyond its field of vision. But the fatal time had arrived, unannounced and largely unanticipated.

---

76. 1856-1929.

77. 1847-1920. One of the leading financiers of Wall Street and a traditional, if not completely observant, Jew. He was one of the leading supporters of the Jewish Theological Seminary.

78. 1870-1938.

79. 1856-1941. He later became a leader of American Zionism.

80. 1843-1923. Together with Marshall, he was one of the founders of the American Jewish Committee.

81. His companies were in the forefront of producing modern farm-machine equipment, and thus revolutionized American and world agriculture.

26
The Great War, 1914-1918

Destruction and Defeat

HE ASSASSINATION OF THE Archduke Ferdinand of Austria and his wife in Sarajevo,[1] in June 1914, was the catalyst for the greatest bloodletting until then known to man. In hindsight, it was clear from 1910 onwards that war was inevitable in Europe. The combination of the Kaiser's personality, Austria's weakness, Russia's instability, Balkan turmoil, Turkish corruption, and British and French imperial interests spelled doom. But no one imagined the cost and carnage that would be involved.[2] Germany remembered its lightning victory over France in 1870.[3] France smarted for revenge. Britain cast covetous eyes on the territories of the Ottoman Empire, as did the Czar. It was a war that everyone was convinced could be won easily and cheaply.[4] In fact it would be a war that all participants lost ruinously.

The war would also change the Jewish world irrevocably. If the Second World War (which was in effect the sequel of the first conflict of 1914-1918) was the end of European Jewry, the First World War was the beginning of that end. It is striking that war was declared on the Ninth of Av, the day that has historically been associated with Jewish

---

1. Bosnian town, located in present-day Yugoslavia.

2. Lord Edward Grey, the British foreign minister, did sense the tragedy that was impending. "The lamps are going out all over Europe; we shall not see them lit again in our lifetime" was his prophetic comment.

3. The Kaiser told his troops in August 1914, "You will be home before the leaves have fallen from the trees." See S.L.A. Marshall, *The American Heritage History of World War I,* (Dell Publishing Co., New York, 1966) p. 62.

4. General Franz Conrad Von Hotzendorf, the Austrian chief of staff, openly agitated for "a bright, brisk little war." Ibid., p. 109.

tragedy and mourning. The destructive changes wrought by the World War affected European Jewry so profoundly that it was unable to respond competently to its new and more dangerous post-war situation. The virtual breakdown of the established community structure, caused by the dislocations and upheavals of the war, rendered the Jewish nation completely defenseless in an age of unmitigated terror and violence.

All the major combatants — Germany, Russia, Austria, France and England — attempted to win the war in the first month of combat.[5] All failed. The result was a bloodbath unprecedented in the history of war.[6] Casualties were counted in the millions and the ordinary foot soldier sensed what the generals did not — that stalemate was at hand and the war, instead of being "bright, brisk, and little," was open ended, catastrophic, and indecisive.

The German drive to Paris was held back at the Marne; the Anglo-French counterattack floundered at the Aisne and Ypres; the Austrian invasion of Russian Poland was smashed; the Russian invasion of Prussia ended in debacle at Tannenberg; and the Turkish invasion of the Caucasus and Southern Russia was, in turn, thrown back. Nowhere, and to none of the participants, was victory visible. By the middle of 1915, one year after the war began, the war of attrition was in full

5. For details, see Barbara Tuchman's great work, *The Guns of August*.

6. Sir Arthur Conan Doyle, the creator of Sherlock Holmes, called it, "The most terrible August in the history of the world. One thought that God's curse hung heavy over a degenerate world." See Marshall, p. 95.

Nicholas II holding an icon before his soldiers

flower.[7] Malaise, despair, and death engaged all of Europe.

Hundreds of thousands of Jews participated in the war as members of the component armies. As such, they fought and killed each other. The Russian army had the largest number of Jews (approximately 350,000), next the Austrian army (100,000), and then the German army (40,000). The British and French armies also had many Jews in their ranks, but because of the relatively small Jewish populations of those countries, only about 20,000 Jews were in the Allied Forces until the entry of America into the war in 1917. Unlike the Second World War, Jews and Judaism were not a major issue in World War I. The war did, however, provide the backdrop, and serve as the reason, for tremendous events and fundamental changes which overcame the Jewish world.

In the wake of the Russian defeat at Tannenberg, the German army invaded Russian Poland, an area dense with Jewish population. Most Russian Jews welcomed the Kaiser's forces as saviors. In fact, most of world Jewry initially was sympathetic to Germany and its aims in World War I, mainly because of its attempt to destroy the Czar and his anti-Semitic government. The Russians were not unaware of this Jewish bias, and responded ruthlessly.

Even though hundreds of thousands of Jews served in the Russian army, the government and a large section of the Russian populace

---

7. Joffre's felicitous phrase on this type of war was "nibbling." Marshal Joseph Jacques Joffre was the head of the French army for most of the war.

Russian soldiers in 1915

viewed the Jews as being actively disloyal. Thus pogroms followed every Russian defeat. The "Zhid" became the convenient scapegoat for the shortcomings of the Russian government and its military. Early in the war, the Russian government exiled hundreds of thousands of Jews from their homes in the Pale to internal Russia. These poor, homeless, defenseless people died in the thousands — of disease, hunger, exposure, and violence — on the dusty or muddy roads of Russia. They were preyed upon by outlaws, deserters, Cossacks, and peasants. Of the exiles who resettled in eastern Russia, tens of thousands more died during the war. Great and ancient Jewish communities were destroyed. The yeshivos of Lithuania were forced to disband and flee to the interior of Russia. Many of them returned to their homes after the war,[8] but many did not. The great rabbinic leaders, the heads of the yeshivos, the Chassidic *rebbeim,* all lost their bases of operation and support.

Conflicts

T HE SPIRITUAL TOLL WAS as great as the physical loss for European Jewry. Everything now became fluid, mobile, uncertain, and unstable. This naturally led to a further weakening of traditional Jewish life, since the necessary infrastructure for such a religious life system was washed away by the torrent of war. The war intensified the trend towards secularization and radicalism already present in Jewish society in the late nineteenth century.

---

8. For example, the *Chofetz Chaim* split his yeshivah into three parts, and they all went through many exiles before returning to Radin in 1921.

The very nihilistic, violent nature of the war propelled many Jews to decide that their future, if they survived, lay with a new Europe, or a new world, or with emigrating to a new locality — in short, in escaping the society that preceded the war. Sadly, many Jews would "discard the baby with the bathwater," and decide that the traditional forms of Judaism and Jewish life also no longer contained any meaning for them. The unraveling of the world of the Eastern European Jew, which began with Napoleon's march towards Moscow, was speeded apace a century later by the arrival of the German army in Russia.

On the whole, the German occupation of Poland and Russia during World War I was benign. Assimilated Jewish German officers and soldiers met traditional Jews for the first time in their lives. Many were positively influenced and became less assimilated.[9] The German authorities in Warsaw appointed two Orthodox German Jews as liaison with the Jewish community in Poland. These two men, Dr. Pinchas Kohn and Rabbi Dr. Emanuel Carlebach, supported traditional Jewry

9. Perhaps the most dramatic example of this was Franz Rosenzweig, the famous German-Jewish philosopher. An officer in the German army, Rosenzweig was engaged to be married to a non-Jewish woman, and had agreed to convert to Christianity. His visit to a Polish synagogue on the night of *Yom Kippur* so touched him that he broke the engagement, and began a return to traditional Jewish life.

A Jewish family in Galicia celebrates Passover, 1915, with two members of the Austrian Imperial Army

Lord Balfour

and saw to its spiritual and physical needs as best they could. They also strengthened the organization of Agudath Israel in Poland.[10]

As stated, Jews the world over were initially not averse to German victory. Most German-speaking Jewish intellectuals supported Germany's effort in the war.[11] Nevertheless, it began to dawn upon many elements of world Jewry that an Allied victory could be of greater benefit to the Jews, even if it meant that the hated Czar would also prevail. This was especially true of the leaders of the Zionist movement. To them, an Allied victory, especially an English triumph, was essential to their hopes for Palestine.

The Balfour Declaration

A S THE CARNAGE ON both the Western and Eastern fronts continued in 1915, England desperately searched for a way to break the stalemate. The solution proposed by Winston Churchill was a campaign against the Ottoman Empire, an attack that would outflank and jeopardize Germany and Austria, and that would thrust through the "soft underbelly of Europe." This ill-fated campaign at Gallipoli ended with the ignominious retreat of the British from Turkish soil. Nevertheless, it shifted the attention of the Allies to the Middle East and to its strategic importance.

At the time of World War I there were almost 100,000 Jews living in Palestine and approximately 500,000 Arabs.[12] Of these Arabs, 350,000 had migrated to Palestine only in the previous thirty years,[13] mainly to gain the economic benefits accompanying the new Jewish development of the country. This pattern of Arab

The Balfour Declaration

Foreign Office,
November 2nd, 1917

Dear Lord Rothschild,

I have much pleasure in conveying to you, on behalf of His Majesty's Government, the following declaration of sympathy with Jewish Zionist aspirations which has been submitted to, and approved by, the Cabinet

"His Majesty's Government view with favour the establishment in Palestine of a national home for the Jewish people, and will use their best endeavours to facilitate the achievement of this object, it being clearly understood that nothing shall be done which may prejudice the civil and religious rights of existing non-Jewish communities in Palestine, or the rights and political status enjoyed by Jews in any other country".

I should be grateful if you would bring this declaration to the knowledge of the Zionist Federation

---

10. Chaim Koolitz, *Sorbanei Geulah,* (Jerusalem, 1987) p. 83.

11. Paul Johnson, *A History of the Jews,* (New York 1987) p. 423.

12. Johnson, p. 430; Joan Peters, *From Time Immemorial,* (New York, 1984) p. 244.

13. Peters, p. 245.

immigration to Palestine would be characteristic of the entire century of Jewish settlement in Palestine. As the Jews built a Western-style agricultural and industrial society, the poor, oppressed Arabs of the neighboring areas of the Ottoman Empire flocked to Palestine in numbers greater than Jewish immigration to Palestine itself. "The Arab population of Palestine was small and limited until Jewish settlement restored the barren lands and drew to it Arabs from neighboring countries."[14]

The Jews in Palestine suffered terribly under the Turkish rule during 1915. The Turks expelled many of the leaders of the *Yishuv*,[15] and refused to allow others to return to their homes in the Land of Israel.[16] Jews were hanged on the walls of Jerusalem, their property was confiscated, and their bodies abused and violated. Hunger, disease, and poverty racked the country. Hundreds of Jews in Jerusalem died of starvation. The enmity of the *Yishuv* to the despotic rule of Kemal Pasha, the Turkish governor, and his cohorts who ruled Palestine, was deep and deserved. A small spy organization, run by the Aronson family and named *Nili*,[17] fed information to British intelligence, but the spies were caught and executed by the Turks.[18]

Lionel Walter Rothschild, English baron, recipient of the Balfour Declaration.

The major rebellions against Turkish rule were mounted not by the Jews but by the Arabs. Under the guidance of the famed Col. T.E. Lawrence,[19] the Hashemite tribe of the Arabian peninsula rose against their Turkish masters and drove them out. The British made grandiose promises to the Hashemites, and those promises would have to be

---

14. A statement made in 1953 by Dr. Carl Herman Voss, then chairman of the American Christian Palestine Committee, quoted by Peters, p. 425.

15. Including Ben Gurion and Ben Tzvi, among others.

16. Rabbi Kook, who had been in Europe when the war broke out, was forced to spend the war years first in Switzerland and later in London.

17. The acronym for the verse in Samuel, "*Netzach Israel Lo Yeshaker* — The Eternal One of Israel will not prove false."

18. Their graves were not discovered until Israel gained sovereignty over the Gaza Strip in 1967.

19. "Lawrence of Arabia" (1888-1935).

redeemed when the wreckage of the Middle East was dealt with at the conclusion of the war.

The major thrust of the war against the Turks in the Middle East came from a British invasion of Sinai and Palestine in 1917, and a complementary attack in Iraq that captured Baghdad. Under the command of General Sir Edmund Allenby,[20] in the summer of 1917, the British drove the Turks from Gaza, Beersheba, and Jerusalem, and eventually out of Palestine completely. In December 1917, Allenby, walking humbly on foot,[21] entered Jerusalem — and a new era in Jewish history began.

Chaim Weizmann had assiduously cultivated English friends for Zionism during the pre-War and War years. The Asquith government, dominated by the Liberal party, was not overly friendly to Jews generally and Zionism particularly. Since 1906, however, Weizmann had met and conversed with Arthur Balfour[22] on matters of Jews,

---

20. 1861-1936.

21. Unlike the Kaiser who visited Jerusalem in 1898 "mounted on a black charger, wearing white ceremonial uniform, his helmet surmounted by a burnished gold eagle." See Allan Palmer, *The Kaiser*, New York, 1978, p. 91. Legend also has it that the Kaiser forced his Turkish hosts to break a passage through the city walls next to the Jaffa Gate in Jerusalem in order to accommodate him, his horse, and his helmet and the Prussian eagle on top of the helmet, without requiring him to bow his head!

22. 1848-1930. A leader of the Conservative Party, a former prime minister of England, and a member of the War cabinets of both Asquith and Lloyd George.

General Allenby

Palestine, the Bible and Zionism. He also lobbied for the Zionist cause with David Lloyd George,[23] Winston Churchill, C.P. Scott,[24] Lord Curzon,[25] Mark Sykes,[26] and Herbert Samuel.

At the end of 1916, Prime Minister Asquith's government fell and he was replaced as prime minister by David Lloyd George, with Arthur Balfour as foreign minister. Weizmann had made a minor contribution to the British war effort as a chemist, by perfecting a new production method for a chemical used in a timing fuse for artillery shells. He sensed the opportunity presented by the new British government and Allenby's successful offensive in Palestine. Both Lloyd George and Balfour felt that out of the terrible carnage of World War I, at least one major achievement could be salvaged: to give the Jewish people their homeland.[27] Weizmann asked for a statement by the British government supporting the establishment of a Jewish home in Palestine.

Weizmann's greatest opponent on this matter was an assimilated British Jew, Edwin Montagu,[28] a member of the cabinet and a noted Liberal politician. He advanced all of the reasons usually associated with the objections of assimilated Jews to the adoption of pro-Jewish policies by their government.[29] Though he did not prevail, he did weaken the eventual language of the government's statement on Palestine. On November 2, 1917, the Balfour Declaration was proclaimed in England. It stated:

> His Majesty's government view with favor the establishment in Palestine of a National Home for the Jewish people, and will use their best endeavors to facilitate the achievement of this object, it being clearly understood that nothing shall be done which may prejudice the civil and religious rights of existing non-Jewish communities in Palestine, or the rights and political status enjoyed by Jews in any country.

How to reconcile the first part of the declaration with the second part was never explained; clearly the establishment of a Jewish home in Palestine would have an adverse effect on non-Jewish communities

23. 1863-1945.

24. Editor of the most influential paper in England, *The Manchester Guardian.*

25. 1859-1925. Former Viceroy of India.

26. 1879-1919. Chief Political Officer of the British army in the Middle East.

27. Johnson, p. 431.

28. 1879-1924.

29. He called such a declaration "anti-Semitic"! See O'Brien, p. 128.

there. In spite of its equivocation, the Balfour Declaration was universally regarded as a commitment by England to a Jewish Palestine.

Its issuance made a deep impression on the Jewish people, even on its sizable non-Zionist component.[30] It galvanized the Zionist movement into intense efforts — political, diplomatic, and organizational — and made Zion a real option for many Jews. It electrified the Jews of Russia and Poland, still suffering through the brutal war that engulfed them, and helped intensify their support of Zionism. It also served to legitimatize the Zionist movement in the United States, where the movement then began the long struggle to mobilize public opinion on behalf of the cause of a Jewish state.[31] The impractical dream began to take on real form.

The Jewish Brigade

 N 1917 THE ENGLISH WAR Cabinet approved the formation of a Jewish legion, composed of volunteers from the *Yishuv* in Palestine, to fight in the Allied cause. This was a plan originally advocated by Vladimir Jabotinsky,[32] a Russian Jew who founded the Revisionist Zionist Party as an alternative to the political Zionism of Herzl and Weizmann. Jabotinsky introduced a new element of nationalist militarism to Zionism. This militance found a responsive chord in the hearts of many Jews, tired of their seemingly passive acceptance of a very unhappy lot. Somehow, the participation of Jews as a unit in a Jewish military brigade, and not merely as individual members of fighting units of the countries of their residence, fired the Jewish imagination and marked a turning point in their attitude

---

30. The *Chofetz Chaim* saw in the Balfour Declaration "a heavenly sign regarding the forthcoming redemption of Israel." However, he feared that secular Jewry could yet abort this possible redemption by their behavior. See *HaChofetz Chaim,* by his son Rabbi Aryeh Leib HaCohen Poupko, Warsaw, 1937, p. 178. Also see there on p. 43 that in the 1890s the *Chofetz Chaim* felt that the "time was then that of the footsteps of the Messiah, and that Jews should prepare to return to the Land of Israel and reinstitute the study of those Torah subjects particularly applicable to life in the Land of Israel."

31. See O'Brien, p. 128, for a description of the indirect role that Louis Brandeis played in bringing about the publication of the Balfour Declaration.

32. 1880-1940. He was also the founder of Betar and the ideological father of the Irgun.

The Zion Mule Corps

towards their destiny. The gun would become a viable, if not yet preferable, option among certain elements of Zionism.

The experience of soldiering in the Jewish Brigade (Zion Mule Corps) would provide a cadre of officers for later Jewish para-military units in Palestine. The violence engendered by World War I permanently entered internal Jewish life. Henceforth, the story of the development of the Jewish *Yishuv* in Palestine would be accompanied by force of arms, acts of violence, and the constant necessity for defensive watchfulness.

The Russian Revolution

HE YEAR 1917 ALSO BROUGHT the Russian Revolution. Jews rejoiced at the downfall of the hated Czar; there was little sympathy for the Romanovs among his Jewish subjects. In the forefront of the revolution were many Jews. The "February Revolution" which installed Kerensky's Provisional Government was popular among the Russian Jews. "Jews supported the Provisional Government to the hilt . . . There were no differences of opinion in the Jewish world. Class interest disappeared."[33]

---

33. Ben Khayim, as quoted by Zvi Gittelman, *A Century of Ambivalence,* (New York, 1988) p. 89.

*Leon Trotsky
as Commissar
of Foreign Affairs*

However, the "October Revolution" of the Bolsheviks, led by Lenin and Trotsky, eventually changed all of this. Jews generally felt that "the essence of the February Revolution was freedom; the essence of the October Revolution was dictatorship . . . the premature dictatorship of the minority over the majority."[34] Nevertheless, Jews were prominently represented in the Bolshevik hierarchy. Trotsky,[35] Yakov Sverdlov,[36] Liev Kamenev,[37] Gregorii Zinoviev,[38] and Semen Dimonshtain[39] were only some of the many Jews who rose to power in the Bolshevik upheaval. These Jews were not only non-Jewish Jews, they were anti-Jewish Jews.

The Jewish section of the Communist Party, known as Yevesektsia,[40] was ruthless and fanatical in its treatment of Jewish society and Judaism. The Jewish Bolsheviks persecuted observant Jews, closed the religious schools and synagogues, exiled and executed leading rabbinic and lay persons, confiscated religious artifacts, and made it almost impossible to adhere to a halachically acceptable lifestyle. By 1919 all local religious *kehillos,* which were the agencies for Jewish self-government for centuries, were abolished, and their assets and functions taken over by the Yevesektsia. Religion was characterized as "superstition and cant."[41]

The attitude of the Yevesektsia was aptly expressed by a ferocious woman Communist, Esther Frumkin,[42] when she said: "The danger is

---

34. Ibid., p. 95.

35. 1879-1940. Born Leib Bronstein. Purged and assassinated in exile by Stalin.

36. 1885-1919. Born Nachmantes.

37. 1883-1936. Born Rosenfeld. Purged and executed by Stalin.

38. 1883-1936. Purged and executed by Stalin.

39. 1888-1938. He was the first Commissar for Jewish Affairs. He was a former student of the yeshivos of Telshe and Slobodka and later received rabbinical ordination from the famed Rabbi Chaim Ozer Grodzenski of Vilna. But he was radicalized in the unsuccessful revolution of 1905, and from then on became an implacable foe of Judaism, though he was less fanatic in his attitudes towards religious Jewry than were the other Jewish leaders of the Bolsheviks. See Gittelman, pp. 96-97.

40. Stalin dissolved this Jewish section of the party by 1931.

41. Gittelman, p. 119.

42. She was a former leader of the Bund who joined the Bolsheviks. She came from a traditional home and was once married to a rabbi. For her loyalty to Bolshevism, Stalin exiled her to Siberia, where she died in a labor camp in 1943.

the masses may think that Judaism is exempt from anti-religious propaganda and, therefore, it rests with the Jewish communists to be even more ruthless with rabbis than non-Jewish communists are with priests."[43] Jewish farm cooperatives and agricultural colonies made a special point of raising pigs in order to prove that Jewish farmers had broken with their religious tradition.

The Yevesektsia also targeted Zionism as its mortal enemy. The communist Jews were determined to prove themselves "more Bolshevik than Lenin,"[44] and thus all organized Zionist activity in Russia was soon forced underground and eventually ceased. The Hebrew language was also forbidden; though, strangely, Yiddish was permitted and encouraged. In the eyes of the communists, Hebrew was a holy, religious tongue and as such had no place in the new utopia of Russia, while Yiddish was a secular, proletarian, progressive language and thus became, with Russian, the language of the Jewish "progressives."[45]

43. Gittelman, p. 120.

44. Ibid., p. 111. See there also pp. 112-121 for a chilling account of the suppression of the "bourgeois-clerical-Zionist camp."

45. By the 1930s the communists mounted an anti-Yiddish campaign and this "proletarian, progressive language" also fell into official disfavor.

Jewish communists present a play mocking traditional Jewish ritual. Note the Hebrew word "kosher" painted on the backsides of the actors.

However, most dangerous of all to the Jews of Russia was the persecution by Jewish commissars of Russian Orthodox Christianity. The Jews were more vicious in this behavior than were many non-Jewish commissars, though their persecution of Christianity was still mild when compared to their anti-Judaism activities. Maxim Gorky, the noted Russian author and supporter of the Revolution, nevertheless lamented that "Jewish communists were purposely put in the ranks of those persecuting the Russian Church and priests, in order that the Russian peasants should see with their own eyes that the Jews are desecrating their holy places."[46] It was not surprising, therefore, that one of the leading priests of the Russian Church exhorted the faithful to "Bless yourselves, beat the Jews, overthrow the People's Commissars."[47]

The barely latent, always nearly overt anti-Semitism of the Russian masses flamed against the Jews generally because of the behavior and prominence of the relatively tiny communist fraction of the Jewish community. The Jews of Europe would find themselves hated as "Bolsheviks" by the non-communists and as "capitalist provocateurs" by the communists. The ancient religious hatred of Jews now was transformed and legitimatized into political and social abhorrence and isolation. The Revolution, which Jews in Russia had welcomed, turned into decades of death and nightmare for them.

Armistice

 HE REVOLUTIONARY GOVERNMENT in Russia, desperate for an exit from the war, signed an unfavorable peace agreement with Germany on March 3, 1918, in the city of Brest-Litovsk. Under the terms of the treaty Russia yielded 34% of her population,[48] 32% of her farmland, 50% of her industrial holdings, and 90% of her coal mines. Said Trotsky: "This is a peace that Russia, grinding her teeth, is forced to accept."[49]

Russia would regain all of this with a vengeance twenty-five years

---

46. Gittelman, pp. 117-118.

47. Ibid., p. 99. See there, p. 153, that Russian Orthodox priests "[prayed] to God to save us from the Jewish nemesis."

48. Included were over three and one half million Jews.

49. Marshall, p. 296.

later, but by then the Jewish population of Eastern Europe would have been largely annihilated. Even after the peace was signed, the Germans continued to occupy large sections of Russia. This would eventually contribute to the defeat of Germany in the war, since these troops were not in the West when desperately needed, and eventually many of them were subverted by Bolshevik propaganda, thus rendering them useless to the Kaiser and his generals.

In March 1918, the German army launched its final great offensive in the West. By then, however, the entrance of the United States into the war in 1917, and the subsequent arrival of the American Expeditionary Force in France in 1918, made German victory impossible. The Germans came close to Paris and breakthrough, but by the summer of 1918 they were spent. The German population at home was hungry, war weary, demoralized, and mutinous.

The great Allied counter-offensive now began, and by the fall of 1918 the Kaiser abdicated, and the German government that replaced him[50] signed the Armistice agreement that ended the war. Germany was in ungovernable chaos, Russia was engaged in a bloody civil war, France, England, Austria, and other antagonists in the war were bled white. "Almost ten million men and women had been killed in the fighting. More than six million had been crippled or invalided for life. There had been a victory of sorts, but what the victors celebrated chiefly was that mass death, after four years, had taken a holiday. The illusion was that all of humanity would profit by the great lesson."[51]

At the beginning of the century, Theodor Herzl had been told by a leading British statesman that in order for a Jewish state to rise in Palestine, history would first require the demise of the Ottoman, Russian, German, and Austro-Hungarian empires. Herzl was also assured that there was no reasonable chance of this occurring. The First World War destroyed all of these empires and then some, and changed the world in an unpredictable and irrevocable manner. The ancient, permanent rulers of Europe and the world were being swept away. The Jewish world would have to deal with this startling new reality.

---

50. Which had Jewish representation, thus fueling Hitler's later lie that the Jews sold out Germany in the Great War.
51. Marshall, pp. 398-9.

Section VI

Treacherous Hopes

1920-1930

27

After the Conflict

New Countries, Old Problems

HE GREAT WAR LEFT EUROPE prostrate. Both victor and vanquished lived in cold, hunger, disease,[1] and uncertainty. The German Army was so exhausted and immobile it could not immediately return to German soil. The victorious Allies sent thousands of occupation troops into Germany. The presence of these occupiers served to make their unexpected[2] defeat more galling to the Germans. The "short, brisk war" had turned into an endless nightmare and many Germans plotted revenge rather than reconciliation. The shape of the new Europe was to be decided upon at the peace conference in Versailles, France.

This conference began on January 18, 1919 and was attended by all of the major world figures of the time. Woodrow Wilson, the American President, came to see his idealistic hopes of self-determination, protection of minorities, and open treaties translated into action. Though all of the major participants paid lip service to Wilson's altruistic plans, none of them were prepared to sacrifice national interest or ambition to effectuate them. Thus, the Treaty of Versailles, when finally produced, was a product of vengeance, greed, cynical power-plays, secret treaties, and shrewd trading among the victors, all at the expense of the losers. This vindictive treaty, with its unrealistic and fictitious blueprint and map for the new Europe, guaranteed the onset of World War II only twenty years later. Wilson, who had the power to save the

---

1. The great influenza epidemics of 1919-23 afflicted hundreds of thousands, if not millions, of victims worldwide.

2. As late as the summer of 1918, the German General Staff and the nation at large were still confident of at least partial victory, or, at worst, a draw.

day, was bested by Lloyd George of England, Clemenceau of France, and Orlando of Italy. He left for home a sick and beaten man.

Out of the wreckage of the war, the treaty of Versailles created nine new European countries: Finland, Estonia, Latvia, Lithuania, and Poland were carved from Russia (and some German territory), while the newly dismantled Austro-Hungarian Empire yielded Austria, Hungary, Czechoslovakia, and Yugoslavia. In addition, major territorial adjustments were made for Rumania, Greece, and Turkey. France took back Alsace-Lorraine from Germany. The German colonial empire, as well as most of the Ottoman Empire, were divided between England and France, with England receiving the lion's share.

The professed ideal of self-determination fired the imagination of Europe's minorities, including those of the new countries, nearly all of which were conglomerations of various ethnic groups, many of which were antagonistic to one another. It was ironic that most of these new countries, though inherently weak, militarily and economically, were themselves immediately faced with the specter of minority defections, fragmentation, and even civil war. With the exception of Finland and Estonia, all of these fledgling countries contained significant Jewish populations. The ensuing turmoil would have devastating consequences on these Jewish communities, already mortally weakened by the war itself.

Polish Jewry

 HE LARGEST JEWISH COMMUNITY in Europe outside of Russia resided in Poland. Jews constituted ten percent of the Polish population and in certain major urban centers such as Warsaw, Lodz, and Cracow were almost thirty percent of the population. The Poles took to their new independence with a vengeance. Declaring "Poland for the Poles," they rapidly moved to subdue any minority unrest within their new borders. On November 3, 1917, Poland declared its independence. By 1921 its army, under the command of General Jozef Pilsudski,[3] had engaged in

---

3. 1867-1935. He was the Polish national hero during the 1920s and 1930s, and eventually became the country's dictator. His anti-Semitic, right-wing nationalist policy was actually seen as moderate within the context of the virulent xenophobic and blatantly violent anti-Semitic Poland of the time.

six different conflicts against its minorities and neighbors. The Jews suffered horribly in all these battles, being the scapegoat for both sides, and providing easy killing for the sadistic mobs.

Poland's first major struggle was with its Ruthenian minority for control over Eastern Galicia, centering upon the city of Lvov.[4] The Ruthenians were ethnic Ukrainians who, for cultural, religious, and social reasons, desired union with their brethren in the Ukraine, then fighting to be independent of Russia. The Jews were officially neutral in the war, though their sympathy was on the side of the Poles, as the lesser of two evils. Nevertheless, the capture of Lvov by the Poles touched off a dreadful pogrom.[5] In an interview given later, Pilsudski dismissed the pogrom by saying, "I don't think the affair was serious, and have not yet received a full report about it. I must inquire. I must say that the Poles are not philo-Semites. That must be admitted. The Jews in Poland form a very large number and are a foreign body whom one would like to get rid of."[6]

---

4. Known to Jews by its German name of Lemberg.

5. See Sanders, *Shores of Refuge*, chapter 38, for a horrific description of the Lemberg pogrom.

6. Ibid., p. 323.

THE SECOND
POLISH REPUBLIC
1921-1939

- Under International control
- Conquered from Lithuania and annexed to Poland

By 1923 Poland would wrest Vilna from its newly independent Lithuanian neighbor, and many Jews would be massacred in that war as well. The Lithuanians accused the Jews of being pro-Polish and the Polish forces viewed them as hostile Lithuanians. The Polish-Lithuanian border became a sealed and dangerous one. This new, artificial border was a strange one to Jews, who had always lived on both sides of it and easily commuted between the cities and towns now located in two different warring countries. It impeded the return of the yeshivos to their Lithuanian base after the war and dislocated the ancient centers of Jewish learning and tradition in Lithuanian Poland and Lithuania proper. Lithuania without Vilna was unthinkable to the average Lithuanian, both Jew and non-Jew; and yet the Lithuanian nationalists, smarting under this shame, were quick to blame the Jews somehow for the debacle.

Strashun Library, Vilna. Established by Matisyahu Strashun, son of the "Rashash", Rabbi Shmuel Strashun, noted commentator to the Talmud

This new nationalism of the small minorities of Eastern Europe brought with it virulent anti-Semitism and violent pogroms. Little wonder, therefore, that mass emigration of Jews from Poland and Lithuania in the early 1920s reached epidemic proportions.

The main arena of war for the Jews, however, was in the Ukraine, where there raged a terrible, tri-cornered contest for domination, between Poland, Red Russia, and White Russia. The Poles reached Kiev by the spring of 1920, leaving in their wake the indescribable ravages of a new war inflicted on the still open wounds of the old one. The Jews suffered horribly as usual, and the Ukraine once again was soaked with Jewish blood.

Street of the Jews, Vilna, 1925

The Russian White Army, which fought the Bolsheviks with great ferocity, and at first with great success, began to wilt in the face of Trotsky's determined Red Army. The Ukranian National Army, allied with the Whites, was commanded by Semen Petluria.[7] Under his rule, the entire Ukraine exploded into one vast pogrom.

---

7. 1879-1926. Petluria was shot to death by a Jewish youth seeking revenge for the Ukrainian pogroms.

A synagogue in Vitebsk, wrecked by the communists

Jewish villages and city quarters were pillaged and razed to the ground. The pogroms were marked by indescribable barbarism and personal cruelty. Children, pregnant women, and young girls were sought out and subjected to horror and torture on an especially vicious plane. Only the later atrocities of the Nazis equaled the fury of this holocaust of hate in the Ukraine. "From 1918-21 more than 2000 pogroms took place; half a million Jews were left homeless; 30,000 Jews were killed directly, and together with those who died of wounds or as a result of illnesses contracted during the pogroms, a total of about 150,000 Jews died."[8] The Jewish heartland in Europe lay wasted, and from the Vistula to the Don, the Pale of Settlement had been transformed into a fiery grave.

The Red Army vanquished the Whites, and by August 1920 had forced its way almost to the gates of Warsaw. There Pilsudski and the Poles rallied and drove the Russians back to Pinsk. It was then that the border between Poland and Russia finally stabilized and remained static until the advent of World War II. The Poles added to the already accepted "Jewish-Bolshevik" myth with fanciful tales of Jewish commissars executing innocent Poles. The tragedy of the Russian Revolution was that, in the mind of the masses of Poland, Lithuania, the Ukraine, and Russia, it equated Jews with Bolshevism, when, in reality, the Jews were overwhelmingly anti-Bolshevist and suffered more than others under its cruel repression.

---

8. Gittelman, p. 106.

Czechoslovakia and Hungary

HOUGH LESS BLOODY, the transition to independence in the other new countries of Europe was also particularly trying for Jews. Only in Czechoslovakia, under the benign leadership of Tomas Masaryk[9] and Edvard Benes,[10] were Jews extended full legal protection and rights. However, Czechoslovakia was involved in constant border disputes with its neighbors, especially Hungary, and the sealed borders proved especially troublesome to Jewish commerce, as well as to the large number of Chassidic Jews whose *rebbe* happened to be on the other side of the international border. The great bastion of learning at Pressburg (now called Bratislava) was in Czechoslovakia, but the hinterland of its influence and support was in Hungary.

Nevertheless, Jewish life in Czechoslovakia and Hungary flourished between the wars, though the native anti-Semitism of the masses was still felt in every facet of life. This anti-Semitism was spurred by the Jewish-communist connection, now fixed in the minds of the populace. Bela Kun,[11] a Jew, was the dictator of the communist regime in Hungary, which held sway until overthrown in the fall of 1919. Kurt Eisner,[12] also a Jew, was the leader of the communist uprising and government in Bavaria in 1918. He was assassinated in 1919. And "Red Rose," Rosa Luxemburg,[13] was the most notorious communist revolutionary outside of Russia. She, too, was murdered in 1919. These secularized, radical, non-Jewish Jews fueled the anti-Semitism that they believed their radicalism would eliminate. Their own blind hatred of their tradition and their people translated itself into a lethal weapon thrust into the heart of the Jewish people. Their guilt in the destruction of European civilization and of the Jewish people in the twentieth century cannot be minimized. As always, the fruits of Jewish assimilation and radicalism were bitter.

---

9. 1850-1937. The first president of Czechoslovakia. A tolerant, noble friend of the Jews and humanity. He visited Palestine in the 1920s and was a supporter of the idea of a Jewish state.

10. 1884-1948. Second president of Czechoslovakia and Masaryk's devoted assistant and disciple, as well as his foreign minister until 1937.

11. 1886-1939.

12. 1867-1919.

13. 1871-1919. See Johnson, pp. 448-50, for an excellent analysis of her political philosophy and Jewish self-hatred.

Jewish Political Divisions

 HE NEW GOVERNMENTS in Europe, all of which were ostensibly democratic, gave their Jewish citizens the right to vote and organize political parties. Unlike the Jews in Western Europe and the United States, who participated in the political process as part of the general political structure and never formed exclusively Jewish political parties, the Jews of Poland, Lithuania, and other Eastern and Central European countries formed individual Jewish parties. These parties competed for the Jewish vote and for representation in the national parliaments and local councils.

In addition, such Polish cities as Warsaw, Lodz, and Cracow had local autonomous Jewish governments, which regulated Jewish communal life. The degree of autonomy and freedom of action extended to these local Jewish councils varied from time to time, but rarely were they free from interference by the national government. In Poland, the Pilsudski government openly connived with certain Jewish political figures and parties to rig the elections, and many times the results of these illegitimate elections were set aside by the Polish courts.[14] But the internal rivalries of the Jewish parties, fanned by these political rivalries, proceeded unabated until the Holocaust.

The three main political groupings of Polish and Lithuanian Jewry were the Bund and other leftist socialist parties, the Agudath Israel, which represented traditional, observant Jewry, and the Zionist parties, both religious and secular, which promoted the cause of settlement in

---

14. *Autonomous Jewish Rule in Poland, Lodz, 1914-39,* by Reuven M. Shapiro, *HaDavar*, Vol. 67, No. 36, p. 17.

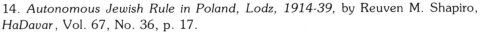

Voters line up at the polls in a Jewish neighborhood in Warsaw to elect representatives to the Polish Parliament

Palestine. In addition, there were splinter parties of all these groupings, which were disproportionately powerful because of the coalition nature of national and local government and its system of strict proportional representation. The disagreements in policy, outlook, and aims between these Jewish parties were intense, personal, and vitriolic. Much of these disagreements stemmed from diverse, firmly held views as to how best to deal with the "Jewish" problem and who would be the best ally to help solve the matter. Jews, who had been shut out of the political system for centuries, now entered the arena of inter-group politics with feverish fervor. At one time or another, their behavior was noble, opportunistic, spiteful, violent, altruistic, positive and counter-productive. Sometimes it was all of these at one and the same time.

The bitter rivalries between the different factions and parties of the Jews of Poland were eventually transplanted to the Israeli scene and survive there as a hardy weed. The Jewish scene in Poland was fragmented and of infinite variety. Jewish Poland was a bastion of tradition and Torah learning, Chassidus and innovative education.[15] It also was a stronghold of Jewish secularism, nationalism, socialism, and nihilism. It was the most fertile ground in the world for recruits to Zionism, and yet it produced some of the strongest anti-Zionist personalities as well. Jewish Poland was alive and vibrant, noisy and quarrelsome, creative and intellectual, numerically strong but very insecure. Instinctively, it felt that its future in Poland

15. The Yeshivah Chachmei Lublin, founded by Rabbi Meir Shapiro, and the Bais Yaakov girls' schools system, founded by Sarah Schenirer, are only two examples of the old wine of Torah in the new vessels of the twentieth century.

Enrollment of Jews in Educational Institutions in Poland, 1934-1935[*]

TYPE OF SCHOOL AND AFFILIATION	NUMBER OF SCHOOLS	ENROLLMENTS
Non-Jewish		
STATE, MUNICIPAL, and PRIVATE		
elementary		425,566
secondary		29,822
vocational		6,994
special (for the disabled)		1,607
university		7,114
Total		481,203
Jewish		
TARBUT & JEWISH SECONDARY SCHOOL FEDERATION (Zionist)		
kindergarten and elementary	255	35,764
secondary and vocational	10	10,857
evening	4	6,229
Total	269	53,080
CYSHO (Bund, Labor Zionist, Folkist, and others)		
kindergarten and elementary	97	10,256
secondary	2	650
evening	70	4,580
Total	165	15,486
SHUL-KULT (Labor Zionist and others)		
kindergarten and elementary	13	2,026
evening	3	317
Total	16	2,343
YAVNEH (Mizrachi)		
kindergarten and elementary	220	
secondary	3	
yeshivah	4	
rabbinical seminary	2	
Total	229	15,923
HOREV & BETH JACOB (Agudas Yisrael)		
cheder and Talmud Toarh	557	81,328
yeshivah	197	18,758
Total	754	100,086
PRIVATE		
cheder		40,000
secondary	147	8,232[**]
Total		48,232
ORT		4,427
ICA		2,942
WUZET		1,933
Total		9,302
Total number of enrollments in Jewish schools		244,452
Total number of Jewish enrollments		725,655

[*] This table is based on Zineman 1938, Chmielewski 1937, Kazdan 1947, and Mauersberg 1968. The number of enrollments is greater than the number of students because one person might enroll at more than one institution; for example, one student might attend a public elementary school in the morning and a Jewish school in the afternoon. According to the census of 1931, the total number of Jews between the ages of three and nineteen in Poland was 1,056,556.
[**] 1937-1938

was uncertain and its reaction to the problems of Poland vis-a-vis its sizable Jewish minority between the wars was diffuse and somewhat confused.

A great many Polish Jews left for America and Palestine after the war (the ratio was ten to one in favor of America), but in the early 1920s, America closed its doors to this immigration. Jewish Polish immigration was reduced from 120,000 in 1921 to 50,000 in 1922. In 1924, the far-more restrictive Johnson Act cut the quotas drastically by stages, so that immigration from Poland was reduced to only 5,982 per year. Jewish immigration to Palestine was also slowly restricted by the changing attitude of Britain towards the establishment of "a national Jewish home in Palestine."[16]

Almost 50,000 Polish Jews became residents of Germany in the 1920s. They were despised by their German hosts and resented even by their German Jewish brethren.[17] In spite of the obstacles they faced, these "Ost-Juden"[18] became a vital force in German Jewish life and brought Eastern European spirit and dedication to Torah study to the German Jewish community. Though they gradually became more "modern" and "German," and less "Polish," they were always viewed as unwanted outsiders in the twenty years between the wars.

The situation of the Jews in Germany after the war was already precarious, but few yet recognized it as such. The Jewish future in Germany was inextricably bound to the triumph of political democracy, financial stability and prosperity, and a peaceful German attitude towards its neighbors. In effect, this was the program of the Weimar Republic that governed Germany from 1920 to 1933. However, that government eventually failed and collapsed, thus sealing the fate of Europe and presaging the destruction of German Jewry.

The true instigators of World War I, and the ones who brought about the terrible defeat of Germany, were "the army, the princes, generals, and landowners, the law-professors who endowed it [the German War drive] with academic legitimacy, and the Lutheran pastors who gave it moral authority . . ." But they were never blamed for the war and its ruinous consequences. Instead, "not only was the truth not told; it was deliberately concealed beneath a myth that the German war

---

16. Sanders, p. 387.

17. Torah study, and public Orthodox life-style generally became more recognized in German-Jewish circles that had never before been exposed to public intensive Orthodox life.

18. Jews from the East.

machine had been 'stabbed in the back' by civilian defeatism and cowardice . . ."[19]

Thus, by a curious piece of national myopia, containing elements of self-deception, the Germans exonerated those who had got the country into the fearful mess in which it found itself.

In Germany's search for scapegoats, blame for the defeat was placed on the communists, the socialists, the social democrats, on democracy, and eventually on the Weimar Republic itself. And, in a sinister and unreasoning fashion, it was also placed on the Jews. The communists, socialists, social democrats, and Weimar republicans would purge themselves by becoming Nazis. Only the Jews would remain as the hated scapegoat.

Walter Rathenau, Jewish German foreign minister. Assassinated by right-wing radicals for having signed the Armistice Treaty

Germany Teeters on the Brink

 ERMANY SUFFERED FEARFUL inflation in the 1920s. It had a very large number of unemployed workers. These conditions spawned many radical political movements and parties. Its parliament was continually deadlocked and its government unstable. There was violence and mayhem in the streets between warring factions of the political Left and Right. "Volkische"[20] parties abounded, including a small Nationalist Socialist Party led by an Austrian, Adolf Hitler, who had served as a corporal in the German army during the war. Lost were the fruits of Germany's eastern triumphs during the first three years of the war; its empire was divided among others and its self-pride severely wounded.

Anti-Semitism, which has always been present in Germany — Martin Luther, founder of the predominant German church, was a fierce anti-Semite — was officially opposed by the Weimar regime. But as a policy of revenge and as a release of frustration, anti-Semitism became more popular and solid among the German masses in the 1920s.

On the surface, Germany floated in a nihilistic, laissez-faire

---

19. *Modern Times,* by Paul Johnson. Harper and Row, 1985, p. 108, 111.

20. Nationalistic, xenophobic political groups.

environment, but just beneath, it seethed with uncontrollable hatred, anger, violence, and lustful ambition. Jewish reaction to this anti-Semitism was ambivalent. Yes, Jews were frightened, but they also felt that despite it they could survive, indeed prosper, in Germany. For after all, what could they do about it? Anti-Semitism in Germany was a fact, just as beer, dueling, and punctuality were facts of German life. A German Jew of the time said: "Moritz Goldstein argued that it was useless to expose the baselessness of anti-Semitic 'evidence': 'What would be gained? The knowledge that their hatred is genuine. When all calumnies have been refuted, all distortions rectified, all false notions about us rejected, antipathy will remain as something irrefutable.' "[21] In Germany, as in Eastern Europe, the Jew was regarded as an alien and a usurper, and served as the natural and most convenient scapegoat for the ills of the post-war society.

Spiritual Revival

 N SPITE OF ALL OF THIS, Jewish life in Europe between the wars remained vital, creative, and optimistic. The yeshivos of Lithuania eventually reestablished themselves — some in newly created Lithuania and some in newly expanded Poland — and such places as Slobodka, Mir, Ponevez, Kaminetz, Radin, Telshe, Kletzk, and Lublin became centers of Jewish learning and Torah scholarship again. Students from Germany, England, Western Europe, and even America enrolled in the Torah academies of Eastern Europe. The Chassidic courts of Poland and Hungary teemed with life and activity.[22] Although many, if not most, of their supporters did not survive the later Holocaust, such vibrant courts as Gur, Belz, Bobov, Munkacz, Satmar, Vizhnitz, Spinka and others that are familiar names today were fruitful and active in the interwar years. The *Rebbe* of Gur, leader of hundreds of thousands, spearheaded the successful effort to establish and finance hundreds of schools in Poland. The combined leadership of the *Chofetz Chaim* and

---

21. Johnson, Modern Times, p. 121.

22. The national Polish Railway System built a special spurline from Warsaw to Gura Kolwaria, where the *Rebbe* of Gur resided and from where he guided hundreds of thousands of chassidim. The rail line facilitated travel to the *Rebbe,* and made a handsome profit for the railway.

Rabbi Chaim Ozer Grodzenski resulted in the establishment of the Vaad HaYeshivos (Committee of Yeshivos) that accomplished the same end for the Lithuanian academies. Rabbi Meir Shapiro[23] of Lublin called for new yeshivos and new ideas in Torah education and methods.

Rabbi Meir Shapiro

Sara Schenirer[24] founded the Bais Yaakov system of girls' schools in Cracow in the 1920s. She was bitterly opposed by some, rabbinic leaders but with the help and support of the *Chofetz Chaim*, Rabbi Chaim Ozer Grodzenski, and the *Rebbes* of Gur and Belz, she wrought a major revolution in traditional Jewish life. Women's education, in all of its variety and depth and popularity, is one of the major areas of accomplishment in the Jewish world over the past sixty years.

In spite of poverty, bigotry, governmental oppression, and severe internal divisions, Jewish life and numbers in Europe strengthened and grew during this period. This central, vital core of Judaism in Europe nurtured and helped sustain and expand Jewish life in Palestine and America in the 1920s. On the eve of its extinction, European Jewry enriched its tradition in all forms of scholarship and human service, and remained essentially loyal to its instincts of intelligence, compassion, and morality.

In the face of the unremitting enmity exhibited by the new governments of Europe to their Jewish citizens, traditional Jewry did not flinch. In spite of the beatings, humiliations, taxes, restrictions, and petty harassment[25] of the Jews by the new governments ostensibly pledged to equal rights and non-discrimination, religious Jewry persevered. The religious Jew rarely felt demeaned by the hatred directed against him. He pitied the perpetrator and felt morally superior to his vulgar foe. Orthodoxy expected only minimal benefits from the new Poland, Lithuania, or Austria, and therefore was neither surprised nor overly

Rabbi Chaim Ozer Grodzensky

---

23. One of the leading rabbinic figures of the time. He was an elected member of the Polish Parliament, a leader of Agudath Israel, the founder of the great Yeshivah Chachmei Lublin. His historic, lasting achievement was the origination of the world-wide Talmudic study project *Daf HaYomi*, which called for all Jews to study the same folio-page of the Talmud every day. Rabbi Shapiro intended this as a way to unify Jews through shared study and as a way to elevate the lives of its individual participants. Now in its tenth $7^1/2$ year cycle, *Daf HaYomi* has many tens of thousands of adherents.

24. 1882-1935.

25. Letters to rabbis or yeshivos in Poland, on which the name of the addressee was slightly misspelled (Shapiro instead of Szapiro, etc.), were routinely returned to the sender or sent to the dead letter office.

depressed when the promised rosy new world of post-Versailles Europe did not materialize. The spiritual strength of traditional Torah life and of the deep-rooted Jewish historical experience served to solidify Jewish strength and to nurture Jewish pride.

Secular Jewry, however, was badly shaken by the new anti-Semitism that manifested itself in the 1920s in Europe. Having invested all of their idealistic capital in the national and international movements of the time, they were depressed and confused at finding themselves still despised by their erstwhile idealistic allies and fellow citizens. Their program of fighting this new anti-Semitism only seemed to provoke new anti-Semitism. Their fierce defense of Jewish rights in Parliament and in the streets was met by even fiercer enmity and hatred.

The hopes of the Jewish socialists, trade-unionists, social-democrats and others were dashed by the mid-1920s, and these groups thrashed about to find a new path of hope for themselves. Many of them despaired about Jewish life in Europe and joined the Zionist movement, looking towards the Jewish national home in Palestine for comfort and pride. The Zionist movement grew stronger in Poland and other European countries in the 1920s as a result of the bankrupt policies of the other secular Jewish parties. But the feeling of betrayal, worthlessness, anger, and deep frustration never left secular Jewry, until the Jewish tragedy in Europe culminated in World War II.[26]

---

26. For a detailed description of the different attitudes of religious and secular Jewry towards anti-Semitism in the 1920s in Poland, see *Jewish Jews* in *Jewish Poland Between the Wars*, by Ceille Heller.

28

Palestine for Whom?

The New Rulers

HE JEWS GENERALLY, AND THE Zionists particularly, were convinced that the Balfour Declaration gave them a national home in Palestine. The San Remo Conference in April 1920 supported this conclusion by granting England, the author of the Balfour Declaration, mandatory control over Palestine,[1] thus giving England the legal and practical means to implement the promises of the Balfour Declaration. The total population of Palestine, which in 1914 had reached 800,000, had shrunk to a little over 600,000 by 1919. Of this number, approximately 66,000 (11% of the total population) were Jews.[2] The Zionists planned to expand immigration, make large-scale land purchases, and build the infrastructure of a nation, all under the administration, protection, and even encouragement of England. They would be sadly disappointed.

The Arabs were quick to resort to violence in opposing the Balfour Declaration and the Jewish *Yishuv*. Rioting by Arabs had been a fact of life in Palestine for the last century of Turkish rule. The English were interested in a stable society and realized early on that enforcing the pro-Zionist tone of the Balfour Declaration would result in further and continuing Arab violence. The military administration of the English mandatory government of Palestine had a decided pro-Arab, anti-Zionist, if not anti-Semitic, bias.[3] The main villain in the

---

1. At that time, Palestine included the eastern bank of the Jordan River, currently the Hashemite Kingdom of Jordan, and the Golan Heights. England transferred the Golan to Syria, then under French mandate, in 1923.

2. O'Brien, *The Siege,* p. 133.

3. See O'Brien, page 139. Some of the comments of the leading British generals in charge of Palestine were: "Balfour, Lloyd George, and their long-nosed friends;" "Jewish clannishness;" "The Jews are so clever and the Arabs so stupid and childish, that it seems only sporting to be for the Arabs."

field was Sir Ronald Storrs, who was the English governor of Jerusalem from 1917 to 1925. An able, clever administrator, he was an Arabist, typical of the British colonial forces and diplomats of the time, who tended to romanticize the Arab cause and people, thus granting the Arabs a great deal of unearned sympathy. The Jews eventually classified him as their worst enemy in Palestine and developed an attitude of paranoia regarding his pronouncements, activities, and even his presence.

Storrs and the English subtly gave the impression to the local Arabs that violence could abort the Balfour Declaration and the Arabs gladly responded to the hint. On April 1, 1920, an Arab pogrom against the defenseless, religious, anti-Zionist Jews[4] of the Jewish quarter of the old city of Jerusalem took place. Nine people died, and 244 were wounded. The Arab police sided with the rioters and the British Army did not respond for five days. This pogrom set the pattern for life in Palestine: Arab violence, Jewish indignation, and British neutrality on the side of the Arabs were the story of Palestine from 1919 to 1948.

---

4. The Arabs never were sophisticated enough to differentiate between Zionist and non-Zionist Jews when it came to violence and terrorism. This plain fact, somehow, was lost upon the divisive Jews themselves.

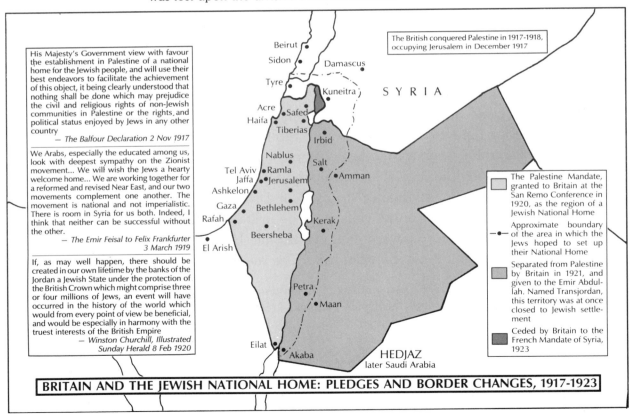

His Majesty's Government view with favour the establishment in Palestine of a national home for the Jewish people, and will use their best endeavors to facilitate the achievement of this object, it being clearly understood that nothing shall be done which may prejudice the civil and religious rights of non-Jewish communities in Palestine or the rights and political status enjoyed by Jews in any other country
— The Balfour Declaration 2 Nov 1917

We Arabs, especially the educated among us, look with deepest sympathy on the Zionist movement... We will wish the Jews a hearty welcome home... We are working together for a reformed and revised Near East, and our two movements complement one another. The movement is national and not imperialistic. There is room in Syria for us both. Indeed, I think that neither can be successful without the other.
— The Emir Feisal to Felix Frankfurter 3 March 1919

If, as may well happen, there should be created in our own lifetime by the banks of the Jordan a Jewish State under the protection of the British Crown which might comprise three or four millions of Jews, an event will have occurred in the history of the world which would from every point of view be beneficial, and would be especially in harmony with the truest interests of the British Empire
— Winston Churchill, Illustrated Sunday Herald 8 Feb 1920

The British conquered Palestine in 1917-1918, occupying Jerusalem in December 1917

Beirut
Sidon
Damascus
Tyre
Kuneitra
SYRIA
Acre
Safed
Haifa
Tiberias
Irbid
Nablus
Salt
Tel Aviv
Ramla
Jaffa
Jerusalem
Amman
Ashkelon
Gaza
Bethlehem
Rafah
Kerak
Beersheba
El Arish
Petra
Maan
Eilat
Akaba
HEDJAZ
later Saudi Arabia

The Palestine Mandate, granted to Britain at the San Remo Conference in 1920, as the region of a Jewish National Home

Approximate boundary of the area in which the Jews hoped to set up their National Home

Separated from Palestine by Britain in 1921, and given to the Emir Abdullah. Named Transjordan, this territory was at once closed to Jewish settlement

Ceded by Britain to the French Mandate of Syria, 1923

BRITAIN AND THE JEWISH NATIONAL HOME: PLEDGES AND BORDER CHANGES, 1917-1923

In 1920, Sir Herbert Samuel,[5] an assimilated Jew, was appointed High Commissioner of Palestine by George Curzon, Balfour's successor at the English Foreign Office. Samuel, a noted Liberal party politician, and apparently pro-Zionist in inclination, was hailed by the Jews as a modern Nehemiah. On his first Sabbath in Jerusalem he walked to a synagogue in the Old City of Jerusalem[6] and recited the *Haftarah*[7] of comfort and consolation of Israel. However, Samuel was dogged by the eternal problem faced by assimilated Jews in national government service, when forced to deal with a Jewish problem. His loyalty to English policy and goals, and the necessity for cool "even-handedness" in dealing with the Jew-Arab conflict, contrasted painfully with his own Jewish origins and instinct.

Sir Herbert Samuel

A believer in the political democracy and liberalism of England, Samuel set about to reconcile, by democratic process, the Jewish and Arab communities; to establish representative bodies to rule the country; and to build a social and economic infrastructure that would benefit all. His goals were lofty and his intentions worthy, but his judgment was hopelessly naive. Samuel's Immigration Ordinance, published in September 1920, encouraged Jewish immigration into Palestine. Almost 12,000 Jews arrived in Palestine during the following year, in what was known as the Third Aliyah. They came from Eastern Europe and they were young, dedicated, trained, and prepared for the ordeal that faced them. Although many traditional Jews arrived in Palestine then as well, the Third Aliyah was overwhelmingly secular, socialist, and fiercely loyal to their belief in the creation of the new, secular Jew as envisioned by Zionist culture. They were to become the backbone of the new *Yishuv* and eventually the second group of leaders of the state they would help create twenty-five years later.

---

5. 1870-1963. See Johnson's bitter assessment of him in *A History of the Jews*, p. 436: "He wanted to be a Jew without believing in God. He wanted to be a Zionist without joining any Zionist organization. He wanted to promote a Jewish national home without offending the Arabs." The Jewish view of him was much more charitable.

6. A long and hot walk in the Jerusalem summer sun.

7. Sabbath morning reading from the Prophets.

Arab Unrest

OR EVERY JEW WHO IMMIGRATED to Palestine in the 1920s, two Arabs arrived.[8] These Arabs were attracted by the development of the new agricultural and industrial infrastructure financed by the Zionist movement. Ironically, the very success of the Zionists in developing their old-new homeland insured their permanent minority status there, since it attracted constant and large Arab immigration. Palestine was not crowded, but it contained two wholly different groups who viewed each other with suspicion, and sometimes outright hatred. In such a situation, reason, tolerance, and accommodation become endangered species.

The pro-Arab bias of much of the British military in Palestine, coupled with Samuel's typically reticent Jewish "even-handedness" in matters effecting his brethren, gave the Arabs ample cause for optimism. In 1920 they rioted, but were unable to then achieve their goals. A year later, they placed the Jewish High Commissioner Samuel in an untenable position. They were confident that his Jewishness would prevent him from taking decisive action against their lawlessness and terror. The new Nehemiah could be transformed into the new Herod. On May 1, 1921, Arab rioters in Jaffa killed 27 Jews and

The Union Club —
League for
Jewish-Arab friendship
in Hebron, 1923

8. See Peters, p. 232, 269.

wounded 104 others.[9] The terror soon spread throughout Palestine. By the next week another 20 Jews were killed and many more wounded. As the situation rapidly deteriorated, the Jews now armed themselves for self-defense. In spite of its pro-Arab bias, the British Army was prepared to put down the riots with crushing force, but Samuel vacillated, as the Arabs were sure he would.

In order to stop the rioting, he finally made two far-reaching concessions to the Arabs. Thus was the precedent of appeasement of Arab rioting established as Western policy. Samuel ordered a temporary halt to Jewish immigration and he acquiesced to the appointment of the wily, violent, bitterly anti-Jewish, Jerusalem Arab, Haj Amin el-Husseini,[10] as Grand Mufti of Jerusalem.[11] This man, convicted of rioting and murder in 1920, was pardoned, rehabilitated, and appointed to this important position. His appointment foreclosed the opportunity for any meaningful Arab moderation or cooperation for the next twenty-five years. He was hated and feared, not only by the Jews but by many of the Arabs, as well. He eliminated his Arab rivals by intimidation and assassination. He would become an early and die-hard supporter of Hitler and the policy of genocide against the Jews. He was the heir to the Arab tradition of violence and terror, and would impress those methods irrevocably on the Arabs in Palestine.

Samuel now attempted to create a Palestine Parliament which would help England run the affairs of Palestine. Because of their numbers, it was obvious that the Arabs would dominate such a parliament or "national democratic institution," as Samuel called it. The Jews were forced to accept this idea because of their dependence on Britain and their own naively idealistic commitments to the forms of Western liberalism, no matter how inappropriate those forms were to their actual situation in Palestine, and inimical to their physical survival. But the Arabs, as they would do so many times in the future, saved the Jews from their own foolishness.

The Arabs refused to cooperate in the venture, vetoed any idea of cooperation with the Jews, and effectively forced Samuel to withdraw the proposal. From now on, there would be many governments in Palestine. The British controlled the country through the police and their immigration policies. The Zionist organization, through the Palestine

---

9. O'Brien, p. 160.

10. 1893-1974.

11. A position created by the British mandatory rule to give them a "leader" of the Arabs to deal with.

National Council, the Haganah,[12], the Histadrut[13], and other Jewish groups, governed the Jewish community and represented the Jewish interests to the mandatory government. In addition, there was a sizeable group of Jews of the *Yishuv HaYashan* and Agudath Israel who autonomously governed themselves outside of the control of the Zionist framework. The Arabs formed a Supreme Moslem Council, under the domination of the Mufti, and this group now became all powerful in Arab affairs in Palestine. Thus, the *modus operandi* of life in Palestine from 1921-48 depended on the balancing of the interests and goals of these disparate "governments." It would be a most daunting experience.

The First Partition

IN THE EARLY 1920S, Winston Churchill, then the British Colonial Secretary, broke off the eastern section of Palestine, renamed it Trans-Jordan, and awarded it to Emir Abdullah, one of the Hashemite sheiks who had supported the Allied-sponsored insurrection against the Turks during World War I. This new, artificial country, with a small, nomadic Bedouin population, was completely dependent on England for its survival.

The Jews were disappointed, feeling that this amputation of territory was a betrayal of the spirit of the Balfour Declaration. But since no major Jewish economic commitment to the development of the eastern bank of the Jordan had occurred, and the Zionists had enough problems to occupy their efforts and attention west of the Jordan, the protest was weak and ineffective. Abdullah and his descendants would henceforth become inextricably involved in the Arab-Jewish struggle in Palestine. The indulgence of the Hashemites by Churchill and England would further complicate an already volatile situation.

In 1924 and 1925, after Samuel rescinded his temporary ban on Jewish immigration, almost 50,000 new Jewish immigrants reached

---

12. Jewish self-defense militia which would later become the nucleus of the Israel Defense Forces.

13. The left-wing trade union organization, which was the most powerful economic and social force in the country.

Winston Churchill during his visit to Jerusalem in 1921. On his right is Sir Herbert Samuel

Palestine. This Fourth Aliyah coincided with the closing of America's doors to Jews from Eastern Europe. The terrible condition of Jews in Poland inspired many Jews, especially the young, to leave, and Palestine became one of the few viable options for immigration. These new immigrants settled mainly in the Jewish cities of Haifa, Tel Aviv, and Jewish Jerusalem, where they were a vital additional force in the building of the country. The Arabs viewed this new wave of immigration with suspicion and hate, but this time, instead of responding with riots, they attempted to increase their own rate of immigration into the

Polish Jews leaving for Israel, 1922

country. By 1930, the Arabs still held a 5 to 1 majority in population in Palestine,[14] but this was down from their 9 to 1 majority at the end of World War I. Because of this, continuing Jewish immigration to Palestine would remain the chief Arab issue of complaint to the mandatory government until 1948.

---

14. In 1931, there were 175,000 Jews in Palestine, 760,00 Moslem Arabs, and 100,000 Christians, most of whom were also Arabs.

Hebron Pogrom

THE NEW IMMIGRATION OF 1924 also contained a fresh and historic element. The great yeshivah of Slobodka, headed by Rabbi Nassan Tzvi Finkel and Rabbi Moshe Mordechai Epstein, decided to open a branch of the yeshivah in Palestine. These two great rabbis, with over one hundred of the leading students of Slobodka, left Lithuania and established a great yeshivah in 1924 in Hebron, the City of the Patriarchs. Known universally as the Hebron Yeshivah, it made an important contribution to Jewish life in Palestine. It also signaled the eternal commitment of the yeshivah world to the Land of Israel, and its willingness to undertake positive steps to insure the traditional Jewish character of the *Yishuv*.

The Arab assault on the old Jewish quarter of Hebron in August 1929 was one of the many anti-Jewish outbreaks inspired by the Mufti of Jerusalem

Many other great rabbis and yeshivah students of Poland and Lithuania, inspired by the example of Slobodka, left for the Land of Israel. The yeshivos of Palestine were revitalized by these newly arrived scholars, and a number of new yeshivos were established. The horizon of Torah study in Palestine, restricted in the minds of many to certain neighborhoods of Jerusalem, was now expanded, intensified, and publicized. Many of the secular leaders of the *Yishuv* did not take notice of this new force, and those who did, dismissed it as unimportant in the long-term development of the new Jewish society in Palestine. But time would prove this assessment wrong, for the yeshivos in Palestine, as in the Diaspora, would prove expert at surviving, and would wield influence far disproportionate to the then small numbers of their student bodies. These yeshivos contained brilliant scholars and idealistic leaders, and many of them became the rabbis, educators, and builders of a revitalized Torah *Yishuv* in the future.

However strong the propaganda for Jewish immigration to Palestine was, the results in terms of numbers of immigrants were disappointing. The 1920s were years of opportunity for Jewish immigration to Palestine, since

British restrictions were relatively benign, in spite of Arab pressure. Samuel's successor as High Commissioner, Lord Plumer, assumed office in 1925, and was efficient, able, fair, and brooked no nonsense as far as Arab rioters were concerned. Nevertheless, relatively few Jews arrived in Palestine from 1925 to 1933.[15] There are many reasons for this — economic hardship in Palestine relative to the Jewish condition in other countries; the intensely secular, socialist orientation of the Jewish Agency and the Histadrut, which proved unappealing to many Jews, especially the Orthodox; the constant threat of Arab violence; and finally, the inertia of life that governs us all. The next decade would reveal how harmful this error of non-immigration to Palestine was for European Jewry.

In 1929, the Arabs once again mounted major pogroms against the Jews in Palestine. Over 150 Jews were slaughtered and many hundreds more maimed.[16] The Jewish community in Hebron,[17] together with the newly arrived Slobodka Yeshivah, was brutally destroyed. Jewish property over all of Palestine was looted and expropriated. Belatedly, the British army quashed the insurrection, but the vindication of the Mufti's policy was clear. The Arabs would use systematic terror and violence to drive the Jews from Palestine. This policy remained unswervingly consistent for the next six decades.

Internal Divisions

 HE JEWS THEMSELVES in Palestine were divided into three basic groups comprising the new *Yishuv*. Ben Gurion and his group, who were socialists and secularists, envisioned a Jewish state based more on Marx than on Moses. They were determined to create a "new Jew" who would discard all of the "baggage" of the exile. Their attitude towards the Arab inhabitants of Palestine was ambivalent. They hoped somehow to come to a peaceful

---

15. In 1927, 2713 Jews arrived and more than 5000 left. See Johnson, p. 444. The problem of Jews leaving Palestine — *yeridah* — has plagued the Jewish *Yishuv* there throughout its existence.

16. In his autobiography, *Trial and Error*, p. 411, Weizmann records that the wife of the British foreign secretary told him, "I can't understand why the Jews make such a fuss over a few dozen of their people killed in Palestine. As many were killed in London in traffic accidents and nobody pays attention."

17. Fifty-nine Jews, including twenty-four students of the yeshivah, were slaughtered.

accommodation with them based on a vague formula of shared territories and a common humanistic destiny. Though they prepared to defend themselves physically from Arab violence, they preferred to ignore the political message and consequences of the Arab terror.

The second group, the Revisionist Zionists, was oriented to capitalism and toward the creation of a completely Jewish state, and they saw no way to accommodate the Arabs of Palestine in that Jewish state.[18] Zev Jabotinsky, the leader of the Revisionists, saw the new Jewish state emerging only from war and not from diplomacy, and thus advocated para-military groups within his party. He scorned Ben Gurion, personally and ideologically, and his rancor was repaid in kind with venom and even violence. Jabotinsky and his followers were also secular and saw religion in the new Jewish state as unnecessary and anachronistic. However, since they were not grounded in Marx and his anti-religious diatribes, their public pronouncements were far less anti-religious than were those of the socialists, and thus Jabotinsky was able to gain a following within the Orthodox camp.

The third group were the Orthodox Jews who attempted to see the proposed Jewish state in religious and historic context. The Mizrachi, which was part of the Zionist movement, and Agudath Israel, which was not, quarreled among themselves as to the tactics, policies, personalities, and even goals of the religious *Yishuv*.[19] But they agreed that any future Jewish state, however and whenever formed, could not survive as a purely secular state. In addition, there were many Orthodox Jews who opposed the idea of the formation of any Jewish state — even a religiously observant one — on religious and ideological grounds.[20] This

---

18. Part of their ideology was to undo Churchill's partition of Palestine and reclaim the eastern bank of the Jordan — Trans-Jordan — as part of the ancient Jewish homeland and the new Jewish state. The anthem of the Revisionists contained the passage: "There are two banks to the Jordan. This one (the west one) is ours. That one (the east one) is ours, too."

19. Agudath Israel did not support a Jewish state as a soluation to the "Jewish problem." It wanted to create a physical refuge for Jews in Palestine, but was not committed to the idea of statehood. The redemption of Israel would be achieved by spiritual greatness and repentance and this would lead to the messianic redemption and state foretold by the prophets. The Diaspora, in this view, was not a politico-military phenomenon and would not be ended by politico-military means. Mizrachi saw statehood as a necessary step on the road to redemption and therefore even a secular state was a positive event. This basic difference of ideology lay at the root of their dispute regarding tactics, attitudes, and programs vis-a-vis the Zionist movement.

20. This view had been au courant in Eastern Europe for the previous century. It has been expounded in the works of Rabbi Yoel Teitelbaum, the Satmar *Rav*, the physical and ideological descendant of Rabbi Moshe Teitelbaum, mentioned previously in the same context.

group, though small, was very vocal and insistent, and not without influence.

Apart from these groups living in Palestine was Chaim Weizmann. He represented the large and powerful General Zionist faction of Zionism, which disagreed with Ben Gurion's socialism, and wanted a secular, capitalist state. All through the 1920s, Weizmann continued to play the "English card," hoping that England itself would somehow help establish a Jewish state in Palestine and include it under the protective umbrella of the British Empire. Weizmann viewed the Balfour Declaration as only the first step in the march of Anglo-Jewish cooperation that would later result in a Jewish state under British auspices. However, history shows that the Balfour Declaration was in fact the high-water mark of the Anglo-Jewish relationship, and that the cooperation between the Jews and His Majesty's government would deteriorate steadily from 1917 to 1948.

Weizmann stubbornly refused to recognize this. He was thus in open confrontation with Ben Gurion and Jabotinsky on policy,[21] and with the Orthodox groups on religion, for Weizmann's Zionism and vision of the Jewish state was then a purely secular one. Nevertheless, in one of the great political tightrope-walking feats of the ages, Weizmann remained the head and effective leader of the Zionist movement for most of the time between the Balfour Declaration and the actual declaration of the independence of Israel. In the eyes of the non-Jewish world, and even much of the Jewish world, it was Weizmann who represented Zionism and Jewish aspirations. His main power base was among the General Zionists, outside and within Palestine, and his personality, shrewdness, and tenacity enabled him to retain control of the funding and direction of the world Zionist movement for most of the time, despite Ben Gurion's personal and political opposition and occasional victories. As such, he was always a force to be reckoned with.[22]

---

21. Ben Gurion felt that diplomacy and good relations with England were secondary to Jewish labor and efforts in Palestine itself. He bitterly opposed Weizmann as impractical and naive. Ben Gurion was committed to socialism and the triumph of labor over capital. Weizmann was personally hostile, stemming from their ideological differences. Jabotinsky felt Weizmann to be too docile and accommodating to the British. He ridiculed Weizmann's pacifism and "ghetto mentality." Jabotinsky's expulsion/defection from the Zionist movement between the wars inevitably led to his antagonism towards Weizmann. Ironically, Ben Gurion and Jabotinsky despised each other with the same gusto that they expressed in opposing Weizmann.

22. Both Ben Gurion and Jabotinsky found it difficult to reconcile themselves to this reality.

29

Assimilation Forever!

The Roaring Twenties

HE 1920S BROUGHT TO FULL realization the attempt first begun by Reform and the *Haskalah*/Enlightenment a century earlier to redefine Judaism and the Jewish people. Until the First World War, neither *Haskalah* nor Reform were able to command the loyalty and approval of the vast majority of world Jewry. In fact, the pogroms and persecutions of the Jews of Russia in the 1880s sounded the death-knell of the original program of *Haskalah*.[1] But the emergence of Zionism revitalized *Haskalah*, for now it gave it a practical purpose and allowed it to tap into the age-old religious dream of the return to Israel. The Hebrew language, popularized and secularized by the nineteenth-century *Haskalah*, became the spoken vernacular of the new *Yishuv* in Palestine and of the Zionist movement the world over.[2] Jewish literature, art, song, and drama all took the return to Palestine as their main motif.[3]

The idea of Zionism was a powerful magnet for all Jews, except for the communist and Bundist Left. Even the Orthodox Jews, who opposed political Zionism, were always supportive of efforts to allow

---

1. See O'Brien, p. 47, and Johnson, p. 335.

2. This amazing feat was tenaciously pursued by Eliezer Ben Yehudah (1858-1922) who wrote the definitive dictionary of modern Hebrew and created "The Committee for [the Development of] Language," which institutionalized and formulated Ivrit (modern Hebrew, spoken in a modified Sephardic pronunciation) as the language of the *Yishuv*. This new dialect was meant to be a conscious rejection of the Eastern European ghetto, which spoke Ashkenazic Hebrew.

3. The establishment of the Bezalel School for Art in Jerusalem in the early 1900s is an example of this trend.

Jewish settlement in the country. In fact, it was the Orthodox alone who had maintained a strong Jewish presence in Palestine throughout the centuries, though their primary goal was religious and spiritual growth. Yet, Zionism proved to be the main vehicle for the transformation of a large segment of Jewry to a secular way of life and value system.

Reform Judaism was anti-Zionist in the extreme. It opposed a Jewish state, fearful that Jews would be accused of being somehow disloyal to the states in which they resided. Reform became a societal "minimum religion" that gave its members a socially acceptable religious affiliation without demanding from them ritual, discipline, or even faith.[4] But it soon deteriorated into a conduit that led to complete assimilation and even baptism.

By the 1920s, Reform was in the forefront of anti-Zionist activities. In the euphoria of the 1920s, Reform was convinced that the ultimate solution to the "Jewish problem" lay in assimilation. It advocated no meaningful Jewish education, no substantive ritual, and adopted a universalistic agenda of social welfare goals. As such, it encouraged and legitimated the forces of cultural and social assimilation in Jewish Western Europe. In the 1920s, Orthodoxy, traditional Jewish observances, intensive Jewish education — all were on the wane in Western Europe, and the wave of Jewish assimilation and intermarriage there rose steadily and seemingly inexorably.

Jewish Secularism

HOWEVER, THE MAIN CATALYST for change in Jewish society both in the Diaspora and in the Land of Israel was the institutionalization of the secular Jew in leadership roles in Palestine. The secular Jew differed from his non-Jewish secular counterpart. In the non-Jewish Western world, secular people saw humanism, liberalism, and agnosticism as a means of escape from the ancient binding forms of the church. They were fleeing from religion to their brave new world. But the Jewish secularists were fleeing from one religion to another one.

Their new orthodoxy of Jewish secularism was just as binding and demanding as the old orthodoxy of Torah observance, for the new

---

4. See above, Chapter 6.

secular Jew believed in atheism with all the fervor of a religious zealot. In discarding old ritual and forms, the new secular Jew merely substituted new ritual and forms. The costume of the open-necked shirt and shorts to him was as much a uniform as was the Chassidic black caftan and the fur hat. Being bareheaded was as necessary for the new Jew, as having one's head covered was for his father. It was on the basis of this new secularist religion that the foundation for the new Jewish society in Palestine was laid in the 1920s.[5]

Traditional Jewry's response, again both in the Diaspora and Palestine, to the new secularism in the 1920s varied greatly. Most Orthodox leaders opposed the new society vehemently, and openly fought against it. Some Orthodox leaders ignored this new and growing secularist phenomenon entirely and continued in their traditional ways, outlook, and agenda. Others attempted to reconcile their communities and programs to accommodate the new Jewish secularism, especially since it appeared that the secularists were destined to dominate Jewish society.[6]

The continuing institutionalization of secularism as the controlling force in Jewish affairs in Palestine had far-reaching consequences, for the future of Jewish life would now begin to shift from Eastern Europe to America and the Land of Israel. A secular Jewish society in Palestine would certainly have a dramatic effect on the Jewish Diaspora, and speed the process of secularization and assimilation that had begun in the nineteenth century.

Defining Relationships

HROUGH ITS EXECUTIVE ARM — the Jewish Agency, in Jerusalem — the Zionist movement pursued its goal of power over the policies and direction of the new *Yishuv*.

Its first step was to gain control of the Jewish community. The great majority of Jerusalem's Jewish population — both Sephardic and

---

5. Article by Pinchas M. Peli, *HaDoar*, April 22, 1988, p. 3.

6. In Palestine, the secularists controlled the effective leadership of the *Yishuv* and were recognized as the leaders of the Jewish community by the British mandatory powers. In addition, the secular Jewish parties in Poland and Lithuania were very popular (over thirty percent of the Jewish electorate there voted for them) and also occupied positions of leadership and control in Jewish life (many Jewish communal councils — such as Warsaw's — were controlled by the secular Jewish parties).

Ashkenazic — was Orthodox, and it dominated the elected community councils. As Jerusalem went, so would the country go. But thanks to its virtual monopoly of foreign financial support, superior political organization, and control of the press, the Zionist organization had powerful leverage on its side. This was especially true since Turkish-controlled Palestine had suffered from a famine imposed by British siege during the war. The secularists who controlled emergency relief supplies from abroad at that time allocated these resources in such a way as to increase the power of those who shared their vision of secular Zionism.

The next step was to increase non-Orthodox representation in communal bodies under the guise of equal representation for all. The result was that the majority Orthodox community soon found itself a minority in all the decision-making bodies, except for its own limited community council. Under Chaim Weizmann's active leadership, the Zionists attempted to gain control over the Jewish schools and the rabbinate and, although they were fiercely resisted, they made substantial inroads, in great measure due to their sheer economic power. In all of these endeavors, the British rulers lent their prestige to this effort to dislodge the "backward" clerics from power.[7]

The traditional Jewish community itself now lacked cohesion and direction. It had already been in upheaval for two centuries. And by 1920, the struggles within that community focused on three main issues: 1) messianism 2) secularism, and 3) the return to the Land of Israel.

From before the time of the Chassidic revolution in the eighteenth century, overtones of open messianism were heard in the Jewish world. One of the fears that impelled the misnagdim to oppose Chassidus so strongly was the chassidic emphasis on the supernatural and the messianic. But the belief that the Messianic Era was at hand was not restricted to the chassidim. Many later disciples of the Gaon of Vilna were also of the opinion that the Messianic Era was at hand.[8] But any overemphasis of the idea of messianism after the Shabtai Tzvi debacle was viewed as dangerous by much of traditional Jewry. Belief in the coming of Messiah is a principle of Jewish faith, but Jews recoiled in

---

7. True to their "divide and conquer" method of colonial rule, at the same time that the British permitted the Zionists to gain power, they allowed certain Jewish communities in Jerusalem and other parts of Palestine to exempt themselves from the rule of the Zionists.

8. See Rabbi Menachem Kasher's book *HaTekufah HaGedolah* (Jerusalem, 1969) which incorporates within it the work, *Kol HaTor,* by Rabbi Hillel of Shklov, a disciple of the Gaon of Vilna.

fright at the identification of any particular time or circumstances as being unquestionably messianic. Thus a description of the nineteenth and twentieth centuries as being definitely messianic was of itself controversial.

Added to this controversy, traditional Jewry was confused and defensive in relating to the new secular society that surrounded and engulfed it. Should traditional Jewry adapt itself to the new reality of secularism? And if so, how? Could the apparent benefits of life in the new secular world be advantageous to the Jew, or would those very benefits lead to the assimilation and extinction of the Jew and Jewish life? Opinions differed widely and bitterly.

Finally, what was to be the attitude of traditional Jewry towards the Zionist movement and the philosophy of national Zionism? Was Zionism — apart from its secular leadership and philosophy — a positive development, or was it merely another disappointing and dangerous mirage in Jewish history? Was it to be encouraged and channeled, or fought and opposed at all costs? All of these questions were to be personalized in the remarkable career of Rabbi Avraham Yitzchak Kook,[9] for he served as the lightning rod that attracted all controversies that focused on these problems.

Rabbi Kook

Rabbi Kook

 FTER SERVING AS THE RABBI of Boisk, a small community in Lithuania, Rabbi Kook arrived in Palestine, as the rabbi of Jaffa in the early 1900s. He immediately gained fame as a great rabbinic scholar and Talmudic sage, as well as an ambassador to the secular farmers and colonists of the new Jewish settlements. He was a poet, philosopher, Kabbalist, mystic, organizer, and political leader. He was also a dreamer, controversial and given to polemics. He became the central figure of Religious Zionism and everyone responded to him. Rabbi Kook was convinced that the Messianic Era was at hand and this belief governed all of his actions. In his view, everything in the Messianic Era was necessarily positive and all problems could be overcome. Only this

---

9. 1865-1935.

viewpoint could justify many of his actions and statements.[10]

The opponents of Rabbi Kook were shocked by some of his writings and policies. They were led by Rabbi Yosef Chaim Sonnenfeld,[11] the rabbi of the *Yishuv HaYashan* of Jerusalem, and most of the rabbinic leaders of Agudath Israel, worldwide. Rabbi Sonnenfeld in particular had a warm, personal relationship with Rabbi Kook. In 1913-1914 the two of them had led the historic pilgrimage known as the "Teshuvah Campaign" through the northern settlements. Though his personal respect for Rabbi Kook remained unshaken, Rabbi Sonnenfeld felt compelled to oppose vehemently the views espoused by Rabbi Kook, especially those he advanced after World War I, when the Zionists gained control of the *Yishuv*.

Though Rabbi Sonnenfeld never recognized Rabbi Kook as the rabbi of Jerusalem, and certainly not as the Chief Rabbi of Palestine, he nevertheless recognized his personal greatness. He, however, characterized Rabbi Kook's messianism as the major point of contention between them, and from this conflict all other differences in attitude and policies between them flowed.[12] For his part, Rabbi Kook often commented that he was able to pursue his policies and agenda because he knew that Rabbi Sonnenfeld was fighting the battles for the preservation of tradition that otherwise he, Rabbi Kook, would have had to fight.

Even among the Mizrachi, there were those who were wary of Rabbi Kook's theories and shied away from his messianism.[13] Rabbi Kook's seemingly benevolent attitude towards the new secularism also aroused opposition. His slogan "To renew the old and to sanctify the

R' Yosef Chaim Sonnenfeld receiving Professor Masaryk

10. For example, his statement that "I believe that the greatest atheists (*apikorsim*) of Israel possess greater faith than can be found in the houses of prayer of other peoples" (quoted by Shmuel Avidor, in *HaIsh Neged HaZerem*, Jerusalem, 1970, p. 219).

11. 1848-1932.

12. *HaIsh Al HaChomah*, Vol. 3, p. 414.

13. Included in this group was Rabbi Yehudah Leib Fishman-Maimon, later the first minister of religion for the State of Israel. He was a supporter of many of Rabbi Kook's programs, including the formation of the Chief Rabbinate, but he differed sharply with him in his view of the messianic nature of the times and was often annoyed by Rabbi Kook's seeming lack of political sophistication. This is clear from his biography, *Rabbi Maimon B'Dorotav*, by his daughter Geulah Bat Yehudah, Jerusalem, 1979.

new"[14] was received coldly by the "old" who felt no need for renewal as well as the "new" who were fleeing from sanctification. And finally, his whole-hearted support of the Zionist movement and its program of rebuilding Jewish Palestine polarized the opinions of traditional Jewry regarding him and this issue.

Thus, for the later decades of his life, Rabbi Kook was engaged in unremitting controversy, and was subjected many times to public and private rebukes, threats, calumnies, and physical and verbal abuse. By nature he was reclusive, shy, gentle, and sensitive to a fault — hardly the personality for a warrior. Yet he was strong, principled, undaunted, and persevering in pursuit of his goals for the Jewish people. He was convinced that his fathomless, all-encompassing love for his fellow Jews would triumph.[15] And because his life was a living exhibition of that supernatural love, he was able to take central stage in Jewish life in his time.

Ashkenazic Chief Rabbi

 ABBI KOOK WAS IN EUROPE when World War I broke out. Since the hostilities made it impossible for him to return to Palestine, he spent the war years in Switzerland and London, and did not return to Palestine until 1920. He was then elected Rabbi of Jerusalem over the opposition of the *Yishuv HaYashan,* who saw his election as part of a general attempt by the Zionist leadership to gain political, economic and now religious control of the city.[16] In 1921, he prevailed upon the mandatory government of Palestine to establish an "official" rabbinate to govern Jewish religious

---

14. *"L'chadesh et hayashan v'lekadesh et hechadash."* Rabbi Kook issued a letter justifying the Zionists' creation of sports teams, especially soccer leagues, though certainly not for the leagues to operate on the Sabbath. These teams nevertheless performed on the Sabbath and were universally condemned by the traditional camp. Rabbi Kook opposed vigorously their desecration of the Sabbath but saw in them the new physical resurrection of Israel which would eventually be followed by spiritual renewal. Others saw these sports leagues only as a further step in the secularization process of Israel from which no positive spiritual gain would ever occur.

15. One of his most famous statements was that "Jerusalem was destroyed because of unwarranted intramural hatred among Jews, and it would be rebuilt because of unwarranted intramural love among Jews."

16. Since his election implied the politicization of the Rabbinate, it was never accepted by the *Yishuv HaYashan,* and they intended to accept only Rabbi Yosef Chaim Sonnenfeld as their rabbi.

matters in the country and he was elected to the post of Ashkenazic Chief Rabbi of Palestine.[17] Many of the leading rabbis of Palestine were members of the Chief Rabbinate, though the rabbis of the *Yishuv HaYashan*, and many of the more distinguished rabbis who arrived later, refused to participate in this new organization.

The Zionist movement itself was ambivalent towards the new Rabbinate. On one hand, the Chief Rabbinate promised a positive, cooperative attitude towards the new *Yishuv* on the part of rabbinic leadership. Yet, on the other hand, it also entrenched in power the forces of traditional Jewry who would certainly continue to oppose the creation of the "new" Jew and the "new" Jewish society that the Zionists so desired. This ambivalent attitude towards the Chief Rabbinate on the part of the Zionist leadership would continue indefinitely.

In 1923, Rabbi Kook also established his yeshivah called "Mercaz Harav," which was intended to produce spiritual leaders in the mold of their mentor and to advance his ideas of Torah and redemption among the Jewish people. Rabbi Kook also traveled to America that year to raise funds for the destitute yeshivos of Europe. His visit[18] to the United States took on the trappings of a triumphal tour.

Returning to Jerusalem, he remained an officially recognized spokesman for his people in matters regarding Jewish rights in Palestine. He campaigned vigorously for unrestricted rights of Jewish prayer at the Western Wall — where it had been subject to Arab violence and harassment, and British restriction during the 1920s — for freer immigration of Jews to Palestine, and for matters of social justice and fair play between the different economic and social strata of Jews, as well as between Jews and Arabs. He roundly denounced the Grand Mufti of Jerusalem and his terrorist policies, and staunchly supported Jewish efforts at self-defense.

Even though Rabbi Kook differed markedly in political view and philosophy from many of the great leaders of Orthodoxy of the time, he

---

17. His Sephardic counterpart was Rabbi Yaakov Meir. The Sephardic Chief Rabbi carried the title "Rishon LeZion" as part of his official status. In this he was seen as the successor to the "Chacham Bashi," which was previously the institution of the Sephardic Chief Rabbinate in Palestine and had been in effect for many generations under the Turks. Thus, the Sephardic Chief Rabbinate was not the subject of bitter Orthodox opposition, as was the Orthodox Chief Rabbinate.

18. He was accompanied by Rabbi Moshe Mordechai Epstein of Slobodka and later of Hebron, and Rabbi Avrahom Dov Ber Kahane Shapiro, the rabbi of Kovno, Lithuania.

19. *HaIsh Al HaChomah,* Vol. 3, p. 414.

was on friendly and good terms with almost all of them. Rabbi Chaim Ozer Grodzensky, Rabbi Yisrael Meir Kagan (the *Chofetz Chaim*), Rabbi Avraham Alter of Gur, and many others corresponded with him regularly.

During Rabbi Alter's visit to the Holy Land in 1923, he attempted to resolve the dispute between Rabbi Kook and the leaders of the *Yishuv HaYashan*, Rabbi Yosef Chaim Sonnenfeld and Rabbi Yitzchak Yeruchem Diskin. The three great rabbis cooperated in this effort and Rabbi Kook agreed to retract some of his writings that the others regarded as too radical. However, the peace effort failed due to outside opposition and long-standing organizational and idealistic differences.

Hostility Breeds Violence

Jacob deHaan

URING THIS PERIOD OF TIME, two murders shocked the Jewish settlement in Palestine. In the early 1920s a young Jewish assimilated intellectual by the name of Jacob deHaan[19] began a tortuous return to Judaism. From being a bohemian and an atheist, and living a dissolute life, he eventually rehabilitated himself and rose to become the "foreign minister" of the *Yishuv HaYashan*, representing this element of Jewry before the official commissions of England and the world.

A sophisticated, worldly person since his earlier career was as an influential, well-connected journalist and lawyer in his native Holland, deHaan articulated brilliantly the essence of the case against secular Zionism and was unsparing in his words and relentless in his presentation. It was learned that he was carrying on secret negotiations with the Emir Abdullah, ruler of Trans-Jordan, which, if successful, would have established the *Yishuv HaYashan* as a dominant factor. His skills and success infuriated his opponents and incurred their hatred.[20] In June 1924, deHaan was shot dead leaving the synagogue in Shaarei Zedek Hospital in Jerusalem. His assassins were never apprehended. Many pointed the finger of blame at his political enemies.

The murder shocked the *Yishuv*, for if it was politically motivated,

---

19. Born in Amsterdam, Holland in 1881.

20. For a thorough discussion of his life and achievements see Friedman, *Chevrah V'Daath,* Jerusalem 1978, pp. 230-252, and Sonnenfeld, *Guardian of Jerusalem,* New York, pp. 379-83 and 440-44.

it introduced into Jewish life a violent force almost unknown since the time of the destruction of the Second Temple. Rabbi Kook refused to believe that the murder was perpetrated by Jews and attempted to still the religious community's outcry over this murder. Forty years later, however, in books, articles, and in a radio documentary on Israel Radio, it was revealed that deHaan's killing was, in fact, a political assassination, carried out under the orders of high officials in the Jewish Agency leadership and the Haganah.[21]

During the 1920s the rivalry between the socialist forces in Palestine and those of the Revisionist movement[22] surfaced and intensified. One of the leaders of the socialist group, second only in influence and power to David Ben Gurion, was Chaim Arlozoroff.[23] On a summer's Friday night in 1933, on the beachfront of Tel Aviv, Arlozoroff, walking with his wife, was gunned down by unknown assailants. Three members of the Revisionist party were arrested, and the socialist press clamored for their conviction and execution. After long and protracted legal processes, Avraham Stavsky, one of the three arrested Revisionists, was convicted and sentenced to hang for the murder of Arlozoroff.

Rabbi Kook was convinced of his innocence. "No Jewish hand participated in Arlozoroff's murder,"[24] was his contention. He moved heaven and earth to free Stavsky, and incurred the wrath of the socialist camp, which vilified him in a most shameful manner.[25] Against all political wisdom and friendly advice, he championed the cause of Stavsky's innocence. Eventually he triumphed, for Stavsky's conviction was reversed and he was freed.[26]

By then Rabbi Kook was dying of cancer, but this last struggle of his exemplified his entire career. His inner beliefs, shaped by his personality and motivated by his love of Israel and Jews, often brought him into sharp conflict with the grim realities of the society in which he

---

21. Shaul Avigur, *Toldoth HaHaganah*, part 1, Vol. 2, pp. 251-2; *Zarkor* broadcast on *Kol Israel*, Nov. 21, 1971.

22. *See* above, Chapter 24.

23. 1899-1933.

24. *See Halsh Neged HaZerem*, p. 272. The truth of this statement has been argued for over fifty years without any definitive proof.

25. "Shame on the Rabbis, the Accomplices of Murderers" was one of the more moderate headlines in the socialist press of Palestine of the time.

26. In one of history's ironies, Stavsky was to die of bullet wounds inflicted on him by the Haganah when it attacked and sank the Irgun boat, Altalena, off Tel Aviv harbor in 1948.

lived. As always, he refused to retreat, to accommodate, to moderate his stand, and thus, till the end, this kind, pious, gentle soul remained embroiled in controversy and bitterness.

Rabbi Kook saw Jewish secularism and assimilation as a passing phase in Jewish life. Once the Jewish state was established on the soil of the holy land, he believed that spiritual renewal and return to tradition would follow automatically, if slowly. Thus assured by his faith of eventual triumph, he could afford to be sanguine about the "temporary" heresy that engulfed Israel. His opponents, both in the secular and religious camps, differed with him on this point of view regarding the "temporary" nature of secular Judaism. His fellow rabbis were convinced that it was a serious and permanent movement that would reshape the Jewish world if allowed to proceed unchecked. They were therefore less charitable, and more suspicious and contentious towards their opponents.

The hostility evinced in future decades by the secularists toward religion, even Religious Zionism, tends to bear out the fears of those of the old *Yishuv* who opposed Rabbi Kook. His softer approach was overwhelmed by the events of the next decades which would themselves irrevocably change the Jewish people and the fate of the *Yishuv* in Palestine.

30

American Jewry in the 1920s

Help for Other Jews

HE FOCUS OF ATTENTION in the new Jewish world was now seemingly the Land of Israel, but the Jewish community in America was soon to become the largest and most influential component of that new Jewish world. By the middle of the 1920s, the Jewish population in the United States numbered over four and a half million.[1] However, the Jewish community in the United States, and especially its assimilated leaders and organizations, were yet wary about the relationship of this large community to the non-Jewish majority in the United States. Long experience in exile had trained Jews instinctively — secular Jews as well — to expect the worst, even when the government guaranteed equal, favorable, and non-discriminatory treatment. Most of the Jews in the United States in the 1920s were foreign born, self conscious, and susceptible to the blandishments of American assimilation on one hand and to Jewish paranoia on the other hand.

This decade of the 1920s was to be the last "normal" decade for the Jewish people in the twentieth century, and the euphoria of the "Roaring Twenties" in America engulfed its Jews with the rest of American society. Jews looked to cast away their old ways in the hope that they would achieve in the New World what they never could have in the Old World — societal acceptance and upward

---

1. It is interesting and frightening to note that in the last sixty-five years the Jewish population in the U.S.A. has barely increased by a fifth while the general population has doubled! Such is the toll of assimilation, low birth rate, and restrictive immigration policies.

Felix M. Warburg

Jacob H. Schiff

social mobility. This became the main objective of Jewish communal life in America in the pre-Hitler era, and it colored Jewish attitudes and behavior in American public life.

At the conclusion of the First World War, Jewish Europe, especially Eastern Europe, lay devastated and impoverished. It needed vast amounts of money, logistical support, technical skills, and human encouragement to restore itself. To a great extent, this was supplied by American Jewry and its various organizations. This effort of relief and help placed American Jewry in the role that it has fulfilled ever since — of being the "big brother" for all segments of world Jewry. Indeed, many American Jews view this as the prime reason for the existence of an organized American Jewish community.

The major vehicle for this relief and help was the Joint Distribution Committee.[2] The "Joint" operated then, as later, efficiently and compassionately, distributing millions of dollars to the needy, without recourse to the cumbersome bureaucratic machinery usually associated with governmental aid and welfare programs. It also distributed food, clothing, and medical help and, perhaps most importantly, established a system for transferring funds directly from American Jews to their relatives in Europe.[3] Though it cannot be proved statistically, it is reasonable to assume, based on the later Israeli experience, that more help reached Eastern European Jews from private sources than from any organized communal aid programs or governmental efforts. It was during the 1920s that American Jewry established its reputation for generosity and help to its less fortunate brethren.

A smaller, but also important relief organization was organized by the Union of Orthodox Rabbis at this time. Known as Ezras Torah,[4] it provided life-saving help to the destitute scholars, rabbis, and yeshivah leaders of Eastern Europe. The founder and first president of Ezras Torah Relief Society was Rabbi Yisroel Rosenberg. He was also ther prime force in the organization and strengthening of teh Union of Orthodox Rabbis of thre United States and Canada. A man of vision,

---

2. This was an amalgamation of three organizations: The American Jewish Committee, the Orthodox-sponsored Central Committee for the Relief of Jews Suffering Through the War, and the secular labor group, People's Relief Committee — hence its title "Joint" Distribution Committee.

3. *Shores of Refuge*, by Ronald Sanders, p. 370.

4. The Torah Relief Society.

energy and action, he was a powerful force in the American rabbinate in the first half of the twentieth century. Administered by Rabbi Yosef Eliyahu Henkin,[5] Ezras Torah concentrated on help to individuals and similar needs that were not within the purview of the Joint.

In addition to these efforts that linked American to European Jewry, great rabbinic figures from Europe began to visit America regularly during the 1920s to raise the necessary funds to sustain yeshivos and other facets of Jewish life in Europe.[6] Such visits proved beneficial to the American Jewish community as well, for these great men provided much-needed inspiration, directional advice, and constructive criticism regarding the American Jewish scene. They also initiated a slow trickle of American young men who journeyed to Eastern Europe to study in the great yeshivos of Poland and Lithuania. Many of these American students returned to the United States and occupied positions of importance in the Jewish community and in its rabbinate.

The effect of relief and charitable work on American Jewry was inestimable. For, to a great extent, and for better or worse, philanthropy and aid to fellow Jews became "Judaism" to most American Jews, replacing Judaism in the traditional halachic sense. Desiring acceptance and assimilation into American society, convinced that the new world also meant a new Judaism, American Jewry, in the main, chose to remain Jewish by helping fellow Jews and becoming the self-appointed protector and benefactor of world Jewry. This attitude of solidarity and help to Jews and Jewish causes, coupled with further flight from personal Jewish observances, lifestyle and values, produced the basic American Jewish prototype: a Jew with little or no religious commitment or personal Jewish life, who was nevertheless nostalgic regarding the beauty of Jewish life in the "old home"and who possessed a "Jewish heart," an open hand to help Jewish causes, and a great deal of inner angst, guilt, and confusion. Just as the State of Israel would become the unofficial religion of American Jewry in the second half of the century, charitable work and good deeds on behalf of European and Palestinian Jewry was the foundation of organized American Jewish commitment in the 1920s.

---

5. 1881-1973. A scholar and holy man who was a quiet hero in American Jewish life.
6. Among the distinguished visitors in the 1920s were Rabbis Meir Shapiro of Lublin, Avraham Y. Kook of Jerusalem, Moshe Mordechai Epstein of Slobodka, Avraham Dov Ber Kahana of Kovno, Yosef Cahaneman of Ponevez, and Shimon Shkop of Grodno. Other great leaders came in the 1930s.

Movie Industry

O F VAST, BUT OFTEN IGNORED, influence on American Jewry was the rise of the entertainment industry as a powerful medium in American life. In nineteenth-century Europe, individual talented Jews found their way to the conductor's podium and the soloist's spotlight in music. But in spite of their talents, Jews were not easily accepted in the genteel Gentile society that frequented the concert halls of Vienna, Berlin, Paris, and London.[7] In the United States, many Jews found an opportunity in the entertainment and communication fields to express their talent, drive, creativity, and energy, but it gave them an outlet for their baser side as well. Any undercurrents of vulgarity and bawdiness in nineteenth-century Eastern European Jewry were controlled there by the Jewish tradition and halachic propriety. In the United States, however, these undercurrents became major factors in the Jewish influence on American entertainment, leisure, and fashion. In effect, the Jews created Hollywood.[8] And Hollywood, more than any other social force, formed American general opinion and influenced assimilating Jewish life in the 1920s.

Wilshire Boulevard Temple. This was the temple of the Jewish Hollywood moguls.

The major movie studios were almost all headed by immigrant Jews who clawed their way to success — innovators, fighters, and single-minded men all. In the process they attempted to erase their past and heritage. They despised Judaism, forsook tradition, and preached ultra-assimilation as the American dream. These men, Adolph

---

7. As mentioned before in this book, Gustav Mahler, the greatest composer and conductor of his time, was forced to convert to Catholicism in order to receive the appointment as conductor of the Vienna Symphony Orchestra. He was nevertheless hounded and persecuted — mainly because of his "Jewishness" — and eventually moved to New York.

8. Neal Gabler's book, *An Empire of their Own — How the Jews Invented Hollywood* (New York, 1988), provides a detailed description of this phenomenon.

Zukor;[9] William Fox;[10] Louis B. Mayer;[11] Carl Laemmle;[12] Marcus Loew;[13] Harry, Sam, Albert, and Jack Warner;[14] Sam Goldwyn;[15] Irving Thalberg,[16] and other Jews were the creators of the movie industry.

The most striking similarity among the Hollywood Jews, however, wasn't their Eastern European origins. What united them in deep spiritual kinship was their utter and absolute rejection of their pasts and their equally absolute devotion to America . . . The Hollywood Jews embarked on an assimilation so ruthless and complete that they cut their lives to the pattern of American respectability as they interpreted it . . . They would fabricate their empire into the image of America as they would fabricate themselves in the image of prosperous Americans. They would create its values and myths, its traditions and archetypes. It would be an America where fathers were strong, families stable, people attractive, resilient, resourceful and decent. (This in marked contradistinction to the movies of Hollywood in the 1960s and later which invariably mocked, criticized, and vulgarized traditional American life and values. These later movies were no longer the product of immigrant Jews but rather of pampered, non-ethnic Americans. BW.)

This was "their" America, and its invention may be their most enduring legacy . . . [The religious community to which they contributed almost disowned Judaism entirely]; but by its lights Jews were to be seen and not heard. As the rabbi[17] who guided the Hollywood Jews put it, "For God's sake, I'm living in America. I have to be part of my environment. I don't want any ghettos here for myself . . ." Ultimately, by creating their idealized America

---

9. A Hungarian Jew born into a rabbinic family in 1873. He built Paramount pictures.

10. 1879-1952. Another Hungarian Jew. He founded the Fox Film Corp., later Twentieth Century Fox.

11. 1885-1957. A Russian Jew, he headed the largest studio in Hollywood, Metro-Goldwyn, Mayer.

12. 1867-1939. A German Jew, he created Universal Studios.

13. 1872-1927. American-born of Eastern European Jewish parents, he organized and owned the largest theater group in the United States and was one of the founders of Metro-Goldwyn, Mayer.

14. Warner Brothers.

15. 1882-1974. Born Samuel Goldfish in Warsaw, he was a founder of Metro-Goldwyn, Mayer.

16. 1899-1936. A native New Yorker, pioneer producer of acclaimed films and discoverer of numerous stars.

17. Rabbi Edgar Magnin of the leading Reform Temple in Los Angeles.

on the screen, the Jews reinvented the country in the image of their fiction."[18]

If the influence of these Jews on American society generally was profound, its effect on the American Jewish community was devastating. In the manner that they portrayed Jews, Judaism, and Jewish values, the movies tore apart the already fraying thread of Jewish community and commitment, and provided justification and added impetus to the flight to assimilation, intermarriage, and Jewish extinction. The movies caricatured traditional Judaism and observant Jews. It showed them always as being anachronistic, foreign, threatening, obdurate, and doomed. Towards the old generation, it exhibited a great deal of nostalgia, and even pathos, but the movies made it clear that they were not role models for the new American Jew and that the traditional way of Jewish life had no place in American society, as Hollywood imagined it.

It is no wonder that most of the Hollywood Jews were therefore anti-Jews, fearful, insecure, defensive, and never in the forefront of Jewish causes or commitment.[19] Indicative of this is that from 1933-1945, when the Holocaust was in progress, Hollywood was completely silent about the persecution of Jews, although it led the country in opposition to Hitler and Nazism, and in using film to arouse patriotism and support for the war effort. The vast majority of Jews in America were inveterate moviegoers. What they saw on the screen imprinted images on them and their children which would not easily be discarded. The generation of American Jews raised in the 1920s was, in the main, convinced that living in America required total and rapid assimilation of Jews, and the movies deserve an Oscar for their subliminal impact in reinforcing and confirming that belief.[20]

---

18. Gabler, pp. 4,5,6 and 7.

19. Later generations of Hollywood Jews were little different.

20. Al Jolson's role in "The Jazz Singer" is the prototype of the Jewish "hero," who intermarries, discards his Jewishness, and nevertheless is somehow accepted by the Jewish synagogue.

Upward Mobility

Benjamin Cardozo

HE 1920S ALSO SAW JEWS continue their rise to high position in other areas of American life. Building upon grudging acceptance accorded them in pre-war American society, Jews began to appear in the upper strata of American professional life. Though burdened by discrimination, quotas, and lack of funds, Jews nevertheless flooded American colleges, universities, and professional schools. The ancient Jewish love of learning and the poignant lullaby of "Torah will you learn, a scholar will you be," was now distorted to say "To college will you go, a professional will you be" — figurative but true. Such schools as City College of New York, which provided a free college education, became overwhelmingly Jewish in student population. A college education became the springboard for continued upward mobility for Jews in the professions. Most American Jews were merchants, entrepreneurs or laborers in the 1920s. But they shared an aspiration that their sons become professionals, and a college education for their children became the goal of Jewish parents in America.[21] Jewish doctors, lawyers, accountants, and administrators appeared in increasing numbers in spite of the efforts of the non-Jewish society to limit their numbers. Benjamin Cardozo and Louis Brandeis were on the Supreme Court, and many leading academicians, authors, and men of letters were Jews. But again, it was the drive of men like David Sarnoff,[22] William Paley,[23] George Gershwin,[24] Irving Berlin,[25] and Jerome Kern[26] that brought Jews to the forefront of American life.

Louis Brandeis

---

21. A situation little changed through the 1980s.

22. 1891-1971. He was the founder of RCA and the NBC radio (and later television) network.

23. Born in 1901, a former cigar-maker who founded and, as of this writing, is still chairman of CBS.

24. 1898-1937. The premier American musical genius of the 1920s.

25. 1888-1989. Born Israel Baline, he became the great songster of America. Unlike Berlin, who at one time converted to Christianity, the others were lapsed Jews who never formally left the community.

26. 1885-1945. A famous Broadway composer, whose most memorable work is "Old Man River."

Planned Assimilation

HE COMMON DENOMINATOR of all these Jews, however, was their flight from Judaism and the Jewish community. They attempted to eradicate their Jewishness; many intermarried, and all refused to be identified with Jewish groups or causes. Nevertheless, non-Jewish leaders of conservative groups in America blamed the Jews as a whole for what they perceived as a weakening of the country's moral fiber. They accused Jews of being the fermenting yeast of the "Roaring Twenties," of the new wild America, of the post-war boom and of the strange and looser morals and mores of the era. This perception raised again the specter of anti-Semitism, as now the old, established system of American values was being threatened by the new times, and with these new times came the continuing erosion of Anglo-Saxon, Protestant influence on American life.

Such prominent Americans as Madison Grant[27] and the Attorney General of the United States, Mitchell Palmer,[28] railed against Jewish influence in the country. A great "Red Scare" engulfed America in the early 1920s, and because so many American Jews were immigrants from Russia, and some Jews were among the leaders of the Communist Revolution, Jews were labeled as being synonymous with socialists, Bolsheviks, and subversives. The 1921 Immigration Quota Act, followed by a much more restrictive act in 1924 — marked the beginning of the end for major Jewish immigration to the United States. These laws were passed largely out of fear that America would be "Judaized" in the near future. Thus, Jewish America in the 1920s was caught in a web of contradictions: America meant unlimited opportunity and unchecked assimilation. It also meant bigotry, discrimination, and insecurity. The rootless, neurotic Jew portrayed so graphically by American Jewish fiction was a product of these crosscurrents.

In the 1920s, Conservative Judaism came of age in the United States. It was confident that it had the solution to the religious

---

27. The author of a boring work of anti-Semitism, *The Passing of the Great Race*, first published in 1915. He decried the "mongrelization" of America and blamed the Jews for the new American culture as well as for World War I and a host of other social evils.

28. Among other calumnies, Palmer claimed that the Russian revolution was bankrolled and even planned by the rich Jewish bankers and financiers of New York!

problems of American Jewry. Orthodoxy seemed doomed and Reform was far too radical. The number, wealth, and influence of Conservative congregations in America grew steadily after World War I. The Jewish Theological Seminary was recognized in both the secular Jewish and non-Jewish world as a leading school of Jewish scholarship. It had an imposing faculty of formidable scholars, many of whom were personally observant and traditional in their daily lives. It aggressively projected itself as an American school of intensive Jewish learning.

Tradition Takes Root

TS MAIN COMPETITION IN THE Orthodox sector came from Rabbi Isaac Elchanan Theological Seminary in New York, headed by Rabbi Dr. Bernard Revel.[29] But RIETS was never as well funded as was the JTS, and Revel was under constant attack by differing groups within the Orthodox community itself, because of his attempts to create an institution that would accommodate the trends of American society without going beyond the pale of Orthodoxy, as had JTS. RIETS encouraged secular studies and was convinced that a synthesis between traditional yeshivah education and the new American world was necessary for Orthodox survival in the United States. It also retained the basic Talmudic curriculum of the European yeshivos, but added courses in history, Hebrew, and philosophy. As such, it was subject to strong attacks from different sections of its Orthodox constituency. It later evolved into Yeshiva University.

Orthodoxy in the United States, as elsewhere, was never monolithic and it was weakened by its lack of unity. The vast majority of rabbis and congregations in the United States were Orthodox in the 1920s, but their European-born constituency was unable or unwilling to have its American-born children follow in their footsteps. Many leading Orthodox rabbis in the United States enrolled their sons (who were interested in pursuing a rabbinic degree)[30] in the

---

29. See Chapter 25, "Social Revolution" for a biographical sketch of him.

30. Most sons of rabbis of the 1920s did not follow the career of their fathers. The poor salaries and low social esteem of the rabbinate at that time undoubtedly contributed to this situation.

Rabbi Chaim Tzvi Rubinstein

Reb Shraga Feivel Mendlowitz

Conservative seminary, thereby personally confirming their opinion that Orthodoxy in America had no future.

However, there was a stubborn minority that exhibited signs of confidence in Orthodox Jewish life as well. The first major yeshivah rabbinical school outside of New York was founded in Chicago in 1921 by Rabbis Chaim Tzvi Rubenstein[31] and Shaul Silber.[32] Called the Hebrew Theological College, it produced a substantial number of American-born rabbis and scholars for the traditional American Jewish community.

The nuclei for Yeshiva Torah Vodaath and Mesivta Chaim Berlin in New York were formed and strengthened in the 1920s. These two institutes would grow into two of the largest and most influential yeshivos in America.[33] Yeshivos such as Rabbi Jacob Joseph School and Mesivtha Tifereth Jerusalem had been operating on the lower East Side of New York since the early 1900s.

Perhaps the leading figure in Torah education in the United States was a self-effacing idealist who, though ordained in Nitra, Czechoslovakia — at the age of 16 — refused to be addressed as Rabbi. "Mister" Shraga Feivel Mendlowitz came to the United States as a young man in the early 1920s and, after a few years as a teacher in Scranton, became the head of the fledgling Yeshiva Torah Vodaath in Brooklyn. His dream was to meet the needs of America by combining chassidic warmth with Lithuanian-type analytical scholarship. In addition to building his own institution, he sent his best students to form the nucleus of other institutions, such as Mesivta Rabbi Chaim Berlin of Brooklyn, Telshe Yeshiva in Cleveland, Ner Israel Rabbinical College in Baltimore, and Beth Medrash Govoha in Lakewood, New Jersey. A practical dreamer, he also fostered the creation of out-of-town day schools, founded Torah Umesorah (National Society for Hebrew Day Schools), and encouraged the establishment by his family of what is now Boys Town Jerusalem.

---

31. 1872-1944. A student of Volozhin who served as *rosh yeshivah* in Jaffa when Rabbi Kook was rabbi there. He arrived in America in 1917 and was one of the leading rabbis in Chicago in the 1920s and the 1930s. The author is his grandson.

32. 1876-1946. One of the leading rabbinic figures in America, he combined the scholarship of his Eastern European education with a pragmatic and gifted insight into the realities of American Jewry. He was a strong administrator and an unforgettable fund-raiser, and was the president of the Hebrew Theological College for its first twenty-five years, while at the same time occupying the pulpit of one of the leading synagogues in Chicago.

33. For details, see "The New Jewish World," below.

Great European scholars came to teach in American yeshivos, especially at RIETS and Torah Vodaath.[34] Books of Talmudic scholarship were written and published by American rabbis. English translations of the Bible and prayer books were prepared, printed, and distributed in the tens of thousands; and the English-speaking Orthodox rabbi was no longer a rare creature. But in the main, Orthodoxy was still predominantly European in character and outlook, Yiddish was its language, and the mores and lifestyle of the *shtetl* still governed its society. The new "Modern Orthodox" format in American Jewry was just emerging.

Rabbinic leaders of American Jewry, 1925

Young Israel had become a national movement with branches over the entire country. It encouraged youth programs, communal prayer with song, English-speaking rabbis, and strong commitment to tradition coupled with a positive attitude toward American life and society. It can be said that Young Israel in the 1920s served as a lifeline to tradition for thousands of young American Jews who otherwise would have been swept away in the avalanche of assimilation. Thus, in the American Jewish spiritual sea of darkness there were islands forming, upon which the foundation for a strong — albeit uniquely American — Orthodoxy would be built. However, the importance of these events and institutions are apparent to us only now in retrospect. They were little noticed and even less appreciated in the society of their contemporaries. No one foresaw the face of American Jewry as it would appear a few short decades later. The Jewish world was now on the verge of an irrevocable moment of change, and that change would, perforce, alter American Jewish life as well.

---

34. At RIETS, Rabbi Moshe Soloveitchik of Brisk and Warsaw, Rabbi Shimon Shkop of Grodno, and Rabbi Shlomo Poliachek, the Progidy of Maitchet, among others. At Torah Vodaath, Rabbi David Leibowitz of Radin, Rabbi Shlomo Heiman of Baranovitch, and Rabbi Elya Chazan of Mir. During the 1930s Rabbi Moshe Feinstein came to Mesivtha Tifereth Jerusalem, where, in a nearly fifty-year career, he became one of the world's leading halachic authorities.

31
Jews Under Moslem Rule

A Protected Minority

I have not discussed the history of Sephardic Jewry at any length in this book until now. Most of the thrust, drama, and changes of Jewish history in the seventeenth, eighteenth, and nineteenth centuries were concentrated in Europe. Therefore, though the Sephardic element was essential to the survival and development of world Jewry, it played a relatively minor role in the Jewish history of these three centuries. This would begin to change in the early twentieth century when the stories of Ashkenazic and Sephardic Jewries would begin to converge, especially with relation to Jewish settlement in Palestine. Thus, the background, attitudes, lifestyle and social forces of Sephardic Jewry must be known in order for the reader to appreciate the development and struggles of the Jewish Yishuv in Palestine in the twentieth century.

 T THE BEGINNING OF THE First World War over one million Jews lived under Moslem rule.[1] Almost 100,000 lived in Iran, and many Jewish communities there were able to trace their roots to the ancient Persia of Mordechai and Esther. Another 500,000 lived in the countries of the *Maghreb*, i.e. Western North Africa — Tunisia, Algeria, and Morocco. The ancient Jewish community of Babylonia still survived in Iraq and numbered 125,000, while 80,000 Jews lived in Egypt, 60,000 in Yemen, and the

---

1. For an excellent and concise survey of the history of Jewish-Moslem relationships and an understanding of the lot of the Jews under Moslem rule, see Bernard Lewis, *The Jews of Islam*, Princeton University Press, 1984.

balance under the direct rule of the Ottoman Empire in Turkey, Syria, Lebanon, and Palestine.[2]

The masses of Sephardic Jewry were pious, loyal Jews, with unswerving allegiance to Torah and its tenets. The position of *chacham*, or rabbi, was prestigious and authoritative. The Sephardim were responsible for maintaining the Jewish presence in Palestine for centuries and were most zealous in protecting their customs and traditions. Even in this century, when the level of religious observance has fallen from its original state, Sephardic Jews tend to be more loyal to tradition than their Ashkenazic brethren, and more respectful of their *chachamim*.

Although Talmudic scholarship among the Sephardic communities had declined from its exalted levels of earlier centuries, late-nineteenth-century Sephardic Jewry produced its share of scholars and authors who were universally respected. Among them were Rabbi Haim Hizkiyah Medini of Jerusalem, author of *Sdei Chemed*, a multi-volume encyclopedia of rabbinic responsa on the entire range of halachic questions; and Rabbi Yosef Haim of Baghdad, known as the *Ben Ish Hai*, after the most popular of his numerous works of responsa, novellae and homiletics.

The attitude of the Moslem rulers to their Jewish subjects had crystallized over thirteen centuries into one of disdain, contempt, cruelty, exploitation — and, yet, wariness. In the translation of this attitude into practical policies, there was a tone of ambivalence. Jews did not, as a rule, suffer from the open, unceasing, and violent anti-Semitism that was the lot of their brethren in Christian Europe. Nevertheless, violence against Jews was always present just below the surface of Arab life. Revolution, social unrest, and religious fanaticism always engendered Jewish casualties. As late as 1941, the overthrow of Rashid Ali as ruler of Iraq was the signal for a pogrom of major proportions in Baghdad, resulting in the death of 150 Jews.[3]

The Moslems practiced the policy of *dhimma*[4] towards all their non-Moslem subjects: the minorities were considered inferior under the law, but they were protected. The Jews were naturally included as one

---

2. See Lewis, p. 191, for slightly more conservative estimates of the Jewish population then under Moslem rule.

3. *The Second World War*, Martin Gilbert, New York, 1989, p. 187.

4. Literally "pact" or "treaty." This was an official agreement between the Moslem governmental authority and the non-Moslem communities under its rule, providing for the regulation of those communities and their rights under Moslem law. The people covered by this *dhimma* were known as *dhimmies*.

of the non-Moslem communities under Moslem rule, but in many cases they were not the major group affected by the discriminatory policies; for many centuries, the Christian minorities in the Moslem world were the primary targets of Moslem hatred.

The Jews suffered greatly as well, however, because in addition to the expected bigotry of the Moslem authorities and population, Jews had also to contend with the enmity of their Christian neighbors. As often happens under tyrannical rule, the victims persecuted each other, rather than uniting against the common despot. Nevertheless, until the nineteenth century, Jewish life, though poverty stricken, primitive, and deprived, was more stable, peaceful, and secure under Moslem rule than it was in Europe.

This situation of the Jews began to change radically in the nineteenth century with the decline of the Ottoman Empire and the encroachments upon it of the European powers. France established its influence and eventually its dominion over Tunisia, Morocco, and Algeria. It also was extremely busy in Syria[5] and Lebanon. It established itself as the protector of the Roman Catholic and Maronite Christian minorities in the Ottoman Empire, and it pursued an active policy of intervention in internal Ottoman affairs, vigorously pursuing its imperial goals under the guise of guarding the interests and human rights of its fellow Christians.

---

5. The infamous "blood libel" of Damascus in 1840 was the product of the instigation and lies of the French consul there.

Traditional Bucharan Jews

Russia, continuing its voracious expansionist policy, drove the Turks out of Crimea, the Caucasus, and other areas of dense Moslem population. In addition, Russia established itself as the protector of the Eastern Orthodox (mainly Greek Orthodox) Christians living under Ottoman rule and, in one of the great ironies of history, also insisted on good treatment and respect for the human rights of the Russian Jews (i.e., the European Jews) then in the Land of Israel. The Czar still claimed these Jews as his wards, even though they lived thousands of miles from the location of his otherwise less-than-benevolent rule. In practice, his policy applied to the Ashkenazic community in *Eretz Yisrael*, which had originated in Russia. The weakness of the Ottoman Empire — its corrupt decadence and governmental inefficiency — was apparent to its Moslem subjects. In frustration at their inferior world position vis-a-vis Christian Europe, the Moslems became increasingly less tolerant of the non-Moslem minorities in their midst.

Contempt Evolves into Hatred

N THE 1800S THE CHRISTIAN minority had strong protectors who were prepared to forcibly intervene on their behalf, but the Jews had no real protection[6] and were powerless. Thus, the indignities and persecution of

---

6. The Czar's protestations against the persecution of "his" Jews in the Moslem countries was viewed by Moslems and Jews alike as hypocritical, laughable, and cynical.

Traditional Bucharan Jewish children

the *dhimma* fell almost exclusively on the Jewish minority. Pious statements on their behalf were issued by some governments, notably England, but since these countries had little presence and weak leverage in the Ottoman Empire, from 1850 to 1920 the Moslems were never deterred from enforcing their brutal decrees.[7]

To make matters worse, Moslem rulers no longer viewed the Jews as necessary contributors to society. They had slowly been displaced from positions of importance in mercantile, medical, governmental, and investment positions by the Christian minority. The Westernized Christians had outstripped their Jewish rivals, as well as the Moslems themselves, in their ability to deal with an increasingly technological and complex European-style society. To a great extent, the Jews were backward and only semiliterate in European terms. Thus, they were expendable, and their main purpose now was to serve as a scapegoat for the ills of the Ottoman society and the Moslem world generally.

The Christians in the Moslem world were also the conduit by which the classical anti-Semitism of nineteenth-century Europe reached the Moslem world. This ominous development went almost unnoticed at the time. The caricature of the "evil Jew,"[8] the calumnies of *The Protocols of the Elders of Zion,* the unreasoning hatred of the Jews as being radical and disloyal — all now reached the Moslem world. The original religion-based contempt of the Moslem world towards the Jews now was transformed into deep social suspicion and, eventually, irrational hate. Jews, under Islam, had not been taken seriously, but the terrible European lies about them were. The Christian minorities of the Moslem world were the sowers of these evil seeds, but they fell on fertile ground.

After the First World War, a great wave of secularization took place in the Moslem world. This was due to the ignominious end of the Ottoman Empire and the now almost complete dominance over the Moslem world by England and France. The Pahlavi family was installed as the rulers of Iran and they secularized — albeit only for sixty years — the fanatical Shiite Moslem population of that country. North Africa was under the French, as were Lebanon[9] and

---

7. See Lewis, pp. 164-168 and pp. 181-3 for details and examples of Moslem contempt and cruelty towards the Jews in their domain.

8. See Chapter 24.

9. Artificially created by France, and with a Christian "majority" in the country.

Syria. Iraq, Egypt, Jordan, Palestine, and parts of Arabia became British responsibilities. Turkey,[10] under the dictatorial rule of Kemal Ataturk, became an officially secular country and discarded Islam as the state religion, even going so far as to ban traditional Moslem dress.

In the main, the Jews welcomed this process of secularization, since it brought with it citizenship, the abolishment of official *dhimma* and discrimination, and new economic and social opportunities. However, as could be foretold, it also brought secularization to the Jewish community.

This great body of Sephardic Jewry had remained sheltered in its traditional ways for centuries. It never experienced any of the great struggles that befell Ashkenazic Jewry in the eighteenth and nineteenth centuries. It was not rejuvenated by Chassidus, challenged by Enlightenment, exposed to the new ideas of the modern world, or driven to Zionism in a search for the solution to the "Jewish problem." It was therefore a politically naive society, never toughened in the fire of controversy nor vitally strengthened in its commitment to Torah Judaism. It had fought few internal battles,[11] and encountered minimal spiritual and intellectual challenges. As such, it was extremely vulnerable to the wave of secularization that swept over the Moslem world in the 1920s through the impetus of the Western powers and the modern world. It would be even more vulnerable to the systematic secularization efforts of the political Zionist movement in the 1940s and 1950s.

The secularization of the Moslem world's leadership during the 1920s led observers to conclude that Islam's medieval backwardness would dissipate, but this surface change masked a deep hatred of Western values by the Moslem masses and clergy. The fact that the Jews joined the secularists so willingly and with such alacrity, and benefited from the new society — ostensibly at the "expense" of the

---

10. During World War I, while on the way to becoming a "better society," Ottoman Turkey had slaughtered one-and-a-half million Armenians for purely ethnic, racial, and religious reasons. Hitler referred to this slaughter as a prototype for his own dark plans.

11. See Lewis, p. 176-7, for one example of a challenge to the traditional role of the rabbi in Moslem countries in the 1860s, and its failure. The Ottoman government had then imposed a new "constitution" on the Jewish community, which severely limited the dominant role of the rabbi in religious and legal matters and made him subject to the limitations of a council of laymen. Within a decade, the "constitution" was a dead letter, unobserved by the Jews and unenforced by the Turks.

Moslem population — further strengthened anti-Semitism[12] among the Moslems.

The emerging Jewish-Arab conflict in Palestine, which the 1920s brought into sharp focus, only served to further undermine the stability of the Jewish communities in the Moslem countries. The Palestinian Arabs and their Moslem co-religionists never differentiated between Zionist and Jew,[13] and thus all the "sins" of the Zionists against the Arabs of Palestine were attributed to all Jews in every Moslem country. The success of Zionism, and the inability of the Arabs to prevent the growth of the new Jewish *Yishuv* in Palestine, only intensified the Moslem hatred of the Jew.

Thus, as the 1930s dawned, the Jewish world was tottering. Russian Jewry was enslaved and isolated; Polish and Lithuanian Jewry were embattled in a struggle, both internal and external, to survive and prosper; American Jewry was still relatively weak and inexorably sinking into the swamp of assimilation; and the Jews in Palestine were struggling against England and the Arabs to retain their foothold in the land of their fathers. The religious, spiritual, and social cleavages in the Jewish world were intense and bitter, and there was no united Jewish people, nor even a commonly agreed-upon agenda for the Jews to pursue. Yet the beast was about to be loosed from its cage, and its Jewish prey was ill prepared to mount any meaningful defense. The dread curses of Deuteronomy[14] were now to become reality.

---

12. To the statement of the Arabs that they cannot be anti-Semites since they themselves are Semites, see Bernard Lewis, *Semites and Anti-Semites*, New York, 1987, p. 16: "The logic of this would seem to be that while an edition of Hitler's *Mein Kampf* published in Berlin or in Buenos Aires in German or Spanish is anti-Semitic, an Arabic version of the same text published in Cairo or Beirut cannot be anti-Semitic because Hebrew and Arabic are cognate languages. It is not a compelling argument."

13. See Lewis, op. cit., pp. 22-3.

14. Deuteronomy 28:15-68 gives a litany of misfortunes that will befall the Jewish people if they disobey the Torah.

Section VII

The Holocaust[1] and the State

1938-1958

1. There are numerous books on this subject. I have found the following to be the most instructive and meaningful:

Lucy Dawidowicz, *The War Against the Jews*, Holt, Rinehart, and Winston, N.Y. 1975

Martin Gilbert, *The Holocaust*, Holt, Rinehart, and Winston, N.Y. 1985

William L. Shirer, *Berlin Diary*, N.Y. 1941, and *Twentieth Century Journey*, Vol. II, *The Nightmare Years*, Little Brown, and Co., N.Y. 1984

Gideon Hausner, *Justice in Jerusalem*, Harper and Row, N.Y. 1966

Rabbi Michael Dov Weissmandel, *Min HaMaytzar*, Emunah, N.Y. 1960

Abraham Fuchs, *The Unheeded Cry*, Mesorah Publications, N.Y. 1984

Elie Weisel, *Night*, Hill and Wang, N.Y. 1960

Steiner, *Treblinka*, Simon and Schuster, N.Y. 1967

Arthur Morse, *While Six Million Died*, Random House, N.Y. 1968

David Kranzler, *Thy Brother's Blood*, Mesorah Publications, N.Y. 1987

David S. Wyman, *The Abandonment of the Jews*, Pantheon, 1984

Monty Noam Penkower, *The Jews Were Expendable*, Univ. of Illinois Press, 1983

Moshe Prager, *Sparks of Glory*, Mesorah Publications, N.Y. 1975

32

Hitler Comes to Power

Blueprint for a New Germany

I N 1933, ADOLF HITLER was appointed Chancellor of Germany. That single act sealed the doom of European Jewry. Hitler, a wounded veteran of World War I, was an Austrian by birth, a frustrated painter by vocation, and a psychopathic hater by nature. His main demon was the Jewish "race," which he believed responsible for all of the ills of the world generally and Germany particularly. In his warped mind, the Jews had betrayed the "Fatherland" in forcing the Armistice upon it in 1918; they had destroyed the German economy after the war and were actively abetting either a Communist takeover or a capitalist exploitation of Germany.

In the early 1920s he gained control of a tiny, insignificant group, the National Socialist Party,[1] which was viewed by most as a lunatic, right-wing, fringe group. It was this party, however, that was to provide his springboard to power. In 1923 he attempted to overthrow the Munich city government, but failed ignominiously in what was derisively called the "Beer Hall Putsch." Hitler was arrested, convicted of sedition, and sentenced to a five-year prison term, but was paroled after only nine months.

He used his time in prison to organize all of his racial, national, and political theories into an almost incoherent, rambling diatribe of a book called *Mein Kampf*.[2] In it he drew the blueprint for his new Germany and Aryan-dominated Europe. He would rid the world of Jews,

---

1. Nazi was the popular name of the party, a contraction of the German words for "National Socialist."

2. Literally, *"My Struggle."* The book sold millions of copies and made Hitler an independently wealthy man.

Communists, Gypsies, and other "sub-human races." Other "inferior races," such as the French, Dutch, and especially the Slavs, would not be destroyed but rather be enslaved to the master Aryan race which was German. But his primary fury was reserved for the Jews, whom he regarded as a racial pollutant that degraded, diluted, and destroyed the purity of all with whom they came in contact. In *Mein Kampf*, Hitler also declared that the Western world would have to scrap the Treaty of Versailles and provide Germany with *lebensraum*,[3] or "living space," and a "place in the sun."

Hitler often stated that no one should have been surprised by his policies when he came to power. "'No human being has ever declared or recorded what he wanted more often than I.' So Hitler said, and it was true."[4]

The Nazi party never won a majority in any free election in Germany, but by 1930 it had become the largest single German political party, winning 37% of the vote. Although its vote dipped somewhat in the 1932 election, it remained the largest party by a solid margin. Under the spellbinding oratory and leadership of Hitler, its fanatically loyal adherents numbered in the millions, and his Brown Shirts[5] were a private army of many hundreds of thousands. The continuing pressure of Nazi terror on the streets and in the *Reichstag*,[6] the worldwide economic depression of 1929-30, the specter of Stalin's ruthless Bolshevization of Russia, Hitler's bellicose threats upon his neighbors, and the malaise and ineptitude of the democratic parties of Germany — all these allowed Hitler to maneuver his way to the top of the political heap.

All of the forces in German life — political, economic, and military — underestimated and misjudged Hitler. Somehow, they thought that they would be able to manipulate him, or, at the very least, moderate his views when he came to power. After meeting Hitler for the first time, President von Hindenburg said privately that "at most, he could be a postmaster." They were wrong, and in many cases, they were dead wrong. Hitler's use of propaganda, his appeal to the basest

---

3. Literally, "room to live." By this, he meant territorial expansion of Germany, mainly at the expense of Poland and the Baltic States.

4. *Modern Times*, Paul Johnson, p. 351.

5. The Brown Shirts, officially known as the *Schutzabteilung* (SA) or Security Force, officially a para-military Nazi organization headed by Ernest Roehm, was the instrument of Nazi street terror. Roehm was purged by Hitler in the mid-1930s and the organization absorbed into the German army and the SS.

6. The German parliament.

instincts of the German population, and his terror machine allowed him to consolidate power rapidly.

In January 1933, he assembled a coalition government and became the Chancellor of Germany. Capitalizing on his position, he moved quickly to take full control of the country. Almost immediately he began to persecute the Jews, through discriminatory legislation, organized boycotts, and officially sanctioned violence. By the end of 1934 Germany was completely in the grip of Hitler's dictatorial rule, and its Jewish population of over half a million was on the way to disenfranchisement, pauperization, and, eventually, destruction.

Hitler had noted that Italy's aggression in Libya and Abyssinia in the 1930s had brought no concerted action against it from the democratic powers of Europe or the League of Nations. He was convinced that the democracies were weak of will. Even though they were still immeasurably stronger militarily than was Germany, he knew that they would never dare confront him directly.

Steadily and vigorously, he pushed his program of unilaterally abrogating the Treaty of Versailles. That treaty, which had formally ended World War I, forced humiliating terms on Germany, requiring it to pay reparations to the victors and severely restricting Germany's armed forces, among other things. The treaty provided a convenient target for Hitler, who blamed it — and the Jews — for all of Germany's ills. First he canceled all reparations payments. Then he began a massive rearmament of Germany, in direct and public violation of the Versailles Treaty.

Thanks in great measure to his program of rearmament, Hitler was able to produce full employment. Not one of the major powers remonstrated with him over this violation of the Treaty of Versailles. Under Hitler, Germany was the first major industrial power to emerge from the Depression. He provided Germans with jobs and economic stability, albeit at the cost of their personal rights and civil liberties. Emboldened by his success and the weakness of his antagonists, Hitler ruthlessly destroyed all internal opposition to his rule and policies. The Gestapo,[7] the SA and later the SS,[8] all became the law in Germany. The underworld, the sadists and criminals, now were in charge. All of

---

7. Acronym for *Geheimestaatspolizei,* the Nazi Secret Police organization.

8. The *Schutzstaffel,* Security Force, known as the Black Shirts. Headed by Heinrich Himmler, members of this group swore loyalty to Hitler personally and not to Germany. Although parallel to the army, it had its own command, and Himmler was responsible directly to Hitler, not to the military command. It was an elite organization,

the dreams of human progress nurtured in the nineteenth and twentieth centuries were dashed by the demon state controlled by Hitler. The darkest chapter of the human story was about to be written.

The World Ignores the Threat

S NOTED, THE DEMOCRACIES were war weary, badly divided among themselves, and given to unbelievable naivete as to Hitler, his motives, and his goals. Many even agreed that he had a right to unilaterally nullify what they also considered to be the unduly harsh Treaty of Versailles.[9] Others thought that his "ferocious statements were mere rhetoric intended for home consumption."[10]

England slept, oblivious to the danger facing it. France, with a socialist Jewish premier, Leon Blum,[11] was wistfully looking the other way, convinced that Hitler was bent only upon rectifying the injustices of Versailles, and was really a man of peace. The United States, gripped in the throes of a terrible economic Depression, locked in the political struggle over Roosevelt and his New Deal, had little interest in foreign affairs. Such pro-German and anti-Semitic American organizations as the German-American Bund and the Silver Shirts, and such individuals as Henry Ford,[12] Gerald L.K. Smith,[13] and Father Coughlin,[14] all had created a climate in the United States of toleration of, if not support for,

---

and eventually was charged with the destruction of European Jewry. It also comprised the most feared units in the German military and was infamous for its sadistic and ruthless behavior towards friend and foe alike.

9. Johnson, pp. 348-9.

10. *The Times of London*, July 10, 1934. Fifty-five years later, the *Times* continues to write about the PLO in the same vein.

11. Another example of the danger some Jews pose to their people when they achieve political power. In response to his Jewishness and socialism, many Frenchmen proclaimed, "Better Hitler than Blum."

12. The legendary automobile manufacturer was strongly anti-Semitic. He founded a newspaper in Dearborn, Michigan to propagate his views.

13. A rabid evangelist preacher who was an avowed anti-Semite, and an erstwhile presidential candidate.

14. A Roman Catholic priest from metropolitan Detroit, whose weekly national radio program was openly anti-Jewish. He commanded a wide following until the United States entered World War II.

Hitler. Coupled with the ingrained isolationist tendencies of the American public, a powerful counter-reaction to the heavy casualties of World War I, this mood prevented any effective response to Hitler and his program. Thus he had a free hand in the 1930s to implement his cruelties.

First Hitler occupied the Saar basin in early 1935. Then, after a plebiscite, the Saar was reunited with Germany. Immediately thereafter, he officially repudiated the Treaty of Versailles. In late 1936, he threatened to move his army into the demilitarized Rhineland, and in early 1937 he did so. The French and English could have easily repulsed him at any time during this period, and even toppled him from power. Hitler himself admitted as much: "If even the French police had marched into the Rhineland, we would have had to withdraw with our tails between our legs."[15] But the French did not march.

Hitler then demanded that Austria be annexed to Germany, because it was a "Germanic" country. He browbeat the Austrian Chancellor, Kurt von Schuschnigg, into submission, and in March 1938 the *Anschluss*[16] took place.

Insatiable, he now claimed the Sudetenland section of Czechoslovakia for the Reich, on the grounds that it, too, had many German-speaking citizens. Czechoslovakia had treaties with England and France guaranteeing its territorial integrity. It also had a large, well-trained and well-equipped army and a strong defense line, anchored by fortresses on its border. Nevertheless, the prime ministers of England and France, still terrified at the prospect of war, and under the delusion that "Herr Hitler is a reasonable man who wants peace," met with him at the infamous Munich Conference of 1938. Giving in to Hitler's demands without even inviting the Czechs to the conference, they forced Czechoslovakia to concede the Sudetenland to Germany.

---

15. Paul Schmidt, *Hitler's Interpreter* (London, 1951), p. 320, quoted by Johnson in *Modern Times*, p. 353.

16. The reunification of Austria and Germany to form the new German Reich. Hitler proclaimed that this "Third Reich would last 1000 years." It lasted seven.

"Peace for Our Time"

PPEASEMENT OF HERR HITLER was seen somehow as a positive foreign policy by British Prime Minister Neville Chamberlain. He promised "peace for our time," but his craven duplicity at the Munich Conference guaranteed war. In March 1939, contemptuous of England and France, Hitler occupied Prague and dismembered Czechoslovakia. Germany then seized the port of Memel from Lithuania, again to resounding silence from the Western democracies. This made Hitler certain that Britain and France would fight for no one in Europe. Now, the British and French finally began to prepare for war, but Hitler did not take them seriously, in light of their past lack of performance.

Immediately after Munich, Hitler began to threaten Poland, which, like Czechoslovakia, was "protected" by treaty with England and France. From Poland he demanded impossible territorial concessions. Having defeated Russia in the 1920s, Poland had a false sense of security and misplaced trust in its armed forces, which still relied on cavalry and horse-drawn artillery. Although it seems incredible in retrospect, high officers of the British and French military agreed that the Poles could defeat Germany in a war. Thus Poland prepared for battle, confident in its own strength and in its alliances with the West. In his first major miscalculation, Hitler was convinced that England and France would not go to war over Poland, but he misjudged the mood of the populations of the Western democracies, who were fed up with their timid leaders. Hitler would now be resisted by force at the next provocation.

Neville Chamberlain arrives in Cologne on September 22, 1938

In May 1939, Hitler and Mussolini entered into an agreement — "The Pact of Steel" — forming the Axis alliance. Mussolini attacked and eventually conquered Albania. In the Far East, Japan continued its relentless war against China and also came into combat with Russian troops. Poland and Hungary each tore off a piece of Czechoslovakia. The world had gone mad. But the agreement that com-

pleted the diplomatic scenario for war was the Russo-German Treaty of 1939.

Hitler and Stalin, even though they represented conflicting ideologies and had always professed hatred and contempt for one another, had great similarities in outlook, Realpolitik, and pragmatic ruthlessness. They learned from one another's methods, achievements, and mistakes, and had a grudging admiration one for the other.

In May 1939, Stalin signaled his willingness to join Hitler by discharging his Jewish foreign minister, Maxim Litvinov, and replacing him with the dour hard-liner, V.M. Molotov. For his part, Hitler realized that his Polish campaign was dependent upon Russia giving him a free hand on its frontier. Thus, in August 1939, Joachim von Ribbentrop, Hitler's foreign minister, visited Moscow to negotiate and execute a "non-aggression" treaty between Germany and Russia. Included in it was a secret protocol dividing Poland between Germany and Russia, and permitting Russia to annex the Baltic republics of Lithuania, Latvia, and Estonia. The treaty was signed on August 25, giving Hitler the green light to unleash his fearsome machine of war against Poland. On September 1, 1939, the blitzkrieg against Poland began. England and France, honoring their commitment to Poland, gave Hitler an ultimatum to withdraw or they would declare war against Germany. He ignored them, convinced that they were bluffing. This time he was wrong, and two days later Armageddon had arrived.

Reaction at Zionist Congress, 1939, upon word of the German-Russian non-aggression treaty signing

33

Hitler's War Against the Jews

All the Doors Are Closed

ITLER'S WAR OF ANNIHILATION against the Jews began on the day he assumed power. The Nazis celebrated their ascension to government with violent attacks on Jews, concentrating initially on the upper strata of German Jewry. Jewish professors, doctors, lawyers, and other professionals and academicians were beaten and arrested; then, gradually, they were restricted and forbidden to practice their professions. This brought home, clearly and brutally, the message that no matter how assimilated or valuable a Jew was to society, there was no such creature as a "German" Jew.

On April 1, 1933, a general one-day boycott of all Jewish shops and enterprises was implemented by the government and observed by the entire populace.[1] The first of the infamous concentration camps, Dachau, was opened in March, 1933. Book-burnings on a mass scale began in May, 1933. Jews were eventually dismissed from the universities, the press, and the theater. Jews were also prevented from continuing in scientific research and planning,[2] lest they infect true Aryan science with the Jewish bacillus.

---

1. To people who were not there at the time, lack of any response by the "good Germans" to the anti-Jewish activities of the Nazis has always remained one of the most troubling and perplexing problems in this tragic matter. Yet eyewitnesses who lived in Germany during that time recall that the Nazi terror was so brutal and dominating that effective protest was impossible.

2. The irony of this is that the exclusion of Jewish physicists, mathematicians, and scientists from German scientific life set back Germany's nuclear capability for years. Thank God!

*Barbed wire fences in
a concentration camp*

The Jews reacted to this horror slowly and cautiously. They held to their Jewish identity as a badge of honor.[3] At first, world Jewry reacted with demonstrations and counter-boycotts against Germany, but the Nazis made it starkly clear to the Jews in Germany that it was they, not the country, who would pay a heavy price, unless the foreign outcries were stopped. German Jewry attempted to maintain a low profile, remaining apart from the rest of the German population, and wait out the tide. Most people thought that they were living through nothing more than another episode of European anti-Semitism, and that Hitler would soon pass from the scene. However, many Jews in Germany, both Zionists and non-Zionists, realized that the only solution to their problem was emigration. At first the Nazis encouraged this course, pushing the Jews hard to leave; their initial goal was to make Germany *Judenrein*,[4] rather than to physically exterminate the Jews.

Over 75,000 Jews left by August, 1935. Thirty thousand of them came to Palestine, and almost 14,000 came to the United States and Canada, neither of which had liberal immigration policies. To the contrary, both countries put every possible impediment in the way of the desperate Jews. American immigration quotas, which were very small to begin with, were never filled, and were overzealously protected by unsympathetic bureaucrats. Many Jews fled to England, South Africa, and Australia. Others fled, but not far enough, and settled in France, Belgium, Holland, Austria, and Czechoslovakia. However, there were German Jews who were proud of their nationality and insisted that they were entitled to live in Germany; such people stubbornly refused to

---

3. The *Judische Rundschau*, a German-Jewish newspaper, published an article called "Wear the Yellow Badge with Pride," on April 1, 1933.

4. Literally, "clean of Jews."

leave. By the time they were finally ready to go, after the traumatic events of 1938, the opportunities to do so had evaporated. No one wanted the Jews.

In 1938, President Roosevelt called a conference of thirty-one countries in Evian, France to deal with the refugee crisis. The result was resounding apathy. As one nation put it, "We do not have a 'Jewish problem' and we do not wish to import one." The American contribution to the solution of the refugee crisis was a pledge that it would do everything permitted by existing law — which law was in itself a significant part of the problem. Hitler, crowing that he was only doing what the democracies themselves would have liked to do, was convinced that he could destroy the Jews with impunity.

The "Nuremberg Laws," enacted in September, 1935, stripped Jews of German citizenship, denied them civil rights in Germany, and forbade Jewish sexual contact with non-Jews. Thus, even the intermarried and baptized Jews were now forcibly returned to the fold of their people. A succession of laws forced the removal of Jews from most businesses and the divestiture by Jews of most of their property. The Jews of Germany had been made defenseless and brought to economic and social ruin. Jewish emigration now became more frenzied, and before the doors finally shut, an additional 100,000 Jews left Germany in 1938, mostly to neighboring countries including Poland. The 220,000 Jews remaining in Germany were destroyed in the Holocaust.

During the course of the decade, Jewish children were excluded from the schools, whether by official fiat or because the persecution was more than the children and their parents could bear. As a result, many more Jews were exposed to their heritage, albeit in a watered-down form, because the Jewish community now assumed the responsibility for education. To Orthodox Jews, the events were not as traumatic, because they viewed anti-Semitism as a natural phenomenon of the long history of exile. Their historic faith helped sustain them. However, the ninety percent of the Jews who were more German than Jewish, were shattered, because they had suddenly been excluded from the society to which they had convinced themselves they belonged.

After the Anschluss with Austria in 1938, Adolf Eichmann of the S.S. established an "Emigration Office" in Vienna, to intimidate the Austrian Jews into leaving the country. He brought about the expulsion of 110,000 Jews from Austria and an additional 35,000 from Moravia and Bohemia. Jews were terrorized, beaten on the streets, forced to clean public latrines and driven into economic destitution. This pattern of behavior, repeated in the Sudetenland — which had been taken from Czechoslovakia, thanks to Western capitulation at Munich — produced the desired result of forcing the Jews to flee from the German "homeland," and also established Eichmann's grim reputation as an "expert on Jewish affairs."

Reign of Terror

T HE EVENT THAT CAME TO CHARACTERIZE the 1930s reign of terror was *Kristallnacht,* or the Night of Broken Glass, in November, 1938. On the pretext of "spontaneous" national outrage for the killing of a junior German diplomat by a Jew in Paris, the worst pogrom of the decade broke out in Germany. It was so well orchestrated that it began almost simultaneously throughout the country. Nearly all synagogues were burned, stores were looted, individuals were beaten, terrorized, and arrested. The atrocity received its name from the tens of thousands of windows that were smashed in the course of the pogrom. More than any single event before the outbreak of the war, *Kristallnacht* created international public outrage regarding the plight of Jews. Even Roosevelt felt the sting, and immigration regulations were somewhat liberalized in the United States: the exclusionary immigration laws were finally reinterpreted so as to let Jews into the country, rather than keep them out.

This phase of German treatment of the Jews — humiliation and terror to effect emigration — came to a close at the beginning of World War II with the invasion of Poland. Then Hitler was no longer content with only Germany being *Judenrein.* He wanted all of Europe, which he felt was now within his grasp, to become *Judenrein,* but emigration would not be the means. His ally, the Mufti of Jerusalem, then in exile in Berlin, complained long and hard to Hitler about the increased Jewish immigration to Palestine in the 1930s. All the world was closed to the Jews, and Hitler therefore set about to solve the "Jewish problem" permanently on the killing fields of Eastern Europe.

The German invasion of Poland culminated in complete victory within six weeks. The Polish army was overwhelmed, outgunned, and outmanned. It sent horses against tanks and fought bombers with machine guns. Thus 3,250,000 Jews fell under German domination. In Hitler's words, "the breeding grounds of Jewry" were now in the hands of their executioners. Meanwhile, the eastern provinces of Poland were annexed by Russia; Lithuania, not realizing that its own days were numbered, pounced on Polish Vilna, its ancient capital, and annexed it.

As noted above, less than a week before the invasion, Germany and the Soviet Union astounded the world by signing the infamous Molotov-Ribbentrop Pact. Ostensibly it would be a treaty of friendship between the two sworn enemies, but on September 1, 1939 it became clear that Hitler's intention was simply to clear the way for his attack on Poland by neutralizing Russia. On September 17, the secret clause of the treaty became obvious: Hitler and Stalin had agreed to partition Poland. The Nazi troops stopped their advance, and even withdrew from some areas, in order to allow the Russians to move in. Only much later did it become known that the treaty also allowed the Soviet Union to annex the three tiny Baltic states of Lithuania, Latvia, and Estonia.

Letter from Ribbentrop

Indirectly, the Molotov-Ribbentrop Treaty resulted in an important turning point in Jewish history: The Russian move into Poland caused virtual anarchy on the Polish-Lithuanian border, making it possible for large numbers of Jewish refugees — about 25,000 — to pour across the border to "safety." Rabbi Chaim Ozer Grodzensky, head of the Vilna rabbinical court, sent urgent word to the yeshivos under Russian domination to escape to Vilna. Miraculously, the Russians had curried favor with Lithuania by returning Vilna, its ancient capital, to Lithuanian control after it had been occupied by the Poles for nearly twenty years. Many of the major yeshivos, such as Mir, Kletzk, Kaminetz, Baranovitch, and others crossed the border secretly, even traveling on the Sabbath in obedience to Rabbi Grodzensky's orders.

In Vilna, the academies continued to function, supported by the heroic efforts of Rabbi Grodzensky, who, beneath his sparkling smile, was in constant pain from terminal cancer. Supported by the hospitality of the poor Jews of Lithuania and the generosity of the American rabbinate and the Joint Distribution Committee, the rabbi became the major relief agency for all the refugees. Many major Torah leaders were able to escape to the free world during the months between Germany's conquest of Poland and its invasion of the Baltic countries. Among them were Rabbi Eliezer Yehudah Finkel of Mir, Rabbi Reuven Grozovsky of Kaminetz, Rabbi Aharon Kotler of Kletzk, and Rabbi Yitzchak Zev Soloveitchik of Brisk. They, and others like them, succeeded in establishing major Torah institutions in the free world, which were successful transplants of the European Torah world. Nearly the entire Mir yeshivah and remnants of other academies succeeded in escaping to Kobe, Japan, and eventually to Shanghai, China, where they survived the war. They, too, were instrumental in rebuilding the Torah world in America and Israel after the war's end.

Traumatized, Isolated and Defenseless

EANWHILE, THE KILLINGS BEGAN early and often, but they were still only sporadic acts of violence and sadism, and not yet the organized extermination that would later descend upon Jewish Poland, the Baltic countries, and Russia. Thousands of Jews had been killed in the wanton German bombings of the major Polish cities. The German bombers concentrated their fury on the Jewish neighborhoods, and were particularly cruel on the Jewish holy days.

In the first fifty-five days of the German occupation of Western Poland, over five thousand Jews were murdered by the "master race."[5] The Jews were consistently and systematically harassed, brutalized, and humiliated. Beards were shorn, ear-locks were pulled off, women were stripped, children were beaten before the eyes of their parents — and vice versa — and laws which were impossible to fulfill were enacted, thus making all Jews criminals. All Jewish property was confiscated and the goods that the Germans were unable to reach were looted by the local Polish population. The Jews found themselves traumatized, isolated, and defenseless.

Their Polish neighbors turned against the Jews with a fury barely exceeded by the Germans themselves. The German anti-Semitism was racist, based on the lies of secular humanism, Marxism, and the insane theories of Hitler and the Nazi race theoreticians. The Polish reaction

---

5. Gilbert, *The Holocaust*, p. 87.

was the traditional, basically religious, anti-Semitism — the Jews were the "Christ-killers" — and thus the Poles, and later the Ukrainians, enacted an expanded replay of the horrors of 1648-9.[6]

This combination of the ancient and modern anti-Semitism, blended with the twentieth-century technology of mass murder, doomed European Jewry. Aside from those Jews killed at random by the Germans and the Poles, six thousand Jews had been killed in the war while fighting as members of the Polish army.[7] Whenever possible, the Poles assigned Jewish soldiers to the most dangerous parts of the front. But these numbers were mere drops in the sea of blood that would soon wash away Eastern European Jewry.

The German policy was to expel all Jews from western Poland eastward to Warsaw, Lodz, and Lublin. Also, Jews from the smaller towns and villages were driven into newly established ghettos in the larger cities. There, the refugees found little shelter, food, or hope. Their fellow Jews attempted to help them but had neither the freedom nor the resources to do so. The Nazis embarked on a policy "of concentration of Jews in cities," i.e. the reestablishment of the medieval ghettos. Jews were to be gathered in cities which were situated at railway junctions "so that future measures may be accomplished more easily,"[8] a euphemism for storing Jews in places that would make it more convenient to exterminate them, through disease and starvation, slave labor, or wholesale murder.

Life in the Ghetto

 HE NEXT INSTRUMENT OF German control was the establishment of a Jewish town council — *Judenrat* — in every major Jewish community. These councils, which were allegedly formed to give the Jews some measure of autonomy and self-government, were in reality designed to be the tools that would greatly simplify the task of eliminating the Jews, by making them the executors of their own destruction. Requisitions for hostages, forced labor, taxes, goods, and even entertainment for German soldiers were all funneled through the Jewish councils.

---

6. See chapter 1.

7. Gilbert, p. 91.

8. Heydrich's memo as quoted by Gilbert, p. 89. See page 363 below.

Life in the ghetto

Many, if not most, council members were conscientious, idealistic people who truly thought that they would be able to ease the plight of their brethren by serving; the alternative, they thought, was that the Germans would exercise all control, with unpredictable random barbarity. The councilmen were themselves terrorized by threats to themselves and their families. When they finally realized that they were merely pawns doing the Germans' grisly work of torture and extermination, many members of the councils committed suicide, unable to bear the horror of their role. But most continued and rationalized their behavior by convincing themselves that somehow things would be worse for the Jews if they withheld their cooperation with the Germans. Some justified their work by believing that at least they and their families would survive. Ironically and tragically, the councilmen and their families, almost to a man, were all executed anyway.[9]

The ghettos were formalized by the Germans. Walls were built and all Jews were forced to live within prescribed areas; Jews who were found outside the ghetto were subject to immediate execution. Contact with the outside world was forbidden. The ghettos were overcrowded, dirty, disease ridden, and terror filled. Hunger, sickness, depression, and hopelessness aided this Nazi program of extermination — which was designed as the first step in the campaign of genocide. The Jewish population was being "thinned." The old, the weak, the young, and the delicate were systematically being killed off by "natural" means. The survivors would be destroyed by more diabolical, "technologically advanced" methods.

In spite of all this, however, the ghetto teemed with life. Even Jewish culture and education existed in abundance. In addition to religious life and relief activities, there were concerts, dramatic presentations, lectures, debates, newspapers, and books. And in spite of the unbelievable oppression, the Jews remained Jewish. Under-

---

9. See Isaiah Trunk, *Judenrat*.

ground yeshivos were maintained, rabbis taught and ruled on questions of Torah law, people attempted to keep the commandments as meticulously as possible, and to help one another with the pitifully small means still in their possession. Thus, there were schools of Torah, synagogues, ritual baths (*mikvaos*), and faith.

The people were vibrant, industrious, fractious, studious, naively optimistic, and in the main attempted to remain faithful to themselves and their heritage. They hoped that France and England would soon crush Germany and end their torture. They prayed that the God of their fathers would yet save them. They believed that somehow they would survive.[10] Their hopes and belief often contributed to their willingness to make peace with situations that were otherwise completely intolerable. This made the German task of extermination easier in the short run, but in the final analysis, it made no difference. The Jews were doomed and no change in their attitude would affect their ultimate fate. The Jews were unarmed, weakened by starvation, surrounded by a hostile population, and had nowhere to run. The world had gone mad and hell was now on earth; the devil wore German black and grey, and escape was impossible.

Jews attempted to flee the country, but the German policy toward Jewish emigration had changed. Hitler was no longer interested in exporting Jews. He was now determined to annihilate them. No Jew was too small or insignificant to escape the notice of the Nazis. Anyone who delivered a Jew — any Jew — to the Nazis was rewarded. Anyone caught harboring or protecting a Jew in any way was killed. Yet, there were heroic individuals among the Germans, Poles, Russians, and others who saved Jews at the risk of their own lives.[11] The heroism and morality of the few served only to highlight the guilt and brutality of the many. And a number of Jews did somehow escape and some even reached Palestine.[12]

---

10. The song of the Jewish Resistance was "Say not that this is our final road."

11. I find that the tree-lined "Avenue of the Righteous of the Nations" at the Israeli Holocaust Museum *Yad Vashem* is one of the most moving sights in the world.

12. Among them, some of the leading Jewish religious leaders of Polish Jewry such as Rabbi Avraham Mordechai Alter, the *Rebbe* of Gur; Rabbi Yitzchak Zev Soloveitchik, the Rabbi of Brisk; Rabbi Eliezer Yehudah Finkel, *Rosh Yeshivah* of Mir; and Rabbi Aharon Rokeach, the *Rebbe* of Belz.

The War Accelerates

N MAY, 1939, ENGLAND had issued its infamous White Paper,[13] limiting Jewish immigration to Palestine to a maximum of 75,000 over the next five years. Although the new policy permitted a maximum of 20,000 "exceptions" a year to be granted admission, the effect of the White Paper was to virtually ban further significant Jewish immigration to Palestine, because the British kept such immigration far below even the 75,000 Jews envisioned in the White Paper. In reality, only 27,561 Jews had gained entry to Palestine in 1939, though over 80,000 had arrived since 1936.[14] But the British had finally decided that it was more important for them to appease the rebellious Arabs than to save the lives of the endangered Jews. For now there would be no more immigration. The Jews could no longer leave Europe and the doors of the world were barred against them. There was no exit and no entrance. The trap was closed.

England and France were paralyzed in the face of the German conquest of Poland. Though they were officially at war with Germany, they made no threatening moves on the German western border. The period came to be known as the "Phony War," with good reason; it was a war without hostilities. The only heartening development was the substitution of Winston Churchill as prime minister of England for Neville Chamberlain.

Churchill rose mightily to the occasion and became the spokesman for the free world against Nazi tyranny. When Germany invaded Norway in 1940, England countered by sending its own expeditionary force to fight the Germans. This was an attempt to deny Hitler the North Sea ports and the mineral resources of Scandinavia, but the offensive was unsuccessful and the English were forced to withdraw. The string of German victories only seemed to confirm Hitler's contemptuous assessment of the West as being soft and unwilling to fight. He turned his troops westward, and the "Phony War" was about to end.

In May 1940, Germany invaded France, Denmark, Holland, and

---

13. The name for official policy statements issued by the British Foreign Office. These policy statements were printed on white paper — hence the name. Other official documents were printed on papers of a variety of different colors.

14. Gilbert, p. 108.

At the eve of the "final solution" to the "Jewish problem," the Mufti and Adolf Hitler confer

Belgium. In a most astounding military campaign, the Wehrmacht crushed its enemies and overran all of Western Europe in six weeks. Tens of thousands of Jewish refugees who had fled Germany and Austria now found themselves trapped again in the grip of the Nazis. The only ray of light in the otherwise totally dismal picture was the miraculously successful evacuation of 350,000 British and French troops from the port of Dunkirk to safety in England. But as Churchill wryly remarked, "victories are not achieved by [successful] evacuations." Germany seemed invincible and Hitler was convinced that he had a free hand in reshaping the world.

Part of his plan — if not the main part — was to make Europe, and eventually the world, *Judenrein*. In order to do this he would need to dominate Russia. And thus, like all megalomaniacal dictators, he overreached. In doing so, he would eventually seal the doom of the Third Reich, but first he would bring more millions of unfortunate Jews under his brutal control. Hitler was convinced that after the conquest of Western Europe, England — outnumbered and outgunned — would sue for peace. Thus, when he was ready to invade Russia he would be free of the necessity of fighting a two-front war, for the British would hardly fight to save the hated Communist government of Stalin. Rather than pursue the demoralized British Army immediately after Dunkirk and invade Britain when it was ripe for the taking, Hitler ordered his generals to prepare for the invasion of the Soviet Union.

When the British lion continued to roar, Hitler was convinced by Goering, his air commander, that aerial bombings would crush

England, enabling the German Army to invade with minimal resistance. The Luftwaffe unleashed a tremendous air attack against British air defenses and then against London. The Battle of Britain raged from August to October, 1940, and the Germans lost it decisively, forcing Hitler to scrap his plans to invade Britain. Britain suffered major destruction, loss of life and nine hundred planes, but the Germans lost 2,300 planes, and ceased their attacks. In retrospect, it was one of the major turning points of the war. Again, in Churchill's words, "Never . . . had so many owed so much to so few (the airmen of the Royal Air Force)." Yet this lonely victory was the only thread of hope for those suffering under the Nazi occupation; the war was far from over and Germany still had the upper hand.

Hitler and Mussolini completed their conquest of continental Europe in 1940 and 1941 by occupying Greece, Yugoslavia, Albania, and by dominating Rumania and Hungary through treaty. This again brought additional hundred of thousands of Jews under the domination of the Axis powers. Hitler began to sense that the time for the implementation of his "final solution" to the "Jewish problem" — the annihilation of European Jewry — was at hand. Only Russia stood in his way, and he would now attend to her.

34
War and Holocaust

Terror

O N JUNE 22, 1941, GERMANY invaded Russia.[1] By the end of October, the Russian army was decimated and in retreat, and the spires of Moscow were sighted through German binoculars. Leningrad was besieged and cut off, and Russian losses in men and materiel were staggering. And Hitler now dominated an additional two million Jews.

On July 31, 1941, Goering ordered the SS second in command, Reinhard Heydrich, "to make preparations for the general solution of the Jewish problem within the German sphere of influence in Europe." The Nazi hierarchy knew exactly what that euphemistic statement meant: genocide! The first step was the implementation of the plan for mass murder by the *Einsatzgruppen*.[2] Their mission was to follow on

---

1. Hitler invaded Russia six weeks later than he had originally planned. Because he was personally stung by the overthrow of the pro-German government of Yugoslavia, he first invaded and subdued that country. This delayed his invasion of Russia, and as it turned out, defeated him, because the delay prevented him from sweeping into Moscow before the coming of winter. As a result, his invasion bogged down in the face of two implacable foes: resistance and weather. "Pride cometh before a fall."

2. Mobile killing units who worked at their task with fanatical and cruel zeal and precision. They were composed of SS men and police, local citizens and militia members, and numbered from 500 to 1000 men in each group. There were four groups, each assigned to a different section of the Russian front. Their killing operations were carried out according to a prepared plan. Generally, a large trench was dug by the victims themselves. Then the victims were lined up on the edge of the trench and shot from behind by machine guns. Layer upon layer of victims filled the trench, moved into close position by Jewish slave laborers, who were themselves killed at the end of the operations. Finally the trench was covered up, and those few still alive were thus buried alive and suffocated. It was estimated that 1,250,000 Jews were killed by the *Einsatzgruppen* .

the heels of the conquering army and slaughter every single Jewish man, woman, and child. This marked a decisive new departure in the war against the Jews. Up to then, the German campaign against them had been based on intense persecution, hunger, and disease, rather than organized, quick extermination. In Russia, the focus was changed to murder — quick, brutal, and wholesale.

Lithuania, Poland, White Russia, and the Ukraine were the major areas of activity for the *Einsatzgruppen*. However, after about eight months of continuous shooting, the Germans became convinced that this method of annihilation was too inefficient, as well as being too taxing on the psyche of the killers. The non-stop, point-blank, cold-blooded murder took a toll on many of the German soldiers. Some of them needed alcohol to overcome their distaste for the continuous brutality while others enjoyed their role so much that the army complained they were a bad influence on regular troops! Even Heinrich Himmler, commander of the SS, became nauseous the one time he witnessed a mass murder.[3]

So it was decided that a less gory method had to be instituted. The killing would now move to death camps, where it could take place more privately, efficiently, and on a scale never previously imagined. The *Einsatzgruppen* themselves attempted to insulate the killers from the bloody sight of the victims by using mobile gassing vans, which were specially altered trucks. The victims were herded into the sealed cargo areas and then the engine's carbon monoxide exhaust was directed into the vans. But this killing method also proved inefficient and incapable of achieving the needed scale of mass murder. Only later in the war was the gas chamber-crematorium mass murder process developed and perfected.

The Germans employed hundreds of thousands, if not millions, of Jews, Russian prisoners of war, and other "subhumans," **as slave laborers**. These unfortunates were literally worked to death.[4] Construction jobs, factory work, heavy labor, as well as skilled tasks and

---

3. See Raul Hilberg, *The Destruction of the European Jews* (New York, 1985, revised edition pp. 332-3), for the record of how shaken Himmler himself was upon witnessing the killing of 100 Jews by an *Einsatzgruppen* squad. The commander said to the craven Himmler, "Reichsfuhrer, those were only a hundred!"

4. The official language of Fritz Sauckel, the head of the Allocation of Labor Office, was: "Jews are to be exploited to the highest possible extent at the lowest conceivable degree of expenditure." This meant that they would be worked to the limits of their endurance and fed so little that they would die in a matter of weeks or months.

"entertainment projects,"[5] were all serviced by the slave laborers. IG Farben, Daimler-Benz, Krupp, and other major German industrial concerns availed themselves liberally of this pool of laborers, whom they did not have to pay or care for. These major corporations, which still thrive, paid a minimal fee to the German government for each slave. Post-war attempts by the Jewish survivors to sue these companies for compensation for their work ended in humiliating failure.

Special labor camps, eventually to reach the number of 900, were established, and Jews and others were deported there to work and to die. Some of the more infamous of these, such as Auschwitz[6] and Mauthausen,[7] became synonymous with sadism and unbelievable cruelty. The conditions of the camps reached such terrible proportions of suffering that many inmates regretted that their agony had not been ended quickly by the relatively merciful shootings of the *Einsatzgruppen*. The use of Jewish labor was part of the policy of the Rumanian army on the Russian front as well, where Jews were used to clean out mine fields, dig trenches, and serve as beasts of burden for heavy weapons. Not many survived these labor battalions.

The crematorium furnaces of Majdanek

5. These included musical concerts, sports exhibitions, dramatic presentations and other forms of amusement for their German masters. Also, thousands of Jewish girls, women, and boys were collected and installed in German Army and SS houses of prostitution.

6. Auschwitz was in reality two installations: the labor camp called Auschwitz and the death camp called Birkenau.

7. Located in Austria near Hitler's birthplace in Linz, Mauthausen was especially noted for barbarity. Many American pilots who were shot down over Germany were killed there. The "work" at that camp consisted mainly of carrying heavy chunks of granite from a stone quarry up 186 narrow and slippery steps to the work camps at double-time pace. Most inmates were dead before six weeks of such work had elapsed.

Turmoil

ITLER'S MILITARY CAMPAIGN in Russia ran into severe problems in the late fall of 1941. A bitter early winter arrived in 1941, and the German army and its war machinery was unprepared for the snow and sub-zero tempertures. The days of blitzkrieg were over, defeated by "General Winter." The Russian army, which the Germans were convinced that they had destroyed, reappeared in overwhelming numbers and ferocity. The later spring thaw drowned the German armor in a sea of mud. Moscow and Leningrad were never captured.

Russian industry rebuilt itself east of the Ural mountains, and produced planes, tanks, guns, and vehicles at a prodigious rate. Stalin, who had temporarily lost his spirit in the initial phase of the German onslaught, regained his iron will and composure and pursued the war relentlessly and ruthlessly. Forced to cope with long supply lines from Germany, a ferocious Russian counter-attack, armed partisan groups harassing them from the rear, and difficult weather and terrain, the German offensive ground to a halt. The war would now become a German disaster, but it would nevertheless last another four years and consume many more millions of lives.

On December 7, 1941, Japan attacked the major United States Navy base at Pearl Harbor, Hawaii. In suicidal glee, Hitler immediately declared war against the United States, though his treaty with Japan did not require him to do so. Naturally, the United States responded in kind. Roosevelt, whom Hitler hated and believed to be Jewish, was freed of the isolationist forces that had hampered his efforts to aid England, and now, with the country united behind him, committed himself to win the war. Even though the Allies would face many hardships and defeats, it is clear in retrospect that Hitler had lost his gamble by the end of 1941. He had been confident that the West was cowardly and Russia would crumble; he was wrong on both accounts.

The war waged by the new "Thousand Year Reich" for world domination was doomed to defeat. But Hitler's parallel war against the Jews was still capable of a victorious end. And the Germans would now devote themselves to this anti-Jewish war with a fury and commitment that guaranteed success — even at the cost of neglecting the other German war.

The Final Solution

N January 20, 1942 a conference was held in Wannsee, a suburb of Berlin. The sixteen participants were the heads or high officials of the main ministries of the German government. All of the transport, manpower, and material resources of Germany were now to be harnessed for the "Final Solution of the Jewish Problem." Heydrich gave the number of 11,000,000[8] as the Jewish population in Europe subject to annihilation. The Jewish population of Europe was to be shipped to the East and there destroyed in the major killing camps; Sobibor, Chelmno, Belzec, Treblinka, Majdanek, and Auschwitz. They were all located in Poland, in the heartland of Jewish Eastern Europe, so that their victims could be funneled to them conveniently.

On December 8, 1941, even before Wannsee, the first gassing took place at Chelmno, using carbon monoxide gas from truck engines. Chelmno was the killing camp for the Jews in the ghetto of Lodz. It was closed in April 1943, having killed 360,000 Jews. On March 1, 1942, the extermination by gassing began at Sobibor. By October 1943, 250,000 Jews had been murdered there. On March 17, Belzec, a larger and more efficient death camp, began operations. By January 1943, over 600,000 Jews had died there. Treblinka, the destroyer of Warsaw Ghetto Jewry, was opened on June 1, 1942. By the time it was closed in August 1943, nearly 900,000 Jews had been killed there. In November 1941, Majdanek, in the Lublin area, opened. Before it was closed in 1944, 1,380,000 Jews had been put to death.

At the largest and most efficient[9] death camp, Auschwitz, nearly 2,000,000 Jews and hundreds of thousands of non-Jews were killed. Auschwitz itself was a huge slave labor camp; the gas chambers were in adjacent Birkenau; but the word Auschwitz has entered the human

Soap, made from Jewish human fat

---

8. Barely 5,000,000 Jews in Europe survived the war. Of these, three million were in Russia, with the balance mainly in Western Europe, England, parts of the Balkans, Hungary, and Rumania.

9. Rudolf Hoess, the commander of Auschwitz, boasted that his efficiency at Auschwitz was such that 60,000 human beings could be killed in a 24-hour period.

language as a synonym for mass murder. "For many months in 1942, 1943 and 1944, the Nazis were each week killing in cold blood over 100,000 people, mainly Jews."[10] The trains to the death camps continued running even while the German army was desperately short on transport. In fact, while his generals on the Russian front were pleading for reinforcements, Hitler refused to divert the trains that were then deporting the Hungarian Jews to Auschwitz — eloquent testimony to his priorities.

It must also be noted that the trains to the death camps were never interfered with by Allied planes, also eloquent testimony to Allied lack of concern for Jewish lives. In the spring of 1944, when Hungarian Jewry was being destroyed in Auschwitz, at the rate of over 12,000 people a day, Rabbi Michael Dov Weissmandl came into possession of a map of the gas chambers and crematoria. He sent urgent requests to the Allies asking that those facilities, and the rail lines from Budapest to Auschwitz, be bombed. His requests were ignored. Jewish leaders, who repeated them to Washington, were told by the American government that bombers and fighter support were not available, among other excuses. Subsequent historical research has proved that all the reasons were false. In fact, American bombing raids were conducted a scant fifty miles from Auschwitz, and American bombardiers reported seeing flaming smoke coming from the smokestacks of the crematoria, but the plan to bomb the death camp was not even considered. Apparently there was no interest in saving Jewish lives.[11]

Train Ride to Hell

HE TRAIN RIDE TO THE death camps was in itself hell. Overcrowded into cattle cars and sealed freight wagons, without water, ventilation, or sanitation facilities, many unfortunates went mad. Many others died on the trip and most of the survivors of the trip were gassed within twenty-four hours of their arrival at the death camp. The arrivals, dazed, hungry, thirsty, and terrorized, were subject to a welcome of whips, attack dogs, and random shootings. When finally lined up properly on the train landing, they were subject to "selection." The old, weak, young, most women, and others

10. Johnson, *A History of the Jews,* p. 498.

11. See David S. Wyman, *Abandonment of the Jews* (New York, 1984); Martin Gilbert, *Auschwitz and the Allies* (New York 1981); and Monty Noam Penkower, *The Jews Were Expendable* (New York, 1983).

who were deemed unable to be worked to death efficiently in the adjoining labor camp were immediately sent off to "paradise," "the rose garden," or the "synagogue" — the German euphemisms for the gas chamber.

Even in death, the Jews were not freed of their Nazi oppressors. The gold fillings from their teeth were extracted, their hair was shorn for use as mattress stuffing, their clothing and goods were collected, sorted, and distributed throughout Germany.[12] This was in addition to all of the other Jewish property stolen, pillaged, and confiscated by the Nazis and the native populations at the time of the deportation of the Jews.

The deportation of Western European Jews and the extermination in the East were done in the midst of populated areas with — in most countries — the cooperation of the local people. The Poles, Lithuanians, Latvians, Austrians, Slovakians, Rumanians, Hungarians, and many French all willingly cooperated with the methods and aims of the Germans. They too wished to solve the "Jewish problem" permanently.

Switzerland, too, was a bitter disappointment, turning away 85% of escaping Jews at the border, and even deporting to Nazi-occupied France many Jews who had succeeded in illegally entering the country. Until 1944, the International Committee of the Red Cross turned its back on opportunities for aid and relief. The Catholic Church ignored the plight of the Jews, and many individual priests under the Nazis even cooperated in the Holocaust. The Pope, too, was silent. In response to a plea from the head of the American mission to the Vatican that he condemn the slaughter of Jews, Pope Pius XII replied that he had said enough and that, in any case, he could not condemn the Nazis without condemning the "Bolsheviks" as well.

There were exceptions, however. The Danes, and to a lesser extent, the Dutch, Belgians, Norwegians, Bulgarians, and surprisingly, the Italians, attempted to save and aid their Jewish populations. The Danes were the only ones who were almost completely successful in saving their Jewish neighbors, rescuing almost 90% of them in a daring overnight sea lift to Sweden, the climax of their unanimous refusal to cooperate with the Nazis. But in the main, the destruction of European Jewry was a community project, aided and abetted by many nations and millions of people. The events of 1941-45, the killing and the complicity, remain the strongest indictment of modern man and his society.

---

12. In one six week period alone, 222,269 sets of men's suits and underclothes, 192,652 sets of women's clothing, and 99,922 sets of children's clothes collected from the gassed at Auschwitz were distributed on Germany's Home Front.

Genocide Downplayed

A T FIRST, PEOPLE IN THE WEST had no idea of the extent of the tragedy. When word of genocide finally filtered through the Nazi news blackout in mid-1942, the governments of the United States and Great Britain tried to suppress or deny it. Authoritative word of the Final Solution — that is, that the German goal was genocide rather than persecution — arrived in August 1942, in the form of a cable to Stephen Wise from Gerhart Riegner, a World Jewish Congress official in Switzerland. Instead of making the hair-raising news public, Wise deferred to the request of the State Department and agreed to keep silent until the Administration could verify the news — a process that took nearly three months.

A few days after Riegner's cable, a second, more detailed report came from the Swiss Orthodox activists, Isaac and Recha Sternbuch.[13] It was addressed to Jacob Rosenheim, president of the World Organization of Agudath Israel. He prevailed upon Wise to convene meetings of Jewish leaders, which put further pressure on the State Department and the British Foreign Office. Although these Jewish leaders honored Wise's pledge of silence, this initiative led to the first united Jewish efforts to save the Jews. The broad spectrum of Jewish organization in America initiated joint proposals and demands for rescue programs. Unfortunately, these initiatives produced few results.

Even when the American and British governments finally announced official confirmation of the genocide in November 1942, they still tried to downplay it. They stressed that the only way to save the Jews was to win the war. They neglected to answer the inconvenient question, "What good would victory do for Europe's Jews if they were all dead?" The press in the United States was equally culpable. News of the Holocaust went virtually unreported. Even the press conference in November 1942, that first revealed the slaughter of at least two million Jews, with the pace of murder increasing, was not treated as a major story. And what coverage there was, treated the news as a "claim" and a "Jewish charge" rather than a fact.[14] The result was that

---

13. See David Kranzler, *Heroine of Rescue* (New York: Mesorah Publications, 1984) for the account of their noble rescue work before, during, and after the war.

14. For a fine study of press coverage of the Holocaust, see Deborah Lipstadt, *Beyond Belief* (New York, 1986).

America's and Britain's indifference to the plight of the Jews was abetted by public opinion.

Too Few Rescue Efforts

EGINNING WITH THE GERMAN DEFEAT at Stalingrad in late 1942, the Russian army rolled westward. This defeat and its obvious consequences only increased the rate and fury of the Nazi killings of Jews. Realistic Germans knew now that the war was lost, but their leaders were determined to destroy the Jewish people before their own defeat was final. In this, they were aided by the passive policies of the Allies themselves.

The refusal of England to relax immigration restrictions in Palestine, the shutting of American gates to European Jews, and the inexplicable failure of the Allies to attempt to destroy the killing camps or disrupt the transportation to them, all conspired to help Hitler win the war against the Jews. The Arabist, anti-Semitic officials of the American State Department resisted all efforts to intervene on behalf of the hapless Jews of Europe, as did the officials of the Department of War and most generals of consequence.

Roosevelt himself was "mildly anti-Semitic,"[15] and was not overly disturbed by the reports reaching him of the destruction of European Jewry. He spoke of "the understandable complaints which the Germans have towards the Jews in Germany, namely that while they represented a small part of the population, over 50% of the lawyers, doctors, schoolteachers, and college professors in Germany were Jews."[16] The true figures were 16.3% of the lawyers, 10.9% of the doctors, 2.6% of the schoolteachers, and 0.5% of the professors.[17] Yet, Roosevelt was then idolized by American Jews,[18] and was above criticism and pressure.

---

15. Johnson, p. 504.

16. Wyman, p. 313.

17. Johnson, p. 504.

18. I remember the open weeping in the streets in the Jewish neighborhood of Chicago when Roosevelt died. This scene was repeated throughout the country. An extensive chronicle of the failure to save lives may be found in Wyman, especially his chapter "The Zionists;" and in *Thy Brother's Blood* by David Kranzler (New York: Mesorah Publications, 1987).

*The Einsatzgruppen
at work*

The Allies had convinced their Jewish populations that priority number one was winning the war and that, somehow, efforts to save European Jewry would be a diversion and danger to achieving that priority. Virtually all official Jewish organizations and spokesmen acquiesced in this death warrant. They were afraid to push the "Jewish issue" in the midst of total war, and opted to do nothing that would enable their non-Jewish neighbors to question their patriotism. Thus, they ignored the desperate telegrams, the diplomatic-pouch reports, and their own humanitarian instincts.

Jewish leaders did call for governmental attempts at rescue, specifically well-publicized threats that those participating in the slaughter of Jews would be called to account after the war, and by humanitarian appeals to citizens and Germany's allies. They also asked the Pope to protest and threaten excommunication, redoubled efforts to send food to Jews in the ghettos and concentration camps, called for negotiations with Germany and its allies for the release of Jews, and begged free countries to provide refuge to Jews who gained freedom. All their pleas failed. No one cared. Even so apparently simple a matter as a statement of condemnation by the United Nations[18a] was hampered and eventually diluted by the State Department and the Foreign Office.

But there was a more important impediment to rescue efforts on the part of the Jewish leadership: its own sense of priorities. Under the leadership of Rabbi Stephen Wise and Rabbi Abba Hillel Silver, rescue was relegated to a secondary position in a strategy to help create a Jewish homeland after the carnage of Europe. At the American Jewish Conference, called for August 1943, rescue was not even on the original agenda. Although it was added at the insistence of the Orthodox, the Jewish Labor Committee, and other participants, it was accorded a decidedly minor role and produced an inconsequential resolution. Thus, the official Jewish emphasis during the war was not on saving lives, but on gaining Palestine as a homeland when the war was over.

A significant consideration in this choice of priority was the disheartening refusal of the United Nations to help save lives. Many Jewish leaders simply decided that it was hopeless to fight for rescue, and

18a. This term was coined in 1941 by President Roosevelt to describe the nations allied against the Axis Powers.

instead concentrated on at least winning the peace. But this abdication was a sorry chapter in the history of American Jewry. Not only did the Jewish establishment fail to fight against the government's complicity in the "war against the Jews," it fought its own ferocious battle against some of those who put rescue ahead of all considerations.

There were prominent exceptions to this sorry spectacle, however, in the form of organizations and leaders that *did* put rescue ahead of all other concerns. Vaad Hatzolah (Rescue Committee) was composed mainly of European-born Orthodox rabbis, American laymen, and yeshivah faculty and students. It badgered, cajoled, begged, and pressured American officials on behalf of their European brothers. The Vaad's leadership studiously avoided any organizational or political involvement, lest institutional rivalry jeopardize its effectiveness. Although founded under the aegis of the Union of Orthodox Rabbis it had the cooperation of Agudath Israel, Mizrachi, Orthodox Union, and Young Israel, among others. Its success in terms of numbers was small, but its efforts were prodigious.[19]

A fair statement of world opinion during the Holocaust

Originally, the Vaad Hatzolah had been founded at the urgent behest of Vilna's Rabbi Chaim Ozer Grodzensky, in order to provide for the huge influx of rabbis and scholars who had managed to flee to Vilna and its environs. Consequently, it envisioned its mission as the preservation of European Torah heritage, but as the Holocaust progressed, the Vaad broadened its focus. The primary driving forces behind the Vaad's work were Rabbi Eliezer Silver of Cincinnati; Rabbi Avraham Kalmanowitz, head of the Mir yeshivah in New York, and the one who assumed responsibility for the yeshivah's support during its long exile in Shanghai; and Rabbi Aharon Kotler, who had escaped to America from Vilna. Among the leading lay figures in the Vaad and related rescue work was Irving Bunim.[20]

Operating on a shoestring budget and mostly with volunteers, the Vaad did heroic work. There were times when distinguished rabbis drove on the Sabbath to collect funds when lives were at stake, and

---

19. For a record of their efforts see Kranzler; see also Rakefet-Rothkopf, *The Silver Era*.

20. See his biography by Amos Bunim, *Fire in His Soul* (Jerusalem: Feldheim Publishers, 1988).

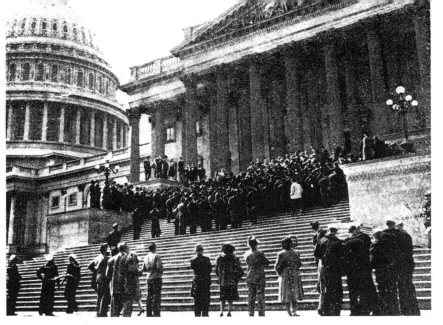

Rabbis head delegation to Congress to take action against the Holocaust

when American yeshivos were closed and the students sent door-to-door and on subway trains to solicit contributions for rescue. Private rescue efforts, organized from Jewish Palestine, America, Great Britain and Switzerland as well as from other neutral countries were mounted, many of them in cooperation with the Vaad.[21]

The Agudath Israel, an Orthodox organization whose main base had been Central and Eastern Europe, was heavily involved in rescue work. Jacob Rosenheim, president of the World Agudath Israel, was a central figure in the ultimately vain efforts to place rescue on the agenda of the Jewish establishment. He and his associates developed valuable contacts in Washington and overseas that gave the Agudah influence out of proportion to its size.

The rescue effort of the American branch of Agudath Israel was headed by Michael Tress, a charismatic and idealistic layman who gave up a promising business career to devote his life to the Orthodox community. Many refugees were brought to the United States thanks to the personal initiatives and financial guarantees of Agudah members. Early in the war, Tress and his associates sent food packages to the Polish ghettos in defiance of a British-declared boycott. In an appalling spectacle, some Jewish establishment organizations actually picketed the Agudah offices to protest the dispatch of food to starving Jews in Europe.

The best known of the groups advocating rescue was informally known as the "Bergson Group," after its leader Peter Bergson, a young Revisionist Zionist who came from Palestine to the United States to raise funds for a Jewish army in Palestine. When reports of genocide were confirmed, Bergson concentrated on rescue. The Bergson Group attracted a sizable following in Congress and among the general public, but the establishment organizations attacked it bitterly as divisive and somehow "unauthorized" to work for rescue. Undeterred, the Bergsonites lobbied in Congress and ran provocative advertisements and rallies to raise funds and ignite public opinion for rescue.

One of the most dramatic of these public demonstrations was the "Rabbis' March on Washington." Undertaken by the Agudath Harabbonim in cooperation with the Bergsonites, the march brought four

---

21. See Kranzler for accounts of many of them.

hundred Orthodox rabbis to Washington, just before *Yom Kippur*, 1943, to plead with the Administration to move on rescue. Though Congress treated the patriarchal group with great respect, the Jewish establishment convinced Roosevelt to "be away on pressing business" and not receive the rabbis.

Despite these considerable hindrances, the Bergson group was instrumental in influencing Congress to exert pressure on Roosevelt until he finally, grudgingly, agreed to the establishment of a War Refugee Board, which received very little governmental aid and almost no Federal fund allocations. Nevertheless, even without these funds, and with only a meager staff and mostly private financial support, the War Refugee Board saved over 100,000 people from the Nazis. Ninety percent of those saved by the War Refugee Board were Jews. Thus, it is clear that although tens of thousands of Jews were saved by these various efforts, millions more perished because of inaction.

Disbelief, Not Despair

 HE JEWISH VICTIMS THEMSELVES could do pitifully little to save themselves. The psychological insight of the rabbis that "A prisoner is unable to free himself from prison"[22] never was so apparent as in the destruction of European Jewry. Above all, Jews were and are life loving, optimistic, and trusting. In this they reflected another rabbinic dictum that "Even if a sharp sword is at one's neck, one should not despair."[23] The Jews refused to believe the worst. And in this they were abetted by the diabolical stage-managing of the Nazis. Never did the Germans acknowledge that they were pursuing a policy of slaughter; everything was camouflaged by lies and euphemisms.

The Jews were told that they would be "resettled," sent to "the East," rehabilitated by "productive labor," but never executed or destroyed; gas chambers were called "shower rooms." Radios and newspapers were forbidden in the ghettos so it was virtually impossible to know what was really happening. The railroad platforms at the killing camps were decorated with flowers, and had performing musical bands, fake station fronts, and clocks. Eternally infamous is the legend emblazoned at the entrance to Auschwitz, *Arbeit Macht Frei* (Work

22. *Talmud Bavli, Berachos* 5b.
23. Ibid. 10b.

Provides Freedom), calculated to reinforce the lie that the Jews had been deported to a life of opportunity and independence.

The Nazis used the Jewish Councils to help lull the Jewish communities into the hope of survival.[24] It was a very successful strategy for the most part, because the Jews — having become experts over the ages in the art of surviving persecution, buying time, giving a little to gain much more — thought they would be able to deal with the Germans and Hitler as they had with the Romans, the Church, the Czars, and the Moslems.

No one imagined a program of annihilation, conducted in the twentieth century in the midst of civilized Europe, to be possible. This disbelief was also a factor in the Allied lack of response: Most people and governments were sure that the first atrocity stories were nothing more than wildly exaggerated propaganda. By the time the true situation was clear to Europe's Jews, millions had already died and the

---

24. See Isaiah Trunk, *Judenrat*.

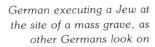

German executing a Jew at the site of a mass grave, as other Germans look on

monstrous machinery of murder was operating with such momentum and efficiency that almost no organized effort to arrest it could now succeed. The holding and executing of hostages, the threat of reprisals against loved ones, collective punishments, and the threat of even greater barbarity were all valued and fearsome weapons in the Nazi arsenal.

The uninhibitedly sadistic behavior of the vicious Germans who had no human or moral compunctions, combined with the traditional, humane, optimistic, and moral inhibitions of their Jewish victims, formed an insurmountable barrier to effective physical resistance. This was true not only as far as the Jews were concerned. It is noteworthy that with the exception of Russia, none of the occupied nations were able to mount effective resistance to the occupation excesses of the Nazis, just as none of the Russian Eastern European satellites could effectively alter the course of post-war Russian behavior on their soil for decades. In the short run of five years the barbarity and ruthlessness of the occupier overwhelmed all efforts at resistance by the occupied.

There was, however, *spiritual* resistance in abundance. One of the German goals was to de-humanize the Jews, to destroy their sense of decency and brotherhood, their faith in God, their compassion for one another. To an astounding degree, the Nazis failed, as attested to in many memoirs of Germans themselves.[25]

Jewish Resistance

 ET, IN SPITE OF ALL of the odds, there was an undercurrent of violent Jewish resistance against the Germans. Jewish partisan groups were already in operation in 1941 in the White Russian and Lithuanian provinces of the new German Empire. In July 1942, Jews fought with guns, hammers and bare fists to prevent the liquidation of the Nesvizh and Mir ghettos in western White Russia.

The main resistance, however, was concentrated in the Warsaw Ghetto in the spring of 1943. After two weeks of fighting, during which a small number of famished, poorly armed Jewish fighters forced the

---

25. See Moshe Prager, *Sparks of Glory*, New York: Mesorah Publications, 1985, for numerous examples of this faith in action.

Germans to fall back and call for reinforcements, the ghetto was completely leveled. The Warsaw Ghetto uprising became the symbol and the legend of Jewish resistance. Revolts occurred in the killings camps as well. In August 1943, a violent mutiny occurred at Treblinka, destroying parts of the killing machinery,[26] as did resistance action at the Krikov labor camp near Lublin. In October 1944, the kapos (Jewish trustees appointed by the Nazis) revolted at Auschwitz. Yet, in spite of all these heroics, the German annihilation machine was barely slowed.

The Warsaw Ghetto

The main Jewish resistance, paradoxically, lay in remaining human in the province of hell. Dignity, faith, kindness, and a sense of solidarity remained Jewish traits in the face of the angel of death. Jews had long practice in dying nobly at the hands of oppressors. But in the long history of Israel, there was no chapter comparable to the events of 1941-45. Typical of this nobility of spirit is a story from the Warsaw Ghetto. In one of the secret, illegal yeshivos that operated in cellars and attics, a little boy said, "We are like Jacob and the Germans are like Esau. I'm glad. I don't want to be like Esau."

Arab Response

HE ARAB RESPONSE TO THE Jewish predicament in Europe was predictable, if deplorable. The Grand Mufti of Jerusalem declared openly for the Axis Powers and took up residence in Berlin. He hoped that the "solution of the 'Jewish problem' advocated [by Hitler] would be applied in the

---

26. See Jean Francois Steiner, *Treblinka.*

Middle East as well." The religious leader of the Arab cause in Palestine protested against allowing Jewish children to leave Bulgaria for Palestine. He suggested they be sent instead to Poland, "under strong and energetic guard."[27]

England had appeased the Arabs since their revolt of 1936-7, on the coldly calculated grounds that the Jews had no choice but to support the West, while the Arabs would try to join the Axis if the British offended them. The result was that the British deservedly lost on both sides: they alienated the Jews and lost the Arabs. England was forced to use force to put down a pro-Axis revolt in Iraq.[28] Despite their persistent refusal to let the Jews arm themselves in self-defense, or to join the war effort in the form of a Jewish Brigade, manpower shortages eventually forced England to use forces from the Jewish Haganah militia in 1941 to invade and occupy Syria, then under the control of collaborationist Vichy France.[29]

Rommel's Afrika Korps

 N 1942, GENERAL ERWIN ROMMEL and his vaunted Afrika Korps stood at the gates of Alexandria, Egypt. German bombers had bombed Tel Aviv, and the *Yishuv* felt then that it was in mortal danger. It is obvious that the *Yishuv* could not have stopped the Afrika Korps had Rommel broken through in Egypt. The Jewish Agency began burning sensitive documents and moving other records out of its headquarters. The Orthodox *Yishuv* declared days of public prayer and fasting. In the midst of the general fear, Rabbi Yosef Kahaneman laid the cornerstone for what would become the great Ponivezh Yeshiva in Bnei Brak. In response to incredulous questioners, he replied that he had faith that God would not forsake His land. Events vindicated his trust. British Field Marshal Montgomery's victory over Rommel at El Alamein ended the direct German threat to Palestine.

In 1944, the Jews of Palestine were finally allowed to form a

---

27. Gilbert, *The Holocaust*, p. 578.

28. David Raziel, the commander of the Irgun, was killed in this battle. The Irgun claimed that he was shot by the British themselves.

29. It was in this action that Moshe Dayan was blinded in one eye.

"Jewish Brigade" and to fight as part of the British army. The Jewish Brigade saw action at the terrible battle of Monte Casino in Italy, where the Germans subjected them to especially fierce bombardment.

Yishuv Provides Limited Aid

HE JEWISH COMMUNITY OF the *Yishuv* would expend herculean efforts to save their brothers and sisters *after* the war, but during the war the main response of Jewish Agency leadership to the destruction of European Jewry was inaction and insistence that rescue, no matter how important, could not be permitted to stand in the way of efforts to establish a Jewish state in Palestine. To help accomplish this, David Ben Gurion determined that the survivors in Europe must be influenced to demand entry into Palestine when the war was over. Partly to achieve this and partly to conduct anti-Nazi guerrilla activities, Jewish parachutists from Palestine landed in occupied Europe during 1944-45, but their efforts to help their brethren were understandably limited. Many of the Jewish parachutists were captured by the Germans and tortured to death by the Gestapo.

Help for Hungarian Jews

N 1944, WHEN THE ALLIES were poised to invade France (Hitler's "Fortress Europa"), the Nazis embarked upon the destruction of the last large Jewish community still extant in Europe — that of Hungary. Frustrated and angry that the Hungarian government had not cooperated sufficiently in the total extermination of its large Jewish community, the Germans occupied the country, and installed Adolf Eichmann to render the country *Judenrein*. Until then, the anti-Semitic excesses in Hungary had been horrendous, but had not extended to genocide. Now the time had come. Even though the war was clearly lost, the Germans continued their methodical destruction of Jews, sending transports of as many as 12,000 Jews a day to Auschwitz.

As the deportations went into full swing, there was an astounding change of Nazi policy. Hungarian Jewish "agent" Joel Brand was summoned by Eichmann and presented with a bloodcurdling offer: "Blood for money, money for blood." Eichmann was ready to spare all the Jews except for those still alive in Poland and Germany — an estimated million Jews — in return for 10,000 trucks. If the deal was struck, the Jews would be permitted to leave Europe in lots of 100,000 each, as the trucks and other goods were delivered.

The "Jews for trucks" offer was a direct outgrowth of a series of initiatives originally undertaken by Rabbi Weissmandl of Slovakia. In 1942, with the close cooperation of his cousin, Mrs. Gisi Fleischman, Zionist leader of Slovakia, and other Slovakian Jews, Weissmandl established a working relationship with Dieter Wisliceny, the Eichmann lieutenant in charge of Slovakia. Wisliceny had begun deporting the Slovakian Jews at the rate of 2,500 per week. Rabbi Weissmandl and Mrs. Fleischmann negotiated an arrangement with Wisliceny whereby the deportations would be halted indefinitely for payment to him of $50,000. Wisliceny was true to his word and, as the destruction continued in other countries, Rabbi Weissmandl had the audacious idea of offering to "purchase" the lives of all the remaining European Jews.

In 1944, Weissmandl made the proposal to Wisliceny. Wisliceny secured Himmler's permission to negotiate, but the small Slovakian Jewish community could not even dream of raising sufficient funds, so Eichmann went to the Zionist leadership in Hungary. He was convinced that they, working through the Jewish Agency, could raise whatever ransom was agreed upon.

To make the deal more palatable to the Americans and British — who would have to supply the trucks — Eichmann guaranteed that the trucks would be used only against the Russians. Eichmann and Himmler, his superior, sincerely believed that world Jewry was in charge of the war against the Axis powers, and that the Jews manipulated and controlled Allied war policy. Germany desperately needed motor transport and therefore was willing to free Hungarian and Rumanian Jews for the trucks, which would be somehow delivered to the German army. Brand brought the news to Rudolf Kastner,[30] leader of the Zionist movement in Hungary, who took over the negotiations with Eichmann. As a good-faith gesture, Eichmann temporarily

---

30. The subject of the famous Kastner-Gruenwald trial described below in Chapter 36, "The Miracle of Survival."

suspended deportations to Auschwitz and allowed Kastner to choose 1,600 Hungarian Jews to be diverted to Bergen-Belsen, rather than Auschwitz. After several months there, they were freed and transported to Switzerland in a sealed train.[31]

Joel Brand was chosen to bring Eichmann's offer to the Jewish Agency and the Allies. To be sure that he would not create artificial delays, Eichmann kept Brand's wife and children as hostages and gave him a strict time limit; if he did not return as promised, his family would be killed and deportations would resume. Brand found no sympathetic ear for his proposal. Aside from the understandable Allied refusal to ship goods that would help the German war effort, the British said quite openly that if so many Jews were freed, "Where would we put them?"

Despite assurances given the Jewish Agency that he would be free to convey his message to the highest authorities, the British arrested Brand as soon as his train arrived in territory they controlled. Brand spent the duration of the war interned in a British camp in Egypt, ostensibly as a "suspected spy," but really to prevent him from publicizing his story. He lived out his years a broken man, convinced that the blood of his loved ones and a million Jews somehow lay on his hands.

Furious that his "generosity" was spurned, Eichmann renewed the deportations to Auschwitz — first killing Brand's family — and all through that awful summer of 1944 the trains rolled north from Budapest to Auschwitz. Even so, the highest percentage of Jewish war survivors from any given Jewish community in Europe was from Hungary. The Nazis had gotten to them last, and time ran out on their extermination schedule.

Seven Stories of Suffering

 HE ARMIES OF THE ALLIES converged on the German Reich, and with their advance, the Russians and the British liberated many of the concentration camps. Thus were the horrors therein revealed to an unbelieving world. An avenging spirit overcame the inmates and the occupying troops, and many of the guards and SS troops were killed on the spot.

---

31. Among those saved on that train, aside from Kastner's own family, was Rabbi Yoel Teitelbaum, the *Rebbe* of Satmar.

Most escaped, however, and few of them ever paid in this world for their crimes. Hundreds of thousands of Jewish survivors were now homeless refugees[32] in Europe.

Hitler committed suicide in his bunker in Berlin barely two weeks after the death of Franklin Roosevelt. The "thousand-year Reich" surrendered on May 7, 1945, twelve years after Hitler came to power. In its bloody history, it brought down with it millions of innocent people, non-combatants and civilians, among them six million Jews, one and a quarter million of whom were children under the age of twelve. Europe had become virtually a closed chapter in Jewish history, sealed shut in the blood, gore and tears of hapless victims by the cold cynicism of modern humanist civilization.

No review of this period can be complete without recounting individual incidents that reduce the overall historical picture to the personal level. Out of the myriad possible stories, these seven will suffice to convey this necessary small picture:

1. The destruction of the books in the Talmudic Academy in Lublin gave so much pleasure to the conquerors that it was recalled with glee more than a year later. "For us," a German eyewitness later reported, "it was a matter of special pride to destroy the Talmudic Academy, which was known as the greatest in Poland!" And he went on to describe how: "We threw the huge Talmudic library out of the building and carried the books to the market place where we set fire to them. The fire lasted twenty hours. The Lublin Jews assembled around and wept bitterly, almost silencing us with their cries. We summoned the military band, and with joyful shouts the soldiers drowned out the sounds of the Jewish cries."[33]

❦ ❦ ❦

2. At Stolpe, on September 23, [1943] the ghetto was surrounded by German soldiers. Pits had been prepared outside a nearby village. Hundreds of Jews hid in cellars. The Germans entered the ghetto shooting. Eliezer Melamed later recalled how he and a female had found a room in which to hide behind some sacks of flour. A mother and her three children followed them into the house. The mother hid in one corner of the room, the three children in another. The Germans entered the room and discovered the children. One of them, a young boy, began to scream, "Mama! Mama!" as the Germans dragged

---

32. The official euphemism for them was "displaced persons," or DP's.
33. Gilbert, p. 101.

the children away. But another of them, aged four, shouted to his brother in Yiddish, *"Zog nit Mameh. Men vet ir oich zunemen.* (Don't say 'Mama,' they'll take her, too.)" The boy stopped screaming. The mother remained silent. Her children were dragged away by the Germans. She was hitting her head against the wall, as if to punish herself for remaining silent, for wanting to live.[34]

⋆ ⋆ ⋆

3. [Rabbi Abraham Maroko ran into his synagogue, which the Germans had set afire, and emerged carrying a sacred Torah scroll.] One of the Germans produced a can of gasoline, knocked the Torah scroll from Rabbi Abraham Maroko's hand, and poured gasoline over the scroll. Then he handed the rabbi a match. "Here! Set that scroll on fire!" . . . "No! No!" he shouted. "Heaven forbid!" He bent and snatched up the scroll from the ground. "I will not burn the Law of God!"

In reply, the soldier picked up the gasoline can, poured the rest of its contents on the rabbi's head, and set him afire along with the Torah scroll. Instantly a sheet of fire flared up and enveloped the rabbi. One of the villagers who witnessed the scene reported afterwards that the rabbi kept on reciting prayers at the top of his voice until he collapsed.[35]

⋆ ⋆ ⋆

4. A rabbi in Lodz was forced to spit on a scroll of the Law. In fear for his life, he complied and desecrated that which is holy to him and his people. After a short while he had no more saliva, his mouth was dry. To the Nazi's question, why did he stop spitting, the rabbi replied that his mouth was dry. Then the son of the "superior race" began to spit into the rabbi's open mouth and the rabbi continued to spit at the Torah.[36]

⋆ ⋆ ⋆

5. High-ranking SS officers, including Himmler himself, would come on inspection visits from time to time [to the death camps], reaching the [killing] compound through the entrance reserved for SS personnel which bore the inscription, "Entrance to the Jewish State." From there they could see the doors of the gas chamber, covered with synagogue curtains that had hung before the Holy Ark, and bearing the Hebrew

---

34. Ibid., p. 465.

35. Zuker, *The Unconquerable Spirit* (New York: Mesorah Publications 1980), p. 48.

36. Gilbert, p. 105.

inscription: "This is the gate to the Lord, into which the righteous shall enter."[37]

❧ ❧ ❧

6. Rabbi Tzvi Yechezkel Michelson, dean of the Warsaw rabbinate, deliberately remained at home while a large roundup was on. He did not go out as the Germans ordered, but put on his praying shawl and phylacteries and stayed inside. He preferred to be shot on the spot, hoping that thus his body would be thrown into one of the wagons that accompanied the roundup and find a last resting place in the Jewish cemetery. So he willingly opened the door to the search party, but when the Germans saw the tall old man, with his long silver-white beard, they became uneasy. One of them mumbled, according to the Jewish policeman who accompanied the search: "This must be Moses in person!" They slammed the door shut and left the aged rabbi alone. He must have decided then that staying with his people in their last moments was even more important than being buried in a Jewish cemetery. He rose, went down to the courtyard and joined the marching ranks of Jews toward the *Umschlag* [roundup area], from which the people were sent to Treblinka.[38]

❧ ❧ ❧

7. The Germans entered all the courtyards in the ghetto and tore away every child they encountered. They tossed them into trucks, while inside music was playing. Mothers would approach the automobiles and plead with the Germans to give the children back. I saw one mother beseech the guards near the hospital. "How many do you have there?" the German asked. "Three," said the mother. "You may have one back," said the German, and climbed into the car with the mother. All three children looked at her and stretched out their little hands — all of them wanted to go with the mother. She did not know which child to select, looked from one to the other, and finally went away alone.[39]

---

37. Gideon Hausner, *Justice In Jerusalem*, p. 167.
38. Ibid., p. 209.
39. Ibid., p. 330.

35
The State of Israel

Time of Turmoil

HE JEWISH WORLD WAS SHOCKED and numbed in 1945. It now knew the worst and was in mourning for its six million dead. The non-Jewish world was also stunned — at least temporarily — and somewhat mortified over what had happened. But this feeling of guilt was not universal, and anti-Semitism — though less vociferous and open — nevertheless survived World War II, alive and intact. Jews attempting to return to their Polish homes were subjected to unwavering hostility, violence, and even death. There was actually a pogrom in the Polish town of Kielce, in which nearly sixty Jews, who had survived Hitler, were murdered by their Polish neighbors.

It became clear to the 250,000 Jews in the DP camps and the other 200,000 Jewish refugees wandering over Europe that organized Jewish life in Europe, as they had known it, was at an end. Europe was not *Judenrein*, but it would no longer play the central role in Jewish life and history. Most of the Jewish survivors, dazed, broken, and pained, wished to go to Palestine. The United States was a strong second choice, but the commitment to attempt to build a new life in a new Jewish state was predominant among the refugees. The *Yishuv* in Palestine sent hundreds of agents into the DP camps to organize their immigration to Palestine and to propagandize on behalf of Jewish immigration and the establishment of the Jewish state. Thus the stage was set for the drama of the birth of Israel.

On a different scale, the stage was being set for the rebirth in Palestine of the Orthodox community as well. As the twentieth century progressed, the traditional community in Palestine was dwindling in the face of the new influences that had infiltrated the once cloistered *Yishuv*. This trend would continue for another few years, but the groundwork for a reversal was being laid.

Rabbi Eliezer Yehudah Finkel had established the Mir Yeshiva in Jerusalem, and Rabbi Yosef Kahaneman had established the Ponivezh Yeshiva in Bnei Brak, both of which would become huge Torah centers. Rabbi Avraham Yeshayahu Karelitz, the *Chazon Ish,* helped build Bnei Brak into a bastion of traditional life. Rabbi Isser Zalman Meltzer, Rabbi Zalman Sorotzkin, the Lutzker *Rav;* and Rabbi Dov Berish Weidenfeld, the Tchebiner *Rav;* together with Rabbi Yitzchak Zev Soloveitchik of Brisk, became forceful religious leaders in Jerusalem. The *Rebbes* of Belz and Gur, both saved miraculously from under the very noses of the Nazis, were beginning to build new communities in Jerusalem and Tel Aviv. These new institutions augmented such existing yeshivos as Etz Chaim, Chevron, Chaye Olam, Porat Yosef, and other less famous academies. Israeli youth and the children of survivors would coalesce into a rejuvenated and dynamic Torah world in future decades. These seeds were barely perceptible in 1945, but they were there.

In the wake of the terrible events in Europe, the Zionist movement had been able to influence American policy toward support of unlimited Jewish immigration to Palestine and the eventual establishment of a Jewish state. As President of the United States, Harry Truman was much more sympathetic to Jewish aims in Palestine than was his predecessor, Franklin Roosevelt. Truman, an uncomplicated, sincere, and hard-working person, was free from personal bigotry and harbored no Arabist romanticism or anti-Jewish bias. Thus, he listened sympathetically to the Zionist argument and was willing to exert American pressure on Britain to help the Zionists achieve their goal. But the British were unwilling to hear the cries of the Jews in Europe or to be pressured by those they considered to be the "do-gooders" of the U.S. government.

In a startling display of ingratitude, the British electorate turned out Winston Churchill in 1945. Clement Atlee, the new Prime Minister, installed Ernest Bevin, a gruff, opinionated, and anti-Semitic labor union leader, as Foreign Secretary. In a revealing aside, Bevin hoped out loud "that the Jews would not [use the destruction of European Jews as a means to] push to the head of the queue." He dismissed America's pressure for increased Jewish immigration to Palestine as being a ploy because the United States "did not want too many of them in New York."[1] In general, it soon became clear that "people who disliked the Jews before the Holocaust generally didn't dislike them any the less because of the Holocaust."[2] The attitude of much of the world was well phrased by one representative of the Vatican, who stated, "I am not anti-Semitic, I just hate them."[3]

The Vatican itself had not done much on behalf of Jews during World War II, and Pope Pius XII was widely viewed as being obsessed by anti-Communism above all and indifferent to Jewish suffering. After the war, thousands of Jewish children were under the control of the Church, having been sequestered in monasteries, nunneries, and churches throughout Europe by desperate Jewish parents. Some were returned to their families and their faith, but most were never released to their Jewish brethren. The Chief Rabbi of Palestine, Isaac Halevi Herzog,[4] journeyed to Rome to plead for the restoration of the Jewish orphans, but in the main his arguments fell on deaf ears. Thus the aftermath of the war dawned bitterly on the remnants of European Jewry.

Palestine Partitioned

 N MAY 1946, THE REPORT of the Anglo-American Enquiry Commission on Palestine was released. Its two main proposals were for the establishment of a bi-national (Arab and Jewish) federated Palestine State to be implemented during a United Nations trusteeship period and for the immediate admission of 100,000 Jewish refugees to the country. The

---

1. Jacob C. Hurewitz, *The Struggle for Palestine* New York, 1950, p. 253.

2. O' Brien, *The Siege*, p. 266.

3. Ibid.

4. 1889-1959. This great person was a renowned Torah scholar, a man of deep piety, a Ph.D. in literature, a gentle humanitarian, and a man of ability and aristocracy. His never-ending care for his fellow Jews, his love of Torah scholars and scholarship, and his concern for the new Jewish State of Israel all were legendary. He wore a formal top-hat, carried a silver-encrusted Bible with him at all times, and his snow-white beard and gentle face combined to make him an unforgettable sight. I saw him in Chicago when I was twelve years old and in my mind I have always retained his image as that of a truly noble representative of the heritage of Israel. His son Chaim eventually became president of the State of Israel, while his younger son, Yaakov, a renowned Torah scholar, served as one of Israel's leading diplomats before his tragic untimely death.

Jews accepted the second proposal, the Arabs rejected both ideas, and the British authorities became increasingly militant in their impatience with the Zionist leaders of the *Yishuv*.

Responding to continuing and increasing anti-British provocations, the British arrested many leading Jews in Palestine and even deported some to East Africa. The Jewish community in Palestine was badly divided in its attitude toward the British. Though the policy of Weizmann and other world Zionist leaders advocating total cooperation with the British was now discredited, the mainstream Zionist leadership in Palestine, mainly under the iron-fisted direction of David Ben Gurion, refused to support acts of open rebellion against the British Army. However, the *Irgun Zvai Leumi,* headed by Menachem Begin, who was the spiritual and political heir of Zev Jabotinsky, began a calculated program of force against the British Army in Palestine, hoping to drive it out of the country. The Lechi,[5] which was the smallest and most daringly violent of the resistance groups, also conducted bloody acts of sabotage and shootings against the British.[6]

These groups of Jews quarreled and even shot at each other. Ben Gurion and the Haganah viewed the two right-wing militias with bitter disapproval and attempted to suppress them. Nevertheless, stunning events forced the British and the Haganah to reckon with the Irgun and Lechi. The bombing of the King David Hotel in Jerusalem, the hanging of British sergeants in Tel Aviv as retribution for British hangings of Irgun members, and the daring prison break from the Acre jail all served to unravel British control over events in Palestine.[7] The Jews of Palestine desperately combed the world for arms for their militias. American Jewry was drawn into the struggle for the first time, and funds and materiel from the United States' Jewish communities began to trickle and then flow into Palestine.

But the main pressure against the continued British rule in

---

5. *Lochamei Cherut Yisrael* — Freedom Fighters for Israel — is better known by the name the British gave it: the Stern Gang.

6. Yitzchak Shamir, later a prime minister of Israel, was the head of this group.

7. A senior British officer summed up the effect of the Jewish resistance groups thus: "The British Army suffered greater losses in traffic accidents than in all the underground operations [in Palestine] put together. But the blows to the Empire's pride and prestige were something which could not be digested. The break-in at the Acre Prison and hanging of the two sergeants were blows to our pride. The break-in at the prison gained the symbolic significance of the fall of the Bastille. And the hangings places us, the rulers, on equal footing with the terrorists." Uri Dan, *To the Promised Land* (New York, 1988), p. 120.

Palestine came from the refugees clamoring for admittance there. Illegal immigration sponsored by the Haganah and the Irgun, though naturally not in concert, reached epic proportions. The British navy intercepted 85% of the incoming boats, boarded them, arrested the "illegals" and deported them to Cyprus, where they were interned in hastily erected camps (which, in the eyes of the prisoners, resembled the concentration camps of Europe). Tens of thousands of Jews languished in these camps until the newly created State of Israel came and fetched them.

The climax of the struggle between the desperate immigrants and the British navy came with the sailing of the ship *Exodus 1947*. This old, fairly unseaworthy boat was crammed with Jewish refugees when it sailed from Hamburg, Germany. Intercepted in the Mediterranean Sea by the Royal Navy, it was towed into Haifa harbor where the immigrants could see their goal but were not allowed to disembark. The ship was then escorted by the British Navy back to Hamburg, where the poor, unfortunate refugees were forced off the boat and onto the shores of Germany. The world was shocked by the callousness of the British, and public opinion now swung in favor of the Jewish dream of unimpeded settlement in Palestine.

The Exodus 1947

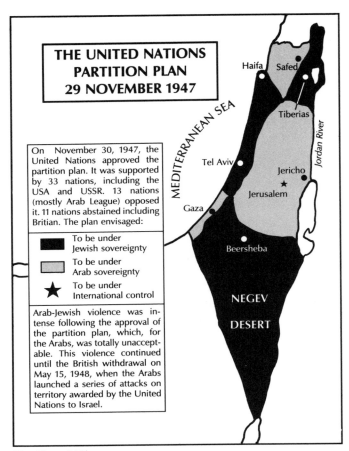

The United Nations
Partition Plan:
November 29, 1947

In February 1947, the British Foreign Office, under increasing pressure at home and abroad, tried a new ploy. It announced that "the only course open to us is to submit the problem to the judgment of the United Nations."[8] England was confident that the U.N. would not be able to arrive at any solution to the problem and that the "Cold War" competition between Russia and the United States would deadlock any possibility of agreement, thus leaving England in Palestine indefinitely. However Stalin, the cruel anti-Semite, coldly changed position and, in his ardor at driving England from the Middle East, cooperated with the United States.[9]

The U.N. devised a partition plan for Palestine, somehow providing for two independent states — one Arab and one Jewish — in that small wedge of land, with Jerusalem as an international city. The Jews, disappointed at the map but elated by the concept, accepted the U.N. plan. The Arabs, always maximalist in their demands and never given to compromise, bitterly rejected the plan and began to conspire for war against the Jews in Palestine. In spite of numerous waverings and diplomatic equivocations, the United States remained the active sponsor of the partition plan[10] and on Nov. 29, 1947, the U.N. passed it by a vote of 33 to 13. On November 30, war erupted in Palestine, with the Arabs determined to murder the new Jewish nation while it was yet in its embryonic state.

---

8. O'Brien, p. 272.

9. Stalin's motive was reminiscent of the Talmudic dictum that, at the time of the Purim miracle, one of the Persian courtiers spoke up on behalf of Mordechai, not because he loved him but because he hated Haman (*Megillah* 16a).

10. Then, and in the next eight crucial months, Harry Truman overruled the Arabists in the State Department and made the Jewish state possible. In early 1948, Eddie Jacobson, Truman's Jewish former partner in an ill-fated haberdashery business, made an impassioned plea to the President on behalf of the Jews, and received a positive response. Out of such sentimentality does God fashion history. See note 15 below.

Arabs Fight or Flee

HE NEXT DAY, NOVEMBER 30, 1947, seven Jews were slain in an ambush on the Jerusalem-Tel Aviv road; snipers from Arab Jaffa shot at Jewish children walking to school in southern Tel Aviv; and an Arab mob set fire to Jewish stores in Jerusalem. The British police, with their usual "even-handedness," prevented the Haganah from coming to the aid of surrounded and beleaguered Jews. Two weeks after the U.N. partition resolution was passed, the Arab League began to send soldiers from the surrounding Arab countries into Palestine. They were called "volunteers"!

"The British did not lift a finger to stop this military invasion. They also refused to cooperate with the U.N. committee charged with supervising implemention of the General Assembly resolution. At the same time, the Arabs living in the district destined to become part of the Jewish state began evacuating their homes and moving to the Arab states neighboring Palestine at the orders of the Arab High Committee."[11] In short, anarchy reigned. Jerusalem was cut off from the rest of the country when Arabs seized control of the road leading to the Holy City. The Arab "riots" were in reality total war against the Jewish civilian population of the country. In the four months between December 1947 and Passover 1948, almost a thousand Jews were killed by Arab violence.[12]

The Haganah, with the cooperation of the Irgun, was able to turn the tide against Arab arms in Jaffa and Haifa. In naivete, coupled with a desperate hope for peaceful accommodation with their enemies, the Jews initially asked the Arab population to remain in their homes and not leave the Jewish areas of Palestine. However, the Arab High Committee, headquar-

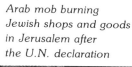

Arab mob burning Jewish shops and goods in Jerusalem after the U.N. declaration

---

11. David Ben Gurion, *Israel, A Personal History* New York: 1971, p. 65.

12. This was one six-hundredth of the entire Jewish population of the country! Translated into terms of the U.S. population today, this would amount to almost a half-million Americans.

tered in Cairo, ordered the Arab population to leave all of the Jewish areas of Palestine immediately. The High Committee announced an impending Arab invasion of Palestine by the regular Arab armies and promised that after the Jews were thrown into the sea, all of the former Arab residents would return and avail themselves of the pick of the homes and property of their former neighbors.

Sixty thousand Arabs fled Haifa, followed by almost 100,000 from Jaffa, Tiberias, Safed, and Beit She'an. This established a pattern of Arab flight that continued throughout the war. As this pattern became clear, the Jewish attitude towards it changed. Fleeing Arabs were no longer begged to remain and, as blood and atrocities mounted, the attitude of the Jews toward them hardened. Eventually, 800,000 Arabs fled their homes — driven by propaganda, fear, hysteria, threats, and the mass psychology of panic.[13]

Later, the scholars would propound theories to explain this emigration.[14] But when it occurred, the Arab flight was a source of amazement and bewilderment to all concerned. It was one of the many inexplicable, illogical, unpredictable events that marked the birth of the Jewish state and gave it an inexplicable cast.

The bitter fighting in Palestine over the winter of 1947 and the spring of 1948 caused American foreign policy to waver in its support

---

13. Ben Gurion himself expressed wonderment and shock at the Arab flight. "Why did tens of thousands of people leave their cities, their homes, and their worldly possessions in such panic, without sufficient cause? What caused this flight? Could it have been simply an order from above? It does not seem possible that the immensely rich — and some of the richest people in the country lived here — would abandon all their material assets just because somebody gave them an order. Was it really fear?" Dan, *To the Promised Land,* p. 153.

14. The Irgun action at Deir Yassin, an Arab village near Jerusalem, is often cited as a contributory cause to Arab flight. The village was used by Arabs as a mounting base for attacks on Jewish Jerusalem, and the Irgun attacked it on April 19,1948. In the ensuing fighting 270 Arab civilians, many of them women and children, were killed. The Irgun was widely condemned by the Haganah and the establishment leaders of Jewish Palestine for the attack at Deir Yassin. The Arab press and radio pounced on Deir Yassin as an example of Jewish brutality, hoping thereby to rouse the flagging morale of the Arab fighters. However, "the publicity which the Arab press gave to the massacre at Deir Yassin, for the purpose of attracting sympathy, greatly accelerated the demoralization and flight of non-combatant Arabs." (George Kirk, *Survey of International Affairs: The Middle East* 1949-50, p. 263, quoted by O'Brien, p. 282). O'Brien continues: "In a reprisal action for Deir Yassin, Arabs ambushed a medical convoy bound for the Hadassah Hospital and the Hebrew University, isolated on Mt. Scopus, and seventy-seven doctors, nurses, university teachers, and students were killed. This incident occurred within two hundred yards of a British military post that made no attempt to intervene, although the attack continued for over seven hours."

for the partition of Palestine and the establishment of the Jewish state. On March 19, Warren Austin, the United States Ambassador to the U.N., told the Security Council that all efforts to implement the partition resolution should be halted. But Chaim Weizmann — old, half blind, and discarded by the Zionist movement that he had led for decades — persevered and prevailed once more. He obtained an appointment with President Truman[15] and presented the case for Jewish history and redemption. Truman was won over by the justness of the argument and the patience and wisdom of Weizmann. The President's support of the creation of the Jewish state, which ran counter to the desires of his Arabist-State Department and many of his political soothsayers, was explained by him in his usual candid and terse manner: "I have Dr. Weizmann as my conscience."[16]

As Truman put it in a personal note:

> "I recognized Israel immediately . . . in 1948 . . . against the advice of my own Secretary of State, George Marshall, who was afraid that the Arabs wouldn't like it . . . but I felt that Israel deserved to be recognized and didn't give a darn whether the Arabs liked it or not."

Jerusalem Under Siege

 N FEBRUARY 1948, ERNEST Bevin encouraged the English client ruler of Trans-Jordan, Abdullah, to invade Palestine and annex the Arab sections as part of his kingdom. In the inter-Arab rivalries, Abdullah set out to triumph over the Mufti, Syria, Egypt, and Iraq. With the commander of his Arab Legion, John Glubb,[17] an able English officer, Abdullah was

---

15. Weizmann's appointment with Truman was secured for him by Eddie Jacobson, the President's former partner. Jacobson was prevailed upon by Zionist leaders, who found all access to the President closed to them, to beg Truman to grant Weizmann an audience. Loyal to his friends to a fault — a trait that often haunted him during his Presidency — Truman reluctantly acquiesced to his old friend's entreaty and thus Weizmann was able to plead the necessity for the establishment of a Jewish state to the one man in the world who could help the cause.

16. O'Brien, p. 286.

17. Commonly known in the Arab world as Glubb Pasha. His memoir, *A Soldier Among the Arabs,* is an illuminating view of the Arab-Jewish conflict from the Arab side. He and his English officer staff fashioned Abdullah's Bedouin warriors into the

Orthodox Jews took up arms to defend their capital

determined to incorporate Jerusalem into Trans-Jordan, and secretly negotiated with Jewish emissaries, attempting to come to an agreement with them about the division of Palestine. However, all the negotiations came to naught, because Abdullah refused to countenance an independent Jewish state, while the Jews were unable to imagine Jerusalem under exclusive Arab control.

Jerusalem, in fact, was the focal point of the military struggle. The Arabs maintained a nine-month siege on the Jewish area of the city. Hunger, thirst, and shortages of ammunition and medical supplies threatened the Jewish hold on their half of Jerusalem. The old Jewish quarter in the walled Old City was completely cut off, and the ragged Haganah defenders were driven from house to house, rapidly losing space and men. But the main struggle for Jewish Jerusalem was fought on the heights and in the valley where the road from Tel Aviv twisted its way up to the Holy City.

Yitzchak Rabin, then a young commander, seeing the limited resources of the Jews, asked Ben Gurion, "What comes first, Jerusalem or the road?" Ben-Gurion answered: "Both."[18] The heights over the Jerusalem road were dominated by the sheer cliff known as the **Kastel**. The Jews tried without success a number of times to dislodge the **Arabs** from the Kastel. The commander of the Arab troops on the Kastel was Abdul Khader El Husseini,[19] the most feared and successful of the Palestinian Arab commanders. The Jews mounted a concerted

---

Arab Legion, the most efficient and professional of all the Arab armies. After Abdullah's assassination, Glubb was rewarded for his efforts on behalf of the Arab cause by being dismissed. He retired to live out his life in his native England.

18. Dan, p. 179.

19. A cousin of the Grand Mufti of Jerusalem.

offensive in early April[20] to open the road to Jerusalem. The fighting was fierce and the casualties high, but the offensive was in the main successful, except for the Kastel, where the Arab defenders held fast under the personal direction of Abdul Khader.

The great Jewish victory finally occurred, and when it did, it was through an unlikely stroke of providential fortune. A young Jewish sniper, born in Yemen and not previously known for his accuracy with a rifle, shot wildly at three Arab men in the vicinity of the Kastel. He killed all three, and one of them was Abdul Khader el Husseini. "Thirty thousand Arabs participated in his funeral at the Dome of the Rock on the Temple Mount. Arab morale was dealt a crushing blow from which it never recovered."[21]

Har HaZeisim, destroyed

The Arabs abandoned their position on the Kastel and the road to Jerusalem was open, albeit only temporarily. Two hundred fifty trucks loaded with nine hundred-fifty life-saving tons of food — a convoy six miles long — arrived in Jerusalem on the Sabbath, April 17, 1948. Jews left their synagogues and, with their prayer shawls still draping their shoulders, helped unload the convoy. The siege of Jerusalem was broken for the moment. The Arabs, however, mounted a strong counterattack, and by the end of April once again cut the Jerusalem road at Shaar HaGai. The road to Jerusalem was now closed again to Jewish traffic, and for the next seven weeks Jewish Jerusalem was isolated.

As the fateful day of formal British evacuation drew nearer, Abdullah sent his forces across the Jordan River to occupy eastern

---

20. Called "Operation Nachshon" after the heroics of Nachshon ben Aminadav, who was the first Jew to plunge into the waters of the Red Sea before they miraculously parted.

21. Dan, p. 167.

Palestine. His Arab Legion surrounded and then captured the four *kibbutzim* of Gush Etzion, which controlled the Jerusalem-Hebron road. Other forces of the Arab Legion entered the Old City of Jerusalem and began to reduce the perimeter of Jewish defense in the Jewish quarter. The Legion also occupied Ramallah, Nablus, Hebron, and other Arab towns in Judea and Samaria. The successes of Abdullah frightened not only the Jews but the competing Arab nations as well. Egypt and Syria were especially offended by Abdullah's bold strokes and refused to coordinate their own armed attacks on the Jews with those of the Arab Legion. Naturally, this helped the Jewish cause materially. The Jewish army, meanwhile, reeled off a string of successes of its own, capturing Ramle, Lod,[22] Nazareth, Tiberias, Safed, and much of the Galilee. But the Jewish situation in Jerusalem remained precarious, and the Jews grimly anticipated an invasion of their territory by the massed armies of seven Arab states now poised on their borders.

British Mandate Ends

N THE DAYS BEFORE MAY 15, 1948, when, in line with the U.N. resolution, it was time to declare the existence of the new state, Jewish resolve wavered. The American State Department, under Secretary George Marshall, withdrew its support for statehood, calling instead for an international trusteeship to administer the country until the Jewish-Arab conflict was resolved. Some among the Zionist leadership, as well, were opposed to a formal declaration of independence, in view of the precarious military and diplomatic situation. Still others were in favor of a provisional government to replace the departing British, but not for statehood. Even among those in favor of statehood, there were divisions. Some wanted the declaration to specify the boundaries decreed by the U.N. partition resolution, while others opposed any specification of boundaries, since a successful war against the Arab attackers could lead to a conquest of more territory.

The division in the Zionist executive about the wisdom of declaring a state and, thereby, certainly precipitating a war to the death with the Arabs, was mirrored in the religious community as well. The famed

22. The site of the large international airport built by the British and designated for incorporation into Arab Palestine. In exultation, Ben Gurion said: "When could we have built such an airport on our own?!"

Elderly Jewish couple fleeing Old Jerusalem
with a few meager belongings

Arab woman carrying three Torah Scrolls
pillaged from a Sephardic synagogue in the Old City

Rabbi Yitzchak Zev Soloveitchik[24] vehemently opposed the declaration of the state. In a personal letter he wrote:

> The Jewish state will create a state of war and no one can predict its consequences even under the most favorable of circumstances, and if it is still possible somehow to influence [the Jewish Agency] that they should not risk the destruction, God forbid, of the entire *Yishuv,* [it should be done].[24]

Ben Gurion fought tenaciously for a declaration of statehood without mention of boundaries. In the Provisional People's Council, the

---

23. The son of Rabbi Chaim Soloveitchik and his successor as the rabbi of Brisk (Brest-Litovsk). He escaped from the Germans and arrived in Jerusalem in 1940. Though he held no official rabbinic position, he was a powerful and influential figure in religious Jewry and his views were always considered seriously, even if not always followed, by his colleagues. His great Talmudic genius, coupled with his frank, direct, and uncompromising stands on difficult issues, earned him his stature as one of the leading authorities in religious Jewish life.

24. From a letter of Rabbi Soloveitchik to Rabbi Yechezkel Abramsky, then head of the British Rabbinical Court in London, written in January 1948, in the midst of the Arab siege of Jerusalem. The letter was published in its entirety in *Yated Ne'eman*, Volume 2, No 2, November 3, 1989.

proposal not to specify boundaries was carried by only five to four. And it was by another slim majority of six to four that the Council approved Ben Gurion's plan to declare the State of Israel on Friday, May 14, 1948 at 4:00 p.m., prior to the entry of the Jewish Sabbath, and eight hours before the time of the official termination of the British mandate over Palestine.

Ben Gurion himself was the driving force; while others wavered, he remained resolute. He refused to accept proposals of an Arab cease-fire in exchange for a delay in the proclamation. His historic sense told him that if he delayed declaring the state now, there might not soon arise another opportunity to do so. He appointed a five-man commission to draw up the declaration of statehood for the new State of Israel. After some wrangling,[25] the document was ready for signature by the appointed deadline of 4:00 p.m., May 14, 1948. The moment had arrived.

Even the secular Ben Gurion saw the creation of the Jewish state as an extraordinary historical event. In a speech to the Central Committee of his worker's party, the Mapai,[26] he said:

> The wonder has arisen and has come into being; the nations of the world have resolved to re-establish the State of Israel. The Jewish people have always believed in this phenomenon and have waited two thousand years for it to come. This belief itself is one of the unprecedented historic wonders of the world. We know no other people that was exiled from its land and dispersed among the nations, hated, humiliated, and oppressed without respite for hundreds of years, but has nonetheless persevered in its special existence and persisted in its belief that the day would come when it would restore its independence in its own state.[27]

---

25. The most bitter controversy concerned the inclusion of the name of God in the declaration of statehood. The representative of Mapam, the leftist Socialist party, was adamant that no reference to the Deity mar the secular nature of the birth of the new Jewish state. The rabbis who represented religious Jewry were naturally horrified at the thought that the first Jewish state in nineteen centuries should be established without acknowledging the God of Israel. Ben Gurion, the supreme pragmatist, compromised the matter by writing in the declaration of statehood, "with trust in the Rock of Israel, we set our hands . . .," leaving the interpretation of the phrase to the differing consciences of the signatories.

26. The acronym of the Hebrew letters of the "Worker's Party of Israel." It was a left-wing party — the most dominant political party in Palestine — but it was much more moderate than the Jewish Communist Party or the Mapam ("United Worker's Party") which were very pro-Soviet in their foreign policy and virulently anti-religious in their general outlook and were doctrinaire socialist in their domestic policy.

27. Dan, p. 131.

Believing Jews were upset that Ben Gurion spoke of the good will of the nations and the persistence of the Jews, but made not even a token mention of God. This sort of tension between the outspoken secularism of the political leadership and the faith of traditional Jews rankles Israeli society to this day.

The Provisional Council convened in Tel Aviv on May 14, 1948, and at the request of the assembled, the veteran Zionist leader, Rabbi Yehudah Leib Fishman-Maimon, rose and recited the *shehecheyanu* blessing: "Blessed are You . . . Who has kept us alive, sustained us, and brought us to this time." Ben Gurion then read the declaration of statehood in his unemotional, flat manner,[28] and those convened immediately dispersed to their homes and to the monumental task they had undertaken — the building of a modern state, with traditional Jewish values, that would gather the Jewish exiles and provide them with physical security in spite of being surrounded by a sea of implacable enemies.

The Jewish State

 ITH THE CREATION OF THE State, much of Orthodox Jewry had to reconsider its policy regarding the Jewish political entity in the Land of Israel. Agudath Israel, the largest non-Zionist Orthodox group, had always rejected Zionism and the idea that the creation of a Jewish state would solve the "Jewish problem." It could not accept the idea that the Diaspora and its dilemmas were purely man made and could be therefore solved solely by human agencies. Nor could it agree with the notion that the "Jewish problem" could be solved by making Jews less Jewish and turning them into a "nation like all the nations."

Yet, while rejecting the Zionist philosophy, Agudath Israel nevertheless subscribed to the desire to rebuild the Land of Israel. Historically, it had strongly supported Jewish settlement in Israel as a fulfillment of the Divine commandment of *yishuv ha'aretz.*[29] In the 1930s and especially during and after the war, the Agudah fought for

---

28. The document itself was a disappointment; it was lacking in emotion and memorable prose. Unlike the American Declaration of Independence, it is neither taught nor quoted.

29. Literally, "settling the Land [of Israel]." Some rabbinic authorities held that this commandment was binding upon individual Jews at all times, circumstances permitting.

such settlement as a physical necessity in order to alleviate the dire economic and persecution problems of Jews in the Diaspora. This positive attitude toward rebuilding the Land of Israel was endorsed by virtually all of the leading Torah scholars of the century.[30]

Until 1937, the question of a Jewish state had, in a sense, been an internal matter of dispute between Zionist and non-Zionist Jews. In that year the British attempted to extricate themselves from the nutcracker of Arab rebellion and pogrom and Jewish pressure for a homeland in Palestine. Under the shadow of Hitler, England floated a trial balloon in the form of a partition plan for Palestine. It was formulated by the so-called Peel Commission after extensive and well-publicized hearings and deliberations about the future of Palestine. The proposed Jewish state would have consisted of tiny, barely viable slivers, but the proposal required a Jewish response. The Zionist establishment itself was divided on this issue. So, too, were Agudath Israel and much of world Jewry.

The Agudath Israel World Congress of 1937, meeting in Marienbad, grappled with the issue. In its final resolutions, the organization rejected the partition plan, since it felt that Jews had no moral or legal right to compromise the historic, Divinely ordained borders of the Holy Land. It also did not look favorably upon the idea of a Jewish state that would reject the Torah. Since the Peel Commission's plan was unacceptable, Agudath Israel preferred the continuation of the British mandate, but it vigorously protested Britain's restrictive immigration and land purchase policies, and called upon Britain to find "means of assuring the historic right of the Jewish people to the Land of Israel, which is based on the Torah." Nevertheless, it concluded that "if the partition plan should be altered and the boundaries will be acceptable to the Jewish people, and if other conditions (mainly religious in nature) are satisfactory, then Agudath Israel will not be opposed to establishing a Jewish government (in the Land of Israel)."[31]

After the Holocaust, however, the saving of the remnant of European Jewry became most prominent in all considerations regarding a Jewish state. Since it was now obvious that the Jews from Europe who had survived Hitler had nowhere to go but Palestine, and that neither the British nor the Arabs were about to allow them free immigration there, the necessity for a Jewish state became clear. Thus, in response to the

---

30. Including the *Rebbe* of Gur, Rabbi Isser Zalman Meltzer, Rabbi Chaim Ozer Grodzenski and Rabbi Yosef Chaim Sonnenfeld. See *A History of Agudath Israel,* by Joseph Friedenson, p. 26, for a fuller explanation of this policy of Agudath Israel.

31. Friedenson, p. 37.

U.N. resolution partitioning Palestine, the Agudah stated: "The World Agudath Israel sees as a historic event the decision of the nations of the world to return to us after two thousand years a portion of the Holy Land, there to establish a Jewish state and to encompass within its borders the banished and scattered members of our people. This historic event must bring home to every Jew the realization that 'The Almighty has brought this about' in an act of Divine Providence which presents us with a great task and a grave test."[32]

In the decade from 1937 to 1947, the Jewish world had been radically altered, and wise men accommodated themselves to the new realities of attempting to save the new Jewish world from the fate that had befallen the old one.

When the State of Israel came into existence, the overwhelming majority of Orthodox Jewry participated fully in its political, social and economic life. In 1948, Rabbi Reuven Grozovsky, then the chairman of the Rabbinic Sages of Agudah in the United States, explained the new policy of participation in the State by non-Zionists as follows:

> The Zionist movement was a voluntary organization and [many] Orthodox Jews refused to be associated with any organization that did not recognize the authority of Torah. It is quite a different case with a state to which everyone belongs de facto. This is the difference between a state and a movement. In a state, for example, should we not participate in the elections, it would mean relinquishing our basic rights and even assisting them [the secularists] to rule over us with even greater strength.[33]

Rabbi Grozovsky, however, declined to accept the State of Israel de jure as *the* Jewish state because of its secular makeup. He, and many others, did not recognize Israel as the messianic harbinger of final redemption. His view of it was prosaic, practical, and limited.

There were those in the Orthodox camp, as well as among the secular groups, who were opposed to the declaration of the State. But, once it was declared and came into being, the question of the wisdom of its establishment became moot. It now had to be sustained, defended, and enhanced. And this realization became the fundamental policy of almost all Jewish groups, parties, organizations, and leaders on that fateful Friday afternoon of May 14, 1948.

---

32. Friedenson, p. 47.

33. Ibid. p. 49.

Arabs Invade Israel

CONCURRENT WITH THE WITHDRAWAL of the British High Commissioner — the "last" British soldier to leave Palestine[34] — the Arab armies of Trans-Jordan, Syria, Lebanon, Saudi Arabia, Syria, Iraq, and Egypt invaded Palestine. The War of Independence, already in progress for six bitter months, now was formalized and intensified. Egyptian bombers struck at Tel Aviv and the Egyptian army attempted to move swiftly up the Mediterranean coast to capture Tel Aviv. Another Egyptian force veered east and threatened Jewish Jerusalem from the south. Syria captured the kibbutz Mishmar HaYarden, attacked Kibbutz Degania, and attempted to move west into the Galilee. The Lebanese army was not a major threat, though it did make threatening, if futile, gestures to menace Dan, Dafna, Metulla, and Rosh Hanikra. The Iraqi army opened an offensive in the Jordan Valley together with Syrian contingents, and the Jewish kibbutzim in the Beit She'an valley were placed

Jewish trucks destroyed on the Tel Aviv-Jerusalem road

34. The final British departure from Palestine did not occur, in fact, until the end of June, 1948.

under massive fire.

Believing their own propaganda, the Arabs were expecting a cake-walk. Instead, the outnumbered, outgunned Jewish army gave them a black eye. At Degania and Tirat Zvi, the Syrians and Iraqis were stopped. The Lebanese soon fled back across the border and the Saudis withdrew from the southern front. The Egyptian Army was slowed and punished at Yad Mordechai and Negba. Their drive toward Jerusalem was repulsed at Ramat Rahel.

Israel purchased weapons on the world market, brought in thousands of new immigrants — many of whom were immediately impressed into the Israeli Defense Forces — and began to strengthen its position militarily. The Arabs were backed by Britain, which hoped to retain its control over Palestine through its surrogate clients, Egypt and Trans-Jordan. But to their shocked surprise, the Arabs suffered mounting defeats. The Arab armies and their foot soldiers, promised an

Jerusalem being attacked at night

orgy of looting and pleasure, found only dust and defeat and rapidly lost heart for the battle.

The situation in Jerusalem was still precarious, however. The Jewish quarter of the Old City fell to the Arab Legion on May 28, and the siege of West Jerusalem continued. All Jewish attempts to open the road at Latrun and Shaar HaGai were repulsed by the Arab Legion. The Jews searched for a way to relieve Jerusalem. They found it by building a "Burma Road" that bypassed the entrenched Arab Legion at Latrun.

This road ran from Kibbutz Hulda, climbed to the deserted Arab village of Saris, and then rejoined the Jerusalem highway at a point where it was under Jewish control. At first, parts of the road were passable only by human porters; but in time it was cleared and paved. Trucks, some pushed uphill by tractors because of the steep grade, climbed the hill at Saris and finally reached Jerusalem. The convoys began to arrive regularly, and by the end of June the siege of Jerusalem was ended. The Jews were unable to retake the Old City, but the Arabs were also unable to breach the defenses of Jewish West Jerusalem. In effect, the battle of Jerusalem was stalemated, with the city divided, Mount Scopus isolated, and the Jewish holy places in the hands of Trans-Jordan. This situation would continue until the 1967 Six Day War.

Barbed wire fences separating the Arab section from Israeli Jerusalem

The Israel Defense Force

HE BITTER FEUD BETWEEN the Haganah and the Irgun continued even during the war.[35] Determined to end any private militias, Ben Gurion proclaimed the formation of the Israel Defense Force at the end of May. He ordered all Irgun and Lechi units to incorporate themselves into the new army and abide by its discipline. When they were slow to comply, Ben Gurion used force against them.

When the ship Altalena, bearing ammunition and supplies for the Irgun, attempted to dock at Tel Aviv at the end of June, Ben Gurion ordered it sunk. The shelling had Jew killing Jew, and the ship with its valuable cargo exploded and sank. In order to avert a potential civil war, Menachem Begin disbanded the Irgun and went into exile in the political desert of the "loyal opposition" for the next thirty years. But the Lechi

---

35. Jewish history has abundant examples of the Jewish people being somehow able to pursue bitter internal struggles while at the same time being forced to wage a war of survival against a powerful external foe.

The Irgun ship Altalena lies damaged off the Tel Aviv beach

still lived and would perpetrate one more violent act that horrified the world and gave Ben Gurion the opportunity to permanently disband it.

Under pressure from Britain and the Arabs, the United Nations ordered a cease-fire in the Arab-Israeli war in the early summer of 1948. Both sides used the month's respite to rearm themselves and plan new military moves. As noted, Russia had inexplicably joined the United States in backing partition of Palestine. It extended diplomatic recognition to the new State of Israel immediately upon its declaration and only hours after the United States had done so. But whereas the United States had an arms-embargo policy which thwarted Israeli efforts to obtain sorely needed weapons from the West, Stalin had no such pious inhibitions.

With funds from the urgently mobilized American Jewish community, Israel was able to purchase large amounts of first-rate military equipment from communist Czechoslovakia's Skoda Arms Works. Thus, at the end of the first cease-fire in August, 1948, the Jews possessed weaponry that could finally match that of the British-supplied Arabs.

The results of the new fighting in the fall of 1948 were disastrous for the Arabs. They were driven from the Negev and Galilee, and a large portion of the Egyptian army was trapped in the "Faluja pocket." In terror, the Arabs appealed again to the U.N. to save them from their own aggressive folly.[36]

The Security Council appointed an official mediator, Count Folke Bernadotte,[37] to devise a solution to be imposed on the warring parties. He was viewed with suspicion by both sides, but Ben Gurion cooperated with him, hoping that peace and stability could be achieved by Israel's sacrifice of some of the gains of its military victories. Israel was rife with rumors that Bernadotte would remove Jerusalem from Jewish control. On September 17, 1948, gunmen of Lechi assassinated him in Jerusalem. Ben Gurion moved quickly, arresting Lechi leaders and sympathizers and permanently ending the organization. A storm of world-wide protest against Israel sobered Israeli public opinion, and Ben-Gurion's tough stance against Lechi

---

36. This scenario of the U.N. with the world powers saving the Arabs from ever having to deal with the consequences of their cruel policies would be repeated on a regular basis during the ensuing years of the Arab-Israeli struggle.

37. A member of the Swedish royal family who had been instrumental in relief and rescue work for European Jews during and after World War II.

and the Irgun was widely praised. The internal struggles of Israel would henceforth be conducted exclusively in the political arena.

The Israel Defense Force pursued the retreating Egyptians into the Sinai Desert. Alarmed at the crushing defeat of its client state, England sent the Royal Air Force into the fray in support of Egypt. The fledgling Israel Air Force[38] shot down two British Spitfires and England threatened war against Israel. Recoiling, Ben Gurion ordered Israeli soldiers out of the Sinai.

In February and March 1949, armistice agreements were negotiated under U.N. auspices between Israel and Egypt, Trans-Jordan, Syria, and Lebanon. Iraq remained in a state of war with Israel. The armistice agreements were viewed as the first step in a peace-making process that Israel was confident would now rapidly occur. But the Arab states chose otherwise. Israel had come into being and had survived a determined effort to annihilate her at birth. It knew freedom and victory, but it was not to know peace and security.

---

38. Flying, among other planes purchased on the world market, German Messerschmidt fighters!

36
The Miracle of Survival

Ingathering of the Exiles

LL OF THE IMPOSSIBLE CONDITIONS of history had been met at the birth of the State of Israel. Russian-American cooperation, British folly and intransigence, Arab unreasonableness and violence, the intervention of the long-lost Jewish ex-partner of an American President, the flight of Arab civilians, and unforeseen, inexplicable military victory. But the cost was prodigious. Six thousand Jews died in the fighting — fully one percent of the entire Jewish population of Israel. Also as a result of the Israeli victory, the Jews living in the Arab countries were placed in mortal danger. Ancient Jewish communities located in Iraq (Babylonia),[1] Egypt, Morocco, and Yemen[2] were subject to violence, persecution, and forced emigration. In effect, the voluntary Arab flight from the tiny Jewish state was matched by a forced Jewish flight to Israel.

The driving force behind the immigration of Jews to Israel from 1948 to 1954 was the violence and persecution directed against them, mainly in Arab countries, but also in the countries of the Communist bloc in Eastern Europe. Stalin's anti-Jewish campaign and his purges of loyal Jewish Communists[3] convinced Jews who survived the Holocaust and remained in the countries behind the Iron Curtain that they had no future there. Great waves of immigration from Rumania and Hungary

---

1. Founded shortly before the destruction of the First Temple by the exiled Judean King Jechoniah, and the prophet Ezekiel.

2. Also dating back to the fifth century before the Common Era.

3. Such as Rudolf Slansky of Czechoslovakia. The Jewish Communists were all charged with being "Zionist agents and capitalist provocateurs." Thus history showed again that Jews disloyal to their heritage paid the ultimate price for this "conversion" and disloyalty at the hand of the new gods and ideologies for which they had sacrificed all.

accompanied those of the Jews of the Levant to Israel. The population of Israel grew from 650,000 Jews in 1947 to 713,000 in 1948 and 965,000 in 1949. From 1950 to 1954 the Jewish population of Israel nearly doubled while the Arab population nearly tripled,[4] reaching over 200,000.

The new immigrants arrived in a desperately poor country. Most of them were housed in sub-standard housing and in mass tent-cities called *ma'abarot*, or transition centers.[5] The problems of integrating diverse cultures and peoples into a unified nation were enormous. The strong secular policy of the government and the immigration authorities succeeded in loosening the bonds of loyalty to Torah observance among the new immigrants, especially among the Sephardic youth. Even when the secular political leaders attempted to mollify religious voters, the career bureaucracy displayed an intense antipathy to religious observance, usually with the covert encouragement of the leadership. The children of poverty-stricken, bewildered immigrants were almost always placed in non-religious institutions where they were taught that the Torah commandments applied only in the Diaspora. Now, in place of their traditional lifestyle and value system, there were planted within many of the newcomers the bitter seeds of spiritual

---

4. This increase was due in the main to a small amount of Arab refugees returning to Israel, a high Arab birthrate, and the absorption of some previously Arab-held territory into the finally negotiated borders of Israel. See Uri Dan, *To The Promised Land*.

5. Many thousands remained in these unfit "temporary" quarters for years on end.

Ma'abarot

emptiness, which would breed violence, despair, crime, and anti-social behavior. These social problems would pollute Israeli life for decades.

The struggle for political control of the new state was reflected in the results of the election for the first Knesset, in 1949. Mapai — Ben Gurion's Labor Party — emerged with a plurality of 46 of the 120 seats in parliament. Mapam — the more left-wing Socialist Party, which followed the Soviet Union's party line — won 19 seats. The United Religious Front[6] gained 16 seats, Menachem Begin's Herut party — 14, and the General Zionists — 7. The other eighteen seats were divided among various splinter groups, including an Arab party and a Jewish Communist party. Thus, in the first Knesset the left wing (including Mapai, Mapam, the Communists and a small Arab party) controlled seventy seats; the religious parties, the right wing, and the Sephardim gained forty seats; and the other ten seats were in the center. This political balance of power would remain in place until 1977 when Menachem Begin and the religious and Sephardic parties would reverse it.

Coalition Government

 EN GURION COULD HAVE formed a left-wing Labor majority of sixty-five seats in coalition with Mapam,[7] but he preferred to form a broader coalition with the religious and other smaller parties. Even prior to the elections, Ben Gurion had held intensive discussions with the leaders of the religious parties regarding the nature of the State. Though he was totally non-observant as a matter of "principle," he perceived the need to temper his antagonism to religion in the interest of national unity. The problems of aggressive Arab states and massive internal difficulties were sufficiently daunting, and as he told his more militant anti-religious associates, the State could not now survive a religious "civil war." In any case, he was convinced that religious observance would fade from the scene in a generation or two.

---

6. In the elections for the first Knesset, the four religious parties — Mizrachi, Hapoel Hamizrachi, Agudath Israel, and Poalei Agudath Israel — united and appeared as one electoral bloc for the one and only time in the history of Israel.

7. This was an opportunity for the left-wing secular parties to control the Israeli government exclusively. Ben Gurion's refusal to do so was based on his hesitancy to adopt Mapam's pro-Soviet, anti-Western foreign policy.

With Rabbi Yitzchak Meir Levin, head of Agudath Israel, Moshe Shapiro, head of Hapoel Hamizrachi, and others, Ben Gurion negotiated the so-called "Status Quo Agreement" governing the official religious tone of the State of Israel. While never formalized in legislation, and though it was regularly criticized and tested, the "Status Quo" has remained the framework of the national modus vivendi. It consists of four points: (1) The maintenance of separate religious school systems; (2) kashruth observance in government, army and public kitchens; (3) the observance of the Sabbath as the official day of rest; and (4) regulation of "personal status," meaning marriage, divorce, and matters regarding religious identity would be left solely in the hands of the Chief Rabbinate of Israel.

However, the government itself and the majority of the citizens of the State of Israel were secular in behavior and belief; even the "Status Quo Agreement" tacitly acknowledged that the nature of Israeli public life and private behavior were to be secular outside of the four points it covered. The government's underlying resistance to religion showed itself in the form of constant and numerous public exceptions to the laws of kashruth and Sabbath; thus the "Status Quo" proved to be only an uneasy truce in the continuing struggle for the definition of the character of the Jewish state.

"Status Quo"

 NE OF THE MOST EMOTIONAL and divisive issues in this secular-religious contest was the issue of army service for women. Because of its prevailing ideological, secular beliefs and a practical necessity for manpower, occasioned by Israel's small population, the State instituted and still maintains a conscription program for women to its armed services. The religious community protested this bitterly, and many announced that they would disobey this law no matter what the consequences. This strongly held view was based on the opinion of virtually all authoritative rabbinic leaders, including Chief Rabbis Herzog and Uziel, who ruled that the draft of women for army service was a cardinal violation of Jewish law and tradition. They held that any law that requires a woman to submit to authority outside of the family was immoral on its face and, therefore, obligated Jews to resist it at all costs.

Rabbi Isaac Herzog and Rabbi Ben Zion Meir Hai Uziel

The Chazon Ish

Moving to prevent incipient civil strife, Ben Gurion traveled to Bnei Brak to meet with Rabbi Avraham Yeshayahu Karelitz, the *Chazon Ish*,[8] who was universally acknowledged as one of the premier sages and halachic authorities of Israel. Calmly and wisely, the *Chazon Ish* explained to the secularist leader the emotional and halachic dimensions and depths of the issue. In a famous, widely quoted metaphor, the *Chazon Ish* cited the Talmudic law that when meeting on a narrow path, an empty wagon must yield the way for a loaded one. So, too, he argued, the new State must accommodate a rich, ancient tradition.

Yielding to practicality, if not Higher Authority, Ben Gurion had the government adopt a compromise whereby religious women could petition to be excused from the Army draft and fulfill their national obligation through voluntary non-army National Service (*Sherut Leumi*) in a variety of public service jobs. Although this compromise satisfied some Orthodox leaders, especially those affiliated with the Mizrachi party, it did not remove the objection of many others. Again the government backed down, conceding that girls who could establish that their religious convictions prevented them from serving would be completely excused.

Further credence has been given to the firm stand of the rabbis by later statements of Ben Gurion and others, that Army and National Service for women have the major function of homogenizing immigrants from scores of countries into a cohesive society with common values, and were not militarily necessary. Quite understandably, therefore, the religious community was opposed to the very concept that the values of its youth should be shaped by the foes of traditional Judaism.

---

8. He was known as the *Chazon Ish*, after the name of his famous series of books on the Talmud and Jewish halachic law. Born in 1879 in Lithuania, he came to Israel in the 1930s. His nobility of spirit, imposing Torah scholarship, compassion, and practical wisdom were the inspiration of his generation. He died in 1954 and is buried in Bnei Brak.

The necessity of having religious life play an important role in the national building of Israel as a modern state (something which secular Jewry attempted to ignore) cannot be overstated. An astute non-Jewish historian saw this very clearly:

> Many of the hundred or more countries which became independent after 1945 had to borrow institutions and traditions from their former colonial rulers or invent them from a past which was largely unrecorded. Israel was fortunate because her past was the largest and richest of all, was copiously chronicled and kept fresh by absolute continuities. . . the living force of a religion which had formed the Jewish race itself and whose present custodians could trace their rabbinical succession back to Moses. The Jews had survived precisely because they were punctilious about their rituals and had been prepared to die for them. It was right and healthy that the respect for strict observances should be a central feature of the Zionist community.[9]

Thus, Ben-Gurion's establishment of the "Status Quo" should not be viewed as merely a political deal to insure his governmental power, but rather as a necessary, almost statesmanlike decision made to guarantee the unity of the people and the survival of the State of Israel. Unpalatable though it was to him, Ben Gurion was shrewd enough to swallow a necessary dose of religion in his political, though not his personal, life.

U.N. Admits Israel

 N FEBRUARY 16, 1949, the Knesset elected Chaim Weizmann to the ceremonial position of first president of Israel.[10] As Weizmann's arch-foe of many years, Ben Gurion would not have permitted him a more substantive post.

On May 11, 1949, Israel was admitted as a member of the United Nations. The country suffered from inflation, a lack of industry and raw materials, forced food and materiel rationing, and a tremendous housing shortage. To alleviate this situation, the Jews of the Diaspora

---

9. Paul Johnson, *A History of the Jews,* pp. 553-4.

10. Not to universal approbation. The Knesset vote was 83-15 with 22 abstentions.

Chaim Weizmann presents a Sefer Torah to President Harry S. Truman at the White House, May 25, 1948

rallied their efforts, talents, and wealth. The United Jewish Appeal organized itself in the United States and in other countries, and raised large amounts of money to help Israel solve its social and economic problems. Founded in 1952, the Israel Bond Organization bent itself to the task of providing large amounts of investment capital to help build the economic and industrial infrastructure of the new country.

In short, Israel now became the "religion" for much of world Jewry, especially for those whose observance of Torah and tradition had waned. The symbiotic relationship between Israel and the Jews of the Diaspora was now formed and formalized, and Israel's survival became the primary goal of the Jews of the Diaspora.

Jews were optimistic about their new state and its future, seeing their personal future as Jews tied to that of the State. Having barely survived the Holocaust of World War II and the trauma of the Arab aggression against the new Jewish state, the Jewish people were reinvigorated by their military victory, the ingathering of the refugees of Europe and the Middle East, and the subsequent muting of anti-Semitism in the world. Israel fully expected its Arab neighbors to proceed from the Armistice agreements to full-scale peace negotiations, and hoped to devote itself to the absorption of the new immigrants and the development of its economic and social life.

The elections to the second Knesset in 1951 resulted in the coalition partners Mapai, Mapam, and the General Zionists electing a total of 80 of the 120 parliamentary members. However, in the inter-party squabbling following the election, Ben Gurion was unable to include either Mapam or the General Zionists in the new government. Instead, he formed a narrow coalition based on Mapai and the religious parties. There can be no doubt that the inability of the secular left and center to cooperate in forming a coalition government helped traditional Jewry maintain its position and influence throughout the decades of the 50s and 60s.

Contrary to the expectations of the socialists and secularists, the religious infrastructure in Israel continued to grow and intensify. The infusion of great chassidic leaders and *roshei yeshivah* who had escaped from Hitler, as well as the generally positive attitude of Sephardic Jewry toward tradition and Torah practice, strengthened the outlook for a stronger religious influence in the country. More yeshivos and chassidic courts were beginning to establish themselves. Religious leaders of Orthodoxy united in establishing and supporting *Chinuch Atzmai,* an independent Torah-school system that did for Israel what the "day school" movement was doing for the United States and Canada.

Barely perceptible at first, these signs of religious strength were nurturing the future groundswell of Torah life that would proliferate in the 70s and 80s. Bnei Brak was beginning to emerge as a center of Jewish life and Torah study, and Jerusalem was, naturally, a bastion of traditional Jewish life.[11] But the basic tension between the secular government and the observant community in Israel remained, with numerous confrontational issues always guaranteeing bitter flare-ups.

Such a situation led Agudath Israel to leave the government coalition. Despite repeated government assurances and legal commitments, it charged the Jewish Agency and Youth Aliyah with taking immigrant children from religious families and placing them in secular institutions, sometimes even by force, a charge that was confirmed by a governmental commission of inquiry. This was typical of the many underlying religious conflicts that simmered, barely beneath the surface, and often erupted into conflict and political turmoil.

German Reparations

A NOTHER BITTER ISSUE WAS raised in 1951 and 1952 throughout the Jewish world. Chancellor Konrad Adenauer of West Germany had agreed to a reparations proposal to compensate the Jewish people for the *financial* horror of German behavior in World War II. Payments were

---

11. The Israeli description of their major cities was that "Tel Aviv dances (*rokedet*), Haifa works (*ovedet*), and Jerusalem studies Torah (*lomedet*)."

to be made over twelve years and in German currency and goods. At no time were the reparations to be anything more than partial financial payment for the robbery of Jewish assets in Europe.

The vast majority of the funds were to be given to the State of Israel for its industrial and transport development. A smaller amount would be paid to an all-Jewish committee representing organized Jewry throughout the world. In addition, money was to be paid directly to the individual victims of the German war against the Jews, in lump-sum or extended-time payments.

Even though both Germany and the Jewish negotiators[12] emphasized the purely economic nature of the compact, many Jews viewed this matter as a moral one. They contended that the Germans would inevitably claim that these reparations payments would absolve them of guilt for the Holocaust. Opponents of the agreement argued passionately that it would be immoral to allow Germany to "buy" vindication for the brutal murder of six million Jews. Thus the Jewish people were bitterly, emotionally, and even violently divided over the reparations agreement. After a vitriolic debate, unprecedented in the annals of the Knesset before or since, the agreement ratifying the reparations payment was passed by a vote of 61 to 50. Menachem Begin, the leader of the opposition to German reparations, was suspended from the Knesset for three months, due to "his unruly and emotional behavior" during the debate.

In his memoirs, Ben Gurion smugly notes,[13] "members of the parties that had opposed the payments willingly have benefited from the goods received." But he missed the point. It was Ben Gurion's cavalier attitude towards the pain of the survivors that Begin found most galling and offensive. The issue of the relationship of German aid to Israel — as well as that of the State's relationship to the non-Jewish world generally — always remained alive in Israeli political and social life. The acceptance of reparations somehow had to be considered as a reconciliation between the Jewish world and Germany. Whether such a reconciliation, so soon after the war, was justified became the crux of the issue.

---

12. Led by Dr. Nahum Goldman, a veteran Zionist leader who had been shouldered aside by his political nemesis, Ben Gurion.

13. *Israel: A Personal History*, p. 400.

The Kastner Trial

ANOTHER EXAMPLE OF THE raw scar left on the Jewish psyche by the horror of the destruction of European Jewry was the notorious "Kastner trial" which took place in an Israeli District Court in 1954. In 1944, when the Nazi army occupied their Hungarian ally and Eichmann undertook the extermination of Hungarian Jewry, Dr. Rudolf Kastner was the president of the Hungarian Zionist organization. Kastner negotiated with Eichmann unsuccessfully for the salvation of Hungarian Jewry, but, as mentioned before, he was able to secure permission for two trainloads, totaling 1618 Jews, to go to Switzerland and safety. One of these refugees was the Satmar *Rav*, who was one of Hungarian Jewry's principal spiritual leaders even before the War, but many of the others were Kastner's relatives and colleagues.

Kastner survived the war and immigrated to Israel. There he was publicly accused by Malkiel Gruenwald, a fellow Hungarian Jew who lost his family in Auschwitz, of collaborating with the Germans by not informing the Jews of what truly awaited them at the hands of the Germans. According to Gruenwald, Kastner purposely lulled his Jewish brethren into cooperating with the Germans, so that he, Kastner, could gain advantages from Eichmann. Other charges of personal gain and unsavory activity were also made. The greater, implied charge was that Jewish leaders in general were ready to connive against their people in order to save their families and their political parties. Kastner responded by suing Gruenwald for libel.

The trial was emotionally wrenching, politically and socially divisive, and nationally riveting. All of the terrible questions were asked, and no adequate answers were forthcoming. It was the first time since the war that such charges were made in a court of law under rules of evidence. The fact that Kastner was part of the Zionist establishment made him a target for political opponents of Ben Gurion.[14]

After laboriously pondering the matter, a lower court judge ruled that Kastner was decisively at fault, but on appeal a higher court reversed the decision and ruled in favor of Kastner, thus clearing his name and restoring his honor in the eyes of the law, if not the people. However, Kastner's triumph was stillborn, for just as the verdict was to be

---

14. See Ben Hecht's bitter account of the trial and the larger issue in his book, *Perfidy*.

announced, he was gunned down in an apparent vengeance attack. The killer was never apprehended. All of Israel was shocked, but the wound was not closed nor the country united.

Ben Gurion Resigns and Returns

T THE END OF 1953, Ben-Gurion resigned as Prime Minister, in response to strife in the government regarding religious and economic issues. He decried the power of small parties, the proportional representation method of electing the Knesset, and the fragmentation of political power in Israel. Claiming to be "unable to bear any longer the psychological strain,"[15] he retired to Sde Boker, a newly formed kibbutz in the Negev desert. The new Prime Minister was Ben Gurion's longtime associate and foreign minister, Moshe Sharett.[16] He, too, governed through a coalition of Mapai, two of the religious parties,[17] and a number of small parties.

At this time the Soviet Union, obsessed by deep and irrational anti-Semitism,[18] assumed an even harder anti-Israel stance in its foreign policy. In retaliation, Jewish fanatics bombed the Soviet Legation in Tel Aviv and, though Israel apologized sincerely and immediately, the U.S.S.R. used the excuse to break diplomatic relations with the Jewish state. Simultaneously, the economic situation in Israel worsened, and new immigration to the country slowed markedly. Another element of instability was the notorious "Lavon Affair,"[19] which further weakened Sharett's ability to govern effectively. By early 1955, the Mapai pined for Ben Gurion's return. He was recalled as Minister of Defense

15. Ben Gurion, *Israel: A Personal History*, p. 404.

16. Originally named Shertok.

17. National Religious Party and Poalei Agudath Israel. Agudath Israel had withdrawn from the government.

18. The "Doctor's Plot" in Russia, the Slansky trial in Czechoslovakia, and other open anti-Semitic outrages were in progress. In all these cases, prominent Jews were accused and convicted in show trials of being traitors to their countries.

19. The "Lavon Affair" was an Israeli spying operation in Egypt in the early 1950s, which was unsuccessful and proved disastrous to Israeli intelligence. The crux of the "affair" was whether the operation was undertaken on the authority of Pinchas Lavon, then the Defense Minister, as the operatives claimed, or on their own initiative, as Lavon claimed. Ben Gurion, an opponent of Lavon, vindictively used the "affair" as a pretext to banish him from Mapai leadership. Bitterness over the "affair" and what many perceived as the injustice done to Lavon roiled Israel's political life for many years.

and eventually replaced Sharett as Prime Minister, with Sharett returning to his previous post of Foreign Minister.

The real reason for Ben Gurion's return to power was the clearly developing threat of renewed war against Israel by its Arab neighbors. The antipathy of the Arab governments towards Israel intensified in the early 1950s. None of the leaders of the Arab states who attacked Israel in 1948 survived in power after their defeat.

The new leaders sought revenge, not peace, and looked to solve their enormous internal domestic problems by waging a "holy war" to destroy the Jewish state. The leader of the Arab world in this matter was Gamal Abdul Nasser,[20] of Egypt. Nasser had overthrown King Farouk in a military coup and immediately adopted a hostile attitude towards Israel. He employed Arab infiltrators — *fedayeen* — who committed atrocious terrorist acts against Israeli citizens. From 1951 to 1955, there were 864 Israeli casualties due to the *fedayeen*. All of the Arab countries disclaimed responsibility, but privately gloated over the Israeli discomfort.

When Israel retaliated with its official army, the governments of the world roundly condemned her, conveniently using the hair-splitting legal argument that, under international law, troops could not be used in the absence of a declaration of war. Thus, the siege mentality that had characterized the Jewish state since its inception intensified and hardened. The people of Israel became convinced that they could not expect impartial justice from the United Nations or the chanceries of the world.

Israel was now ready to participate in a conspiracy to topple Nasser and hopefully free itself from the scourge of the *fedayeen*. It also hoped to gain relief from Nasser's blockade of Israeli shipping in the Straits of Tiran, which effectively closed Israel's southern port of Eilat. Furthermore, Nasser had seized the Suez Canal from England and nationalized it, and closed it to Israeli shipping.

Because of his alliance with Russia, and the enormous amount of Soviet weaponry and advisers in Egypt, Nasser felt he could act against England and Israel with impunity. But his violent rhetoric and

---

20. 1918-1970. A captain in the Egyptian army, he was part of the Egyptian forces beleaguered by Israel in the "Faluja pocket." He was, to a great extent, a prisoner of his own rhetoric and hungered to be the leader of a great Pan-Arab empire stretching from Morocco to Iran. Feared by his fellow-Arabs, he undermined many governments and waged war against his fellow Arabs throughout his mercurial career. However, he eventually convinced himself that the destruction of Israel would be his ticket to dominion over a "Pan-Arab" union of states.

anti-Western behavior unintentionally opened a door of opportunity for Israel, as he provoked the notoriously pro-Arab foreign ministries of England, France, and the United States to become more conciliatory towards the survival efforts of the Jewish State. France supplied Israel with new weapons — tanks, planes, mobile guns and artillery. Though aware of Israel's rearmament, the Arabs nevertheless again overestimated their own military prowess and underestimated the frustration of England, France, and Israel.

In the fall of 1956, Ben Gurion decided to attack Nasser using a strategy coordinated with the British and French. In an elaborate scheme, Israel would invade the Sinai and drive to the Suez Canal, where British and French paratroopers would then land, occupy the canal, topple Nasser and "separate the combatants." Thus Israel would occupy the Sinai — ending the threat of the *fedayeen* , and England and France would regain control of the Suez Canal. On October 29, the Israeli move took place. Israeli tanks drove deep into the Sinai to link up with the English and French paratroopers who had dropped behind the enemy lines. The operation was an astounding military success, but a diplomatic disaster.

The world reaction to the Israeli move and the subsequent Anglo-French intervention was universally hostile. The Soviet Union threatened to flatten Israel with its ballistic rockets. The United States government demanded Israel's immediate and unconditional withdrawal.

In an emergency Security Council meeting, the U.S. and the Soviet Union joined in denouncing all three countries and demanding total and immediate withdrawal. France and England lost their nerve and evacuated Egypt, while Nasser mocked them publicly. Anthony Eden was forced to resign as Prime Minister of Great Britain. It was poetic justice. Eden had been a bitter and vociferous foe of the rescue of Jews from Europe; now his once-distinguished career was in shambles because of his involvement with Israel. It would not be the last time that the Arabs were successful in converting a military defeat into a diplomatic triumph.

America, Russia, and the U.N. recognized Nasser's grab and ownership of the Suez Canal, and forced complete Israeli withdrawal from the Sinai. However, the U.N. created an international peace-keeping force to patrol the Egyptian-Israeli border and prevent *fedayeen* infiltration into Israel. The U.N. also guaranteed freedom of navigation of Israeli shipping in the Gulf of Eilat/Aqaba and the Straits of Tiran. Yet

Nasser still successfully blockaded Israeli shipping in the Suez Canal and continued his propaganda attack, aiming for the destruction of the Jewish state.

Nasser had gained great prestige among the masses in the Arab world, and thereafter attempted to undermine neighboring Arab governments as well. He participated in the Yemeni civil war, fought pitched battles with Saudi Arabian troops, merged Egypt and Syria in the ill-fated United Arab Republic — which never functioned well and eventually broke apart — and fomented instability throughout the Middle East. His cunning and evil dominated Israeli and Arab life for almost two decades.

New Growth of Torah

 S ISRAEL NEARED THE END of its first decade of existence, it had great national accomplishments to its credit. It had become a haven for dispersed and oppressed Jews, built an economic infrastructure, and established a free and vital government. All were major accomplishments. But the greatest reality of all was the usual Jewish miracle of survival.

Many of the countries founded after the Second World War had already sunk into dictatorship, oppression, stagnation — and even extinction — by the mid-1950s. However, in spite of two wars, a flood of impoverished immigrants, unceasing terrorist activity, diplomatic isolation and superpower confrontations, Israel had survived and, in a sense, prospered. "One to whom a miracle occurs, never recognizes the miracle."[21] However, the exclusively secular nature of both the government and the majority of Israelis led them to attribute success solely to their own efforts. This bred hubris and arrogance in the Israeli political establishment, traits which would cost Israel dearly in the future.

An important development in Israeli life was the growth of Torah education in the first years of the State. The independent Torah-school system, *Chinuch Atzmai,* supported by most of the great rabbinic leaders of Israel and the Diaspora,[22] was established and began to flourish. There were privately supported schools of intense Torah study

---

21. *Talmud Bavli*, *Niddah* 31a.

22. Included among its American sponsors were Rabbis Aharon Kotler, Moshe Feinstein, Reuven Grozovsky, Eliyahu Meir Bloch, and Joseph B. Soloveitchik.

on all levels. A government-sponsored religious school system, *Mamlachti Dati,* also existed, as did religiously oriented high schools, trade schools, and even a university under religious auspices.

Not only did religious education develop and expand its enrollment, but it also intensified and assumed greater qualitative goals. The old and revered names of yeshivos destroyed by Hitler were now heard again in the everyday speech of the Jewish state. Ponivezh, Mir, Slobodka, Grodno, Gur, Lomza, Belz, Vizhnitz and Pressburg took their places alongside Hebron, Etz Chaim and Mercaz Harav as premier Torah institutions in Israel.

Of great, yet different, significance was the establishment of yeshivos by the Mizrachi and Bnei Akiva movements. These were oftentimes established in spite of the advice and goals of the "establishment" leaders of these organizations, who previously had rarely supported intensive Torah study as a mass movement, and had generally become more lax in their own approach to religious observance. The movement's new yeshivos became an irritant to many of the political leaders of the party that spawned them. These yeshivos became the core of the *Hesder* yeshivos[23] in Israel, which combined Torah study with military service. They changed the complexion of the religious life in Israel, and intensified religious study and observance in the country generally.

Silently, almost unnoticed, a significant growth in the cadre of Torah-committed Jews was occurring in Israel. This element, and its influence on Israel, would yet become far reaching, intense, controversial, and continuing.

---

23. So-called because of the *hesder* [arrangement] with the Israel Defense Forces. The *Hesder* students would distinguish themselves in the tank and parachute corps of the army, and many also grew into roles of Torah leadership in Israel. The first *Hesder* yeshivah was Kerem B'Yavne, founded in 1942 by Rabbi Chaim Goldvicht, a student of the famed Brisker *Rav* of Jerusalem.

Section VIII

The Modern Jew

1958-1988

37
The New Jewish World

Changing Times

FTER THE DESTRUCTION of European Jewry, the axis of the Jewish world ran through two poles, Israel and America. Though American Jewry was wholeheartedly committed to the development and prosperity of the State of Israel — in fact, Israel became the Jewish "religion" for many American Jews — there was no mass inclination to actually forsake the Diaspora and return home to Israel. The opposite would be true, for in the first four decades of Israel's existence five times more Israelis were leaving for America than American Jews emigrating to Israel.

This disturbing reality caused different reactions among the Israelis. Ben Gurion caustically called for the dismantling of the Zionist movement's *aliyah* apparatus, saying that since it had failed in bringing the Jews of the West to Israel it was a waste of resources.[1] Other Israeli leaders still hoped for a significant *aliyah* from America. Many disparaged American Jewry for its failure to grasp the opportunities that the State presented. However, American Jews, in post-World War II society, were dazzled by the new opportunities presented in America and most — almost all — felt their future to be in the United States. A slight tinge of guilt,[2] however, remained with American Jews, and this would color their attitudes and sacrifices on behalf of Israel.

---

1. His famous riposte was that "the Zionist movement is the first woman in history to continue wearing maternity clothes even after having successfully given birth."

2. This guilt feeling has worked itself out in strange ways. Many American Jews justified their failure to make *aliyah* by denigrating Israeli society, democracy, and accomplishments. This guilt fuels the fire of self-hatred of Israel by the crusading Left, the liberal establishment, and the hard-core assimilationists of American Jewish society. On the other hand, the secularism of the State of Israel and the religious

Jewish life in America underwent radical change after the war. The old established Jewish neighborhoods in almost every urban community in the United States disintegrated. Like their non-Jewish neighbors, Jews embarked on a flight to suburban, or at least to more up-scale urban, neighborhoods in their cities. Jewish synagogues and institutions were abandoned and sold cheaply (if sold at all). The new American-born Jew disassociated himself from his parents' way of life and thought, and the assimilation of the Jew into American life was now nearing completion.

In the wake of this social change, there was also a significant change of attitude toward Judaism and religious behavior. The typical European-born Jew in pre-war America, though not strongly committed to strict observance of religious ritual, was traditional. He attended an Orthodox synagogue, kept a kosher home, ate matzos and only permissible food on Passover, and still retained much of the basic Jewish value system in his outlook and behavior. His American-born son, in the new post-war America, kept a much less kosher kitchen at home (if kosher at all), still ate matzos on Passover but no longer exclusively permissible food, and had a lifestyle and value system hardly different from that of his non-Jewish neighbor. He attended synagogue fewer than five times a year, and was usually affiliated with a Conservative or Reform congregation.

Institutionally, the greatest casualty of the post-war period in American Jewish life was the Orthodox synagogue. Victimized by the loss of its European-born constituency through attrition and the flight of Jews from their old urban neighborhoods, the Orthodox synagogue as an institution seemed doomed to demise.[3] The Conservative movement and its Conservative congregations became the principal beneficiary of the assets,[4] buildings, and families that had previously been associated with the Orthodox camp.

---

tensions existing there seemingly justified the opposition of many religious Jews to immigrating, and thereby soothed their guilt in choosing to stay away from the Holy Land. Finally, the herculean efforts of American Jewry on behalf of Israel may be at least somewhat motivated by these latent guilt feelings.

3. In 1948, there were 42(!) Orthodox synagogues in the Lawndale neighborhood of Chicago, half of them possessing large and impressive buildings, and each with membership rolls of hundreds of families. A decade later, only twelve of them had survived (through relocations and mergers with other synagogues), and only a few of these still could be considered Orthodox.

4. See Boruch Litvin's book, *Sanctity of the Synagogue,* for a record of the legal efforts made by some Orthodox people to save their synagogues' assets from being illegally taken away.

Wave of the Future

I N THE 1950S, CONSERVATIVE spokesmen and institutions claimed to be the wave of the future for American Jewry and confidently predicted the death of Orthodoxy, at least in America. The growth of the Conservative movement during the first two decades after the war was truly phenomenal, though the great majority of its constituents found the movement more convenient than challenging, and were little interested in the theological niceties of the movement's attempts to "conserve" Judaism.

During this period, a large proportion of the rabbis in the Conservative movement were men who were raised in Orthodox homes and even attended Orthodox yeshivos. Many of them still nursed the hope that Orthodoxy would accept the religious legitimacy of Conservatism, and therefore they steered away from the more divisive issues[5] that would, in time, separate their movement completely from mainstream Orthodoxy and eventually place strong internal strains on the Conservative movement itself.

The Reform movement in World War II, but especially in post-war America, began a slow but steady reversal of its long-held anti-Zionist policy. The horrors of the destruction of European Jewry, coupled with the reality of the establishment of Israel, forced Reform to withdraw from its extreme anti-Zionist position. Such leading Reform leaders as Abba Hillel Silver and Stephen Wise were instrumental in the push towards Jewish independence in Palestine. The old and extreme Reform position, represented by the American Council for Judaism and its Arabist head, Dr. Elmer Berger, was repudiated by mainstream Reform.

The Reform movement in America now contained in its **ranks** a sizable number of adherents who were only a generation **or** two removed from being traditional Jews. These "new" Reform Jews had no objection to discarding Jewish ritual, and even belief, but they would

---

5. Among these issues are: driving automobiles to the synagogue on the Sabbath, eating non-kosher food out of the house, granting of Conservative *gittin* (divorces) that do not conform to *halachah,* women being called to the Torah, women rabbis and cantors, and the validity of Conservative conversions, which is at the crux of the "Who is a Jew?" controversy. The movement's stand over the years on these terribly divisive religious deviations have damaged Conservatism since its heyday in the late 1950s.

not agree to play traitor to their people and its physical survival. In the past, Reform had been characterized by the "Pittsburgh Platform," in which Reform repudiated the commandments and any attachment to the Land of Israel. Now this stand was tempered by the new constituency of Reform in America and the new circumstances of world Jewry after World War II, and certainly the establishment of the State of Israel.

Fund-Raising

HE RISE OF THE STATE of Israel projected fund-raising efforts on its behalf to the forefront of American Jewish life. The United Jewish Appeal and the Israel Bond Organization became the major visible factors in American Jewish life. Though they valiantly raised enormous sums of money on behalf of Israel and world Jewry, they also had a passively negative effect on the development of American Jewry. They fostered the impression that American Jewry's sole purpose was to supply funds for Israel.

They advertised Israel as a modern, secular democracy — a second America — and ignored its Jewish roots, and the deeply held religious beliefs of large numbers of its people. In their efforts to tap the wealthy, assimilated Jews, and their non-Jewish friends and corporations, the fundraisers projected a romantic image of the country that would appeal to the givers. This distorted view of Israel would eventually cause strains between Israel and American Jewry when it became apparent that the reality of the Jewish state did not satisfy the vision of the liberal, assimilated, and left-leaning American Jewish establishment.

The UJA and Israel Bonds also denigrated any Jewish projects in America — such as intensive Jewish education — that they felt would seriously compete for those funds that they wished to send to Israel. Eventually, the UJA/Federation fund-raising drives did provide substantial aid to Jewish education in the U.S.A., but many times it was too little and too late. These organizations virtually institutionalized Israel as the religion of American Jewry.

All American Jewish efforts, wealth, and interests were now to be directed solely to Israel. This great cause of Israel, however, was defined in a fashion that ignored other Jewish issues in America, and Judaism now became synonymous not with a Jewish way of life or belief, but rather exclusively with support of the State of Israel. This short-sighted policy led to an acceleration of assimilation, and thus eventually to a reduction in the number of committed Jews who would remain loyal to Israel. In effect, the fund-raising apparatus for Israel was guilty of almost killing the very goose which was laying all of those golden eggs for the State of Israel.

Orthodox Resurgence

Rabbi Dr. Joseph Breuer

UNNOTICED BY THE OFFICIAL leaders of the Jewish establishment in America and by a majority of American Jews, a number of determined people set about to build a more intensive Jewish life in America. They were European-trained scholars who arrived on this continent before the Holocaust and were determined to dedicate their lives to the building of Torah institutions.

Among them were Rabbi Moshe Feinstein[6], Rabbi Yaakov Yitzchak Ruderman[7], Rabbi Yaakov Kamenetzky[8], Rabbi Yitzchak Hutner[9]. The father of Jewish education in America, Reb Shraga Feivel Mendlowitz, also wielded great influence. He assumed the principalship of Torah

Rabbi Yitzchak Hutner

---

6. A rabbi in Russia, he arrived in America in the late 1930s and served as *rosh yeshivah* of Mesivtha Tifereth Jerusalem on Manhattan's Lower East Side for nearly fifty years. He was the acknowledged rabbinic master of halachic responsa for decades, until his death in 1986. A man of gentleness and piety, he was a person of wisdom and innocence, practicality and faith. His home, heart, mind and soul were open for all Jews and Jewish problems. He carried the problems of the Jewish people on his frail shoulders as a badge of honor. Rabbi Feinstein's eight volumes of responsa have become the standard of Jewish law in our time, even for those who disputed some of his rulings. There was hardly a subject in *halachah* and modern life that he did not deal with and expound upon. He had time for everyone and his responsa are a model of logic, knowledge, human understanding, and sweeping command of the halachic tradition. His quiet, measured responsa set policy on internal Jewish matters and his word, even if not always followed, was respected by all. His funeral, the day before Purim, 1986, was attended by over 100,000 people in New York, and the next day by an additional 250,000 in Jerusalem, where he was buried. See his biography, *Reb Moshe*, by Rabbi Shimon Finkelman (Mesorah Publications, Ltd.: New York, 1986).

7. The founder of Yeshivas Ner Israel in Baltimore, who arrived in America in the 1930s.

8. During the war he was a rabbi in Toronto, and in 1945 he became the *rosh yeshivah* of Torah Vodaath. He was famous as a man of profound wisdom and insight, in addition to his vast Torah knowledge.

9. The head of Mesivta Chaim Berlin in New York. He arrived in America in the 1930s.

Vodaath in 1923 and was personally responsible for most of the advances and innovations in American Torah education until his death in 1948. Another pioneer was Rabbi Dr. Joseph Breuer, head of the German *kehillah* in Washington Heights, New York. Rabbi David Leibowitz,[10] his son Rabbi Henoch, and Rabbi Shlomo Heiman,[11] also left their mark on American Jewish youth.

Beginning in the 1930s and early 1940s, these and other great Eastern European scholars and rabbis, many rescued miraculously from Hitler's grasp, arrived in America.

Rabbi Moshe Feinstein and Rabbi Yaakov Kamenetzky

All of these men were unswerving in their loyalty to Jewish tradition and to their faith, and believed that a strong, vibrant, Torah-oriented Jewish life could be created in America. They were undaunted by the failures of their rabbinic predecessors in America and scorned compromise or adjustments of Torah practices and values to America lifestyle. They represented the noblest tradition of Eastern European Jewry, and they firmly believed that they were spared the fate of their families and brethren in Europe so that they could be the instrument for the creation of a new Torah bastion in America. Thus they were driven men, haunted by the horror of Europe, and inwardly impelled to accomplish the impossible in America during the waning years of life left to them. Their spiritual mission was the overriding concern of their lives. Most prominent among them were the last lions, Rabbis Yoel Teitelbaum and Aharon Kotler (see below). Among those who had major influence — not only on their own institutions, but on the development of Orthodoxy in a broad sense — were Rabbi Reuven Grozovsky[12] and Rabbis Eliyahu Meir Bloch and Chaim Mordechai Katz.[13]

---

10. Founder and leader of the Rabbinical Seminary of America, New York, commonly known as the Chofetz Chaim Yeshiva. He arrived in the 1930s.

11. He was appointed *rosh yeshivah* of Torah Vodaath in the mid-1930s, and was recognized as a master educator, until his early death in 1945.

12. The last *rosh yeshivah* in pre-war Kamenetz, *rosh yeshivah* of Torah Vodaath and Beth Medrosh Elyon, Monsey, N.Y., and head of the Council of Torah Sages of Agudath Israel of America.

13. The builders of Telshe Yeshiva in Cleveland, Ohio.

Rabbis Mordechai Rogow, Yisrael Mendel Kaplan,[14] the young Chaim Kreiswirth,[15] Abraham Kalmanowitz[16] and Mordecai Ginsburg,[17] Yeruchem Gorelick, David Lifshitz, and Menachem Mendel Zaks,[18] Eliyahu Chazan[19] and Zelik Epstein,[20] were among the other great teachers of the newly resurgent yeshivah movement in post-World War II America.

The *Rebbes* of Lubavitch — Rabbi Yosef Yitzchak Schneerson and his son-in-law and successor, Rabbi Menachem Mendel Schneerson — led and developed a movement that was unique in its dynamism and ability to reach out to non-observant Jews by the tens of thousands. The great chassidic *Rebbes* of the dynasties of Bobov, Skvere, and others attracted large followings, strengthened observance and education, and influenced the development of post-war American Orthodoxy. Such chassidic-oriented rabbis as the *Rav* of Tzelem and the *Rav* of Mattersdorf built communities and yeshivos and, in the case of the former, elevated the standard of kashruth supervision in the United States.

To this group one should add Rabbi Gedaliah Schorr, brought to America as a child in the 1920s, and described by Rabbi Aharon Kotler as "the first American *gadol*" (great Torah personality).[21]

These men, their names unknown, even today, to the vast majority of American Jews, created a revolution in Jewish life in the United States. They educated generations of American-born Torah scholars, redirected the spiritual priorities of thousands, strengthed kashruth standards, infused the warmth of tradition into the lives of many families,

---

14. *Roshei yeshivah* at Beis Medrash L'Torah in Chicago, Illinois.

15. The head of the Beis Medrash L'Torah in Chicago from 1947 to 1953. He later became the Chief Rabbi of Antwerp, Belgium. The Rabbis listed in notes 14 and 15 were the personal mentors of the author, and though their national standing did not compare with the other rabbis mentioned, their many students occupy positions of great influence in world Jewry. The author includes their names as a point of personal privilege.

16. President of the Mir Yeshivah in Poland and founder of its successor institution in Brooklyn. Rabbi Kalmanowitz assumed full responsibility for the yeshivah's support during its wartime exile in Shanghai, and was a prime figure in rescue work.

17. *Rosh yeshivah* in Mir, Brooklyn.

18. *Roshei yeshivah* at RIETS. Rabbi Gorelick was also the founder of Yeshiva Zichron Moshe in the Bronx and later in South Fallsburg, N.Y.

19. *Rosh yeshivah* of Torah Vodaath.

20. *Rosh yeshivah* at Torah Vodaath and founder and *rosh yeshivah* of Shaar HaTorah, Queens.

21. He studied at Torah Vodaath and later became its *rosh yeshivah*. He also studied under Rabbi Kotler in Kletzk before the outbreak of World War II.

and arrested the encroachments of secularism in the Orthodox camp. Through their students, they influenced the direction of American Jewry in myriad ways, and shaped a new, more militant and assertive Orthodoxy in America.

Although all of the above were great men whose contributions shaped American Jewish life, the Satmar *Rav*, Rabbi Yoel Teitelbaum, and Rabbi Aharon Kotler earned a special place because their scholarship, dedication, charisma, and character made them stand out as leaders and role models, not only for their disciples, but for their rabbinic peers. Both became leaders and teachers in their early 20s, an achievement that was most uncommon in Europe, where great scholarship and piety abounded. The Satmar *Rav* became a dominant figure for most of the chassidic leaders in America, and Rabbi Kotler was the same in the yeshivah world.

Rabbi Yoel Teitelbaum, the Satmar *Rav*, was a member of a major chassidic dynasty, but he did not inherit his father's mantle as rabbi of Sighet; his position was his own. As a young rabbi in Kroli and later in Satmar, Hungary, he was rabbi, *rosh yeshivah*, spiritual mentor, and collector and dispenser of charity to tens of thousands of disciples and admirers. When he arrived in America in 1946, he had barely a quorum for prayers, but he insisted that even in assimilationist America loyalty to traditional chassidic Torah life would prevail, and he provided strength and inspiration to scores of other chassidic leaders. Indeed, he did prevail. Forty years later, Satmar had tens of thousands of adherents,

Rabbi Aharon Kotler

*Satmar Rav
Rabbi Yoel Teitelbaum*

*Beth Medrash Govoha,
Lakewood, N.J.*

dozens of major institutions, and significant political and social influence in the United States.

Rabbi Aharon Kotler succeeded his distinguished father-in-law, Rabbi Isser Zalman Meltzer, as *rosh yeshivah* in Slutzk. The latter was imprisoned by the Russians in the 1920s and left for the Land of Israel upon his release. Rabbi Kotler succeeded in re-establishing the yeshivah in Kletzk, Poland, and soon became regarded as a peer by personages many years his senior. He arrived in America in 1941, hoping that he would be able to save his students who were stranded in Lithuania, but it was too late. When he founded his Beth Medrash Govoha in Lakewood, N.J., it was with the determination that his students would devote themselves solely to Torah study, with no thought of career or societal compromise, and that they would continue to do so even after marriage. These were almost unheard-of concepts in America, and initially there was great resistance to them, but he succeeded. Other institutions emulated his, and his students assumed major roles in Torah education. Beth Medrosh Govoha itself founded many satellite yeshivos and *kollelim*[22] across the United States.

Orthodox Education System

NE OF THE MAJOR CHANGES in Jewish life in America was the appearance of the Jewish Day School. This school was meant to provide a complete religious and secular education in a single institution under the auspices of people whose priority was adherence to the teachings of the Torah. Unlike the traditional American setting that placed a Jewish child in a non-Jewish public school for most of the day and relegated his Jewish education to the drudgery of the afternoon Hebrew School, the day school provided that child with a wholesome, integrated education in an environment that would help shield him from the assimilating trends of everyday American life.

The Day School movement began in earnest in the late 1940s, and the primary organization responsible for its success and growth was the National Society for Hebrew Day Schools — Torah Umesorah. Reb Shraga Feivel Mendlowitz of Mesivta Torah Vodaath was the founder

22. Learning seminars for married men conducted in a post-graduate level, usually providing stipends for their full-time participants.

and mentor of the organization, and his students were the pioneer principals and teachers of the movement. His optimism, personal example, teaching ability, intellectual capacity, and utter selflessness contributed immeasureably to his stature as the premier Torah educator of his era.

Rabbis Aaron Kotler, Yaakov Kamenetzky, Yitzchak Hutner, and Yaakov Ruderman also provided leadership and drive for Torah Umesorah. Dr. Joseph Kaminetzky was its first National Director, and over the next few decades it grew to include a network of schools nationwide, with a student population that approached 100,000. It marked the first major attempt to provide intensive, authentic Jewish education to large numbers of Jewish children in America. Thus, the focus of Orthodoxy shifted from the synagogue, where it had suffered serious reverses, to education and the creation of schools and yeshivos. Schools flourished from Bangor, Maine to Miami, Florida, and from Washington D.C. to Los Angeles, California.

The reaction of the non-Orthodox and secular Jews to the new schools and all that they represented was initially one of indifference. However, after the struggling schools had somehow gained a toehold in their communities, this reaction often changed to one of open hostility. Reform, Conservative, and secular Jewish leadership predicted dire results for the Jewish community in the United States because of the Day School movement. They were certain that the graduates of the schools would be "cripples" — educationally, socially, and professionally. They decried the abandonment of the American public school system by tens of thousands of Jewish children as being somehow un-American, if not outright disloyal.[23]

The local Jewish Federations, which allocated millions of dollars of Jewish money for social projects, hospitals, and other non-sectarian — albeit worthy — endeavors, originally opposed the Jewish Day Schools fiercely and allocated little or no funds towards their maintenance. Yet, the beleaguered little schools hung on in the 1940s and 1950s and began to grow. New yeshivah high schools and rabbinic seminaries were then founded in Philadelphia and Scranton, Pennsylvania; Monsey and Long Beach, New York; and Detroit, Michigan, among other places. Rabbi Kotler's yeshivah in Lakewood, New Jersey grew into a school that rivaled the great yeshivos of Lithuania in size and scope. The senior yeshivah population in America now grew to include thousands.

---

23. This, in a country where *millions* of non-Jewish children regularly attend Catholic parochial schools, Protestant denominational schools, and countless private and special schools.

In the 1950s, intensive Torah education for women was also introduced in Jewish life nationally. The Beth Jacob system of girls' high schools, and learning seminaries for college-age women — who would staff much of the Jewish teaching profession in the ensuing years — came into being. More importantly, the Beth Jacob schools produced women who valued Torah study and were willing to live a lifestyle that would allow their husbands to spend years of intensive Torah study in a *kollel* after marriage, and thereafter as Torah educators. More than was originally recognized, the strength of the revitalization of Orthodoxy in America was due to the quality and idealism of the schools for girls and women in America.

The pioneer of Beth Jacob education was the legendary Rebbetzin Vichna Kaplan, who founded America's first Beth Jacob High School around her dining room table in 1938. With her husband, Rabbi Baruch Kaplan, she overcame the skeptics and her school became the forerunner for scores of other girls' schools throughout the continent.

In spite of the tremendous financial and social problems involved, Jewish young men devoted themselves to years of intensive Torah study and many of them sought thereafter to pursue lifelong careers in the most neglected and maligned modern Jewish profession — teaching Torah to Jewish children. A new spirit of Jewish commitment and idealism was abroad in the land and it would transform long-held attitudes, predictions and perceptions regarding the nature and future of the American Jewish community.

This positive spirit in Orthodoxy would also accelerate the religious polarization of the American Jewish community. Orthodoxy became less tolerant of the assimilation and halachic deviations of the non-Orthodox, and it was no longer prepared to play the role of the terminally ill relative pitied by the rest of the family. It felt itself equal to the challenge of the new opportunities and situations of American life, and protested the compromises and equivocations of the non-Orthodox.

Because the fabric of American Jewish life was fraying, the rate of intermarriage began to skyrocket, Jews observed less and less of their traditions, and the family structure of Jewish America weakened. The new Orthodoxy viewed these threats to Jewish survival with alarm, pain, and trepidation, and it now rejected its previous policy of accommodation and superficial unity. With its new-found self-image, it felt responsible for Jewish survival, and it would not countenance silent acquiescence to policies, groups, and representatives that were destructive to that survival. In light of this changing pattern within

Orthodoxy, it began to insist that federations assume a major role in supporting day schools, as the best guarantor of Jewish continuity.

Another issue — it may have been more symbolic than substantive — reflected the shifting attitudes and powers within American Jewry. Historically, many Orthodox organizations and rabbis had been members of innocuous, communal umbrella-organizations, such as the Synagogue Council of America. Both the Rabbinical Council of America and the Union of Orthodox Jewish Congregations of America belonged to this group, which included Conservative, Reconstructionist, and Reform synagogue and rabbinic groups. Led by Rabbi Kotler, eleven major *roshei yeshivah* demanded the withdrawal of the Orthodox groups from this umbrella-organization, on the grounds that their membership conferred *religious* recognition on movements that denied the Divine origin of the entire Torah and sanctioned the nullification of the authority of *Halachah*. The *roshei yeshivah* did not object to cooperating on Jewish or general social issues with individual non-observant Jews, or with secular organizations, but they would not countenance the American way of giving equal recognition to the "religious validity" of all "trends" in Judaism, or, in the popular cliche, "the three wings of Judaism."

Two Orthodox groups — the Rabbinical Council of America and the Orthodox Union — refused to accept the decision of these rabbis. They marshaled other Orthodox rabbinic opinion, led by Rabbi Joseph B. Soloveitchik, that allowed their continued membership in the Synagogue Council. However, the raising of the issue itself signaled a change in the attitude of Orthodoxy, and even though this issue and others of its kind[24] have never been fully resolved, the hardening of the lines between the various groupings of American Jewry was clear.

Chassidic Movements Resurgent

 NOTHER IMPORTANT ELEMENT beginning to affect American Jewry in the 1950s and 1960s was the growth of a large and strong chassidic population. Though this group was concentrated mainly in the New York area, chassidic enclaves eventually grew in all urban American Jewish communities. The largest and most influential group was that of Rabbi Teitelbaum —

---

24. Orthodox support of local federations, and even support of the UJA, on the grounds that they discriminate against Orthodox causes and education, is such an issue.

the Satmar chassidic community. It was strongly anti-Zionist, hard-working, politically active and astute, and determined to preserve its traditional way of life at all costs — and if this meant that it had to be iconoclastic in terms of the existing Jewish protocol, so be it.

This community was basically self-contained and not given to proselytization or outreach. It was legendary for its charity and good works, and its leader, Rabbi Yoel Teitelbaum, had been recognized as a scholar and holy man even in pre-war Europe. The influence of Satmar over other chassidic groups was very strong and helped shape the policies of American Chassidus regarding many major issues of Jewish life. Not to be minimized is that their strict observances of kashruth and dress became the standard by which many other groups measured their own behavior. Chassidic garb, customs, and practices gradually gained ascendancy in American Orthodoxy and influenced all groups greatly.[25]

The Lubavitcher Rebbe
Rabbi Yosef Yitzchak
Schneerson

Chabad-Lubavitch also prospered in the post-war decades, and from its Brooklyn headquarters, it operated tens of Chabad centers worldwide, and held the loyalty of thousands of adherents. Unlike Satmar, Chabad actively proselytized and fostered the most ambitious outreach program to non-Orthodox Jews, within Orthodoxy. In this, it enlarged upon its European tradition, which was reestablished in America by its sixth *Rebbe*, Rabbi Yosef Yitzchak Schneerson. The charismatic and public figure of his successor, Rabbi Menachem Mendel Schneerson, helped propel Chabad into the public limelight and keep it there for decades.

Other strong chassidic movements in America such as Bobov, Vizhnitz, Skver, and Klausenburg also gained adherents and strength.

In addition to the religious leadership of their *rebbes*, the chassidic groups shaped and influenced entire communities, regarding schools, *mikvaos* (ritual baths), welfare services, and other non-chassidic kashruth supervision. Some chassidic groups became identified with existing neighborhoods, such as Bobov in Boro Park, Chabad in Crown Heights, and Satmar in Williamsburg. Others built communities outside their old neighborhoods, in order to provide not only adequate housing, but also self-contained communities where their children would be insulated against secular influences. The first to build such a new home was Skvere, followed by Klausenburg, Vizhnitz, and even Satmar. Gur and Belz also had strong and growing followings in America, though their *rebbes* and most of their adherents were in Israel.

---

25. Glatt kosher, Jewish milk, separate seating for men and women at public affairs, the emphasis on *shtieblach* (small private prayer groups) over synagogues, all can be seen as evidence of the chassidic influence in American Jewish life, although these matters of halachic practice are not necessarily the exclusive concern of chassidim.

New World of Opportunity

IN THE EARLY 1950s, YESHIVA UNIVERSITY, under the leadership of Rabbi Samuel Belkin, created Albert Einstein College of Medicine, the first medical school in America founded under Orthodox Jewish auspices. The opening of this institution, and the subsequent accommodations made to Orthodox medical students by other medical schools, served to train a generation of Torah-observant physicians, many of whom obtained recognition and honor in their chosen specialties. The doctor wearing a *kippah* on his head was still a rare sight in the 1950s and 1960s. But this lonely prototype proved so attractive to other young students, as well as to hospitals, medical schools, and patients, that such doctors would be a common and welcome sight thirty years later.

The career choices for Orthodox young men suddenly broadened. Medicine,[26] law, financial services, engineering, education, and even politics now replaced the traditional, narrower fields of retailing, textile manufacturing, and journeymen craftsmen. To be an observant Jew was no longer viewed as an impediment to career and financial success in American Jewish life. Certainly amongst the most influential leaders of post-war American Jewry was Rabbi Joseph B. Soloveitchik (1903-1993). He combined the posts of communal rabbi in Boston with that of Rosh Yeshiva of Rabbi Isaac Elchanan Theological Seminary of Yeshiva University. However, these two posts, important as they were, are not truly reflective of his larger role in American Jewry. He was the guide and Halachic authority for a significant segment of American Jews who classified themselves as "modern" Orthodox. His great Talmudic brilliance coupled with his masterful oratory and gifted educational skills helped raise thousands of rabbis and laymen to the level of defenders of tradition and pioneers of Jewish accomplishment. A recognized philosoper and secular scholar, his role nevertheless, was essentially to be the conduit for the great tradition of Torah of his family[27] and Eastern Europe to a modern world. He exemplified the tension inherent between the old Europe and the new America and the swirling controversies, impossible paradoxes and enormous possibilities that this tension created. His influence helped hold

Rabbi Joseph B. Soloveitchik

Photo: Rabbi I. Albert

---

26. The new five-day school week at medical schools, the removal of official and unofficial quotas for admitting minorities to medical schools, and the rise of ethnic pride in the United States, all contributed to this situation.

27. He was the son of Rabbi Moshe Soloveitchik and the grandson of Rabi Chaim Soloveitchik of Volozhin and later of Brisk.

Rabbi Meir Berlin

the line of demarcation between Orthodoxy and other interpretations of American Jewish life, was one of the founders of the Day School and Yeshiva movements in the Unived States in the 1930's and 1940's and described a vision of the modern world and the new Jewish state that somehow reconciled itself with the ancient Jewish dreams of tradition and observance.

The "modern" Orthodox Jew, like his chassidic and yeshivah counterpart, became more assertive of his Jewishness and less open to compromise and reticence. Post-war America afforded Jews maximum freedom and opportunity in life. It also afforded Jews maximum freedom and opportunity to be fully Jewish without fear of persecution or economic deprivation. All American Jews benefited from the first option. Only a small (10-15%) minority seized the second opportunity, which would permit them to be not only successful in their careers, but successful Jews in the same process.

In pre-World War II America, the Mizrachi party commanded the allegiance of most of American Orthodoxy. This religious Zionist party was founded in America by Rabbi Meir Berlin[28] during his stay in New York in the early part of the twentieth century. Most of the distinguished Orthodox rabbis in America identified themselves with this movement and it reached its zenith of power and popularity in the early 1950s. However, the newly arrived European *roshei yeshivah*, and hence their students as well, rejected the ideas, ideals, and organization of the American Mizrachi. They cast their lot with the then smaller, non-Zionist group, Agudath Israel of America.

Although the American Agudah had existed since 1924, it became reinvigorated in 1937 at the urgent request of Rabbi Chaim Ozer Grodzensky. His former student, Rabbi Eliezer Silver of Cincinnati, one of the leaders of America's European-born rabbinate, took the lead in organizing the Agudah. It was during the war years, however, that the young peoples' branch of the Agudah, under the inspired leadership of Michael Tress, came to the fore in its rescue work. Tress gave up a promising executive career in business to devote his life to Agudah activity. Tress's successor as head of the entire Agudath Israel of America was Rabbi Moshe Sherer.[29]

The Agudah slowly gained momentum as a representative organization of American Orthodoxy. By the 1960s it had become a serious force in American Jewish life, while the entrenched Mizrachi party perceptibly

---

28. This youngest son of the *Netziv* of Volozhin, later Hebraicized his name to Bar Ilan, and had a strong presence in American Jewish life just before World War I.

29. One of the most able administrators and organizers in post-World War II American Jewish life.

started to fade. Thus, the religious realignment in American Jewish life reflected itself organizationally, as well. The Agudah now represented Jewish interests at state and national government levels, published magazines, newspapers, and research papers, and gradually began to represent itself as the official spokesman for Orthodoxy in America. Though this claim was hotly disputed by other Orthodox organizations,[30] the strength of Rabbi Kotler's personality brought the *roshei yeshivah*, almost to a man, into the camp of the Agudah, and the Agudah, even if it did not yet represent the majority of Orthodox American Jews, became an effective and articulate champion of the Orthodox agenda in Jewish life.

The new Jewish world was thus full of surprises, contradictions, heartbreak, and hope. American Jewry was still in the ferment of formation, Israel was holding the sword in one hand and the trowel in the other, and the age-old questions of survival and Jewish uniqueness were still being posed. So much had happened in such a short span of time — thirty years — and most of it was still mysterious and unexplained. But one prophecy of the Bible was certainly pertinent to the time: "Peace, peace, but there is no peace."[31] And the absence of peace in the Jewish world, internally and externally, was the one constant of post-World War II Jewry.

---

30. Such as the Union of Orthodox Jewish Congregations of America, Young Israel, and others. The twentieth century has never suffered from a dearth of competing and often-times overlapping organizations.

31. Jeremiah 6:14.

Rabbi Moshe Feinstein, Rabbi Joseph B. Soloveitchik and Rabbi Aharon Kotler at a Chinuch Atzmai Dinner

38

The Six-Day War

Search for Nazi Killers

S THE 1960s BEGAN, there were two bedrock beliefs present in the Jewish world. One was that nothing like the Nazi genocide could ever again happen to the Jews. And the other was the inviolability of the security of the State of Israel. Both of these beliefs were called into question in this decade.

After World War II, many Nazi murderers and criminals avoided prosecution for their crimes. The lower-echelon killers were quickly exonerated by the Allied De-Nazification Commissions. "The Cold War" between the West and the Soviet Union, which began concurrently with the conclusion of the war, took precedence over questions of justice, and thus many of these criminals were found to be useful to the Allies and the Soviets in their new struggle. Of the main Nazis, however, most were tried and imprisoned or executed by the Allied War Crimes Tribunal, chiefly in the trials held in Nuremberg in 1946. Nevertheless, many key Nazis had escaped Europe. The search for three of them — Dr. Josef Mengele,[1] Martin Bormann,[2] and Adolf Eichmann — the SS commander in charge of the Final Solution — was pursued, not by the Allied governments, but by Jewish individuals and organizations. The State of Israel and its secret and most capable intelligence service, Mosad, was also involved in the search.

---

1. Mengele was the sadistic doctor who decreed who would live and who would die in Auschwitz. He also conducted brutal medical experiments on Jewish inmates in the name of "science." His grave would be discovered in Paraguay in the 1980s, although some still refuse to accept the identification of the remains as positive.

2. Hitler's personal assistant, Bormann disappeared immediately after the war. Neither he nor his remains have yet been found.

In the spring of 1960, Israeli agents traced Adolf Eichmann to Argentina, where he was living with his family. They abducted him on a Buenos Aires street and flew him to Israel to stand trial for his crimes. Argentina protested vociferously against the "illegal" kidnapping, and brought the matter to the U.N. for consideration. However, world opinion in this case was on the side of Israel, and the matter was amicably settled between Argentina and Israel.[3]

The Jewish world and a great deal of the non-Jewish world would be preoccupied by the Eichmann trial for the next two years. All of the horror of the Holocaust was relived. Witnesses collapsed, demonstrators battled to quicken the pace of justice, and the civilized world was again appalled at the description of the greatest crime in the history of man. A distinguished German jurist, Dr. Robert Servatius, led the Eichmann defense team, while the Israeli prosecutor was Gideon Hausner.[4]

The trial was a shattering catharsis for the Jewish people. It also served to convince many that "it" could happen again. The Eichmann trial fostered within world Jewry a renewal of tension and fear as to the relationship of Jews to the civilized non-Jewish world. The unanswered question — "How could it have occurred?" — brought to Jewry a foreboding that it could occur again. Spawned by the Eichmann trial, Jewish groups and organizations, formed in the 1960s and 1970s, were increasingly militant and even violent in their attempt to show the world "never again!" But it was all bravado. Only those who know that it can happen again need shout, "Never again!"

Adolf Eichmann died on the gallows of an Israeli prison on May 31, 1962. He went to his death calmly, "believing in Nature rather than God." Mounting the scaffold he gave his blessing to Germany, his native Austria, and Argentina. His body was cremated and on June 1 "his ashes were carried three miles offshore by a police cutter and thrown into the sea."[5]

The trial had an effect on Germany itself. The truth was finally out. "So it was from Jerusalem that the Germans were reminded that all

3. The masterful diplomatic communique stated in part ". . . [Argentina and Israel] have decided to regard as closed the incident that arose out of the action taken by Israel nationals that infringed fundamental rights of the State of Argentina." Thus, Israel acknowledged its "guilt" and Argentina, in return, dropped its charges.

4. Hausner's book, *Justice in Jerusalem*, New York 1966, is the best record of the trial proceedings. It is also an excellent description of the events of the Holocaust itself.

5. Ben Gurion, *Israel: A Personal History*, p. 603.

branches of their authorities, including the army, had played an active part in their crimes . . . The emerging facts are not confined to a new assessment of the past, but strongly penetrate into our present."[6] Perhaps the best judgment on the Eichmann trial was written by Martha Gellhorn in *The Atlantic,* February 1962. She said:

> No one who tries to understand our times, now or in the future, can overlook this documentation of a way of life and death which will stain our century forever. No one will see the complete dimensions of twentieth-century man — and that includes all of us, I insist — without studying the Eichmann trial.

Arab Extremism

EANWHILE, IN 1961 AND 1962, Syria, which was the most implacable of all of Israel's enemies, pursued a policy of keeping the northern borders of Israel "hot." Settlements on the Kinneret were shelled and Jews were killed and maimed.[7] Israel finally retaliated and a Syrian military position was demolished in November 1960. The Syrians brought the matter to the U.N. Security Council where, with its typical "even-handed approach," the Council censured Israel. This set the pattern for all later U.N. resolutions in the 1960s. Thereafter, Israel chose to ignore U.N. resolutions and became even more convinced that it could not rely on the good will of the world for its preservation.

In 1960, Israel announced the operation of its first nuclear reactor. Since then, it has steadfastly maintained that it did not possess nor manufacture nuclear weapons. But the existence of the possibility of nuclear weapons in the Middle East made a volatile military situation even more unstable. Syria and Iraq, the more militant Arab states, goaded Nasser and King Hussein into a more aggressive stand against Israel.

In Arab politics and rivalries, extremism towards Israel was always a litmus test issue, and only in confronting Israel could a true Arab

---

6. Hausner, p. 467.

7. Syria also attempted to divert the headwaters of the Jordan River so that Israel would be deprived of the river's irrigation and power capacity. Israeli air power and artillery responded strongly to this insidious threat and aborted the project.

leader prove himself valorous and charismatic. Thus, as the Arab countries underwent political and economic turmoil in the 1960s and as Russia's penetration into Egypt and its army intensified, it became more evident that Israel would again be faced with the bleak prospect of war. But even though the Israeli military planners prepared their strategies for war, the politicians and the country in general were preoccupied with lesser matters.

In 1963, David Ben Gurion resigned as prime minister for "personal" reasons.[8] The bitter split in the Labor party over the "Lavon affair," the problems of religion in the state, and age and its infirmities began to take a toll on Ben Gurion. His silly experiment with Buddhism, his petty and vitriolic personal vendettas with old colleagues, his ever more dictatorial style of governing — all served to dim the luster of the grand old man of Israeli politics.

Ben Gurion eventually retired[9] to Sde Boker, a small kibbutz in the Negev desert, where he would live out his life. He was succeeded as prime minister by Levi Eshkol, a Yiddish-speaking technocrat and a veteran Labor Zionist. Eshkol's government would be efficient but uninspiring, and — as originally constituted — would eventually prove incapable of facing the challenge of renewed Arab belligerency.

Church's Attitude Towards Israel

 HE EARLY 1960s BROUGHT a temporary softening of the attitude of the Vatican towards Jews, Judaism, and the State of Israel. After the death in 1958 of Pius XII — the wartime pope whose passive stance against Hitler and Mussolini, and whose silence in the face of the Holocaust added little honor to the Church — a new pope, John XXIII, was elected. John was one of the few important churchmen who had worked to save Jewish

8. Ben Gurion would yet help found another splinter Labor party called Rafi, led by him and Moshe Dayan. Eventually Rafi rejoined the Labor party and it, together with Mapai, Mapam, and Achduth Avodah, became the Labor party of the 1970s and 80s.

9. Before his resignation, Ben Gurion made a very prescient comment about the Arabs living in Israel, which would prove just as accurate regarding the Arabs who later would be under Israeli control in the West Bank. Ben Gurion stated: "Many members of the [Arab] minority here do not look upon themselves as a minority but

lives during the war. He unexpectedly attempted to reform the Church's teachings on many matters, including the accusation of deicide against the Jews in the crucifixion of Jesus, and the use of pejorative words, such as "perfidious Jews," against Jews and Judaism in the liturgy of the mass.

The Vatican Council that he convened did make adjustments toward that end in the liturgy, and many Jews hoped that basic attitudes of the Church toward Jewry had finally changed.[10] However, after the death of John XXIII in 1963, his successor, Paul VI, arrested the process of Church liberalization, though he convened a second Vatican Council which confirmed much of the work of John's first Vatican Council. But upon his visit to Israel and Jordan[11] in 1966, Paul took a very strong anti-Israel stand on such matters as Arab refugees, Jerusalem, and the inherent right of the Jewish state to exist. Thus, Jews still questioned the Church on the moral issue of its commitment to Jewish survival. What had been John's era of hope became Paul's reversion to traditional Vatican antagonism to Jews.

Again, Gideon Hausner summed up the matter clearly:

> The Church acts very slowly, through its century-old [sic] channels, but there is positive evidence that the revelations of the Jerusalem [Eichmann] trial have had a deep impact on its liberal elements which are resolved to withdraw the ancient, terrible and false accusation of deicide against Jewry. At the Ecumenical Council held in the Vatican in 1964-1965 some steps were taken in this direction . . . Only the future can tell whether these steps will ever be carried to their logical conclusion. It is a

---

rather consider us a minority — a foreign usurping minority. This is the difference between the Arab minority here and minorities elsewhere. In our case the facts make it possible to think it is not the minority but the majority who constitute a minority, since the minority is surrounded by tens of millions of its fellow countrymen beyond the borders." Quoted by O'Brien, *The Siege*, p. 422.

10. Jewish reaction was very divided on the Vatican Council. The Orthodox, in the main, ignored the entire process, while the leaders of the Reform and Conservative movements traveled to Rome with alacrity and participated in the sessions to the extent that the Church allowed.

11. One of the ironic factors in the visit of the pope to Jordan and Israel was the allocation of a large sum of money by the United States to Jordan for the construction of a modern, proper road leading from Jerusalem to Nablus (then controlled by Jordan) in order to facilitate the pope's travel to Jerusalem. This road proved vital to the Israeli tanks in the 1967 Six-Day War and helped seal the doom of the Jordanian Arab Legion on the West Bank. Just as one does not always realize for whom the bell tolls, it is not always obvious for whom the road winds.

historic test for the Church itself. Actually, it is Christianity which needs exoneration.[12]

War Erupts Once Again

I N MAY 1967, FOR REASONS best known to itself, Russia informed Egypt and Syria, falsely and maliciously, that it had learned of a forthcoming Israeli attack. The Arabs began to mobilize and, worse, to make bellicose speeches. Their rhetoric of violence would again prove to be self-fulfilling, for the respective leaders of their countries had now to implement their bellicosity with deeds. The barrage of martial rhetoric ignited a volatile mix of internal Arab feuds and hatred of the Jews, and culminated in an Egyptian demand that the U.N. peace-keeping forces in the Sinai be withdrawn. The then Secretary-General of the UN, U Thant, surprised even Egyptian President Nasser by agreeing to his preposterous demand.

On May 23, Nasser announced that he was closing the Gulf of Eilat to Israeli shipping. President Lyndon Johnson had pledged that the U.S. would honor its old commitment to keep the high seas open, but it was an empty promise. No American ships steamed to Eilat, and Israel was isolated. King Hussein of Jordan flew to Cairo and signed a military pact with his erstwhile arch-enemy, Nasser. Finally, on May 28 Nasser announced his goal: "We intend to open a general assault against Israel. This will be total war. Our basic aim is the destruction of Israel."[13]

Israel mobilized its civilian army while the U.N. and the democratic world equivocated. Presidents Johnson and DeGaulle,[14] Prime Minister Wilson of England and other world leaders all urged restraint and — shades of the betrayal of Czechoslovakia at Munich in 1938 — urged Israel to consider territorial concessions to the Arabs. The Arabs and Russia chortled in delight at their easy diplomatic victory, while the mobs in the streets of Cairo, Damascus, East Jerusalem, and Amman demonstrated for the death of the Jews.

---

12. Hausner, p. 450.

13. General S.L.A. Marshall, *Swift Sword*, New York 1967, p. 19.

14. He would never forgive Israel for ignoring his advice to avoid a pre-emptive strike.

The desert littered with Egyptian vehicles

In a radio speech to his people, Prime Minister Levi Eshkol mumbled, lost his place while reading the speech, and, in general, did little to inspire confidence. A groundswell of public opinion in Israel demanded a government of national unity to replace the then ruling coalition. Menachem Begin was recalled from political oblivion and made a Minister Without Portfolio, and Moshe Dayan became the Defense Minister.

On Monday morning, June 5th, 1967, the Six-Day War began. Israel had decided not to wait passively for its destruction but to strike first, hard and effectively. In an unprecedented strategic air strike, the Israel Air Force destroyed the Arab air forces in the first four hours of the war. Most of the Arab planes were caught on the ground at their bases in Egypt, Syria, Iraq, and Jordan. Israel destroyed 452 planes that morning, with a loss of nineteen of its own.

The Israeli tank corps then crossed into the Sinai to engage the massed Egyptian army. Lacking any effective air cover, the Egyptians were doomed by the thrust of the armed fist of the Israeli army and air force. The Israeli strategy was to knock out Egypt first. Fighting with innovative tactics, the Israeli army destroyed the Egyptian forces in the Sinai and were astride the eastern bank of the Suez Canal by late Thursday, June 8. Egyptian stragglers struggled over the sands of the Sinai that entire week. Nasser's bluff had been called and his aggression frustrated.

The Western Wall Reclaimed

WHILE NASSER WAS WELL aware at the beginning of the war that his air force had been destroyed and that this negated any chance of victory, he purposely misled his Syrian and Jordanian allies with false claims of triumph and boasts that his bombers had left Tel Aviv and Haifa in flames. King Hussein of Jordan imprudently entered the fray by ordering Jordanian troops to occupy U.N. headquarters, which was located in a south Jerusalem's no-man's land marking the 1948 truce lines between the belligerents.

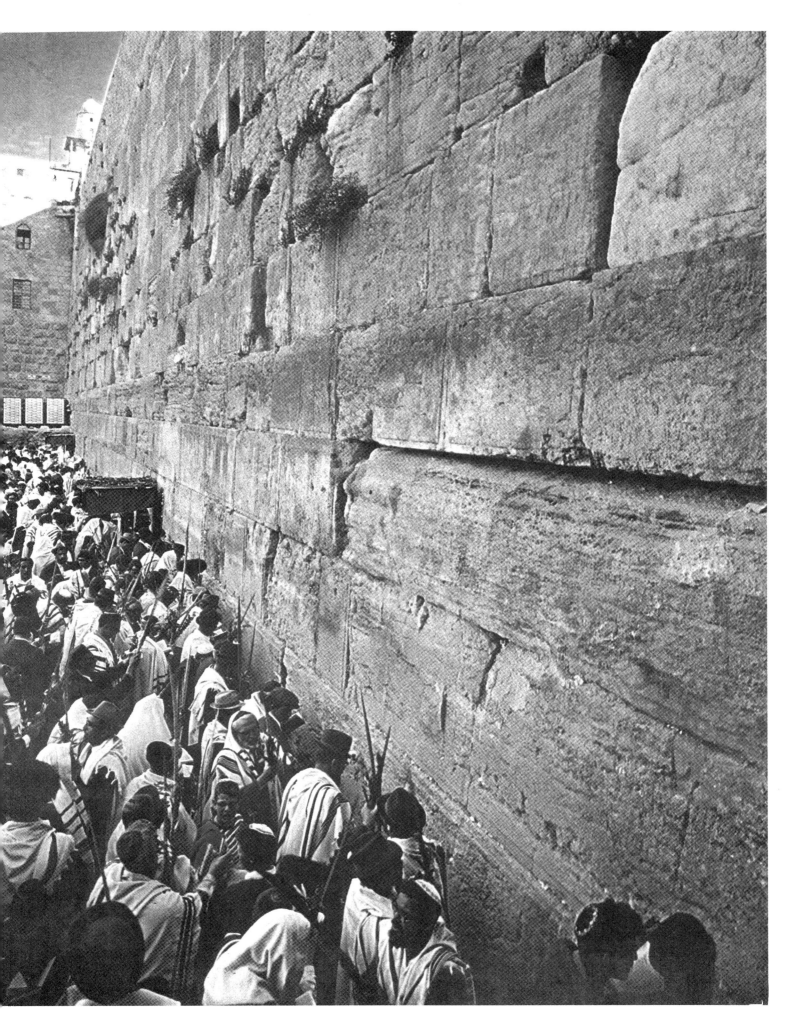

Soldier praying at the Western Wall after its capture

Israel had sent Jordan a message early in the day that it would take no action on the Jordanian front if the Jordanians did not attack, but Hussein could not restrain himself. Misled by Nasser's claims of victory, Hussein seized what he thought was a golden opportunity to occupy all of Jerusalem. Jordanian artillery shelled Jewish Jerusalem indiscriminately. But he had miscalculated badly. The Israeli army moved against Jordanian positions in East Jerusalem and the rest of the West Bank, and within three days had severely punished the Jordanian army, pushing it out of pre-war Palestine, east of the Jordan river. The Gaza Strip, Jenin, Tulkarm, Nablus, Bethlehem, Hebron, and all of the West Bank now came under Israeli control. And most importantly, the Old City of Jerusalem, with its sacred Western Wall, returned to Jewish hands.

Israeli gunner returns to Hebron

The moment of the recapture of Jerusalem was an electric one throughout the Jewish world. The Wall seemed to shed tears of joy together with the Jewish soldiers who stood before it in awe and reverence. It was not only a historic moment — it was a moment of faith and religious experience, even for hardened secularists. It was perceived as a vindication of the Jewish historic experience and had a profound effect upon Jews everywhere. As soon as the military situation permitted, a steady stream of Jews filled the Old City's narrow alleyways, walking to the Wall, from which they had been barred since 1948, and countless Jews from the Diaspora flocked to Jerusalem that summer and fall.

The war was not yet over. On Friday and Saturday, June 9 and 10, the Israeli army smashed their Syrian tormentors and drove them from the Golan Heights. The ferocious onslaughts of the Israelis broke through the well-entrenched, Soviet-designed, mine-infested Syrian defense lines, and the road to Damascus was open. But as soon as the Arab rout became obvious, the U.N. Security Council rushed in to limit the Israeli victory. The Security Council voted a cease-fire to which the Arabs grudgingly agreed, and Israel had no choice but to observe it as well. Israel had suffered over 700 dead and more than twice that many wounded, but the halo of victory blinded the pain of loss.

The week that began in despair for the Jewish world ended in exhilaration and triumph. The specter of a second Holocaust in the twentieth century had temporarily disappeared and Israel had gained international respect as a mini-superpower. Its army's exploits were often described as miraculous.[15] Tens of thousands of Arabs now fled the West Bank to the squalor of the refugee camps of Lebanon and Jordan. Russia again broke diplomatic ties with Israel and was followed in this policy by the other communist countries, with the exception of Rumania.

Hope for Peace In Vain

HE VICTORY HAD ENGENDERED a dangerous euphoria in the Jewish world and especially in Israel, a euphoria that the cold reality of the harsh world would soon dispel. Israel naively believed that the Arabs would now come to their senses and make peace. Moshe Dayan said that he was waiting for Hussein's phone call. The telephone never rang. Meeting that fall of 1967 in Khartoum, the Arabs developed their response to Israel in the formulation of the three "nos": no peace, no war, no negotiation.

At that time, Israel undoubtedly would have been prepared to return the West Bank to Jordan — with minor border corrections, and with Jerusalem remaining a united city under Israeli administration — but no one on the Arab side was willing to talk to Israel. Thus Israel took the fateful step of integrating the West Bank into Israel. This step, which circumstances forced upon Israel, would have far-reaching consequences, as yet unseen in 1967.

A shadow organization created by Egyptian propaganda offices and named the Palestine Liberation Organization (PLO) had come into being in the 1960s. Its first head was a charlatan by the name of Ahmed Shukeiry, who made a great deal of noise before the Six-Day War and disappeared from sight immediately thereafter. Its new leader after the war was Yassir Arafat, a shadowy figure, wily, cunning, and clever, and he carved out a new role for this group: that of sponsoring a local war of liberation. Arafat recruited young Arabs for the uprising throughout Gaza and the West Bank.[16]

The Israeli army and police fought a clandestine war against this

15. "[The army soldiers] told one another that superior shooting accounted for the smash victory. But as did their [civilian] neighbors, they also spoke of the miracle. Many things about the way they did it transcended technical explanation and mortal understanding." Marshall, p. 131

16. See O'Brien, p. 449.

PLO uprising and by 1972 had gained the upper hand, driving the PLO from the West Bank and into the neighboring Arab countries. Simultaneously, Israel found itself engaged in a new war with Egypt[17] — a war of attrition. Bombs and shells fell across the Suez Canal on a daily basis and the Israeli newspapers published pictures of their young fallen soldiers on a sickeningly regular basis. The Israeli Air Force exacted a gruesome price from the Egyptian forces west of the canal. Israel estimated that over 10,000 Egyptian soldiers died in this undeclared war of attrition, until it finally ended in 1970, through American diplomatic intervention.

The PLO and the Arabs introduced a new wrinkle in their war against Israel. They had always employed terror against civilians, but now airplane hijacking, indiscriminate airport shooting massacres, and hostage taking became the staple tools of the PLO terror worldwide. Israel refused to capitulate to or negotiate with the terrorists, and developed highly sophisticated defensive methods to counteract this new type of evil. But Nasser, the PLO, and the Arabs continued to exhibit their talent for somehow achieving diplomatic progress in spite of military defeats.

Israel had made the public relations mistake of winning the war, and thereby it forfeited world sympathy reserved for the victim. The former Jewish David had become the Goliath; the aggressive and violent Arabs somehow transformed themselves into the underdog, the persecuted party. DeGaulle publicly castigated Israel in sophisticated anti-Semitic tones. Israel was now almost wholly dependent on the United States for diplomatic support, Security Council vetoes, and modern weapons. It was an uncomfortable position for the Jewish state, but most Jews were simply grateful there still *was* a Jewish state.

The harrowing experience of the Six-Day War was a further scar on the psyche of twentieth-century Jewry. The war, its origins and results, was yet another watershed in modern Jewish history, and the resulting strains, confusion, messianic hopes and paranoiac fears that it engendered were to be the stuff of Jewish life for the foreseeable future.

---

17. Russia had rearmed Egypt fully within six months of its defeat in the Six-Day War.

39

The Changing Face of Jewry

Orthodox Resurgence Continues

HE EICHMANN TRIAL AND THE Six-Day War combined to increase Jewish consciousness in the 1960s. Many Jews who had been neutral and passive towards Israel, the Jewish people, and Jewish tradition, began to reexamine their position and lifestyle. A search for a meaningful life, for roots and stability, and for an understanding of Jewish heritage, as well as growing disillusion with Western secular life, caused a steady — though not yet large — stream of assimilated young Jews to return to Jewish life, observance, and study. This phenomenon, called the "*Baal-Teshu-vah* movement,"[1] born in the 1960s, would be a major factor in Jewish life for the next few decades. It heartened traditional Jewry, injected new blood and talent into the ranks of the religious community, and frightened secular Jewry.

The secular Jewish organizations, from the government of the State of Israel itself to the liberal left-leaning Jewish labor and peace parties, maligned the movement and the individual *baal-teshuvah*. They identified the trend of return to Jewish life and observance as cultist, bizarre, and a temporary aberration. Their odious comparison of the *baal-teshuvah* to the cultist followers of maharishis and gurus or hippies only served to harden the resolve of traditional Jewry not to make any further accommodations to the agenda of secular Jewry.

Both in Israel and the Diaspora, Orthodoxy became more aggressive in asserting the primacy of tradition in Jewish life and in bitterly opposing the programs and goals of Reform and secular Jewry.

---

1. The Hebrew term describing one who has "returned" to the traditional observances of Jewish life.

The secular Jewish world in America and Israel, accustomed to the Orthodox cooperation and subservience of the 1930s, was slow to react to the new circumstances. A wide, but previously unpublicized, rift in Jewish life was now becoming wider and more public. Secular Jewry was impatient and frustrated with Orthodox Jewry. The predictions of Orthodoxy's imminent demise, or at least its "modernization" and acceptance of the secular values of general society, had been proven false. Even though the hemorrhage of assimilation and intermarriage in the 1960s and 1970s continued unabated, the major casualties now were the Conservative and Reform movements.

From the 1960s onwards, Orthodoxy not only held its own in terms of numbers of adherents, but was able to enhance the quality of Jewish commitment and observance in daily and public life, both in Israel and the United States. The chassidic movement continued to grow. The yeshivos, again both in Israel and in the United States, continued to increase their enrollments and to expand their influence. The *kollel*,[2] once derided as an aberration and not even

---

2. A "graduate school" of Talmudic studies, providing stipends for married young men, allowing them to continue their intensive Torah studies after their marriage. In 1985 there were approximately 1500 such students in the United States and 4000 in Israel.

Shmuel Yosef Agnon, Orthodox writer and author, receives the Nobel Prize for Literature in 1966

introduced in the U.S. until the 1940s, became an accepted part of Orthodox Jewish life.

The new and continuing resurgence in Orthodox life was based on a deeper level of observance of ritual and commitment of spirit. Consequently, as previously noted, Orthodoxy moved towards a more demanding pose. The first generation of post-war day school and yeshivah graduates was no longer meek, nor satisfied with minimal goals and observance.

Such modern Orthodox organizations as Young Israel, Yeshiva University, Hebrew Theological College, and the Union of Orthodox Jewish Congregations of America came under increasing pressure from a new and more militant Orthodox world to disassociate themselves from Jewish religious "umbrella" organizations and from accommodations that lent recognition to Reform and Conservative Jewry as legitimate expressions of the Jewish religion. The Mizrachi party[3] — which in the 1930s, 40s and 50s was the leading group in numbers and power in Orthodox Jewry — continued its precipitous slide in popularity and influence. By the 1980s, Agudath Israel had replaced it as the mainstream Orthodox group in America, while in the Israeli elections of 1988, the combination of Shas,[4] Degel HaTorah[5] and Agudath Israel far outpolled the National Religious Party (Mizrachi).

Success Breeds Imitators

THIS NEW ORTHODOXY WAS PAID the ultimate compliment by its erstwhile detractors, the Conservative and Reform movements — the compliment of imitation. The Conservative movement established its own day school movement,[6] mainly limited to the elementary school level, and gained thousands of students. Even the Reform movement created pilot day

---

3. Religious Zionists of America in the United States, and the National Religious Party in Israel.

4. A Sephardic religious party, founded by Rabbi Eliezer Shach, the *rosh yeshivah* of Ponivezh, Bnei Brak, and Rabbi Ovadiah Yosef, the former Sephardic Chief Rabbi of Israel.

5. An Ashkenazic religious party also founded by Rabbi Shach.

6. Called Solomon Schechter Schools.

schools, though most Reform families continued to send their children to secular public and private schools.

However, the Conservative movement embarked on a new and far-reaching course of change. New "rabbinical courts" were established to issue *gittin*,[7] which were unacceptable according to the traditional standards of *Halachah*. Conversions to Judaism were performed, again without the necessary prerequisites of *Halachah*.[8] Women rabbis and cantors became acceptable, as did the inclusion of women in a *minyan*[9] and their being called to the Torah.

Thus Conservatism, which was founded as a movement that claimed to attempt to conserve the halachic process, moved closer to Reform in spirit and practice. These innovations caused a split in the Conservative movement itself, with a sizable minority of rabbis and synagogues dissenting from these new departures. Not to be outdone by their Conservative competitors in innovation, Reform made a catastrophic departure from Jewish tradition by discarding the rule of matriarchal descent in determining who is a Jew. These new policies of Reform and Conservative movements further divided the Jewish people and prevented any common religious effort in Jewish life.

Religious Revolution in Russia

THE 1960s ALSO MARKED the emergence on the Jewish scene of the problem of Russian Jewry. In 1959, the Soviet census listed 2,267,814 of its citizens as being Jewish. However, it is clear that the census under-counted the Jewish population, which in reality was approximately 3,500,000.[10] These Jews had lived under atheistic, anti-Semitic Communism for over four decades. They were deprived of all opportunities to observe their rituals, study their heritage, and know their history and destiny. The situation of Russian Jewry in the 1960s was summed up succinctly by an eyewitness:

---

7. Jewish divorces.

8. These were contributing factors in the later "Who is a Jew?" controversy of the late 1980s.

9. The quorum of Jewish males necessary for public prayer.

10. Ben Ami, *Between Hammer and Sickle*, (Philadelphia 1967), p. 107.

The big stick wielded by the regime against the Jewish religion takes many forms. Jews are forbidden to organize; they cannot maintain a line of continuity for religious leadership (training of rabbis); synagogues are shut down gradually but relentlessly, and those still open are defamed; the government also tries to interfere with, or prevent the observance of the fundamental religious practices of Judaism.[11]

Circumcision, the Sabbath, Jewish calendars and prayer books all were non-existent in Russia, except in tiny and dwindling pockets of underground loyalty to tradition. The situation was desperate and it seemed inevitable that this ancient, honorable, and noble branch of the Jewish people would disappear. That certainly was the conventional wisdom of the Jewish "experts," both inside and outside the Soviet Union. An old Jew wrote an "obituary of the Jews of the Soviet Union," saying among other things:

> We suffer from an incurable disease which no doctor and no medicine will help. We do not agonize day by day, but from one hour to the next. We are lost forever. We do not have anyone to say *Kaddish* [prayer over the dead]. There is no one to set a tombstone over us and no sign of us will be left. We will be lost like the shadow of a passing bird and like a stone that is hurled into the abyss . . . I would have wanted to say *Kaddish* for myself and for my generations; in the last moments of my life to say my

Golda Meir, Israel's ambassador to the Soviet Union, in Moscow in 1948

11. Ibid., p. 52.

confession from the depths of my heart; to pronounce the *Yizkor* [memorial service] and the last *Kel Moleh Rachamim* [a memorial prayer], and leave a will. But, alas, there is no one to read my will and it would be a useless effort. The Messiah will not come to the Jews of our generation in Russia. And if he should, he would be too late. He will come when there is no one left to save from the darkness of our exile . . .[12]

But this pessimism was unwarranted. If there is anything to be learned from Jewish history, it is that no one should ever despair of the survival of the Jewish people. There existed within Russian Jewry the unquenchable Jewish spark of eternity. When Golda Meir, the first Israeli ambassador to Moscow, arrived in 1948 to present her credentials at the Kremlin, she was mobbed by thousands of Jews who came to express their Jewish "solidarity with the hopes of the people of Israel." Through all of the twists and turns of Russian anti-Israel diplomacy and policy, the masses of Russian Jewry remained loyal, if silent,[13] supporters of the Jewish state.

Russian Jews clandestinely began to study Hebrew and Torah. A *Baal-Teshuvah* movement arose in Russia itself. Jews gathered by the thousands in front of the main synagogue in Moscow annually on Simchas Torah to identify themselves with the Jewish people and its Torah. In the 1960s and for the next two decades, new names were entered on the rolls of Jewish heroism — Joseph Mendelevitch, Natan Scharansky, Eliyahu Essas, and Yosef Begun, among others — and world Jewry responded to the plight of their brothers.

---

12. Ibid., pp. 276-7.

13. Eli Wiesel's book on Russian Jewry is aptly titled *"The Jews of Silence."*

Ilya (Eliyahu) Essas, now in Israel, teaching two young men in Moscow, Aryeh Katzin (left) and Michael Karaivanov

Haunted by their inaction during the destruction of European Jewry in World War II, American Jewry organized itself on behalf of its Russian brothers. Soviet Jewry became a matter of negotiations between the governments of the United States and Russia. Economic and diplomatic pressure was exerted against Russia in an unprecedented fashion to force it to permit Jewish emigration.

In the 1960s there was slow but steady emigration of Jews from Russia, mainly to Israel. At first, the immigrants were motivated by strong Jewish feelings and a desire to live in the Land of Israel, but as time went on, the Jews of Russia yearned more for the opportunity and comfort of America. In the 1970s, more than 250,000 Jews left Russia, with almost 65% of them settling in America and the balance in Israel. However, the increase in emigration was coupled with a more virulent anti-Jewish, and especially anti-Israel, campaign in Russia. Show trials, shameful emigration procedures, the exclusion of Jews from the professions and academia — all were part of the intensified Russian anti-Jewish program.

> In 1966 Jews accounted for 7.8 per cent of academics, 14.7 per cent of doctors, 8.5 per cent of writers and journalists, 10.4 per cent of judges and lawyers and 7.7 per cent of actors, musicians and artists. But in every case the percentage was being pushed down by party and bureaucratic action. Thus Jews provided 18 per cent of Soviet scientific workers in 1947, only seven per cent by 1970 . . . The number of Jewish students [in Russian universities] declined in absolute terms, from 110,900 in 1968-9 to 66,000 in 1975-6, and still more heavily relative to the population as a whole. In 1977-8 not a single Jew was admitted to the Moscow University.[14]

The attempt to help Russian Jewry was augmented by continuing personal visits to Russia by leading rabbis, scholars, and educated laymen. Coming mainly from the United States, England, and Israel, these Jews helped train a cadre of Russian teachers and activists who disseminated Judaism and Torah — albeit on a small scale — to other Russian Jews. Jewish prayer books, Bibles, and scholarly Torah works also began to arrive in Russia, though Soviet Customs confiscated them at sporadic intervals. Matzoh for Passover, *esrogim* for Succos, and other religious items also were shipped to Russia in greatly increasing numbers.

---

14. Johnson, *A History of the Jews*, p. 571.

The Soviet Union grudgingly allowed this "interference in their internal affairs," mainly under pressure from the American government. But the viciously anti-Semitic government propaganda intensified.

Trofim Krychko, a notorious Jew-hater, published in 1968 a poisonous diatribe, *Judaism and Zionism,* which was distributed widely in Russia. In it he reiterated all of the calumnies of the ancient Czarist anti-Jewish lies, and began for the first time the insidious Judaism = Zionism = racism equation that eventually was adopted by the U.N. in 1975, when it passed its notorious resolution equating Zionism with racism. The Russians and Arabs introduced Zionism as the acceptable code word to identify and vilify Jews, and to make open, arrogant anti-Semitism legitimate fare in the civilized world. Russia also escalated the shipment of arms and the sending of military advisers to Egypt and Syria, and did all in its power to cancel the security and military supremacy that flowed to Israel from its sweeping victory in the Six-Day War.

Breakdown of Basic Values

 ENERAL WESTERN SOCIETY, especially in the United States, underwent a radical change in the 1960s, signaled by the election in 1960 of President John F. Kennedy, the first President born in the twentieth century. Bringing to the office a vigor and a vision of sweeping change and progress, Kennedy was a catalyst for many of the forces that had been simmering beneath the placid surface of American life for decades.

Powerful forces for social change were about to be unleashed. Underlying them was a rebellion against the class and political order upon which American life had been based for decades. The immediate provocations for this drive for change were two national crises that were popularly viewed as requiring radical change. The first was the fight for minority civil rights and the second, later in the decade, was the Vietnam War. The results caused major turmoil in American life, affecting all elements of society, including Jews.

For a century after the Emancipation Proclamation freed the slaves, the black citizens of America accommodated themselves to the "separate but equal" policy that had kept them segregated and bereft of hope of any major social and economic improvement. In the early 1960s, the civil rights movement in the United States, led by Dr. Martin

Luther King, forced America to remove all legal protection for racial segregation. The Jewish community in America was in the forefront of the civil rights movement, and Jews were beaten and killed in the struggle.

Jews had traditionally fought for equality for blacks and were important supporters of the successful attempt to enforce equality of opportunity. However, this positive accomplishment began to turn sour in the very decade of its achievement. Understandably, "morally justified" violation of the law in the cause of civil rights spilled over into other areas of life. Once they lose their sanctity, respect for tradition and obedience to the law are hard to restore.

The assassinations of John and Robert Kennedy and Dr. King, together with the attendant riots, ghetto burnings, lawlessness and rage, triggered a new type of American society, one which eventually influenced the entire world. Permissiveness and violence became the new hallmarks of Western civilization.[15] Sexual promiscuity became open and accepted. Basic values of society were torn down and radicalism became chic.

All of this was intensified by the escalation of U.S. involvement in the Vietnam War, which resulted in a passionate protest movement against the war. Student protests turned violent, outrageous public behavior became common, and the fabric of general society unraveled. The new America also spawned numbers of non-Jews — and even leftist Jews — both blacks and whites, who virulently attacked Jews, Judaism, and Israel, all under the guise of anti-racism/Zionism. By the end of the decade, tensions between blacks and Jews were apparent in many major urban areas. The new radicalism, too, contained many Jewish figures as leaders, and thus Jews were thrust in the limelight of public controversy.

Against this backdrop, a growing section of American Jewry began to turn more conservative. Famous secular Jewish intellectuals such as Irving Kristol, Norman Podhoretz, and others became neo-conservatives.[16] But the main swing away from liberal positions in American Jewry took place in the Orthodox camp, which was upset by the eroding moral values in American life. The new America was turning anti-religious,

---

15. See Paul Johnson, *Intellectuals* (New York, 1988). The chapter "The Flight of Reason" gives an insightful description of how permissiveness laced with violence became the symbol of the 60s.

16. Prof. Kristol, of New York University, and Podhoretz, editor of Commentary Magazine, were leaders of the neo-conservatives, many or most of them Jewish, who became disillusioned with the liberalism to which they had subscribed.

immoral, hedonistic, mobile, violent, and rebellious. All of these trends were disturbing to Orthodox Jewish life and inimical to traditional Jewish goals and lifestyle.

This new political attitude of Orthodoxy coincided with its own continuing intensification and self-confidence. The influence of the yeshivos and their heads continued to grow.

The main leaders of Orthodoxy in the yeshivah world after the death of Rabbi Aharon Kotler in 1962 were Rabbi Moshe Feinstein[17] and Rabbi Yaakov Kamenetzky.[18] Under their guidance the yeshivos continued to grow. The Satmar *Rav* suffered a crippling stroke, but he continued to be a commanding presence and his disciples grew in numbers and strength, as did many other chassidic movements. Their influence was felt even in the non-yeshivah circles of Orthodoxy. Higher standards of Torah knowledge and halachic observance became the norm in all sectors of Orthodoxy. Behavior acceptable in Orthodox circles in the 1920s and 1930s was no longer normative in the same circles in the 1960s. American Orthodoxy was coming of age and it would play an ever-increasing role in American Jewish life over the next decades.

Thus American Jewry was slowly becoming more polarized. The traditional became more traditional, while the secular became more assimilated. The yeshivos grew and prospered, but the intermarriage rate for American Jewry soared. Many assimilated Jews searched for a way to return to their heritage but many more dropped out of Jewry forever. Judaism was stronger in America than it had ever been (or ever imagined that it could be), but millions of American Jews were unaffiliated and estranged to their people and beliefs. Israel, Russia, America — these were the arenas of change in Jewish life. An ancient people was renewing itself again, all in the face of unremitting enmity and hostile environments.

---

17. See "The New Jewish World," footnote 6.

18. A graduate of Slobodka and the Kovner *Kollel,* he arrived in America in the 1930s. He served as a rabbi in Seattle and Toronto. In the 1940s he was invited to New York to become *rosh yeshivah* of Mesivta Torah Vodaath where he served for nearly thirty years. He "retired" to Monsey, New York, but was active until his last day (he died at the age of 95) in leading, advising and shaping American Jewish life. A sagacious, compassionate person, he was scholar, leader, counselor, and inspiration for hundreds of American Jewish leaders, lay and rabbinic. To know him was enough to give one a new understanding of human wisdom and empathy.

40

The Yom Kippur War

Sadat's Year of Decision

N SEPTEMBER 28, 1970, Gamal Abdel Nasser died and was succeeded by Anwar Sadat.[1] Nasser had mortgaged the Egyptian economy and military to Russian domination. He was ensnared by his own stubbornness and could not bring himself to make a reasonable offer of peace to Israel. The bitter and costly War of Attrition had forced Egypt to conclude a new cease-fire with Israel, but Nasser used the cover of the cease-fire to increase his war potential and to install a screen of anti-aircraft missiles over the Suez Canal.

After Nasser's death, Sadat searched for a way out of the grinding war situation. In February 1971, he made a dramatic proposal to break the impasse. This included Egyptian recognition of Israel, coupled with Israeli withdrawal from the Canal and later from Sinai. Israel countered with initial distrust and scorn.[2] Eventually, Israel did make a peace proposal to Egypt through the U.N., which approximated much of the later 1979 Camp David Israel-Egypt peace agreement.

In 1971, however, the negotiations floundered and Sadat made the fateful decision for war. He announced that 1971 was to be the "Year of Decision." Syria, Egypt's competitor for leadership of the Arabs, mocked this announcement and Israel ignored it. As 1971

1. A supporter of Germany in World War II, Sadat was an unlikely partner for peace with Israel when he first ascended to power. He was consistently underestimated by his contemporaries, both allies and enemies, during the early years of his administration.

2. Israeli Prime Minister Golda Meir, when questioned regarding Sadat's willingness to make peace, stated, "That will be the day. I don't believe it will happen." Chaim Herzog, *The War of Atonement* (New York 1975), p. 18.

passed, it appeared that Sadat was all bravado and bluff in the classic mold of many Arab leaders. But this assessment proved to be a fatal miscalculation.

Sadat had set three prerequisites for his mission to end the state of war with Israel. First, he had to wean Egypt from its military, diplomatic, and economic dependence on Russia and instead ally it with the United States, the only country that had sufficient leverage with Israel to force it to a settlement. Secondly, he had to restore Arab pride, for only then would it be safe for him to engage in peace negotiations with Israel.[3] Thirdly, he had to impress upon Israel that an uncomfortable and cold peace was preferable to a hot, bloody, albeit successful, war.

The true "Year of Decision" was 1972; that was when Sadat would begin the complicated process of accomplishing all three necessary conditions for the success of his long-range diplomatic goal of removing Egypt from the Israeli-Arab struggle. He expelled the Russian advisers from Egypt, but only after being certain that the latest Russian weaponry had been delivered to Egypt and installed effectively among the Egyptian forces. He concluded a secret pact with Haffez Al Assad, the Syrian dictator, to coordinate a surprise attack against Israel. Assad's hatred of Israel overcame his antipathy to Sadat.

Israel was able to read all of the warning signs regarding the impending attack. Intelligence reports and aerial reconnaissance indicated concerted military activity in Syria and Egypt. In August 1972, in a bitter aerial dogfight over the Golan Heights, the Israel Air Force shot down thirteen Syrian planes. Israel mobilized its army in late August, convinced that this would be enough to expose the Arab bluff and prevent war, and then demobilized these same forces shortly thereafter. The Israeli leadership was blind to the threat facing it.

Hubris, arrogance, overconfidence, and unpreparedness were the ingredients of the witch's brew of Israel's near-disaster. The Bar-Lev Defense Line on the Suez Canal was ill conceived, poorly maintained, and vastly undermanned. Fewer than sixty Israeli tanks on the Golan Heights facing Syria were battle ready on the morning of Yom Kippur 5734, October 6, 1973.[4] Convinced that the Arabs would not dare attack the Jewish state again, Israel's leaders ignored all of the aggressive movements that were clearly evident, and instead trusted

---

3. Poor Sadat — like other Arab leaders before him — would learn that it is apparently never safe for an Arab to make peace with Israel.

4. The war is known in Israel and the Western World as the Yom Kippur War, while the Arab world calls it The October War.

their vaunted intuition that Sadat was bluffing. It would now take more than 3,500 Jewish casualties to bring them to sober reality.

The Egyptian army included 800,000 battle-ready troops, 2,200 tanks, 2,300 artillery pieces, 150 anti-aircraft missile batteries and 550 modern war planes.[5] It was a strong and well-prepared army that had held maneuvers dozens of times to rehearse its well-planned attack against the Israeli line east of the Suez Canal. The Syrian army was also well trained and superbly equipped, its armament consisting of over 1,500 tanks, 1,000 artillery pieces, and 50,000 infantrymen massed on the Golan, with substantial reserves protecting the road to Damascus. To neutralize the Israel Air Force over the field of battle, Syria concentrated Russian-supplied missiles on the Damascus plateau.[6]

Israel Wins the Battle but . . .

T 2:00 P.M. ON YOM KIPPUR, 5734/1973, Egypt and Syria simultaneously attacked Israel. The Egyptian army easily established a foothold east of the Suez Canal and succeeded in breaching and capturing most of the Bar-Lev line on the canal. The Israelis scrambled to recover from their shocked surprise, and mobilize their forces. Men in their prayer shawls left their synagogues and mounted the trucks that brought them to their army bases. The prayers of the Holy Day assumed even more intense proportions as Israel realized that it was gravely hurt.[7]

The situation in the North was even more serious than in Sinai. In the Golan, Israel had little room to maneuver and limited ground to yield. Syrian forces were close to Tiberias and for a brief moment, even the road to Haifa was open. The heroism and sacrifice of the few Israeli defenders on the Golan somehow stemmed the Syrian rush until sufficient reinforcements arrived, on the third day of battle, to turn the struggle against Syria.[8]

---

5. Chaim Herzog, *The Arab-Israeli Wars* (New York, 1982), p. 239.

6. Ibid., p. 241.

7. When Moshe Dayan, the Minister of Defense, realized the gravity of the initial military situation, he told Prime Minister Golda Meir, "The Third Temple is falling!"

8. A young Israeli tanker, Tzvi'ka Gringold, miraculously put out of service an entire Syrian tank battalion all by himself! For a recounting of his exploits, see Herzog, *The War of Atonement*, pp. 84-92.

Even hardened secularists spoke of miracles as the only explanation for the ability of the outnumbered, unprepared Israeli forces to blunt the Syrian assault. Slowly, but then steadily, the Israelis pushed the Syrians back past the original attack lines, and finally formed a "box" well within Syrian territory. Israeli artillery advanced to within shooting range of Damascus. Israeli aircraft slowly regained mastery of the Syrian skies after their initial heavy losses. Now that the danger from Syria was diminished, Israel turned to Sinai and the Egyptian front.

Over the holiday of Succos, large tank battles took place in the Sinai. An apparent stalemate was developing on the Egyptian front. The Egyptian army could push no farther into the Sinai, nor could the Israelis dislodge them from their early gains. On October 15, in a brilliant military maneuver, under the command of General Ariel Sharon, a strong Israeli force broke through the Egyptian lines, splitting the seam between the Egyptian Second Army to the north and the Third Army to the south, and reached the Suez Canal.

On October 16, Israeli troops crossed the canal, fanned out on its western shore, and threatened the Egyptian Third Army with encirclement and disaster. The road to Cairo was now open, and the Israel

Soldier on leave from Sinai carrying lulav, hitchhiking home to celebrate the Succos holiday with his family

Air Force pounded the suddenly desperate Egyptians mercilessly. The military phase of the Yom Kippur War, which began with Israeli defeats, ended with Arab demoralization, flight, and death. However, the Arabs, and especially Sadat, had achieved the goal of breaking the status quo. Sadat had succeeded in restoring Arab pride by his early victories. And the Arabs were able to turn their later military defeat into a diplomatic and political victory.

The unpreparedness of Israel at the onset of the Yom Kippur War was most evident in the lack of ammunition and supplies for a war that would last longer than six days.

> The intensity of the war took the quartermaster staffs by surprise. The expenditure of ammunition was inordinately high, the losses of aircraft were serious, the figures of tanks destroyed were alarming. General Dayan was to make an ill-advised public admission that Israeli forces had run out of certain items of ammunition and that, but for American supplies, the country would have been in a very serious situation.[9]

Beginning on October 14th, a major resupply of military materiel to Israel by the United States took place. A continuing airlift was undertaken by United States and Israeli cargo planes, under the direct orders of President Richard Nixon.[10] This placed Israel directly in the debt of Nixon and his Secretary of State, Henry Kissinger,[11] and they immediately exploited this Israeli dependence.

Kissinger made a midnight flight to Moscow to forge a united stand with the U.S.S.R. As long as the Arabs were winning the war, the superpowers and the U.N. were silent, but as soon as Israel turned the tide, Russia and the United States forced a cease-fire resolution through the Security Council, and the fighting stopped, thus saving the Egyptian Third Army from the humiliation of defeat and surrender.

---

9. Ibid., p. 227.

10. Nixon's own administration was at that very time beginning to unravel. His vice-president, Spiro Agnew, resigned in the midst of the Yom Kippur War, accused of accepting bribes. The Republican Watergate scandal was surfacing. It was a time of terrible turmoil for Nixon and his leadership, and he felt that he needed a foreign policy victory to salvage his presidency.

11. A German-Jewish refugee, brilliant, egotistic, and widely regarded as devious. Claiming that he "would never harm the interests and security of Israel," he fit the latter-day pattern of Jews in power in non-Jewish societies, who claimed to help their brethren by being "evenhanded" in Jewish matters. This attitude inevitably proved inimical to Jewish interests. Kissinger's later marriage to a non-Jew was an emotional barrier and a source of estrangement with much of the American Jewish community and even Israeli leadership.

Over the next several months, Kissinger shuttled between Washington, Cairo, Damascus, and Jerusalem and achieved accord on "disengagement" compacts between Israel, Egypt, and Syria. The Arab countries received territorial concessions[12] in return for a commitment to fully observe the cease-fire and the exchange of Israeli prisoners of war.

But more than that, the Arabs achieved a stunning psychological victory and the momentum of world opinion now shifted strongly in their favor. Israel had been proven physically vulnerable and its enemies in the world, of whom there were many, rejoiced in its discomfiture. This change in world opinion had begun slowly after the Six-Day War, when Israel shed its image of a perpetually threatened underdog and began to be called a "mini-superpower." The creditable performance of the Arabs in the Yom Kippur War helped remove the contempt in which the Western world held them. Now traditional anti-Semitism took a stronger hold.

. . . Loses the War of World Opinion

HE ARAB OIL-PRODUCING COUNTRIES used the Yom Kippur War to triple the price of their oil on the world market. In solidarity with their demand for Israeli concessions and withdrawals, an Arab oil boycott of the United States and other Western countries was implemented. Long lines at gasoline stations, limited oil supplies, dimming of decorative lights in cities, plus the outbreak of a serious price inflation shocked complacent America. The fact that the Arabs — very active and anxious to limit any Israeli victory — were able to connect their price-and-supply extortion to the "Israel problem" also contributed to an erosion of public support for Israel.

Anti-Israel and anti-Jewish slogans appeared publicly and the Jewish community throughout the world squirmed uncomfortably. Anti-Semitic propaganda and distortions flooded the world, stemming mainly from Russian and Arab sources. The worst excesses of the lies of the Czar and Hitler were recirculated, and very little critical response countered its dissemination. It is sobering that there was more

---

12. Egypt received one-third of the Sinai, and Syria regained a sliver of land in the Golan as well as the city of Kuneitra.

resentment against Israel, the victim, than against the Arab countries, which actually imposed the boycott. Anti-Semitism is a hardy virus, eternally present, if sometimes dormant, in the non-Jewish world.

The worst travesties of fairness and justice were perpetrated by the U.N., the world organization allegedly committed to fairness and justice. Yassir Arafat, the head of the PLO, strode up to the General Assembly podium — wearing a gun! — to tumultuous applause. In 1975, Idi Amin, the butcher of Uganda, who had earlier applauded the acts of the Nazis in destroying European Jewry, was officially welcomed by the U.N. General Assembly. There he denounced the "Zionist-American conspiracy" and called for Israel's expulsion from the UN and its eventual extinction.[13] He received a standing ovation from most of the assembled diplomats.

In November 1975, the U.N. General Assembly passed the infamous resolution equating Zionism with racism.[14] Thus was anti-Semitism legitimized in the post-Auschwitz world. All of the horrible statements of the 1920s and 30s were now repeated to a new generation. Having survived the harrowing military experience of the Yom Kippur War, the Jewish people were now suffering through the agony of diplomatic isolation and almost universal condemnation for their crime of surviving the latest effort to destroy them.

The Arab governments, meeting at Rabat in October 1974, declared the Palestine Liberation Organization as the "sole legitimate representative of the Palestinian people." Flushed with this inter-Arab victory and savoring his triumph at the U.N., Arafat unleashed his murderous terrorists against Israel.[15] Airplanes were hijacked, little children murdered at a school in the Galilean town of Maalot, Israeli Olympic athletes were assassinated during the Munich Olympics of 1976, and Israeli diplomats and representatives were threatened and abused worldwide.

The PLO's terrorism became the new, accepted, condoned version of the age-old pogrom. Typical of the world's response was that of the International Olympic Committee to the cold-blooded murder of the

---

13. Johnson, *A History of the Jews*, pp. 578-579.

14. The Arabs and Russians mobilized the "Third World" countries and passed the resolution with only 35 countries voting against it.

15. But not exclusively against Israel. PLO terrorism and war against fellow Arabs was extensive and continuing. In 1975, the PLO was the main catalyst for the outbreak of civil war in Lebanon. This terrible, unending war destroyed the most prosperous and stable Arab country in the Middle East. More than any other series of events, the PLO's activities in Lebanon exposed it as a murderous, divisive, lawless group.

eleven Israeli athletes in 1972. The IOC refused to halt the games, even for a perfunctory minute of silence. Yet Israel fought back valiantly and, on the whole, effectively. The 1976 rescue operation of airplane hostages held by Arab terrorists and Idi Amin, at the Entebbe airport in Uganda, thrilled the world. Israel became the world leader in counter-terrorist activity and know-how. But the flow of Jewish blood was never completely staunched.

The Begin Era Begins

SRAEL CONDUCTED ELECTIONS in the wake of the Yom Kippur War. The new Knesset which met in January, 1974, had fifty-one Labor members, with thirty-nine Likud deputies, and fifteen representatives of the religious parties.[16] Golda Meir formed a government and remained as Prime Minister. But a few months later, when the commission conducting an inquiry into the conduct of the war issued a scathing indictment of her and Moshe Dayan for permitting Israel to be so woefully unprepared for the Arab attack, she resigned and was replaced by Yitzchak Rabin. At the end of 1976, domestic issues[17] and personal scandal brought down the Rabin government.[18]

The results of the ensuing 1977 election were startling. After winning only fifteen seats in the first Knesset and suffering through twenty-eight years in the political wilderness, Menachem Begin's Likud emerged as the largest party in Israel with 43 seats, while Labor dropped precipitously to 32 — an unprecedented loss of 19 seats. Likud combined with the religious parties to form the new government, and Begin, against all odds, had finally become the Prime Minister of Israel. Likud attracted to its list a vast number of Sephardic Jews who had previously voted Labor. It also held great popularity among religious Jewry.

Begin was a traditional Jew, who spoke in the religious accents of

16. National Religious Party (Mizrachi), ten, and Agudath Israel, five.

17. New planes were accepted from the USA into the Israel Air Force at a ceremony held so late on Friday afternoon as to guarantee desecration of the Sabbath. The NRP left the government in protest.

18. Rabin hid from the Israeli public his wife's illegal savings account in the amount of $23,000, held in a bank in Washington, DC.

Eastern European Jewry, and not with the secular voice of the Labor leaders, who had governed Israel for twenty-eight years of statehood, and, under the British, for nearly thirty years previously. Begin's upbringing was apparent in his opening words to the Knesset upon being installed as Prime Minister:

> We were granted our right to exist by the God of our fathers at the glimmer of the dawn of human civilization nearly four thousand years ago. For that right, which has been sanctified in Jewish blood from generation to generation, we have paid a price unexampled in the annals of the nations. Certainly, this fact does not diminish or enfeeble our right. To the contrary. Therefore, I reemphasize that we do not expect anyone to request on our behalf that our right to exist in the land of our fathers be recognized.[19]

Whereas the exile and the past were ignored by the secular socialist leaders who were determined that the "new" Israel would have no truck with the ancient faith of the Jews, to Begin the past was real, important, instructive, and intimately bound to the future of the State of Israel. His ascension to power worked a profound turning point in Israeli politics and life.

Camp David

 EGIN'S RISE TO POWER coincided with Jimmy Carter's election as President of the United States. Carter relentlessly pursued a settlement in the Middle East, but Anwar Sadat proved to be the key in bringing about that settlement. After successful secret negotiations, Sadat flew dramatically to Israel and presented the Egyptian case before the Israeli Knesset. Begin responded conciliatorily, but after two years of intensive and often acrimonious negotiations, little progress was achieved.

Finally, President Carter summoned Begin and Sadat to Camp David, the presidential retreat in Maryland. Free from media involvement and the glare of the spotlight, the three leaders engaged in marathon discussions, and finally concluded the Camp David agreement, making peace between Israel and Egypt. Egypt regained the entire Sinai, while Israel gained diplomatic recognition and a final peace

---

19. Eric Silver, *Begin: A Biography* (London, 1984).

treaty from its largest and most powerful adversary.[20] It was the first peace treaty between Israel and an Arab state.

For their efforts, Begin and Sadat were awarded the Nobel Prize for Peace. Unfortunately, Sadat was ostracized by his fellow Arab leaders for his boldness and practicality. He would eventually be assassinated, thus continuing the melancholy procession of slain Arab leaders who had attempted to make peace with the *Yishuv* and Israel.

All who witnessed Begin place a *yarmulka* on his head to recite the ancient Jewish blessing of good tidings hoped that somehow another fundamental change in Israel's life had occurred. Begin's gesture was symbolic of part of his political appeal. Though not a fully observant Jew, he recognized that the Jewish nation did not come into being with Herzl. His respect and sensitivity for Jewish tradition gained him the support of many who, nevertheless, held serious misgivings about some of his policies.

Though Begin would go on and win another election mandate, make war to drive the PLO out of Lebanon, bomb an Iraqi nuclear reactor, and attempt to strengthen Israel diplomatically, his finest hour was the signing of the Camp David Accord. The agreement with Egypt led only to cold peace, but a cold peace was certainly preferable to a

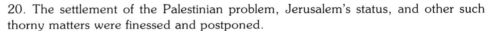

20. The settlement of the Palestinian problem, Jerusalem's status, and other such thorny matters were finessed and postponed.

Begin, Sadat, and President Carter shaking hands at Camp David

warm war. Even during the Israeli war in Lebanon in 1982, which Egypt vociferously opposed, Egypt kept to the letter of the treaty, if not to its spirit.

The fact that the Camp David agreement took hold and survived even in times of great stress proved to be of basic comfort to Israel. The 1970s was a most turbulent decade for Israel and world Jewry. War and peace, terror and rescue, change and continuity were the hallmarks of that decade. But the basic underlying problems[21] of Jewish life in the modern era were still unsolved.

---

21. Among them: external anti-Semitism, internal divisiveness, the struggle for the sustaining of Torah life and values, and the ravages of secular assimilation.

41
Towards Peace?

In the Shadow of Camp David

s mentioned in the previous chapter, the Camp David agreements brought Israel and the Jewish people a very cold peace indeed. Even though Egypt, in the main, lived up to its formal agreements, its heart was not in it, and a spirit of true peace and cooperation between Israel and Egypt was absent. There were many reasons for this indeterminate state of affairs, but the chief problems were that Egypt did not want to appear to have deserted its Palestinian brethren in making a separate peace with Israel, and that more than half a century of vicious anti-Jewish and anti-Zionist/Israel propaganda had poisoned Egyptian public opinion, so much so that true acceptance of Israel and Jews as peaceful equals proved impossible. The Jews, too, had their misgivings about the agreement. Israel gave up the lucrative and strategically valuable oil fields that it had developed in the Sinai desert. It also committed itself to evacuate the beautiful Jewish settlement of Yamit on the Sinai's Mediterranean coast, and forcibly evict its settlers. The eviction was traumatic and Israel leveled Yamit to the ground. The Begin government, though apparently idealistically committed to settlement of the total Land of Israel and to a "greater Israel" concept of territorial annexation, thus set the pattern for all later Israeli governments in peace negotiations with the Arabs by accepting and implementing the "land for peace" formula of the Arabs.

Anwar Sadat was a complex, wily, cunning, and heroic figure. He genuinely wished to end the war with Israel, which had proved so disastrously draining to Egypt for decades. He tied the future of Egypt to American economic and military aid, and hoped to build the Egyptian economy to a self-sufficient level. Egypt, however, was faced with horrific problems of crumbling and inadequate infrastructure, and after decades of mismanagement and corruption, its economy was in shambles. In addition, its population rise was enormous, compounding its problems. Nevertheless, Sadat hoped that his peace with Israel would provide the open door he needed to the West and its technology and allow Egypt to experience growth, peace, and rising prosperity. But Sadat himself was not long for this world. Egypt, like all the other Arab countries, had a large and violent Islamic opposition, which opposed all peace overtures and any acceptance of Israel, and felt that Western technology and ideas were subversive of the true aims and values of the Moslem religion. In Egypt it was called the Moslem Brotherhood. This group had been persecuted, though not eliminated, during the reign of Gamal Abdel Nasser, Sadat's predecessor, and remained a dark and dangerous force in Egyptian society. Leading officers in the Egyptian army, clandestine members of this group, conspired to assassinate Sadat and impose an "Islamic" regime on the country. In October 1981, while reviewing Egyptian troops parading in commemoration of the beginning of the Yom Kippur War eight years earlier, Anwar Sadat was shot and killed by these officers.

Into Lebanon

enachem Begin, Sadat's partner in the Camp David agreements, also did not fare well.[1] The Lebanese civil war drove the country into ruinous chaos. The Syrians had come to dominate Lebanon in the early 1980s, and well-organized terrorist groups under Syrian protection, if not initiative, used Lebanon as a base for constantly bloodier incursions into Israel. The large Palestinian element, confined to refugee camps and hovels and embittered for decades, joined forces with Moslem forces in opposing the Christian Maronite Arabs' political dominance over the country. Bloody and bitter civil war was the result, with Beirut, the "Paris of the Middle East," being reduced to rubble. The Middle East

---

1. The third partner to the Camp David agreement, President Jimmy Carter, also did poorly, losing the 1980 presidential election to the Republican challenger, Ronald Reagan.

A Palestinian refugee camp destroyed by Shiite Moslem militias

rule of life, that "my enemy's enemy is my friend," brought Israel into open support of the Maronite Christians in this war. This proved to be a major policy blunder on Israel's part. Syria had attempted to balance the Moslems, Christians, and Palestinians against each other, thus allowing Syrian hegemony and control to take away Lebanon's political independence. But at times even Syria found the going rough, as it slowly became impossible to identify the true interests and allied forces of the many contestants for Lebanese control. As terrorist raids and regular artillery and Katyusha rocket attacks into northern Israel mounted in intensity, the Begin government was goaded into a massive war of intervention in Lebanon. Dubbed "For the Peace of Galilee," the war began in the summer of 1982 with a large-scale Israeli invasion of Lebanon. The PLO/Fatah camps in the south of Lebanon were comparatively easily eliminated, and after more severe tank and plane warfare, the Syrians were also dislodged from their positions in south Lebanon and driven back to the border of Syria deep in the Bekaa Valley.

Faced now with a decision on whether to limit or expand the Israeli incursion into Lebanon, Begin and Defense Minister Ariel Sharon decided to go all the way. The Israeli army drove up the

Mediterranean coast of Lebanon, capturing the Biblical cities of Tyre and Sidon and reaching the outskirts of Beirut itself. Yassir Arafat and 12,000 of his PLO fighters were trapped in Beirut. The Christian militias began to dominate the area and Israel made an alliance with the dominant Christian militia leader to impose a new government on Lebanon; one which would shut out Syrian and PLO influence and sign a peace treaty with Israel. Such a plan was far too ambitious and simplistic, given anti-Israel world opinion and the interests of the Arab world. The militia leader was soon assassinated, the UN imposed a cease-fire, and Arafat and his fighters evacuated Beirut under UN protection to a temporary refuge in Tunis.[2] The grand design that was the *raison d'etre* for the war began to unravel. The culminating disaster of the war was the massacre of over 300 Palestinian men, women, and children, in the refugee camps of Sabra and Shatilla outside of Beirut, by Christian Lebanese militia members. While Israel was not directly involved in this atrocity, it bore the brunt of world condemnation.[3]

The United States, under President Ronald Reagan, sent Marines to keep the peace. Soon Arab terrorists blew up the American Marines' compound in Beirut, killing over 250 men in the process. America soon withdrew from Lebanon and the chaos and killing resumed unabated. Israel was faced with an untenable and impossible situation. It could not remain in Lebanon as an occupying power unless it dispatched a large and permanent army of occupation, and by so doing, risk world condemnation, UN sanctions, and a possible war with Syria and other Arab states. On the other hand, if it did withdraw from Lebanon, it had to persuade Israeli public opinion that something valuable had been accomplished and that it justified massive expenditure of blood, wealth, and firepower. Either way, Israel was again faced with the familiar situation of having won a war and yet accomplished little, strategically or diplomatically.

Burdened by the disappointing results of the "Peace in the Galilee" war, Menachem Begin suffered personal tragedy when his beloved wife, Aliza, died. He depressed, retreated into being a virtual

---

2. The Fatah terrorists soon returned to Lebanon from their Tunisian exile and resumed their murderous raids against northern Israel.

3. Menachem Begin's plaintive comment on the massacre was: "*Goyim* kill *goyim* and the Jews are blamed." This analysis of the situation, accurate as it may have been technically, was ill received in the world press and in the foreign ministries of the world.

Menachem Begin (left) and Yitzchak Shamir.

recluse, and resigned his leadership and political roles. The leadership of the Likud party now passed to Yitzchak Shamir, a hard-line former head of Lechi.[4] In the 1984 Knesset elections Likud and Labor ran an almost dead heat and a government of national unity was formed, with rotating prime ministers, first Shimon Peres of Labor and then Yitzchak Shamir. Peres was successful in extracting the Israeli army from the morass of occupying Lebanon, but he left Israel and its Christian militia allies to occupy a small "security zone" in the southern part of Lebanon hard against the border of Israel. In spite of the presence of the Israeli forces in that "security zone," the Arab terrorist/guerrilla organizations[5] were able to continue their periodic attacks on northern Israel, always provoking a strong Israeli military response and, usually, an attendant international diplomatic crisis. Shimon Peres was also able to rein in the runaway inflation in the Israeli economy that, in the early 1980s, threatened the basis of Israel's economic and social foundations. As Yitzchak Shamir became the prime minister, however, a new and unexpected danger soon struck the Israeli society.

---

4. See p. 390 above.

5. Hezbollah, Islamic Jihad, and Organization for the Liberation of Palestine were some of the public names of these shadowy groups, financed and supported mainly by Syria and Iran.

The New Face of Terror

T he Arab residents of the West Bank had become increasingly restive as it became obvious to them that the Arab countries had no real solution for their frustrations at being, at one and the same time, inextricably bound to Israeli society and yet not sharing in its achievements and benefits. An entire generation of Arab youth had grown up under Israeli rule and were disaffected, sullen, and prone to violence. Whereas the older Arab generation recognized that Israeli rule, no matter how politically unpopular, was an improvement over the previous Jordanian administration of the West Bank and that the Palestinian Arab standard of living now surpassed what it had been in the past, the generation coming of age under Israeli administration would have none of that. Furthermore, the older generation had felt Israel's overwhelming military superiority and had no taste for tangling with this superpower; their young offspring had not had the humbling experience of defeat. Beginning at the end of 1986 and gaining vicious momentum during 1987, Arab riots, stabbings, burnings, stone-throwing, and low-grade guerrilla warfare broke out throughout the country. The new revolt became known as the "Intifada."[6] Though apparently grass roots in origin, the Intifada became part of Arab and PLO strategy. Armed conflicts between Arabs and Jewish settlers in the West Bank and between Israeli soldiers and Arab gangs, often composed of pre-teen-age, stone-throwing youths, became regular occurrences. In spite of the boast of then-Defense Minister Yitzchak Rabin that "we will break their bones," the Intifada continued to flicker at various rates of intensity for the next five years. The response of the Shamir government was to encourage increased Jewish development and settlement in the West Bank and to continue to fight the Intifada with the Israeli Army and the intelligence infrastructure of the "Shin-Bet"[7] and to continue to stonewall international and especially American pressures to be diplomatically more forthcoming to the Arabs.

---

6. The Intifada, in retrospect, was a logical and apparently unavoidable consequence of the continuing Israeli settlement policy in Yehudah, Shomron and Gaza. The feeling of desperation among the Palestinian Arabs increased after the "Peace in the Galilee" war and the continuing Israeli-Arab diplomatic deadlock.

7. The Hebrew letters' abbreviation of "Sherut Bitachon" — Security Service — the famed Israeli counterpart of the CIA.

A vociferous element of Israeli society objected to these policies of the Shamir government. Left-wing groups such as the Meretz party,[8] the "women in black,"[9] and "Peace Now"[10] demonstrated regularly in the country. They visited foreign countries to attempt to have those countries and their Jewish communities bring pressure against the policies of the Shamir government. In November 1988, George Bush was elected president of the United States. His Secretary of State, James Baker, enunciated the basic U.S. policy of "land for peace" and took a strong anti-settlement line against the expansion of Jewish towns on the West Bank. George Bush and Yitzchak Shamir did not like each other and relations between the United States and Israel were strained, if correct, between 1988 and 1992. Even though settlement in the West Bank continued apace, the continuing Intifada and the outspoken disapproval of such settlement by the United States, the UN, and many governments served to temper the optimism of Israeli society regarding the eventual success of its policies towards the Palestinian Arabs and their foreign allies.

Palestinian youths throwing stones at Israeli troops

8. A combination of anti-religious, civil libertarian, environmental "greens," and peace-at-all costs groups, headed by such disparate personalities as Shulamit Aloni, Yossi Sarid, and Ron Cohen. It was a merger of three parties, all of which had been either in decline or were static. Meretz played a disproportionately major role in the Rabin/Peres government of 1992-6.

9. A group of women who wore black mourning clothes while protesting the Israeli presence on the West Bank. These protests were mounted in growing intensity every Friday on the streets of Jerusalem, Tel Aviv, and other Israeli cities, always occasioning counter-demonstrations. These confrontations sometimes turned violent.

10.This group pressed for immediate and unconditional withdrawal of Israeli troops from the West Bank, the dismantling of Jewish settlements built beyond the pre-1967 existing borderlines of Israel, and the recognition of a Palestinian state on the West Bank.

The Fall of Communism

hese issues were in a certain sense completely over-shadowed by the unforeseen, though long-hoped-for, collapse of the Soviet Union and its Eastern and Central European empire. A cornerstone of Ronald Reagan's American foreign policy was the placing of nuclear missiles in Western Europe, directly counterbalancing the SS-20 missiles placed in western Eastern Europe by the Soviets. Reagan also embarked on an ambitious technological arms race,[11] which was given the highest priority as to American funding and resources. At the very same time, the Soviet Union was beginning to undergo an internal breakdown, social and economic, which was as yet unrecognized in the West.

In the mid-1980s, Mikhail Gorbachev became General Secretary of the Communist Party of Russia and soon afterwards its head of state. He found before him an economy that was hopelessly outdated and inefficient; a crumbling industrial infrastructure;[12] a disheartened and apathetic population, cynical of the ideas and policies that had ruled them for seven decades; a military that had been fought to a bloody standstill in Afghanistan; ever more restive and unhappy Eastern European satellite nations;[13] and a technological arms race with the West that the Soviet Union could not possibly win. Gorbachev attempted a harrowing tight-rope balancing act. He loosened political repression, liberalized the economy to include the private sector,[14] signed arms-control treaties with the West, pleaded

11. This program — the Strategic Defense Initiative — was known to the general public by its derisive Hollywood-type title, "The Star Wars Program."

12. The nuclear disaster of the radiation breakdown in the Chernobyl power plant in the early 1980s contaminated vast sections of the Soviet Union and brought untold grief to hundreds of thousands of innocent Soviet citizens. This disaster exposed the growing breakdown of Soviet industry and the unreliability of its much-vaunted technology.

13. By the middle 1980s, though still nominally ruled by the Communist Polish General Jaruzelski, Poland had already gone her own way, distancing itself in its economic structure and society from Soviet norms and standards. The revolution of Lech Walensa and the Solidarity labor union he headed had — with the unrelenting pressure of the Catholic Church — been successful in turning Poland towards the West. Gorbachev realized that only massive forceful intervention by the Red Army could restore the Soviet situation in Poland. He was unwilling and unable to use such force.

14. The private, shadowy, illegal, "parallel economy" had always existed in the Soviet Union, many times providing the necessary wherewithal for Soviet economic survival. Gorbachev was the first to officially recognized its existence and its importance and at-

for massive infusions of Western investment capital to shore up his sinking economy, all the while maintaining Russia's facade of being a superpower and the vanguard of world Socialism.

Gorbachev soon fell off the high wire. The Soviet Empire collapsed. The satellite countries, Czechoslovakia, Poland, Romania, Hungary, all went their separate ways. Yugoslavia broke up into Croatia, Bosnia, and Serbia and fell into a horrendous bloody civil war. Estonia, Latvia, Lithuania, Ukraine, and Byelorussia all seceded from the Soviet Union. The hated "Berlin Wall" was torn down and East Germany collapsed, eventually becoming reunited with West Germany, at great economic and social cost and angst. Gorbachev himself faced a coup and was rescued only by the resoluteness of his rival, Boris Yeltsin, a Communist turned democrat, who eventually became the first freely elected Russian head of state in its thousand-year-old history. The Soviet Union was no more. In its place there arose the Confederation of Independent States (CIS), an amalgamated group of different states of the former Soviet Union, led by Russia. The red hammer and sickle flag that represented the inexorable march of the "progressive future" disappeared. The Czar, Trotsky, Zinoviev, Bukharin, and the millions of "counter-revolutionists" executed by Lenin and Stalin were rehabilitated, while Stalin and Lenin themselves moved toward oblivion. And the Jewish dissidents, the "Prisoners of Zion," the tenacious "zeks" of the "Gulag," triumphed.

Mikhail Gorbachev (left) and Ronald Reagan at an October 1986 summit at Reykjavik, Iceland

tempted to combine it with the Marxist "centralized command economy" that officially existed in Russia. The task was to prove too daunting for any hope of success.

Starting in the late 1980s a veritable flood tide of Jewish immigrants arrived in Israel from the former Soviet Union.[15] A much smaller number of Soviet Jews also came to the United States. Those Jews who remained in the former Soviet Union now could be reached by their brethren from the West and Israel. Jewish schools, camps, tours, and even yeshivos were founded and maintained. They expanded in number and size, and an unimagined renaissance of Jewish life began in the states of the former Soviet Union. The "dead bones" of Jewish Russia now began to revive and multiply. The triumph of Jewish survival had again been demonstrated by the Divine hand, against all expectations and odds. History repeated itself — yet again!

Iran and Iraq

n the Arab world of the 1980s, a bitter and costly war was fought between Iraq and Iran. Sadam Hussein, the brutal dictator of Iraq, sought to capitalize on the chaos of Iran in the late 1970s and early 1980s, when the Shah was deposed and the Ayatollah Khomeini installed a militantly theocratic, fundamentalist, Shiite Islamic regime in Iran. After initial successes in capturing strategic land at the mouths of the Tigris and Euphrates Rivers, where they empty into the Persian Gulf, Iraq was fought to a standstill by waves of Iranian suicide squads. The carnage produced hundreds of thousands of casualties. Long-range Scud missiles bombarded both Teheran and Baghdad, wreaking enormous havoc among the civilian population. Poison gas, a weapon eschewed even by the Germans in World War II, was employed against Iran by

---

15. Approximately 700,000 immigrants from the former Soviet Union arrived in Israel in the decade of 1986-96. As many as 200,000 of them may not have been truly Jewish, thus causing untold personal, political, and communal problems in Israeli society. Nevertheless, on the whole, the absorption of the immigration from the former Soviet Union into Israeli life was remarkably successful and beneficial, although, unavoidably, most could not find employment commensurate with their educational and professional background. The new immigrants brought skills, technical and scientific knowledge, and a sense of purpose with them to their new home. Many were now exposed to Torah knowledge and a Jewish life-style for the first time ever. While most of the immigrants remained secular and non-observant of Jewish daily ritual, it must be said that the vast majority of them also became much more Jewish, spiritually and intellectually, than they were in the former Soviet Union.

Sadam Hussein. The war eventually became a deadlock, with daily killing and maiming, but no strategic advantage being gained by either side. Seemingly exhausted, both sides, in spite of slogans to fight to the last man, agreed on a cease-fire and armistice. This now left both Iran and Iraq free for more major mischief, which would not be long in coming.

Iran became the center of Arab-sponsored terror in the world. The terror was directed not only against Israel but at Western countries as well. The United States, Khomeini's "great Satan," was a particular target. Iran, Libya, and Syria became "rogue states," sponsoring, supporting, and maintaining terrorist groups. A Pan Am plane was blown out of the skies over Scotland by Libyan and Syrian operatives. The terrorist organizations in south Lebanon received active and continuing Iranian and Syrian support. In Egypt, Moslem terrorists attacked tourists, police, and the government, in an attempt to destabilize Mubarak's regime. King Hussein of Jordan uncovered assassination plots against him. In spite of enormous bribes paid by the Saudi royal family to the backers of these terrorist groups, Saudi Arabia also became the target of increasing tensions and terrorist plots and attempts. Iran was the leading destabilizer of the Middle East, with the avowed purpose of destroying Israel and eradicating any Western influence and culture from the area.

The Persian Gulf War

raq, meanwhile, planned an even more violent and audacious act of aggression. Just south of its border lay the small but enormously oil-rich emirate of Kuwait. Sadam Hussein coveted the defenseless state and was convinced that no one would oppose his rapacious grab. In the summer of 1990 he massed his army at the Kuwaiti border and, ignoring international and especially American warnings not to invade Kuwait, the Iraqi army captured the country. Stung by Sadam Hussein's arrogance, President George Bush cobbled together an alliance of countries to oppose him and to reverse his conquest.[16] The United

---

16. England, France, Saudi Arabia, Syria(!), and the Gulf States joined the United States in forcibly opposing Sadam Hussein.

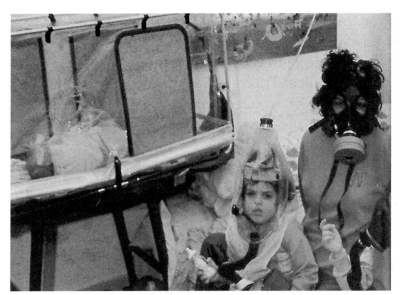

An Israeli family in their "sealed room"

States sent a large expeditionary land force, a tactical wing command of its air force, together with a major aircraft carrier flotilla to the Persian Gulf. Saddam Hussein refused to budge and in the winter of 1990-91, the Gulf War took place. American, British, French, and Saudi airpower pounded Iraqi forces and destroyed major installations in and around Baghdad. The Iraqis retaliated by unleashing Scud attacks against Israel! Most of the Scuds were aimed towards the Tel Aviv area, and even though they were wildly inaccurate, they sowed panic in Israel. The threat of Scuds carrying poison gas warheads, or other chemical or biological warfare weapons, had all of Israel living in "sealed rooms" and never straying far from their gas masks. The sight of little Israeli schoolchildren walking to school carrying their gas masks in their hands or pouches, all this at the end of the 20th century, is a scene that remains firmly embedded in my psyche.[17] Saddam Hussein hoped to draw Israel into retaliating, thereby making it an Arab-Israeli war and changing the whole tenor of the confrontation. The Shamir government, under intense American pressure, did nothing against Iraq, while the American forces desperately attempted to locate the mobile Scud launchers in Iraq and destroy them. Their efforts in this matter were only partially successful and Scuds continued to rain down on Israel almost till the end of the war. Unlike their record in the Iranian war, the Iraqi Scuds caused almost no loss of life, and relatively minor damage when falling in Israel — a miracle. But those Scud attacks and the resulting inaction of the Israel Defense Forces traumatized the country.

General Norman Schwartzkopf, the commander of the allied forces, unleashed "Operation Desert Storm," the land invasion of

---

17. I was "privileged" to be in Israel that winter and to don my gas mask and sit in a "sealed room" during one of Sadaam Hussein's Scud attacks on Israel. It is an experience not easily forgotten.

Iraqi troops surrendering to Allied forces during the Gulf War

Iraq and the encirclement and destruction of Iraqi armed forces in Kuwait. The Iraqi army was shattered and forced to evacuate Kuwait. A cease-fire was agreed upon and the Scuds stopped falling on Israel. But for inexplicable reasons, the American allies did not topple Sadaam Hussein, though, by the imposition of economic sanctions and the destruction of many of his fearsome weapons by UN inspectors, he and Iraq were greatly weakened. After the Gulf War, many felt that there was now a new Middle East and that the logjam in the diplomatic arena between Israel and the Arabs could now be broken. The American Secretary of State, James Baker, organized a conference in Madrid, attended by Israel and all of the Arab states, as well as the United States and Russia. The Madrid Conference reiterated the "land for peace" formula, but no real positive steps towards peace were advanced. Years later, Yitzchak Shamir stated that he intended to continue to stonewall the issue of settlements in the West Bank and any final

Prime Minister Shamir addresses the Madrid Conference. Seated at the table, far right, is American Secretary of State, James Baker

settlement that conferred recognition on the PLO. But, unknown perhaps at the time, the Madrid Conference did open the door to dramatic events that would come to be known as "the peace process" and provide an opportunity for an eventual Israeli-Arab agreement.

Israel's 1992 Elections

n the 1992 elections for the Israeli Knesset, the Labor party, headed by Yitzchak Rabin, emerged with a narrow victory. The veteran warrior and politician was viewed by most Israelis as being "strong" against the Arab demands and as one who would place personal security of Israelis ahead of all other considerations. Rabin had publicly committed himself in the election campaign not to leave the Golan Heights and to take a strong stand against the PLO. However, upon assuming office, Rabin entered into a very narrow coalition of Labor with Meretz, the most left-wing, anti-religious of Israeli political parties, and the Israeli Arab parties.[18] Thus the Israeli government took on a strong anti-religious, anti-settlements, "peace now" look. Shulamit Aloni, one of the most vociferous anti-religious spokespersons of the Left, became Education Minister,[19] and a wave of secularist, anti-religious, and anti-Zionist proposals emanated from officials of the new government. A strong effort to introduce "religious pluralism"[20] in the country; the import of large amounts of non-kosher meat into Israel; the approval of the opening of a large non-kosher, open on the Sabbath, American chain restaurant in the heart of Jerusalem; a proposal to amend the Israeli national anthem so as not to be "offensive to non-Jews," and other plans and ideas were encouraged. Rabin, who had absolutely no sensitivity towards or knowledge of Jewish tradition, caustically rejected all protest and criticism of the excesses of the Left. His government ministers clashed openly with representatives of the American Jewish community, and the message that his administration communicated to American Jewry was "that we no longer need you."[21]

The question of the place of Reform in the Jewish world took on added urgency during the 1980s and 1990s. Ever eager to discard the past and climb on board any current fashionable social religious bandwagon, Reform took major steps to distance itself from the traditional Jewish community. While calling other Jews intolerant, hateful, and divisive, Reform undertook decisions that caused irrevocable splits in the Jewish world. It stated that patrilineal descent was now sufficient for Jewish identity. It embarked on a mission to the intermarried and non-Jewish, hoping to build its ranks from that population. Non-Jewish cantors, Temple members who remained practicing Christians, and as-

---

18. Shas, the religious Sephardic party whose religious mentor was the great Torah scholar Rabbi Ovadya Yosef, also agreed not to vote against the government, but for most of the rule of the Rabin/Peres administration it did not actually sit as a member party of the ruling government coalition.

19. Her shrill excesses in office were so great that Rabin eventually had to jettison her in favor of the more urbane, but no less secularist, Amnon Rubenstein.

20. "Pluralism" is a euphemism for reversing the "status quo" agreement which had been effect since the founding of the State. This would empower Conservative and Reform in Israel and force the rabbinate of Israel to recognize their conversions and other matters of personal status.

21. The inept phrase of an assistant Foreign Minister of Israel to a gathering of leading New York Jewish supporters of Israel in 1992.

sorted other non-Jews and non-believers were welcomed into the Reform movement and the Temple. Women rabbis in Reform pulpits[22] were soon followed by avowed by lesbian and homosexual rabbis. And when the vast majority of world Jewry rejected these radical and un-Jewish proposals, Reform demanded that they be forced to accept them, through the institution of "religious pluralism" in Israel, a position that could only tear asunder the already fragile fabric of basic Jewish unity. The hardened secularists of the Israeli government thought that they could use "religious pluralism" as a means of further defeating their traditional Jewish brethren and to thereby continue their campaign to turn Israel into a state for Jews but not a Jewish state.

To Oslo and Beyond

ut as important as these issues were, they were temporarily dwarfed by the steps that the Rabin government took in relation to the Arabs. Rabin's former bitter political rival, Shimon Peres, reconciled with him and became Foreign Minister in the government. In a series of secret meetings and negotiations in Oslo, Norway, initiated by Peres' intellectual circle,[23]

---

22. The Conservative movement also allowed women rabbis and cantors to serve in its pulpits since the 1980s.

23. Shimon Peres was undoubtedly the most intellectual and sophisticated of all Israeli leaders. He had a great creative vision of a peaceful and utopian Middle East with Israel as an integral part of it. He was able to convince Yitzchak Rabin of the possibility and necessity of actualizing that dream. However, later, he was unsuccessful in con-

Shimon Peres, standing fourth from left, at the secret signing of the Oslo Accord

Israel came to an agreement with Yasir Arafat and the PLO about the establishment of Arab autonomy in the major areas of the West Bank. Rabin agreed to freeze all Jewish settlement on the West Bank[24] and to transfer to the new Palestinian Authority adminisitrative and police control over Gaza and Jericho. Arafat agreed to end the state of war against Israel, to end the Intifada,[25] to amend the PLO charter that called for the destruction of the State of Israel, and implicitly to help Israel control and prevent terrorist acts against Jews. This agreement, known as Oslo I, was signed with great pomp and circumstance on the White House lawn in Washington, under the watchful eye of President Bill Clinton. When Yitzchak Rabin hesitantly shook Arafat's hand in front of the world's media, the "peace process" was created. Many relied on the

Prime Minister Yitzchak Rabin and Yasir Arafat shake hands after the signing of Oslo I on the front lawn of the White House, as President Clinton looks on

vincing the Jewish electorate of Israel as to that dream's viability. The electorate respected him, but regarded him as unrealistic.

24. Though no new Jewish settlements were founded on the West Bank during the Rabin/Peres adminstration, the large influx into the existing settlements and the building of new housing within those settlements continued apace.

25. By 1993, the Intifada had anyway petered out and was no longer the force it had been even two years earlier. Nevertheless, its end was certainly a major accomplishment for the Israeli government.

hope that perhaps at long last, a way to break the cycle of violence in the Middle East could now be found. Israel entered into direct negotiations with Jordan and with Syria on signing peace treaties. But the euphoria was not to last.

Arafat had many enemies in the Palestinian and Arab world. Israel had no friends among the Palestinians and the other Arabs. Somehow, Israel expected that Arafat and his police would be able to prevent terrorist acts on Israeli territory and citizens. But they could not or would not. In the three years of the Rabin/Peres "peace process," more Israelis died from Arab terrorism than in the entire previous decade, including the years of the Intifada. Suicide bombers, bus bombings, stabbings, and hitch-hiker kidnappings all became part of the norm. After every atrocity, the Israeli government stated that it would not allow the terrorism to halt the "peace process." But Arafat himself continued to send mixed signals. He spoke militantly in Arabic to his Arab constituency, failed to fulfill many points of the Oslo agreement, and never was able to inspire any confidence within the Israeli public. Rabin called the complaining settlers, whose lives were daily endangered by Arab terrorism, "cry babies." The Israeli police exhibited great force in containing continued demonstrations against the Rabin government policies. Every public opinion poll showed the country split on the issue of continuing the "peace process." Nevertheless, Rabin and Peres persevered and pushed forward in order to complete all necessary agreements as soon as possible. The perception existed that the Rabin government would cede the entire Golan Heights to Syria and that Israeli's sole sovereignty over the city of Jerusalem was also negotiable. In the Oslo II agreement, implemented in 1995-6, Israel transferred administration and police control over major Arab towns in the West Bank to the Palestinian Authority. Jenin, Tulkarm, Nablus, Bethlehem, Ramallah and other Arab population centers saw the withdrawal of Israeli forces to be replaced by Arafat's police. In elections held in the West Bank, Arafat and his party won a convincing victory, and Arafat publicly proclaimed the coming establishment of a Palestinian state in the Land of Israel. The Labor Party in Israel amended its platform to allow for the creation of such a state. Arafat also publicly stated that Jerusalem would be the capital of the new state. The response of the Rabin government to that claim was muted.

In the negotiations with Jordan, the Rabin government achieved a great success. The peace treaty with Jordan, again signed with great fanfare at the White House, was well received by all sections of the Israeli public, as well as by the Jordanians. A de facto peace with Jordan had existed for years and many Israeli leaders had met secretly with King Hussein over decades. The official peace turned into a much warmer one than the peace agreement with Egypt. Tourism, transportation, trade, water, and security all became matters of cooperation and mutual development. King Hussein reiterated the Jordanian claim for administration over the Moslem holy places in Jerusalem. Arafat objected bitterly to Hussein's claim but Israel did not. However, the protracted negotiations with Syria made little progress, even after Rabin and Peres made it clear that Israel was prepared to withdraw completely from the Golan Heights. Assad, the head of Syria, preferred to remain at war rather than to reap the benefits of peace, even when those benefits were so obviously one-sided for Syria's benefit. Syria continued to encourage and maintain terrorist organizations in the Middle East, and the Western policy of appeasing Assad had very little to show for itself.

The Rabin Assassination and Its Aftermath

he continuation of the "peace process" brought continued strife and bitterness to Israeli society. After every terrorist outrage, large numbers of Israelis expressed themselves with growing bitterness against the government and against Rabin and Peres personally. Incendiary statements were made, and Rabin's own peculiar brusque abrasiveness towards his critics served to further exacerbate the problem.

The worst nightmare of Israeli society soon came to pass. At a giant Saturday night peace rally in Tel Aviv in the winter of 1995-6, Yitzchak Rabin was gunned down and killed. His assassin was Yigal Amir, a former yeshiva student and soldier in the Israel Defense Forces and a law student at a prominent Israeli university, who claimed he was saving Israel from the doom being brought upon it by the Rabin government. Despite the denunciations of the Moslems by Rabbinic and political leaders across the political and religious spectrum, the mood of the Israeli public and especially its press turned bitterly anti-right wing and anti-religious.

Shimon Peres, who now succeeded Rabin as Prime Minister, pushed ahead with the "peace process," dropping broad hints that he now would be able to come to a final settlement with the PLO regarding Jerusalem, Hebron, and the full West Bank, and even with Syria regarding peace and the Golan Heights. Peres was so confident of his mandate with the people that, riding the crest of sympathy and popularity that he inherited from the Rabin assassination, he advanced the date of the elections for the 14th Knesset from the late fall to the end of May 1996. This election would also be the first one in which the Israeli electorate would vote directly for a Prime Minister. Peres' challenger was Binyamin Netanyahu, the leader of the right-wing Likud party. In a stunning upset, Netanyahu defeated Peres[26] and formed a coalition government based on the religious parties,[27] the new Russian immigrant party, and other smaller factions of the Knesset.

Again, Israel stood at a crossroads. The future remained as always inscrutable and uncertain. But the hope for secure and peaceful peace remained the core idea of the people of Israel and of Jews the world over. Only time would tell of the eventual outcome of all the hopes and prayers of Israel for physical peace and spiritual renewal and rebirth.

---

26. Netanyahu's margin of victory in the overall vote was little more than one percent, though his margin of victory among Jewish voters was over 11 percent. The Arab vote went almost unanimously to Peres.

27. The religious parties elected 23 Knesset members, and a number of members from other parties were also visibly observant Jews.

Epilogue — Jewish Survival

HIS BOOK HAS COVERED 350 years of history. On its pages are found heroes, saints, holy men, and martyrs. Also remembered on its pages are malicious villains, madmen, fools, cowards, and traitors. Great and noble events in human life and Jewish history are described. So are sagas that are so base and bad as to defy the power of literary depiction. The staggering story of Jewish experience from 1640 to 1980 is unimagined truth beyond the scope of any inventive fiction, written by the Providential hand through the events and behavior of mortals — mostly ordinary and some extraordinary.

Secular historians, when viewing the forest and not merely the trees of Jewish history, have stood in awe of the story. Even they have noticed the Divine Presence in this human story.[1] Believing Jews have always seen God's hand in their personal and national lives. All of the events that have befallen Israel in the modern age were alluded to in

---

1. See Cecil Roth, *History of the Jews,* (New York 1963), p. 424: "The preservation of the Jew was certainly not casual. He has endured through the power of a certain ideal, based upon the recognition of the influence of a Higher Power in human affairs. Time after time in his history, moreover, he has been saved from disaster in a manner which cannot be described excepting as 'providential.' The author [meaning Cecil Roth] has deliberately attempted to write this work in a secular spirit; he does not think that his readers can fail to see in it, on every page, a higher immanence."

Also Paul Johnson, *A History of the Jews*, (New York, 1987), p. 586-7: "The historian should take into account all forms of evidence, including those which are or appear to be metaphysical. If the earliest Jews were able to survey, with us, the history of their progeny, they would find nothing surprising in it. They always knew that Jewish society was appointed to be a pilot-project for the entire human race. That Jewish dilemmas, dramas and catastrophes should be exemplary, larger than life, would seem only natural to them. That Jews should over the millennia attract such unparalleled, indeed inexplicable, hatred would be regrettable but only to be expected. Above all, that the Jews should still survive, when all those other ancient peoples were transmuted or vanished into the oubliettes of history, was wholly predictable. How could it be otherwise? Providence decreed it and the Jews obeyed."

the Divine song of Moses which is recorded in the Book of *Devarim* (Deuteronomy).[2] In the perfect vision of hindsight, the dire events forecast by the Bible and the prophets, occasioned by Israel's pursuit of the false gods of modernity, have come to pass in our era. Yet, somehow, the Jewish people and its eternal Torah have survived. In spite of all pressures and blandishments, the core of Israel has remained loyal to this Torah and its precepts, value system and lifestyle. In responding to the modern era, its new technology, hopes, and political systems, the Torah has remained the salvation of Jewry, allowing it to be part of the general world, yet remain separate from it.

The modern world has proven bittersweet to Jews and Judaism. Jews are freer, more affluent and influential than ever before in the history of the Diaspora. But at the same time they are more vulnerable, physically and spiritually, to destruction than ever before. The troublesome dilemma of spirit and flesh, secular and sacred, separate and joined, that marked the dawn of the modern era for Jews, remains yet unresolved. The current historic forces shaping and affecting Israel, the people and the Land, are still not completely understood and evaluated. But the transcendent miracle of the survival of the Jews and of Torah overshadows all other events and facets of the modern era for Jews. The detailed immediate future of the people and the Land of Israel is indiscernible. But the grand, destined vision of the future of the Jews, of peace and joy to the Land of Israel, of purpose and Torah nobility to the people of Israel, of redemption and Messianic blessing to Israel and all mankind is clear and recognizable. History tells the Jew: "To impart knowledge to all the peoples of the earth regarding the strong and exalted hand of God, and by so doing, you — Israel — will revere the Lord, your God, for all time."[3]

---

2. Chapter 28 till the end of the book.

3. Joshua 4:24.

Index